THE BLUE GUIDES

A NOTE ON BLUE GUIDES

The Blue Guides series began in 1915 when Muirhead Guide-Books Limited published *Blue Guide London and Its Environs*. Finlay and James Muirhead already had extensive experience of guide-book publishing: before the First World War they had been the editors of the English editions of the German Baedekers, and by 1915 they had acquired the copyright of most of the famous "Red" handbooks from John Murray.

An agreement made with the French publishing house Hachette et Cie in 1917 led to the translation of Muirhead's London Guide, which became the first *Guide Bleu*—Hachette had previously published the blue-covered *Guides Joanne*. Subsequently, Hachette's *Guide Bleu Paris et Ses Environs* was adapted and published in London by Muirhead. The collaboration between the two publishing houses continued until 1933.

In 1931 Ernest Benn took over the Blue Guides, appointing Russell Muirhead, Finlay Muirhead's son, editor in 1934. The Muirhead's connection with Blue Guides ended in 1963, when Stuart Rossiter, who had been working on the Guides since 1954, became house editor, revising and compiling several of the books himself.

The Blue Guides are now published by A & C Black, who acquired Ernest Benn in 1984, so continuing the tradition of guide-book publishing which began in 1826 with *Black's Economical Tourist of Scotland*. The Blue Guide series continues to grow: there are now over 50 titles in print with revised editions appearing regularly and many new Blue Guides in preparation.

"Blue Guides" is a registered trade mark.

BLUE GUIDE

BOSTON AND CAMBRIDGE

John Freely

Atlas, maps, and plans

A & C Black Limited
London

W. Norton & Company, Inc.
York

Second edition 1994

Published by A & C Black (Publishers) Limited
35 Bedford Row, London WC1R 4JH

Printed in the United States of America

A CIP catalogue record of this book is available from the British Library.

ISBN 0-7136-3170-8

Published in the United States of America by
W. W. Norton and Company, Inc
500 Fifth Avenue, New York, NY 10110

Published simultaneously in Canada by
Penguin Books Canada Limited
10 Alcorn Avenue, Toronto, Ontario M4V 3B2

The text of this book is composed in Egyptian 505.
Composition by The Maple-Vail Book Manufacturing Group.
Manufacturing by The Courier Companies, Inc.

Library of Congress Cataloging-in-Publication Data

Freely, John.
Blue guide : Boston and Cambridge / John Freely.—2nd ed.
p.   cm.
Includes index.
1. Boston (Mass.)—Guidebooks.   2. Cambridge (Mass.)—Guidebooks.
I. Title.
F73.18.F74   1993
917.44′610443—dc20   92-31581

ISBN 0-393-30988-6

1   2   3   4   5   6   7   8   9   0

CONTENTS

MAPS AND PLANS

PREFACE

Boston, the capital of Massachusetts, is by far the largest city in New England although it ranks only 21st in size among cities in the U.S., with a population in 1990 of 630,000. However, there are about five times that many people living in greater Boston, depending on just where the indefinite boundaries of the metropolitan area are drawn, making it the fifth-largest population concentration in the country. According to one definition of the metropolitan area, it consists of the city of Boston itself and 76 smaller cities, towns, and villages, the most populous of which is Cambridge, with 71,101 residents. The present guide describes all of the many monuments and museums in Boston, Cambridge, and contiguous areas, most notably Brookline, which although a city in its own right is to all external appearances an integral part of Boston. (The other cities and towns in the environs of Boston will be described in the forthcoming *Blue Guide New England*.) In addition, the book provides all of the background and practical information that travelers will need to enjoy every aspect of their stay in Boston and Cambridge.

As with all of the Blue Guides, the main body of this book is divided into routes, most of which are designed as walking tours through Boston, Cambridge, and certain parts of Brookline. There are 22 itineraries in all, 16 of them in Boston, five in Cambridge, and one in the outlying parts of those two cities and downtown Brookline. The two largest museums in Boston are treated as separate routes; these are the Boston Museum of Fine Arts and the Isabella Stewart Gardner Museum. The walking tours in the city, aside from the museums, are designed so that they can be covered in a single day. Those who will be staying in the Boston-Cambridge area for a longer span may well want to spend much more time on some of these itineraries, particularly in the large museums, for their collections are so vast and interesting that it would take many months to see all of their exhibits fully. The present guide seeks to give an extremely thorough description of the collections in all the museums in Boston and Cambridge, something that no book about this area has ever before attempted. This is especially advantageous to those travelers who use the *Blue Guide Boston and Cambridge*, for none of the museums in the area except the Gardner has published a comprehensive guide to its exhibits. The historic houses in Boston and Cambridge are also described more minutely than in any other book on the two cities. However, in order to save space, the interior furnishings in these houses are not described in detail, except for items of outstanding interest, because all of those places provide guided tours in which detailed information is given in that field. Finally, the book seeks to communicate to travelers something of the unique spirit and atmosphere of Boston and Cambridge, two cities that have played such important roles in the political and cultural life of the United States.

The second edition of *Blue Guide Boston and Cambridge* takes into account all of the changes that have occurred in these two cities since the publication of the first edition in 1984, including new buildings that have been erected, deleting old ones that have been demolished, updating the descriptions of museum collections that have been rearranged, and giving new listings of hotels and restaurants as well as current information on all other aspects of travel to and within Boston and Cambridge.

EXPLANATIONS

TYPE. The main routes are described in large type. Smaller type is used, in general, for historical, background, and practical information, as well as for the description of subroutes and diversions.

ASTERISKS (*) indicate places of special interest or importance. Double asterisks (**) denote monuments or exhibits of extraordinary interest, those that should not be missed on a visit to Boston and Cambridge.

ABBREVIATIONS. In addition to generally accepted and self-explanatory abbreviations, the following are used in this guide:

AAA: American Automobile Association
Assocs: Associates
BRA: Boston Redevelopment Agency
c.: *circa* (approximately)
C: Century
exc.: except
fl.: *floruit* (flourish, or the active period of an artist's career)
Hol.: Holiday(s)
l.: left
MBTA: Massachusetts Bay Transit Authority

MDC: Metropolitan District Commission
MFA: Museum of Fine Arts
Pl.: Place
r.: right
Rte: Route
Sc.: school of art
SPNEA: Society for the Preservation of New England Antiquities
SS: Saints
St.: Saint
T: MBTA (see above)

BACKGROUND INFORMATION

Introduction to Boston and Cambridge

Boston is often called the Hub, and Bostonians sometimes indulge themselves in the thought that they and their intellectual cousins in Cambridge constitute the cultural nexus of the U.S. Boston's nickname stems from an article that Oliver Wendell Holmes wrote in 1858 for the *Atlantic Monthly,* where he stated that the "Boston State House is the hub of the solar system." The nickname might now appear to be out of date, for Boston is surpassed in population by a score of cities in the U.S.; the State House is far from the nation's political center in Washington, D.C., now the hub only of one of the smaller states in the country; while the focal point of most other aspects of American life is in New York City. So one might think that Boston and Cambridge are just living on in memories of their illustrious past, when their doughty citizens were leaders in the struggle for American independence and in the political and intellectual life of the early Republic. There are certainly many evocative reminders of that historic period still gracing Boston and Cambridge, perhaps more than in any other cities in the U.S. But the busy streets of Boston and Cambridge are not mere outdoor museums of history, for there is a sense of vitality in their distinguished and influential universities, in their research laboratories, high-technology industries, symphony orchestras, professional and collegiate athletic teams, and in their soaring modern architecture. And so the perceptive visitor inevitably realizes that Boston and Cambridge, though no longer the hub of the solar system, are still two of the most interesting and important cities in the U.S., living links with its history.

Boston's first town house, 1657–1711, drawn by Charles Lawrence (1930)

History

(This section deals principally with Boston, whereas the history and topography of Cambridge are described in Part II of the Routes.)

Prehistory. Anthropologists now generally agree that the first human inhabitants of North America, known as Paleo-Indians, migrated from Siberia to Alaska over ice or by a land bridge now covered by the waters of the Bering Strait. After crossing, they headed southward toward warmer climes, fanning out through North and South America. The first of these Paleo-Indians are believed to have settled in New England between the eighth and the third millennium B.C., where the large variance in the estimated time of their arrival reveals the great uncertainty in the factual evidence. In any event, the first European explorers of New England found its sea coasts and forests inhabited by people who apparently had been long settled there, as evidenced by their advanced agriculture and their mastery of their environment. The chronicles of the early explorers record that virtually all of these people, whom they called Indians, were members of one or the other of two great tribal groups, the Algonquins and the Iroquois, who had since time immemorial been contending for supremacy in the N.E. regions of North America. The first settlers in the Massachusetts Bay area found that the hinterland was inhabited by a numerous Algonquin tribe, the Massachusetts, from which the colony and later the state took their name. The Indian population of New England at the beginning of the 17C is estimated by one authority to have been about 75,000, but this was greatly reduced by a terrible epidemic in 1616–17. This tragedy was undoubtedly caused by the contact of the Indians with the first European sailors, fishermen, and settlers along the New England coast, which exposed them to a disease, perhaps smallpox, for which they had not developed an immunity.

Early Voyagers to Massachusetts. Many so-called Viking remains have been identified in New England, including the Massachusetts Bay area; however, there is absolutely no scientific evidence to support these claims, and they have been rejected by all responsible scholars.

The first European explorer known to have sighted the coast of Massachusetts was Giovanni da Verrazano, an Italian navigating a ship of the Royal French Navy. In 1524 Verrazano explored the coast of North America from Cape Fear in North Carolina to Cape Fogo in Newfoundland, sailing across Massachusetts Bay. The following year Estevan Gomez, a Portuguese captain in the service of Charles V, explored the coast southward from Cape Breton in Newfoundland to Cape Cod in Massachusetts. However, no attempt was made to establish settlements on the New England coast until the first decade of the 17C, when the colonization of America became the avowed policy of the British government. At that time other powers became interested in the region too, and in the years 1602–14 no fewer than seven parties of European explorers sailed along the coast of Massachusetts.

The Colonization of New England. The first attempt to establish a colony in New England was made in 1602, when an expedition led by an English navigator named Gosnold attempted to settle on Cuttyhunk Island in Buzzard's Bay. The attempt failed, as did another expedition in 1607 that tried to establish a settlement in Maine. The abortive Maine colony had been financed by the Plymouth Company, a joint-stock enterprise that had its headquarters at Plymouth in Devonshire. The Plymouth Company was associated with a similar enterprise known as the London Company, which earlier in 1607 had financed an expedition to Jamestown in Virginia, establishing what would be the first permanent English colony in North America.

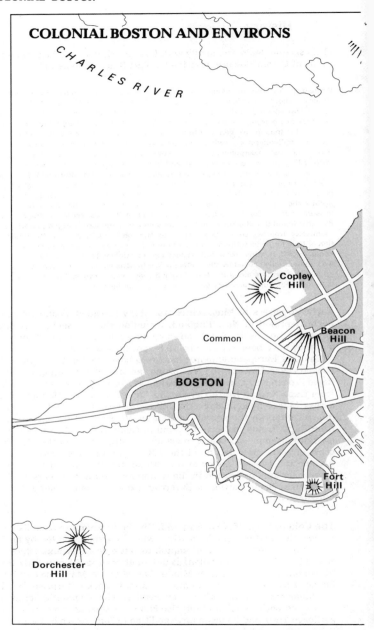

COLONIAL BOSTON AND ENVIRONS

CHARLES RIVER

Copley Hill

Common

Beacon Hill

BOSTON

Fort Hill

Dorchester Hill

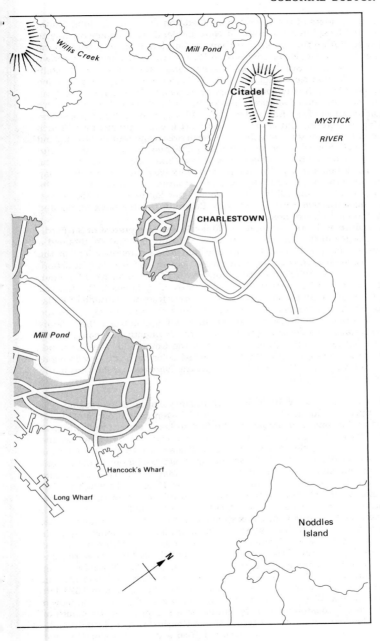

One of the leaders of the Jamestown expedition was Captain John Smith, who in 1614 explored the coast of New England from Penobscot Bay to Cape Cod. During the course of the voyage Smith and his men entered the bay that in time would become Boston Harbor, the first Europeans known to have explored it. Smith was enthusiastic about the possibility of establishing a colony in New England, and on his return to England he applied for a patent from the Plymouth Company, receiving financial backing from a group of merchant-adventurers headed by Sir Ferdinando Gorges. Smith's expedition set sail from England in March 1615; however, his ship was first disabled in a storm, and after a second start it was captured by a French cruiser. Smith spent some months in a French prison and returned to England only in 1616. Shortly after his return he published a work called *Description of New England . . .* where for the first time he gave the region the name that it bears today. This pioneering work was illustrated with a map that became the basis for New England cartography, and which would be used by all of the expeditions that would later journey out to that coast. Smith himself never returned to New England, but his book stimulated much interest in the region.

The failure of Smith's expedition did not lessen the interest of Sir Ferdinando Gorges in the colonization of New England. In 1620 he obtained a new patent for the Plymouth Company that made it independent of the London Company, thus giving him greater power and freedom of action. This document established a body known as the Council for New England, a corporation of 40 patentees presided over by King James I. The Council was given title to all the land in North America from the latitude of Philadelphia to that of Quebec, and extending from the Atlantic Ocean to the Pacific. For the next 15 years all settlers in New England based their claims on territorial rights conveyed to them by the Plymouth Company, acting through Gorges and the other members of the Council for New England. This proved to be a great stimulus for the British colonization of New England, most notably those settlements founded by the Pilgrims and Puritans in the third decade of the 17C.

The First Permanent British Colonies in New England. Increasing religious oppression in the early years of the 17C eventually brought about an exodus of Puritans from England. The first to leave were a tiny group of Separatists from Scrooby in Nottingham, who came to be known as the Pilgrims after they fled from England to Holland in 1606. The Pilgrims remained in Holland until 1620, when they obtained a patent from the London Company and set sail for America in the *Mayflower*. They eventually set up a colony at Plymouth late in December 1620, and though half of them died during the first winter the others survived and prospered, making theirs the first permanent British colony in New England.

During the first decade of its existence the Plymouth Plantation grew in population from 50 to 390, as the original settlers were joined by their brethren from the Pilgrim community in Holland, along with a number of outsiders. By the end of that decade other English settlements were scattered along the shores and islands of Massachusetts Bay. The first settler on what later came to be the site of Boston was the Rev. William Blaxton (his name is often given, but incorrectly, as Blackstone) who in 1624 left the settlement at Wessagusett, an abortive foundation of Gorges, and moved off by himself. Blaxton eventually settled on a peninsula at the mouth of the Charles River opposite the future site of Charlestown, a place the Indians called Shawmut. He found a spring of good water on the slope of what is now known as Beacon Hill, built a cabin there, and cleared land for a garden and orchard. Blaxton lived there alone for the next five years, trading with the occasional Indians who crossed over to Shawmut from the mainland, passing his time reading from the library of some 200 books that he had brought with him to the New World from Cambridge.

The Massachusetts Bay Colony and the Founding of Boston. The prelude to the first large-scale Puritan colonization of New England began in 1628, when a group of about 90 of them formed the Massachusetts Company, headed by John Endicott. Endicott and five of his associates received from the Council for New England a grant of land that included all of the territory between three miles N. of the Merrimack to three miles S. of the Charles, extending from the Atlantic to the Pacific. In the summer of 1628 Endicott led an advance party of Puritan colonists on an expedition to found a colony within the land granted to them. They landed at Naumkeag, joining a group of Puritans headed by Roger Conant that had settled there five years before. At first the earlier settlers tended to dispute Endicott's authority, but the two groups were soon reconciled, and in token of this they decided to rename the colony Salem, the Hebrew word for "peace."

In March 1629 the Rev. John White of Dorchester, a leading spirit in planning the Puritan exodus, succeeded in obtaining for himself and his associates a charter from Charles I setting up the Massachusetts Bay Colony, which would include the land given to the Massachusetts Company. The affairs of this corporation were to be managed by a governor, a deputy governor, and a General Court, sometimes called the Court of Assistants. This Court, which originally consisted of 18 assistants elected annually by the Company, had the power to regulate the affairs of the Colony, provided that they did not run counter to English law. Within weeks after its formation the Company financed an expedition in which 300 Puritan settlers were embarked on six small ships under the leadership of the Rev. Francis Higginson of Leicester. In summer 1629 this group joined the colony in Salem, thus making it the most populous settlement in New England. In the summer of 1629 the General Court of the Massachusetts Bay Colony, meeting first in London and then in Cambridge, discussed the possibility of bringing their charter and government out with them to New England, agreeing that it was far better to do so than having their affairs directed by an absentee council in England. When they found that there were no legal obstacles to doing so, the Court, on Aug. 29. of that year, drew up and signed the Cambridge Agreement, the first official step in bringing about the great Puritan migration to New England. The Court then elected as governor John Winthrop, a wealthy lawyer who was manor lord of Groton in Suffolk, after which they chose Thomas Dudley as deputy governor and then went on to select the 18 assistants, the most prominent of whom were John Endicott, who was then in Salem, Sir Richard Saltonstall, and Isaac Johnson, whose wife, Lady Arbella, was a daughter of the Earl of Lincoln.

In the five months after his election Winthrop and the others in the Company were fully occupied with preparations for their departure. A dozen ships were chartered for the voyage, and in early spring of the year 1630 four of them were ready to sail from Southampton. These were the *Talbot,* the *Ambrose,* the *Jewel,* and the *Eagle,* the largest and best appointed of the vessels, which was renamed the *Arbella* in honor of Lady Arbella Johnson. On March 22 some 700–800 Puritans boarded the four ships, with Winthrop and the other leaders and their families berthing down on the *Arbella.* They set sail the same day, beginning what proved to be an uneventful but extremely long voyage; with the *Arbella,* the fastest of the ships, not arriving in Salem until June 22, and the others following over the course of the next several days.

When Winthrop and the others from the *Arbella* landed at Salem they were appalled at what they saw, for the people there had just undergone a winter as terrible as that which the Pilgrims had endured when they first set up their colony at Plymouth. Five days after their arrival Winthrop led a party of exploration up the Mystic River, and a few days later Dudley took another group up the Charles, both of them seeking a better place to settle. When they returned they argued for a few days concerning which of the sites each of them had chosen was the most suitable. By that time the other ships of the Puritan flotilla had arrived and all of the passengers were anxious to move on, for Salem was now hopelessly overcrowded. Winthrop and Dudley were forced to compromise and agreed upon a site midway between those they had each chosen. This was a peninsula, now known as Charlestown, at the confluence of the Charles and Mystic Rivers, linked to the mainland by a thin neck. Endicott had founded a small colony of 50 settlers there the year before, so the site at least had the advantage of affording shelter until they could build their own homes. When they arrived there Winthrop and several of the patentees moved into the Great House, the central building of the settlement, while the rest of the multitude set up crude shacks and tents on the eminence known as Town Hill. The First Church of the Colony gathered together in the tent village for the first time on July 30 of that year, and on Aug. 23 Governor Winthrop called the General Court into session, its first meeting on American soil. Two months after their arrival in the New World the Puritans had set up their basic civic and religious institutions.

But that first summer was an awful one for the settlers, with a frightful epidemic breaking out in the overcrowded shantytown on Town Hill, which was littered with garbage and completely devoid of sanitation. Food was becoming scarce, and the single brackish spring at Charlestown seemed about to run out.

The abysmal conditions in Charlestown forced many settlers to leave, and during that summer groups went off to found the towns of Watertown, Medford, Saugus, and Roxbury. While this diaspora was taking place, a party of 140 Puritans who had no connection with Winthrop's group arrived in Boston Harbor in a vessel called the *Mary and John,* an expedition sent out by the Rev. John White of Dorchester. The new arrivals sent out their own exploratory parties and soon decided to settle on a peninsula S. of Shawmut, at a place the Indians called Mattapan, and which they renamed Dorchester after their native town in England. Winthrop contacted the settlers at Dorchester and tried to persuade them to join his own community, but the people there decided to make a go of it on their own.

Meanwhile, Winthrop himself had become attracted to the Shawmut Peninsula, just across the river from Charlestown. The Puritans called it Tramount, or sometimes Trimountaine, because of the three-peaked eminence (the present Beacon Hill), which was its most prominent feature as seen from Charlestown. The Rev. Blaxton, still the only resident on Shawmut, had already made himself acquainted with the Puritans in Charlestown, for he had rowed across the Charles on several occasions to see his old friend Isaac Johnson. Blaxton invited the Johnsons to come and live on Shawmut near him, pointing out that he had an excellent spring of fresh water, but both of them died before they could take advantage of his offer,

Arbella in late August and Isaac on Sept. 30. Blaxton also extended his invitation to the other Puritan leaders who remained in Charlestown, and Governor Winthrop was one of the first to accept his offer and move there. Winthrop's removal to Shawmut convinced many others in Charlestown to do the same, and by early autumn it had a population of some 150 souls. On Sept. 17 the Court of Assistants, meeting in Charlestown, issued a decree stating "That Trimountaine shall be called Boston," naming it after the town in Lincolnshire from which Isaac and Arbella Johnson had come. The Court continued to meet in Charlestown until the end of Sept. 1630, but on Oct. 29 it began to convene in Boston. Later that autumn a crude meeting-house was erected for the First Church of Boston, where the Rev. John Cotton became the minister in 1633. The Rev. Cotton had for 20 years previously been rector of the magnificent Church of St. Botolph in Boston, Lincolnshire. And thus it was that St. Botolph became the patron saint of Boston in New England.

The Topography of Old Boston. The Shawmut Peninsula, where the Puritans settled in 1630, bore little resemblance to the modern city of Boston. One can best appreciate this by consulting the next map, showing Shawmut as it was in 1630. The Shawmut Peninsula was then almost an island, connected to the mainland at Roxbury to the S. by a narrow strip of land called the Neck, which was sometimes awash at times of especially high tides or in gales. To the W. of the Neck was Back Bay, an area of mud flat and marshland that was inundated at high tide. Beyond Back Bay the Charles River separated Shawmut from the mainland to the N. and E., flowing past the northern end of the peninsula as it emptied into Boston Harbor. Near the northern end of the peninsula two deep indentations, Mill Cove to the N. and Town Cove to the S., divided the town into what came to be known as the North and South Ends. The most conspicuous feature of the North End was Windmill Hill, now known as Copp's Hill, which stands at the northernmost end of the peninsula, while the most striking feature of the main part of Shawmut was Trimountaine, a high ridge with three peaks that ran from near the shore of the Charles halfway across the peninsula at its broadest part. These were for the most part leveled during the urban development of the town, and only the truncated base of the central one survives as Beacon Hill. Another eminence, named Fort Hill, now totally leveled, dominated the promontory that jutted out into the sea at the S. end of Town Cove. The first settlers in Boston built their homes on the land that sloped down from Trimountaine to the Town Cove, where a large spring gave them a plentiful supply of fresh water. There they were sheltered from the cold N.W. winds of winter and had access to the sea, which early on became the principal source of their sustenance through fishing and trade. In fact, the first ship built in Boston, the *Blessing of the Bay,* was launched as early as 1631. Boston was very fortunate in having a bay deep enough for even the largest vessels to anchor close inshore to the peninsula, from which wharves could be built out over the shallow waters by the shore to load and unload vessels. This process of "wharving out" and the filling in of the shallow waters between that went along with it soon changed the shape of the Shawmut Peninsula, as can be seen from John Bonner's map of Boston in 1722 on p. 30. There one can also see the manner in which the town spread as it grew in population, with the densest concentration of houses around and inland from Town Cove, the main port, and also in the North End, whose shore was also serrated with wharves. Bonner's map is a striking illustration of how Boston faced to the sea and crowded its dwellings close to the wharves, for that was where the town derived its living. The golden emblem of a codfish still hangs prominently in the State House in Boston, symbolizing the principal source of income for the town and the Bay State since the beginning of their history.

Boston: 1630–1649.

The first two decades in Boston's history witnessed intense political and religious discussion—these two areas being intimately related to one another—as the townspeople strove to work out a way of life in their new and unique situation. When the Bay Company was first formed

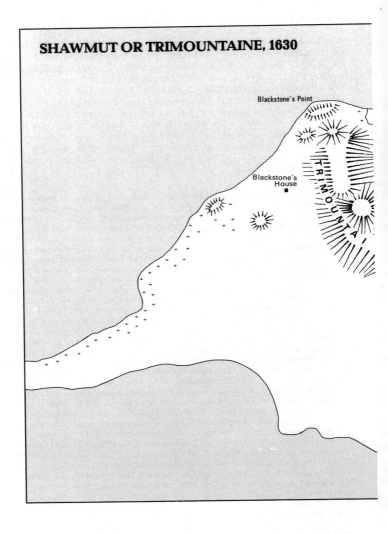

SHAWMUT OR TRIMOUNTAINE, 1630

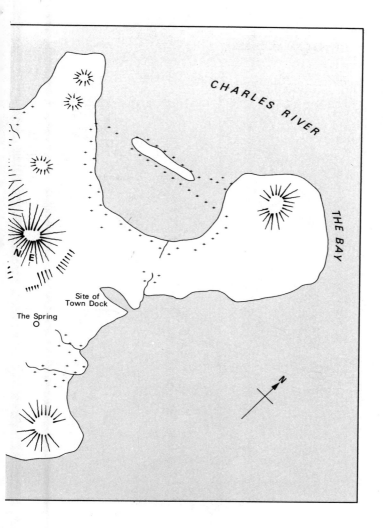

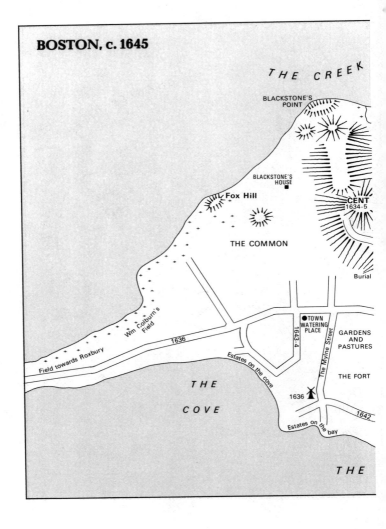

BOSTON, c. 1645

THE CREEK

BLACKSTONE'S POINT

BLACKSTONE'S HOUSE

Fox Hill

CENT
1634-5

THE COMMON

Burial

TOWN WATERING PLACE

Wm Colburn's Field

1636

GARDENS AND PASTURES

THE FORT

The Mylne Street

1843-4

Field towards Roxbury

Estates on the cove

THE COVE

1636

1642

Estates on the bay

THE

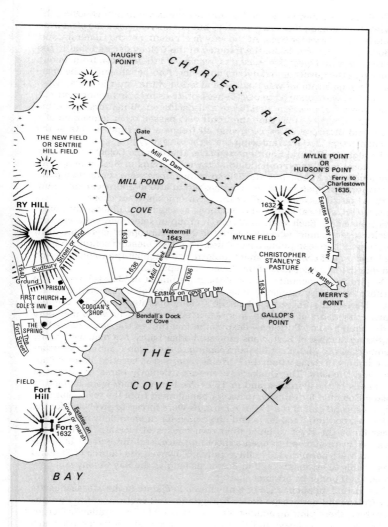

in England the patentees alone had formed the government, choosing the officials from among their own number, but in Massachusetts the electorate would have a far wider base. At the very first meeting of the General Court in Boston, on Oct. 29, 1630, the freemen of the Colony decided that in the future they would elect the assistants, who would then choose from among themselves the governor and deputy governor. Another change in the character of the government was made at a meeting of the Court in 1634, when the freemen were allowed to elect representatives in their various districts, giving them full power to deliberate and decide on all matters that came before the Court. At that time the Court also passed other legislation of a liberal and democratic nature, giving all freemen the right to vote at the annual election, and guaranteeing the right to trial by jury.

Although the General Court enacted laws affecting the Colony as a whole, purely local matters were handled at town meetings in Boston and other communities in Massachusetts. The town meetings were completely democratic forums, open to anyone who wished to attend and speak his mind. At these public assemblies all of the town officials were chosen, all local taxes levied, all local laws and regulations enacted, and all local civic business transacted. Each year, in March, a group of selectmen were elected, usually seven to nine, who dealt with the day-to-day operations of the town government between public assemblies. The town meeting continued to be the basic unit of civic government in Boston throughout the colonial period and into the early decades of the American Republic.

Despite the democratic nature of the government in Massachusetts, the Puritans were very intolerant when it came to religious beliefs and practices. During the 56 years when the Colony operated under its original charter the status of freeman was restricted to those who were members of the church—i.e., Puritans—despite the fact that as the years passed an increasing number of Bostonians professed other faiths. Not only were many members of the Church of England coming to the Colony, but also substantial numbers of those whom the Puritans regarded as heretics, namely Baptists and Quakers. The Quakers received particularly harsh treatment at the hands of the Puritans, and in 1649–51 four of them were hanged in Boston Common for refusing to accept banishment from the town. But during the second half of the 17C the Puritans were forced to give way, for the town was becoming too large and diversified for them to deny members of other faiths the right to build their own houses of worship. In 1677 the Quakers were allowed to open a meeting place, and three years later the Baptists were permitted to build a church. However, the Church of England was unable to establish itself in Boston as long as the Bay Colony still governed itself under its original charter.

The virtual independence of both church and state in the Massachusetts Bay Colony did not escape notice in England, and enemies of the Puritans were busy there plotting against them, most notably Sir Ferdinando Gorges and Captain John Mason. In February 1635 Gorges and Mason concocted a scheme in which the moribund Council for New England surrendered its charter and all of its territorial rights in America, on condition that the King should nullify all other grants of land there, including that of the Massachusetts Bay Colony. The King concurred and granted a new charter to Gorges, Mason, and six other notables, who divided the whole of New England up among themselves, with Sir Ferdinando to act as viceroy. When news of this scheme reached Boston and the other towns of the Bay Colony the settlers immediately sprang to arms and prepared to resist the attempted takeover by Gorges and Mason. Militia companies were organized and began training in Boston and in all the other towns of the Bay Colony, and at town meetings decisions were made to fight in defense of their charter. In the end the military preparations of the colonists proved to be unnecessary, for the attempted land grab by Gorges, Mason, and their group never came about. The King's increasing political difficulties led him to withdraw his active support in the venture, and when Mason died later that year the corporation was dissolved. The Bay Colony faced another crisis in 1638, when the Lords Commissioners of Plantations demanded that the Puritan settlers return their charter, for the Crown was now fully aware that a virtually independent state had emerged on the shores of New England. The people of Massachusetts once again armed themselves and prepared to defend their liberty. However, Governor Winthrop blunted the threat through diplomacy, sending a humble petition to England pledging the loyalty of the settlers, and the charter was saved for the time being.

Early in the spring of 1649 John Winthrop died, after which he was buried with "great solemnity and honour" in what is now the King's Chapel graveyard. His passing marked the end of the first stage of Boston's history, for he had directed the affairs of the town since the day of its founding. At the time of his death Boston was no longer a mere settlement struggling for existence on the hostile shores of the New World, but a thriving town with an international trade and commerce, the acknowledged capital of a virtually independent state.

Boston: 1649–1675. After the death of John Winthrop leadership of the Bay Colony passed to John Endicott, who governed for the next decade. One of the first events of note during Endicott's tenure was the construction in 1650 of a second church, the Old Meeting-House having accommodated the entire populace until that time, but with some 3000 people now resident in the town this was no longer possible. The Second Church of Boston, which was built of wood, was erected at North Sq. in the North End and thus was called Old North, a name it passed on to the other churches that succeeded it in the same area. Then, in 1669, a dispute over broadening the electorate to include all Christians caused a split in the First Church of Boston, with the more liberal members leaving to form their own congregation, the Third Church. A wooden meeting house was built in the South End and thus came to be called the South Church; half a century later, after the erection of a second church in that area, it came to be called the Old South. The Old South, rebuilt in brick in 1729, was in the years before the Revolution the scene of some of the most important town meetings in the history of Boston.

Massachusetts had been relatively free of interference from the mother country during the Protectorate of Cromwell, but after the restoration of the monarchy in 1660 the Crown set out to take a more direct hand in the government of its American colonies. The first move was the re-enactment in 1660 of the Navigation Act, which had been passed during the Protectorate but never enforced. The Navigation Act was part of England's mercantile policy, according to which the colonists were to ship raw materials to the mother country and to buy from England manufactured goods, with this commerce to be carried on only in British vessels with English navigators; besides that, no produce could be sent from one American port to another unless a duty was paid equal to that which would be levied upon it in England. The Act also stipulated that each colonial governor should, at the time of his election, swear an oath that he would uphold this and all other legislation enacted in Parliament. However, as long as the Bay Colony continued to function under its original charter, the governor of Massachusetts never once took the required oath. And so, by sheer defiance, the people of Massachusetts succeeded in evading compliance with the Navigation Act, which would have totally destroyed Boston's trade and commerce.

King Philip's War. In 1675 the colonists of New England were faced with the greatest threat to their existence since they landed on the shores of the New World. Early in that year rumors reached Plymouth that the chief sachem of the Wampanoags, Metacom, whom the colonists called King Philip, was planning to go to war against the white man, breaking a treaty that his father, Massasoit, had agreed with the Pilgrims more than half a century earlier. The war began on June 20, 1675, when a horde of Indians led by King Philip massacred all of the settlers in Swansea, a hamlet of 40 houses on Narragansett Bay. This was the first atrocity in a war that kept New England in a state of siege for three years. Boston itself was never attacked, although there was a massacre at Weymouth, just 12 miles S., but it was the center from which the militia of the New England Confederation was dispatched against the Indians. King Philip himself was defeated and killed on Aug. 12, 1677, but other Indian sachems continued the struggle until midsummer of 1678. By that time most of the Indian braves in New England had been killed and the survivors driven deeper into the wilderness, finally ending the threat to the colonists. But the people of New England had suffered grievously, particularly in Massachusetts, and it was decades before the region fully recovered. Of the 90 towns in Massachusetts at the beginning of the war, 12 were utterly destroyed and more than 40 others suffered death and destruction. With a population of about 25,000, Massachusetts had some 600 of its militia killed in battle, not to mention civilian deaths, a far greater casualty rate than the U.S.A. would suffer in any of the wars in its history to date. More than 100 of those killed were men from Boston, which as the capital of the New England Confederation paid a disproportionately high price in the war, both in blood and money.

The Loss of the Charter. Throughout the course of King Philip's War, Edward Randolph, the Crown's agent in New England, had been gathering information to discredit the Bay Colony and plotting to have its charter revoked. He found allies among a growing faction in Boston, most of them wealthy merchants, who preferred to be ruled by the King rather than by the strict and intolerant Puritan elders and clergy. The leader of this Tory party was Joseph Dudley, a son of Thomas Dudley, who had been deputy governor under John Winthrop. Such was the power of the Tory party in Boston at the time that Dudley was chosen to represent the Bay Colony in England in 1682, after King Charles II had sent a letter to Massachusetts, demanding submission on several issues and threatening to revoke the charter. However, Dudley's mission was a failure, and he returned to Boston to tell the colonists that their charter would be revoked and that they would be governed henceforth by the Crown. The people of Boston gathered in the Old South Meeting-House to decide whether they should submit to the King. After a stirring address by the Rev. Increase Mather, president of Harvard College, they decided unanimously that they would not willingly surrender their charter. But matters were soon taken out of the colonists' hands, for on June 18, 1684, the Court of Chancery issued a decree annulling the charter of the Massachusetts Bay Colony. The colonists appealed the decision, but the Lord Keeper refused the motion and rendered final judgment. When news of this decision reached Boston in January 1685 the General Court ordered a day of prayer and fasting. The decision was not enforced for another year and a half, during which time the colonists continued to govern themselves, but then, on May 15, 1686, Edward Randolph arrived in Boston with the authority to set up a new government under the Crown, appointing Joseph Dudley as president. So, after more than a half-century of freedom, the Massachusetts Bay Colony lost its independence, and within the next few years all of the other English colonies in New England would suffer the same fate.

Massachusetts as a Crown Colony. Joseph Dudley's tenure as president of the Bay Colony proved to be of short duration, for on December 19, 1686, a British warship arrived in Boston with the new royal governor, Sir Edmund Andros. Sir Edmund, a favorite of James II, had been given jurisdiction over all the English colonies from Maine to the Delaware River, and he chose to set up his headquarters in Boston. One of the first measures he took after his arrival was to initiate the construction of an Episcopal church, on the site of the present King's Chapel. At the same time he met with the ministers of the Old South Meeting-House and told them that Episcopal services would be held there until the new church was ready. The ministers flatly refused, but on Good Friday in 1687 Andros forced the sexton to open the building, and members of the Church of England then held services there. For the next two years, the duration of Sir Edmund's rule in Boston, Episcopal services were held in the Old South Church, alternating with the meetings of the regular congregation, who were outraged and humiliated by this arrogant intrusion.

Andros ruled like a despot, issuing decrees and levying taxes without any consultation with the colonists, granting huge tracts of lands to his friends, including common lands and farms already cultivated by homesteaders. Through his principal aide, Joseph Dudley, he kept the populace of Boston completely in check, arresting any who objected to his rule. The autocratic regime of Andros soon brought the colonists to the point of rebellion. On April 4, 1689, word reached Boston that Prince William of Orange had landed in England the previous November and that James II had fled, so it was obvious that Sir Edmund's days as governor were numbered. Two weeks later the people took matters into their own hands, as 1500 militia from Boston and surrounding towns forced the British garrison in the town to surrender without bloodshed, after which they arrested and imprisoned Andros, Dudley, and other officials of the royal government. At the end of that day, April 18, 1689, the bloodless revolt was over and the colonists were once again in control of Boston and the Bay Colony, at least for the time being.

Immediately after the revolt Simon Bradstreet resumed his role as governor, a post from which he had been removed when the charter was revoked in 1686, and on May 26 he and the other members of his Council proclaimed their allegiance to King William and Queen Mary. Six months later Bradstreet received word from the Crown that he should send Andros and Dudley back to England, along with the other officials who had been imprisoned in the revolt, and in February 1690 they were duly shipped off from Boston.

King William's War. In May 1689 William III went to war against France, and early in the following year the conflict spread to America, when Count Frontenac, governor of New France, launched an offensive against the English colonies. In January 1690 the French and their Indian allies attacked several English settlements in New York and New England, massacring many of the villagers and carrying off the survivors, mostly women and children, into captivity in Canada. This was the beginning of what came to be called the French and Indian Wars, an intermittent struggle that would last for 73 years. The first phase of this conflict was known in America as King William's War, a bloody struggle that did not end until 1697.

Massachusetts was the first colony to launch a counterattack against the French. This expedition was commanded by Sir William Phips, a colorful character who later became governor of Massachusetts. In April 1690 Phips led an expedition from Boston to attack the French naval base at Port Royal in Acadia (now the town of Annapolis, in Nova Scotia). The governor of Port Royal surrendered without a struggle, after which all of Acadia fell to the colonial forces. In Aug. of that same year Phips led an even larger force against Montreal. However, because of his inept leadership the expedition failed. Phips was forced to lift his siege and return ignominiously to Boston, and the French regained control of Acadia. Shortly afterward Phips left Boston and returned to England. Less than two years later King William appointed Phips to be governor of the newly organized Province of Massachusetts, which included the territory of the old Bay Colony along with those of Maine and the Plymouth Colony. The King had been much influenced in his decision by the Rev. Increase Mather, pastor of the Old North Church in Boston, of which Phips had been a member. Phips and Mather then set sail from England in March 1692, and on May 14 they landed in Boston, beginning a new chapter in the history of Massachusetts.

Boston as a Royal Provincial Capital. During the period 1692–1774 Boston was the capital of a royal province that extended from Narragansett Bay to Penobscot Bay, excluding only the territory of New Hampshire. Under the new provincial charter, the governor and the lieutenant governor were appointed by the King. The Legislature met in Boston and consisted of two houses, the lower one made up of 75 delegates from towns in the provinces, while the upper chamber had 28 members, with five designated by the King and the others nominated by the delegates. The Crown had veto power over the selection of members of both houses and also over all legislation, while magistrates were appointed by the governor and his Council. Although the people had little real political power under this charter they continued to hold town meetings, and these popular assemblies represented the principal opposition to the Crown during the remainder of the colonial period.

Sir William Phips was the first in a series of eleven royal governors who ruled the Province of Massachusetts from 1692 until 1775. In every case the governor was at constant odds with the Legislature of Massachusetts. The main issue was the refusal of the Legislature to pay the governor a regular salary, on the grounds that he was representing the Crown and not the people of Massachusetts. The governor on his part invariably responded by vetoing the prospective members of the Legislature nominated by the delegates, and also on several occasions proroguing the General Court, so that for long periods the government of the Province came to a standstill.

The Witchcraft Trials. Governor Phips arrived in Boston in the midst of the most extraordinary episode in the history of Massachusetts, the witchcraft hysteria, which began in

Salem in the winter of 1691–92. The drama began when a group of girls and young women in Salem started behaving in a bizarre manner, and a local doctor, after examining them, pronounced them possessed by the Devil. This diagnosis was confirmed by several ministers in Salem, and a number of women were accused of being in league with Satan and having practiced witchcraft on the girls. A wave of hysteria then swept through Salem and other towns in the area, as scores of people were accused by their enemies or the superstitious of being witches. Since Governor Phips had to leave Boston on colonial business, he appointed his lieutenant governor, William Stoughton, to act as chief justice in the ensuing trials. The first of these trials took place on April 11, 1692, in which the General Court found six women from Salem guilty of witchcraft. During the months that followed, a series of such trials resulted in the conviction of some 150 people as witches, and 20 of them were executed. By the spring of 1693 the hysteria had subsided, and when Governor Phips returned to Boston in May of that year he ordered that all of those still imprisoned for witchcraft be released. The General Court later ordered that a day of prayer and fasting be held throughout Massachusetts in atonement for the shameful witchcraft trials, and the surviving victims of the hysteria were given compensation.

Boston: 1700–60. In 1701 the War of the Spanish Succession broke out in Europe, and in 1703 it spread to North America, where it was called Queen Anne's War. This bloody conflict, the second phase of the French and Indian Wars, was fought out mainly in New England, with Massachusetts bearing the brunt of the struggle for a decade. Governor Joseph Dudley organized two expeditions against the French in Port Royal, but both were unsuccessful, as was a third force sent out from England by the Crown in 1712. The war in Europe finally ended in 1713 with the Treaty of Utrecht, in which England received the Hudson Bay region, Newfoundland, and Acadia, after which Port Royal was renamed Annapolis.

In the winter of 1720–21 a terrible smallpox epidemic broke out in Boston, killing 1000 people out of a total population of 16,000. An even worse epidemic of smallpox hit the town in the winter of 1729–30, this time leaving 2000 dead. Boston took a long time to recover from these calamities, and its population remained static at about 15,000 for the next quarter-century, while other towns in Massachusetts were doubling in size.

Then, in 1734, the whole basis of Boston's economy was threatened when Parliament passed the Molasses Act; this was a new step in England's mercantile policy, putting prohibitive duties on imported molasses, rum, sugar, and sugar products, which the colonists had been buying cheaply from the French colonies in North America. The Molasses Act was successfully evaded by the merchants and shippers of Boston, through smuggling and the bribery of customs officials, and it was never strictly enforced. Nevertheless, the hindrance on trade that it represented caused a sharp decline in Boston's ship building industry, so that by 1740 the number of vessels launched annually in the city fell to one-half of what it had been before the Molasses Act was enacted. This in turn caused a decline in all of the other industries that depended on ship building, so that in the 1740s Boston entered a prolonged economic depression.

In 1740 the third phase of the French and Indian Wars began; this was known in Europe as the War of the Austrian Succession and in America as King George's War. The high point of this war for Boston came in 1745, when Governor William Shirley organized a great expedition against the French fortress of Louisbourg, on Cape Breton Island. The expeditionary force, which was commanded by Colonel William Pepperell of the Boston militia, finally captured Louisbourg on June 15, 1745, after a six-week siege. However, it proved to be a hard-won victory, for more than 1000 of the colonial troops did not live to return to Boston, with more than 100 dying in action and the others perishing in an epidemic during the siege. Nevertheless, the people of Massachusetts took considerable pride in this first great victory of colonial arms against a European power, a harbinger of the future. The Crown rewarded Massachusetts by reimbursing it for all of the expenses it had incurred, a payment that helped Boston to recover from its long economic depression and to start the town on the road to recovery. But all of the colonial military efforts came to nothing when the War of the Austrian Succession ended with the Treaty of Aix-la-Chapelle in 1748, for Louisbourg was returned to France in exchange for Madras, which the French had captured during their campaign in India.

The final phase of the French and Indian Wars reversed the previous pattern of that long conflict, for it began in North America in 1754, and in 1755 it spread to Europe, where it was called the Seven Years' War. The conflict arose out of English colonial expansion into the upper valley of the Ohio River, beginning in 1753. The following year the Marquis Duquesne, governor of New France, sent an expedition of 1500 men to occupy that territory and defend it with a line of fortresses. The advance of the French into the Ohio Valley convinced the royal governors of the English colonies that they should join forces and agree on a joint plan of military action. Thus began a war that dragged on for a decade, finally coming to an end with the Peace of Paris in Feb. 1763. The last phase of the French and Indian Wars had been a great drain upon Massachusetts and the other English colonies, but at the same time the Americans had acquired military experience that would prove invaluable to them in the coming struggle for independence. This was particularly true in the case of those who had held positions of leadership in the allied British-colonial armies, most notably George Washington, who would later command the Continental Army in the Revolutionary War.

Meanwhile, another smallpox epidemic had hit Boston in the winter of 1759–60, although fortunately it was not as severe as those of 1720 and 1730. Then, just as Boston was recovering from the epidemic, a great fire that began on the morning of March 20, 1760, burned out part of the town, destroying 150 shops and houses and leaving 220 families homeless. No one died in the conflagration, or in a second fire, a month later, that destroyed Faneuil Hall, the large market building that served as the principal place of assembly for town meetings at the time. These catastrophes lowered morale in Boston, and several ministers lectured to their congregations that their miseries had been visited upon them by God as punishment for their sins.

Prelude to Revolution: 1760–1765. Such was the state of Boston when Sir Francis Bernard arrived on Aug. 2, 1760, to take up his post as governor, with Thomas Hutchinson serving as his lieutenant governor. Sir Francis, in his first address to the Massachusetts Legislature, tactlessly informed the representatives that "they derived their blessing from their subjugation to Great Britain," which hardly endeared him to the people of Boston. Soon afterward there was further cause for aggravation when the chief custom officer, Charles Paxton, petitioned the General Court for Writs of Assistance, documents which would enable his officials to enter homes, shops, and warehouses in order to carry out their duties and to seize any smuggled goods that they found. The people of Boston were outraged by this, and soon afterward their leaders chose a brilliant but erratic young lawyer named James Otis to contest the Writs of Assistance before the General Court. The Court convened in Feb. 1761, with Thomas Hutchinson acting as chief justice, to hear the arguments for and against the proposed regulations. Otis argued against the Writs in an impassioned speech that lasted for four hours, swaying both the packed audience and the members of the Court with his eloquence. This historic address convinced many in the audience that the time had come for the colonies to break away from England and form their own nation. Among those present who felt this way was John Adams, a young lawyer who later succeeded George Washington as President of the United States of America. As Adams later wrote, describing the popular reaction to the speech by James Otis: "Then and there the child Independence was born."

The next steps on the road to revolution were taken after the conclusion of the final phase of the French and Indian Wars. In April 1763 George Grenville became prime minister of England, with Charles Townshend acting as trade minister. Townshend had made a thorough study of American affairs, and he proposed some drastic measures. Among other things, he found that it cost England more than three times as much to maintain customs houses in America as it received from all the American colonies in customs fees. He resolved to correct this imbalance, for the Crown was in need of revenue to administer and defend the vast territory it had obtained from France in North America, as well as for the expenses it had incurred in the last phase of the French and Indian Wars. Grenville set Townshend's program into motion in 1764 by having Parliament pass the Sugar Act, a re-enactment of the Molasses Act of 1734, whose avowed purpose was not only to raise money in the colonies but also to reform their governments to give the Crown more control. In that same year Parliament passed the Colonial Currency Act, which prevented the colonies from paying their debts in depreciated colonial currency. This act created an acute shortage of money in the colonies at a time when the Sugar Act was ruining the colonial trade to the West Indies, a commerce that had originally supplied the revenue necessary for Americans to pay their debts in England.

In 1765 Grenville persuaded Parliament to pass the Stamp Act, which was designed to raise money for the Crown by requiring stamps to be placed on all legal documents, newspapers, and pamphlets, as well as on almanacs and playing cards. That same year Parliament also passed the Quartering Act, which allowed British troops to be put up at public hostels in the colonies if there was not sufficient room for them in the local barracks.

This legislation, particularly the Stamp Act, alarmed and enraged the colonists. When news of the Stamp Act's passage reached Boston the populace rioted, causing such a disturbance that Governor Bernard and Lieutenant Governor Hutchinson fled for safety to the fortress on Castle Island. In the Massachusetts Legislature a series of 14 resolves were prepared by Samuel Adams, asserting that the inherent and inalienable rights of the colonists had been violated by the Stamp Act, and these were published and distributed throughout the 13 colonies. One of the resolves called for a congress of the American colonies to form a united front against the Stamp Act and other such legislation. Delegates from nine of the colonies, including Massachusetts, met in Albany in Oct. 1765, at which time they drafted addresses to the King and both houses of Parliament, petitioning for the repeal of the Stamp Act. The petition was ignored and the Stamp Act went into effect on Nov. 1, 1765, and on that day all of the church bells of Boston tolled mournfully while a procession of 3000 townspeople marched in protest against the legislation. The people of Boston refused to use the stamps, and since these were needed on legal documents Governor Bernard ordered all courts in Massachusetts to be closed. The following day, at a town meeting the citizens of Boston appointed John Adams, Samuel Adams, and John to present their case for the reopening of the courts. The Sons of

Captain John Bonner's map of Boston, 1722

Liberty, a group of patriotic Bostonians, wrote letters to similar groups in other colonies, asking them to consider actions that might be taken to repeal the Stamp Act. Then, in the spring of 1766, the colonists received news that Parliament had in fact repealed the Stamp Act, but at the same time they were informed of the passage of the Declaratory Act, which stated that the King, with the consent of Parliament, had authority to make laws to bind the colonies in all respects. This legislation was not long in coming, for later that year Parliament passed the Townshend Acts, which levied duties on imported glass, paper, painters' colors, and tea. Governor Bernard refused to call the Legislature into session to discuss the issue, so the

people of Boston called a series of town meetings under the leadership of Samuel Adams, convening in either Faneuil Hall or the Old South Meeting-House. When the Massachusetts Legislature finally reconvened in January 1768 popular feeling against the Townshend Acts was so widespread that the delegates carried on the struggle in the same spirit as did the citizens in the town meetings, led here too by Samuel Adams. On February 11, 1768, Adams introduced in the House of Representatives a letter protesting against the Townshend Acts, asserting that they were "infringements on the natural and constitutional rights" of Americans, since they had no representation in the Parliament that passed the legislation. The House approved

John Adams, 1783, a portrait by John Singleton Copley (Courtesy of the Harvard University Portrait Collection, Bequest of Ward Nicholas Boylston, 1828, to Harvard College)

the letter by a large majority, whereupon copies were sent to the King and to the other colonial assemblies. The circular letter brought encouraging replies from the other colonies, and the leading merchants in most of the towns entered into an agreement not to import English goods until the repeal of the Townshend Acts.

The vehement opposition to the Townshend Acts in Boston led to increased tension between the townspeople and the British authorities, and it was inevitable that this would eventually erupt into violence. On the morning of June 10, 1768, the director of customs, Joseph Harrison, tried to seize a sloop owned by John Hancock on a charge of smuggling. A mob of more than 1000 men tried to prevent this and in the ensuing riot Harrison and

The second Faneuil Hall, built apparently to the same design as the original structure of 1742 (1789 engraving)

his son were beaten up and their house was sacked. The mob ran amuck and Governor Bernard was forced to flee to his country estate in Roxbury, while the royal commissioners took refuge on Castle Island. Soon afterward Hancock was arrested and arraigned, but in March 1769 the charges were dropped, undoubtedly because of fear of the violent public reaction that would occur if he were put on trial.

The riot and the subsequent frantic reports of Governor Bernard alarmed the Earl of Hillsborough, secretary of state for the colonies. He dispatched orders to General Thomas Gage in New York, telling him to send two regiments of British troops to Boston, after which he ordered still more soldiers to be sent there from Ireland. The first of these arrived in Boston Harbor on Sept. 30, 1768, aboard 18 troop transports, and by the time General Gage himself appeared, on Oct. 15, there were 4000 British soldiers occupying the town, an enormous number considering that the population was then only about 16,000.

As soon as the soldiers were quartered in Boston, Samuel Adams published a series of letters of protest against the British occupation, and these were circulated throughout the colonies. In June 1769 the House of Representatives protested to Governor Bernard because their meeting place, the Town House, was surrounded by British troops, with two cannon aimed directly at the front door. But Bernard ignored their protest and shortly afterward vetoed 11 delegates whom the Legislature had nominated for the Council. The Legislature was outraged by this and sent a petition to the King asking for Bernard's recall. Bernard retaliated by proroguing the Legislature until Jan. 1770, after which he departed for England. In Jan. 1770 the King himself prorogued the Legislature for another six months, and later in that year he appointed Thomas Hutchinson to be governor of the Province, the last civilian to hold the post under the Crown. Hutchinson was unwilling to face the same kind of popular opposition that his predecessor had endured, so soon afterward he moved the seat of the Legislature to Cambridge, where it remained for the next two years.

Bonner's new map of Boston, 1769

During the winter of 1769–70 tension between the people of Boston and the British army of occupation grew, with almost daily altercations between the townspeople and the redcoats. By the end of winter public opinion in Boston was so bitterly anti-British that it needed only a spark to bring about an explosion, and this was not long in coming. On the evening of March 5, 1770, a squad of eight British soldiers under the command of Captain Thomas Preston fired into a crowd of hostile townspeople, killing five and wounding five others. This incident, which came to be called the Boston Massacre

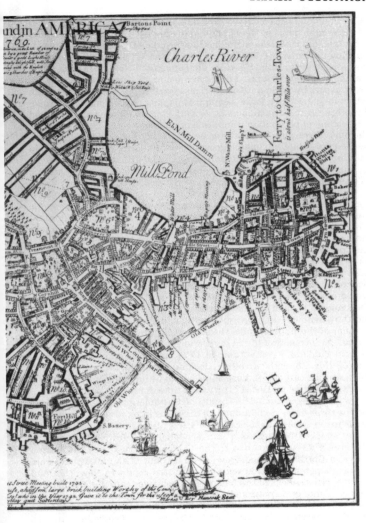

(see below), was the point of no return in relations between the people of Boston and the Crown, and from that time on revolution was inevitable.

The American boycott of English goods that began in 1768 was so effective that it caused serious financial losses to British merchants and shippers. As a result Lord North, who became prime minister in April 1770, that same month persuaded Parliament to repeal all of the Townshend Acts except for that which imposed a tax on tea. By this action he hoped to revive British trade to America, and also to weaken the spirit of united opposition to the Crown among the colonists. In this he was partially successful, for in July 1770 the merchants of New York began importing British goods again, except for tea, and they sent a circular letter to the other colonies suggesting that they do the same. But the people of Massachusetts and the other colonies refused to do so and angrily denounced the New York merchants as cowards. At a town meeting in Boston the circular letter from New York was torn to pieces by Samuel Adams and flung contemptuously to the ground, after which he published a letter saying that popular opposition to the Crown would continue until all such legislation as the tax on tea was repealed and the British army of occupation removed from Boston.

So the boycott continued over the issue of the tax on tea, which thereafter became the focal point for popular opposition to the Crown. At a town meeting in Boston on Oct. 30, 1772, Samuel Adams moved that a Committee of Correspondence be formed for the purpose of communicating with patriotic groups elsewhere in the colonies. The motion was carried by a nearly unanimous majority, after which Samuel Adams and Dr. Joseph Warren prepared a statement of the rights and grievances of the American people. That same day the Committee sent this statement in a circular letter to 80 towns in Massachusetts, suggesting that they too form committees of correspondence, and soon the idea spread to all of the other colonies.

In the spring of 1773 the East India Company applied to Parliament for assistance in solving its financial problems, which were largely due to the American boycott on tea. Parliament passed an act allowing the Company to import tea from China without paying duty when it arrived in England. This would enable the Company to sell its tea in America at a lower price than the smuggled Dutch tea that was available there, even with the added tax, and they believed that the colonists would then buy their stocks and relieve them of the huge surplus that had built up since the beginning of the boycott. After passage of the legislation several ships loaded with tea set sail from England in the autumn of 1773, and the first of these arrived in Boston on Nov. 28, with two others docking shortly afterward. According to regulations, the cargoes of these ships had to be unloaded and registered at the Customs House by Dec. 17, by which time the tea tax had to be paid. But on the evening of Dec. 16 a group of Bostonians dressed as Indians boarded the three ships and dumped all of the tea into the sea, an operation that came to be called the Boston Tea Party. Governor Hutchinson was profoundly shocked by this act of brazen defiance of British law, and he immediately wrote a report of it to the Crown. The next day the Boston Committee of Correspondence drew up an account of the affair, and Paul Revere was dispatched to ride with copies of the report to New York and Philadelphia, where news of the Boston Tea Party was received with joyous celebrations. Among the patriots in Boston there was a mood of calm pride, and the feeling that a final break with England was now inevitable. As Samuel Adams wrote at the time: "the Dye is cast: The People have passed the River and cutt away the Bridge."

When news of the Boston Tea Party first reached England, on Jan. 20, 1774, there was a furor, and in both the ministry and Parliament the consensus was that the Bostonians should be severely punished for their actions. In March, Lord North persuaded Parliament to pass the Port Act, which decreed that Boston Harbor should be closed to all shipping as of June 1, 1774, unless the townspeople agreed to make restitution to the East India Company and to pay the tax on the tea that had been destroyed. This was followed by a series of bills which in America were called the Coercive

Acts, whose purpose was to impose additional punishments on the colonists for their rebellious actions, particularly in Massachusetts, and also to take virtually all power away from the colonial legislatures and popular assemblies such as Boston's town meetings. As a final step Lord North dismissed Thomas Hutchinson as governor and replaced him with General Gage. Simultaneously, the British admiralty ordered all available troop transports and men-of-war to sail to Boston, while the War Office issued orders for 11 more regiments of troops to occupy the town.

On May 5, 1774, Boston received official notice of the Port Act, and eight days later General Gage officially took office as military governor of Massachusetts. On June 1 Boston Harbor was ordered closed, since restitution had not been made to the East India Company nor had the tea tax been paid. The British navy then enforced an embargo on Boston, allowing no shipping of any kind to enter or leave the harbor, even closing down the ferry to Charlestown. The embargo completely cut off Boston from its principal source of income—sea borne commerce—resulting in widespread bankruptcy, unemployment, and impoverishment. But as soon as news of Boston's plight spread through the colonies, towns from Maine to Georgia sent help in the form of money and food supplies, along with messages of support from all of the committees of correspondence. On May 27 the Virginia Legislature sent a circular letter to the other 12 colonies calling for a Continental Congress, inviting Massachusetts to set the time and place of the meeting. The Continental Congress convened for the first time on Sept. 5, 1774, with Massachusetts represented by Samuel and John Adams, Thomas Cushing, and Robert Paine. By that time the last of the Coercive Acts had gone into effect, nullifying the Charter of 1692 and depriving the people of Massachusetts of virtually all forms of self-government.

When Samuel Adams and the other delegates left for the Continental Congress, Dr. Joseph Warren took charge of the patriotic movement in Boston, where events were moving rapidly toward a crisis. On Sept. 5 General Gage began fortifying the Neck, so as to cut off the only approach to Boston by land. On Sept. 30 Gage prorogued the Legislature, but the representatives ignored his dismissal, and a week later they convened in Salem. There they organized themselves into a provincial congress, electing John Hancock as president, after which they moved to Concord. On Oct. 27 the Massachusetts Congress elected a Committee of Safety, with Dr. Joseph Warren serving as chairman, and charged the members with the task of acquiring and storing arms and ammunition for use by the provincial militia. The first Massachusetts Congress dissolved itself in December, but a second one convened in Cambridge on Feb. 1, 1775, at which time it began organizing and staffing the provincial militia. Part of this militia, an elite force later to be known as the minutemen, volunteered to be ready at a moment's notice if General Gage attempted to take military action against the colonists.

In Feb. 1775 the Crown declared that the Province of Massachusetts was in a state of rebellion, after which legislation was passed closing all the ports of New England and prohibiting American fishermen from using the Newfoundland fishing grounds. Parliament also voted to increase the British army of occupation in Boston to 10,000 troops. In the meantime every community in Massachusetts was organizing and drilling its local militia, many of whom had seen service in the French and Indian War. The Coercive Acts were defied, and there was tremendous public pressure applied to prevent anyone from serving in any official capacity under the Crown, bringing the government of Massachusetts to a standstill. By the spring of

1775 the Crown and the people of Massachusetts were so totally alienated that there was no hope of reconciliation, and only a spark was needed to set off a war. This would not be long in coming.

Boston During the Revolution. The Provincial Congress of Massachusetts met again at Concord on March 22, 1775, remaining in session until April 15. After its adjournment Samuel Adams and John Hancock went to Lexington to visit their friend the Rev. Jonas Clark, intending to stay in his house for a few days before going on to Philadelphia, where the Second Continental Congress was scheduled to begin on May 10. During the previous winter General Gage had received orders from the Crown to arrest Adams and Hancock and other leaders of the patriots in Boston, but he had refrained from doing so in fear that it might provoke a violent reaction on the part of the populace. But when Gage received word from his spies that Adams and Hancock were in Lexington he decided to send a detachment of troops to arrest them there. On April 18 Gage ordered Colonel Francis Smith to take a detachment of 800 troops to Lexington to arrest Adams and Hancock, after which he was to proceed to Concord to seize the provincial arms and ammunition that his spies had reported to be stored there.

After sunset on April 18 Colonel Smith marched his men across Boston Common to Back Bay, where boats were waiting to transport them across the Charles River to Cambridge. When news of this came to Joseph Warren he dispatched William Dawes and Paul Revere to warn Adams and Hancock, and also to alert the minutemen along the way that the British were coming. Dawes and Revere did so, and Adams and Hancock made their escape the next morning, just before the advance guard of the British army reached Lexington. When the British marched into Lexington they found waiting for them on the village green 130 militiamen under the command of Captain John Parker. There was a brief exchange of fire in which ten Americans were killed and ten more wounded, whereas only two of the redcoats suffered minor wounds. The British then marched on to Concord, where they made a house-to-house search for colonial armaments, destroying or damaging what little they found. While the search was in progress some 400 American militiamen attacked a British unit of 90 troops that had been guarding Concord Bridge, and after a brief exchange of fire the redcoats broke and ran. This too was only a brief skirmish, with three British soldiers killed and nine wounded, whereas the Americans had two dead and two wounded. But, minor though it may have been, the Battle of Concord Bridge has great historical significance, since it was the first victory for the Americans over the British in the Revolutionary War, which had now begun in earnest.

The British march back from Concord soon turned into a running battle, with militiamen from all the towns along the route firing on the British from cover on both sides of the road. The British reached Lexington, where they met a relief force of 1200 redcoats commanded by General Percy. They stopped to regroup and make a stand against the Americans. Percy then decided to march to Charlestown rather than cross on the bridge from Cambridge to Brighton, for he knew that the span would have been dismantled by the local militia. The running battle continued after the British resumed their march, and the redcoats suffered heavy casualties before they crossed Charlestown Neck at nightfall, after which they were ferried across to Boston by the British navy. Before the night was through all of the surviving redcoats were back in their barracks, and when roll call was taken the next morning the toll was recorded: 73 British soldiers dead and nearly 200 wounded, with officers making a disproportionately high percentage of the casualties. It was another and even greater victory for the Americans, who had 49 killed and 41 wounded. There was great pride throughout Massachusetts as news spread of these first victories of provincial arms against the King's troops, but at the same time there was the very sobering realization that there could now be no turning back from the abyss of war.

While the British soldiers were being ferried across the Charles on the night of April 19—20, provincial militia were converging on Boston from all of the surrounding towns for 100 miles around. Those who stood on Copp's Hill or Beacon Hill that night could see watchfires burning beyond Charlestown Neck, Roxbury, and Boston Neck, where the provincial militiamen had already set up their advance lines; the siege of Boston had begun. General Artemas Ward was given command of the provincial forces, and Joseph Warren succeeded John Hancock as president of the Provincial Congress, which soon assembled in Watertown. Within a few days some 16,000 provincial militiamen had taken up positions in a great arc about 16 miles long from Charlestown Neck to Boston Neck, cutting off the town from the mainland and penning up the British inside. But the provincial forces had virtually no military training or organization, and ammunition supply was very limited. General Gage was aware of this and yet he made no move to mount a counterattack against the Americans, for he had sent a message to England asking for reinforcements and intended to remain where he was until they arrived.

While the siege of Boston was ending its third week the provincial delegates were arriving in Philadelphia for the Second Continental Congress, which convened there on May 10. The most important decision taken at the Congress was the formation of a Continental Army under the command of General George Washington. Washington left Philadelphia on June 19 to set up his headquarters in Cambridge, so that he could command the forces besieging Boston, not knowing that just two days before the American forces there had just engaged in one of the most important battles of the Revolutionary War.

While the Continental Congress had been meeting in Philadelphia, events had been moving slowly but inexorably ahead in Boston and its environs. In the weeks following the fighting at Lexington and Concord there was a great movement of people to and from Boston, with Tories from the surrounding communities seeking the protection of the British army in Boston, while those in sympathy with the rebels left to join the militiamen or to take refuge with families or friends in the countryside. The exodus from Boston was so great that by the end of May there were fewer than 7000 civilians left in Boston of the pre war population of 16,000.

On May 25 the reinforcements requested by Gage arrived in Boston, bringing the total number of British troops there to about 10,000. With the new troops came three of the highest-ranking generals in the British army: Sir William Howe, Sir Henry Clinton, and John Burgoyne, popularly known as Gentleman Johnny. General Howe brought with him orders to reorganize the military command structure in Boston; thenceforth he was to be commander-in-chief of the British troops in the town, with Clinton and Burgoyne as his principal aides, while Gage was to serve strictly as the military governor of the province. Then, just a few days later, Howe formulated a plan for routing the American forces besieging Boston, beginning with the British occupation of Bunker Hill in Charlestown and Dorchester Heights, on the mainland, just beyond Boston Neck.

While Howe was making preparations for this campaign, news of his plan reached the Committee of Safety in Cambridge, and they immediately took steps to forestall it. They organized a force of 1200 militiamen and placed it under the command of Colonel William Prescott, with orders to occupy Bunker Hill before the British made their move. Prescott's force assembled on Cambridge Common at sunset on June 16, after which they marched off to Charlestown under cover of night. Prescott's instructions were to fortify Bunker Hill, the eminence that ran down the ridge of the peninsula from Charlestown Neck, but his aides argued that the lower hill, near the far end of the peninsula, would be far more defensible. This was Breed's Hill, and Prescott finally agreed that they should build their main fortifications there. But in the confusion of combat and in the years to follow it came to be called Bunker Hill, giving that name to the battle fought there the next day.

Prescott spent the night directing his men in building a fortification atop Breed's Hill, while General Israel Putnam entrenched himself on Bunker Hill, to defend against any British force that might try to land farther up the peninsula or attack across Charlestown Neck. At dawn the British spotted the hordes of men digging on Breed's Hill, and soon the battery on Copp's Hill began bombarding the American position, as did all of the British warships anchored in the Charles. However, the bombardment did little damage to the fortifications and killed only a single American militiaman.

Early that morning General Howe decided that he would lead an immediate and direct attack on the American position, but it was 3 p.m. before his entire force of 2000 men was landed in Charlestown and ready for battle, with General Pigot as second-in-command. The first British assault against the fortifications on Breed's Hill failed, as the Americans held their fire until the last moment, so that their vollies had a devastating effect. Both sides of the British line broke and ran in the face of this withering fire, retreating back to the landing place. While he re-formed his men for a second assault Howe ordered the battery on Copp's Hill to begin bombarding the town of Charlestown, since Pigot had reported that he had been fired on from snipers in the houses there, and soon the town was a smoking ruin. Howe ordered a second assault on the American position on Breed's Hill, but this was driven back with even greater casualties. Howe now sent word for a detachment of 400 marines to be ferried over from Boston, and when they arrived and formed their ranks he ordered a third assault. The Americans were almost completely out of ammunition, and when the British began to penetrate their defenses Prescott ordered a retreat. He himself was the last American to get out alive, but Joseph Warren was killed in the hand-to-hand fighting that took place when the redcoats swarmed into the fort. Prescott led his men in an orderly withdrawal from the peninsula, with Putnam covering his retreat until all of the surviving Americans had crossed Charlestown Neck and marched to safety behind the provincial lines at Prospect Hill, near Cambridge.

After the Battle of Bunker Hill, as it came to be called, both sides took stock of their losses. According to Gage's account, 2600 British troops took part in the battle, of whom 254 were killed outright and 830 wounded, with 250 men dying later of their wounds. The number of Americans who took part in the battle was somewhere between 1500 and 1700, and their casualty toll was 140 killed, 271 wounded, and 30 captured by the enemy. Although the British technically won the battle, since they succeeded in driving the Americans out of Charlestown, it was a Pyrrhic victory for them because of their extremely high casualty rate. It was also a political defeat for the Crown because of the enormous uplift that it gave to American morale, to learn that colonial militiamen could hold their own against the King's troops. When George Washington received news of the battle a few days later, en route to his new headquarters in Cambridge, he expressed his satisfaction at its outcome, saying that "the liberties of the country are now safe."

Washington arrived in Cambridge on July 2, 1775, and on the following day he officially took command of the Continental Army. At that time this consisted almost entirely of the 16,000 New England militiamen who were engaged in the siege of Boston, of whom 11,500 were from Massachusetts, but during July the Continental Congress sent Washington an additional 3000 men from Pennsylvania, Maryland, and Virginia. Washington spent the summer and autumn of 1775 trying to form the disorganized and undisciplined militia units into a regular army, an extremely difficult task that so frustrated him that he almost despaired of ever being able to accomplish it. Meanwhile, he had to keep the Continental Army in their defense lines around Boston, as the siege of the town continued through the winter of 1775–76. By that time General Gage had been recalled to England, leaving General Howe in complete charge of both the civilian administration and the Boston garrison, which now numbered some 13,500 troops, almost double the civilian population. Despite the large force under his command, Howe made no move to break the siege or to attack the American troops surrounding Boston; in fact, he suggested to the Crown that his army should abandon Boston and occupy New York. On the other side, many American leaders became impatient with Washington's failure to attack the British army; John Hancock even urged him to burn Boston down if that was the only way he could drive the redcoats out. But Washington bided his time, for he had already formulated a plan to capture Boston, he hoped without bloodshed or destruction. The plan began to take form on March 1, 1776, when General Henry Knox arrived in Cambridge with many cannon that had been carted on sledges from Fort Ticonderoga after the Americans had captured it from the British. On the night of March 4–5 Washington assembled a force of 2000 men under the command of General Ward to haul the cannon to Dorchester Heights and build a fortification there. In order to cover the movements of these soldiers and to distract the British, Washington ordered his artillery batteries in Somerville, East Cambridge, and Roxbury to bombard Boston, a furious cannonade that continued throughout the night, with the British on their part keeping up a lively fire in return. While this thundering artillery fire was going on, General Ward's men were busy building the fortifications on top of Dorchester Heights and dragging the siege guns into position on the summit of the hill. After dawn Howe saw with astonishment what the Americans had done. Soon afterward the commander of the British fleet sent word to Howe that he would have to leave Boston Harbor unless the Americans were dislodged from Dorchester Heights, for from there their siege guns could easily destroy his warships. At first Howe made plans for General Percy to take 3000 men and attack the American position in an amphibious operation, but a violent storm on the night of March 5–6 prevented him from doing so. By that time Howe could see that the fort on Dorchester Heights was virtually unassailable, and so he sent word to Washington that he would withdraw his troops from Boston, and promised that he would not harm the town or its inhabitants if he was not attacked during the evacuation. Washington agreed, though unofficially, and Howe immediately began to prepare for the evacuation. Howe's preparations were complete by March 17, and on that morning all of the British troops, who numbered 8900, boarded 78 vessels that had assembled in Boston Harbor. Along with them embarked more than a thousand Tory civilians, who left with the British for fear of what might become of them when the rebels took over the town. The flotilla left the harbor during the course of the day and headed for Halifax; while they were doing so, General Ward entered the town with 500 American troops. General Washington arrived the following day, and though he gravely acknowledged the cheers of the townspeople he did not mark the occasion by speech-

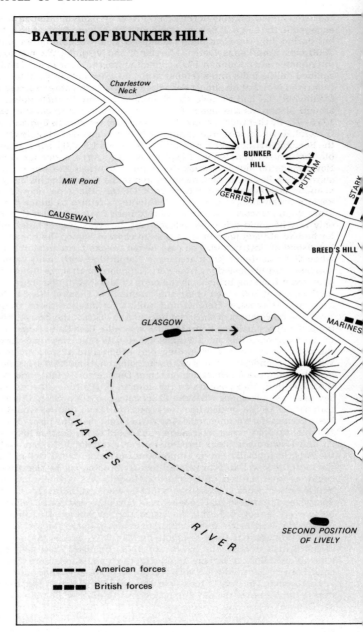

BATTLE OF BUNKER HILL

Charlestow Neck

Mill Pond

CAUSEWAY

N

GLASGOW

CHARLES

RIVER

BUNKER HILL

PUTNAM

STARK

GERRISH

BREED'S HILL

MARINES

SECOND POSITION OF LIVELY

- - - American forces
▬▬▬ British forces

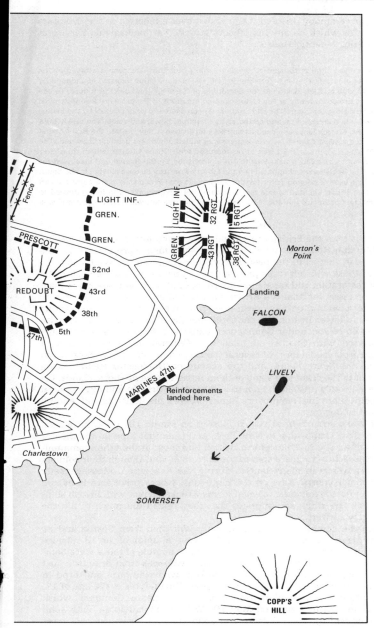

making or ceremony. Instead, he presided over a meeting at the Old State House, after which he and his officers attended a thanksgiving service at the Old Brick Meeting-House.

Boston was a sad sight at the end of the siege. Many buildings had been destroyed by the American bombardment just before the British evacuation. Other houses, abandoned by the patriots who had left Boston at the beginning of the siege, had been torn down by the redcoats for firewood. Many of the historic public buildings of Boston were also destroyed or damaged during the siege. The Old South had been used as a riding school by the British Cavalry, who had chopped up and carted away its pulpit, pews, and seats. The newly built Brattle Street Church had been used as barracks for British troops, as had the Hollis Street Church and the West Church, whose steeple was pulled down and used for firewood. The Old North Church on North Sq (not to be confused with Christ Church, which thereafter took the name of the Old North) was totally demolished by the British and also used for firewood. The British even chopped down the Liberty Tree, the historic old elm in the South End that had been a rallying point for the Sons of Liberty. When they were cutting down the tree the British shouted taunts and insults at the townspeople who had gathered to watch, but the Bostonians had the last laugh: one of the redcoats fell from the tree and was killed.

A few days after the British evacuation a town meeting was held in the Old Brick Meeting-House, at which time the selectmen were chosen for the coming year, just as in the past. Boston then began to resume its old way of life, as those who left it the previous spring began to return and start the work of restoration and repair. But there was still a general feeling of insecurity, for many felt that the British fleet would appear at any moment to attack the town and perhaps even attempt to reoccupy it. A British flotilla remained in lower Boston Bay for three months after the evacuation, with several men-of-war under Commodore Banks escorting seven troop transports loaded with Scottish Highlanders. General Benjamin Lincoln of Hingham organized a force of several thousand militiamen from Boston and towns on the South Shore, and the cannon on Dorchester Heights were hauled out to the coast and some of them ferried to the offshore islands. On June 14 Lincoln's artillery began to bombard the British, and after several of his ships were hit Commodore Banks ordered his flotilla to sail, ending the threat to Boston.

After Washington's brief visit to Boston on March 18, 1776, he moved his army from Cambridge to New York, and from that time on the theater of war shifted south. Thenceforth Boston and most of the other communities in Massachusetts were spared the horrors of war, though their soldiers fought elsewhere in many battles during the Revolution. Massachusetts made a major contribution on the high seas, where privateers built and manned in Boston and other coastal towns wreaked havoc with British shipping, while the ships and supplies that they seized did much to aid the American war effort.

During the course of the Revolutionary War men from Boston and its environs played an important part in the eventual union of the 13 colonies and their emergence as a new nation. The most notable of these were Samuel Adams, John Hancock, and John Adams, who was from Braintree, just S. of Boston, along with Benjamin Franklin, who was born and bred in Boston before going off to begin a new life in Philadelphia at the age of 17. All four of them were leaders in the Second Continental Congress, which convened for the first time on May 10, 1775, in Philadelphia, with John Hancock presiding. John Adams and John Hancock were the two most influential members of the committee that drafted the American Declaration of Independence, and both of them made significant changes in the original document drafted by Thomas Jefferson before it was signed by Congress on July 4, 1776. John Adams was a leader in the movement to have the 13 states frame their individual constitutions as preparation for writing a federal constitution. In 1778 a popularly elected convention in Massachusetts accepted a constitution drawn up largely by John Adams, and this was ratified on June 7, 1780, by which time all of the other states had done the same. The following year the first federal constitution, called the Articles of Confederation, came into effect. Though it proved a weak and ineffective form of government, it did bind the states together until the framing of the present Constitution of the U.S., which was signed in Philadelphia on Sept. 17, 1787. John Adams and Franklin spent the latter years of the war in France, looking after American interests there. On Feb. 6, 1778, Adams and Franklin signed an agreement with the French foreign minister, the Comte de Vergennes, in which the French and the Americans became military allies and agreed to a commercial treaty. This brought France into the war against Britain and was a major factor in the final surrender of Cornwallis at Yorktown on Oct. 19, 1781. Adams and Franklin, with John Jay of New York, stayed on in France for the long and difficult negotiations that led up to the signing of the Peace of Versailles on Sept. 3, 1783, officially ending the Revolutionary War and establishing the United States of America as an independent nation.

Boston: 1783–89. The six years that followed the end of the Revolutionary War are known as the critical period in the history of the U.S. The Articles of Confederation did not really bind the 13 states into a firm union, and during those years centrifugal forces threatened to tear the new nation asunder. This was particularly true in Massachusetts, where in Sept. 1786 the farmers in the western part of the state began an insurrection under the leadership of Captain Daniel Shays. Shays and his followers were rebelling against the federal government's financial policy, which had ruined many farmers in New England and sent hundreds of them to debtors' prisons. At the outset of Shays' Rebellion, as it came to be called, Governor James Bowdoin organized a force of 4400 militiamen under General Lincoln to put down the rebels. The insurrection, widespread though it was, was suppressed within a matter of weeks without serious casualties on either side. Shays, along with all of the other leaders of the rebellion, was eventually granted amnesty when John Hancock succeeded Bowdoin as governor in April 1787. Shays' Rebellion greatly alarmed George Washington and other American political leaders, and gave considerable impetus to the formation of a stronger central government with a more effective constitution. Public opinion in Boston was at first divided, with Samuel Adams and John Hancock lukewarm. But the Federalists, those who favored a stronger union of the states, eventually won over Adams and Hancock to their side, and with their support the new federal Constitution was on Feb. 6, 1788, ratified by Massachusetts. On June 21 of the same year New Hampshire became the ninth state to ratify the Constitution, whereupon it officially came into effect throughout the new nation. The first election under the new Constitution was held on April 6, 1789, when electors from the states that had ratified the covenant unanimously chose George Washington to be the first President of the U.S., after which John Adams was elected Vice-President by a large majority. In the autumn of 1789 Washington made a state visit to Boston, where the townspeople greeted him with great enthusiasm and warmth, in recognition of his determined leadership in the struggle for American independence.

By the time of Washington's visit Boston had completely recovered from the stagnation into which it had sunk during the British occupation, and once again its merchants and shippers were engaged in the ocean-borne commerce that had always been the basis of the town's prosperity. But now the ships of Massachusetts sailed even farther abroad in their search for profit, and in 1786 a merchant ship from Salem, *The Grand Turk,* circumnavigated the globe on a trading venture to China. Within the next two years *The Grand Turk* was followed by other ships from Salem and Boston, and the China trade was in full progress, pouring wealth into the coffers of merchants and shippers in the two ports. Dramatic evidence of Boston's economic resurgence was the completion in 1786 of a bridge across the Charles from Boston to Charlestown, an enormous span 1053ft long and 42ft wide, which at the time was described as the greatest feat of engineering ever undertaken in America. This was the first of four bridges to be constructed across the Charles in the following quarter-century, ending Boston's virtual insularity and linking the town more intimately to the mainland. The town suffered a temporary setback the following year, when, on April 24, a great fire in the area leading to Boston Neck destroyed 100 buildings, including the Hollis Street Church. But the town soon recovered from the disaster, and the burned-out area was quickly rebuilt. A new Hollis Street Church was completed in 1788 from plans drawn by Charles Bulfinch, a young Bostonian who had just returned after an 18-month tour of Europe, in which he had been profoundly influenced by the architecture of England and the Continent. The design of the Hollis Street Church marked the beginning of a brilliant career that was to span four decades, in which Bulfinch would create a distinctive architectural style appropriate to the prosperous new town of Boston that developed during the Federal period.

Boston in the Federal Period: 1789–1829. The first census in the U.S. was taken in 1790, revealing that Boston then had a population of 18,039; this was only about 2000 more than it had been at half-century earlier, when it was the most populous town in America. During that same period New York and Philadelphia had grown from populations of 13,000 each to 46,000 and 55,000 respectively, making them the largest towns in the 13 states. (Vermont, which had formerly been claimed by New York, became the 14th state on March 4, 1791). Boston, which had always been in the forefront of the struggle for independence, now found itself after victory far from the center of political power in the new nation, whose capital was first in New York City and then, after 1801, in Washington, D.C. Nevertheless, Boston's influence on national affairs was still considerable during the career of John Adams, who was Vice-President during both of Washington's terms of office, becoming President himself in 1797 and serving until 1801.

John Adams was succeeded as President in 1801 by Thomas Jefferson, who served two terms in office. During Jefferson's second term the renewal of war between England and France caused both nations to intercept neutral shipping to their enemy's ports, as a result of which U.S. merchant ships were stopped on the high seas by warships of both sides, their cargoes confiscated, and their seamen taken prisoner. This led Jefferson to order all English and French vessels to leave American ports and to impose a total embargo of U.S. shipping to foreign ports, a measure ratified by Congress on Dec. 22, 1807. The embargo proved to be a very unwise and futile policy, and its effect on Boston and the other seaports in New England was catastrophic. The lucrative China trade was abruptly cut off, and the merchants and shippers of the New England seaports went bankrupt, as did the farmers in the hinterland. However, their vehement opposition to the Embargo Act eventually brought about its repeal by Congress on March 15, 1809. This was just 11 days after the inauguration of James Madison as the fourth President of the U.S., whose Vice-President was Elbridge Gerry of Cambridge.

During the first three years of Madison's administration relations between the U.S. and England grew steadily worse, and aggressive American Westerners known as the "Warhawks" called for the President to declare war and to invade Canada. Madison was finally led to declare war on June 1, 1812, and by June 18 his declaration was passed by both houses of Congress, with the New England representatives casting most of the dissenting votes. The vast majority of the people in Boston and elsewhere in New England were opposed to what they called "Mr. Madison's War." Massachusetts, Rhode Island, and Connecticut refused to send their state militias to join the federal army, using them instead for local and coastal defense. In 1814 the British began making punitive raids along the coast of New England, capturing four villages in Maine. On two occasions they even succeeded in sending raiding parties into Boston Harbor under cover of night, burning sloops and schooners at their berths. When the federal government seemed unwilling to help New England defend its coast, the state governments of Massachusetts, Rhode Island, and Connecticut called for a convention to be held in Hartford to discuss common defense and political problems. The delegates of the three states met there in secret session for three weeks in December 1814, with the more radical of the Federalists calling for the New England states to secede from the Union. The moderate delegates, led by Harrison Gray Otis of Boston, eventually gained control of the convention and drafted a final report calling for amendments to the U.S. Constitution that would redress the grievances of the New England states. But before the report could be delivered to Congress the delegates learned that the war between the U.S. and Britain had already ended with the signing of the Peace of Ghent on Dec. 24, 1814. And so the ending of the war came as an anticlimax for the people of Boston and elsewhere in New England, but they could at least take pride in the fact that the peace treaty had been negotiated from the U.S. by John Quincy Adams, son of John Adams, who later became the sixth President of the U.S. (1825–29). The administration of John Quincy Adams marked the end of an age as far as Massachusetts was concerned, for it would be another century before another citizen of the state would rise to the nation's highest office. Also, by the time Adams left office the political party that had elected his father to the presidency of the U.S. a generation earlier was no longer in existence, and so the year 1829 serves as a convenient date to mark the end of the Federalist period, particularly as regards the history of Boston.

In the meantime, Charles Bulfinch and other architects, builders, and developers had been transforming the face of Boston during the Federalist period. As early as 1787 Bulfinch had submitted plans for a new State House, since the old Town House was too small to accommodate both the town and commonwealth governments, as it had throughout the 18C, as well as housing the State Supreme Court. On May 13, 1795, the town decided to buy a plot of land on the slope of Beacon Hill above the Common, on what had been the pasture of the late John Hancock's estate, and Bulfinch was selected as the architect. The cornerstone was laid on July 4, 1795, and on Jan. 11, 1798, the new State House was occupied for the first time. Harrison Gray Otis, who had headed the town committee that bought the land for the new State House, realized that the erection of this huge public building, in what had been rural surroundings, would soon attract people to live in its vicinity. Not long after the cornerstone of the State House was laid Otis and his associates formed a corporation called the Mount Vernon Proprietors, to buy and develop land in the vicinity of the new State House. John Singleton Copley, the painter, had emigrated to England in 1774, leaving behind a large tract of upland pasture on the western slope of Beacon Hill. Otis and his group purchased the land from Copley's agent and in the summer of 1799 they began the work of surveying the land, laying out plots, and cutting streets for the development. In the course of this development Mount Vernon, the western peak of Beacon Hill, was gradually truncated by some 50ft to level the land for the housing project, with the excavated earth being dumped into the mud flats along the adjacent shores of the Charles River. This development, which one historian of Boston has described as a "cutting down of the hills and filling up of the coves," combined with the constant "wharving out" to increase the land area of Boston and to transform it from a peninsula to an arm of the mainland. In 1804 the area of Boston was further augmented by the annexation of Dorchester, and later that year a bridge was constructed between the Neck and the new district of the town, which came to be known as South Boston. The Neck was then widened out as the mud flats on either side were filled in, and later the Mill Pond underwent the same transformation, increasing the area of the northern part of the peninsula. This expansion of the land area of Boston was due to the large increase in the population of the town during the Federalist period, so that by 1820 it numbered 43,298, more than twice what it had been in the first U.S. census, in 1790.

The City of Boston in the 19—20C. The Massachusetts State Convention of 1820 had made provisions for the incorporation of cities, and in 1822 the town government of Boston was replaced by a city charter. John Philips was elected as the first mayor of Boston, and the following year he was succeeded by Josiah Quincy, who held that office until he in turn was replaced by Harrison Gray Otis in 1829. During his five-year tenure as mayor Josiah Quincy transformed Boston from a colonial town into a 19C city, organizing its police and fire departments, its sanitation system, social services, and public school system. Mayor Quincy also initiated a major project in town planning that involved filling in the Town Dock and building over the piers between it and the Long Wharf, a project that he assigned to the architect Alexander Parris. In the newly created area, which was directly in front of Faneuil Hall, Parris designed a two-story market hall 550ft long and 50ft wide, flanked on either side by a series of warehouses of comparable dimensions. The cornerstone of the Quincy Market was laid on April 27, 1825, and the first shop in the complex opened for business on Aug. 26, 1826, inaugurating an institution that continues to be a vital center in the life of modern Boston.

In summer 1835 three railway lines began operating from Boston, connecting the city with Lowell, Providence, and Worcester, respectively, and by the middle of the 19C three more lines were added to these. The line from Boston to Worcester eventually developed into the Western Railway, which by the winter of 1841—42 stretched as far as Albany, linking the city to the American West for the first time. The Boston and Worcester Railway brought about a great change in the topography of Boston. When it was first built the viaduct for the railway ran across Back Bay on a dike, the Mill Dam, that extended from the foot of Mount Vernon to Sewall's Point in Brookline. About halfway along its length the Mill Dam was intersected by the Cross Dam, a dike that extended from Gravelly Point in Roxbury and divided the Back Bay into two parts. The western basin was maintained at a higher level than the eastern one, the Lower Basin, and this hydrostatic differential was used to power a series of mills on the Cross Dam. In 1857 work began on filling in the Lower Basin, and by the end of the 19C the entire Back Bay was *terra firma*. This and other filling projects in South Cove, South Bay, and Dorchester Flats dramatically altered the topography of Boston. Not only did they add 450 acres to the original 783-acre peninsula, but they fused Boston to the mainland by increasing the width of the old Neck so that it was more than a mile across. At the same time similar projects were taking place on the other side of the Charles, as 416 acres of that side of the Back Bay were filled in to connect Charlestown and East Cambridge.

The filling operations were a direct result of the land hunger created by the accelerated growth of Boston's population, which by 1860 numbered 136,881. A large part of the population increase was brought about by the Irish famine of 1845—50, which led to a tremendous exodus from Ireland. Boston was one of the principal ports of entry for the Irish immigrants who came to the U.S., and by 1850 about 35,000 of them had settled in Boston. Political upheavals on the Continent in the mid-19C brought immigrants to Boston from all over Europe, as well as French Canadians from the N., but the Irish continued to make up the vast majority of the new arrivals in the city. Most of the Irish and other immigrants lived under appalling conditions for years after their arrival in Boston, eking out a miserable existence in the slums that festered in large areas of the city. These immigrants provided the bulk of the labor force that was needed to staff the workshops and factories that sprang up in Boston and other towns in eastern Massachusetts in the 19C, when the economy of the state shifted from shipbuilding and farming to industry. Boston itself was less industrialized than the surrounding towns, as it became one of the financial centers of the U.S.

The 19C was a time of great intellectual and political activity in Boston. In 1831 William Lloyd Garrison published a newspaper called the *Liberator,* advocating unconditional emancipation of the slaves. This marked the beginning of the Abolitionist movement in the U.S., and led directly to the founding of the New England Anti-Slavery Society in 1832 and the American Anti-Slavery Society the following year. Nevertheless, the Abolitionists were still a minority in Boston at that time, and Garrison was on one occasion beaten, tarred, and feathered by an angry mob. During this period Boston was also the scene of religious controversy, centering on the rise of the Unitarians, who denied the existence of the Trinity and held that God existed as a single person. During the period 1815—36 the leading Unitarian minister in Boston was the Rev. William Ellery Channing, who held that reason and conscience were the only guides to religious truth, and who believed in the innate goodness of man and the need for complete religious freedom. Channing's thought was one of the factors that gave rise to the philosophical school of Transcendentalism. The most systematic expression of this philosophy was given in the works of Ralph Waldo Emerson, who was born in Boston, educated at Harvard, and lived out the latter years of his life in Concord, Mass. Emerson was the central figure in the cultural renaissance that took place in Boston and its environs in the 19C, a phenomenon that the critic Van Wyck Brooks called "The Flowering of New England."

This renaissance gave rise to important works in many fields of scholarship and other areas of human endeavor, including the writings of George Ticknor, Henry David Thoreau, Nathaniel Hawthorne, Henry Wadsworth Longfellow, Emily Dickinson, Louisa May Alcott, Harriet Beecher Stowe, John Greenleaf Whittier, Oliver Wendell Holmes, Charles Francis Adams, Henry Adams, James Russell Lowell, and William Dean Howells. (Howells was a native of Ohio, and came to Boston in 1866 to become an editor on the *Atlantic Monthly,* the most prestigious literary journal in the U.S. during the second half of the 19C.) The 19C renaissance in Boston also produced five of the greatest American historians in that period: George Bancroft, William Hickling Prescott, John Lothrop Motley, Francis Parkman, and John Fiske.

Many important figures in Boston's 19C renaissance were leaders in the Abolitionist movement, making important contributions toward freeing American blacks from slavery. Harriet Beecher Stowe's novel *Uncle Tom's Cabin* did much to arouse sympathy for the slaves and indignation against the barbarous institution of slavery. The most powerful opponent of slavery in the U.S. Senate was Charles Sumner of Boston, and in the city itself William Lloyd Garrison's most articulate follower in the Abolitionist movement was Wendell Phillips. Other Bostonians of the period devoted their energies toward bringing about much-needed reforms in different areas: Horace Mann modernized the public school system of Massachusetts, an example that was followed elsewhere in the U.S.; Elizabeth Peabody, a prominent author and educator, founded in Boston the first kindergarten in the U.S.; Samuel Gridley Howe, his wife, Julia Ward Howe, and Dorothea Dix campaigned to provide better care for the deaf, blind, and insane; Margaret Fuller was an ardent advocate of feminism and was also one of the leading social critics of her day; Bronson Alcott, father of Louisa May Alcott, was an apostle of progressive education. Alcott's unconventional ideas led him to become a member of the two idealistic communes that were founded in Massachusetts in the 19C; these were New Eden, at Fruitlands, and Brook Farm, now in West Roxbury. (Hawthorne lived at Brook Farm for a time, and later satirized the community in his novel *The Blithedale Romance.*)

A very important factor in the 19C intellectual renaissance in Boston and its environs was the high level of education that had existed in the area since its earliest days. Harvard College, founded in Cambridge in 1636, was the first institution of higher learning to be established in the English colonies in America, and during the presidency of Charles William Eliot, who held that office from 1869 until 1909, it emerged as one of the truly great universities in the world. One of the renowned members of the Harvard faculty during that period was William James, who there began his pioneering researches in human psychology, culminating in the publication of the two volumes of his magisterial work, *The Principles of Psychology* (1878, 1890). (His brother, the novelist Henry James, lived for a time in Cambridge, but spent most of his life abroad.) The Massachusetts Institute of Technology (M.I.T.) was founded in Boston in 1861 by the geologist William Barton Rogers as a small school "for practical science." M.I.T. moved to its present site in Cambridge in 1916, since which time it has developed into what many believe to be the world's foremost technical and engineering school. But M.I.T. was just one of some 40 universities and four-year colleges that were founded in the city and its environs after 1869, giving metropolitan Boston the greatest concentration of institutions of higher learning in the U.S.

During the second half of the 19C the whole face of Boston changed completely, as most of what was left of the old colonial and Federal town wa swept away in the building boom made necessary by the rapidly grow population. Then, on the night of Sept. 9–10, 1872, a great fire swept thr the center of the business district, destroying 770 buildings and leav acres of the city in ruins, though fortunately there were relatively fe alties. The most historic structure destroyed in the fire was Trinity which had been founded in 1733. Soon after the fire the congr Trinity, whose minister was the Rev. Phillips Brooks, decided new church at Copley Sq in the Back Bay, appointing Henry Ho

Boston in 1844: the "Boynton" map

ardson as architect. The new Trinity Church was completed by Richardson in 1877, and it stands today as one of the masterpieces of this great Victorian architect. In 1888–95 the Boston Public Library was constructed on Copley Sq, as the center of the town shifted westward with the development of the Back Bay. In 1900 Horticultural Hall and Symphony Hall were built, even farther to the W. in Back Bay, on the corner of Massachusetts and Huntington Aves. In 1903 Mrs. John L. Gardner completed work on Fenway Court, the palace in the Back Bay Fens that became the Isabella Stewart Gardner Museum, and in 1909 the Boston Museum of Fine Arts moved into its monumental new quarters in the same area. During the first decade of the 20C other large building complexes were erected in the southwestern part of Back Bay, including the new Harvard Medical School and several hospitals and colleges.

By 1900 the population of Boston had reached 560,892, as hordes of immigrants continued to pour into the city, the majority of them Irish. By that time some 24,000 acres of adjacent countryside and neighboring villages had been annexed to Boston in order to contain its rapidly increasing population. Roxbury was annexed in 1868, Dorchester in 1870, West Roxbury (including Jamaica Plain and Roslindale) and Brighton in 1874, and Hyde Park in 1912. (The town of Brookline, which was founded in 1705, somehow managed to escape annexation, though to all appearances it is an integral part of Boston.) This enormous influx of Irish and other foreigners completely altered the power structure of Boston, and a new political machine was created out of this constituency by the local bosses of the Democratic Party, most of whom were Irish Americans. On January 1, 1885, Hugh O'Brien became mayor of Boston, the first person of Irish descent ever to hold that office, and he was subsequently re-elected three times. The two most famous Irish Americans to become mayor of Boston during the early years of the 20C were John Fitzgerald ("Honey Fitz"), who was first elected to that office in 1905, and James Michael Curley, who defeated Fitzgerald in the mayoralty election in 1913. Curley was subsequently re-elected mayor three times and also served a term as governor of Massachusetts, as well as representing the state in the U.S. Congress. Curley's terms as mayor were marked by charges of malfeasance and corruption, and in 1947, during his fourth and last term, he served five months in a federal prison on charges of fraud.

The first half of the 20C was a difficult time for many in Boston, particularly during the Great Depression of the 1930s. Large parts of the inner city were showing serious signs of urban blight and had decayed into slums, with the dockside area falling into ruins because of the sharp decline of the shipping industry in Boston after sail gave way to steam in the second half of the 19C. After World War II people began leaving the inner city in large numbers to seek better housing and living conditions in the suburbs of Boston and its surrounding towns. In the 1950s the population of the city of Boston declined from 801,440 to 697,000; by 1970 it had dropped to 641,071, and in 1980 it had gone down to 562,994, as the exodus from the city continued.

Bostonians once again became prominent on the national scene after World War II, with the rise of the Kennedy political dynasty. The dynasty began with John F. Kennedy, grandson of former Mayor John Fitzgerald, who was born in Brookline in 1917. Kennedy was first elected to the U.S. House of Representatives in 1947, and served two terms in that office before being elected to the U.S. Senate in 1952. In 1960 he was elected President of the U.S., the first Roman Catholic and the first Irish American ever to hold that office, facts in which the Boston Irish took great pride. This pride grew during the hope-filled months of Kennedy's administration, in which his younger brother Robert Kennedy served as his attorney general. Then, in 1962, the Boston Irish had another occasion to celebrate, when Edward Kennedy, the youngest of the brothers, was elected to the U.S. Senate at the age of 30. But all of this pride was shattered on Nov. 22, 1963, when President Kennedy was assassinated, and Boston was plunged into grief again when Robert Kennedy suffered the same fate on June 4, 1968, during a campaign that many thought would win him election to the presidency. Edward Kennedy continues to serve in the U.S. Senate and is one of the leading figures in the Democratic Party.

In 1960 Mayor John F. Collins began a campaign to revive Boston, appointing the city-planner Edward J. Logue to be administrator of the Boston Redevelopment Authority. This program has been continued by his successors as mayor, Kevin H. White and Raymond L. Flynn, and it has succeeded in remaking large areas of downtown Boston, creating Government Center in the midst of the business district, Prudential Center in Back Bay, restoring Faneuil Hall and the Quincy Market, as well as many of the handsome old warehouses along the waterfront, where a pretty park has been created. These projects were completed in time for the celebration of the Bicentennial Anniversary of American Independence in 1976, an event in which Boston took particular pride because of the leading role that its citizens had played in the struggle for freedom. Four years later, in 1980, Boston celebrated the 250th anniversary of its own founding, a resurgent city with justifiable pride in its distinguished history and venerable traditions.

Glossary of Architectural Terms

The following is a glossary of some of the architectural terms that are used in the text.

ADAM / ADAMESQUE. Building style influenced by the Scottish architects Robert Adam (1728–92) and his brother James (1732–94).

APSE. Semicircular end of a building projecting from an exterior wall and forming a niche within.

ARCADE. Series of arches supported by columns, piers, or pillars, often in the form of a vaulted walkway.

ARCHITRAVE. Beam or lowest member of the entablature, which extends from column to column.

ARCHIVOLT. Decorated molding carried around the outside face of an arch.

ASHLAR MASONRY. Regular masonry of squared stone, with horizontal courses and vertical joints.

BARREL VAULT. Continuous arched roof or ceiling of semicircular or semielliptical form.

BAY. Space between a series of columns, piers, or wall panels.

BAY WINDOW. Polygonal window element projecting outward from the exterior wall, usually with three windows.

BLIND ARCADE. Closed arcade indicated by pilasters against a wall surface.

BLIND ARCH. Arch built into a wall to distribute the weight above it.

CAPITAL. Crowning feature of a column, pier, or pilaster.

CASEMENT WINDOWS. Windows hinged on the side so that they can be opened inward or outward.

CHANCEL. Space around the altar reserved for the clergy.

CLAPBOARD. Horizontal wooden siding, radially cut.

CLERESTORY. Upper wall of the nave, transepts, and choir of a church, containing windows; also the uppermost windows in a church.

COFFER. Recessed panel in a ceiling, wall, or dome, often decorated.

CONSOLE. Projecting bracket, often spiral-shaped, used to support overhanging upper stories or balconies; sometimes called a CORBEL.

COPING. Top course of a wall, usually designed with rainspouts or gutters, often ornamental.

CORNICE. Uppermost and most prominent member of an entablature.

COURSE. Row of bricks, stones, or building blocks extending the full length and thickness of a building.

CROSS VAULT or GROIN VAULT. Vaults characterized by arched diagonal groins, which are formed by the intersection of two barrel vaults.

CURTAIN WALL. Enclosing wall attached to the frame of a building.

DENTILS. Line of small rectangular blocks in the bedmolding of a cornice.

DRUM. Cylindrical structure that supports a dome.

EAVES. Overhanging surfaces of a roof, designed to shed water.

ENGLISH BOND. Pattern in which all the bricks in one course have their ends facing outward (headers), while the courses above and below have their sides facing outward (stretchers). In the FLEMISH BOND pattern headers and stretchers alternate in each course.

ENTABLATURE. Upper part of a Greek order of architecture, comprising architrave, frieze, and cornice, supported by a colonnade.

EXEDRA. Semicircular niche.

EXTRADOS. Outside face or edge of an arch.

FANLIGHT. Semicircular or semi-elliptical window over a doorway.

FEDERAL STYLE. Architectural style popular in New England c. 1790–1830.

FENESTRATION. Arrangement of windows in a building.

FRET. Continuous ornamental band of stonework, usually with geometric designs.

FRIEZE. Middle element in the entablature. Applied also to any horizontal band adorned with sculpture or other decoration.

GABLE. Triangular upper part of a building.

GAMBREL ROOF. Double-pitched roof, with the lower plane rising more steeply than the upper one.

GEORGIAN ARCHITECTURE. In the U.S. the architectural style that flourished from the reign of George I (1714–27) until the Revolution.

GREEK CROSS CHURCH. Church whose plan forms a cross with equal arms.

GREEK REVIVAL. Architectural style that was popular in the U.S. in the first half of the 19C, when ancient Greek structures were used as prototypes.

HIP ROOF. Roof with roofs sloping up from all four walls.

IMPOST. Block from which an arch springs.

IN ANTIS. Arrangement in which columns are in line between the extended ends of two walls.

INTRADOS. Inner curve of an arch.

LANCET WINDOW. Tall window topped by a sharply pointed arch.

LINTEL. Horizontal member that spans an opening.

LUNETTE. Small round or half-round window or wall niche.

MANSARD ROOF. Similar to the gambrel roof, but with the lower plane much more sharply pitched than the upper, which is often nearly flat, and with windows in the lower plane.

MULLION. Upright member dividing a wall opening into two contiguous windows, or separating a window from a door.

OCULUS. Circular opening or window in a dome, usually small and eyelike.

ORIEL WINDOW. Bay window projecting outward on a corbel.

PALLADIAN. Style influenced by the Italian architect Andrea Palladio (1508–80).

PALLADIAN MOTIF. Arrangement in which a round-arched window or panel is flanked by lower square-topped windows or panels, all separated by columns or pilasters.

PEDIMENT. In ancient Greece the space under the raking cornice at the two ends of the temple; in modern houses the triangular space at the gable ends of the building.

PENDENTIVES. Triangular over-hanging spherical segment by means of which the transition is made from a square or polygonal chamber to the circular cornice on which rests the dome.

PENT ROOF. Small roof over a first-floor window.

PERISTYLE. Array of columns surrounding a courtyard.

PIANO NOBILE. Main floor of a mansion, usually on the first floor above the ground.

PIER. Mass of masonry, as dis-tinct from a column, from which an arch springs.

PILASTER. Rectangular feature in the shape of a pillar, but engaged to a wall and projecting by only about one-sixth of its breadth.

PLINTH. Square block supporting a column or statue.

PORTICO. Colonnaded space, with a roof supported on at least one side by columns.

POST AND LINTEL. Structure consisting of vertical members, or posts, supporting horizontal members, the lintels.

QUEEN ANNE STYLE. Style of architecture popular in the sec-ond half of the 19C, patterned on that of the reign of Queen Anne (1702–14).

QUOIN. Beveled corner of a building.

RAKING CORNICE. Cornice that forms the upper part of the pedi-mental triangle.

REREDOS. Decorated screen behind an altar.

REVEAL. Surface formed when a window or door is set into a wall.

REVETMENT. Facing of stone, marble, or tile upon a wall.

RIBS. Cusps separating the seg-ments of a dome.

RIDGE LINE. Line of intersection of two opposite roof slopes.

RIDGE POLE. Topmost horizontal roof member.

RINCEAU. Vinelike decoration in low relief.

RUSTICATION. Masonry con-structed in a rustic style, with joints emphasized externally, and with wooden members made to appear as stone.

SALTBOX. Type of American farmhouse of the 17C.

SASH WINDOW. Window that slides up and down in a grooved frame.

SHED ROOF. Roof with only one slope.

SHINGLE STYLE. Type of shin-gled New England house that became popular in the 1880s.

STICK STYLE. Type of timbered building that was prevalent from the 1850s to the 1880s.

SOFFIT. Ceiling or underside of any architectural member.

SPANDREL. Curvilinear triangle space between two adjoining arches and a line connecting their crown. Also, in modern high-rise buildings, the space between the top of one window and the sill of the one above it.

SQUINCH. Small arch, corbel, or lintel built across each angle of a square or polygonal structure to form a suitable base on which to rest the cornice to support the dome.

STRING COURSE. Narrow hori-zontal band of masonry, project-ing slightly from the wall, which extends across a brick facade. Also called a BELT COURSE or BAND COURSE.

TRABEATE. Post-and-lintel con-struction.

TRANSEPTS. Lateral arms of a cross-shaped church.

TRANSOM. Horizontal bar over a door or window opening at the top.

TYMPANUM. Triangular wall enclosed by the raking cornice of the pediment and the horizontal cornice of the entablature beneath.

VAULT. Arched covering in stone or brick over any part of a building.

VOLUTE. Spiral scroll of an Ionic capital.

VOUSSOIRS. Truncated wedge-shaped blocks forming the segments of an arch.

WAINSCOT. The protective wall lining of a house.

WEATHERBOARD. Lapped horizontal wood siding using boards often of parallel faces.

WEATHERING. Slope given to any exposed surface so that it will shed water.

Bibliography

The following is a selective list of books about Boston and its environs. This is not meant to be a complete bibliography, but, rather, a listing that will provide introductions to the history, topography, art, architecture, and life of the city and its surrounding area.

Early Chronicles. John Winthrop: *History of New England, 1630–1649* (rep. 1908). William Bradford: *History of Plimouth Plantation* (rep. 1856). Thomas Hutchinson: *History of the Colony and Province of Massachusetts Bay* (3 vols., rep. 1936). William Wood: *New England's Prospects* . . . (1634, rep. 1898).

Topography. Nathaniel B. Shurtleff: *A Topographical and Historical Description of Boston* (1872). Annie Haven Thwing: *The Crooked and Narrow Streets of Boston, 1630–1822* (1920). Walter Muir Whitehill: *Boston: A Topographical History* (1968).

History. Justin Winsor (ed.): *The Memorial History of Boston* (4 vols., 1880). Howard S. Russell: *Indian New England Before the Mayflower* (1980). Wallace Notestein: *The English People on the Eve of Colonization, 1603–1636* (1962). Samuel Eliot Morison: *Builders of the Bay Colony* (1930). John Fiske: *The Discovery of America* (2 vols., 1895); *The Beginnings of New England* (1889); *The American Revolution* (2 vols., 1897); *The Critical Period in American History* (1888). Charles McLean Andrews: *The Colonial Period in American History* (1934). James Truslow Adams: *Revolutionary New England, 1691–1771* (1922); *New England in the Republic, 1776–1850* (1926). Darrell B. Rutman: *Boston; Portrait of a Puritan Town, 1630–1649* (1965); *The Morning of America* (1971). Roland G. Usher: *The Pilgrims and Their History* (1977). G. B. Warden: *Boston, 1689–1776* (1970). James Duncan Phillips: *Salem in the Seventeenth Century* (1933); *Salem in the Eighteenth Century* (1937). Marion L. Starkey: *The Devil in Massachusetts: A Modern Enquiry into the Salem Witch Trials* (1949). Cass Canfield: *Samuel Adams's Revolution, 1765–1776* (1976). Catherine Drinker Bowen: *John Adams and the American Revolution* (1956). Bernard Bailyn: *Ideological Origins of the American Revolution* (1967); *The New England Merchants in the Seventeenth Century* (1957). Hiller B. Zobel: *The Boston Massacre* (1976). Benjamin Woods Labaree: *The Boston Tea Party* (1964). Richard B. Frothingham: *History of the Siege of Boston* (1851). Allen French: *The Day of Concord and Lexington* (1925). Page Smith: *A New Age About to Begin: A People's History of the American Revolution* (2 vols., 1976). Charles Francis Adams: *Three Episodes of Massachusetts History* (2 vols., 1896). Richard D. Brown: *Massachusetts: A History* (1978). Walter Muir Whitehill and Norman Kotter: *Massachusetts: A Pictorial History* (1976). Walter Muir Whitehill: *Boston in the Age of John Fitzgerald Kennedy* (1969).

Maritime History. Samuel Eliot Morison: *The European Discovery of America* (2 vols., 1974); *The Maritime History of Massachusetts* (1921). David Beers Quinn: *England and the Discovery of America, 1481–1620* (1971). Bernard Bailyn: *Massachusetts Shipping, 1647–1714* (1959). William Henry Bunting: *Portrait of a Port: Boston, 1852–1914* (1971). Bettina A. Norton: *The Boston Naval Shipyard, 1800–1974* (1974). Tyrone G. Norton: *A Most For-*

tunate Ship: A Narrative History of the U.S.S. Constitution (1980). Thomas P. Horgan: *Old Ironsides: The Story of the U.S.S. Constitution* (1963).

Social and Intellectual History. Samuel Eliot Morison: *The Intellectual Life of Colonial New England* (1956); *Three Centuries of Harvard, 1636–1936* (1936). Alice Morse Earle: *Home Life in Colonial Days* (1926). Clifford K. Shipton: *New England Life in the Eighteenth Century* (1963). Robert Gross: *The Minute Men and Their World* (1976). Edwin Powell: *Crime and Punishment in Early Massachusetts, 1620–1692* (1966). Percy Miller: *The New England Mind: The Seventeenth Century* (1939); *The New England Mind: From Colony to Province* (1953); *The American Transcendentalists: Their Prose and Poetry* (1957). Van Wyck Brooks: *The Flowering of New England, 1815–1865* (1936); *New England Indian Summer, 1865–1915* (1940). Geoffrey Blodgett: *The Gentle Reformers: Massachusetts Democrats in the Cleveland Era* (1966). Paula Todisco: *The North End, Boston's First Neighborhood* (1976). Sam Bass Warner: *Streetcar Suburbs: The Process of Growth in Boston, 1870–1900* (1962). Brett Howard: *Boston: A Social History* (1976). James R. Coreen and Hugh Carter Donahue: *Boston's Workers: A Labor History* (1979).

Biography. Edmund S. Morgan: *The Puritan Dilemma: The Story of John Winthrop* (1958). Robert C. Winthrop: *Life and Letters of John Winthrop . . .* (2 vols., 1864, 1867). Dorothy Brewster: *William Brewster of the Mayflower: Portrait of a Pilgrim* (1976). Bernard Bailyn: *The Ordeal of Thomas Hutchinson* (1974). John M. Galvin: *Three Men of Boston* (Thomas Hutchinson, James Otis, and Samuel Adams) (1976); *The Minute Men* (1967). James K. Hosmer: *Samuel Adams* (1889). William M. Fowler: *The Baron of Beacon Hill: A Biography of John Hancock* (1979). Arthur Bernon Tourtellot: *Benjamin Franklin: The Shaping of Genius; The Boston Years* (1977). Leonard B. Labaree et al. (eds.): *The Autobiography of Benjamin Franklin* (1964). Page Smith: *John Adams* (2 vols., 1964). Lyman Butterfield et al. (ed.): *The Book of Abigail and John; Diary and Autobiography of John Adams* (4 vols., 1965). John Adams: *Familiar Letters of John Adams and His Wife Abigail Adams* (1876). Charles Francis Adams: *John Adams: Life and Work* (1913). John Quincy Adams: *Memoirs* (undated); *An Autobiography* (1919). Jack Shepherd: *The Adams Chronicles* (1975). Esther Forbes: *Paul Revere and the World He Lived In* (1942). Jules P. Prowse: *John Singleton Copley* (2 vols., 1961). Ellen Susan Bulfinch: *The Life and Letters of Charles Bulfinch, Architect* (1894). Edward Wagenknecht: *Nathaniel Hawthorne: Man and Writer* (1961); *John Greenleaf Whittier: A Portrait in Paradox* (1967); *Harriet Beecher Stowe: The Known and the Unknown* (1965); *Henry Wadsworth Longfellow: Portrait of an American Humanist* (1966). Gay Wilson Allen: *William James* (1967); *Waldo Emerson* (1981). Richard B. Sewell: *Life of Emily Dickinson* (1980). Joseph Wood Krutch: *Henry David Thoreau* (1948). David Donald: *Charles Sumner and the Coming of the Civil War* (1961); *Charles Sumner and the Rights of Man* (1976). Henry Adams: *The Education of Henry Adams* (1938). Ferris Greensleet: *The Lowells and Their Seven Worlds* (1946). Joseph F. Dineen: *The Purple Shamrock: The Honorable James Michael Curley of Boston* (1949). Theodore Sorenson: *Kennedy* (1965). Arthur M. Schlesinger, Jr.: *A Thousand Days* (A history of the JFK administration) (1965); *Robert Kennedy and His Times* (1978).

Architecture. G. E. Kidder Smith: *The Architecture of the U.S.*, vol. 1: *New England and the Middle Atlantic States* (1981). William H. Pierson, Jr.: *American Buildings and Their Architects: The Colonial and Neo-Classical Styles* (1976). William H. Jordy: *American Buildings and Their Architects: Progressive and Academic Ideals at the Turn of the Twentieth Century* (1976). Joseph L. Eldridge: *Architecture Boston* (1980). Marjorie Drake Ross: *The Book of Boston: The Colonial Period* (1960); *The Federal Period* (1961); *The Victorian Period* (1964). Douglas Shand Tucci: *Church Building in Boston* (1974); *Built in Boston, City and Suburb* (1978). Walter Muir Whitehill: *Back Bay Churches and Public Buildings* (1967); *Boston: Distinguished Buildings and Sites Within the City and Its Orbit* (1975). Henry Russell Hitchcock: *The Architecture of H. H. Richardson and His Times* (1936, rev. ed. 1961); *Boston Architecture, 1637–1954* (1954). Harold Kirker: *The Architecture of Charles Bulfinch* (1969). Harold Kirker and James Kirker: *Bulfinch's Boston, 1787–1817* (1964). Raymond W. Stanley (ed.): *Mr. Bulfinch's Boston* (1963). Walter H. Kilham: *Boston After Bulfinch* (1946). Robert Bell Rettig: *A Guide to Cambridge: Ten Walking Tours* (1969); *The Architecture of Richardson and His Contemporaries in Boston and Vicinity* (1974). Bainbridge Bunting: *Houses of Boston's Back Bay . . .* (1967). Bainbridge Bunting and Robert H.

Nylander: *Survey of Architectural History in Cambridge: Report 4, Old Cambridge* (1973). Pauleen Chase Harrell and Margaret Supplee: *Victorian Boston Today: Ten Walking Tours* (1975). A. McVoy McIntyre: *Beacon Hill: A Walking Tour* (1975). Joan E. Goody: *New Architecture in Boston* (1965). Carl J. Weinhardt, Jr.: *The Domestic Architecture of Beacon Hill, 1800–1856* (1958). John Harris, *Historic Walks in Old Boston* (1982). Donlyn Lyndon: *Boston: A Guide to the Architecture of the Hub* (1982). George M. Cushing, Jr. (photos) and Ross Urquhart (text), *Great Buildings of Boston: A Photographic Guide* (1982); Peter Vanderwarker, *Boston Then and Now* (1982). John Harris: *Historic Walks in Cambridge* (1986). *Susan and Michael Southworth:* A. I. A. Guide to Boston (1984). *Naomi Miller and Keith Morgan:* Boston Architecture 1975–1990 (1990).

Major Libraries and Art Museums. Walter Muir Whitehill: *Boston Public Library: A Centennial History* (1956); *Museum of Fine Arts, Boston: A Centennial History* (1970). Mable Munson Swan: *The Athenaeum Gallery 1827–1873: The Boston Athenaeum as an Early Patron of Art in Boston* (1940). Jane S. Knowles: *Change and Continuity: A Pictorial History of the Boston Athenaeum* (1976). Morris Carter: *Isabella Stewart Gardner and Fenway Court* (1925). Denys Sutton (ed.): *Fogg Art Museum, Harvard University* (1978). Charles Haxthausen (ed.): *The Busch-Reisinger Museum, Harvard University* (1980). Mary Ann Tighe and Elizabeth E. Lang: *Art America* (1977). Kristin A. Mortimer: *Harvard University Art Museums: A Guide to the Collections* (1985).

General and Local Color. Samuel Adams Drake: *Old Landmarks and Historic Personages of Boston* (1872, rep. 1971); *Historic Mansions and Highways Around Boston* (1873; rep. 1971). Samuel Eliot Morison: *One Boy's Boston* (1962). Walter Muir Whitehill: *Boston: Portrait of a City* (1964); *Boston Statues* (1970). David McCord: *About Boston* (1948). George Weston: *Boston Ways* (1957). Paul Hogarth: *Walking Tours of Old Boston* (1978). Jane Holtz Kay: *Lost Boston* (1980). Cleveland Amory: *The Proper Bostonians* (1947). Lucius Beebe: *Boston and the Boston Legend* (1935).

PRACTICAL INFORMATION

Approaches to Boston

Most travelers coming to Boston from outside the New England region make the journey by air. Some visitors may want to stop over in New York to see the sights there before going up to Boston; some prefer to make the journey overland, traveling by train, bus, or rented car. Information on travel from New York to Boston can be obtained from the agencies listed below.

Transport from the Airport into Boston

Arrival in Boston by Air. Logan International Airport is across the Inner Harbor in East Boston. It is very close to the downtown area, and unless there are traffic jams, which are frequent during morning and evening rush hours, the trip into town is very short. Transportation is available in the form of taxis, public or airline buses, private limousine services, and the subway. There is also a Share-a-Cab service, in which each passenger pays only the appropriate fraction of the fare. This service is available not only into Boston but to 139 communities in its suburbs and environs. There is a Share-a-Cab booth in each of the baggage-reclaim areas. Massport (the state transportation agency) provides a shuttle bus to take passengers to the MBTA Blue Line Airport station on the subway. The Massport Shuttle stops at all terminals, and runs every six to ten minutes from 5:30 a.m. to 1:00 a.m.; from the Airport subway station it is only three stops to the center of downtown Boston. There are also several car-rental agencies with desks at the Arrivals terminals. Another alternative is the Airport Water Shuttle (tel. 1-800-235-6426; in Boston, 330-8680), which takes seven minutes to cross Boston Harbor from the airport to Rowes Wharf.

Arrival in Boston by Surface Transport. Passenger trains to and from the S. and W. arrive at South Station, which is located at the corner of Summer St and Atlantic Ave, while those coming from the N. arrive at North Station, at 100 Causeway St. There are two bus terminals in downtown Boston. Greyhound / Trailways, at Park Square (tel. 423-5810), connects Boston with all major cities in the U.S.; Peter Pan Bus Lines, Atlantic Ave, opposite South Station (tel. 426-7838), operates services to all the New England states except Vermont.

Hotels and Motels

The following is a selected list of hotels and motels in Boston and environs. Omission of a hotel from this list does not imply any adverse judgment by the author or publisher of the *Blue Guide Boston and Cambridge*. Information on the prices of hotels and the amenities they offer can be obtained from any travel agent. Hotels in Boston are very heavily booked during the summer months, and if a trip there is planned during that season it is advisable to book well in advance.

HOTELS IN BOSTON, BROOKLINE, AND CAMBRIDGE (unless otherwise noted, the address is in Boston)

Anthony's Town House, 1085 Beacon St, Brookline (566-3972).
Back Bay Hilton, 40 Dalton St (236-1100).
Beacon Inn (furnished apartments), 1087 & 1750 Beacon St (566-0088).
Bostonian Hotel, North & Blackstone Sts (523-3600).
Boston Marriott Copley Place, 110 Huntington Ave (236-5800).
Boston Marriott Long Wharf, 296 State St, Long Wharf (227-0800).
Boston Harbor Hotel, 70 Rowes Wharf (439-7000).
Boston Park Plaza and Towers Hotel, 50 Park Plaza (426-2000).
Cambridge Center Marriott, Cambridge Center, Kendall Sq, Cambridge (494-6600).
Chandler Inn, 26 Chandler St (482-3450).
Charles Hotel at Harvard Square, One Bennett St, Cambridge (864-1200).
Charles River Motel, 1800 Soldiers' Field Rd, Brighton (254-0200).
The Colonnade, 120 Huntington Ave (424-7000).
Copley Plaza Hotel, Copley Sq (267-5300).
Copley Square Hotel, 47 Huntington Ave (536-9000).
Eliot Hotel, 370 Commonwealth Ave (267-1607).
Four Seasons Hotel, 200 Boylston St (338-4400).
Guest Quarters Suite Hotel, 400 Soldiers' Field Rd, Brighton (783-0090).
Harvard Manor House, 110 Mount Auburn & Elliot Sts, Cambridge (864-5200).
Hilton Inn at Logan, Logan International Airport (569-9300).
Holiday Inn—Government Center, 5 Blossom St (742-7630).
Holiday Inn Boston at Brookline, 1200 Beacon St, Brookline (277-1200).
Home Away (furnished apartments), 66 Mount Vernon St (523-1423).
Homestead Motor Inn, 220 Alewife Brook Parkway, Cambridge (491-1890).
Howard Johnson, 407 Squire Rd, Revere (just north of Logan Airport) (284-7200).
Howard Johnson Hotel, 200 Stuart St (482-1800).
Howard Johnson Hotel—Kenmore, 575 Commonwealth Ave (267-3100).
Howard Johnson Motor Lodge, 575 Commonwealth Ave (267-3100).
Howard Johnson Motor Lodge—Cambridge, 777 Memorial Drive, Cambridge (492-7777).
Howard Johnson Motor Lodge—Fenway, 1271 Boylston St (267-8300).
Howard Johnson Motor Lounge—Southeast, 5 Howard Johnson Plaza, Dorchester (288-3030).
Hyatt Regency Cambridge, 575 Memorial Drive, Cambridge (492-1234).
The Inn at Children's, 342 Longwood Ave (731-4700).
Lafayette Hotel, 1 Avenue de Lafayette (Washington St & Lafayette Pl) (451-2600).
Lenox Hotel, 710 Boylston St (536-5300).
Logan Airport Hilton, Logan Airport, East Boston (569-9300).
Meridien Hotel, 250 Franklin St (451-1900).
Midtown Hotel, 220 Huntington Ave (262-1000).
Milner Hotel, 78 Charles St (426-6220).
Northeast Hall Residence, 204 Bay State Rd (247-8318).
Omni Parker House, 60 School St (227-8600).
Quality Inn, 275 Tremont St (426-1400).
Quality Inn of Cambridge, 165 Massachusetts Ave, Cambridge (491-1000).
Ramada Inn—Airport, 225 McClennan Highway, East Boston (569-5250).
Ramada Inn of Boston, 1234 Soldiers' Field Rd, Brighton (254-1234).
Ritz Carlton, 15 Arlington St (536-5700).
Royal Sonesta Hotel Boston / Cambridge, 5 Cambridge Parkway, Cambridge (491-3600).
Sheraton Boston Hotel and Towers, 39 Dalton St, Prudential Center (236-2000).
Sheraton Commander Hotel, 16 Garden St, Cambridge (547-4800).
Sonesta Hotel, 5 Cambridge Parkway, Cambridge (491-3600).
Susse Chalet Inn, 211 Concord Turnpike, Cambridge (661-7800).
Susse Chalet Motor Lounge and Inn, 800 Morrissey Boulevard, Dorchester (287-9100).
Terrace Motor Lodge, 1650 Commonwealth Ave, Brighton (566-6260).
Tremont House, 275 Tremont St (426-1400).
Westin Hotel—Copley Place, 10 Huntington Ave (262-9600).
YMCA—Central Branch, 316 Huntington Ave (536-7800).

Restaurants

The ancestors of most Bostonians came to the city in the past century from all over the world. For that reason Boston has a greater variety of ethnic restaurants than any other city in the U.S. except New York. It is also a cosmopolitan city with many people who can afford to eat well and who have an educated taste, and so there are a number of distinguished restaurants that serve the best of both Continental and traditional American cuisine. Boston has long been famous for its seafood, and there are many good restaurants of that type, particularly along the waterfront. The following is a selective list of restaurants in Boston, Brookline, Cambridge, Somerville, and Watertown, grouped by area. Omission of a restaurant from this list does not imply any adverse judgment by the author or the publisher of the *Blue Guide*. For a more detailed and extensive review of restaurants in the Boston area consult Robert Nadeau, *Guide to Boston Restaurants;* Dennis Fitzgibbons, *Phoenix Guide to Dining Out;* or Steven Raichlen, *Boston's Best Restaurants.*

RESTAURANTS

DOWNTOWN BOSTON

Bay Tower Room, 60 State St (723-1666).
Blue Diner, 150 Kneeland St (338-4639).
Boston Proper, 53 State St (723-6440).
Brandy Pete's, 267 Franklin St (439-4165).
Cafe Fleuri, Meridien Hotel, 250 Franklin St (451-1900).
Cafe Suisse, Lafayette Hotel, 1 Ave de Lafayette (451-2600).
Cafe Tremont, Omni Parker House, 60 School St (227-8600).
Cornucopia, 15 West St (338-4600).
Dakota's, 101 Arch St (737-1777).
Dini's Sea Grill, 94 Tremont St (227-0380).
Julien, Meridien Hotel, 250 Franklin St (451-1900).
Le Marquis de Lafayette, Lafayette Hotel, 1 Ave de Lafayette (451-2600).
Locke-Ober Cafe, 3 Winter Pl (542-1340) (founded in 1875).
Maison Robert, 45 School St (in the Old City Hall) (227-3370).
Marliave, 11 Bosworth St (423-6340).
Milk Street Cafe, 50 Milk St (542-3633).
Nara, 85 Wendell St (338-5935).
Parker's, Omni Parker House, 60 School St (227-8600).
Sakura-Bana, 57 Broad St (542-4311).
Schroeder's, 8 High St (426-1234).
Weylu's Wharf, 254 Summer St (423-0243).

FANEUIL HALL / QUINCY MARKET

Aegean Fare, Faneuil Hall Marketplace (742-8349).
Brasserie Les Halles, North Market Building, Quincy Market (227-9660).
Cricket's, 101 South Market Building, Quincy Market (720-5570).
Durgin-Park, 5 Faneuil Hall Market Place (227-2038).
Houlihan's Old Place, 60 State St (367-6377).
Lily's, Faneuil Hall Marketplace (227-4242).
Seasons, Bostonian Hotel, North & Blackstone Sts (523-3600).
Tatsukichi, 189 State St (720-2468).
Union Oyster House, 41 Union St (227-2750) (Boston's oldest eating place, founded in 1826).

NORTH END

Bella Napoli, 425 Hanover St (720-2811).
Bernardo's, 24 Fleet St (723-4554).

Carlo Marino's Ristorante, 8 Prince St (523-9109).
Circle Pizza, 361 Hanover St (523-8787).
Daily Catch, 323 Hanover St (523-8567).
Davide, 326 Commercial Ave (227-5745).
Dom's, 10 Bartlett Pl (523-9279).
The European, 218 Hanover St (523-5694).
Fedele's, 319 Hanover St (523-0734).
Felicia's, 145A Richmond St (523-9885).
Florence Restaurant, 190 North St (523-4480).
Giacomo's, 355 Hanover St (523-9026).
G'Vanni's, 2 Prince St (720-3663).
Jasper, 240 Commercial St (523-1126).
Joseph's Aquarium, 101 Atlantic Ave (523-4000).
L'Osteria, 109 Salem St (723-7847).
Lucia's, 415 Hanover St (367-2353).
Mama Maria's, 3 North Sq (523-0077).
Mother Anna's, 211 Hanover St (523-8496).
Pagliuca's, 14 Parmenter St (367-1504).
Piccolo Venezia, 63 Salem St (523-9802).
Polcari's, 283 Causeway St (742-4142).
Regina Pizzeria, 11½ Thatcher St (227-0765).
Sabatino's, 14 Parmenter St (367-1504).
Villa Francesca, 150 Richmond St (367-2948).

WATERFRONT
Anthony's Pier 4, 140 Northern Ave (423-6363).
Chart House, 60 Long Wharf (227-1576).
Cherrystone's, 100 Atlantic Ave (on Commonwealth Pier) (367-0300).
Daily Catch, 261 Northern Ave (next to Boston Fish Pier) (338-3093).
Jimbo's Fish Shanty, 245 Northern Ave (next to Boston Fish Pier) (542-5600).
Jimmy's Harborside, 242 Northern Ave (next to Boston Fish Pier) (423-1000).
No Name, 15½ Fish Pier (off Northern Ave) (338-7539).
Rowes Wharf Restaurant and Cafe, 70 Rowes Wharf (439-3995).
Sally Ling's, 256 Commercial St (227-4545).

BEACON HILL
Another Season, 97 Mount Vernon St (367-0880).
Bel Canto, 42 Charles St (523-5575).
Hampshire House, 84 Beacon St (227-9600).
The Hungry I, 71½ Charles St (227-3524).
Il Dolce Momento, 30 Charles St (720-0477).
The King and I, 145 Charles St (227-3320).
La Trattoria, 288 Cambridge St (227-0211).
Paramount Steak House, 44 Charles St (523-8832).
Rebecca's, 21 Charles St (742-9747).
Ristorante Toscano, 41—43 Charles St (723-4090).
Tangiers, 37 Bowdoin St (367-0273).

CHINATOWN
Carl's Pagoda, 23 Tyler St (357-9837).
Chau Chow, 52 Beach St (426-6266).
Dong Khanh, 83 Harrison Ave (426-9410).
Dynasty, 33 Edinboro St (350-7777).
Golden Palace, 14 Tyler St (423-4565).
House of Toy, 14 Hudson St (426-5587).
Ho Yuen Ting, 13A Hudson St (426-2316).
Imperial Tea House Restaurant, 70 Beach St (426-8439).
Maxim's House, 84—86 Harrison Ave (451-5282).
Moon Villa, 15—19 Edinboro St (423-2061).
Pho Pasteur, 8 Kneeland St (451-0247).

Shanghai, 21 Hudson St (482-4797).
Viet Restaurant, 21 Tyler St (350-6615).

THEATER DISTRICT
Bennigan's, Stuart & Charles Sts, City Pl in Transportation Building (227-3754).
Bnu, 123 Stuart St (367-8405).
Downtown Cafe, 12 LaGrange St (338-7037).
Jacob Wirth, 31 Stuart St (338-8586) (an old German beer-hall, founded in 1868).
Mandalay, 63 Stuart St (338-5600).
Montien Thai Restaurant & Lounge, 63 Stuart St (338-5600).
Rocco's, 5 South Charles St (723-6800).
Stage Deli of New York, 275 Tremont St (523-3354).
Suntory, 212 Stuart St (338-2111).

BACK BAY
Acapulco, 266 Newbury St (247-9126).
Agatha, 142 Berkeley St (262-9790).
Arne's, Copley Pl (267-4900).
Atlantic Fish Company, 793 Boylston St (267-4000).
Aujourd'hui, 200 Boylston St (451-1392).
Back Bay Bistro, 565 Boylston St (536-4477).
Biba Food Hall, 272 Boylston St (426-3500).
Boodle's of Boston, Back Bay Hilton, 40 Dartmouth St (266-3537).
Cafe Budapest, Copley Hotel, 90 Exeter St (266-1979).
Cafe Plaza, Copley Plaza Hotel, Copley Sq (267-5300).
Cafe Rouge, Park Plaza Hotel, 50 Park Plaza (426-2000, ext. 35).
Casa Romero, 30 Gloucester St (536-4341).
Charley's Eating and Drinking Saloon, 284 Newbury St (266-3000).
Ciaobella, 240A Newbury St (536-2626).
Copley's Restaurant & Bar, Copley Plaza Hotel, 138 St James Ave, Copley Sq (267-5300).
Dartmouth Street, 271 Dartmouth St (536-6560.
Davio's, 269 Newbury St (262-4810).
Division Sixteen, 955 Boylston St (353-0870).
Du Barry, 159 Newbury St (262-4445).
57 Restaurant, 200 Stuart St, Park Plaza (423-5000).
Fox & Hounds, Park Plaza Hotel, 40 Park Plaza (426-0555).
Genji, 327 Newbury St (267-5656).
Grill 23 and Bar, 161 Berkeley St (542-2255).
Gyuhama, 827 Boylston St (437-0188).
Harvard Bookstore Cafe, 190 Newbury St (536-0095).
House of Siam, 21 Huntington Ave (267-1755).
J. C. Hilary's, 793 Boylston St (536-6300).
Kebab-N-Kurry, 30 Massachusetts Ave (536-9835).
The King and I, 259 Newbury St (437-9611).
Kyoto Steak House, 267 Huntington Ave (536-9295).
Legal Sea Foods, Boston Park Plaza Hotel, 64 Arlington St (426-4444).
L'Espalier, 30 Gloucester St (262-3023)0.
Mass. Bay Co., Sheraton Boston Hotel, 39 Dalton St (236-2606).
Mr. Leung, 545 Boylston St (236-4040).
Miyako, 468 Commonwealth Ave (236-0222).
Morton's of Chicago, 1 Exeter Plaza (266-5858).
Newbury's Steak House, 94 Massachusetts Ave (536-0184).
Oceanic Chinese Seafood, 91 Massachusetts Ave (353-0791).
Ritz Cafe, Ritz Carlton Hotel, 15 Arlington St ((536-5700).
Ritz Carlton Dining Room, Ritz Carlton Hotel, 15 Arlington St (536-5700).
Siam Cuisine, 961 Commonwealth Ave (254-4335).
Skipjack's, 199 Clarendon St (536-3500).
Stage Deli of New York, 725 Boylston St (859-9747).
Star of Siam, 93 Church St (451-5236).
A Steak in the Neighborhood, 30 Dalton St (262-1822).

Top of the Hub, Prudential Center (536-1775).
Turner Fisheries, Westin Hotel, 10 Huntington Ave, Copley Sq (424-7425) (best chowder in Boston).
Twenty-Nine Newbury Street, 29 Newbury St (536-0290).

SYMPHONY
Arirang House, 162 Massachusetts Ave (536-3141).
Bangkok Cuisine, 177A Massachusetts Ave (262-5377).
Cafe Promenade, Colonnade Hotel, 120 Huntington Ave (424-7000).
Ethiopian Restaurant, 333 Massachusetts Ave (424-1132).
Kyoto, 267 Huntington Ave (536-9295).
Oceanic Chinese Seafood, 91 Massachusetts Ave (353-0791).
Saint Botolph, 99 St. Botolph St (266-3030).
Thai Cuisine, 14A Westland Ave (424-7000).
Zachary's, Colonnade Hotel, 120 Huntington Ave (424-7000).

SOUTH END
Bob the Chef, 604 Columbus Ave (536-6204).
Buteco II, 57 W. Dedham St (247-9249).
Capriccio Piu, 550 Tremont St (338-6252).
Chef Chandler's, 329 Columbus Ave (247-7874).
Club Cafe, 209 Columbus Ave (536-0966).
Commonwealth Grille, 111 Dartmouth St (353-0160).
Hamersley's Bistro, 578 Tremont St (267-6068).
Icarus, 3 Appleton St (426-1790).
Legal Sea Foods, Park Plaza Hotel, 35 Columbus Ave (426-4444).
Nadia's Eastern Star, 280 Shawmut Ave (338-8091).
St. Cloud, 557 Tremont St (353-0202).

KENMORE SQUARE / FENWAY
Buteco I, 130 Jersey St (247-9508).
Cornwall's, 510 Commonwealth Ave (262-3749).
Gardner Museum Cafe, 280 The Fenway (at the rear of the museum on the ground floor) (566-1088).
India Quality, 536 Commonwealth Ave (267-4499).
Miyako, 468 Commonwealth Ave (236-0222).
Museum of Fine Arts Restaurant, 465 Huntington Ave (on the ground floor of the new wing) (267-9300).

BROOKLINE / CHESTNUT HILL (unless otherwise stated, the address is in Brookline)
B & D, The Deli, 1653B Beacon St (232-3727).
Bertucci's Pizza & Bocce, 4 Brookline Pl (731-2300).
Caffe Luna, Chestnut Hill Star Market Shopping Center, 11 Boylston St (734-8400).
Chef Chang's House, 1006 Beacon St (277-4226).
Chef Chow's House, 230 Harvard St (739-2469).
Ciro's, 239 Harvard St (277-7112).
Colorado Public Library, 111 Washington St, Brookline Village (734-6772).
Dover Sea Grille, 1223 Beacon St (566-7000).
Golden Temple, 1651 Beacon St (277-9722).
Harvard Street Grille, 398 Harvard St (734-9834).
Legal Sea Foods, 43 Boylston St, Chestnut Hill (277-7300).
Masada, 1665 Beacon St (277-3433).
Matt Garrett's, 299 Harvard St (738-5635).
Ming Garden, 1262 Boylston St, Chestnut Hill (232-4848).
Open Sesame Macrobiotic Restaurant, 48 Boylston St (277-9241).
Papillon, 1353B Beacon St (566-8495).
Rubin's Kosher Deli and Restaurant, 500 Harvard St (731-8787).
Sawsdee Thai Restaurant, 320 Washington St, Brookline Village (566-0720).
Skipjack's, 2 Brookline Pl (232-8887).
Sol Azteca, 914A Beacon St (262-0909).

Tam O'Shanter, 1648 Beacon St (277-0982).
Village Catch, 22 Harvard St, Brookline Village (566-3474).

ALLSTON / BRIGHTON
Barbeques International, 129 Brighton Ave, Brighton (782-6669).
Cafe Brazil, 420 Cambridge St, Brighton (789-5980).
Cao Palace, 137 Brighton Ave, Allston (783-2340).
Korea House, 111–117 Chiswick Rd, Brighton (783-7030).
Sculler's Grille, Embassy Suites Hotel, 400 Soldiers' Field Rd, Allston (783-0090).
Siam Cuisine, 961 Commonwealth Ave, Allston (254-4335).
Siam Palace, 379 Cambridge St, Allston (783-2434).
Thai House, 1033 Commonwealth Ave, Brighton (787-4242).

CAMBRIDGE: HARVARD SQUARE
The Acropolis, 1680 Massachusetts Ave (492-0900).
Ashoka, 991 Massachusetts Ave (661-9001).
Asmara, 714 Massachusetts Ave (497-9635).
Bartley's Burger Cottage, 1246 Massachusetts Ave (354-6559).
Bennett Street Cafe, Charles Hotel, 1 Bennett St (864-1200).
The Black Rose & Corrigan's, 50 Church St (492-8630).
Border Cafe, 32 Church St (864-6100).
Cafe Sushi, 1105 Massachusetts Ave (492-0434).
Casablanca, 40 Brattle St (867-0999).
Casa Mexico, 75 Winthrop St (491-4552).
Changsho, 1712 Massachusetts Ave (547-6565).
Chez Jean, 1 Shepard St (354-8980).
Chez Nous, 147 Huron Ave (864-6670).
Cottonwood Cafe, Porter Exchange Building, 1815 Massachusetts Ave (661-7440).
Dolphin Seafood, 1105 Massachusetts Ave (354-9332).
Elsie's, 71A Mount Auburn St (354-8781).
Grendel's Den, 89 Winthrop St (491-1050).
The Harvest, 44 Brattle St (492-1115).
Iruna, 55 Boylston St (868-5633).
Lucky Garden, 282 Concord Ave (354-9514).
Mexican Cuisine, 1682 Massachusetts Ave (661-1634).
The Peacock, 5 Craigie Circle (661-4073).
Rarities, Charles Hotel, 1 Bennett St (661-5050).
Roka, 1001 Massachusetts Ave (661-0344).
Shilla, 95 Winthrop St (547-7971).
The Skewers, 92 Mount Auburn St (491-3079).
The Spaghetti Club, 93 Winthrop St (576-1210).
Upstairs at the Pudding, 10 Holyoke St (864-1933).
The Wursthaus, 4 John F. Kennedy Drive, off Harvard Sq (491-7100) (the oldest eating place in Cambridge).
Yenching, 1326 Massachusetts Ave (547-1130).

CAMBRIDGE: INMAN SQUARE
Cafe China, 1245 Cambridge St (868-4300).
Cajun Yankee, 1193 Cambridge St (576-1971).
Casa Portugal, 1200 Cambridge St (491-8880).
East Coast Grill, 1271 Cambridge St (491-6568).
Haveli Classical Indian Cuisine, 1250 Cambridge St (497-6548).
New Korea, 1281 Cambridge St (876-6182).
S & S Deli & Restaurant, 1334 Cambridge St (354-0777).
Sunset Cafe, 851 Cambridge St (547-2938).

CAMBRIDGE: CENTRAL SQUARE
Bel Canto, 928 Massachusetts Ave (547-6120).
Bertucci's Pizza & Bocce, 799 Main St (661-8356).
Gandhi, 704 Massachusetts Ave (491-1104).
Green Street Grill, 280 Green St (876-1655).

Indian Globe, 474 Massachusetts Ave (868-1866).
India Pavilion, 17 Central Sq (547-7463).
Jonah's, Hyatt Regency Hotel, 575 Memorial Drive (492-1234).
Kabuki, 24 Pearl St (491-4929).
La Groceria, 853 Main St (547-9258).
Lai Lai, 700 Massachusetts Ave (876-7000).
Mary Chung, 447 Massachusetts Ave (864-1991).
Middle East, 472 Massachusetts Ave (354-8238).
Oh Calcutta, 468 Massachusetts Ave (576-2111).
Panache, 798 Main St (492-9500).
Peppercorn's, 154 Prospect St (661-2022).
Sally Ling's, Hyatt Regency Hotel, 575 Memorial Drive (492-1234).
Viceroy, 569 Massachusetts Ave (354-0611).

CAMBRIDGE: KENDALL SQUARE
Bisuteki Japanese Steak House, 777 Memorial Drive (492-7777).
Daily Catch, 1 Kendall Sq (225-2300).
Legal Sea Foods, 5 Cambridge Center (864-3400).
Michela's, 1 Athenaeum St (225-2121).
Milk Street Cafe, 101 Main St (491-8286) (a branch of the downtown Boston cafeteria).

CAMBRIDGE: FRESH POND
Joyce Chen's, 390 Rindge Ave (492-7373).
Little Osaka, 465 Concord Ave (491-6660).
The Lucky Garden, 282 Concord Ave (354-9514).
Pentimento, 344 Huron Ave (661-3878).

CAMBRIDGE: PORTER SQUARE
The Acropolis, 1680 Massachusetts Ave (354-8335).
Averoff, 1924 Massachusetts Ave (354-4500).
Passage to India, 1900 Massachusetts Ave (497-6113).
Tapas, 2067 Massachusetts Ave (576-2240).

SOMERVILLE
Bertucci's Pizza & Bocce, 197 Elm St, Davis Sq (661-8356).
Dali, 415 Washington St (661-3254).
Neighborhood Restaurant and Bakery, 25 Bow St, Davis Sq (623-9710).
P.A. Seafood, 345 Somerville St, Union Sq (776-1557).
Rudy's Cafe, 250 Holland St, Davis Sq (623-9201).

WATERTOWN
Le Bocage, 72 Bigelow Ave (923-1210).
Glenda's Kitchen, 45 Lexington St (926-3222).
Stellina's, 47 Main St (924-9475).
Taste of India, 91 Bigelow Ave (926-1606).

CHARLESTOWN
Barrett's on Boston Harbor, 2 Constitution Rd (242-9600).
Olive's, 67 Main St (242-1999).
Roughan's, 10 City Sq (242-3380).
Sorelle, 1 Monument Ave (242-2125).

CHELSEA / EAST BOSTON
Blazing Saddles, 940 Saratoga St, East Boston (569-2020).
New Bridge Cafe, 650 Washington Ave, Chelsea (884-0134).
Rita's Place, 88 Winnisimmet St, Chelsea (884-9010).
Sablone's, 107A Porter St, East Boston (567-8140).

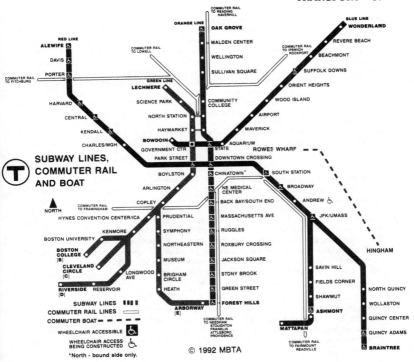

SUBWAY LINES, COMMUTER RAIL AND BOAT

SUBWAY LINES
COMMUTER RAIL LINES
COMMUTER BOAT
WHEELCHAIR ACCESSIBLE
WHEELCHAIR ACCESS BEING CONSTRUCTED
*North - bound side only.

© 1992 MBTA

Transport

Boston and its environs have one of the most extensive public transportation systems in the U.S., and also one of the most inexpensive. Public transport is under the control of the Massachusetts Bay Transportation Authority,
which is referred to as the MBTA, or simply as the T. Besides the T, which
operates both the subway and the public bus system, the Boston Metropolitan area is served by 28 private bus carriers. The Greater Boston Region,
as it is officially known, is served by Commuter Rail, which is operated by
the Boston & Maine R.R. under the jurisdiction of the MBTA. Rail service
from Boston to points S. as far as Washington, D.C., is provided by Amtrak,
an organization of several railroad companies that is heavily subsidized by
the U.S. government to provide fast and efficient rail service between the
major cities on the Eastern Seaboard. There are also commuter ferries
between Boston and points on the South Shore, as well as summer cruises
to the Harbor Islands, Provincetown, and the North Shore and Cape Ann.
Information on all of these transport services is given below. More detailed
information about transportation in Boston and its environs can be obtained
by calling Travel Information, tel. 722-3200.

The MBTA City Rail System consists of four lines: the Orange, Red, Blue, and Green. The
first three of these are subway trains, which surface and run on elevated viaducts along
part of their routes, while the Green Line operates two-car trolleys that travel underground

in the center of the city and then emerge to run at street level to their final destination. Both trains and cars bear a sign at the front giving their destination. On the Green Line the final stop is indicated by a letter as well as the destination, because the line forks into three branches: **B** denotes Boston College, **C** is Cleveland circle, **D** is Riverside, and **E** is Arborway, and a red slash through the letter indicates that the car does not run to the end of the line. At present the Green Line trolleys only go as far as Brigham Circle, where one must transfer to a bus that goes to the end of the line. Alternatively, if one is taking the Green Line to Arborway one can transfer at the Copley Sq station and take a Green Line bus that follows the same route to the final stop. At street-level stops on the Green Line there are no token booths, so travelers must board at the front of the trolley and put the exact change into the coin box. (The driver will not give change.) Children under 12 and handicapped persons pay half fare. The T fares have changed repeatedly in the past few years and will undoubtedly continue to do so, and thus there is no point in giving information about fares in this guide.

The MBTA Bus System is designed to supplement the rail system. Since the MBTA trains and trolleys radiate out from the center of the city many of the buses provide crosstown communication between the T train stations. Some buses provide local service in the city and suburbs, while others connect suburban areas with the last stops on the T train lines. There are also express buses that connect some of the suburban towns with Boston; these leave either from a lot beside the South Station or from Copley Sq, on the Dartmouth St side of the Boston Public Library. Bus-stop signs vary. Many are "No Parking" signs with the T logo in the middle, and some also say "Bus Stop" as well. In some places the only indication of a bus stop is a wide red-and-yellow band painted on an adjacent telephone pole. Signs at the front of the buses give the route number and the final stop. Enter at the front and put the exact change in the coin box.

Private Bus Companies connect downtown Boston with most of the towns in the metropolitan area. Most of these buses leave from the Greyhound / Trailways terminal on Park Sq, or from the area around South Station. Information concerning the routes and schedules of these private bus companies can be obtained by calling Travel Information, tel. 722-3200.

The Commuter Rail System also connects Boston with many of the towns in the Metropolitan Area. Trains going to the southern and western suburbs depart from South Station, while those going to the N. and N.W. depart from North Station. Information on routes and schedules can be obtained by calling Travel Information, tel. 722-3200.

Amtrak provides frequent intercity service to points S.: Providence, New Haven, New York, Philadelphia, and Washington, D.C. A daily train from South Station travels direct to Chicago via Worcester, Springfield, and Albany. Information on schedules and fares can be obtained by calling Travel Information, tel. 722-3200.

Commuter Ferry Boats to Hull and Hingham leave from Rowes Wharf and Long Wharf near the Aquarium stop on the Blue Line. In the summer there are cruises to Provincetown from Long Wharf, and from Rowes Wharf there are cruises of Boston Harbor and its islands, as well as day trips to the Harbor Islands and Nantasket Beach. Several companies offer cruises around the harbor and to the Charlestown Navy Yard. For information about all of these cruises consult the Yellow Pages in the Boston Telephone Directory under the heading Boats—Excursion. The A.C. Cruise Line offers a cruise along the North Shore from Boston to Gloucester, leaving daily at 9:30 a.m. from Pier 1 on Northern Ave; for information call 426-8419. There are also "Whale Watch" cruises to Gloucester and Cape Ann.

The MBTA Pass Program. The MBTA sells a monthly pass for unlimited rides on the T. One pass allows unlimited rides on the T trains, another on the T buses, and a third on both trains and buses. Passholders also receive discounts at the New England Aquarium and the Institute of Contemporary Art. For information call the Pass Program Manager at the MBTA; tel. 722-5218.

MBTA Information. There is an Information Center at the Park St T station where maps of the T train and bus routes as well as routes and schedules for the Commuter Rail are obtained; tel. 722-3200, 722-5657 (evenings and weekends).

Shoppers' Shuttle. A number of old London double-decker buses have been pressed into service to take passengers across the downtown area, a particularly convenient itinerary for shoppers. For information call 739-0100.

General Information and Addresses

Information. The National Parks Service operates an Information Center on the ground floor of 15 State St, directly opposite the Old State House and the State St T station (on both the Blue and Orange Lines). At the State House on Beacon St there is a Boston and Massachusetts Information Desk; in summer this is located to the left of the entrance to the East Wing (the section to the r. of the main entrance); in winter it is in Doric Hall, the main entrance lobby.)The public entrance to Doric Hall is to the l. of the main entrance.) The *Boston Visitors and Information Center* is located on Boston Common, at the corner of Tremont and West Sts. There are recorded telephone messages giving the following information: *Time:* 637-1234; *Weather:* 936-1234; *Boston Garden* (forthcoming events): 237-3200; *Children's Museum:* 522-5444: *Gardner Museum:* 734-1359; *Museum of Fine Arts:* 267-9377; *Museum of Science:* 742-6088; *New England Aquarium:* 742-8870; *Franklin Park Zoo:* 442-0991.

Information pertaining to the Commonwealth of Massachusetts can be obtained from the Massachusetts Tourism Office, Department of Commerce & Development, 100 Cambridge St, Boston 02129 (tel. 727-3221). The Visitors' Center in the Prudential Center is open daily, 9—5. Information can also be obtained from the following: Greater Boston Convention & Visitors' Bureau, Box 490, Boston 9-02199 (tel. 267-6446 for recorded information); or Superintendent, Boston National Historical Park, Charlestown Navy Yard, Boston 02129. For additional information on Boston as a place to visit, work, or study, call 1-800-858-0200 every day, 9—5, or 536-4100 for specific information.

Rest Rooms. There is a Visitor Hospitality Center located on the fourth floor of Boston City Hall; this is open from May through Oct. and includes rest rooms and associated facilities, for both children and adults, and includes a playground and baby-care facility (ages three to six). There are also rest rooms at the National Parks Information Center at 15 State St. In Boston Common there is a men's room near the tennis courts, and in the Boston Public Gardens there is a ladies' room near the Charles St entrance.

Emergency Telephone Numbers. *Ambulance, Fire, Police* (emergency only): 911, or any of the following numbers for specific cases: *Boston Police:* 247—4200; *Cambridge Police:* 542-5500; *Massachusetts State Police:* 566-4500; *Fire Dept.:* 442—8000 or 536-1500; *Poison Control Center:* 232-0000; *Alcohol Abuse:* 426-9444 or 524-7884; *Drug Abuse:* 536-0279; *Rape Crisis Center:* 492-7273; *Personal Crisis Support:* 267-9150; *Child at Risk Hotline:* 1-800-792-5200; *Suicide:* 247-0220; *Mayor's Office Night Line:* 725-4000; *Dental Emergency:* 969-6663; *24-Hour Pharmacy:* Phillips Drug Store, 155 Charles St, Boston, 523-1028; *Hospitals:* Beth Israel, 735-3337; Boston

City, 424-5000; Brigham & Women's, 732-5636; Cambridge City, 498-1000; Children's, 735-6611; Massachusetts General, 726-2000; New England Medical Center, 956-5566; St. Elizabeth's, 789-2666.

Travelers in distress can contact the Travelers Aid Society at the following locations: Main Office, 711 Atlantic Ave, Boston (542-7286), open Mon.– Fri. 8:45 a.m.–4:45 p.m.; Greyhound / Trailways Bus Terminal, Park Sq, Boston (542-9875), open Mon.–Sat. 11 a.m.–7 p.m.; Logan Airport, 567-5385, open daily 11:30 a.m.–7:30 p.m.; South Station, 423-7766. American Automobile Association (AAA): Information Service, 723-9666; Emergency Road Service: 723-9666.

Twenty-four-Hour Services. *Restaurant:* Mondo's, 14 South Market St, behind Faneuil Hall. *Food Market:* The Store, 24 Main St, across from City Hall in Watertown. *Service Station:* Gulf Service Station, 188 Summer St, at Atlantic Ave. *Post Office:* Main Post Office at Post Office Sq. *Taxis:* Checker, 537-7000; Independent, 426-8700; Green Cab, 628-0600; Town Taxi, 536-5000.

Telephone: Instructions for using the telephones are posted in the telephone booths.

Opening & Closing Times. *Banks:* generally open weekdays 9–4; some branches open Sat. 9–12 (or 1 p.m.). *Post Offices:* generally open weekdays 8–5, Sat. 9–12. The General Post Office at 25 Dorchester Ave, behind South Station, is open weekdays 8:30–8:30, Sat. 8–5; a self-service machine there is open 24 hours. Public buildings are open weekdays 9–5. Shops are generally open Mon.–Sat. 9 (or 9:30)–6 (or 7); some, particularly in touristic areas or in shopping malls, are open Sun. 12–5.

Liquor Laws. Packaged spirits and beer are sold at licensed liquor stores and at some grocery shops Mon.–Sat. 8 a.m.–11 p.m., closed on Sun. Bars, restaurants, hotels, and nightclubs sell by the drink Mon.–Sat. 8 a.m.–Sat. midnight, Sun. 2 p.m.–2 a.m. Liquor stores are closed on Memorial Day, Thanksgiving Day, Christmas Day, and New Year's Day. The minimum legal age for drinking in Massachusetts is 21.

Newspapers & Magazines. The two daily newspapers published in Boston are the *Boston Globe* and the *Boston Herald American.* The *Boston Phoenix* is a weekly newspaper that specializes in the arts and entertainment. Foreign and out-of-town newspapers and magazines are sold at a kiosk in Harvard Square. *Boston* magazine, a monthly, reports on the city's cultural, social, and sports scenes.

Tipping. In restaurants, bars, and taxicabs the normal tip is 15 percent.

Houses of Worship. (Whenever possible, these have been selected because of their historical or architectural interest, otherwise because of their central location.) *Roman Catholic:* St. Stephen's, 401 Hanover St. *Unitarian:* King's Chapel, Tremont and School Sts. *Episcopal:* Christ Church ("The Old North"), 190 Salem St; Trinity Church, Copley Sq. *Congregational:* Church of the Covenant, 67 Newbury St. *Congregational-United Church of Christ:* Old South Church, 645 Boylston St. *Baptist:* First Baptist Church of Christ, Commonwealth Ave at Clarendon St. *Friends:* Beacon Hill Friends House, 6 Chestnut St. *Greek Orthodox:* Cathedral Church of the Evangelismos, 514 Parker St. *Armenian Gregorian:* Armenian Holy Trinity Apostolic Church of Greater Boston, 145 Brattle St, Cambridge. *Russian Orthodox:* Russian Orthodox Cathedral, 165 Park Drive. *Albanian Orthodox:* 529 Broadway, South Boston. *Christian Science:* Christian Science Mother Church, Massachusetts Ave and Huntington Ave. *Armenian Catholic:* 100 Mount Auburn St, Cambridge. *Mormon:* Church of Jesus Christ, 132 Pleasant St, Cambridge. *Lutheran:* First Lutheran Church of Boston, 299 Berkeley St. *Jewish:* Temple Israel, 260 The Riverway. *Moslem:* American Muslim Mission, 35 Intervale Ave, Dorchester.

Holidays. The official holidays in Boston are: New Year's Day (Jan. 1); Martin Luther King's Birthday (Jan. 15)., observed the third Mon. in Jan.); Washington's Birthday (Feb. 21, observed the third Mon. in Feb.); Evacuation Day (March 17); Patriots Day (April 19, observed the third Mon. in April); Memorial Day (May 30, observed the last Mon. in May); Bunker Hill Day (June 17); Independence Day (July 4; if this falls on a weekend the following Mon. also becomes a holiday); Labor Day (first Mon. in Sept.); Columbus Day (Oct. 12, observed the second Mon. in Oct.); Thanksgiving Day (last Thur. in Nov.); Christmas Day (Dec. 25).

Orientation Programs. At the National Parks Visitors' Center at 15 State St there are brochures available and an audiovisual program describing the city and its historic past. At the Old State House Museum there is a continuously showing audiovisual program on the history of Boston. At 60 State St, on the Freedom Trail next to Faneuil Hall, there is a multimedia show and exhibition entitled "Where's Boston?" These shows are given hourly from 10 a.m. onward and last for 50 min; an admission fee is charged.

Sightseeing Tours.

By Bus: Boston Double Deckers (629-2300) offer one-hour sightseeing tours of Boston every day, with frequent stops along the Freedom Trail, a route that takes one to the major Revolutionary War sites in Boston and Charlestown. The Brush Hill Transportation Co., 109 Norfolk St (236–2148), offers city tours aboard "Beantown Trolleys"; one can board at the Sheraton, Westin, or Copley Square Hotel for a 90-minute tour or extend it over a whole day by pausing at stops en route. Another, similar service is the Blue Trolley, P.O. Box 267 (tel. TROLLEY). The Gray Line, 420 Maple St., Marlboro (426-8805), offers three-hour bus tours of Greater Boston, starting from several downtown hotels; another three-hour tour takes one to Lexington, Concord, and Cambridge; a seven-hour tour combines the above with a visit to Sudbury.

By Boat: Bay State Spray and Provincetown Steamship Co., general offices at 66 Long Wharf, ticket office at 20 Long Wharf (723-7800), offers several cruises. One cruise goes from Boston to Provincetown on the tip of Cape Cod, a three-hour voyage each way. A second cruise goes out to the Harbor Islands as well as to see the USS *Constitution* in Charlestown and the site of the Boston Tea Party. Carefree Cruises, 433 Hanover St (723-6446), offers fully narrated tours of inner Boston Harbor aboard the *Sans Souci.* Mass Bay Lines, offices at 344 Atlantic Ave, ticket office on Rowes Wharf, offers sightseeing cruises of Boston Harbor and trips out to George Island, as does Boston Harbor Cruises, whose offices are at One Long Wharf (227-4321). When down on Long Wharf, one might recall that it was from here that Captain Joshua Slocum set out on his epic voyage in 1897 in the *Spray,* a little sailboat in which he single-handedly circumnavigated the world. Whale Watch tours to Gloucester and Cape Ann are offered by A. C. Cruise Line, 290 Northern Ave (426-8419).

Walking Tours. There are a number of groups that offer walking tours around Boston. A self-guided tour can be done along the Freedom Trail, a 1½-hour walk, guided by a red stripe along the sidewalk, which takes one to the major sites in Boston and Charlestown associated with the American Revolution. (There is another such self-guided tour in Cambridge, the Heritage Trail.) The tour begins at the Freedom Trail Information Center on the Tremont side of Boston Common, where one can obtain a map of the trail. Another such self-guided tour is the Black Heritage Trail; this takes one to 14 sites on Beacon Hill that have associations with the history of Boston's black community; a leaflet and map describing this tour can be obtained from the National Park Service at 15 State St. Other walking tours are offered by the following: *Historic Neighborhoods Foundation,* 2 Boylston St (426-1885), is a nonprofit organization that offers guided walks through the city. *Boston by Foot,* 77 North Washington St (367-2345), offers a variety of guided walks, and once a month it has a special tour for children. *Fine Arts Tours,* Box 206, Newton 02159 (655-8532), offers guided tours of the city's art museums and galleries as well as to the studios of local artists. *Boston Walkabouts* is a cassette tape, available at hotels, bookshops, and gift shops, designed for a 64-minute walk along the Freedom Trail. *Harborwalk* is a self-guided tour beginning at the Old State House and ending at the Boston Tea Party site; map and brochure are available at the Boston Common information kiosk. *Victorian Society in America,* Gibson House Museum, 137 Beacon St (282-9830), evenings only), sponsors walking tours of sites in Boston and Cambridge with associations in the Victorian era. *The Society for the Preservation of New England Antiquities* (SPNEA), 141 Cambridge St (227-3956), occasionally organizes guided tours of some of the historic houses on Beacon Hill.

Panoramic Views. A number of places in Boston provide a panoramic view of the city. In downtown Boston there are three skyscrapers with observation decks; these are, in order of increasing height: the *Customs-House Tower,* State & India Sts, open Mon.—Fri. 9—11:30 and 1—4:30, free; the *Prudential Tower Skywalk,* Prudential Center, open Mon.—Sat. and Hol., 9—midnight, Sun. 1 p.m.—midnight; fee; the *Observatory of the New John Hancock Building,* St. James Ave & Trinity Place, open May—Oct., 9 a.m.—11 p.m.; Nov.—April, noon—11 p.m., fee. The John Hancock Building is the tallest skyscraper in New England, with a height of 740ft, and the Observatory commands a breathtaking view of all of Boston and its environs. There are a number of telescopes which are focused on some of the major monuments of Boston, and others which can be used to observe any part of the city and its vicinity. The Observatory also has four programs which deal with the history, topography, and architecture of the city. "Boston 1775" is a sound-and-light show that recreates Boston in the Revolutionary period, showing some of the dramatic events that took place there during the struggle for American independence. "City Flight" is a seven-minute color motion picture filmed from a helicopter, focusing on the landmarks of the city. "Skyline Boston" is a program illustrating the changes in the topography and skyline of Boston since its founding in 1630, with a narration by the late Walter Muir Whitehill, the distinguished historian and authority on the topography and architecture of the city. "Photorama" is an exhibition of 110 photographs of historic monuments and landmarks of the city, each accompanied by an informative caption.

Shuttles. Two services shuttle back and forth between the harborside approach to Quincy Market, where it crosses the Central Artery, and various sites of interest. One of these, "The Shuttle" (fee,) goes to 14 sites in Boston and Charlestown. The other, the "Boston Tea Party Courtesy Shuttle" (free), which also leaves from the Congress St side of the Old State House, goes to the Boston Tea Party Museum.

Museums, Monuments, and Historic Sites

The descriptions of the museums, monuments, and historic sites in Boston and Cambridge are prefaced by a paragraph entitled **Admission,** giving the days and hours that these places are open. Times of admission are subject to change, and those listed are the ones posted when this guide was written. The cost of admission to these sites is constantly changing, invariably upward, and so information regarding these and other prices has not been listed below, other than to note "fee" if there is an entrance charge. Unless indicated otherwise, all of the places described in the guide are closed on July 4, Thanksgiving Day, Christmas Day (and many on Christmas Eve as well), and New Year's Day; some are closed on other days besides these.

Calendar of Events

The dates for some of these events vary from year to year. Some of these movable dates are listed in the *Boston Travel Planner,* published twice a year by the Greater Boston Convention and Visitors' Bureau, P.O. Box 490, Boston, MA 02199; tel. 267-6446.

January
1–6:   Christmas Festival of Lights continues in Boston Common.
19:    Benjamin Franklin Day; ceremony at Franklin statue in front of Old City Hall.
Third Mon.: Observance of Martin Luther King's Birthday (actual date Jan. 15); ceremony at City Hall.
Movable Events: Art Boston, Park Plaza Expo & Conference Center (536-5049). Ice Festival, Faneuil Hall Marketplace (523-3886). Boston Boat Show, World Trade Center (536-8152).

February
12:    Lincoln's Birthday; ceremony at Lincoln statue in Park Sq.
Third Mon.: Observance of Washington's Birthday (actual date Feb. 22); ceremony at Washington's equestrian statue in Boston Common.
Black History Month: check newspaper and magazine listings for special programs.
Movable Feast: Chinese New Year (soon to be celebrated in Jan.); celebration in Chinatown.
Movable Events: Boston Sailboat Show, World Trade Center (536-8152). New England Home Show, World Trade Center (536-1852).

March
5:    Boston Massacre Day; the Charlestown Militia leads a parade from the Massacre site to City Hall Plaza.
17:    St. Patrick's Day and Boston Evacuation Day (if a weekday, then observed the Sun. prior to that date); parade by the Irish community beginning at Andrew Sq in South Boston and proceeding to East Broadway.
Movable Events: Boston Globe Jazz & Heritage Festival, Opera House, Berklee Performance Center (929-2649). New England Spring Flower Show, Bayside Exposition Center (265-5800). International Boston Seafood Show, Hynes Convention Center (954-2200). Easter Parade (March or April): Promenade along Commonwealth Ave to the Public Garden.

April

Third Mon.: Observance of Patriots' Day (actual date April 19); On the eve of this day a lantern service is held in Old North Church to commemorate the beginning of Paul Revere's ride. Re-enactments of the rides of both Paul Revere and William Dawes are held, the first beginning at Paul Revere Mall in the North End and the second in John Eliot Sq in Roxbury, with both rides ending on Lexington Green. On Patriots' Day there is a parade in Back Bay by the Ancient and Honorable Artillery Company. The first two battles of the American Revolution are re-enacted, the first on Lexington Green and the second at North Bridge in Concord. The high point of the day is the running of the Boston Marathon, a race of 26 miles 385 yards from Hopkinton Green to the Prudential Center.

Movable Events: Azalea Festival, Faneuil Hall Marketplace (523-2980). Power Boat Show, World Trade Center (439-5000). Artists' Ball, Boston Center for the Arts, Cyclorama (227-2443).

May

20:   Lafayette Day; ceremony at Lafayette monument on Boston Common.

Last Mon.: Memorial Day; ceremony in Copley Sq.

Movable Events: Beacon Hill Hidden Gardens Tour. Art Newbury Street, Newbury St between Arlington St and Massachusetts Ave (267-9416). Lilac Sunday, Arnold Arboretum. New England Street Performers' Festival, Faneuil Hall Marketplace (523-2980). Kite Festival, Franklin Park Zoo. *The Revels,* Sanders Theater, Harvard (426-0889). John F. Kennedy Regatta, Boston Harbor (847-1800).

June

Festival of Art throughout the month in Boston Common.

First Mon.: The Ancient and Honorable Artillery Company musters in Faneuil Hall and parades to Copley Sq.

17:   Bunker Hill Day; parade in Charlestown beginning at the corner of Vine and Tufts Sts and proceeding to Monument Sq; re-enactment of the Battle of Bunker Hill at the Monument.

25–28: Festival of St. Peter in Gloucester; blessing of the fishing fleet on June 28.

Movable Events: Cambridge River Festival, Memorial Drive in Cambridge (498-9033). Dairy Festival, Boston Common (734-6750). Saint Botolph Street Fair, St. Botolph St. Dorchester Day Parade, Dorchester (725-4000). Victorian Parade in the Public Garden. Back Bay Street Fair, Marlborough St. Festival of St. Anthony, Prince St.

July

The Boston Harborfest is celebrated throughout the month, beginning with ceremonies in the Faneuil Hall Marketplace. Events in the Harborfest include the annual ceremonies listed below as well as guided walks on the Harbor Islands; port visits of U.S. Navy ships, tours of Coast Guard ships, the Constitution Cup Regatta, bell-ringing in the Old North, the Chowderfest, the Great Harbor Hunt, the Wind and Water Festival on Gallups Island, and concerts at Columbia Point and City Hall Plaza.

The Festival of Art continues throughout the month in Boston Common; free esplanade concerts begin in the Hatch Shell on the Charles

River Esplanade, continuing throughout the summer.

4:    Independence Day. Parade begins at City Hall and proceeds through the historic neighborhoods of the city to Faneuil Hall, ending with a ceremony there. Declaration of Independence read from balcony of Old State House. Annual "Turnaround Cruise" of "Old Ironsides." Concert by Boston Pops Orchestra at Hatch Shell climaxed with a performance of Tchaikovsky's *1812 Overture,* followed by fireworks over the Charles River.

Movable Feasts: Italian street festivals in the North End every weekend during the summer; also festivals of other ethnic groups at churches throughout the Boston area, including several Greek *paniyeria* and Latin American fiestas.

August

Art Festival and Hatch Shell concerts continue throughout the month, as do ethnic festivals, including the Festival of the August Moon in Chinatown. Other events include the Fishermen's Festival on North St and Kidsfair on Boston Common.

26:    Faneuil Hall Marketplace Birthday Celebration and Parade.

September

1:    Muster Day, Plimoth Plantation, Plymouth.

Movable Events: Charles Street Fair, Beacon Hill Civic Association. New England Apple Fair, Faneuil Hall Marketplace. Greek Heritage Festival, Waterfront Park. Footlight Parade, Park Plaza Hotel. Art Newbury Street, Newbury St between Arlington St and Massachusetts Ave (267-9416). "Taste of Boston," festival on Boston Common. Oxfam America's Annual International Harvest Fair. Artsmart, Wang Center (482-2595).

October

9:    Leif Eriksson Day; ceremony at Leif Eriksson statue on Commonwealth Avenue.

Second Mon.: Observance of Columbus Day (actual date Oct. 12); ceremony at statue of Christopher Columbus in Louisburg Sq; parade by Italian community in North End.

Sun. after Columbus Day: Head of the Charles Regatta.

Movable Events: Boston Globe Book Festival, Children's Museum. Octoberfest Street Fair, Harvard Sq. Harvest Celebration, Plimoth Plantation. Halloween Costume Ball, Hammond Castle Museum, Gloucester (283-2080). Monsterdash, Halloween fun run (523-2980). New England Interior Design Show, Bayside Expo Center (528-1912). International Sportsfishing Boat Show, Bayside Expo Center (265-5800). Fish Expo, Bayside Expo Center (265-5800). New England Fall Home Show, World Trade Center (536-8152). Northeast Computer Fair, Bayside Expo Center (449-6600).

November

11:    Veterans' Day; parade goes around Boston Common and the Public Garden.

Third Fri.: Christmas Festival of Lights begins on Boston Common.

Fourth Thurs.: Thanksgiving; Pilgrim's Progress and other ceremonies at Plimoth Plantation; Thanksgiving celebration at Sturbridge Village.

Movable Events: South End Historical Society Fleamarket, South End (536-

4445). New England Crafts Festival, World Trade Center (439-5000). Harvard Square Light Procession and Tree Lighting, Massachusetts Ave, Cambridge (491-3434). Faneuil Hall Marketplace's "Bells of Boston."

December
1: Prudential Center's Annual Tree Lighting & Carol Sing (236-3302).
1–3: Festival of Trees, Plimoth Plantation.
9: Annual Charlestown Christmas Walk.
10: Boston Tea Party Re-enactment, Boston Tea Party Ship (338-1773).
13–15: Festival of Lights and Song, Tremont Temple (861-0649).
14–30: *Christmas Revels,* Sanders Theater, Harvard.
24: Candlelight and Caroling Service, Trinity Church. Handel & Haydn Society's *Messiah,* Symphony Hall (266-1492). *The Nutcracker Suite,* Boston Ballet, Wang Center (542-1323).
24–31: Christmas Festival of Lights in Boston Common.
31: Boston Pops New Year's Eve Concert, Symphony Hall.

Entertainment

I. The Performing Arts Boston is second only to New York City in the number, variety, and quality of its cultural activities, particularly in the performing arts. Information on current cultural events can be best obtained from the entertainment section of the *Boston Globe,* which every Thursday publishes a special "Calendar" section, which has articles and listings of all of the coming week's cultural events and entertainments. Information on these activities can also be obtained from the *Boston Herald-American* and from the *Boston Phoenix.* Information on cultural affairs and entertainments currently being sponsored by the city of Boston can be obtained by calling City Hall (725-4000).

Many of the theaters in Boston are near the Boylston St T station on the Green Line, an area which has thus come to be called the "Boylston Theater District." Some theaters there often put on productions of plays before they appear in New York or performances by national repertory companies, while others have their own companies of performers or put on new productions and original plays. Tickets may be purchased at the box offices of the theaters or at the following ticket agencies: BOSTIX, the ticket booth at Faneuil Hall; *Hub Ticket Agency,* 240 Tremont St (426-8340); *Tyson Ticket Agency,* 201 Tremont St (426-2662); *Out of Town Ticket Agency* (can obtain tickets for N.Y. productions), Harvard Sq, Cambridge (492-1900). Unless indicated otherwise below, the addresses given are in Boston, and the telephone numbers are given in parenthesis. Some of the more famous theaters, theatrical groups, and symphony orchestras are described in more detail in the various Routes later in the text.

THEATERS
Alley Theater, 1253 Cambridge St, Cambridge (491-8166) (new and experimental plays).
Aquarius Theater, 413 Washington St (482-0650).
Boston Center for the Arts, 539 Tremont St (426-5000).
Boston Repertory Theater, Inc., One Boylston Place (423-6580).

Cambridge Ensemble, Old Cambridge Baptist Church, 1151 Massachusetts Ave, Cambridge (876-2544).

Caravan Theater, Harvard-Epworth Church, 1555 Massachusetts Ave, Cambridge (868-8850).

Charles Playhouse, 76 Warrenton St (423-2255).

Charles Playhouse Stage II, 74 Warrenton St (426-5225) (cabaret setting for Boston's longest-running comedy hit, *Shear Madness*).

Charlestown Working Theater, 442 Bunker Hill Rd, Charlestown (242-3534) (experimental).

Colonial Theater, 106 Kennedy Drive (426-9366).

Fenway Theater, 136 Massachusetts Ave (426-6390).

Hasty Pudding Theatricals, 12 Holyoke St, Cambridge (495-5205).

Hub Theater Co., Old West Church, 131 Cambridge St (227-3532).

Little Flags Theater, 22 Sunset St, Roxbury (232-2666) (original leftist drama).

Loeb Drama Center, 64 Brattle St, Cambridge (864-2630).

Lyric Stage, 54 Charles St (742-8703).

Massachusetts Center Repertory Co., 541 Tremont St (262-0340).

Musical Theaters I & II, 400 Commonwealth Ave (536-4011).

Music Hall Theater, 268 Tremont St (423-3300).

National Center of Afro-American Artists Drama Program, 122 Elm Ave, Roxbury (442-8820).

New Erlich Theater, 551 Tremont St (482-6316).

Next Move Theater, 1 Boylston St (423-5572).

Open Circle Theater, 76 Warrenton St (542-0392).

Peoples' Theater, Church of the Covenant, 67 Newbury St (247-9000).

The Proposition, 241 Hampshire St at Inman Sq, Cambridge (876-0088).

Sanders Theater, Memorial Hall, Harvard (495-1591).

Shubert Theater, 265 Tremont St (426-4520).

Stage I, 539 Tremont St (426-7193).

Terrace Room, Boston Plaza Hotel, 64 Arlington St (357-8384) (setting of the long-running spoof of Broadway musicals, *Forbidden Broadway*).

Theater Co. of Boston, 551 Tremont St (423-7193).

Theater Workshop Boston—OM Theater, 539 Tremont St (482-7193).

Wang Center for the Performing Arts, 268 Tremont St (482-9393) (home of the Boston Ballet, and used for other large-scale productions of dance, drama, and opera).

Wilbur Theater, 252 Tremont St (426-5827).

CHILDREN'S THEATER
Boston Children's Theater, New England Life Hall, 225 Clarendon St (536-3324).

The Cambridge Ensemble, 1151 Massachusetts Ave, Cambridge (542-3945).

National Theater for Children, 73 Park Drive (353-1225).

Puppet Show Place, 30 Station St, Brookline Village (731-6400).

BALLET
Boston Ballet Company, 551 Tremont St (542-3945).

National Center of Afro-American Artists Dance Company, 122 Elm Hill Ave, Roxbury (442-8820).

FOLK DANCING
Beacon Hill Neighborhood Arts Council, Hill House, Inc., 74 Joy St (227-0845); free.

Country Dance Society, 3 Joy St (523-5695).

Folk Dancing Around Boston,l 62 Fottler Ave, Lexington (862-7144).

MIT Campus Activities Service, 77 Massachusetts Ave, Cambridge (491-7071).

Scottish Country Dance Society, Cambridge YMCA, 7 Temple St, Cambridge (491-6084).

OPERA
Associate Artists Opera Company, 551 Tremont St (542-0308).

Boston Conservatory Opera Company, 8 The Fenway (536-6340).

Boston Summer Opera Theater, Peabody School Auditorium, Cambridge (734-9181).
New England Chamber Opera Group, First & Second Church of Boston, Marlborough & Berkeley Sts (969-5186).
New England Conservatory of Music, 290 Huntington Ave (262-1120).
New England Regional Opera, 539 Tremont St (267-8050).
Opera Company of Boston, 172 Newbury St (267-2876).
Wang Center for the Performing Arts, 268 Tremont St (482-9393).
Gilbert and Sullivan operas are given each year by students of Harvard and Radcliffe at the *Agassiz Theater* in Harvard (732-1000); and also by the *Boston University Savoyards*, 855 Commonwealth Ave (353-3341).

ORCHESTRAS AND CONCERT HALLS

Berklee College of Music, 1140 Boylston St (266-1400).
Boston Civic Symphony, 12 Ellsworth St, Cambridge (566-0367).
Boston Conservatory of Music, 8 The Fenway (536-6340).
Boston Philharmonia Orchestra, National Theater, Boston Center for the Arts, 551 Tremont St (426-2387).
Boston Pops Orchestra, Symphony Hall, 251 Huntington Ave (266-1492).
Boston Symphony Hall, 251 Huntington Ave (266-1492).
Boston Symphony Orchestra, 251 Huntington Ave (266-1492).
Harvard-Radcliffe Orchestra, Harvard University, Cambridge (459-5730).
M.I.T. Symphony Orchestra, M.I.T., Cambridge (864-6900, ext. 3210).
New England Conservatory of Music, 290 Huntington Ave (235-4156).

CHAMBER GROUPS

The Annex Players, Museum School of Fine Arts, 230 The Fenway (267-9300).
Bach Society Chamber Orchestra, Harvard University, Cambridge (495-2791).
Boston Musica Viva, 25 Huntington Ave (353-0556).
Boston Philharmonia, 416 Marlborough (536-6311, 495-1591).
Boston University Celebrity Series, 420 Boylston St (536-6037).
Boston Symphony Chamber Players, Symphony Hall, 251 Huntington Ave (266-1492, ext. 31).
Cambridge Society for Early Music, Box 336, Cambridge (495-1591).
Collage, Symphony Hall, 251 Huntington Ave (266-1492).

CHORAL GROUPS

Camerata Players, Museum of Fine Arts, 465 Huntington Ave (267-9300).
Cecilia Society, All Saints Church, 1773 Beacon St, Brookline (277-4115).
Chorus Pro Musica, Old South Church, 645 Boylston St (267-7442).
Handel & Haydn Society, 140 Boylston St (266-3605).
Harvard University Choral Groups; Collegium Musicum (495-5730); *Harvard-Radcliffe Chorus* (495-5730); *Memorial Church Choir* (495-1591).
M.I.T. Choral Society, M.I.T. Music Dept. (864-6900, ext. 3210).

FREE CONCERTS AND ORGAN RECITALS

Berklee College of Music, 1140 Boylston St (266-1400).
Cambridge Common (sponsored by Polyarts), concerts every Sun. at 2 p.m. in summer.
City Hall Plaza, Boston, concerts every noon in summer.
Esplanade Concerts, Hatch Shell on the Charles River Embankment; schedule can be obtained from Symphony Hall, 251 Huntington Ave (266-1492).
Isabella Stewart Gardner Museum, 280 The Fenway (566-1401).
King's Chapel, 58 Tremont St (523-1749).
M.I.T. Music Dept., M.I.T., Cambridge (864-6900, ext. 3210).
Peabody-Mason Music Foundation, P.O. Box 153, Back Bay Station (262-4848) (the Foundation puts on free concerts in Sanders Theater, Harvard).

CINEMAS

Allston Cinemas, 214 Harvard Ave, Allston (277-2140).
Astor, 1 Beacon St (542-5030).

Boston Cinerama, Washington & Essex Sts (482-4515).
Brattle Theater, 40 Brattle St, Cambridge (876-4426).
Center Theater, 686 Washington St (426-0889).
Charles 1, 2, 3, 185 Cambridge St (2277-1330).
Cheri, 50 Dalton St (536-2870).
Cinema Brookline, Washington St, R. 9, Brookline (566-0007).
Cinema Cambridge, Freshpond Shopping Center, Cambridge (547-8800).
Cinema 57, Stuart St (482-1222).
Cleveland Circle 1—3, Chestnut Hill Ave (566-4040).
Coolidge Corner, 290 Harvard St (734-2500).
Exeter, 26 Exeter St (536-7067).
Galeria Cinema, 57 Boylston St (661-3737).
Garden Cinema, 19 Arlington St (536-9477).
Gary Theater, 131 Stuart St (542-7040).
Harvard Square, 1434 Massachusetts Ave, Cambridge (864-4580).
Loew's Abbey Cinema, 600 Commonwealth Ave (262-1303).
Music Hall, 268 Tremont St (423-3300).
Nickelodeon Cinema, 600 Commonwealth Ave (247-2160).
Off the Wall, 15 Pearl St, Cambridge (354-5678).
Orson Welles Cinema, 1001 Massachusetts Ave, Cambridge (868-3600).
Paramount Theater, 549 Washington St (482-4826).
Park Square Cinema, 31 St. James Ave (542-2220).
Pi Alley, 237 Washington St (227-6676).
Plaza Theater, 111 Washington St, Brookline (566-0007).
Pru Cinema and Cocktail Lounge, 903 Boylston St (262-6200).
Publix Theater, 663 Washington St (482-1288).
Savoy I & II, 539 Washington St (426-2720).
Saxon, 219 Tremont St (542-4600).
Symphony I, II, 252 Huntington Ave (262-8820).
Village Cinemas, 547 VFW Parkway, West Roxbury (365-0303).

II. Art Galleries The largest concentration of art galleries in Boston is along Newbury St, in Back Bay, but there are a number elsewhere in the city, particularly in Cambridge. The hours that these galleries are open and information on their current exhibitions can be obtained by calling the numbers listed below.

Alianaz, 140 Newbury St (262-2385).
Alpha, 121 Newbury St (536-4465).
Arvest Galleries, Inc., 77 Newbury St (247-1418).
Brent Sikkema, Inc / Vision Gallery, 216 Newbury St (266-9481).
Bromfield, 30 Bromfield St (426-8270).
Bunnell, 166 Newbury St (266-6193).
Clay Dragon Studios, 27 Otis St, Cambridge (354-3205).
Childs, 169 Newbury St (266-1108).
The Copley Society of Boston, 158 Newbury St (536-5049).
Cutler / Stavaridis, 354 Congress St (482-4151).
English Gallery, 212 Newbury St (536-6388).
Fox Graphics, 36 Bromfield St (fourth floor) (423-2559).
Gallery in the Square, 665 Boyston St (426-6616).
Gallery Naga, 67 Newbury St (267-9060).
George Lewis, 20 Newbury St (second floor) (267-6306).
The Glass Veranda, 36 Newbury St (267-3779).
Graphics 1 & Graphics 2, 168 Newbury St (266-2475).
Guild of Boston Artists, 162 Newbury St (536-7660).
Harcus Krakow, 7 Newbury St (262-4483).
Impressions, 275 Dartmouth St, at Newbury St (262-0783).
The Kingston Gallery, 129 Kingston St (542-5694).

Magnuson Lee, 8 Newbury St (262-5252).
Mills, 549 Tremont St (426-7700).
Mobilia, 343 Huron Ave, Cambridge (876-2109).
Nielsen, 179 Newbury St (266-4835).
Photoworks, 249 Newbury St (267-1138).
Pucker / Safrai, 171 & 173 Newbury St (267-9473).
Seventeen Wendell Street, 17 Wendell St, Cambridge (864-9294).
Society of Arts and Crafts, 175 Newbury St (266-1810).
Stux, 36 Newbury St (267-7300).
Ten Arrow, 10 Arrow St, Cambridge (876-1117).
Thomas Segal, 73 Newbury St (266-3500).
281 Galleries of Boston, 238 Newbury St (536-6176).
Van Buren / Brazelton / Cutting, 290 Concord Ave (354-0304).
Vose Galleries of Boston, 238 Newbury St (536-6176).
Wellfleet Brownware, 33 Gloucester St (247-1737).
Wenninger Graphics, 164 Newbury St (536-4688).
Westminster, 132a Newbury St (266-6704).

III. Sports and Amusements
AMUSEMENT PARKS
Paragon Park, 175 Nantasket Ave, Hull (925-0144).

ARCHERY
Tepee Archery Tackle Co., Spencer St, Newton (527-0550).
Weymouth Sportsmen's Club, Weymouth (335-9765).

BADMINTON
University Club, 426 Stuart St (266-5600).

BEACHES
The beaches in the city of Boston itself are not particularly good and become extremely crowded in summer. The best public beaches in the environs of Boston are the following (in all but one case directions are given only to the nearest town):
Crane's Beach, Ipswich. Take the train from North Station to Ipswich.
Nantasket Beach, Nantasket. Take the Red Line to Quincy Center; in summer the MBTA operates a bus service from the T-station there to the beach.
Singing Beach, Manchester. Take the train from North Station to Manchester.
Wingaersheek Beach, Gloucester. Take the train from North Station to Gloucester.

BICYCLING
There are excellent cycling paths along both sides of the Charles River Embankment. On the Boston side the path extends from the Eliot Bridge to the Longfellow Bridge, and on the Cambridge side it extends from the Charles River Dam to the Boston University Bridge. There are also cycling paths in the environs of Boston; maps for these can be obtained from the Mass. Dept. of Natural Resources, Division of Forests and Parks, Saltonstall Building, 100 Cambridge St, Boston.
Bicycles can be rented at the following shops:
Beacon Hill Bike Shop, 303 Cambridge St (523-9133).
The Bicycle Peddler, 832 Commonwealth Ave (731-3550).
Herson Cycle Co., 1250 Cambridge St (876-4474).

BOAT RIDES
Charles River Excursion: a boat leaves from behind the Hatch Shell at Charles River Embankment near Revere St.
Concert Cruise: Evening summer concerts on the Bay State Line Boat leaving from Long Wharf (723-7800).

Swan Boats operate in the lake in the Public Garden during spring and summer. (For other boat rides see the section on Transport).

BOWLING
Kenmore Bowladrome, Inc, 64 Brookline Ave (267-8495).
Sammy White's Brighton Bowl, 1600 Soldiers' Field Extension, Brighton (254-6710).

CAMPING
Information on public and private campgrounds in the environs of Boston is given in the brochure entitled *Camping in Massachusetts;* this can be obtained by writing to the Mass. Dept. of Natural Resources, Bureau of Recreation, 100 Cambridge St, Boston 02206.

CANOEING
Information on canoeing in New England can be obtained from the *Appalachian Mountain Club,* 5 Joy St (523-0636). Canoes can be rented for use on the Charles River at *Cambridge Canoe Rental,* on Memorial Drive in Cambridge.

CRICKET
There are two cricket clubs in Boston that have matches in Franklin Field, Dorchester, at the corner of Blue Hill Ave & Talbot Ave: the *Windsor Cricket Club* (387-2699) and the *United Athletic Association* (387-2699).

CURLING
Broomstone, Inc., Rice Rd, Wayland (358-2412).

FENCING
Boston Fencing Club, YWCA, Central Sq, Cambridge (523-4960).

FISHING
For saltwater fishing no licences are needed, but for freshwater fishing licences are required for anyone over the age of 15; these can be obtained from the Division of Fisheries & Game, 100 Cambridge St, Boston (727-3151). In Boston one can fish from the pier at *Castle Island* or take one of the deep-sea fishing boats operated by *Boston Harbor Cruises,* Long Wharf. The Division of Fisheries & Game will give advice on where one can do freshwater fishing.

FOX HUNTING
Norfolk Hunt Club, Dover-Medfield (785-9880).

GLIDING
Yankee Aviation, Plymouth Municipal Airport (275-8199).

GOLF
George Wright Golf Club, 420 West St, Hyde Park (361-0366).

GREYHOUND RACING
Wonderland, Route 1A, Revere (284-1300).

GYMNASIUMS & HEALTH CLUBS
Health Center, Inc., 100 Summer St (542-9662).
YMCA, 316 Huntington Ave (536-7800).

HORSEBACK RIDING
Belliveau Riding Arcades, 1244 Randolph Ave, Milton (698-9637).
Forest Hills Riding Stables, 19 Lotus St, Milton (524-9739).
The Paddock Stables, 1010 Hillside St, Milton (698-1880).

HURLING
Galway Hurling Club of Boston; for information write to John Moynahan, 24 Marion St, Medford.

ICE-SKATING
There is ice-skating on the ponds in the Public Garden and Boston Common when they freeze over. The following rinks are operated by the Metropolitan District Commission (MDC):*Brighton-Brookline Rink, Cleveland Circle (277-7822).*
Brighton-Newton Rink, Nonantum Rd (527-1741).
Cambridge Rink (indoor), Gore & Sixth Sts (354-9523).

JUDO
Northeast Judo Club, 30 Temple St, Somerville (623-9075).

LACROSSE
Boston Lacrosse, P.O. Box 77, Lincoln 01773.

LAWN BOWLING
There are two lawn bowling clubs at Merrymount Park in Quincy:
Boston Bowling Green Club, 20 Ridgeway Drive, Quincy (478-2677).
Quincy Bowling Green Club, 75 Verchild St, Quincy (478-2677).

PING-PONG
Waltham Table Tennis Club, 645 Main St, Waltham (894-7900).

ROWING
Union Boat Club, 144 Chestnut St (523-9717).

RUGBY
Beacon Hill Rugby Club, 6 Mount Vernon St (evenings, 227-7157; days, 357-8000, ext. 356). The Club plays at Columbus Park in South Boston; free.

SAILING
Community Boating, 21 Embankment Rd (523-1038); rents boats for sailing on the Charles April 1–Nov. 1.

SKIING (Cross-Country)
Weston Ski Club, Leo J. Martin Memorial Golf Club, Weston (894-4903).

SKIING (Downhill)
Blue Hills Reservation, SR 138, Canton-Milton (828-5070).

SQUASH
YMCA, 316 Huntington Ave (536-7800).

SWIMMING POOLS
During the summer the Metropolitan District Commission operates swimming pools at all of the rinks listed above under ICE-SKATING. In addition to these there is an indoor pool at the YMCA, 316 Huntington Ave (536-7800).

TENNIS COURTS
The MDC maintains 64 tennis courts in Boston; for information call the Boston Recreation Dept. (722-4100, ext. 145). One centrally located court is in *Charlesbank Park,* Charles St.

COURT TENNIS
Tennis & Racquet Club, 939 Boylston St (536-4630).

TOBOGGANING & SLEDDING
Ponkapoag Golf Club, Blue Hills Reservation, SR 138, Canton-Milton (828-0645).

YACHTING
Marblehead Racing Association, P.O. Box 382, Marblehead 01945.

IV. Spectator Sports (Professional) The following is a list of the professional teams that represent Boston in the various major leagues in sport, along with the places where they play their home matches.

BASEBALL
Boston Red Sox, Fenway Park; ticket office at 24 Jersey St (267-2525).

BASKETBALL
Boston Celtics, Boston Garden (523-3030).

FOOTBALL
New England Patriots, Schaefer Stadium, Foxboro, Mass. (25 miles S. of Boston). In Boston tickets may be purchased at the Out-of-Town Ticket Agency, Zero Harvard Sq.

GREYHOUND RACING27-3206).
Wonderland, SR 11A, Revere (284-1300).

HOCKEY
Boston Bruins, Boston Garden (227-3206).

HORSE RACING
Suffolk Downs Race Track, East Boston (567-3900).

TENNIS
Numerous professional tennis tournaments are played at the *Longwood Cricket Club,* 564 Hammond St, Brookline (731-2900).

V. Spectator Sports (Amateur) The various colleges and universities in the Boston area have very active programs in all sports played in the U.S. Besides those stadiums listed above, the largest is *Harvard Stadium,* North Harvard St, Allston (across the Charles from Cambridge). Harvard plays all of its home games in this stadium, the most popular being the Harvard-Yale game, played there in alternate years. Another very popular amateur sporting event is the *Boston Bean-Pot Hockey Tournament,* which is contested by Harvard, Boston College, Boston University, and Northeastern University. The matches are held in Boston Garden on the first and second Mon. in Feb. Still another popular sporting event involving amateurs is the *Head of the Charles Regatta,* held annually on the Sun. after Columbus Day. This regatta attracts spectators and contestants from all over the U.S. and Canada, with over 150 colleges, schools, and private clubs competing in 18 different events. The race starts at the Boston University Bridge and ends beyond the Eliot Bridge. This event should not be missed by any traveler who is in Boston at the time, for it is an exciting and quite beautiful spectacle. And of course one should not miss the most venerable of all athletic events in the city, the *Boston Marathon,* which is held annually on Patriots' Day (see the **Calendar of Events**). This is a race from Hopkinton Green to the Prudential Center in Boston (the date, course, and finish line may be changed in the near future), and everyone in the city and its environs turns out to cheer on the thousands of runners, a very rousing spectacle.

VI. Night Life Information on night life in Boston can best be obtained by consulting the "Calendar" section in the Thurs. edition of the *Boston Globe* or from the *Boston Phoenix.* Another reliable source is the *Boston in Your Pocket* directory published by Barron's.

The following is a selective list of the various types of night life offered in Boston and Cambridge. (Unless otherwise noted, the addresses are in Boston.)

CAFES AND COFFEEHOUSES
Algiers, 40 Brattle St, Cambridge (492-1557).
Blue Parrot, 123 Mount Auburn St, Cambridge (491-1551).
Cafe Paradiso, 255 Hanover St (742-1768) (Italian).
Cafe Vittoria, 294 Hanover St (227-7606) (Italian).
Nameless Coffee House, 3 Church St, Cambridge (864-1630) (folk music).
Passim's, 47 Palmer St, Cambridge (492-7679) (folk music).

COMEDY CLUBS
Comedy Connection Laugh Line, Charles Playhouse, 76 Warrenton St (426-6339).
Improv Boston, 212 Hampshire St, Cambridge (576-2306).
Nick's Restaurant and Comedy Shop, 100 Warrenton St (482-0930).
Play It Again, Sam's, 1314 Commonwealth Ave (782-5883).
Stitches, 969 Commonwealth Ave (254-2054).

DISCOS, JAZZ, AND ROCK
The Channel, 25 Necco St (451-1905).
The Commons, Copley Pl (437-1234).
The Conservatory, Boston Marriott Hotel, Copley Pl (236-5800).
Hampshire House, 84 Beacon St (upstairs) (227-9600).
Jack's, 952 Massachusetts Ave (491-7800).
Jason's, 131 Clarendon St (262-9000).
Jonathan Swift's Club, 30 John F. Kennedy Drive, Cambridge (661-9887).
The Jukebox, 275 Tremont St (426-1400).
Metro, 15 Lansdowne St (262-2424).
Nine Landsdowne Street, 9 Landsdowne St (636-0206).
The Paradise, 967 Commonwealth Ave (254-2052).
The Rat, 528 Commonwealth Ave (536-2750).
Regattabar, Charles Hotel, Bennett St, Cambridge (876-7777).
Ryles, 212 Hampshire St, Cambridge (876-9330).
Willow Jazz Club, 699 Broadway, Somerville (623-9874).

BARS, HOTEL LOUNGES, AND NIGHTCLUBS (ethnic places are listed separately below)
Back Bay Hilton, 40 Dalton St (236-1100) (Le Papillon nightclub).
Bay Tower Room, 60 State St (723-1666).

Boston Park Plaza Hotel, 64 Arlington St (426-2000) (Captain's Piano Bar). Bull and Finch Pub, Hampshire House, 84 Beacon St (227-9605).

Charley's Saloon, 344 Newbury St (266-3000).

Copley Plaza Hotel, 138 St. James Ave (267-5300) (The Plaza Bar).

Daisy Buchanan's, 240a Newbury St (247-8516).

Eliot Lounge, Massachusetts Ave and Commonwealth Ave (262-8823) (traditional gathering place for runners after the Boston Marathon; filled with Marathon memorabilia).

Embassy Suites Hotel, 400 Soldiers' Field Rd, Brighton (783-0090) (Sculler's Lounge).

Frogg Lane, Quincy Market (720-0610).

Friday's, 26 Exeter St (266-9040).

Gallagher's, 55 Congress St (523-6080) (Truffles piano bar).

Howard Johnson's Motor Lounge, 575 Commonwealth Ave (267-6059) (Starlight Roof).

Hyatt Regency Hotel, 575 Memorial Drive, Cambridge (492-1234) (Pallysadoe Lounge has piano and vocalist nightly, as does the Spinnaker, the revolving lounge on the roof).

Jacob Wirth's, 31 Stuart St (338-8586) (the oldest bar in Boston).

Lenox Hotel, 61 Exeter St (536-5300) (Diamond Jim's Piano Bar).

Marriott Long Wharf Hotel, Long Wharf (227-0800) (Rachel's).

Omni Parker House, 60 School St (227-8600) (Last Hurrah has big band; Parker's has piano bar).

Prudential Center, Boylston St (536-1776) (Top of the Hub has Hub Cap Lounge).

Ritz Carlton, 15 Arlington St (536-5700) (The Ritz Lounge).

St. Cloud Restaurant and Bar, 557 Tremont St (353-0202).

The Salty Dog, Quincy Market (742-2095).

Scotch 'n Sirloin, 77 North Washington St (723-3677) (restaurant with music and dancing).

Sheraton Boston Hotel, 39 Dalton St at the Prudential Center (236-2000) (Doubles Lounge; Third Edition, dancing; Turning Point, piano bar).

Sonesta Hotel, 5 Cambridge Parkway, Cambridge (491-3600) (Charles' Bar).

Westin Hotel, Copley Pl (262-9600).

ETHNIC TAVERNS AND RESTAURANTS WITH ETHNIC MUSIC

Averoff, 1924 Massachusetts Ave, Cambridge (354-4500) (Middle Eastern and Greek).

Black Rose, 160 State St (523-8486) (Irish).

Cantares, 15 Springfield St, Cambridge (547-6300) (Latin American).

Claddagh, Dartmouth St and Columbus Ave (262-9874) (Irish).

Middle East Restaurant, 472 Massachusetts Ave (354-8238) (Middle Eastern and Greek).

Plough and Stars, 912 Massachusetts Ave (492-9653) (Irish).

Purple Shamrock, 1 Union St (227-2060) (Irish).

Sultan's Tent, 100 Warrenton St (482-3229) (Middle Eastern and Greek).

I   BOSTON

Although Boston has grown enormously in size and population since colonial days, its center has remained fixed in place. So far as government, business, and the active everyday life of the city are concerned, the omphalos of Boston is the area extending from *City Hall Plaza* south to the *Old State House* and the head of State St. Not only is this area the focal point of the modern city's life, but it preserves some venerable monuments that were the scene of many of the most historic events in the illustrious past of Boston.

1   Boston Center

The first itinerary through Boston begins at *City Hall Plaza* in **Government Center,** for from there one can orient oneself before setting out. This is also an appropriate place to review the architectural history of this part of Boston, where the oldest of the city's monuments stand side by side with its most modern buildings. The first of these modern buildings is the new *City Hall,* which takes up most of the eastern side of the plaza.

History. Prior to 1960, the area which is now Government Center was part of *Scollay Sq,* a neighborhood of old houses and narrow, winding streets that had been in decay since the second half of the last century. Walter Muir Whitehill described Scollay Sq as "the Boston center of tattooing parlors, shooting galleries and burlesque houses; although dear to the hearts of enlisted men and merchant seamen of many nationalities, it had become a shabby, tumbledown area." In 1957 the Boston Redevelopment Authority (BRA) was established in order to rebuild Scollay Sq and to create a new complex to be called Government Center, which would serve to unify the four intermingled types of buildings in that area: business, government, financial, and historic-residential. The BRA began to implement the program in 1958, during the last months in the tenure of Mayor John B. Hynes. Most of the program was carried out during the administration of his successor, John F. Collins, mayor from 1959 until 1967. In 1960 Mayor Collins hired Edward J. Logue of New Haven to be chairman of the BRA, and it was he who guided the project through to completion by the end of the decade. Logue's first move was to hire the New York architectural firm of I. M. Pei & Assocs to design the new Government Center as a whole. Pei was guided by the principle that the huge new buildings should relate harmoniously to the smaller structures of earlier periods around them, particularly the historic monuments. The core of Pei's plan was the new City Hall, and such importance was attached to this building that a national competition was held to choose the most appropriate design. The competition was won by the New York firm of Kallman, McKinnel & Knowles, who, in collaboration with the firms of Campbell, Aldrich & Nulty, and Le Messurier Assocs, completed the new City Hall in the period 1962–68.

Exterior. The ground here slopes sharply down to the E., so that City Hall has nine stories on the Congress St side and six on the side that faces the plaza. The top three stories are cantilevered out above the floor below them, with all four supported by massive concrete piers. Between some of the piers cubical elements of the middle floors protrude outward over the semi-separate four-story brick building that forms the inner core of the City Hall, a structure without window openings. This building houses the city's tax, registration, and licensing bureaus, while the upper floors, which form a rectangles about a central light-shaft, house Boston's actual seat of government, including the mayor's office and the chambers of the City Council.

Interior. Doors at the S.W. corner of City Hall give entrance to that part of the building which is used for other than governmental purposes. The floor of the entrance lobby is a continuation of the brick pavement of the plaza. From the lobby a series of stairways lead up into the vast central volume of the building, which rises 126ft from the ground, illuminated by windows in the uppermost level. The first floor above the lobby is a gallery, where there are frequent art exhibitions and occasional concerts.

On the fourth floor there is a *Visitor's Hospitality Center,* which is open May—Oct. during office hours; the facilities include toilets, drinking fountains, public telephones, facilities for changing babies, a playground for accompanied children between ages seven and ten, a child-care center for those between the ages of three and six (fee), an information kiosk for women, a food counter, and picnic tables.

Precincts. The other buildings that stand on the periphery of City Hall Plaza are also part of the Government Center complex, as are several others beyond them. (These latter buildings will be identified on later routes.) The N. side of the plaza is dominated by the *John Fitzgerald Kennedy Federal Building,* built by Architects Collaborative with Samuel Glazer Assocs, and completed in 1966; this complex consists of two 26-story office towers bridged to two long four-story extensions, which house various federal agencies dealing with the public. Directly across from City Hall to the W. is a crescent-shaped private office building known as *Center Plaza.* This structure, which has eight stories and is 875ft long, was completed in three stages (1966—69) by Welton Beckett & Assocs. The smaller and older building that forms part of the S. side of the plaza is the *Sears Crescent,* one of the few structures in Government Center remaining from the old Scollay Sq neighborhood. The Sears Crescent was erected in 1816—17; the building just beyond it at the S.W. corner of the plaza, the *Sears Block,* was added in 1848. Both structures were rehabilitated in 1969 by Stull Assocs, and are presently used to house various commercial enterprises, including a restaurant and a coffeehouse, the latter forming the horn of the crescent.

Sears Crescent formed the S. side of a curving street that in 1816 was laid out from Scollay Sq to Adams Sq, the southern part of Dock Sq, which in colonial times was the area that fronted on the Town Dock. This street was known originally as Cheapside, then as Market St, and finally, after 1829, as Cornhill. Running closely parallel to Cornhill was a narrow lane known in colonial times as Gay Alley; in 1819 this was broadened and renamed Brattle St. Near its eastern end this street opened into Brattle Sq, an area on which the new City Hall now stands. After passing through the square, Brattle St led directly down to Dock Sq, following a course that passed between the present sites of the City Hall and the buildings to the N. of the Sears Crescent. From the top of the stairway there one looks down on the site of Dock Sq, at the far end of which is *Faneuil Hall.*

The S.W. corner of City Hall stands on the site of the *Brattle Square Church.* The first church on this site was a wooden structure erected in 1698—99, housing a congregation whose religious views were more liberal than those of the strict Calvinists elsewhere in Boston. In 1772 the wooden church was torn down and replaced by one built of stone and brick, designed by the architect Major Thomas Dawes. John Hancock, a member of the congregation, contributed £1000 toward the construction of the new church and also had a new bell made for it. Other members of the congregation at that time included John Adams, Dr. Joseph Warren, and James Bowdoin, who in 1785 succeeded Hancock as governor of Massachusetts. In Aug. 1825 General Lafayette attended services in this church, sitting in the pew of his old friend John Hancock. The church continued in use until 1871, when the congregation decided to build a new one in Back Bay, after which the old meeting house on Brattle Sq was demolished.

The narrow alley that leads off to the S. from the E. end of Sears Crescent is Franklin Ave; in the colonial period it was known as Dorsett Alley. The site at the eastern corner of this alley, where the Veterans Administration Outpatient Clinic now stands, was the house of Dr. Zabdiel Boylston, erected in 1712–13. Dr. Boylston was the first physician in America to inoculate his patients against smallpox, having learned of this practice from the letters that Lady Wortley Montagu sent home to England from Istanbul, where the Turks were successfully using such injections in the control of the disease. There was violent opposition in Boston to this unorthodox practice; angry mobs gathered outside Boylston's house and threatened violence unless he ceased innoculating his patients. But Boylston persevered, and in the terrible smallpox epidemic of 1720–21 only 2 percent of the patients whom he had inoculated died, while 15 percent of the population of Boston perished from the disease that winter. As a result, inoculation against smallpox soon became the general practice among physicians in America.

At the western end of Brattle St, where it entered Scollay Sq, there was an estate that had been laid out soon after the foundation of Boston in 1630. In 1743 this estate and the house and barn that stood on it were inherited by Mrs. Mary Smibert, née Williams, wife of John Smibert, the painter and architect. (The house stood on or near the site of the brick kiosk housing the entrance to the Government Center T station.) Smibert, who was born in Scotland in 1688, came to Boston in 1728 and married Mary Williams two years later. He designed the original Faneuil Hall, built in 1741–42. He was also a professional artist, and after his wife inherited the house on Brattle St he set up his studio there. The house became America's first art gallery, as Smibert gave several public exhibitions of his paintings there. After Smibert's death his studio was used by two other famous American painters, John Trumbull in 1777–79, and Washington Allston in 1809–11. While Allston was in residence here one of his art students was Samuel F. B. Morse, inventor of the wireless telegraph, who became one of the most prominent American painters of the 19C.

Along the western side of the plaza a colonnade of trees stretches in front of the low extension of the Kennedy Building, and a short way beyond them to the W. there is a small sunken park. The trees mark the former course of Old Hanover St, another of the historic streets that ran through the present site of City Hall Plaza. This street formed the S.W. end of the present Hanover St, which is still the main thoroughfare through the North End. One of the houses that stood on Old Hanover St in the Revolutionary period was that of Dr. Joseph Warren, the patriot leader who was killed at the Battle of Bunker Hill. (His house stood on a site between the row of trees and the sunken park.) On the eve of the Revolution, Warren was in command of the patriot organization in Boston, since John and Samuel Adams and John Hancock were absent from the city. On the evening of April 18, 1775, Warren received word that the British forces were leaving Boston to march on Concord, and it was from here that he dispatched Paul Revere and William Dawes to ride to Lexington to warn John Hancock and Samuel Adams.

On the porch in front of the entrance to the twin towers of the Kennedy Building there is a monumental abstract bronze statue by Dimitri Hadzi. The statue, which is 14ft high and weighs 2½ tons, is entitled *Thermopylae*, after the battle in which the Spartans went down to heroic defeat against the Persians in 480 B.C. One occasionally sees passersby looking at the statue with puzzlement, trying to find some resemblance between the tortured mass of bronze and the historic battle.

At the N.W. corner of the plaza a small monument commemorates the invention of the telephone by Alexander Graham Bell, assisted by Thomas Watson. The laboratory in which Bell and Watson first began to develop the telephone was on the fifth floor of a building that stood on this site, at what was then 109 Old Court St. The inscription on the plaque states that Bell and Watson "first transmitted sound over wires here on Jan. 2, 1875"; this was just the first step in the invention of the telephone, with the second coming on June 3 of that year, when they succeeded in transmitting a musical tone. Bell and Watson then moved their laboratory to a new site, an apartment at 3 Exeter Place where on March 10, 1876, the final step in the invention of the telephone was made, when the sound of Bell's voice was transmitted to Watson in another room. He said, "Come here Watson, I want you!"

The monument honoring Bell and Watson stands on the place where Old Hanover St terminated at the head of Treamount St, as it was known in colonial times. Two well-known taverns stood here, one on either side of Old Hanover St. The one on the r. (as one faces Cambridge St) was the *Orange Tree Tavern*, named after the colorful tree painted on the sign above its door. The land on which it stood was bought in 1678 by Bozoon Allen, who built an inn and tavern there some time before 1700; in that year it was sold to Francis Cook, whose heirs retained it until 1785. The earliest-known hackney-coach service in Boston was established here in 1712 by Jonathan Wardwell, who was at that time the tavern-keeper.

The tavern on the other side of Old Hanover St at this point was known as the *Crown and Comb*, opened in 1754 by the brothers Louis and Gilbert Deblois. On the upper floor of the tavern the Deblois brothers opened a ballroom called the *Concert Hall*, where the first regularly scheduled performances of music in Boston were given. In the years prior to the Revolution the tavern was a favorite gathering-place for the Sons of Liberty, with Dr. Joseph Warren and Paul Revere among the regular patrons. On Oct. 29, 1778, Governor Hancock gave a gala ball at the Concert Hall to welcome Count D'Estaing and the officers of the French fleet, and in Oct. 1789 a celebration was held there to welcome George Washington at the time of his last visit to Boston, six months after his inauguration as first President of the U.S.

Scollay Sq itself was situated at the present intersection of Court and Tremont Sts. At the center of the square, which was about where the little traffic island is now located, there was a bronze *statue of John Winthrop*. This was sculpted by Richard S. Greenough, and was placed in Scollay Sq in 1880, on the occasion of the 250th anniversary of the founding of Boston. Because of traffic congestion, the statue was removed from the square in 1903 and placed in the side yard of the First and Second Unitarian Church on Marlborough St (see below). On the traffic island there is now a piece of twisted metal that at first glance looks like a fragment from a wrecked automobile; it is actually an abstract sculpture (1978) by Rick Lee and entitled *Nancy*.

Before Scollay Sq itself was built there stood on its site the *Free Writing School*, founded in 1683–84. This was the second school to be established in Boston, the first one being the *Latin School*; it later came to be known as the *Central Reading and Writing School*, and continued in existence until 1793.

Directly across the street from the traffic island stands the *Sears Block*, at the S.W. corner of City Hall Plaza. The Sears Block now serves as a coffee shop, above the front door of which there is one of the very few old Boston shop signs still in its original location, a huge *copper kettle* with steam issuing from its spout. (The steam is fed to it by a pipe leading from the boiler room of the Sears Block.) The kettle was fabricated in 1873 by Hicks and Badger, the largest firm of coppersmiths in Boston at the time, and was used as a shop sign by the Oriental Tea Co., which was then housed in the Sears Block.

A notice beside the door of the coffee house reproduces articles from several Boston newspapers dated 1875, describing the contest that the Oriental Tea Co. held to guess the volume of the kettle, with the prize winners to receive large quantities of the firm's tea and coffee. According to one account, some 3000 people gathered in front of the shop on

Jan. 1, 1875, when the volume of the kettle was measured to be 227 gallons, 2 quarts, 1 pint, and 3 gills.

The building directly across the street from the Sears Block, at 46 Court St, now occupied by the State Street Bank, was in the Revolutionary period a large four-story inn owned by Joseph Ingersoll. After Ingersoll's death his widow continued to run the inn, and it was here that Washington stayed during his six-day visit to Boston in Oct. 1789. On the day of their arrival President Washington and Vice-President Adams dined here together; on the following day they were visited by Governor John Hancock, who had to be carried to the inn by his servants because he was suffering from a severe attack of gout. Hancock apologized to the President for not having been on hand to greet him when he arrived in Boston, giving as his excuse his very obvious ailment, and Washington very graciously accepted the governor's invitation to have tea with him on the morrow.

Court St extends from the head of Tremont St to the adjacent heads of Washington and State Sts, between which stands the *Old State House*, the venerable red-brick building at the end of the street to the r. on Court St. This was originally known as Prison Lane, for halfway along on its r. side it passed the *Old Prison* of colonial days. The name was changed to Queen St in 1708 and then to its present name in 1784, after a new courthouse was built on the site of the Old Prison, replacing an older tribunal that had stood nearby since colonial times. The presence of the courthouse led many lawyers and law students to rent lodgings or offices on the street. Among these there were several who became political leaders in the U.S., most notably John Adams, Harrison Gray Otis, and Daniel Webster.

The area around the intersection of Court and State Sts was the birthplace of American journalism, and it was the center of Boston's newspaper industry from colonial times up until 1958, when the *Boston Globe* closed its offices in this quarter and moved elsewhere. The first newspaper in America was published in Boston by Benjamin Harris in 1690; this was called *Publick Occurrences Both Foreign and Domestick*, and was printed in a shop on State St (then known as King St). However, Harris did not have a license to publish, and his newspaper was shut down by the authorities after the first issue and never reappeared. The first issue of a regularly published newspaper in America appeared in Boston on April 4, 1704, put out by John Campbell. At that time Campbell as post master and the Post Office was in the Town House, the public building that preceded the Old State House on its present site. A plaque at 55 Court St, just beyond the Sears Block, marks the site of America's second regular newspaper, the *Boston Gazette;* this was first published on Dec. 21, 1719 by William Brooker, who succeeded Campbell as postmaster. The *Boston Gazette* was published continuously for 79 years, and during the Revolutionary period it was the principal journal for those patriots opposed to British rule.

The next structure beyond 55 Court St is the *U.S. Trust Building*. A plaque on the wall beside the entrance records the fact that "D. L. Moody, Christian Evangelist, Friend of Man, founder of the Northfield Schools, was converted to God in a shoe-store on this site, 21 Apr. 1855." Dwight Lyman Moody was born in Northfield, Mass., in 1837. His father died when he was four, leaving his mother with nine children to support. Moody left school when he was 13 and hired out as a farm laborer for four years, at which time he went to Boston to seek his fortune. Soon after he arrived he found work as a clerk in a shoe store on this site. The following year, while working in the store, he had the divine vision that inspired him to embark upon his life's spiritual mission, during the course of which he became the most famous and influential evangelist in the Christian world. He also founded two schools in his native Northfield as well as the Moody Bible Institute in Chicago, an institution to train ministers for evangelical work.

Just beyond the U.S. Trust Building, Franklin Ave cuts through to City Hall Plaza. Looking down the narrow alley, one can see the rear of the Sears Crescent, where offices on the ground floor are framed in a row of granite post-and-lintel construction dating from the original structure of 1817.

On the other side of the alley another historical marker bears the inscription: "Here in 1719 stood the printing office of James Franklin, publisher of the *New England Courant.* Here served as his apprentice his brother Benjamin Franklin. Here from 1769 to 1776 Edes and Gill published the *Boston Gazette.*" When William Brooker first began publishing the *Gazette* he hired James Franklin to be his printer. Seven months later Brooker was succeeded as post master by Philip Musgrave, who dropped Franklin and hired Samuel Kneeland to print the *Gazette*. Since this took away Franklin's main source of income he decided to print his own newspaper, and on Aug. 7, 1721, the first issue of the *New England Courant* appeared. His brother Benjamin, who was then only 15 years old, worked on the paper both as an apprentice printer and as its only journalist, writing under the pseudonym of "Silence Dogood." Benjamin Franklin worked here for his brother until 1723, when he left Boston to seek his fortune in Philadelphia, at the age of 17.

The two publishers of the *Boston Gazette* mentioned in the inscription are Benjamin Edes and John Gill. The paper that Edes and Gill published was actually called the *Boston Gazette and Country Journal*, though it may have been a continuation of the one first put out by William Brooker. Besides the *Gazette*, Edes and Gill also published here a pamphlet giving the text of the Stamp Act, copies of which were distributed widely throughout the American colonies. Among those who wrote anti-British articles in their paper were Samuel Adams, James Otis, Dr. Joseph Warren, and Josiah Quincy, Jr.; they, together with their publishers and other patriots, most notably John Hancock and Paul Revere, met secretly in a chamber above the press to discuss their revolutionary activities, calling themselves the Long Room Club. The members of the club are believed to have been the leading conspirators in planning the Boston Tea Party, and several of them took part in that affair.

The site directly across the street from Franklin Ave was occupied by a jail and courthouse from the early days of Boston. The building presently standing on the site, an imposing neoclassical edifice with a portico of extremely tall Corinthian columns, was erected in 1912 as an annex to Boston's Old City Hall, whose rear end is in the street behind. This building, which now houses the Boston School Committee, replaced an equally monumental courthouse designed by the architect Solomon Willard and erected in 1833–36. A plaque to the r. of the entrance bears an inscription honoring John Augustus, a philanthropist who was active in the mid-19C; his principal concern was to protect the unfortunates brought before the court, providing them with bail money and legal counsel, as well as rehabilitating those who had been imprisoned.

A plaque on the l. side of the entryway concerns the old jail that stood on this site; the inscription reads: "Old Prison: First Prison in Boston stood on this site. Hawthorne thus describes it in *The Scarlet Letter.'* The rust on the ponderous iron work of its oaken door looked more antique than anything else in the New World . . . but on one side of the portal was a wild rose bush.' " The lines quoted on the plaque are from the first chapter of *The Scarlet Letter*, where Hawthorne describes Hester Prynne's release from the Old Prison, in which she had been imprisoned after her conviction on a charge of adultery.

This was where Anne Hutchinson was imprisoned in 1637 on charges of religious unorthodoxy, before she and her followers were banished from the Bay Colony. In 1689 Joseph Dudley and other members of the Andros government were incarcerated here before being shipped off to England. In 1699–1700 the Old Prison housed Captain William Kidd and several of his crew, after they were arrested on charges of piracy by the Earl of Bellomont, governor of Massachusetts. Kidd remained here until he was shipped off to England early in 1700, after which he was convicted of piracy and eventually hanged on Execution Dock, Wapping.

The narrow street that extends around the periphery of the Boston School Committee Building is called Court Square. The back of Court Square is formed by the rear of the *Old City Hall* (see below), and at the far corner on the l. is the *Edward L. Kirstein Memorial Library*, a branch of the Boston Public Library. The library stands at the intersection of two narrow alley-

The Old State House (Amor Towles)

ways, City Hall Ave and Pi Alley, both of which evoke memories of an older and more picturesque Boston.

At the eastern end of Court St stands the ****Old State House**, the most handsome of Boston's monuments of the colonial period, a building which was the scene of some of the most dramatic episodes in the American struggle for independence.

Admission. Open every day 9:30–5; fee (tel. 720-3290).

History. The site on which the Old State House now stands was Boston's first marketplace, established soon after the founding of the town in 1630. The first public building on this site was the *Town House,* erected in 1658, and financed largely on a bequest by Captain Robert Keayne, whose house stood just to the S.W. of the site (see below). The original Town House was a wooden structure set upon 21 pillars each 10ft high, with a merchants' exchange and shops on the lower of the two floors and on the upper level chambers where the General Court of the Bay Colony met when it was in session. After the Bay Colony lost its charter in 1692, the upper floor of the Town House became the seat of government for the royal governors of the Province of Massachusetts. The governor and his Council met in a chamber on the E. side of that floor, the General Court convened in a larger room at the center, while the upper and lower courts of Suffolk County met in chambers at the W. end. The lower floor of the Town House served as a merchants' exchange as well as housing shops and Boston's first Post Office and Public Library, the nucleus of which was a collection of books that had been part of Captain Keayne's bequest. This first Town House was destroyed in the great fire of Oct. 1711, and in May 1712 the cornerstone was laid for the second building, a brick structure completed in April 1713. This was gutted in the fire of 1747, but was rebuilt during the following year. The most important incidents in the history of the Old State House occurred in this rebuilt structure during the half-century that followed. It was here in 1761 that James Otis made his impassioned speech in protest against the Writs of Assistance. Here on March 6, 1770, just after the Boston Massacre, Samuel Adams confronted Governor Hutchinson and demanded that both of the British regiments be removed from the town, and shortly thereafter they were transferred to Castle Island. On the morning of June 17, 1775, Generals Gage, Howe, and Clinton held a council of war here after word reached them that the Americans had fortified the heights in Charlestown, just prior to the Battle of Bunker Hill. On July 18, 1776, the text of the Declaration of Independence was read from the E. balcony of the building by William Greenleaf, the sheriff of Boston, after which the Continental troops in the vicinity of Boston passed in parade, pausing before the Town House to fire 13 volleys, one for each of the American colonies. In 1780 John Hancock was inaugurated here as first governor of Massachusetts, and in the same year the State Legislature began convening here, at which time it came to be called the State House. At the time of George Washington's visit to Boston in Oct. 1789 a great parade was held in his honor, which he reviewed from a temporary balcony on the W. end of the State House, before which a triumphal arch had been erected.

The building continued to be the seat of the Massachusetts government until Jan. 1798, when Charles Bulfinch's new State House on Beacon St was opened. Soon afterward the town government decided to lease the Old State House to commercial enterprises to gain revenue. But then, in May 1830, the City Council reclaimed the building and it once again served as the City Hall, until in 1841 it reverted to commercial use. In 1876 a number of Boston city officials recommended that the Old State House be demolished because it obstructed traffic. The city of Chicago then made a bid to purchase the historic old building and to remove it stone by stone for reconstruction on the shores of Lake Michigan. These developments shocked many Bostonians and led, in 1881, to the formation of the Bostonian Society, whose principal aim was to preserve the Old State House. In Sept. of that year the Society succeeded in persuading the City Council to evict the commercial enterprises and to appropriate sufficient funds for restoration, a project that was completed in June 1882. At that time the city leased the Old State House to the Bostonian Society, which converted the building into a museum with exhibitions dealing with the history of Boston. In 1909–10 the building underwent another restoration, intended to give it the same external appearance that it had in colonial times. Since then the Old State House has undergone additional repairs and alterations, resulting in today's handsome edifice—

Exterior. The entrance to the Old State House Museum is on its S. side, but before entering walk round the building to examine its exterior. At the apex of the stepped gable on the E. side there is a sundial, a replica of the original emplaced there in colonial times. At the l. and r. corners of the E. gable, respectively, there are the figures of a crowned lion and a unicorn, the royal symbols of Great Britain. These are reproductions of the originals, which were pulled down on July 18, 1776, when news of the signing of the Declaration of Independence first reached Boston. At the apex of the W. facade there is the figure of an eagle perched on a globe, both of them gold-plated, an American emblem to counterbalance the British symbols on the E. facade.

Interior. The Old State House contains a very interesting collection of objects associated with Old Boston. One group of exhibits consists of old Boston shop signs. One of these once hung above the shop of Thomas Childs, house-painter, which he opened at the corner of Hanover and Marshall Sts in 1701. The sign bears that date and the initials of the owner and his wife, Katherine; below are the arms of the Honourable Company of Painters-Stainers of London, to which Childs had been admitted in 1679. Another exhibit is known as the *Sign of the Blue Ball*. This sign was first hung over his shop on Milk St in 1698 by Josiah Franklin, father of Benjamin Franklin, who was a tallow-chandler and soap-maker. Benjamin Franklin was born

Shop sign of Thomas Child, housepainter (Amor Towles)

in the house on Milk St on Jan. 17, 1706, and in later years he remarked to an old Boston friend that "he had first seen the light of day at the 'Sign of the Blue Ball.' " Six years later Josiah Franklin and his family moved to the corner of Hanover and Union Sts, where the Sign of the Blue Ball was hung over the door of his new shop, there to remain until the building was demolished in 1858.

A number of other shop signs, figureheads, and emblems are works of some of the renowned wood-carvers of Old Boston. One such is a figure in gilded wood representing *Mercury*, carved in 1792 by John and Simeon Skillin, Jr. This sign was made for the new Post Office established in Boston in 1792. The sign hung over the entryway until the Post Office was moved elsewhere in 1808; in 1839 it reappeared on the Commercial St shop-front of Frederick W. Lincoln & Co., instrument-makers, where it remained until 1916. The sign called the *Little Admiral* was carved before 1770 by Simeon Skillin, Sr. The sign hung over the entrance to the Crown Coffee House at One Long Wharf, where William Williams opened an instrument shop in 1770; this was two doors away from the Admiral Vernon Tavern, from which the sign took its name. The tavern itself was named after Admiral Edward Vernon (1684–1757), whose nickname, Old Grog, stemmed from the fact that he ordered rum and water for his men instead of straight spirits. The figurehead known as the *Lady with the Scarf* was made c. 1820 by Isaac Fowle, shipcarver. Fowle opened his shop on Commercial St in 1807, and his descendants continued to work there until 1869. This figurehead is thought to have been the inspiration for Nathaniel Hawthorne's story, "Drowne's Wooden Image," which was one of the tales in *Mosses from an Old Manse,* published in 1846. The wooden *Eagle's Head* was carved in 1808 by the architect Solomon Willard (1783–1861), and hung above the entrance to the U.S. Custom House on State St. A number of interesting signs and figures have no inscription to identify the craftsmen who made them. The *Bell in Hand* is a sign made c. 1795 for the tavern of Samuel Adams, who was town crier. The tavern, later acquired by James Wilson, was housed in the Exchange Coffee House on Congress St, where it remained until 1853. A *watch sign* in painted wood was made c. 1846 for the shop of David B. Hastings, a maker of clocks and watches as well as jewelry. A painted *wooden pineapple* was made in 1817 for the Commercial Coffee House, which was located at the E. corner of Milk and Liberty Sts. This coffeehouse was a popular meeting place for shipmasters from 1817 until after 1838. The gilded tin globe known as the *Golden Ball* was made c. 1740 for the Golden Ball Tavern, founded c. 1700 on Merchants' Row. The sign was later used at other places, and in 1833 it became the property of Henry Cabot, painter and gilder, whose shop it advertised until 1858.

Besides the shop signs, there are a number of other exhibits associated with the tradesmen and artisans of colonial Boston. Among these are the banners that belonged to four of the town's craft guilds; these were carried in the great procession of townspeople who greeted George Washington in Boston in Oct. 1789, after he had been elected President. One of the banners belonged to the Worshipful Company of Cordwainers, or shoemakers, which was founded in London in 1271.

Another group of interesting objects includes a *drum* carried by John Robbins at the Battle of Bunker Hill, which was used by Daniel Simpson in the War of 1812; a *protractor* and a *set of calipers* used by Paul Revere for measuring cannonballs and the bores of cannon, which he employed in 1778–79, when he was in charge of the artillery unit at Castle Island. There is also a *bell* from Castle Island. This was a gift of Captain Thomas Cromwell, a pirate who arrived in Boston in May 1646 with three captured Spanish vessels; he died soon afterward and left the ships' bells to the town of Boston, which hung this one in the fortress at Castle Island. Other exhibits in this group include a *musket* and *bayonet* from the Battle of Bunker Hill, a large *flag* that once hung from the Liberty Tree, and a *cocked hat* and *knee breeches* that belonged to Major Thomas Melvill, who is represented along with his wife Priscilla in portraits painted by Francis Alexander (1800–90). The Melvills were grandparents of Herman Melville, the novelist. Thomas Melvill was one of the leading patriots in Boston during the Revolution, a Son of Liberty, a member of the Long Room Club, and a participant in the Boston Tea Party. During the Revolutionary War, Melvill was a major in an artillery unit of the Continental Army; from 1786 to 1820 he was chief U.S. naval officer in Boston, and in 1829 he was elected to the U.S. House of Representatives, where he served until shortly before his death in 1832. One of the paintings in the collection of the Old State House shows the Melvill House on Green St at the time of the major's funeral, with the men of Fire Company No. 15 forming a guard of honor in the street outside, while his wife stands forlornly in the doorway.

One notable painting in the collection is *Washington at Dorchester Heights,* painted in 1886 by Jane Stuart (1812–88), after the original by her father, Gilbert Stuart. Two paintings by an anon. artist represent *Isaac Harris* (1779–1869) and *Mrs. Isaac Harris* (1781–1849). Harris was renowned in his time as the Hero of the Milk Street Fire, a title he received for his heroic efforts in saving the Old South Meeting-Place from destruction by fire on Dec. 29, 1810.

A number of prints and paintings depict the harbor of Old Boston. The finest of the maritime paintings are the *Wharves of Boston, 1829,* by Robert Salmon, and *View of Boston Harbor, 1853,* by Fitz Hugh Lane. Among the colored engravings are a *View of Boston Harbor from the Ship House, 1833,* by W. J. Bennett, and *Southeast View of the Great Town of Boston in New England, America,* done c. 1765 by John Carwitham, after the Burgis view of 1722.

Another collection includes objects associated with the mariners of Old Boston. One collection includes superb old *instruments used in navigation.* Another is a collection of *carved ivory objects* and *scrimshaw,* objects carved from whale and fish bones by sailors to pass the time on long voyages.

One room in the Old State House Museum is devoted to objects belonging to John Hancock and his family. Among these are a *silver pepper box* belonging to John Hancock and a *Bible* dated 1721, which was given to him by his father, the Rev. John Hancock of Braintree.

As part of the exhibition on the Revolution, there are objects associated with the Boston Massacre. These include a *musket* found near the site of the incident; a *coroner's report* on Michael Johnson, better known as Crispus Attucks, the Black Bostonian who was killed in the Massacre; the bill of indictment of Captain Thomas Preston, the British officer in charge; and a colored engraving of the *Redcoats Firing on the Crowd,* by Paul Revere, after the original by his half-brother Peter Pelham. The site of the Boston Massacre is close to the E. end of the Old State House, marked by a circle of cobblestones in the traffic island at the corner of Congress and State Sts.

Directly opposite the entrance to the Old State House, at 15 State St, there is a *Visitors' Information Center* operated by the National Parks Service. Free leaflets are available here with information on Boston's monuments and activities, and there are also on sale books about the city and its history. In addition, the Center has toilets, water fountains, public telephones, and comfortable seats for foot-weary strollers.

Elevators on the ground floor of the Center ascend to the premises of the *Bostonian Society,* whose offices and library are on the third floor. The library is open Mon.–Fri. 9:30–4:30, and visitors must sign in at the entrance. The Society has an important collection of books, manuscripts, maps, prints, and photographs, all connected with Boston, which are available for examination by anyone who is doing research on the city.

2 The Old State House to King's Chapel Burying-Ground

The second itinerary begins where the first one ended, opposite the entrance of the Old State House. Before starting out on this itinerary, which will go as far as King's Chapel Burying-Ground, one might pause to identify some of the sites in the immediate vicinity of the Old State House, as this was the center of Boston in early colonial times.

On the facade of 15 State St, opposite the T entrance, a plaque commemorates the fact that the *Rose and Crown Tavern* stood on that site in colonial times. This was one of several taverns that stood on King St, which was one of the busiest thoroughfares in town, leading as it did from Boston's first market square down to the Long Wharf. In the earliest days of the Puritan town the stocks, the whipping post, and the pillory stood in this square, and in c. 1680 a cage was added so that violators of the rigid Sunday laws could be confined and vilified by the populace. This remained a popular gathering-place throughout the colonial period. It was here that the Bostonians rallied together at the beginning of the bloodless revolution that overthrew Governor Andros in April 1689, and here in 1765 a copy of the Stamp Act was publicly burned. At the opposite end of the mall, beside the Old State House, at the near corner on Washington St, another plaque marks the site on which stood the *house and garden of Captain Robert Keayne,* the principal benefactor in the founding of Town House. In 1637 Captain Keayne founded and became the first commander of the militia unit now known as the *Ancient and Honorable Artillery Company of Massachusetts,* which still has its headquarters in Faneuil Hall (see below). Just prior to the Revolution *Daniel Henchman* had a *bookshop* on the site, and it was here that the first Bibles printed in America were sold. (Edgar Allan Poe's first volume of verse, *Tamerlane and Other Poems,* was published here in May 1827.) At that time Henchman's young apprentice was Henry Knox, who became Washington's commanding general of artillery during the Revolution and afterward served as the first President's secretary of war.

Just to the W. of the Old State House, towering over the intersection of Washington and Court Sts, is the *Boston Co. Building,* a 41-story skyscraper completed in 1970 by Emory Roth & Sons, with Pietro Belluschi. The skyscraper stands on the site where the *First Meeting-House of Boston* was relocated in 1640, moved from its original site on what is now Quaker Lane, the little L-shaped alleyway that cuts through from Devonshire St to Court St, near the S.E. corner of the Old State House. The original meetinghouse, a small mud-walled hut put up in 1632, was replaced in the new location by a large wooden structure. This was destroyed in the great fire of 1711, and soon afterward a still larger brick structure was erected on the site, one which in time would be called the *Old Brick Meeting-House.* It was in the Old Brick that George Washington and his officers attended a thanksgiving service after the British evacuation of Boston on March 17, 1776.

Just N. of the church site there originally stood the *house of John Leverett,* who served as governor of the Bay Colony from 1672 to 1679. And N. of that, at the present intersection of Washington and Court Sts, was the site of the *house of Henry Dunster,* first president of Harvard College. The site of the Dunster homestead is now occupied by the *Ames Building;* this handsome Victorian office building was completed in 1892 by Shepley, Rutan, and Coolidge, who succeeded to the architectural practice of H. H. Richardson after his death in 1886.

The first stage of the itinerary goes from the Old State House S. along the r. side of Devonshire St, which at the first intersection crosses Water St. After crossing Water St, one sees on the r. the *Winthrop Building,* an extremely narrow but very long structure that occupies the entire block, bounded on the E. by Devonshire, on the W. by Washington, on the S. by Spring Lane, a pedestrian railway, and curving out in a graceful concave arc along Water St. This handsome edifice was designed by Clarence H. Blackall and completed in 1894, the first steel-framed building erected in Boston. The building takes its name from the fact that it stands on a site that in the years 1643–49 was part of the estate of Governor John Winthrop.

A short way along the l. side of Spring Lane there is a plaque with this inscription: "Mary Chilton, the only *Mayflower* passenger who removed from Plymouth to Boston, died here in 1679. John Winslow and Mary Chilton were married in Plymouth c. 1624, came to Boston c. 1657, and bought a house on this site in 1671. As a passenger on the *Mayflower* in 1620, Mary Chilton came to America before any white woman who settled in Boston."

Farther along the alley and on the r. there is another historical plaque, inscribed: "Here was the *Great Spring,* which for nearly two centuries gave water to the people of Boston." This spring and the one at the foot of Beacon Hill were the principal sources of water for the people of Boston. The Great Spring was the more important of the two, because of its convenient location near the Town Cove, and for that reason many of the early settlers built their homes in its vicinity.

On the l. side of the intersection of Spring Lane and Washington stands the *Old South Building,* with its entrance on the latter street. This was built in 1902–04 by the architect A. H. Bowditch, and stands on the site of Governor Winthrop's mansion. This was Winthrop's second house in Boston; his first residence stood on the site now occupied by 53 State St (see below). After a l. turn onto Washington, on the next corner to the l. is a handsome colonial church; this is the ****Old South Meeting-House,** one of the most historic buildings in Boston.

Admission. April 1–Oct. 31 open every day 9:30–5; Nov. 1–Mar. 31 open every day 10–4; fee (tel. 482-6439).

History. The origins of the Old South Meeting-House go back to 1669, when doctrinal difference led 29 members to split off from the First Church to form their own congregation, which gathered as the Third Church that same year. The first church on the site, which was built in 1670, was a two-story cedar structure with a steeple. It was this church that Governor Andros took over in 1687 to be used by members of the Church of England for services, forcing the regular congregation to share the building with them, a state of affairs that lasted until Andros was overthrown in the bloodless revolt on April 18, 1689. In 1697 in this church Samuel Sewall made a public confession for the part that he had played in the infamous Salem witchcraft trials, in which he had been a judge five years earlier. And it was in this church that Benjamin Franklin was baptized on Jan. 17, 1706, the day of his birth.

The old cedar meeting house was demolished in 1729 to make way for the present structure; this was designed by Robert Twelves and built by Joshua Blanchard, later chief mason in the construction of the original Faneuil Hall. This was the structure that was destined to become one of the focal points in the dramatic events that preceded the American Revolution. On March 6, 1770, the day after the Boston Massacre, a town meeting was held in the Old South and a committee, headed by Samuel Adams, was appointed and instructed to demand from Governor Hutchinson that the British troops stationed in Boston be removed, a commission which Adams successfully carried out. For the next five years on March 5 the anniversary of the Boston Massacre was commemorated by a mass meeting in the Old South, which was the occasion for patriotic speeches calling for an end to British tyranny. The most dramatic meeting held in the Old South took place on Dec. 16, 1773, when several thousand people from Boston and the surrounding towns gathered in and around the building after Faneuil Hall had proved too small to hold them. The meeting then convened here under the chairmanship of Samuel Adams, and a last-minute petition was sent to Governor Hutchinson appealing to him to have the hated tea sent back to England. When the messenger returned to say that the governor had refused to intervene, Samuel Adams stood up and exclaimed, "This meeting can do no more to save the country!" Then all at once there were excited shouts in the street outside the Old South, and as those inside looked out they saw a bunch of men disguised as Mohawk Indians rushing past the door, beginning the Boston Tea Party. As Samuel Adams wryly said at the time: "Depend upon it, those were no ordinary Mohawks."

Another dramatic incident in the history of the Old South took place on March 5, 1775, on the fifth anniversary of the Boston Massacre. The principal orator on the occasion was to be Dr. Joseph Warren, who less than four months later was killed at the Battle of Bunker Hill. By the time Warren arrived at the Old South it was so packed with people that he could not make his way inside, and friends were forced to fetch a ladder so that he could climb through a window into the gallery. There were many British soldiers and officers in the audience, and one of them shouted "Fie! Fie!" as Warren began to speak, holding up a handful of bullets as an implied threat. However, Warren ignored him and went on with his oration, the last he was to make before his death.

At the beginning of the British occupation of Boston, Old South was commandeered by

The Old South Meeting-House

General Burgoyne, who converted it into a riding school for the Light Horse Dragoons. All but one of the old box pews were ripped out and used for firewood, while the remaining one was converted into a pig sty. The floor was then covered with sand, a jumping bar was set up at one end, and one of the galleries was converted into a bar for the British officers. The pulpit was also chopped up and the books and manuscripts in the library of the meeting house were looted, some of them of great historical importance.

After the British occupation Old South was restored and its pews and pulpit replaced, and beginning in 1782 it once again became a house of worship. On the evening of Dec. 29, 1810, Old South was almost destroyed when its roof caught on fire, but Isaac Harris saved it by climbing a ladder to the roof and putting out the flames. The Old South ceased to be a house of worship in 1872, when its congregation leased it to the U.S. for use as a post office, to replace the one destroyed in the great fire that year. When a new post office was built the Old South was threatened with destruction to make way for the construction of a commercial building. This immediately aroused a number of public-spirited Bostonians, who in 1876 formed the Old South Preservation Committee and succeeded in raising enough money to save the historic old building. Today the Old South Meeting-House is part of the Boston National Historical Park, managed by the Old South Association in cooperation with the National Park Service of the U.S. Department of the Interior. It has been restored to much the same appearance that it had during the Revolutionary period, and it now serves as a museum with exhibits connected with its own history and that of old Boston.

Exterior. The exterior design follows the usual style for a colonial church, with the belfry rising from a porch on the entrance facade, topped by a wooden spire. The clock on the r. side of the belfry dates to c. 1770 and is a work of Gawen Brown; when it was first installed many considered it to be the finest in America. There are two round-arched windows in the front of the belfry above the round-arched entryway, and shuttered openings of the same shape on all four sides of the top of the belfry. Two courses of windows of the same type as those in the belfry flank the door and lower window of the porch and run around the other sides of the building. The brickwork, by Joshua Blanchard, is laid in Flemish bond.

Interior. Pass through the entrance porch, where the admission window is located, to the great meeting hall. As noted above, this has been restored to the appearance that it had in the Revolutionary period, with the box pews, the elevated pulpit on the l., and the sounding board above, replicas of originals destroyed by the British.

In cases and frames around the meeting room are exhibits concerned with the past history of the Old South and of Boston. Starting along the back wall of the room to the l. of the entryway one sees in the first case various objects once used in the church, including a foot warmer, footstool, tithing pole (to nudge members who might have nodded off at collection time), and a chart showing the allocation of the various pews. In the other three cases in that corner are weapons and cannonballs from the Battle of Bunker Hill; photos of the Old South at various stages in its history: as a church, a Post Office, and finally as a museum; and behind the last pew on the l. an old spinning wheel. In the far left-hand corner of the room there is an extremely interesting *model of the town of Boston* c. 1775, constructed by Annie Haven Thwing, whose book on the topography of the colonial town, *The Crooked and Narrow Streets of the Town of Boston, 1630–1822,* is one of the definitive works on that subject. Among the other items displayed in the room the most interesting is in a case along the front of the hall; this is a volume of poems by Phyllis Wheatley, America's first black poetess, who was a member of the congregation of Old South in the second half of the 18C. Her book is entitled *Poems on Various Subjects, Religious and Moral,* and was published in London in 1773.

Elsewhere in cases and frames along the front and r. side of the room are: portraits of Benjamin Franklin; Samuel Sewall; Thomas Thacher, first minister of the Old South; Thomas Prince, who became minister in 1718; a plan of the old cedar meetinghouse; a print showing Benjamin Franklin's birthplace, which was just across the street from the church (see below); a picture of Governor Andros demanding the keys of the church; and a print showing the building when it was being used as a riding school by the British army. There are also numerous prints, engravings, old photos, newspaper articles, and hand bills associated with the historic old building.

A multimedia exhibition is presented at frequent intervals. This is entitled "In Prayer and Protest, Old South Remembers," a presentation that leads visitors back through Old South's past, highlighting its role as host to the Boston Tea Party.

The site of *Benjamin Franklin's birthplace* is just around the corner from the church, less than halfway down Milk St on the r. side. The site is now occupied by the building at 17 Milk St, where a bust of Franklin has been placed on the facade. (This building, which was designed by Gridley J. F. Bryant and completed in 1873, formerly housed the *Boston Post.*)

Franklin was born in a house on this site on Jan. 17, 1706 (New Style; Old Style Jan. 6, 1706). His father, Josiah Franklin, was a tallow-chandler, soap-maker, silk-dyer, and skilled mechanic, and as early as 1698 he had set up his shop in the house on Milk St., under the *Sign of the Blue Ball* (see above). The Franklins lived in the house on Milk St until 1712, when they moved into a new home on the corner of Hanover and Union Sts (see below). The old house on Milk St remained standing until Dec. 29, 1810, when it was burned down in the fire that almost destroyed the Old South Meeting-House.

Directly across the street from Franklin's birthplace, at the back of the Old South, there is a branch of *Goodspeed's Bookshop,* which actually occupies the basement of the Meeting-House. The original bookshop of this firm was founded in 1898 by Charles E. Goodspeed, who began business at 5A Park St; the branch here on Milk St opened in 1927, replacing an earlier bookshop founded in 1879.

Return along Milk St to the corner of Washington St. In good weather a small flower-market is set up beside the belfry of the Old South. Directly across the street there is a pleasant little park laid out in 1972 by the builders of the *Boston Five Cents Saving Bank,* the large glass-walled modern building behind the park at the corner of Washington and School Sts; this was built in 1971—72 by Kallman & McKinnell.

The bank here stands on the site of the old *Province House,* which ranked with the Old State House as being one of the two most important public buildings in colonial Boston. The house was originally built as a private residence in 1679 by Peter Sergeant, a wealthy merchant. It was a massive building three stories high with a pitched roof surmounted by an octagonal cupola, atop which there was the large copper figure of an Indian. This was the finest mansion in colonial Boston, both in the grandeur of its dimensions and the sumptuousness of its interior decoration and furnishings. After Sergeant's death the provincial government of Massachusetts bought the mansion and in 1716 it became the official residence of Governor Samuel Shute. The Province House continued to be the official residence of the royal governors for the remaining 60 years of British rule. After the Revolution it was at first used by the treasurer of the Commonwealth of Massachusetts, and later it became the governor's official residence, a function it ceased to serve after 1800. In 1817 it was leased to David Greenough, who rented it out to various commercial enterprises, and in time it became a tavern and later a minstrel hall, before being destroyed in a fire in Oct. 1864.

On the corner just across School St from the park is the venerable building known as the **Old Corner Bookstore,* one of Boston's most famous literary landmarks.

Admission. The Old Corner Bookstore is open Mon.—Fri. 9—5:30; Sat. 10—6.

History. The Old Corner Bookstore is one of the very oldest brick buildings in Boston; it still retains its original form, with 2½ stories and a gambrel roof. It was built in 1712 for

Thomas Crease, who that same year opened Boston's first apothecary shop on the ground floor. In 1828 the building was bought by Carter and Hendon, booksellers, the first of ten firms of booksellers and publishers housed there during the next 75 years. The first four firms to succeed Carter and Hendon were owned wholly or in part by William D. Ticknor, who began his career here as a publisher and bookseller in 1832. In 1842 Ticknor entered into a partnership with James T. ("Jamie") Fields, who had started work as an apprentice in the bookshop 15 years before, at the age of 14. Three years later the firm officially became known as Ticknor and Fields, a name it retained until Ticknor's death in 1865, after which Fields assumed full ownership and moved the business to more spacious quarters at 125 Tremont St. During the two decades 1845–65 the Old Corner Bookstore became the center of literary Boston, as Jamie Fields gathered around him in his office in a curtained alcove on the ground floor most of the leading writers in Boston and several from England as well, most notably Dickens and Thackeray. Oliver Wendell Holmes wrote that Fields was his "literary counsellor and friend," and George William Curtis, in his work *The Easy Chair*, called the Old Corner Bookstore "the Exchange of Wit, the Rialto of current good things, the hub of the Hub." And referring to the group that gathered around Fields, Curtis wrote that "It was a very remarkable group of men, indeed it was the first really great group of American authors which familiarly frequented the corner as guests of Fields," the most renowned being Holmes, Hawthorne, Whittier, Longfellow, and Thoreau. The last of the publishing firms to occupy the Old Corner Bookstore moved out in 1903 and the building became a tobacconist's shop, after which it went into decline before being restored to its original condition in the 1960s. The ground floor was then used as an office for the classified-advertisements section of the *Boston Globe*, which in 1982 opened up a bookshop there, specializing in works dealing with Boston and New England.

The Old Corner Bookstore stands on the site of a house built in 1634 by William and Anne Hutchinson, who lived there until they were banished from Boston in 1638 for their unorthodox religious views.

After leaving the Old Corner Bookstore by the front door, turn l. and walk N. on Washington St as far as the first turning on the l. This is Pi Alley, which leads to the S.W. corner of Court Sq., through which the last itinerary passed. From there another alley, City Hall Ave, leads back out to School St, passing the Kirstein branch of the Boston Public Library at the corner.

One might pause at the corner of City Hall Ave and School St, with Province St just opposite, for there are several minor historical sites of some interest in the immediate vicinity. To the l., at what is now 19 School St, there was a famous inn called *Cromwell's Head,* where *George Washington* was a guest during his stay in Boston in 1756. Just to the r., at the corner of City Hall Ave and School St, there was a *house* in which *James Otis* lived c. 1750–80; later this became the rectory of King's Chapel, and in 1783, after his appointment as pastor of that church, this became the *home of the Rev. James Freeman*, the first Unitarian minister in America. And across the street, a plaque at 24 School St commemorates the fact that the first *church of the French Huguenots* in Boston stood on that site. This was a small brick structure built in 1704, and it remained in the hands of the Huguenots until 1748, when it was taken over by the Eleventh Congregational Society. In 1788 the building was acquired by the Roman Catholics, and on Nov. 2 of that year a Mass was celebrated here by the Abbé François Matignon. Matignon was joined in 1796 by Father John Cheverus, a French priest who became Boston's first Roman Catholic bishop and subsequently, after his return to France, a cardinal. The Catholics continued to hold services here until 1803, when they moved into their new *Church of the Holy Cross* on Franklin St (see below).

Province St, which extends for just one block, from School St to Bromfield St, takes its name from Province House, the headquarters for the governors of Massachusetts during the last six decades of British rule. All that is left of Province House today are its garden steps, which are next to the Marliave Restaurant, at 10 Bosworth St.

Walk up the r. side of School St for a few steps to the gate of the court-

The original Old City Hall, with (right) the U.S. Bank

yard of the **Old City Hall,** one of the more picturesque sights in Boston, with the tables and umbrellas of a French restaurant, *Maison Robert,* set out in the sunken patio beside King's Chapel, partly shaded by the trees in the quaint old graveyard behind it.

History. The Old City Hall stands on the site of a building designed by Charles Bulfinch and erected in 1810; this served as the Suffolk County Court House until 1841, and from 1841 to 1862 it was used as the City Hall. This building proved to be too small for the needs of Boston's rapidly growing population, and in 1862–65 the present building was erected according to the design of Gridley J. F. Bryant and Arthur Gilman. This served as the City Hall until the opening of the present City Hall in Government Center in 1968. The city government then considered demolishing the Old City Hall, but in 1970 they contracted with Anderson Notter Assocs to restore the building and convert it to commercial usage, a project that was completed in 1972. Besides the restaurant, the Old City Hall now contains offices of various commercial firms.

Exterior. The architecture of the building is in the style of the French Second Empire, with a projecting three-story portico of three double columns each rising above the entryway, surmounted by a cupola, with the facades on either side having three tiers of round-arched windows between three pairs of double pilasters.

Courtyard. On the sides of the courtyard there are bronze statues commemorating two great figures from Boston's past. The statue on the l. is of *Benjamin Franklin* (1706–90), a work of the sculptor Richard S. Greenough (1809–94). Erected in 1856, this was the first portrait statue ever set up in Boston; it was paid for by public subscription and dedicated on the 150th anniversary of Franklin's birth. The four panels sculptured in bas-relief on the base show scenes from different phases of Franklin's life: as a boy working in his brother's print shop; signing the Declaration of Independence; experimenting with a kite to detect the electrical charge generated in a thunderstorm; signing the peace treaty that ended the Revolutionary

War. The first and third are by Greenough and the other two are by Thomas Ball. The statue on the r. is of *Josiah Quincy* (1772–1864), second mayor of Boston (1823–29) and president of Harvard College (1829–45), a work of Thomas Ball (1819–1911). The statue represents Quincy as he appeared in his middle years, as mayor of Boston, a period when he created for the city the great marketplace that bears his name.

Franklin's statue stands upon the original site of the *Boston Public Latin School*, the first public school to be founded in the American colonies. The school was established on April 13, 1635, by a vote taken by the people of Boston. According to the town records: "At a meeting upon public notice, it was generally agreed that our brother Philemon Pormont shall be entreated to become schoolmaster for the teaching and nurturing of children with us." Pormont agreed, and for the first years of its existence the school met at his house, which was at the present site of the Boston Co. Building, at 1 Boston Place. The school moved into a building erected beside King's Chapel in 1645, and in 1748 it was transferred into a new and larger structure on the other side of School St. Many of the leading patriots in the American Revolution attended Boston Latin, most notably Samuel Adams, John Hancock, and Benjamin Franklin, who went for only a year. Graduates of the school in the half-century after the Revolution included some of the most renowned figures in the life of Boston during that period, men such as Charles Bulfinch, Harrison Gray Otis, Henry Ward Beecher, Edward Everett Hale, Charles Francis Adams, and Charles Summer. Boston Latin remained on School St until 1844, when it moved to a new location; in the century after that it had moved four more times before settling into its present quarters in the Fenway.

**King's Chapel stands at the corner of School and Tremont Sts. This handsome and distinctive buildings is one of the landmarks of downtown Boston, a venerable and historic edifice that stands in sharp contrast to the characterless modern buildings in its vicinity.

Admission. King's Chapel is open Tues.–Sun. 10–4; Sun. service at 11; music program Tues. 12:15–12:45.

History. Construction of King's Chapel was begun in 1687 by Sir Edmund Andros, the royal governor, who wanted a permanent place of worship for Boston's Anglicans. The structure was nearing completion in the spring of 1688, but on April 18 Andros was overthrown and the church building was damaged by an angry mob. Nevertheless, construction continued and on June 30, 1689, the church was dedicated and began serving as an Anglican chapel. This first chapel was a small wooden structure, occupying only about the front half of the area taken up by the present church. The first minister was the Rev. Robert Ratcliffe, a young Oxford graduate who had come out to Boston in 1686 to serve the Anglican community there. Soon after the dedication of the church he was succeeded as minister by Samuel Myles, a native of New England and a graduate of Harvard. But Myles had not yet been ordained, and so he was forced to travel to England in order to prepare for this. Myles remained in England for four years preparing for his ordination, and while there he was treated with great favor by the King and Queen. When Myles returned to Boston in 1696 he brought with him a number of rich presents that William and Mary had given him for the chapel, and in the next two years more gifts were sent by them; these included sumptuous furnishings for the church and vestments for the clergy, a Bible and prayer book, an altar table, an extremely valuable set of communion silver, and an extensive library of theological works. The King's Chapel Library is now in the possession of the Boston Athenaeum and is on display there.

By the beginning of the 18C the increasing number of Anglicans in Boston made it evident that the church would have to be expanded. In 1710 additional land was purchased and the church was enlarged, doubling its seating capacity. In time even this proved inadequate, and in 1747 the congregation decided to build a new and larger church. This decision was largely due to the influence of the Rev. Henry Caner, who earlier that year had become minister of King's Chapel. The Rev. Caner started a fund-raising drive in Sept. of the same year, with Governor William Shirley heading the subscription list. When sufficient funds had been obtained additional land was acquired adjacent to the church, and Peter

Harrison of Newport, Rhode Island, agreed to draw the plans for the new buildings, free of charge. The cornerstone was laid by Governor Shirley on Aug. 11, 1749, and construction began the following year, when Harrison's plans arrived. The congregation continued to attend services in the old church while the new one was being built about it. By March 1753 the construction had reached the stage where the congregation had to abandon the chapel and attend services at Trinity Church, and soon afterward the old wooden church was broken up and thrown out through the windows of the new building. The new King's Chapel finally opened on Aug. 21, 1754, even though the interior decoration was not yet complete. Several features called for in Harrison's plans had been omitted for lack of funds, principally the front portico and the "elegant and lofty steeple of two square storeys and an octagonal spire." The portico was not added until 1787–89, but the steeple and spire were never built, resulting in the somewhat truncated appearance that the front of the church presents today.

The Rev. Caner continued as Rector of King's Chapel for the remaining years of British rule in Boston. On March 10, 1776, he conducted his last Sunday service in King's Chapel, and a week later he and nearly half of his congregation left Boston with the British fleet, most of them never to return.

King's Chapel remained closed for a month after the British evacuation. It reopened then only for a single service, the funeral of General Joseph Warren, whose body had just been recovered from the battlefield at Bunker Hill and brought back to Boston for reburial. The building reopened on a permanent basis 18 months later, at which time the remaining Anglican congregation shared the church with the members of Old South, whose meeting-house was under repair after the damage caused by the British army. After Old South reopened in 1782 the Anglicans once again had the church to themselves, and the congregation pondered the future of King's Chapel. In the autumn of 1782 the vestry of King's Chapel met and decided to re-establish their church, but with a different character from before, since those of the congregation with close ties to the British had left. Therefore the old role of King's Chapel as a link with the Crown was obsolete; instead the feeling among the congregation was that the church could fulfill a role of leadership in the movement toward religious liberalism that was beginning to develop in New England, particularly among the Anglicans in Boston. In the autumn of 1782 the vestry chose as the new pastor James Freeman, a Harvard graduate who was then preaching in Salem, though he was not yet ordained. Freeman accepted the post, and on April 21, 1783, he was made pastor of King's Chapel. Since the Episcopal Church in the U.S. had no bishops, those who wanted to become priests had to journey to England to be ordained. But the new spirit of independence that had arisen in the congregation of King's Chapel made this repugnant to them, so on Nov. 18, 1787, they took matters into their own hands. Dr. Thomas Bulfinch (father of Charles Bulfinch), who was senior warden and acting for the congregation, ordained James Freeman "to be Rector, Minister, Pastor, Public Teacher, and Teaching Elder of the Episcopal Church." This unprecedented action was condemned by a group of Episcopal clergymen, who denounced the congregation of King's Chapel in a handbill distributed throughout their churches in the U.S., an action which was considered to be one of excommunication. King's Chapel was now completely on its own, and under the leadership of James Freeman the congregation went its own way, making changes in its liturgy and doctrine, eventually becoming the first church in the U.S. to espouse openly the Unitarian theology that had been spreading in New England. Thus developed the unique character of King's Chapel, which its historian André Mayer has described as being "unitarian in theology, Anglican in liturgy, and congregational in church government," characteristics that this distinguished old church still possesses.

Exterior. The church is built of cut blocks of granite from Quincy (then Braintree), the first monumental building in the American colonies to be constructed with cut stone. The most remarkable feature is the tower that rises from its vestibule, looking more like a medieval fortress than a belfry, lacking the two-tiered steeple and the spire that were omitted for lack of funds. The portico, as was noted, was added in 1787–89, but the columns and the balustrade are not stone but wood, carved by Thomas Clement, and painted gray to resemble the dark marble in the rest of the structure. The original bell was cracked while tolling for the evening service on May

King's Chapel (Amor Towles)

8, 1814, after which it was broken up, melted down, and recast in Paul Revere's foundry in Canton, Mass.; it was reinstalled in 1816 and is still in use today. The main structure of the church is unexceptional: a two-story building with two courses of windows; the lower ones small and capped by segmental arches; the upper ones, which open into the galleries, large and round-arched; covered with a hip roof with tiny dormer windows at the top.

Interior. The plain gauntness of the exterior is compensated for by the richness of the nave, which many consider to be the finest Georgian church interior in the U.S. The nave, which is patterned on that of St. Martin's in the Fields, London, a work of James Gibbs, is particularly distinguished by the colonnade of double Corinthian columns that separate the central area of the nave from the side aisles, resting on pedestals that rise to the top of the box pews. (The pedestals are hollow, with shelves for prayer books and hymnals inside.) The capitals of each pair of columns support a small entablature from which members in the form of four spherical segments curve out on one side to meet the flat ceiling over the central aisle, on the inner side to form a groin vault in the gallery, and on the two transverse sides to join the corresponding segments from the adjacent entablatures in a flaring arch, together forming a lovely fanlike array of intersecting surfaces. A pair of intersecting piers frame the apse, whose wall curves from them around to the straight back wall of the chancel.

Gone now are the escutcheons that were once affixed to the walls and columns of the church; these included the coats-of-arms of the King, Sir

Edmund Andros, and Governors Dudley, Shute, Burnet, Belcher, and Shirley. However, there do remain a number of funerary monuments and plaques, some of which have artistic merit. One of these is just to the l. of the entry to the nave: an elaborately carved stone honoring Samuel Vassall, surmounted by his bust and inscribed with his history; this was done by the English sculptor William Tyler in 1760.

Along the l. (N.) wall four plaques honor former members of the congregation at King's Chapel, the most famous of whom is Oliver Wendell Holmes, Sr. (1809–94), physician and author, which is between the first two windows from the back, with the three following belonging to Joseph May, Samuel Appleton, and Charles Apthorp. Apthorp's monument, with its weeping cherubs, is by Henry Cheere, one of the leading sculptors in London during the second half of the 18C.

Within the chancel is the original altar table presented to King's Chapel in 1696 by William and Mary. On the wall behind it are four tablets presented by the King and Queen at the same time; these are inscribed with the Lord's Prayer; Exodus I, II, III, and IV; the Ten Commandments; and the Apostles' Creed. (The Apostles' Creed was omitted from the King's Chapel Prayer Book during the ministry of the Rev. James Freeman.) The four busts around the periphery of the chancel are portraits of the first four Unitarian ministers of King's Chapel; they are, from l. to r., with the years of their ministry in parentheses: Henry Foote (1861–89), Francis Greenwood (1824–43), James Freeman (1782–1824), and Ephraim Peabody (1846–56). In front of the chancel at the l. side of the center aisle is the pulpit, with its sounding board above. This was built in 1717 for the first wooden church on this site, and most of it is still made up of the original wood; it is the oldest pulpit in the U.S. in continued use on the same site. Along the southern wall, starting at the front, there are funerary plaques honoring Frances Shirley, wife of Governor Shirley; Thomas Newton, one of the founders of King's Chapel; John Lowell; and William Sullivan. Mrs. Shirley died shortly before the present church was erected, and she was buried in the crypt, where her husband was laid to rest beside her in 1771. Her funerary monument, which one authority has called "one of the finest examples of 18C monumental sculpture in the U.S.," was carved by Peter Scheemakers, a Fleming who ranked with Henry Cheere as one of the best sculptors in London during the second half of the 18C. Oliver Wendell Holmes wrote a touching poem about Mrs. Shirley on the occasion of the Bicentenerary Celebration of the gathering of the King's Chapel congregation in 1886, calling her "the fair Francesca on the southern wall."

In the southern side aisle is the large canopied pew used by the royal governors of Massachusetts, as well as by visiting dignitaries. Washington sat in this pew with Governor Shirley when he came to Boston in Feb. 1756, and he used it again on Oct. 27, 1789, listening to a concert held to raise money for the construction of the portico. (According to the annals of King's Chapel, the President contributed £7.) The chair within the pew belonged to Governor Thomas Hutchinson, who used it during his term of office, 1770–74.

The organ in the loft above the entry is a modern one, dating to 1964, but structurally and acoustically it is a replica of one made for King's Chapel in 1756. (King's Chapel was the first church in New England to use an organ.) The clock on the front of the organ loft dates to 1853 and was made by Ebenezer Oliver; it is wound by the sexton every Sat. morning.

To the l. of the door leading from the nave there is a monument to the 14 men of the congregation who died in the Civil War, and above the door are inscribed the names of three who were killed in World War I. The Civil War monument replaced a single isolated pew where, during the days of the royal governors, condemned men sat to attend their last church service before execution.

On leaving the church, notice the funerary monument to the r. just outside the portico, a curious stele in the form of a tapered obelisk resting on four stone balls at the corners of a pedestal. This is a monument to the memory of the Chevalier de Saint Sauveur, an officer on the warship *Tonnant* in the French fleet commanded by D'Estaing, which anchored in Boston in late Aug. 1778, after the first phase of the Battle of Newport. There, on Sept. 8, 1778, a violent quarrel broke out between the French sailors and American civilians. Two French officers tried to stop the fight and one of them, the Chevalier de Saint Sauveur, was badly wounded and died a week later, after which he was buried in the crypt of King's Chapel.

The next stop on the itinerary is the ****King's Chapel Burying-Ground,** the oldest graveyard in Boston and one of the most picturesque spots in the city. The entrance to the graveyard is on Tremont St, a short distance to the N. from King's Chapel.

Admission. The graveyard is open daily 8—4:30.

History. The graveyard beside King's Chapel was Boston's first "burying place". After 1659—60, when the North Burying-Ground (Copp's Hill) and the South Burying-Ground (Granary) were established, the graveyard here came to be known as the Old Burying-Place. This is where virtually all of the early settlers of Boston were interred, as well as many of the great men who played a prominent part in the subsequent history of the Bay Colony. The first one to be buried here was Isaac Johnson, husband of Lady Arbella, daughter of the Earl of Lincoln. Johnson was the first of the colonists to settle on the Shawmut Peninsula after the Rev. Blaxton, his classmate and friend at Emmanuel College, who had invited him to take a plot of land near his own. In Aug. 1630 Johnson began to build a house somewhere in the area of the present graveyard, while his wife waited in Salem. But she died in Salem later that month, and Johnson himself passed away on Sept. 30 of that year. As Governor Thomas Hutchinson wrote in his *History of Massachusetts:* "Mr Johnson . . . was buried at the southwest corner of his lot, and the people exhibited their attachment to him by ordering their remains to be buried near him. This was the origin of the first burying-place." Two old bronze tablets on the entrance gateway name some of the people who are interred in the graveyard, along with the year of their death. Among those whose names are recorded on the tablet there are four governors of colonial Massachusetts: John Winthrop, 1649; John Endecott (the modern spelling is Endicott), 1665; John Leverett, 1679; and William Shirley, 1771; along with two governors of Connecticut: John Winthrop, 1676; and Fitz-John Winthrop, 1707. However, Endicott is almost certainly interred in the Old Granary Burying-Ground, while the location of Shirley's last resting place remains a mystery. Other prominent persons listed on the tablet are: John Winslow, 1674; his wife, Mary Chilton, the *Mayflower* passenger, 1679; Lady Andros, 1688; Captain Roger Clap, 1690; Thomas Brattle, 1713; the Rev. John Cotton, 1652; Captain Robert Keayne, first commander of the Ancient and Honorable Artillery Company, 1638; William Dawes, patriot and Son of Liberty, 1799; and Charles Bulfinch, the architect, 1844. But the tablet is also in error on that last name, for Bulfinch is interred in the Mount Auburn Cemetery in Cambridge.

A number of the better-known tombs and gravestones can easily be found, and some have been identified by plaques affixed to them in recent years. To find them, begin by turning r. at the entryway and then turn l. onto the path that leads down the side of the graveyard past King's Chapel. (The large pit surrounded by a grating is a ventilation shaft for the subway line below.) A few paces along is a tombstone marked by a modern plaque (now almost illegible) bearing the name of *Elizabeth Pain,* buried in 1704, who is thought to be the prototype for Hester Prynne, the heroine of Hawthorne's *Scarlet Letter.* (Hawthorne loved the romantic atmosphere of the graveyard and often strolled through it, and it was undoubtedly on one of those occasions that he noticed the tombstone of Elizabeth Pain, who is thought to have been imprisoned for adultery and publicly vilified.)

Continue along the path and turn l. at the end to walk along the lower path. A plaque halfway along marks the grave of *Captain Roger Clap*, one of the first settlers of Dorchester. Turn l. at the end of the lower path and walk up the side path for about half of its length, where a side path to the r. leads to the tomb of *Captain Robert Keayne*. Another path leads back to the center of the graveyard and the tomb of *William Dawes*, surmounted by a large obelisk; the family tomb of the *Winthrops;* and to the grave of *John Winslow* and his wife, *Mary (Chilton) Winslow.*

Before leaving the King's Chapel Burying-Ground, notice the tombstone propped up against the fence to the r. of the gate, for on it is carved one of the finest coats-of-arms extant in Boston.

3 King's Chapel Burying-Ground to City Hall Plaza

This itinerary begins at King's Chapel Burying-Ground, starting from there along the l. side of Tremont St toward the Common. On the corner of Tremont and School Sts, across the street from King's Chapel, stands the *Parker House,* the oldest hotel in continuous operation in the U.S. The first hotel on this site was opened in 1856 by Harvey D. Parker, a native of Maine who had arrived in Boston a quarter-century earlier with less than $1 to his name. Since then the hotel has been rebuilt several times, each time on a larger scale than before, with the present building dating to 1927. After the first Parker House opened it was frequented by a group known as the Saturday Club, which included among its members most of the leading writers and intellectuals of mid-19C Boston. Charles Dickens stayed at the Parker House during his visit to Boston in 1867–68, and he joined the Saturday Club in their convivial meetings. John Wilkes Booth booked in here on April 4, 1865, just ten days before he shot Abraham Lincoln, and during his stay he spent some time practicing at a shooting gallery down the street.

Before the Parker House was built Boston's grand hotel was the *Tremont House;* this stood on the opposite side of Tremont St, extending from Beacon St as far as the Old Granary Burying-Ground. Dickens stayed there on his first visit to Boston, in 1842, and Congressman Abraham Lincoln was a guest in 1848, while on a speaking tour to support the presidential campaign of Zachary Taylor.

In the middle of the block beyond the Parker House stands the *Tremont Temple,* now the *Tremont Temple Baptist Church.* The Tremont Temple stands on the site of the *Tremont Theater,* which opened in 1827.

The first performances of grand opera in Boston were held in the Tremont Theater, and all of the famous thespians of the era trod its boards. In 1842 the building was bought by the Baptist Temple of Dr. Colver, who in 1838 had split from the Charles Street Baptist Church in order to take a stronger stand in favor of the abolition of slavery, and from that time on it was called the Tremont Temple. Nevertheless, the building was still leased out for political meetings and for musical and theatrical performances. Lincoln gave a speech at a Free Soil rally here on Sept. 22, 1848; Jenny Lind sang here in the autumn of 1850, and in Dec. 1867 Dickens packed the theater every time he gave a reading of his works. The present Tremont Temple, the third building to bear that name, was designed by Clarence A. Blackall and built in 1894–96.

Farther on along Tremont St and on the opposite side one comes to the ****Old Granary Burying-Ground,** which in historic interest is the most important of all of Boston's graveyards. Its setting is just as picturesque as that of the burying ground beside King's Chapel, with rows of old tombstones shaded by a copse of trees, the handsome edifice of the Boston Athenaeum looming in the background, and the graceful spire of the Park Street Church soaring above it to the left.

Admission. The graveyard is open daily 8–4:30.

History. The plot of land here was first authorized for use as a place of burial in 1660, just a few months after the burying ground at Copp's Hill was established. The reason for laying out two new cemeteries in a single year was that there was no longer room for additional interments in the Old Burying-Ground at the corner of Tremont and School Sts. The graveyard here, which was originally part of the Common, took its name from a huge building called the *Granary,* which was erected on the present site of the Park Street Church in 1737. The building was moved elsewhere in 1809, but its name survives in that of the graveyard, which since the early 19C has been known as the Old Granary Burying-Ground. Many of the great men of the colonial period and heroes in the struggle for independence are buried here, along with ordinary townspeople; more than 1600 of their graves have been identified.

Interior. The massive gateway to the Burying-Ground dates to c. 1830 and is a work of Solomon Willard. On the two leaves of the entrance gate bronze tablets name some of the notables interred here. The tablet on the l. gate reads: "Within this ground are buried: The Victims of the Boston Massacre, Mar. 5, 1770; Josiah Franklin and Wife (Parents of Benjamin Franklin); Peter Faneuil; Paul Revere; and John Phillips, first Mayor of Boston." The table on the r. reads: "Within this ground are buried: John Hancock, Samuel Adams, and Robert J. Paine, Signers of the Declaration of Independence; Governors: Richard Bellingham, William Dummer, James Bowdoin, Increase Sumner, James Sullivan, and Christopher Gore; and Lieutenant Governor Thomas Cushing; Chief Justice Samuel Sewall; Ministers John Baily, Samuel Willard, Jeremy Belknap, and John Lothrop." John Endicott's name should be added to the list of governors of Massachusetts who are buried in the Old Granary, since an entry in the town records for March 5, 1721, mentions his tomb being located here. General Joseph Warren was buried in the Old Granary in 1776. However, in 1825 his remains were removed to the Warren tomb under St. Paul's church on Tremont St; later still, in 1855, they were again disinterred and finally placed in the family vault in the Forest Hills Cemetery in West Roxbury.

As in the other old burying grounds of Boston, the tombstones here have been rearranged on several occasions, so that there is no certainty that they actually mark the graves of those whose names they bear. The more famous tombs and tombstones can be found easily. Going r. from the gateway along the front of the graveyard, one sees in turn the following tombstones and grave-markers: *John Phillips,* first mayor of Boston; the five *victims of the Boston Massacre,* who are buried here along with *Christopher Snider,* a 12-year-old boy who was killed in an altercation with a Royalist on Feb. 22, 1770, just 11 days before the Massacre; and *Samuel Adams,* whose supposed grave site is marked by a tablet set into a boulder, a monument put in place in 1898. Outside the fence at this point a tablet honors *John Smibert,* the painter who designed the original Faneuil Hall; he is known to have been buried in the Old Granary, but the actual site of his grave is unknown. Walking l. from the entrance gate one then sees the following tombstones: *Dr. David Townsend,* an American surgeon who fought at the Battle of Bunker Hill; *Benjamin Woodbridge,* killed by Henry Phillips in a duel with swords on the Common on July 3, 1728, when the victim was just 19 years of age; and *James Otis,* whose grave is marked by a tablet set into a stone, also set up in 1898.

A pathway leads from the gate to the center of the graveyard. There stands the most prominent funerary monument in the Old Granary, a large obelisk that marks the graves of *Benjamin Franklin's parents.* The original monument here was a marble stone that Franklin himself had placed above the grave of his parents. In time this became badly eroded, and so in 1827 a group of public-spirited Bostonians raised funds to erect the present granite monument, designed and built by Solomon Willard.

The epitaph was written by Benjamin Franklin for the original monument: "Josiah Franklin and Abiah his wife, lie here interred. They lived lovingly together in wedlock fifty-five years. Without any estate, or any gainful employment, by constant labor and industry, with God's blessing, they maintained a large family comfortably and brought up thirteen children and seven grandchildren reputably. From this instance, reader, be encouraged to diligence in thy calling and distrust not Providence. He was a pious and prudent man; she a discreet and virtuous woman. Their youngest son, in filial regard to their memory, places this stone. J.F. born 1665, died 1744, aged 89; A.F. born 1667, died 1752, aged 85."

Another prominent monument is that of *John Hancock* (1737–93), which is next to the mall midway along the l. side of the graveyard, at the end of the path leading in that direction from the Franklin monument. The monument in the form of an ancient Greek funerary stele bears an inscription stating simply that it was erected in honor of John Hancock in 1895 by the Commonwealth of Massachusetts. Hancock's actual tomb, which bears no legible inscription, is close by.

Walk along the path toward the back of the graveyard past the Hancock monument, to a large monument honoring *James Bowdoin* (1726–90), who in 1787 succeeded Hancock as governor of Massachusetts. The pathway continues past the Bowdoin monument up to the far left-hand corner of the graveyard. There a stone table stands over the Faneuil family tomb, where *Peter Faneuil,* builder of the original Faneuil Hall, was buried on March 10, 1742. The surface of the monument is so badly eroded that the coat-of-arms and the inscription are only partly legible, and it is identified principally by the name "P. Funel" on the base of the stone, perhaps scratched there by a mason.

Another very prominent monument is that of *Paul Revere,* which is above the center of the path that runs across the top of the graveyard. Revere's actual tomb is in front of the monument, which bears this simple inscription: "Paul Revere, Born in Boston January 1734, Died May 1818." On the lower side of the path opposite Paul Revere's tomb is the grave of *Chief Justice Samuel Sewall,* who was one of the judges at the Salem witchcraft trials. Below and to the r. of this is the table monument marking the tomb of Sewall's father-in-law, *John Hull,* who minted the famous "pine-tree shillings" of the Massachusetts Bay Colony, the first local coinage in New England.

Walking back along the path that leads down toward the gate, one might turn l. about halfway along and walk to the wall on that side, where a plaque honors the memory of *Robert Treat Paine,* one of the signers of the Declaration of Independence. If one walks straight back toward the path, on the r. is an old tombstone marked with the following inscription: "Here

The Old Granary Burying-Ground and the obelisk marking the graves of Benjamin Franklin's parents (Peter Amory)

lyes ye Body of Mary Goose, Wife to Isaac Goose, Aged 42 Years, Deceased 19 Oct. 1690." Popular tradition has it that this is the grave of the fabled Mother Goose, and that the stories that bear her name are the tales that Mary Goose told her many children and grandchildren, but folklorists are skeptical.

The next stop on this itinerary is the ***Park Street Church,** which stands on the corner of Tremont and Park Sts. This handsome church is one of the landmarks of central Boston, and its graceful spire has been hovering in view through much of this stroll through the town.

Admission. From the last week in June until the third week in Aug. the church is open to visitors Tues.–Sat. 9:30–3:30; year-round there are Sunday services at 10:30 a.m. and 6 p.m.

History. According to its own public statement, the "Park Street Church was founded in 1809 by a group of concerned laymen who had resolved to build a witness to trinitarian and evangelical Christianity in the midst of the general religious apostasy of the day." The cornerstone of the church, which stands on the site of the Old Granary, was laid on May 1, 1809, and the meetinghouse was dedicated on Jan. 10, 1810. The building was designed by Peter Banner (fl. 1794–1828), an English architect who planned it in the style of the London churches of Christopher Wren, particularly its superb spire. During the War of 1812 gunpowder was stored in the crypt, and thenceforth the intersection of Tremont and Park Sts, on which the church stood, was called "Brimstone Corner," although some scholars hold that the name comes from the fiery sermons that were preached from the pulpit of the Park Street Church. Even more fiery than the sermons of its early ministers were the speeches given from its pulpit by orators speaking on matters of public concern. One of the most memorable of these was the speech given on July 4, 1829, by William Lloyd Garrison, then 23 years old, his first public denunciation of slavery. Another was the speech given in 1849 by Senator Charles Sumner, entitled "The War System of Nations," which was addressed to the Second Annual Convention of the American Peace Society. Throughout its history the Park Street Church has been active in religious, political, cultural, and humanitarian activities, and continues to be so today.

Exterior. The most remarkable feature of the church is its steeple, the pinnacle of which is 217ft above ground. This consists of a brick tower enclosing the vestibule of the church, above which is the three-tiered wooden steeple, surmounted by the slender, tapering spire. The capitals of the columns were carved by Solomon Willard, who was also chief carpenter in the construction of the church. A curving colonnade joins the facade of the tower to the main structure of the church, with three columns on either side joined by curtain walls. Old prints show that the cornice of the colonnade originally joined the main cornice, which is now 12ft higher than that of the portico. This is due to the fact that in 1838 the height of the main building was increased by 12ft so that the basement level of the church could be enlarged and thereby become more useful. At the same time the upper tier of windows in the side walls, which originally had been rectangular and only slightly taller than those in the lower tier, were increased in height and topped by round arches, greatly adding to the grandeur of the building.

Interior. The front steps lead up to the vestibule, from where one passes directly into the basement. This is now used as a lecture hall, and during the summer a continuously running film is presented here, dealing with the history of the Park Street Church. The church itself is on the second floor, reached by a pair of staircases that wind up from the vestibule. The interior is a disappointment, totally lacking in artistic or architectural interest, and one lingers there only long enough to reflect upon the active part that this place has played in the social history of Boston.

On leaving the church, pause on the top of the steps and look across to the far end of Hamilton Pl, the cul-de-sac that opens up on the opposite side of Tremont St. The building that forms the far end of Hamilton Pl, now used for commercial purposes, was once the old *Music Hall.*

The Music Hall, which was built in 1852 by the Harvard Musical Association, was Boston's first large concert hall, seating an audience of some 2000. The Harvard Orchestra gave its first concert there on Dec. 28, 1865; the Boston Symphony Orchestra, founded by Henry Lee Higginson, opened its first season in the Music Hall on Oct. 22, 1881; and the Promenade Concerts, now known as the Boston Pops, had their first season there in 1885. The Music Hall was also used for lectures and political rallies. Among the notables who spoke there on such occasions were Theodore Parker and Wendell Phillips, both of whom gave impassioned speeches advocating the abolition of slavery in the U.S., and Oscar Wilde, who entertained a packed house in Jan. 1882, while on a lecture tour to promote a D'Oyly Carte production of Gilbert and Sullivan's *Patience*. Part of the Music Hall was incorporated into the now somewhat derelict Loew's Orpheum, which has an entrance on Hamilton Pl.

Park St is but one block long, extending from Tremont St to Beacon St along the northeast corner of the Common. At the beginning of the 19C Park St was a squalid alley on the outskirts of the town, bordering the Common, with the Old Granary adjoining an almshouse and a workhouse, all three of which catered to the poor of the town, unfortunate wretches who dwelt there under appalling conditions. All of this changed after the new State House opened early in 1798, for Park St now led to what would in the Federal period be the center of the town. Charles Bulfinch, the designer of the State House, in 1804 drew plans for a series of eight attached houses on Park St, stretching from the Old Granary to Beacon St, and to make way for them the almshouse and the workhouse were torn down. Then, in 1809, the Old Granary was moved elsewhere so that the Park Street Church could be erected, and when that was completed in the following year Park St became one of the most elegant thoroughfares in town, with the mansions of wealthy and powerful Bostonians lining one side of the principal approach to the new State House and, stretching off on the other side, the bucolic vista of Boston Common. When Thackeray looked at the mansions on Park St, at the time of his visit to Boston in 1852, he remarked that they "could hardly be surpassed, for elegance and the appearance of comfort, even in London!" Virtually nothing now remains of the block of houses that Bulfinch built on Park St, for, with one exception, they have been either replaced or altered beyond recognition. The single exception is the *Amory-Ticknor mansion*, which stands at the corner of Park and Beacon Sts. Charles Bulfinch built this in 1804 for Charles Amory, a wealthy merchant and shipowner, and later it was acquired by George Ticknor, a distinguished professor of literature at Harvard. Lafayette stayed here as a guest of Mayor Quincy during his visit to Boston in 1824. The building was reconstructed in 1885, when its appearance was considerably altered.

The new ****State House,** a splendid gold-domed edifice, crowns the eminence rising from the intersection of Park and Beacon Sts. It is approached by the long flight of steps leading up from the front gate on Beacon St, entering through a door on the balcony to the l. of the main entryway. (The main doors are opened only when a governor of Massachusetts leaves the State House at the end of his term in office, or when an incumbent President of the U.S. pays a state visit to the Massachusetts Legislature.)

Admission. Guided tours of the State House are given as follows: April 1–Oct. 31 daily 9:30–5, Sat. 9:30–5, Sun. 11–5; Nov. 1–Mar. 31 daily 10–4; fee (tel. 727-3676).

History. After the ratification of the Massachusetts constitution in 1780, the State Legislature began meeting in the Old State House, but it soon became apparent that the building was too small for that purpose. In 1787 the Legislature appointed a committee to study the possibility of creating a new State House, and in Nov. of that year Charles Bulfinch submitted plans for the proposed structure, which were accepted by the committee. However, the project did not begin until 1795, when the committee chose the present site on the southern slope of Beacon Hill. This had originally been a pasture on the estate of John Hancock, whose mansion stood in what is now the garden in front of the W. wing of the State House. The plot was purchased from Hancock's heirs by the town of Boston, and was then sold to the state of Massachusetts for the nominal price of 5 shillings. The cornerstone of the building was laid on July 4, 1795, by Governor Samuel Adams, with Paul Revere assisting in his capacity as grand master of the Grand Lodge of Masons. The building was completed by the beginning of 1798, and the Massachusetts Legislature moved in on Jan. 11 of that year, during the tenure of Governor Increase Sumner. A number of additions to the building have been made since that time. The first of these, a structure designed in 1831 by Isaiah Rogers, was a small addition built out from the central part of the N. facade of the Bulfinch building. The second addition, designed by Gridley J. F. Bryant and built in 1853–56, was also on the N. side, doubling the size of the State House. Both additions were demolished in 1889, when Charles E. Brigham designed the present northern extension of the State House, which increased the area of the site some sevenfold, a project that was completed in 1895. The E. and W. wings, which frame the original Bulfinch State House, were constructed in 1914—17 by Chapman, Sturgis and Andrews. The most recent addition was the Archives Museum, a subterranean building to the W. of the Bulfinch State House, constructed in 1959—60. The dome of the Bulfinch building has twice been reconstructed, in 1859 and 1897.

Exterior. The earliest description of the original Bulfinch building was published in the *Columbian Centinel* on Jan. 10, 1798, the day before the Massachusetts Legislature moved into the new State House. The description of the exterior given there (retaining the original spelling) is as follows: "The new State House is an oblong building, 173 feet front and 61 deep; it consists externally of a basement story, 20 feet high, and a principal story 30 feet high. This in the center of the front is crowned with an Attic 60 feet wide, 20 feet high, which is covered with a pediment. Immediately above this rises a dome 50 feet in diameter and 30 feet high, the whole terminated with an elegant circular lanthorn, supporting a gilt pine cone, an emblem of one of our principal stapels. The basement story is finished plain on the wings with square windows. The centre is 94 feet in length, and formed of arches which project 14 feet; they form a covered wall below, and support a Colonnade of Corinthian columns of the same extent above. The outside walls are of large patent bricks, with white marble fascias, imposts and keystones.

To this description it need only be added that the dome of the Bulfinch State House was made of wood, which was originally painted the color of lead. In 1802 Paul Revere and Sons covered the dome with copper sheathing; it was then gilded in 1861, and in 1874 it was covered with the gold leaf seen today. The brick structure of the Bulfinch State House was painted white in 1825, and then later done in yellow, but in 1928 the paint was removed to recreate the original appearance of the building.

Interior. After entering the building by the door at the l. end of the balcony, turn r. to pass into *Doric Hall,* the main room on the ground floor of the original Bulfinch State House. This noble chamber is square in plan, 55ft on each side, divided into three aisles by a double colonnade of Doric columns, five in each row. (The present columns are made of iron, replicas of the original wooden ones.) At the center of the rear wall there is a statue of *George Washington* done in 1826 by the British sculptor Sir Francis Legatt Chantrey (1781—1841). In the l. corner of the hall there is a statue of *John Albion Andrew* (1818—67), governor of Massachusetts throughout the American Civil War; this is a work of Thomas Ball and was unveiled on Feb. 14, 1871. On the wall to the r. there is a large portrait of *President Abraham Lincoln,* beneath which there are a pair of American cannon from the Revolutionary War. In the center of the wall to the l. a bust of *John Hancock* is flanked by two British cannon captured during the Revolution. On either side of Hancock's bust are paintings; to the l. is a portrait of *General Artemas Ward,* c. 1775, a copy by E. G. Crane of the original by Charles Willson Peale; and on the r. a portrait of *General Thomas Gage,* by John Singleton Copley (1738—1815). In the hallway to the r. of Doric Hall there is a scale model of the Bulfinch State House, and facing it there is a large portrait of *Senator Charles Sumner* by James Wormley.

An archway at the far end of Doric Hall opens into *Senate Staircase Hall,*

Charles Bulfinch's State House (Peter Amory)

so called because of the two winding staircases that lead to the second floor, where the Senate Chamber is located (see below). Below the stairway to the r. a bronze group by the sculptor Bela Pratt shows a nurse tending a wounded soldier, a memorial to the volunteer nurses who served in the Union Army during the Civil War. At the center of the S. wall (to the rear) there is a bronze statue of *General William Francis Bartlett* by Daniel Chester French (1850–1931).

The next chamber, officially called *Memorial Hall*, is better known as the *Hall of Flags*. This is a monumental room with a circular portico of 16 columns, supporting a gallery. The hall takes its name from the banners displayed in the glassed-in alcoves around the room, presented by Massachusetts regiments that have fought in every conflict in which the U.S. has been involved from the Civil War onward. Overhead in the dome is the Seal of Massachusetts, encircled by those of the other 12 original states of the U.S. Four paintings in panels in the gallery depict scenes from the history of Massachusetts.

After passing through Memorial Hall, one enters the vast chamber with the prosaic name of *Main Staircase Hall,* where a double flight of stairs leads up to the second floor. On a landing halfway up the staircase there are stained-glass windows decorated with the original Seal of Massachusetts, dated March 4, 1628, and with the coats of all of its governors up to the Revolution.

At the center of the W. side of the upper floor is the elegant oval chamber of the Massachusetts House of Representatives; this dates to 1895, and prior to that the representatives convened in the room that now houses the Senate. On the frieze below the dome are engraved the names of 53 distinguished citizens of Massachusetts. In panels below the frieze are five large paintings by Albert Herter entitled *Milestones on the Road to Freedom in Massachusetts.*

The visitors' gallery is at the E. side of the chamber, and in front of it is suspended the *Sacred Codfish,* the gilded wooden emblem that was originally placed in the Old State House as "a memorial of the importance of the Cod Fishery to the welfare of this Commonwealth." The Sacred Codfish was brought to the new State House when it was opened in 1798, and since then it has always hung over the meeting place of the House of Representatives.

At the center of the landing on the upper floor is a seated bronze statue of *Governor Roger Wolcott,* a work of Daniel Chester French. Wolcott was governor during the Spanish-American War, and his statue is also a memorial to the men of Massachusetts who fought in that conflict; it was dedicated on Dec. 31, 1906. (Governor Wolcott's r. foot is very shiny, for visitors are continually rubbing it to bring them good luck.)

The present *Senate Chamber* is directly over Doric Hall, and is best approached by the corridor that leads to the S. from the main landing (i.e., to the l. of Governor Wolcott's statue). The entrance to the chamber is to the r. near the end of that corridor. This is the most historic room in the State House, where Presidents of the U.S. from Monroe to Taft have addressed the Massachusetts Legislature, as did John F. Kennedy four days before his own inauguration, and where Lafayette made his farewell address at the end of his last visit to Boston in 1825. As noted above, this was originally the chamber where the House of Representatives met; its appearance is almost identical to what it was when it first opened on Jan. 11, 1798, except for the absence of the four fireplaces that were then used to heat the chamber. The chamber is described thus in the account printed in the *Columbian Centinel* on the day before the State House opened: "The rooms above are: The Representatives' Room, in the center 55 feet square, the corners formed into niches with fireplaces; this room is furnished with Doric columns on the sides, at 12 feet from the floor, forming a gallery; the Doric entablature surrounds the whole, from this spring four flat arches on the side, which are united by a circular cornice above which are four large pendants ornamented with trophies of Commerce, Agriculture, Peace and War. The dome is finished in compartments of stucco in a style of simple elegance. The center of the dome is 50 feet from the floor. The seats for the Members are arranged semicircularly, and the Speaker's chair faces the whole."

On the walls of the chamber on the l. side there are displayed two muskets, one of them belonging to Captain John Parker, who commanded the American militia at the Battle of Lexington, and the other the first British weapon captured during the Revolutionary War. Among the busts in the alcoves of the chamber are portraits of *Abraham Lincoln* and *George Wash-*

ington (flanking the chair of the president of the Senate), of *Benjamin Franklin* (W. wall), and of *Lafayette* (E. wall), the only foreigner to be honored by a monument in the State House.

The large room directly across the corridor E. of the entrance to the Senate Chamber is the *Senate Reception Room.* During the period 1798–1895 this served as the Senate Chamber. This handsome room is also part of the original Bulfinch State House; it too has changed little over the years, as one can see from this description in the *Columbian Centinel:* "The Senate is 55 feet long, 33 wide, and 30 high; highly finished in the Ionic order; two screens of columns support with their entablatures a rich and elegant carved ceiling. This room is also ornamented with Ionic pilasters, and with the arms of the State and of the United States, placed in opposite panels." On the l. side of the wall facing the entrance there is a portrait of *Calvin Coolidge* (1872–1933), president of the Massachusetts Senate in 1914–15, governor of the state in 1919–20, and President of the U.S. 1923–29.

The only other room on the upper floor that dates back to the original Bulfinch structure is the *Governor's Office,* which is to the W. of the Senate Chamber. This splendid suite of rooms, which served as the Council Chamber from 1798 to 1937, is normally not open to the public.

The *Massachusetts State Archives* are located in a subterranean structure to the W. of the Bulfinch State House; the museum there is approached either by an elevator from the second floor of the main building or by a separate entrance from the outside, to the l. of the main staircase leading up from Beacon St.

Admission. The Archives Museum is open to the public Mon.–Fri. 9–5.

Interior. The Massachusetts Archives, as its staff states in a prospectus, is "responsible for the custody, preservation, and management of important non-current records of the Commonwealth. Its holdings include the original Massachusetts Archives (a series of 328 volumes of colonial papers); an outstanding collection of documents including Executive Orders and Proclamations; administrative records of many state agencies; constitutional papers; and a wide assortment of treaties, charters, and maps, some dating back to the earliest settlement period."

The most important document on display in the museum is in a case at the center of the room; this is a copy of the *Charter of the Massachusetts Bay Company,* which the Puritans brought with them when they sailed to New England in 1630. The greatest treasure in the archives is Governor Bradford's *History of Plimoth Plantation,* which was originally in the library of the Rev. Thomas Prince at Old South; this disappeared when the building was looted by the British, but it was returned by an anonymous source toward the end of the 19C. Other historic documents are exhibited in the cases arrayed around this. In case No. 1 is Governor Bradford's copy of the *Mayflower Compact,* which the Pilgrims drew up and signed even before they landed at Plymouth in 1620; No. 2: records of the General Court of the Bay Colony for its earliest years; No. 2A: the charter given by King James II to Sir Edmund Andros in 1686; and No. 3: the charter drawn up in 1691 by William and Mary establishing the royal Province of Massachusetts.

Precincts. Bronze statues of historical figures stand in the precincts in front of the State House. At the far l. of the garden, as one faces the State House, there is a statue of *Henry Cabot Lodge* (1850–1924), who served in the U.S. House of Representatives 1886–93 and in the U.S. Senate 1893–1924;

this is a work of Raymond Porter and was dedicated on Oct. 26, 1932. (Notice the old cannon mounted in the garden a short distance to the r. of Lodge's statue. Inscriptions on the cannon record that it was made in Spain, and that it was captured by American forces in Cuba during the Spanish-American War.)

At the rear of the garden in front of the W. wing there is a statue of *Anne Hutchinson* (1591–1643); this is a work of Cyrus E. Dallin and was dedicated in 1922 as a memorial to a heroine in the cause of religious freedom. To the l. of the stairway there is a statue of *Horace Mann* (1796–1859), who is honored here for his pioneering work in educational reform; this was sculpted in 1860 by Emma Stebbins (1815–82). To the r. of the stairway there is a statue of *Daniel Webster* (1782–1852) by Hiram Powers. Powers, who at the time worked in Italy, shipped the original version of this statue from Leghorn in 1857, but it was lost at sea; he then did the present work, which arrived safely in Boston in 1859. At the foot of the stairs leading to the E. wing of the State House there is an equestrian statue of *General Joseph Hooker* (1814–79), one of several generals who served as commander-in-chief of the Union Army during the American Civil War. Hooker's statue is a work of Daniel Chester French; the horse is by Edward C. Potter. At the rear of the garden in front of the E. wing there is a fine statue of the Quaker martyr, *Mary Dyer,* who was hanged in Boston in 1660 because of her religious beliefs. Her statue, sculpted by Sylvia Shaw Judson, was dedicated in 1959, honoring another heroine in the struggle for religious toleration in Puritan Boston. On the pedestal of her monument are inscribed the last words that she spoke before her execution: "My life availeth me not in comparison to the liberty of the truth."

The last part of this itinerary goes up to the head of Beacon St, heading in that direction along the r. side of the street. After the Amory-Ticknor mansion at the corner of Beacon and Park Sts is the *Claflin Building* (No. 20). This was designed by the architect William G. Preston and erected in 1883–84; it originally housed the College of Liberal Arts of Boston University and was named after the Claflin family, prominent benefactors of that institution. During the years 1936–81 the Claflin Building housed Goodspeed's Bookshop, which now occupies No. 7, at the end of the block on the other side of Beacon St. The charming little building at No. 16 was built in 1809 by Robert Fletcher; it is called the *Harding House,* because in the years 1827–30 it was the home and studio of the artist Chester Harding, some of whose works are on display just down the street at the Boston Athenaeum. The house is now the headquarters of the Boston Bar Association, and is not open to the public.

The next building, at No. 14, is the *Congregational House,* designed by Shepley, Rutan and Coolidge and built in 1897–98 for the American Congregational Association. The Association now uses much of the building to house their extensive and unique library, which specializes in the religious history and literature of New England. On the facade of the second floor four panels of sculpture in relief illustrate the early religious and intellectual history of New England. These were begun by the Spanish sculptor Domingo Mora, but he left the U.S. at the outbreak of the Spanish-American War and the reliefs were completed by the Swiss sculptor Stadler, using Mora's original designs.

The long and massive building beyond the Congregational House, with its entrance at 10½ Beacon St is the ****Boston Athenaeum,** one of the greatest cultural institutions in the city.

Admission. The Boston Athenaeum serves primarily its members. Qualified nonmembers are welcome to use specific Athenaeum collections on the premises for short- or long-term research. The Athenaeum is open 9–5:30 Mon.–Fri. throughout the year, and also 9–4 Sat., Oct.–May. Visitors who would like to see the Athenaeum's library and works of art are invited to join guided tours given on Tues. and Thurs. at 3; those wishing to go on these tours should apply at the front desk a day in advance (tel. 227-0270).

History. The Boston Athenaeum began as the *Anthology Club,* founded in 1803 by a small group of Bostonians who were interested in literature. In 1805 the Club began publication of the *Monthly Anthology and Boston Review,* the first literary magazine in the U.S. The first editor of this journal was the Rev. William Emerson, father of Ralph Waldo Emerson, one of the many Boston literary figures who became members of the Athenaeum. On Feb. 17, 1807, ten members of the Anthology Club formally incorporated themselves as the *Boston Athenaeum,* describing their association as one "designed to serve its subscribers as a library of literature and science, a museum of natural and artificial curiosities, a repository for models of machines and works of art, and a laboratory for natural philosophical inquiry and geographical improvements." The Athenaeum was first housed in a building on Congress St, and over the next four decades it moved several times before the present site on Beacon St was acquired. On April 27, 1847, the cornerstone of the new Boston Athenaeum was laid, a three-story structure designed by Edward Clarke Cabot and built by George Minot Dexter. The new building on Beacon St had four levels: the basement was at first rented out to the American Academy of Arts and Sciences and also to the Massachusetts Medical Association; on the first floor there was a sculpture gallery and a reading room for newspapers and periodicals; the second floor housed the library; and the third was used as the painting gallery, with the first art exhibition opening there on May 27, 1850.

Within two decades of its opening it became apparent that even the new building on Beacon St was not large enough to serve the dual function of the Athenaeum, which was then both a library and a museum of art. In Jan. 1866 the Fine Arts Committee of the Athenaeum suggested in a report that a separate building be erected to house the institution's works of art, the germ of the idea that on Feb. 4, 1870, led to the founding of the Boston Museum of Fine Arts, which opened at its first home in Back Bay six years later. During those six years the gallery on the third floor of the Athenaeum was used to give exhibitions of works of art and antiquities that had been acquired by the new museum. And after that museum opened the nucleus of its collection consisted of works of art loaned to it by the Athenaeum, many of which are among the principal exhibits of the MFA at its present home on the Fenway.

After the opening of the MFA the Athenaeum became primarily a library, and although works of art continued to be acquired the main expenditure was on books. By the end of the first decade of the present century the book collection had grown to the point where more space was needed, and in 1913–15 two more floors were added, a project carried out by Henry Forbes Bigelow, producing the handsome edifice seen today.

Despite the great number of art works loaned or passed on to the MFA, the Athenaeum still possesses a large and distinguished art collection, including works by some of the most prominent American painters and sculptors of the 19C; these are exhibited throughout the building, in reading rooms, galleries, stacks, and stairwells. In addition, the Athenaeum Gallery on the second floor is used for monthly exhibitions of the works of local artists, photographers, and sculptors. But today the Athenaeum is primarily a research library. According to a recent report issued by Rodney Armstrong, the present director and librarian of the Athenaeum, "Its collection today includes some 600,000 volumes, being particularly strong in history, biography, English and American literature, and the fine and decorative arts. Special collections include such rarities as Confederate States imprints, books from the libraries of George Washington, General Henry Knox, and Bishop Cheverus, the King's Chapel Collection (1698), Gypsy literature, private press publications, 19C tracts, early U.S. Government documents, and the Charles E. Mason Print Collection. . . . The unique print collection is particularly strong in 18–19C Boston and New England made prints, and is a major scholarly resource."

Interior. In the following, only the most prominent and important works of art will be described. This is partly in the interests of brevity, but also

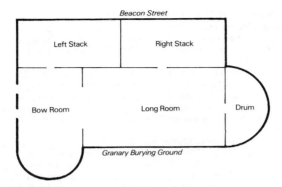

THE BOSTON ATHENAEUM

because many of the objects exhibited here, particularly the portrait busts, are more in the nature of commemorative monuments than works of art.

On the l. side of the lobby the large standing statue of *George Washington* is an 1847 copy by Francesco Cecchi of the 1785 original by Jean-Antoine Houdon; and on the r. side the equally large seated statue of *Nathaniel Bowditch* of 1833 is by John Frazee (1790–1853). On either side of the inner doorway there are huge portraits by Chester Harding (1792–1866): (l.) *Chief Justice John Marshall*, 1830; (r.) *Daniel Webster*, 1828, repainted in 1849. Enter the vestibule, on the r. side of which there is a marble group entitled *Adam and Eve After Their Expulsion from Eden*, a work done in 1855 by Thomas Crawford (1814–57).

Pass through the vestibule to enter the *Delivery Room*, where visitors must check in with the librarian on duty and sign the visitors' book. To the r. of the entryway there is a statue of *Ceres*, c. 1800, by Baron Francois Joseph Bosio (1769–1845); on the pedestal there is a relief showing the *Judgment of Paris*, a work done c. 1840 by Horatio Greenough. On the wall to the l. of the librarian's desk there is a portrait of *Mrs. James ("Jamie") Fields (Ann West Adams)*, painted in 1890 by John Singer Sargent (1856–1925).

The door to the l. of the librarian's desk opens up into the reading room for periodicals, with windows looking out onto the Old Granary Burying-Ground, and to the l. of that is the reading room for newspapers, whose windows overlook Beacon St. On either side of the entryway to the first of these rooms there are large statues, both of which are anon. copies done in the mid-19C of Graeco-Roman originals. The statue to the l. of the door portrays *Demosthenes*, from the original by Polyeuktos (4C B.C.); the one on the r. is of *Sophocles*, a copy of a statue found at Terracina in 1839 and now in the Vatican Museum; this is known as the *Lateran Sophocles*, and is possibly a replica of one that Lycurgus placed in the Athenian Theater of Dionysos in the period 338–26 B.C. On the wall to the l. there is a painting entitled *Flower and Fruit Piece*, by Peter Boel (1622–84). To the r. of the entryway, beside the window, there is a portrait of *Patience Lovell Wright* (1725–86), by John Hoppner (1758–1810), and on the wall to the r. beyond the windows there is a painting showing the *Porcelain Gallery of the Boston MFA*, 1876, by Alice M. Frye. On the l. side of the room, standing on a pedestal, there is a particularly lovely bust of *Elizabeth Barrett Browning*

(1806–61), done in 1886 by William Wetmore Story (1807–86). At the far end of the periodicals reading room there are four paintings; those of interest are the two in the center: (l.) *Joshua Winslow* (1694–1769) and (r.) his wife, *Elizabeth Savage Winslow* (1704–78), both attributed to John Smibert (1688–1750).

At the far right-hand corner of the room there is a delightful little alcove, where one can sit and look out over the Old Granary Burying-Ground. In the corner to the l. there is a large statue of *Mercury* (in Greek, Hermes), c. 1857, a copy of the *Hermes of Andros,* 4C B.C. Facing the entryway is a large portrait of *Thomas Handasyd Perkins* (1764–1854), by Thomas Sully (1783–1876).

Entering the reading room facing onto Beacon St on the l. is a large statue known as the *Discobolus (The Discus Thrower),* an anon. copy c. 1857 of the original by Myron, c. 450 B.C. The huge canvas on the wall to the r. of the windows is *The Golden Age,* attributed to Luca Giordano (1632–1705).

Returning to the Delivery Room, pass into the reading room to the r. of the entrance. The two paintings of greatest interest here are the second and third from the l. of the entryway: (l.) *Self-Portrait of the Artist,* and *The Artist's Wife,* both by Adriaen van der Werff (1659–1722). The two sculptures flanking the staircase to the gallery are (l.) *Little Nell,* c. 1851, by Robert Ball Hughes; and (r.) *Puck and the Owl,* c. 1856, by Harriet Goodhue Hosmer. In the corner of the gallery above the alcove a delightful little reading room has been set aside for children.

The basic layout of the second, third, and fourth floors is much the same, and in describing the works of art exhibited there the following terminology will be used. On entering, either from the stairs or the elevator, one finds oneself in a Bow Room, the r. side of which curves out with windows overlooking the Old Granary Burying-Ground; this opens into a Long Room; and at the far end there is a room of semicircular plan called the Drum; with the stacks opening off to the l. of the first two of these rooms. The second floor differs from this plan only in that it has an exhibition hall opening off from the Long Room, while on the third floor the Long Room takes up the full width of the building, with windows on both sides. All of the floors have galleries, which can be reached either from within or from the stairwell or elevator; of the paintings in the galleries, the only ones that will be described are a few visible from the Bow Room of Floor Two.

Floor Two. The paintings of greatest interest in the Bow Room are: over a door in the rear wall, the *Capture of a French Ship by the Constitution,* by Robert A. Salmon; in the corridor to the r. leading into the Long Room, *The Opening of the Casket,* 1807, by Washington Allston (1779–1844); in the gallery above this, portrait of *John Parker, Jr.* (1783–1844) by Chester Harding; at the foot of the stairs leading up to the gallery a portrait of *John Parker* (1757–1840) by Gilbert Stuart. Look back up to the gallery over the entrance to the Bow Room to two portraits by Washington Allston: (l.) *Benjamin West,* 1814, and (r.) *The Student.*

The first door to the l. in the Long Room leads into the exhibition hall. At the beginning of the stacks leading to this room stands a pair of half-draped marble statues of young women; the one to the r. is by Richard S. Greenough and is entitled *The Carthaginian Girl,* while the one to the l. is a statue of *Venus* by an anon. sculptor, after Canova. Just beyond the Venus there is a unique double-painting on cloth (a fragment of the artist's shirt) done by Washington Allston (the painting is on a hinge; turn it to see both sides); on the front there is a landscape, and on the back a caricature of the *Rev. Joseph Willard,* president of Harvard.

The lower walls of the exhibition hall are used for changing displays, but the paintings higher up generally remain on permanent display; they are, starting with the canvas to the l. of the entrance and continuing in the clockwise direction: *John Brown of Osawatomie* (1800–59), c. 1859, by Nahum Ball Onthank; *James Perkins* (1761–1822), 1822, by Gilbert Stuart; the *Interior of St. Peter's, Rome,* 1756 / 7, by Giovanni Paolo Pannini (1691–1765); *Admiral Sir Isaac Coffin* (1759–1839) by Samuel Stillman Osgood (1808–85); *Benjamin West,* by C. R. Leslie, after Sir Thomas Lawrence; *Fanny Kemble and Her Aunt Mrs. Siddons,* c. 1832, by Henry Perronet Briggs; *William Wirt,* by Henry Inman (1801–46); a *landscape* attributed to Jacob van Ruisdael (1628 / 9–1682); *Pat, the Independent Beggar,* 1819, by Samuel Lovett Waldo (1783–1861); *Thomas Dowes,* 1859, by Moses Wight (1827–95); (above the door) *Landscape with Cattle,* anon., after Albert Cuyp (1620–91).

The main area of the Long Room is flanked by portrait busts of prominent Bostonians, while at the end of the room are a number of copies of ancient Graeco-Roman works. In the center at the far end there is a statue of *Venus* (in Greek, Aphrodite), an anon. copy of the *Medici Aphrodite,* from an original of the early 3C B.C. In the corner to the l. there is a bust of the *Apollo Belvedere,* an anon. copy, c. 1800, of an original of the 4C B.C.

Floor Three. On entering the Bow Room to the l. of center an ornate wooden case contains the **King's Chapel Library.* This collection of books, mostly theological works, was presented to King's Chapel by King William III; it was transferred in 1823 to the Athenaeum, which was given title to the library in 1911. This is the third-largest American colonial library in existence, being surpassed in size only by those in Annapolis and Philadelphia.

The exhibit of greatest interest in the Long Room is the equestrian statue of *George Washington* standing on a pedestal in the center; this is by Thomas Ball, and was made as a model for his monumental work that now stands in Boston Common. At the far end of the room, over the door leading into the Drum, there is a particularly interesting painting by Enrico Meneghilli, showing the *Picture Gallery of the Boston Athenaeum,* 1876.

Floor Four. The central aisle of the Bow Room is flanked by a half-dozen portrait busts, with two more off to the r. side. The best of these is on the last case to the r.; this is a bust of *William Hickling Prescott,* the historian, done in 1844 by Richard S. Greenough. In front of this there is a statuette of *Ganymede and the Eagle,* c. 1838, by Berthel Thorwaldsen.

In the archway leading from the Bow Room to the Long Room on the r. is a bronze *death mask of Napoleon I,* by François Autommarchi (1780–1832); and to the l. a bronze head of *Walter Muir Whitehill,* c. 1977, by Janet Gregg Schroeder. In the first alcove to the l. there is a *Self-Portrait* by Cephas Thompson (1775–1856), and in the next three alcoves on that side there are cases containing the *library of General Henry Knox,* many of the works in which come from the bookshop that he had opened on Washington St in 1771. At the ends of the stacks framing these alcoves are portrait busts of three women, the most striking of which is the one in the center. This is a representation of *Emily Marshall,* who in 1831 wed William Foster Otis, son of Harrison Gray Otis, then mayor of Boston. Emily was generally considered to be the greatest beauty in Boston in her day; the bust is by Horatio Greenough, and it was probably done shortly before she died in childbirth in 1836, when she was just 28 years of age.

At the r. side of the room near the far end there are four fine portraits by Cephas Thompson, at least three of which depict members of his family;

these are, from r. to l.: the *Mother of the Artist; Portrait of a Young Man; Marietta Tintoretto Thompson, Daughter of the Artist; Lucy Thompson: Wife of the Artist.*

The Drum on the fourth floor serves as the Trustees' Room. The portraits arrayed around the room are, beginning at the l. of the entryway: *William Tudor* (1779–1830) by Thomas Sully (1783–1872); *Martha Washington* and *George Washington,* both copies of the originals by Gilbert Stuart; *Hannah Adams* (1755–1831), c. 1827, by Chester Harding (Miss Adams was the first woman to be admitted to membership in the Athenaeum; she was a writer of historical works and was the first professional woman author in the U.S.); *John Adams,* c. 1788, by Mather Brown; the *Rev. John Sylvester John Gardiner* (1765–1830) by Gilbert Stuart (Gardiner was one of the founders of the Athenaeum); *William Smith Shaw,* c. 1826, by Gilbert Stuart (Shaw was the first librarian of the Athenaeum); the *Rev. Joseph Stevens Buckminster* (1784–1812), c. 1810, by Gilbert Stuart; *Gardiner Greene* (1753–1832) by Francis Alexander (1800–81). The room also contains three portrait busts by Jean-Antoine Houdon; to the l. of the central window is one of *Benjamin Franklin,* c. 1788; to the r. of the window is *Lafayette,* c. 1785; and on the mantel of the fireplace is *George Washington,* c. 1787. The bust of Washington was done for Thomas Jefferson and was displayed in his library in Monticello. The bust was inherited by Jefferson's granddaughter Ellen Randolph, and in 1828 it was presented to the Athenaeum by her husband, Joseph Coolidge. On the l. side of the room there is a case filled with books from the personal library of George Washington.

Floor Five. As noted above, the layout of the fifth floor is different from that of the other levels. After passing through the vestibule and stacks, one enters a splendid barrel-vaulted room with windows opening off on either side from barrel-vaulted alcoves, and with the open Drum Room at the far end. There are no paintings exhibited in this room, just the flanking portrait busts and a number of bronze statues. The best of the bronzes is on a pedestal at the far end of the room; this is entitled *The Boy and the Eagle,* done in 1853 by Richard S. Greenough. In the Drum Room at the end there are pastel portraits of George and Martha Washington, after the Gilbert Stuart originals. There are also a number of prints depicting events in the life of George Washington.

This completes a tour of the Boston Athenaeum. In the outer lobby the plaques inside the door to the street record the history of the Athenaeum and its present home. The inscription ends with this singularly appropriate statement: "Here remains a retreat for those who enjoy the humanity of books."

Directly across the street from the Athenaeum there is a fine old residence hotel called the *Bellevue,* whose present structure was erected in 1898. Among those who lived in the Bellevue in times past were Louisa May Alcott, who resided here in the 1870s, and in later times it was the home of Mr. and Mrs. John F. Fitzgerald, the maternal grandparents of the future President John F. Kennedy. The Bellevue stands on the site of the great *mansion of Governor James Bowdoin,* appropriated by General Burgoyne during the British occupation. At the time of Washington's visit to Boston in 1789 he was twice a guest of Governor Bowdoin in this house.

Now turn r. on Beacon St and at the next corner cross Somerset St. On the near corner to the l. is the new home of *Goodspeed's Bookshop,* which has an extensive collection of old maps and prints as well as books on genealogy. Across the street is the attractive skyscraper at *No. 1 Beacon St,* built by Skidmore, Owings & Merrill and completed in 1972. Looking to the r. at the corner, one sees a picturesque view of the Park Street Church framed in the alleyway.

At the next corner turn l. on Tremont St, passing King's Chapel and its Burying-Ground. At the next corner is City Hall Plaza.

4   Faneuil Hall, Quincy Market, and the Blackstone Block

Begin at the S.E. corner of City Hall Plaza, at the top of the steps between City Hall and the New England Bank. There is an excellent view of the two principal monuments on this itinerary: *Faneuil Hall* and the *Quincy Market,* with the enormous tower of the *Custom House* looming dramatically off to the r. After taking in the view, walk down the steps and cross Congress St to the cobbled mall behind Faneuil Hall.

The open area between Congress St and Faneuil Hall was for long known as *Dock Square,* since as early as 1634 the principal landing place in Boston was here, where later the Town Dock would be built out into Town Cove. This was one of the focal points in the life of the early town, because for most Bostonians of that period this was the first spot in the New World upon which they set foot, and through this seaside square passed all of the goods that sustained their life. When the first centennial of American independence was celebrated in 1876, the southern part of this area was named *Adams Sq,* in honor of Samuel Adams. The bronze statue of *Samuel Adams* (1722–1807) that stands there today was done by Anne Whitney (1821–1915) in 1880, and it was erected on its present site in 1928. It is a replica of the marble statue of Samuel Adams that the Commonwealth of Massachusetts commissioned Miss Whitney to create in 1873, a work that was designed to stand in the Statuary Hall in Washington, D.C. On the base of the statue to the r. a bronze plaque honors *Walter Muir Whitehill* (1905–78), author, scholar, and longtime director of the Boston Athenaeum. On the plaque there is a portrait in relief of Whitehill, based on a drawing by his friend Rudolph Ruzicka, and the following inscription: "Dedicated to Walter Muir Whitehill, Historian and Preservationist, who helped Boston shape its Future by Rediscovery of its Past."

Faneuil Hall, the first monument, is one of the most historic buildings in Boston and a center of its life from colonial times to the present.

Admission. Open every day 9–5. (tel. 242-5642).

History. As early as 1708 the site on which Faneuil Hall now stands was used as a market place, and its location at the head of the Town Dock made it more frequented than the one by the Town House. The town records mention that a market building was erected on this site in 1734, but in 1737 it was torn down by a mob disguised as clergymen. The townspeople seemed evenly divided on the question of whether there should be a central market, with many wishing to keep one from being built either because of innate conservatism or, in the case of farmers and merchants, to avoid prying inspectors and regulations. In July

1740 a town meeting was called to discuss the merits of erecting a central market. When the citizens met on the 14th of that month at the Town House they proved to be too numerous to fit inside, and so they reconvened in the Brattle Street Church. There a wealthy Huguenot merchant named Peter Faneuil offered to put up the building at his own expense, if the town would give it legal authorization, regulate the merchants who used it, and keep it in good repair. Despite the great generosity of Faneuil's offer it barely passed, by a vote of 367 to 360. Nevertheless, the selectmen decided to go ahead with the project, and on Sept. 2 of that year it began, with the painter John Smibert serving as architect, Samuel Ruggles as builder, and Joshua Blanchard as mason. The building was completed in Aug. 1742, and included not only a market hall on the ground floor but a meeting hall and offices for the town officials in the upper story. On Sept. 13 the town officials officially accepted the building and named it Faneuil Hall, out of gratitude to its donor. Just a month later the selectmen held their first meeting in Faneuil Hall, by which time the market on the floor below was already in successful operation. (As Francis W. Hatch wrote, in a piece of doggerel describing the dual nature of Faneuil Hall: "Here orators in ages past have mounted their attack / Undaunted by proximity of sausage on the rack.")

The original building, 100ft long and 40ft wide, was completely gutted by a fire on Jan. 13, 1761, which destroyed all except the exterior brick walls. Faneuil Hall was rebuilt during the next two years, apparently to the same design, a project financed by a town lottery. The new hall was so far completed by March 14, 1763, that James Otis, moderator of the meeting, delivered an address remarking on the great success of the rebuilding project. The decade that followed was the most brilliant in the history of Faneuil Hall, when the fiery speeches of Otis, Samuel Adams, and other patriot leaders earned it the title "Cradle of Liberty." But in fact the crowds that gathered there from Boston and the surrounding towns in protest against British tyranny were sometimes so huge that they were forced to reconvene in the Old South Meeting-House, as was so on the momentous evening of Dec. 16, 1773, just prior to the Boston Tea Party. During the siege of Boston, Faneuil Hall was used as a storehouse for the excess furniture of those Loyalists who had fled their homes in the countryside to take refuge in Boston, and also for the firearms of those Bostonians whose loyalty was held suspect by the British. It was also used as a theater for the entertainment of the British and their supporters, and General Burgoyne even wrote a farce, *The Blockade of Boston,* to entertain them while they were besieged by the Continental Army. During one performance of Burgoyne's farce, its last, one of the actors emerged from the wings to announce that "the Yankees are marching on Bunker Hill," and the audience laughed until they realized that he was in earnest, whereupon they departed hurriedly. In the spring of 1777 Faneuil Hall once again became the usual place for town meetings, while the selectmen met in the Old South to conduct official business. During the two decades after Independence the Hall was the scene of gala balls, banquets, and receptions to honor leaders in the Revolution when they came to Boston, both French and American: Count D'Estaing and the officers of the French fleet in 1778, Lafayette in 1784, President George Washington in 1789, and President John Adams in 1797.

During the opening years of the 19C many leading Bostonians came to realize that Faneuil Hall was no longer spacious enough to hold the increasingly large crowds that gathered there for town meetings, something that had already happened on several occasions just prior to the American Revolution. In March 1805 the selectmen issued a report recommending that the building be enlarged, and in May of that year Charles Bulfinch was chosen to be the architect in charge. It took Bulfinch just a year to complete the project, during which time he vastly enlarged the building by increasing the gable ends from three bays to seven by adding four bays on the northern side, erecting a third story, and enclosing the ground-floor market, which previously had been open to the air.

The new Faneuil Hall continued to be the scene of public meetings to discuss the affairs of Boston, and many of the nation's political leaders spoke from its rostrum. One of the most memorable of these speeches was the one made by Daniel Webster in 1826, when he delivered a eulogy in honor of Presidents John Adams and Thomas Jefferson, both of whom had died on July 4 of that year. That was the final echo of the American Revolution, and in the generation that followed, Faneuil Hall resounded to the speeches of those who addressed the newly emerging issues in U.S. politics. The most dramatic of these were the addresses denouncing slavery, most notably the maiden speech of Wendell Phillips in 1837 and the stirring oration of Senator Charles Sumner in 1846. The building itself remained unchanged from 1806 until the summer of 1898, when a program was started to rebuild it in faithful

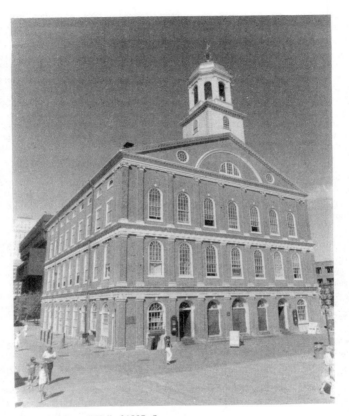

Bulfinch's Faneuil Hall of 1805–6

adherence to Bulfinch's design, a project that was completed in Oct. 1899. In 1925 the building was redecorated, inside and out, and on April 17 of that year it was rededicated by Vice-President Dawes. More recently, in the 1970s, Faneuil Hall received a face-life in connection with the restoration of the Quincy Market.

Exterior. One change made in the recent face-life of Faneuil Hall was the removal of the market stalls that surrounded the building. This allows one to see the exterior form of the lower floor and gives a better view of the whole building. The side that faces Adams Sq is actually the rear of the building, with the front, surmounted by a tall turret, facing the central building of Quincy Market. Notice how the height of the pilasters increases from the first to the second to the third floor, a device used by Bulfinch to give greater elevation to the exterior of the building for aesthetic reasons, and also to provide greater height for the grand Assembly Room that he planned within. In the earlier structure the turret was in the center of the building, but Bulfinch moved it to its present location to emphasize the fact that the front of the market hall was in fact on that side. He also put back on the weathervane the *gold-plated grasshopper* that Deacon Shem Drowne made in 1742 for Smibert's original Faneuil Hall.

Interior. The ground floor of the building is given over to the shops of the Faneuil Hall Marketplace. The main entrance to the upper floors of the building is on the side facing Quincy Market. A broad staircase leads up to the entryway to the *Assembly Room,* which has been restored to much the same appearance that it had when completed by Bulfinch in 1806. A balcony runs around the back and the two sides of the room, carried on a colonnade of wooden Doric columns. At the center of the back balcony an ornate clock is flanked by miniature figures of a pine tree and an Indian, symbols of the Commonwealth of Massachusetts; this was presented to the city in 1850 by the schoolchildren of Boston.

The wall behind the stage and speaker's rostrum is dominated by a huge oil painting entitled *Liberty and Union, Now and Forever* by George P. A. Healy (1813—94). This is a depiction of the reply by Senator Daniel Webster of Massachusetts to Senator Hayne of South Carolina on Jan. 25, 1830, in which he defended New England against the attack of the Southerner.

The picture was commissioned by King Louis Philippe of France, who thus thought to have in one frame all of the great Americans of his day, for the artist not only depicted the famous politicians of the era on the floor of the Senate, but also represented the prominent members of Washington society looking on in the audience. The painting took seven years to complete, and before it was ready to be shipped off to France, Louis Philippe lost his throne, in 1848. Soon afterward the artist sold the picture to a group of wealthy Boston businessmen, who in 1851 presented it to the city. It was then put on display in Faneuil Hall, where it has remained to this day.

Elsewhere in the chamber there are portraits and portrait busts of men who figure prominently in the history of Faneuil Hall, most of them copies of original works, some by famous artists. One of the most interesting of these is a large painting just to the l. of the stage; this is a portrait of Peter Faneuil, founder of the original market hall here, a work by Henry Sargent.

A double flight of stairs leads up to the third floor, which houses the *Ancient and Honorable Artillery Company of Massachusetts,* with the main room serving as its meeting place, the chamber to the rear its headquarters, and the rooms to the l. a museum devoted to its history.

History. The Ancient and Honorable Artillery Company of Massachusetts is the oldest military organization in the Western Hemisphere. Many of its charter members, who were among the original settlers of Boston, had been members of the Honourable Artillery Company at London, which had been organized and chartered in 1537. After the founding of Boston these men decided to form a similar militia unit in the New World, and in 1637 they petitioned Governor Winthrop for a charter. Winthrop at first refused their petition, fearing that such a military force might overthrow the civil government and usurp power for itself. But in March 1638 he finally granted them a charter, and on the first Mon. of June in that year the Company assembled in Boston Common and elected its officers, choosing Robert Keayne as their first captain. (The Company still holds its annual muster in the Common on the first Mon. in June.) The Company first had its headquarters in the Town House, but in 1746 it moved into Faneuil Hall, where it has remained. Members of the Company fought in virtually every battle of the American Revolution, and they have served in all of the other wars in which the U.S. has been engaged since then. Four members of the Company have received the highest military decoration given by the U.S. Armed Forces—the Congressional Medal of Honor—and four others have served as President of the U.S.: James Monroe, Chester Alan Arthur, Calvin Coolidge, and John F. Kennedy.

Along the walls of the main room on the third floor are displayed prints and photographs of the former commanders of the Company, along with its weapons, banners, trophies, medals, and other memorabilia. The most interesting of these exhibits is in the far right-hand corner of the room: a cannon captured from the British at the Battle of Yorktown on Oct. 19, 1783, reused by the Confederate forces during the Civil War, and recaptured by the Union Army at Williamsburg, Virginia, on May 4, 1862. On the risers of the steps that lead up to the headquarters room at the rear are bronze plates bearing the names of the original 13 states of the U.S. in the order in which they adopted the Constitution, and on the steps their state flags are displayed. Also displayed along the walls of the room are paintings, not of any artistic value, depicting the early military history of Massachusetts and the other colonies. In the museum housed in the rooms to the l. of the main hall are innumerable exhibits associated with the Company, including souvenirs from every war fought by the U.S. At the rear of the museum are displayed on racks old prints, newspapers, letters, proclamations, and other documents connected with the history of the Company and of Boston.

While descending the stairs from the armory, there is a good view of the buildings of the *Faneuil Hall Market,* better known as ****Quincy Market.**

History. When Boston was incorporated as a city in 1822, one of the first matters of public concern to be considered by its government was the enlargement of the Faneuil Hall Market, which by then had proved to be too small for the needs of the rapidly growing populace. But the tenure of John Phillips, first mayor of Boston, ended before anything could be done about the matter. However, when Josiah Quincy was inaugurated as the second mayor of Boston on May 1, 1823, one of his first orders of business was to plan a new marketplace as an extension of Faneuil Hall. The necessary legislation was passed in 1824, and the following year Alexander Parris was appointed as the head architect. The cornerstone of the new marketplace was laid on April 27, 1825, and on Aug. 26, 1826 it was formally opened. As Mayor Quincy himself described this enormous project: "A granite markethouse, two storeys high, 535ft long, 50ft wide, covering 27,000 square ft of land, including every essential accommodation, was erected at a cost of $150,000. Six new streets were opened, and a seventh greatly enlarged, including 167,000 square feet of land; and flats, docks, and wharf rights obtained to the extent of 142,000 square ft. All of this was accomplished in the centre of a populous city, not only without any tax, debt, or burden upon its pecuniary resources, but with large permanent addition to its real and productive property. One must add to Mayor Quincy's description the fact that the market house was flanked on either side by rows of handsome warehouses built on a unified plan to correspond to the architecture of the central building.

This complex was at first known as the New Faneuil Hall Market, but in time the townspeople came to call it by the name by which it is known today, the Quincy Market, after the man whose vision brought it into being. These three buildings served as the principal mart of Boston for nearly 150 years, but in the early 1970s they fell into decline when the central market was relocated outside the downtown area to relieve traffic congestion. The Boston Redevelopment Authority then included the Quincy Market in its overall project to revamp the downtown area, and in the period 1974–78 it was restored by Benjamin Thompson & Assocs, who produced the splendid civic center that one sees today.

Exterior. The central building of the complex was designed to be the marketplace proper, while the two rows of structures flanking it were to serve as warehouses. The *Central Building,* which is made of granite, has at its center a squarish building surmounted by a dome, the Rotunda, and from this two immensely long wings with gable roofs extend to E. and W., giving the structure a total length of 512ft, with a width of 52ft. It is designed in the Greek Revival style, with impressive porticos at either end formed by four massive Doric monoliths with a plain entablature and a gable pierced by a circular window. (At that time the Doric columns were the largest single pieces of granite ever quarried and cut in the U.S.) The central market building is in two stories, with round-arched windows below and rectangular ones above, except in the Rotunda, where the upper windows are round-arched and where the lower ones have their arches filled in. The buildings flanking the central one are built of brick with granite facing on the main arcade (but only on the ground floor on the side facing the outer streets and not at all on the ends). They have four main stories, with a steeply pitched roof giving room for two more floors in the attic, the lower of which has dormer windows and the upper skylights, with round-arched windows on the second floor of the side facing the main arcade and rectangular ones elsewhere.

Interior. In the original design by Alexander Parris, the central market building had on its street level 108 stalls opening off from a continuous central hall that ran the full length of the building. The plan is much the same today, though the internal divisions of space are now different and irregular, with at last count some 72 establishments sharing that floor of the building, some of them facing in toward the central aisle, others out toward the arcades, and a few of the larger ones facing both ways. The wooden sheds that once housed the outside stalls along the sides of the building have been replaced by glassed-in enclosures or canopies, which now shelter cafes, restaurants, bars, and shops, while in the inner hall there are mostly foods stalls, food shops, and speciality stores of various kinds. There are another score of firms in the basement level, mostly bars and restaurants, some of which are extensions of those on the street level. The upper floor originally consisted of the Rotunda and three chambers in each wing. Each wing is now divided into two chambers, a large one next to the Rotunda and a smaller one at the end. The two chambers in the W. wing house restaurants, while those in the E. wing now serve their original function as a banquet hall. The chamber over the E. end is called the Parris Room, and above the entryway there is a large reverse portrait in crayon on glass of *Alexander Parris,* a copy of the original made c. 1845 by W. E. Chickering.

The interior layout of the buildings on the N. and S. sides of the arcade are quite different, in keeping with their original character as individual warehouses. These remain separate buildings, although some partition walls have been removed in a few of the larger firms. At last count there were 54 separate establishments in the North Market Building and 53 in the South, mostly boutiques and specialty shops of all conceivable types, along with a number of restaurants. The most renowned of these is the *Durgin-Park Restaurant,* which has become something of a Boston landmark.

Durgin-Park is one of the very oldest restaurants in Boston, surpassed in years of continuous service only by the Union Oyster House, and it is still one of the very best. Not only does it have good food, generous servings, and reasonable prices, but its informal hurly-burly atmosphere is reminiscent of what the market area might have been like in times past.

Precincts. The precincts of Faneuil Hall and Quincy Market have also been very well restored, creating a pedestrian mall with a brick-and-cobble pavement on which park benches have been set out under colonnades of locust trees, allowing one to sit and rest in the shade, to watch the passing parade of tourists, shoppers, and celebrants. The center of life in the mall is the open area between Faneuil Hall and the central building of Quincy Market, where a greenhouse and a large flower-market add nature's colors to the city scene. There are two restaurants with outdoor tables here, and also an outdoor bar, pleasant places to dine and drink in good weather. Or one can sit on the steps of the West Portico and enjoy the musicians and entertainers who put on impromptu shows at noon for the crowds, giving an additional lift to the already lively ambience. The Quincy Market restoration must be counted as one of the most successful projects of its kind, for it has restored not only the splendid buildings of this historic place but also its spirit and atmosphere.

The old market area that once centered on Faneuil Hall and Quincy Market has now almost vanished, except for a small area a short distance to the N. called the *Blackstone Block,* which has several interesting old buildings and other sites and relics of Boston's colonial past.

The best approach to the Blackstone Block is to start in the open area between Faneuil Hall and Quincy Market and cross over to the far side of North St. Pause there at No. 16 to look at the historic plaque to the r. of the entrance to the building. The inscription records that on this site stood the *house of William Dawes,* who on the evening of April 18, 1775, rode out to Lexington to warn John Hancock and Samuel Adams that the British were coming, he taking one route and Paul Revere another.

Turn l. here and walk to the corner of North and Union Sts, crossing to the little park that has been laid out between Union and Congress Sts. At the near end of the park there is a unique and charming memorial to *James Michael Curley* (1874–1958), the most colorful and controversial politician in the history of Boston.

The memorial, a work of Lloyd Lillie (b. 1932), consists of two life-sized bronze statues of Curley in characteristic poses, one standing with his hands behind his back, the other seated on a park bench as if he were carrying on a conversation with an invisible companion. A plaque on the central pathway leading to the statues gives a brief record of the political career of this remarkable man, who first ran for political office at the age of 17.

The houses and alleyways on the r. side of Union St, of which only a short stretch now remains, are collectively known as the **Blackstone Block.** This is the sole surviving fragment of one of the oldest quarters in Boston, with historical associations going back to the early colonial period. The names of the first two alleyways that lead off to the r. from Union St, Salt Lane and Marsh Lane, are reminders that this was part of the neck that led out from the Shawmut Peninsula to the North End, with the Mill Pond to the l., Town Cove to the r., and Mill Creek just a short distance ahead, on the site of the present Blackstone St. The third turning to the r. from Union St is Marshall St, a short and narrow alley that cuts diagonally across to Hanover St. This street takes its names from Thomas Marshall, a shoemaker, who built a house at what is now the corner of Hanover and Marshall Sts soon after the founding of Boston in 1630. He was a selectman of the town in 1636, at which time Hanover, Union, and Marshall Sts were laid out, and in that same year he was given permission to start a ferry service between Boston and Charlestown.

The oldest surviving house of the Blackstone Block stands on the corner of Union and Marshall Sts. (It is actually a pair of houses, one on Union St and the other forming the corner with Marshall St.) Since 1826 this has been occupied by the *Union Oyster House,* which correctly advertises itself as "the oldest restaurant in continuous service in America."

History. The house at the corner of Union and Marshall Sts was built c. 1714. In 1742 the house was bought by Thomas Stoddard, and when he died it passed to his daughter Patience and her husband, Hopestill Capen, a sergeant in the Ancient and Honorable Artillery Company. After they moved in, Capen set up a dry-goods shop on the ground floor, a profitable enterprise which would be operated by his family for two generations. In autumn 1769 Capen hired an apprentice named Benjamin Thompson, a brilliant and ambitious young man from Woburn, Mass. He later became Sir Benjamin Thompson and later still Count Rumford, renowned for his discoveries in science and technology, including the principle of the Conservation of Energy.

During the years 1771–75 the upper floors of the building at the corner of Union and Marshall Sts housed the press and office of the *Massachusetts Spy,* a newspaper published by Isaiah Thomas. The motto of the paper was "open to all parties but influenced by none." But the *Spy* was so openly in favor of American independence that Thomas was forced to flee from Boston in April 1775, moving to Worcester, Mass., where he set up his press again and resumed publication.

The Duc de Chartres (later King Louis Philippe of France) was a guest in this house in 1798, and gave French lessons here to support himself while waiting for a remittance from home.

The house remained in the hands of the Capen family until 1819. In 1826 it was acquired by a Mr. Atwood, who opened up a clam-and-oyster bar on the first floor, the ancestor of the present restaurant. Tradition has it that Daniel Webster dined here frequently during his several residences in Boston. A plaque in one of the booths on the second floor of the restaurant records that this was where President John F. Kennedy frequently dined.

The second-oldest building in the Blackstone Block stands at 10 Marshall St, at the near corner of Creek Square and Salt Lane. This house was built c. 1760 by Thomas Hancock, John Hancock's uncle. John Hancock inherited the house in 1764, and later it passed on to his younger brother Ebenezer. During the Revolutionary War, Ebenezer Hancock served as deputy paymaster of the Continental Army, and in 1778 he here received a huge shipment of silver coins that Count D'Estaing had brought over from France. These were soon disbursed to the local troops of the Continental Army, greatly raising their morale. The Ebenezer Hancock house has been very well restored in recent years, and today it serves as a small office building; it is not open to the public.

The undistinguished building just across the alley from the Ebenezer Hancock Building dates to c. 1835. Set into the base of its wall on the alley is the famous *Boston Stone,* a memento of the colonial period. This is a spherical stone affixed to the top of an hexagonal slab, on the latter of which is inscribed the name BOSTON STONE and below it the date 1737.

The stones were used as a paint mill and grinder by Thomas Child, who set up his shop at the corner of Hanover and Marshall Sts in 1701. Child's specialty was painting shop signs, but, according to Harriet Ropes Cabot, he also provided "hatchments, badges, and funeral trappings." This latter trade was what Judge Samuel Sewall was referring to when, on Nov. 10, 1706, he wrote this note in verse in his diary: "This morning Tom Child, the Painter, died / Tom Child had often painted Death / But never to the Life, before: / Doing it now, he's out of Breath; / He paints it once, and paints no more."

After Child and his wife died the building was acquired by another owner, and in the second quarter of the 18C a tavern opened up there. In 1737 the tavern owner discovered Child's paint mill and grinder half-buried in his back yard. He thereupon inscribed the date 1737 and the name of Boston Stone on the remaining fragment of the grinder, in imitation of the London Stone, and set them into the outer wall of his tavern. When the house was demolished c. 1835 the Boston Stone was preserved and placed in the wall of the present building.

The corner of Union and Hanover Sts was the site of two buildings with important links to the past of Boston; unfortunately not a trace of them remains. At one corner of that intersection Josiah Franklin rented a house in 1712, after having moved his family from their earlier residence on Milk St, and here he once again hung out over his shop the "Sign of the Blue Ball" Benjamin Franklin worked for his father in the shop here until 1719, when he became an apprentice in the print shop of his brother James. Young Ben walked from here to the Boston Public Latin School during his single year of study there, in 1713–14. During his few idle hours he and his friends played and fished for minnows on the shore of Mill Pond, which was then just a short distance away.

On the N.W. side of the intersection of Union and Hanover Sts stood one of the oldest and most famous inns of colonial Boston, the *Green Dragon Tavern*. This inn, which was founded c. 1680, was originally known as the Baker's Arms, and at some time before 1714 it came to be called the Green Dragon Tavern. On the eve of the Revolution this was the principal gathering-place for the Boston patriots who planned the local opposition to British rule, most notably the Boston Tea Party. As Paul Revere wrote in later times: "In the fall of 1774 and winter of 1775 I was one of upwards of thirty, chiefly mechanics, who formed ourselves into a committee for the purpose of watching the movements of the British soldiers and gaining every intelligence of the movements of the Tories. We had our meetings at the Green Dragon Tavern." Paul Revere and the mechanics to whom he referred were members of group called the *North End Caucus*, which met secretly at the Green Dragon and at another tavern called the *Salutation*. (The word "caucus" is believed to be a corruption of "caulkers," a name chosen for the political club because many of those who founded it worked in the shipbuilding industry.) The Green Dragon also played an important part in the development of Freemasonry in America; the Grand Lodge of Massachusetts was founded there in 1774, with Dr. Joseph Warren as grand master and Paul Revere as one of the subordinate officers. The Green Dragon continued in existence until 1828, when the tavern was torn down to make way for a new building. The last tavern-keeper at the Green Dragon was Daniel Simpson, who had been a drummer in the War of 1812, and who would use the same drum as a Union soldier in the Civil War. That drum, which John Robbins had carried at the Battle of Bunker Hill, is today on show at the Old State House. Simpson himself lived on until 1886, dying at the age of 96, the last living link with the old tavern that Daniel Webster called the Headquarters of the Revolution.

The present itinerary comes to an end at the corner of Hanover and Blackstone Sts, where on the r. is the last of the *street markets* in downtown Boston. This is one of the liveliest and most colorful spots in Boston, particularly on Sats., when people come from all over the city to shop at the stores and stalls here, when peddlers hawking their products over the din of the traffic and the passing throng. There has been much discussion in the city government about closing this street market, because of the traffic congestion it is said to cause. One hopes that this will not come to pass, for this is the last remnant of the market that was established in this area in the very first years of Boston's existence.

Before going on, do not fail to notice the curious *bronze reliefs* set into the asphalt at the intersection of Hanover and Blackstone Sts, representations of the real trash and garbage of the street market: squashed fragments of fruits and vegetables, bottle caps, a piece of pizza, crumpled pages from the *Boston Globe,* etc. This clever and amusing work was done by the sculptor Mags Harries and is entitled *Asaraton,* which is the ancient Greek word for unswept floors, or for the mess left over after a banquet, an appropriate form of commemoration for a street market.

5 The North End

This itinerary begins where the last one ended, at the corner of Hanover and Blackstone Sts. In colonial times this was one of the two points from which one crossed over into the *North End,* at that time by a bridge over the Mill Creek, today by a pedestrian underpass beneath the Central Artery, the scabrous expressway that here follows the same course in which that stream once flowed.

History and Topography of the North End. During the early years of Boston, when the town was still limited to the Shawmut Peninsula, the North End was itself a secondary peninsula, joined to the main one by a narrow neck. The narrowest part of this neck coincided with the present Blackstone St, extending from North St to Sudbury St. Blackstone St coincides with the former Mill Creek, built over it in 1834. This was a combination of two creeks, one of which flowed into Mill Pond, the tidal estuary to the N., while the other emptied into Town Cove. Early in the colonial period a canal was cut between the two creeks, so that the water flowing between Mill Pond and Town Cove could be used to power grist mills. Thus, after Mill Creek was cut through, the North End was in fact isolated from the rest of the Shawmut Peninsula, and in colonial times it was often referred to as the "island of North Boston." Consequently, a sense of insularity early on developed in the North End, as if it were a little town within a town, a characteristic that it retains. During the colonial period an intense rivalry grew up between the North Enders and South Enders, as the residents of the main part of the town were called. The annual culmination of this rivalry took place on Guy Fawkes' Day, or Pope's Day, as it was called in Boston. During that wild festival, which was held on Nov. 5, there were parades in both the North and South Ends in which a stuffed figure of the Pope was carried through the streets. At the climax of the festival the North Enders and South Enders inevitably engaged one another in a free-for-all, each trying to capture the Pope of the other group. If the South Enders were successful they burned the enemy Pope in the Common; if the North Enders won they did the same on Copp's Hill. This annual fracas continued until the eve of the Revolution, when the leaders among the patriots persuaded the factions to end their rivalry and unite against the British, a peace pact that was celebrated when John Hancock gave a gala dinner for them on Nov. 5, 1774, at the Green Dragon Tavern.

Since the North End was topographically isolated from the rest of Boston during the colonial period, the residents there early on felt the need for a church in their part of town. They were finally able to achieve this aim in 1650, when the *Second Church of Boston* was built in North Square. The meeting house on North Square, which in time came to be called *Old North,* was the only Congregational church in the North End until 1714, when the *New North* was erected, followed by the *New Brick* in 1721, and then by the Anglican *Christ Church* in 1723. In 1776 the Old North Church on North Square was torn down by British troops; New North was demolished in 1802 to make way for a new church, as was New Brick in 1845. Thus, by the middle of the 19C, Christ Church was the oldest church in the North End, and so in time it came to be called Old North, the name by which it is most commonly known today.

On March 17, 1776, more than a thousand Tories from the North End departed with the British fleet, including most of the wealthy and influential people of the quarter. Those who remained were principally shopkeepers, tradesmen, and "mechanics"—i.e., the artisans, craftsmen, and workers in the shipping and shipbuilding industries. As time passed these two industries and the various mercantile enterprises took up more and more space in the North End, so that its residential area diminished. Also, an increasingly large number of transient workers and sailors moved into the quarter, making it less desirable as a place to raise a family. The first Irish immigrants came to the North End in 1824, and by 1850 they made up half the population of the quarter, which by then had degenerated into a sordid slum. Other waves of immigrants followed, first Eastern European Jews and then Italians, who by 1920 made up 90 percent of the population of the North End. During the years since then the Irish and Jewish populations of the North End have dropped virtually to zero, and the permanent residents of the quarter are now almost exclusively of Italian birth or descent. During the past generation these industrious and communal people have restored the North End so that it is once again the decent working-class quarter that it was two centuries ago, making it one of the most vital parts of modern Boston.

The underpass beneath the Central Artery leads to the corner of Cross and Salem Sts, where the tour of the North End proper begins. This is quite a different Boston, almost a different country, with signs advertising Italian restaurants, cafes, and shops; all of the older people conversing in Italian, and many of the younger ones too; the air heady with Mediterranean aromas.

Salem St is the westernmost of the three main N.-S. thoroughfares in the North End, the other two being Hanover St and then North St. As laid out in colonial times, Salem St led in from the neck of the North End a short distance in from the Mill Pond; Hanover St (or Middle St, as it was originally called) ran along the spine of the peninsula; and North St extended along the shore of Town Cove. Because of landfill and wharving out, both Salem and North Sts are now a good way in from the shore, but are reminders of what the topography of this part of the North End was like in colonial times.

From Salem St walk E. along Cross St and take the first l. onto Hanover St. Ahead is the golden-domed spire of *St. Stephen's Church,* one of the monuments that will be visited on this itinerary. Then at the next corner turn r. onto Richmond St, whose name in early colonial times was Beer Lane.

The N.E. corner of Hanover and Richmond Sts was where the *New Brick Church* was built in 1721. This church came into being because of a dispute in the congregation of the New North Church, some of whom objected to the ordination of the Rev. Peter Thacher as their minister. Thacher and his followers split from the congregation and founded their own church here on the corner of Hanover and Richmond. It was called the New Brick Church to distinguish it from Old Brick in Cornhill. New Brick stood until 1845, when it was torn down to make way for a new church, and that in turn was demolished in 1871 when Hanover St was widened.

The itinerary continues along Richmond St, which at the next corner intersects North St. On the far corner to the l. there is a modern brick building that has affixed to its facade the oldest sign in Boston still on its original site. This is known as the *Wadsworth Tablet:* a shield with the letter "W" above "TS," below that the date 1694, and beneath the shield the legend "REBUILT 1850." The initials are those of Timothy Wadsworth and his wife Susannah, who in 1694 took possession of an estate that extended from this corner into Town Cove, including a tavern, a warehouse, a wharf, and several shops. Susannah Wadsworth had inherited this property from her grandfather Nicholas Upshall, one of the original members of the Ancient and Honorable Artillery Company.

The Wadsworth Tablet marks the site of the *Red Lion Inn,* the tavern that

Paul Revere, a portrait by John Singleton Copley in 1768–70 (Courtesy Museum of Fine Arts, Boston)

Nicholas Upshall founded soon after he obtained title to his estate in 1637. In 1656 Upshall was arrested for trying to smuggle food to two Quaker women who were starving to death in Boston's jail, and after his conviction he was banished from the town. He returned six years later and reopened the Red Lion Inn, but he was arrested on charges of allowing Quaker refugees to stay there without payment. He was treated so harshly that he died two years later, after which the Red Lion passed to his descendants, remaining in the family until 1790.

After its intersection with Richmond St North St leads into North Sq, one of the most picturesque spots in the city. To the l. at 19 North Sq stands the quaint old wooden building now known as the ****Paul Revere House,** the oldest dwelling place in Boston and one of the most important historical monuments in the city.

Admission. April 15–Oct. 15 open daily 9:30–5:15; Oct. 16–April 14 daily 9:30–4:15. Guided tours of the Paul Revere House are given at frequent intervals. Guided tours of the Pierce-Hichborn House (see below) are given daily at 12:30 and 2:30; fee includes both houses (tel. 523-2338).

History. The area around North Sq was the first part of the North End to be settled, and by the middle of the 17C it was already a well-developed community of artisans, tradesmen, and shopkeepers. The land on which the present house stands was acquired as early as 1651 by Bartholemew Barnard, a carpenter, who in 1663 sold part of his plot to Anthony Chickly. Chickly built a house on the plot, and a decade later this became the property of the Second Church, the original Old North, which stood at the northern end of the square. Soon afterward the house was occupied by Increase Mather, minister of the Second Church, who lived there until the building was destroyed in the great fire of 1676. By 1680 a new house had been built on this site by Robert Howard, a wealthy merchant. Howard lived in the house until 1718, after which it passed to a succession of heirs and other owners before being purchased by Paul Revere on Feb. 15, 1770, to remain his property for the next 30 years.

When Paul Revere and his family moved into the house on North Sq he was 35 years old and earned his living as a silversmith, a trade he had learned from his father as a small boy. (His father, a Huguenot refugee from France, was originally named Apollos Rivoire, but changed his name to Paul Revere after coming to Boston in 1715, when he was 13 years old.) Young Revere married Sara Orne in 1757, and before her death in May 1773 she bore him seven children, six of whom survived. Early in the autumn of 1773 Paul Revere married

Rachel Walker, who not only raised the six surviving children of his first marriage but would during the next 14 years bear him eight more children, three of whom died in infancy. The Reveres lived in the house in North Sq until early in the 1790s, when they rented it out to another family, while they themselves moved to a larger house on Charter St. Then, in 1800, the Reveres sold the house on North Sq and bought the one on Charter St, where they lived for the rest of their days, Rachel passing away in 1813 and Paul in 1818.

During the 19C the house on North Sq was used first as a tenement, then as a candy factory, a cigar factory, and a grocery store. It decayed in the process, for there was little regard for the fact that it had been the home of a national hero and was an important historical and architectural monument. Then, in 1905, a group of public-spirited Bostonians formed the Paul Revere Memorial Assoc. and acquired the house. In 1907 the Assoc. hired the architect Joseph Chandler to restore the house to the appearance that it had in colonial times, both externally and internally, afterward opening it to the public as a national historical landmark.

Exterior. The house now has essentially the same external appearance that it had when it was built by Robert Howard c. 1680. It is 2½ stories high, with a sharply peaked roof, from the r. side of which projects the huge chimney. The roof has an overhang, not only in the front and back but on the gable end as well, and it is covered with wooden shingles. The front facade of the second floor projects on corbels out over the ground floor, with carved pendant drops at the corners of both floors and also at the corners of the gable. The house is faced with clapboard, with an Early American nail-studded door on the r. and seven quaint diamond-paned casement windows, three on the lower floor and four on the upper. Behind, in the courtyard, there is an unusual ell of similar structure, but with the roof less sharply peaked and thus slightly lower at the apex, and with sash windows instead of casements. (The latter were installed by Howard some time after the house was built.) Early in the 18C, before the Reveres moved in, the roof in the front part of the house was raised so that there were three full stories there, while the rest of the building remained unaltered. This was the form of the house up until 1907, when the front part of the structure was rebuilt in the original manner.

The entrance to the site is at the kiosk inside the courtyard gateway. At the kiosk one purchases admission tickets for both the Revere House and the *Pierce-Hichborn House* (see below), the brick building to the l. of the courtyard.

On the l. side of the courtyard is a large bronze *bell*, weighing 931 pounds. This was cast by Paul Revere in 1804 for the East Parish in Bridgewater, Mass. Revere made nearly 200 church bells in all, beginning with the one he cast in 1792 for the New Brick Church, with the one on display here being No. 65. Revere's bells are generally considered to have been the finest made in the U.S. during the first decades of its history, and 41 of them still survive in the churches and museums of New England.

Interior. The entrance to the Paul Revere House museum is by the door at the rear of the ell, which opens into the small room that served as the kitchen. Around the fireplace are displayed *kitchen utensils* of the colonial period, and to the r. of that there is a pine-ash *cradle* made from a molasses cask, an example of the technical ingenuity of the early settlers in New England. In the case to the r. of the entryway are the *saddle bags* that Paul Revere used on his midnight ride to Lexington and also on his many trips as a courier for the patriots and the Continental Army. On the wall to the r. of the fireplace is a reproduction of the *portrait of Paul Revere* that John

Singleton Copley painted c. 1765, the original of which is in the Boston MFA. On the l., as one passes through the room, there is a balustrade on the upper side of which there is a "time-line," giving a chronology of Paul Revere and his family, and also providing information about the architecture and furnishings of the house; this continues in the next room and in the two rooms on the upper floor.

One then enters the great hall of the house, with a large fireplace on the l. and the dining room and parlor on the r. (This fireplace was used for heat in the winter and not normally for cooking, which was done only in the kitchen and in the cellar.) The great hall is furnished with objects dating from the late 17C, the period when it was first occupied by Robert Howard and his family. In a case to the r. of the fireplace are exhibited several objects belonging to Paul Revere; among these is a letter of introduction signed by James Otis and dated Nov. 12, 1775, allowing Revere to pass through the lines of the Continental Army.

A narrow staircase leads to the room directly above, which has exactly the same dimensions as the great hall; this is known as the Best Room, the bed chamber and sitting room of the master and mistress of the house. It is laid out in the same fashion as the great hall, with the fireplaces at one end and the living area on the other side. The furniture of this room is all of the 18C, some dating to the period when the Reveres were in residence here, and some earlier but of a type they might well have used. To the r. of the fireplace there is a case with a few more exhibits connected with Paul Revere; the most interesting of these is the document box in which he carried letters and official papers while serving as a courier.

Visitors now enter the small chamber at the back of the house, which was used as the children's bedroom. (There were actually two more bedrooms for children on the upper floor when the Reveres were living here, but these were eliminated in the restoration because they were not part of the original 17C house.) On the side wall to the l. are reproductions of portraits of Paul and Rachel Revere; the originals were done by Gilbert Stuart in 1813 and are now in the Boston MFA. These are the last likenesses ever made of the Reveres, for Rachel died just a few weeks after the portraits were completed, and Paul did not sit for another portrait in the remaining five years of his life.

The ***Pierce-Hichborn House** is within the same enclosure as the Revere House. This is believed to be the oldest brick dwelling place in Boston. The house is open to the public.

Admission. See Paul Revere House p. 136.

History. The house was built c. 1711 by Moses Pierce, a glazier, and a founder of the New North Church. At the time it represented the new type of grander brick buildings that were being built in the North End, replacing the humbler wooden buildings that had perished in the fire of 1676, and whose construction was being discouraged by a town ordinance seeking to prevent another such conflagration. In 1781 the house was bought by Nathaniel Hichborn, a boat-builder, who was a cousin of Paul Revere. The house remained in the Hichborn family until 1864, when it was converted into a multifamily tenement, at a time when the North Sq area had degenerated into a pitiful slum. The building continued to be used as a tenement until 1949, decaying in the process, until it was rediscovered by Carleton Walker, an antiquarian. This led to the restoration of the house, and in 1970 it was acquired by the Paul Revere Memorial Association, who have since been restoring it so that it can take its place beside the Paul Revere House as another fine example of colonial architecture in the North End of Boston.

Across the street from the Revere and Pierce-Hichborn Houses there is a
little park that has been created in recent years by the Massachusetts Charitable Mechanics Association, who dedicated it to Rachel Revere. This phi-
lanthropic organization, which had its origins among the "mechanics" of
the North End, was founded in 1795, with Paul Revere as its first president,
and it continues in existence to the present day. The park is a pleasant place
to sit and rest for a while, and from there one can locate the sites of some
of the monuments that once stood in and around this historic square.

At the apex of the park North St veers off to the r., following the course
of the ancient shoreline. The street that forms the W. side of the square is
called North Sq, and continues on as Garden St (formerly known as Garden
Court), with Moon St running along the E. side of the square. At the far
right-hand corner of the square, which is really triangular, a short street
named Sun Court runs off to the r. from Moon St, producing the uniquely
celestial intersection of two byways named Sun and Moon!

The northern end of the square, on the block between Garden and Moon Sts, was the site
of the *Second Church of Boston*, the original Old North. The Old North, founded in 1650,
was one of the most influential churches in New England, and during the colonial period it
was a bulwark in the Puritans' effort to maintain their religious freedom. It was often called
the "Church of the Mathers" after the three famous men of that family who served as
ministers there; these were, with the dates of their tenures: Increase Mather (1664–1723);
his son, Cotton Mather (1685–1728); and Cotton Mather's son, Samuel Mather (1732–40).

At the right-hand corner of North Sq, at the intersection of Moon St and
Sun Court, stands the *Roman Catholic Church of the Sacred Heart*. The
church, a modern structure, stands on the site of a seamen's church, or
bethel, founded in 1833 by Father Edward T. Taylor, a sailor-priest who
was famous for his eloquent sermons. Directly across the street from the
church, at 11 North Sq, there is a *seamen's bethel* founded in 1848 by the
Boston Port Society, the last remnant of the maritime life that once flourished in this colorful and historic square.

In Paul Revere's time this was known as *Clark's Sq,* named after William Clark, a wealthy
shipowner, who in 1711 built a mansion at the corner of Garden Court and Prince St, the
cross street that leads out from the far left-hand corner of the square. After Clark's death
his estate passed to his son-in-law, Thomas Greenough, who in 1758 sold it to Sir Henry
Frankland, who had been the royal customs collector of the port of Boston and was one of
the richest men in the Province. The *Clark-Frankland house* was one of the most splendid
in colonial Boston, rivaled only by the *Hancock mansion* on Beacon St and the *Hutchinson
mansion* on Garden Court. The latter mansion was built early in the 18C by Thomas Hutchinson, a descendant of Anne Hutchinson and father of Governor Thomas Hutchinson, who
was born in the house on Garden Court in 1711 and lived there until he left Boston in 1774,
to spend the remaining six years of his life in exile in England. A plaque on a modern
building halfway down Garden St on the l. side identifies the site of the Hutchinson mansion, although it states, incorrectly, that it was built in 1687. Directly across the way, at 4
Garden St, there is another historical marker, recording that John F. ("Honey Fitz") Fitzgerald once lived there. Fitzgerald and his family lived in a house on this site from 1886 to
1894, until his election to the U.S. House of Representatives, the first step in a career that
would eventually see him elected as mayor of Boston. His daughter Rose, the mother of
President John F. Kennedy, was born in this house in 1890.

After leaving North Sq, turn l. onto Prince St and walk one block to the
corner of Hanover St. Across the way, on the r. corner of Hanover and
Prince Sts, is the Roman Catholic *Church of St. Leonard,* founded in 1872,
with the present building dating to 1891. In front of the church is its pretty

Peace Garden, so named by one of the priests of the church, who had vowed to create it when the war between the U.S. and North Vietnam came to an end.

One might pause at the corner of Hanover and Prince for a moment to locate three nearby sites associated with the Mather family. The first of these is on the opposite side of Hanover St and a little to the l. of its intersection with Prince St, about where the house at No. 298 Hanover now stands. This is the site of the house where Cotton Mather lived with his family from 1685 until his death in 1728. The two other sites are one block farther N. on the same side of Hanover St, one on either side of N. Bennet, the street that leads off to the l. On the l. side of the intersection of Hanover and N. Bennet is the site of the church that Samuel Mather founded in 1741, after he and his followers split off from the Second Church. On the r. side of the same intersection is the site of the house into which Increase Mather and his family moved in 1676, after their home on North Sq had been destroyed by fire. Increase Mather lived in this house until his death in 1723, and it was here that his son Cotton Mather was born in 1685. After Increase Mather died the house was taken over by the Rev. Andrew Eliot, minister of the New North Church, and on his death it passed on to his son the Rev. John Eliot, who succeeded him as minister of the New North. The two Eliots were the most influential ministers who ever served in the New North, holding that post in turn from 1742 until 1813.

The itinerary now continues N. on the r. side of Hanover St, at the next intersection passing N. Bennet on the l. and Fleet St on the r. Halfway along the next block, at No. 383 Hanover, one passes the *Langone Funeral Home,* where on Aug. 23, 1927, the remains of *Nicola Sacco* and *Bartolomeo Vanzetti* were brought after their execution in the electric chair in Charlestown Prison.

At the next corner Clark St leads off to the l., and across the street is ***St. Stephen's Church,** one of the principal monuments in the North End and the only surviving Bulfinch church in the city.

Admission. Open during daylight hours and when services are being held (see bulletin board).

History. St. Stephen's, a Roman Catholic church, stands on the site of the *New North Church,* the second Congregational meetinghouse to be founded in the North End. According to the annals of the original church, the New North Congregational Society was founded by "seventeen substantial mechanics," who in 1714 built a meetinghouse on this site "unassisted by the more wealthy part of the community except by their prayers and good wishes." The original church that they erected was a small wooden building, which in 1730 was replaced by a larger meetinghouse to accommodate its growing congregation. In 1802 this church was pulled down to make way for an even larger church, with Charles Bulfinch serving as the architect. This was completed in 1804, and the following year a bell cast by Paul Revere was hung in its belfry. In 1813 the congregation changed its affiliation and became the Second Unitarian Church of Boston, under the ministry of the Rev. Francis Parkman, father of Francis Parkman, the historian. The Unitarian congregation continued to use the church until 1862, when the Roman Catholic Archbishopric of Boston acquired the building. In 1870 the entire building was moved back 12ft when Hanover St was widened. The church was badly damaged in two fires, the first in 1897 and the second in 1929, after each of which it was repaired and redecorated. Then, in 1965, Richard Cardinal Cushing raised funds to restore the church to its original appearance as completed by Charles Bulfinch in 1804; this project was carried out by Chester F. Wright.

Exterior. The most prominent feature of the church is the monumental towerlike structure that houses the vestibule and supports the belfry. Bulfinch patterned this on the campaniles of the Renaissance churches he had seen during his travels in Italy, but with a sea-change to make the style compatible with the more restrained New England architecture of the Federal period. This structure is of red brick, as is the rest of the building, with all of the woodwork painted white in sharp contrast. The entrance, framed in a projecting porch, has above it a Palladian window. This central section is flanked by two pairs of Ionic pilasters, with two more such pilasters just around each of the two outside corners. These support a pair of entablatures, and above that a balustrade runs around the three sides of the tower and along the shoulders of the main building. The second story of the tower has a lunette window in the center, flanked by much smaller pilasters which continue the line of those below. On each side of the lower story of the tower there are two windows, rectangular below and round-arched above, a pattern which continues around the sides of the main building, a conventional structure of rectangular plan with a pitched roof. Atop the tower a pedestal supports the belfry, above which there is a rectangular turret surmounted by a dome, and above that a cross. During the restoration of 1965 it was discovered that the dome was covered with thin sheets of copper, held in place by handwrought nails; these were the work of Paul Revere, done at the time he installed the bell in the belfry. Some of the sheets and nails are on display in the vestibule.

Interior. The plan of the interior is almost square, measuring 70ft in length and 72ft in width. A gallery extends around the sides and rear of the nave, carried on Doric columns below and with Corinthian columns above, covered by a barrel-vaulted ceiling with a very small curvature. The columns in both tiers are made from single trunks of pine trees, and their capitals were carved from single blocks of wood by Simeon Skillin, Jr. These capitals, along with 80 percent of the other woodwork in the building, are from the Bulfinch church, and much of that was reused from the church of 1730 that preceded it. The elegant chandeliers over the main aisle are replicas of those hanging in Bulfinch's Doric Hall in the State House. The Stations of the Cross along the side walls are works of the sculptor Archangelo Cascieri; these are carved in Italian mahogany and were put in place during the 1965 restoration.

The superb restoration of this historic building was recognized by the Boston Society of Architects, who in 1970 presented its award for Historic Preservation to Cardinal Cushing, a well-deserved honor.

Across the street from St. Stephen's a wide, tree-shaded mall extends from Hanover St through to Unity St, which runs just behind Christ Church. Originally named the Prado but now called the Paul Revere Mall, this was laid out in 1933 to create an open area where the people of the North End could have a breathing space in the crowded confines of their quarter. It has served that purpose admirably, and it is always filled with children playing, teenagers socializing, mothers wheeling their baby carriages, and old people chatting away in Italian, with a few ancients playing cards or checkers, making it the liveliest and most pleasant spot in the North End. At the head of the mall the fine bronze equestrian statue of *Paul Revere* is a work of Cyrus E. Dallin (1861—1944). The statue was modeled in 1885, but no buyer appeared until 1940, when it was cast for the city of Boston at the expense of the George Robert White Fund. The statue was finally installed in its present location and dedicated on Sept. 22, 1940, giving an appearance of some grandeur to the mall.

In passing through the mall, pause to read some of the many historic plaques embedded in its side walls; these commemorate men and women of the North End who have made a mark in the history and culture of Boston.

At the far end of the mall is Unity St, on the other side of which a gate opens into a courtyard behind Christ Church. Unity St was laid out c. 1710 by a syndicate headed by Ebenezer Clough, one of the two master masons who would later lay the bricks of Christ Church. Within the next five years the syndicate built a block of six houses on this street, beginning at the far corner on the l. The only one of these still standing is the three-story building at 21 Unity St, just to the l. of the courtyard behind Christ Church; this is the *Ebenezer Clough House,* in which the master mason himself lived. Two decades ago this house too was in danger of demolition, for it had fallen into an advanced state of decay. However, in 1962 the Rev. Howard P. Kellett, who at that time was vicar of Christ Church, launched a fund-raising drive to save the Clough House, which has since been very well restored. It is now open to the public every Wed. morning from 10 to 12.

The courtyard behind Christ Church occupies the site of another of the houses built by Ebenezer Clough and his group, at what was once 19 Unity St. Benjamin Franklin acquired this house in 1748, the only one he ever owned in Boston. Franklin never lived there himself, since he bought the house only to shelter his two widowed sisters, the youngest of whom, Jane, lived on there until c. 1800. After Jane's death the house was acquired by Noah Lincoln, who lived there until 1820; he was a distant cousin of Abraham Lincoln, sixteenth President of the U.S.

The courtyard above Unity St has at its upper end a passageway that leads out to Salem St and to the entryway of ****Christ Church,** better known as *Old North,* the oldest church in Boston and one of its most venerated historical monuments.

Admission. Christ Church is open daily 9–5; Sunday services at 9:30, 11, & 4 (tel. 523-6676).

History. Christ Church was founded in 1723, the second Anglican church to be established in Boston, after King's Chapel. The cornerstone of the building was laid on April 15, 1723, by the Rev. Samuel Myles, Rector of King's Chapel, and the first service was held there on Dec. 29 of the same year by the Rev. Timothy Cutler, the first rector of Christ Church. The church was designed by William Price, a Boston draftsman and print dealer, and the master builders were Thomas Tippin and Thomas Bennett. The belfry was not completed until 1740, and five years later a set of eight bells was installed in it; this was cast by Abel Rudhall of Gloucester, England, and was the first peal of bells ever hung in an American church. Four or five years after that a group of seven youths, which included Paul Revere, formed a guild and entered into an agreement with the Rev. Cutler to ring the bells "any time when the Wardens of the Church aforesaid shall desire it. . . ." (Paul Revere himself was never a member of Christ Church, for he was a Congregationalist, but his eldest son, Paul, did become a member, and his descendants still maintain a pew there.)

On the eve of the Revolutionary War the belfry of Old North was the scene of the most celebrated incident in the history of the church, one which is recorded on a plaque beside the entrance: "The signal lanterns of Paul Revere displayed in the steeple of this church April 18, 1775, warned the country of the march of the British troops to Lexington and Concord." Another plaque in the yard also honors "Robert Newman, sexton of this church, who hung the lanterns in the belfry April 18, 1775, to warn the patriots of the British march on Concord." Robert Newman lived in a house at the corner of Salem and Sheafe Sts, and at that time some British officers were quartered there. Paul Revere had apparently made prior arrangements with Newman concerning the signal lanterns, and that night he had slipped out of his home through an upper window and was hiding in the dark near Christ Church, waiting for instructions. When Revere got word to Newman that the British were beginning to send troops across the Charles to Cambridge, he entered Christ Church and locked the doors behind him, while Thomas Bernard and John Pulling waited outside to keep watch for passing redcoats. Newman then lighted two lanterns and displayed them

Christ Church, better known as Old North, c. 1790

for a short time in the belfry to alert the partriots in Charlestown, after which he descended and climbed out of the church through a rear window, making his way back over some rooftops before climbing back through his bedroom window.

After the outbreak of the Revolution, Christ Church was closed because of the tensions between the patriots and the Tories in the congregation. According to tradition, General Gage watched the progress of the Battle of Bunker Hill from an upper window in the belfry of the church. The church remained closed even after the British evacuation, because the minister, Dr. Matthew Byles, went off into exile in Halifax. The church finally reopened in Aug. 1778, when the congregation finally found a minister, the Rev. Stephen Lewis, who had been a chaplain in the British army.

The steeple of Christ Church was toppled during a violent hurricane in 1804, and was replaced two years later by one designed by Charles Bulfinch. The steeple fell again and was destroyed during a hurricane in 1954, and in the following year it was replaced by the present one, which is more like the original steeple of William Price than the one designed by Bulfinch.

The dramatic role that Christ Church played in the Revolution was commemorated by two state visits during the celebration of the American Bicentennial. On April 18, 1975, President Gerald Ford inaugurated the local celebration of the Bicentennial with an address from the pulpit of Old North, and on July 11, 1976, Queen Elizabeth II and Prince Philip worshipped at the church.

Exterior. The exterior form of the church is very similar to that of the Old South Meeting-House, which was built just six years later. The most striking feature of the church is its famous belfry. The belfry, along with the rest of the church, is made of brick laid in Flemish bond; it is square in plan, 24ft on each side, surmounted by a white wooden steeple and a brass spire. The weathervane on the spire is in the form of a waving banner surmounted by a five-pointed star, a work of Deacon Shem Drowne. The main church building is a rectangular structure, 71ft long and 51ft wide, with a small rectangular apse at the E. end; the ridge of its peaked roof is 42ft high and it has two courses of round-arched windows.

Architectural historians find strong resemblances between Old North and several churches in London built by Sir Christopher Wren. The interior has been compared to that of St. James's, Piccadilly; the tower to that of St. James, Garlickhythe; and the spire to that of St. Lawrence Jewry. Since William Price, the architect, was also a dealer in prints, he may very well have been familiar with these churches from views he had seen in his shop.

Interior. The interior is rectangular in plan, with a gallery extending around the sides and rear; this is carried by a colonnade of rectangular piers, separating the floor space into a nave and side aisles. An upper range of piers carries entablatures to the outer walls; these support a series of cross-vaults which cover the galleries, while the nave is covered by an elliptical vault suspended from the main trusses of the roof, with a concha over the semicircular apse. There is a large round-arched window in the center of the apse, and below it a painting of *Christ at the Last Supper,* done by John Ritto Penniman in 1812. The painting is flanked by four tablets, on which are inscribed in gilt letters on a black background the Ten Commandments, the Apostles' Creed, and the Lord's Prayer. The pulpit, which is in the form of a huge wineglass surmounted by a sounding board, is a later replacement of the original, which was three-tiered, with the upper level for the minister, the middle for the reader, and the lower for the clerk. The box pews are laid out as they were in colonial times, although their height is less than that of the originals. Each has on its outside a brass plaque giving the name of the original owner, and inside many of them have additional plaques giving the names of prominent later owners.

The two brass chandeliers were gifts of Captain William Maxwell, one of the founders of the church, with electric lights replacing the original 12 candles; these were first lighted on Christmas Day in 1724. The clock at the rear of the gallery was made by Richard Avery and was set in place on June 6, 1726. The present organ was made by Thomas Johnston and was installed in 1759, replacing an earlier instrument of 1736; the case is the original one, with three organ pipes on each side added in 1878. In front of the organ there are four painted wooden statuettes on pedestals, representations of cherubim with trumpets. These were presented to the church in 1726 by Captain Thomas Gruchy, commander of the *Queen of Hungary,* a privateer owned by him and other parishioners of Old North. The statuettes were part of the loot that Captain Grundy took when he and his crew captured a French vessel bound for Canada; these are fine examples of Belgian baroque sculpture of the early 18C, and were undoubtedly intended for a church in one of the French settlements along the coast of the St. Lawrence River.

To the r. of the apse there is a niche in which is enshrined a bust of George Washington; this was modeled from a bust done in 1790 by Christian Gullager, and it was presented to the church in 1815 by Shubael Bell. A nearby tablet in the S. aisle has an inscription giving this anecdote concerning the bust: "'General Lafayette, standing here in 1824 and looking at the bust of Washington, said, "Yes, that is the man I knew, and more like him than any other portrait.' " Before Washington's bust was put in place there was a window in the niche, and tradition has it that this was where Robert Newman made his way out of the church after displaying the signal lanterns.

Other tablets on the walls of the church commemorate distinguished parishioners of Christ Church and record the roles which they played in its history, some of whom have already been mentioned. One tablet bears this poignant inscription: "After one hundred years of peace, British naval and military veterans of Massachusetts commemorate here the King's soldiers and marines who fell before the rail fence and redoubt in the tall grass on Bunker Hill, on June 17, 1775." Another one states that "Major John Pitcairn, fatally wounded while rallying the Royal Marines at the Battle of Bunker Hill, was carried from the field to the boats on the back of his son, who kissed him and returned to duty. He died on 17 June 1775 and his body was interred beneath this church." After the Revolution arrangements were made for Pitcairn to be disinterred for reburial in Westminster Abbey, but church records indicate that the wrong body was sent; the major's remains are believed to be still buried in the crypt, along with those of more than 1000 departed members of the congregation. (The crypt is not open to the public.)

Before leaving the church, do not fail to notice the tablet on the l. side of the vestibule, identifying the 12 old bricks set into the wall there. These bricks were taken from the wall of one of the cells in Guildhall in the town of Boston, England, where William Brewster and other Pilgrims were held in 1607 after they were caught trying to flee the country. They were sent to the rector of Christ Church in 1923 by John Beaulah, mayor of Boston, England, to commemorate the 200th anniversary of the founding of Old North, and "to continue kindly feelings between the old and the new Boston."

There are more commemorative tablets in the courtyard behind the church, with inscriptions honoring other distinguished members of the congregation. The most interesting of these records that "Here on 13 Sept. 1757, John Childs, who had given public notice of his intention to fly from the steeple of Dr. Cutler's church, performed it to the satisfaction of a great number of spectators."

The building just to the S. of Old North serves as a museum and gift shop, whose profits go toward the upkeep of the church. The building was erected in 1917 as a chapel for the small community of Italian-speaking Protestants among the immigrants in the North End. The chapel was closed after World War II, because by that time most of the Italian Protestants in the North End had either joined other churches in the area or moved away. The chamber at the rear of the building serves as the Old North museum. The most interesting exhibit there is the so-called *Vinegar Bible,* one of a number of gifts sent by King George II to Christ Church in 1733. The Bible is so called because of a typographical error on one of its page headings, in which "Parable of the Vinegar" appears instead of "Parable of the Vineyard." This is one of a number of such Bibles sent by the King to the American colonies, of which eight are still extant.

After leaving the museum, one might pause on the street outside to look up at the steeple of Old North, which since colonial times has been the principal landmark of the North End. Visitors to the church are not generally permitted to ascend the stairway in the belfry, so be content to read a description of the venerable bells that hang there. The eight bells range in weight from 620 pounds to 1545, with a total weight of 7272 pounds. They are a "maiden peal," since each of the bells gives a perfect tone without having been filed down or machined, and they are generally considered to be the finest extant set of colonial bells in the U.S. These bells were first rung on Nov. 8, 1745, and they have tolled the death of every departed President of the U.S. since George Washington passed away on Dec. 14, 1799. The bells of Old North, which have recently been restored and rehung, bear the following inscription: "We are the first ring of bells cast for the British Empire in North America."

Directly across the way from Old North, Hull St leads up to the summit of Copp's Hill. The street is named after John Hull, Boston's first mintmaster, the coiner of the famous "pine-tree shillings," for it was laid out on land that had been part of his estate. Near the upper end of the street on the r. is the entrance to ****Copp's Hill Burying-Ground,** the largest of Boston's old graveyards.

Admission. In summer the graveyard is open 8–5; in other months 9–4.

History. Copp's Hill Burying-Ground is the second-oldest cemetery in Boston, after the King's Chapel Burying-Ground. The nucleus of the graveyard, a plateau on the summit of the hill, was purchased by the town of Boston on Feb. 20, 1659. This eminence, which was only slightly lower than Beacon Hill, was originally called Mill Hill, after a windmill that had been erected there in 1632. Later it was called Snow Hill, most probably because of the snow drifts that accumulated there. This name is perpetuated in that of Snowhill St, which borders the W. end of the cemetery. The present name, which seems to have been given to the hill in the mid-17C, came from that of William Copp, who as early as 1643 had a farm on its S.E. slope. The original cemetery was filled up by the beginning of the 18C, after which it was augmented by several successive purchases of contiguous land. The first of these came in 1708, when the town bought a pasture on Copp's Hill from Judge Samuel Sewall and his wife, Hannah, who had inherited it from her father, John Hull, the mintmaster, after whom Hull St is named. Other additions were made up to 1832, when further expansion became impossible because by that time all of the surrounding area was built up with houses. The first attempt at restoring the cemetery came the following year, when the city of Boston planted some 200 trees there. One of these, a willow tree that stood in the N.E. corner of the cemetery, had been brought as a slip from the willow that shaded Napoleon's grave on St. Helena; this was destroyed by a gale in 1888. In 1838 the present walls were built and the paths laid out, and in 1878 another restoration of the grounds was carried out, at which time the cemetery took on much the appearance it has today. During these restorations a number of musket- and cannonballs were found, relics of the British occupation of Boston, when a park of artillery was set up on Copp's Hill. During the Battle of Bunker Hill the British artillery under General Burgoyne from here bombarded the town of Charlestown with red-hot cannonballs, burning it to the ground. The redcoats on Copp's Hill apparently also used the tombstones for target practice, for many of them bear the marks of musket balls.

Interior. Propped up against the fence just to the l. of the entryway is the tombstone of *William Clark,* the wealthy shipowner whose mansion on Garden Court was later occupied by Sir Henry Frankland. The stone is adorned with a finely carved coat-of-arms, and it bears an inscription that ends with an encomium for the deceased, describing him as "a Despiser of Sorry Persons and fiecle Action, an Enemy of Priestcraft and Enthusiasm, ready to relieve and help the Wretched, a lover of good men of Various Denominations, and a Reverent Worshipper of the Deity."

That part of the cemetery along the Snowhill St side was reserved for the burial of black Bostonians. The most prominent funerary monument of the blacks buried there is a short distance to the r. of the path along the Snowhill St side; this marks the grave of *Prince Hall,* the first grand master of the African Grand Lodge of Masons in Massachusetts. A short distance from Prince Hall's grave there is another prominent marker in the form of a broken pillar. This marks the grave of *Major Samuel Shaw,* who fought in the Continental Army throughout the Revolution, serving as an artillery officer under General Henry Knox. In 1784 Shaw became the first U.S. envoy to China, and during the decade he spent in the Far East his reports to his government were extremely influential in establishing the lucrative American China trade. Shaw died on the way home from the Far East in 1794, in his 40th year.

The oldest extant tombstone in the cemetery is near the Prince Hall and Major Shaw monuments. This marks the grave of *David Copp,* d. 1661, and his brother *Thomas Copp,* d. 1678; these were two grandsons of William Copp, after whom the burying ground is named. Elsewhere in the cemetery there is a tombstone marking the grave of *Grace Berry,* with an inscription recording that she was buried on May 17, 1625, five years before the settlement of Boston! According to an old tale, almost certainly apocryphal, Grace Berry was one of the first settlers in Plymouth and died there in 1625; her remains were removed to Boston by her descendants and buried on Copp's Hill. But authorities believe that Grace Berry actually died and was buried in 1695, and that the 9 was changed to a 2 by some prankster, to make it appear that she had been buried before the founding of Boston.

At the N.W. corner of the cemetery, where Snowhill St intersects Charter St, there are two other old tombstones of interest. One of them bears this inscription: "Capt. Thomas Lake, Aged 61 yeeres, an Eminent & Faithfull Servan of God & One of a Publick Spirit, was Perfidiously Slain by ye Indians at Kennibeck, 14 August 1676, Here Interred the 13 of March Following." There is a deep slit in Lake's tombstone, and an old story has it that this was once filled with lead from melted bullets removed from his body after he was killed, but the metal, if it was ever there, has long since disappeared. A short distance from Lake's grave there is a large slate block inscribed with the name of Nicholas Upshall, who died in 1666, aged 70. As noted earlier, Upshall was the original owner of the Red Lion Inn, and he died as a result of the harsh punishment he received for trying to aid the oppressed Quakers of Boston.

The most famous tomb in the cemetery is down near the lower gate, on the Charter St side. This is the *Mather tomb,* a monument in the form of a low table with brick sides and a stone top, on which are inscribed the names of Increase, Cotton, and Samuel Mather, who died in 1723, 1727, and 1785, respectively, after careers that made them among the most influential ministers in the religious history of colonial Boston. Buried along with them are numerous members of their family, including 15 children of Cotton Mather.

Other persons of note buried in the cemetery are *Deacon Shem Drowne,* who carved the emblem of the grasshopper atop Faneuil Hall and the weathervane on the spire of Old North; *Thomas* and *Elisha Hutchinson,* father and grandfather of the last civilian governor of the royal Province of Massachusetts; *Edmund Hartt,* founder of Hartt's Shipyard and the builder of the USS *Constitution;* and five commanders of the Ancient and Honorable Artillery Company.

When leaving the cemetery by the gate on Hull St, notice the extremely narrow old house directly across the way. The date and history of this picturesque dwelling place are unknown, but one might guess that it dates to the late 18C. It is now the only surviving example in Boston of the venerable "ten-footers" portrayed in old prints of the town dating from the colonial period.

After leaving Copp's Hill Burying-Ground, turn r. on Hull St, r. again on Snowhill St, and r. once more on Charter St, walking around the periphery of the graveyard. Charter St is named from the charter that Sir William Phips brought back with him to Boston when he was made governor of Massachusetts in 1692. At that time Phips moved into a mansion at the far end of the block on the r., at the S.W. corner of Charter and Salem Sts, and he lived there until 1695, when he was dismissed as governor and summoned back to England. Paul Revere and his family later lived on the same street two blocks farther along, at the S.W. corner of Charter and Hanover Sts, a mansion into which they moved after leaving the old house on North Sq. Paul Revere lived there until the time of his death in 1818.

The last part of the itinerary returns along Salem St to the point where this route began. There are no additional monuments of note to be seen on this return stroll, but it takes one through a colorful and lively part of the North End, for Salem St rivals Hanover St in the number of its Italian restaurants, cafes, and shops, as well as in the vitality of its street life.

After one has passed Old North, Salem St is intersected on the l. by Tileston St, which in colonial times was known as Love Lane. This street dates from 1708 and took its original name from John and Susanah Love, who deeded to the town the strip of land on which the lane was laid out. One block down Tileston St on the r., just before it intersects Unity Lane, is the site of the *North Writing School,* founded in 1718. At the next corner Sheafe St leads off to the r. from Salem, with N. Bennet leading to the l. At the far corner on the r. is the site of the house where Robert Newman was living when he sneaked off to display the signal lanterns in the steeple of Old North. A short distance on the l. down N. Bennet St is the site of the *North Latin School,* founded in 1711 by Thomas Hutchinson, father of Governor Hutchinson.

At the next corner Salem St crosses Prince St. This has always been the main cross street in the North End, leading from Town Cove out to the N.W. tip of the peninsula, once the dock for the Charlestown ferry and now the Boston end of the Charlestown Bridge.

During and after the Battle of Bunker Hill the British dead and wounded were carried into town along Prince St after having been ferried across from Charlestown, and many of the houses along the street were converted into first-aid stations. Major John Pitcairn, who had suffered two severe wounds, was taken to a house at 138 Prince St, a site now at the S.W. corner of Lafayette Ave, one block to the l., and he bled to death there shortly afterward.

At the next corner a cul-de-sac named Baldwin Place leads off to the r. from Salem St. Beyond the fence at the end of the street there is a large building that presently houses the North End branch of the Knights of Columbus. This building was originally erected as a synagogue by the Jews of the North End, and its great size gives one some idea of just how large that now-vanished community was in times past.

At the next corner on the l. Salem St crosses Parmenter St, and at the following corner on the r. it crosses Stillman St. In colonial times Stillman St was just a little lane that led to the Mill Pond, on the shore of which the First *Baptist meetinghouse* in Boston was opened on Feb. 9, 1680. But on March 8 of that same year the civil authorities ordered the door of the meetinghouse to be nailed shut. The Baptists gathered at other locations in the North End during the decades that followed, until in 1745 they were finally allowed to build a permanent meeting place at the end of Baldwin Place, just a short distance from the site of their first church. The *Second Baptist Church,* as this was called, remained there until 1810, when the meetinghouse was abandoned and the congregation moved elsewhere.

Salem St now reaches Cross St, where the pedestrian underpass allows one to cross safely back into downtown Boston. This is where the present itinerary began, and where it now ends.

6 The Business and Financial District

This itinerary covers the heart of Boston's business and financial district. Earlier routes went around the fringes of that district, whereas the present walk will penetrate its core. There are no historic monuments of any great importance here, and there are few buildings of any great antiquity to be seen, because much of the district was ravaged in the great fire of 1872, and many of the monuments that survived were demolished when the area ceased to be residential and became industrialized. Nevertheless, there are a number of historic sites in the area, and it is an exciting place in which to stroll, particularly during working hours, for it is at the very center of Boston's extremely active commercial life.

The itinerary will begin at the head of State St, which has been at the epicenter of Boston's business and financial life since the founding of the town, as well as being one of its most historic thoroughfares.

History. There is no record of when State St was first laid out, which indicates that it must have been in use as a pathway since the first settlement of the Shawmut Peninsula in 1630. During the early colonial period it was known variously as "the market street," "the water street," "the broad street," "the great street wherein the Town House stands," and the "townsway down upon the great flats." In 1708 it was officially called King St, by which time it was a broad thoroughfare lined with shops, taverns, inns, and other commercial buildings. Two years later the Long Wharf was constructed at the end of King St, and thenceforth it became the main artery of the town, for virtually all of the seaborne commerce passed along the street on its way to and from the docks. In 1788, after the Massachusetts Convention finally ratified the U.S. Constitution, the street was given its present name to commemorate the fact that the former Bay Colony was now a state in the Union.

The head of State St is flanked by two of the most impressive skyscrapers that have sprung up in the business and financial district since the mid-1960s. On the l., looking down the street, is the *Sixty State Street Building,* completed in 1977 (architects Cabot & Forbes; Skidmore, Owings & Merrill); and on the r. is the *Merchants Bank Building* (formerly the New England Merchants Bank), dating from 1969 (Edward L. Barnes and Emery Roth & Sons).

Two more modest office buildings of an older generation stand near one another on the r. side of State St, just beyond the Old State House, separated by a narrow alley named Quakers Lane. (The alley took its name from the fact that it led to a Quaker meetinghouse, built in 1709 and used by the Friends until 1808.) The one on the r. is the *Brazer Building,* at 27 State St, on the S.E. corner of Devonshire St (Cass Gilbert); and on the l. is the

Worthington Building, 33 State St, S.W. corner of Congress St (Carl Fehmer). The Brazer Building was completed in 1897 and the Worthington Building in 1894; they were among the first steel-framed structures to be erected in Boston, predated only by the *Winthrop Building,* which dates to 1893.

The Brazer Building stands on the original site of the *First Church of Boston,* built in 1632, a mud-walled shack with a thatched roof. John Wilson, the first minister, had his house and garden just to the N. of the meetinghouse, on a path called Crooked Lane. The first town meetings in Boston were held in this church, as were held in this church, as were sessions of the General Court. This church was used only until 1639, when the congregation decided to abandon it and build another one elsewhere.

The oldest tavern known to have stood on King St was the *Royal Exchange,* which was located at what is now the N.W. corner of State and Congress Sts. The building in which the tavern was housed is listed in records as early as 1646, and the tavern itself is mentioned by Samuel Sewall in his diary for the year 1690—91. In the years just before the Revolution the Royal Exchange was a favorite gathering-place for British officers and officials of the Crown, particularly those connected with the *Royal Custom House,* just a few steps away. These two buildings formed the background for the dramatic and tragic scene that took place on the evening of March 5, 1770, the *Boston Massacre.* A circlet of cobblestones on the traffic island at the intersection of State and Congress Sts marks the site of that event.

History. Shortly after 8 p.m. on Mon., March 5, 1770, a street brawl broke out in Brattle Sq between a gang of townspeople and a group of British soldiers, who found that their way into Murray's Barracks was being blocked off. The ensign in charge of the redcoats threatened the crowd that his men would charge them with fixed bayonets if they did not make way, but his captain emerged from the barracks and managed to get them inside without bloodshed. Word of this fight spread through the town, and gangs of angry Bostonians converged on the barracks, only to find all of the redcoats securely inside. At about 9 p.m., while the mob swarmed around the barracks in Brattle Sq, a group of boys surrounded a lone British sentry, Private White, who was on guard outside the Custom House. The youths began insulting White and threw snowballs at him, while he ordered them to disperse and threatened them with his bayonet. One of the boys ran down to Dock Sq, shouting that his friends were being attacked by a redcoat, while another made his way into the First Church, just across the street from the Town House, and began ringing the bells in alarm. The bells were heard throughout Boston, and everyone began rushing toward King St, thinking that a fire had broken out. Soon a large and hostile crowd had gathered in King St around the Custom House, where Private White stood his ground with his musket leveled. Suddenly a detachment of eight redcoats appeared on the scene, led by Captain Thomas Preston. Preston formed his men into a tight arc facing the crowd, which pressed in so close to him and his men that those in front were face to face with the soldiers. Preston tried to calm and disperse the crowd, telling those nearest to him that he would not let his men harm anyone. Nevertheless, he ordered his troops to load and prime their weapons and present arms, as the crowd shouted insults at the redcoats, daring them to open fire. So matters stood for a moment, until someone in the crowd threw a stick that hit one of the soldiers, causing him to lose his balance on the icy ground and accidentally discharge his gun. This led the other soldiers to fire point-blank into the crowd, after which they reloaded and fired a second round; one of the redcoats bayonetted a man who lay wounded at his feet. The soldiers reloaded once again and leveled their weapons at the crowd, who were clustered around those who had been shot, four of whom died instantly, two more dying later on, and five others wounded. One of those killed was Crispus Attucks, a black who had occasionally been employed by John Hancock, and witnesses reported that he had not been hit by the fire of the soldiers but by shots fired from the upper story of the Custom House.

After the Revolution the Royal Exchange became the *Exchange Tavern,* and it continued in existence into the early years of the 19C. The tavern took its name from the informal financial exchange that had developed among the shipowners and merchants of Boston in the early colonial period, with its focus at the head of King St. In 1805 an ambitious project was begun to house this exchange in an appropriate building of its own, with amenities to attract merchants and travelers from outside Boston as well. This institution, which was designed by Asher Benjamin, was finally completed in 1808 and named the *Exchange Coffee House*, standing on State St between Devonshire and Congress Sts. The Exchange Coffee House was Boston's first "skyscraper" an immense edifice of seven stories, a height unprecedented in the U.S., with a shallow Roman dome over its center. The main floor was designed to serve as the financial exchange, but Boston merchants ignored it and continued to transact their business in the street outside, so it was eventually converted to other uses. The rest of the building was fitted out as a hotel in the modern sense, a far cry from the humble inns of colonial times, with some 200 bedrooms, a dining room that seated 300 guests, as well as a huge ballroom, drawing rooms and a reading room, meeting halls and offices for various organizations, and any other amenities that a well-off traveler might desire. President James Monroe lodged here during his visit to Boston in July 1817, at which time he was feted by all of the leading citizens of the town, most notably ex-President John Adams. On Nov. 3, 1818, the Exchange Coffee House was totally destroyed by fire. It was rebuilt in 1822 on a more modest scale, and continued to serve as an inn and tavern until 1854. In 1842 a Greek Revival edifice known as the *Merchants' Exchange* was constructed on State St just to the E. of the Exchange Coffee House. This was demolished in 1889 to make way for the *Boston Stock Exchange Building*, built by Peabody and Stearns and completed in 1891. This fine building, whose entrance was at 53 State St, was gutted for the erection of a skyscraper, but at least its facade has been retained as facing for the lower floors of the new structure.

There are three historic plaques on the facade of the building at 53 State St. The first of these, just past the corner of Congress and State Sts, records the fact that Governor John Winthrop's first house in Boston stood on this site. Winthrop and his family lived here from 1630 until 1643, when they moved to a new home on what is now the intersection of Spring Lane and Washington St. The second plaque is just past the entrance at 53 State St and the third is near the corner of the building at Kilby St, both of them recording that a tavern called the *Bunch of Grapes* stood on this site. The Bunch of Grapes was the most famous tavern on this street in colonial times. The building in which the tavern was housed is first listed in town records in 1658, and the earliest reference to the Bunch of Grapes dates to 1680. It was a favorite gathering-place for the patriot leaders, and as such it is associated with many of the historic events that took place in Boston in the 18C. On March 28, 1776, 11 days after the British evacuation of Boston, General Washington and his staff were entertained at the Bunch of Grapes following a thanksgiving service at the Old Brick Church. On July 18 of that same year, during the celebration that followed the first public reading in Boston of the Declaration of Independence, the royal emblems of the lion and the unicorn were torn down from the facade of the Town House and burned in front of the tavern before a cheering crowd. The second plaque records that the members of the Ohio Company met here in 1786 to write the charter for Ohio University, which opened in Athens, Ohio, in 1804, the first institution of higher learning west of the Alleghenies. The third marker records two other events that took place in the Bunch of Grapes Tavern, stating that "Here on 30 July 1733, was instituted under charter from the Grand Lodge of England the first regularly constituted lodge of free and accepted Masons in America, now St. John's Lodge of Boston. Here in 1786 was organized the Ohio Company, pioneers in the development of the Great West under the leadership of General Rufus Putnam, first township laid out at Marietta, Ohio."

The itinerary continues down State St, passing Kilby St on the r. and Merchants Row on the l. In early colonial times King St ended at this point, but after the filling in and "wharving out" involved in the construction of the Long Wharf in 1710 its length was considerably increased. At the near corner of State St and Merchants Row a historical marker states that "Long Wharf was built in 1710 and was the oldest in Boston, extending from Merchants Row into the bay." The marker then quotes Daniel Neal, writing in 1719, where he describes Long Wharf as a "noble pier 1800 ft. long, with a row of warehouses on the North side for the use of merchants."

There is also a quote from Thomas Pemberton, in his *Topographical Description of Boston,* published in 1794, where he describes State St as "The most noted and spacious street in town, until the American Revolution called King Street; it is broad and straight and in length about 800 feet from the State House to Long Wharf. It is the general mart of business."

The far corner of State St and Merchants Row is the site of another of colonial Boston's well-known taverns, the *Admiral Vernon,* whose shop sign is displayed in the Old State House. As noted earlier, the tavern was named after Admiral Edward Vernon, whose nickname was "Old Grog." Admiral Vernon was the commander of the British West India Station, and he won fame by reducing the Spanish fortress at Porto Bello in 1739 with six men-of-war. Among the American troops on this expedition was Captain Lawrence Washington, George Washington's older half-brother. Lawrence Washington greatly admired Admiral Vernon, and when he returned to the family estate on the Potomac he renamed it Mount Vernon in honor of his commander.

Near the end of Merchants Row, on the l. side, there used to be a small yard called *Corn Court.* One of the first public houses in Boston was opened in Corn Court in 1634 by Samuel Coles, a charter member of the Ancient and Honorable Artillery Company. When Governor Vane invited Miantonomoh, the Sachem of the Narraganset Indians, to Boston in Oct. 1636, he entertained the chief and 20 of his braves at Mr Cole's inn. During the years just prior to the Revolution this tavern was one of the favorite gathering-places for the patriots, and both George Washington and Benjamin Franklin dined there. When John Hancock was elected as the first governor of Massachusetts in 1780 the tavern in Corn Court was named after him, with his life-sized portrait displayed on a sign above the door. (The sign once fell from its supports during a gale and killed a passerby.) During the last decade of the 18C the *Governor Hancock Tavern* was frequented by a number of distinguished Frenchmen, among whom were John Cheverus, who became the first Roman Catholic bishop of Boston; Talleyrand, the former bishop who became Napoleon's foreign minister; and the Duc de Chartres, who became King of France, ruling from 1830 to 1848 as Louis Philippe. In the late 19C the name of the tavern was changed to the *Old Hancock Tavern;* it continued to function as a public house until 1903, when it and the other structures on Corn Court were demolished to make way for a new office building.

As one continues along State St, on the l. at No. 114 is the *Richards Building,* an interesting structure with an elaborately molded cast-iron facade; this was built in the 1850s, and it was originally used by the firms that shipped goods to California on the clipper ships. Next to it is the *Cunard Building,* erected by Peabody and Stearns in 1902. This stands on the site of an earlier building that housed the Boston office of the Royal Mail Steam Packet Co., founded in 1839 by Samuel Cunard, the first to establish a regularly scheduled transatlantic passenger service. The first of the Cunard liners to reach the U.S. was the *Unicorn;* this docked in East Boston on June 2, 1840, after a voyage of 14 days and 23 hours, which included a stop in Halifax, Nova Scotia.

On the r. side of State St at this point is the *Board of Trade Building,* a massive structure filling the entire block between Broad and India Sts. This great pile of a building was completed in 1901 by the architects Winslow and Bradlee.

Farther on down the left side of State St, on the block between Butler and Commercial Sts, there is a quaint old building of some interest at No. 152. The date of the building is not known, but it is probably one of the structures erected on Long Wharf soon after that pier was completed in 1710. The present structure, which is in the Tudor Cheshire style, is the result of a renovation (1918) by C. Howard Walker. The original building was at first used as a storehouse and shop by a wine merchant, and later it housed a sailmaker, among other tenants.

At this point State St enters McKinley Sq, in the center of which stands the ***Custom House.** This is one of the most remarkable buildings in Boston, and its enormous tower is the most distinctive landmark on the maritime skyline of the city.

History. The first U.S. Custom House in Boston was located just to the W. of the Merchants Exchange Building on State St, with General Benjamin Lincoln serving as the first collector of customs. In 1810 Uriah Cotton built a new Custom House at what is now 20 Custom House St, a short distance to the S. of Mc Kinley Sq. This five-story brick structure, despite its size, eventually proved to be inadequate to handle Boston's rapidly increasing maritime trade, and a quarter-century later the government decided to build a still larger Custom House. But that took a decade to construct, and during that time the building on Custom House St continued to be used. Nathaniel Hawthorne worked there from 1838 to 1840 measuring cargoes, a position that had been secured for him by George Bancroft, the historian, who was at that time collector of customs. Hawthorne resigned his post at the Custom House on Jan. 1, 1841, after which he moved to Brook Farm and subsequently married Sophia Peabody.
   Work on the present Custom House (minus its tower) was begun in 1837, with the architect Ammi Burnham Young in charge of construction. Its site was originally part of Town Cove, forming the head of the dock between Long Wharf and Central Wharf. It took Young three years to lay the foundations alone, which he began by driving some 3000 piles into the seabed, and the structure was not completed until 1847. The tower is not part of the original building, but was erected in 1913–15 by Peabody and Stearns to provide more office space for the Custom House.

Exterior. Young designed the original Custom House in the Greek Revival style, and it is generally considered to be one of the most outstanding examples of that architectural type in the U.S. Its plan is that of a Greek cross, with each of its four facades in the form of a Greek temple. Each portico has six fluted Doric columns, monoliths of Quincy granite weighing 46 tons apiece, surmounted by an entablature and a pediment. The columns of the front and rear porticos are free-standing, while those flanking them are engaged in the wall, as are the columns at the sides of the building. The building was originally surmounted by a shallow Roman dome, with a large skylight in the center to provide illumination for the rotunda within, but this was enclosed by the tower. The tower has 29 stories and is 495ft high; when it was first built it was by far the tallest building in New England. In recent decades many buildings of considerably greater height have been erected in downtown Boston, but few surpass the old Custom House in grandeur. Walt Whitman, who saw the Custom House while it was still under construction, called it "one of the noblest pieces of commercial architecture in the world."

Interior. The most remarkable features of the interior are the original rotunda and dome, which can be seen from the ground floor of the tower. There is also an observation deck on the 25th floor, with a superb view of the city and its surrounding waters.
   Facing the Custom House across McKinley Sq on the seaward side is the *State St Block,* a massive and quite handsome structure designed by Gridley J. F. Bryant and completed in 1858. Like the Custom House, the State St Block is built on foundations that were set into the waters of the dock between Long Wharf and Central Wharf. Built of rough-hewn blocks of Quincy granite, this complex originally consisted of 16 contiguous warehouses that extended down to the present shoreline, and what remains, impressive though it may be, is only about one-fifth of the original length, the remainder having been destroyed when Atlantic Ave and the Central

The Custom House tower, once the tallest building in New England (Amor Towles)

Artery were cut through the neighborhood. This splendid old building has been refurbished in recent years, as have so many of the old warehouses along the waterfront; like the others, it has shops and offices on the ground floor, with various commercial enterprises and condominiums on the upper stories.

The itinerary now leaves Mc Kinley Sq and goes S. along India St, which after a short way joins Milk St. Looking to the l. down Milk St, which runs into the Central Artery at the end of the block, one sees a venerable row of eight four-story brick warehouses. These are all that remain of a line of 54 contiguous buildings erected in 1816—17 by Uriah Cotting and his partners in the Broad Street Assocs, apparently to designs drawn by Charles Bulfinch. This immense array of warehouses extended from this corner out to the end of *Central Wharf*, and in its time was the longest stretch of such buildings in the U.S.

At the S.E. corner of Milk and India Sts stands one of the most unusual and charming structures in Boston, the *Flour and Grain Exchange Building;* this was built in 1889–92 by Shepley, Rutan, and Coolidge, and originally housed the Boston Chamber of Commerce. The most striking feature of this astonishing structure, built of grayish-pink granite, is the towerlike facade at the corner; notice the elaborately carved entryway, resembling the portal of a Romanesque cathedral; the grand circlet of three-story round-arched windows halfway up to the top; the dormer windows capped by tall triangular stone faces ending with crockets in the form of four-armed crosses; and above all the enormous conical roof above the corner, with a smaller cone above the corner to the rear for good measure.

Continue along Milk St, which crosses Broad St at the next intersection. At the S.E. corner of this intersection, with its entrance at 50–52 Broad St, stands a handsome old building of another era, the sole survivor of others of its type which must once have clustered close around it. It is built of rough-hewn gray granite and is four stories high; with round-arched windows and a door of similar shape at the corner; a gracefully curving mansard roof with peaked dormer windows; the corner on Milk St accentuated by tall chimneys. This charming building has been dated to c. 1860.

This part of Broad St was laid out in 1806–7 by Uriah Cotting and his associates, who included wealthy real-estate dealers such as Harrison Gray Otis. Most of the commercial buildings that were erected along this street were four-story brick structures, at least some of which, perhaps all, were designed by Charles Bulfinch. Some authorities have tried to identify a dozen or so structures along Broad St as Bulfinch buildings, and although many of these have been seriously altered, a few still retain something of their original 19C appearance.

At the next corner Milk St crosses Batterymarch St, which takes its name from the fact that the Ancient and Honorable Artillery Company marched this way when proceeding from the Common to *Fort Hill.*

Fort Hill no longer exists, for what remained of it was leveled in 1866–72 to provide earth for filling Town Cove. Its site is two blocks down Batterymarch to the l., roughly on the block bounded by that street and by Franklin, Oliver, and High Sts. This hill, along with Beacon Hill and Copp's Hill, was one of the three principal eminences on the Shawmut Peninsula. It was originally called Corn Hill, but on May 24, 1632, the General Court issued an order to fortify its summit, and thereafter it was known as Fort Hill. This fortress was eventually abandoned, and the hill was not fortified again.

Turn r. onto Batterymarch. After crossing Milk St, one passes on the l. the *Samuel Appleton Building,* built in 1924 by Coolidge and Shattuck; and on the r. the 22 *Batterymarch Building,* erected by Ball and Dabney in 1893. These two buildings take up the entire block between Milk St and Water St, where one turns l. to enter Liberty Sq. This is an irregular area at the intersection of Batterymarch, Water, and Kilby Sts, with the latter leading off to the r. Liberty Sq, contrary to expectation, does not take its name from the American War of Independence, but commemorates a great feast held here on Jan. 24, 1793, to celebrate the success of the French Revolution. There are a number of fine Victorian buildings standing around the square, most notably those at Nos 44, 45, and 55 Kilby St, all of which date from the last quarter of the 19C.

At the next intersection Water St crosses Congress St, the principal N.-S. thoroughfare through this part of downtown Boston. In the early colonial period this was called Leverett's Lane, because in 1667 it was laid out on land that was part of the estate of Governor John Leverett. In 1709 the Quakers built a meetinghouse on this street, just opposite Exchange Pl, a small wooden structure with a graveyard behind it. The meetinghouse was destroyed in the great fire of 1760, and it was rebuilt shortly afterward. In the first decade of the 19C the congregation had diminished to the point where the Quakers decided to abandon the meetinghouse on Congress St, and in 1827 they sold the land, at which time the remains of the departed Friends in the graveyard were removed to the Quaker Burying-Ground in Lynn.

Turn l. off Water St to enter Post Office Sq, a triangular area bounded on its l. side by Pearl St, on the r. by Congress, and at its base by Water St. The square takes its name from the massive skyscraper that looms over its r. side between Water and Milk Sts; this is the *Boston Post Office and Federal Building*, erected in 1930–31 by Cram & Ferguson and James A. Wetmore. At the center of the square a pleasant little park has been laid out with stone benches and shade trees around a fountain, from which rises a commemorative column surmounted by the golden figure of an eagle. The plaza and the column are a memorial to *George Thorndike Angell* (1823–1909), who is honored here as the founder of the Massachusetts Society for the Prevention of Cruelty to Animals, and also the American Humane Education Society.

The itinerary continues along Pearl St, passing on the l. a new skyscraper and the gleaming four-square edifice of four stories that now houses the *Meridien Hotel*. The hotel occupies part of the *Old Federal Reserve Bank Building* (to distinguish it from the new home of the bank, on Atlantic Ave); this was completed by R. Clipston Sturgis in 1922, and it was renovated for use as a hotel in 1981 by Jung-Brannan Assocs.

At the next corner Pearl St crosses Franklin St. On the far side of the street to the l. is the *State Street Bank,* which takes up the entire block between Pearl and Oliver Sts; this was built by the Pearl Street Assoc. in 1966. And on the far side to the r. is the *New England Telephone Headquarters Building,* built by Cram and Ferguson in 1947, which extends from Pearl to Congress St.

In the lobby of the latter building, whose main entrance is at 185 Franklin St, there is an interesting display concerned with the invention of the telephone by Alexander Graham Bell; this is in an alcove just to the r. of the entryway (open Mon.–Fri., 9–5).

Interior. The exhibition chamber is an authentic reconstruction of the room in which the first telephone was invented by Alexander Graham Bell, assisted by Thomas A. Watson; this was in an attic of the fifth floor of a building at what was then 109 Court St and is now in City Hall Plaza, near the Kennedy Office Building. When the building was demolished in the early 1920s, the attic workshop was carefully dismantled and stored, with the thought that it might be reconstituted in the future. This was done in 1959, and the display opened on June 3 of that year, on the 84th anniversary of the invention of the telephone. The room is recreated to look exactly as it was in Oct. 1875, when Bell was preparing sketches and models for the first telephone patent, which was granted to him on March 7, 1876. All of the models and replicas were constructed by the Bell Telephone Laboratories from original drawings made by Bell himself, and the books and reference materials are those he actually used; these include one of his own works, *The Standard Elocutionist.* In the display case are objects connected with the early history of the telephone. Among these are the world's first telephone switchboard, operated by E. T. Holmes at 342 Washington St, in Boston, in May 1877; and the first commercial telephone, which was located in the shop of Charles Williams, Bell's landlord at 109 Court St, and connected to the Holmes switchboard. The window behind the laboratory bench is one of the originals from the attic workshop, and behind it a diorama represents the same Scollay Sq street scene that Bell and Watson looked down upon in 1875.

After leaving the Telephone Building, turn l. and continue along the l. side of Franklin St, crossing Congress St. The l. side of the block between Congress and Federal Sts is taken up by the *First National Bank of Boston Building,* completed in 1971 by Campbell, Aldrich and Nulty. This building, which is faced in gleaming red granite that almost looks like porphyry, is one of the most unusual of the modern skyscrapers in Boston. Its lower floors are cantilevered out on tiers above one another until they reach the plane of the street below, above which the next eight stories rise vertically, and then the outward projection abruptly ends to recede to a vertical tower of 24 stories, producing that bulge in its abdominal region that has led Bostonians to refer to this edifice as the "pregnant building."

On the facade of the bank, at the corner of Franklin and Federal Sts, a plaque records that "Here stood the *Long Lane Meeting-House* (later the *Federal Street Church*), in which the Massachusetts State Convention met to ratify the United States Constitution on 6 Feb. 1788." The plaque goes on to say that the American Unitarian Assoc. originated in the Federal Street Church on May 25, 1825, and that the Rev. William Ellery Channing preached there from 1803 to 1842.

The meetinghouse referred to in the inscription took its name from the fact that Federal St was originally known as Long Lane, and was given its present name only after the federal Constitution was ratified in this church. The first church on this site was founded by Scotch-Irish Presbyterians, who originally congregated in a barn before they built a more suitable meeting place in 1744. The church eventually became a Congregational meetinghouse, and that was its status in 1788, when the delegates convened there, after having found that the Old State House was too small for their number. As recorded in a popular ditty of the time, sung to the tune of "Yankee Doodle": "The 'Vention did in Boston meet / But State House couldn't hold 'em / So then they went to Federal Street / And there the truth was told 'em." John Hancock presided over the Convention, which was split over the question of ratifying the Constitution. Samuel Adams, the most influential of the delegates, would at first not support the Constitution, but when Paul Revere brought him news from the Green Dragon Tavern that the great majority of the mechanics were in favor of ratification he changed his position, saying "Well, if they must have it, they must have it," and this proved crucial in the final vote that approved the document.

Soon after the Rev. Channing became minister of the Federal Street Church, in 1803, he and his congregation decided to build a new and larger meetinghouse. Charles Bulfinch was chosen to be the architect, and in 1809 he completed the structure, his only church in the Gothic style. The church stood only until c. 1859, when it was abolished after its congregation moved to a new church they had built on Arlington St in Back Bay.

Diagonally across the way from the Federal Street Church stood the *Federal Street Theater,* the first to be established in Boston. The first Federal Street Theater, designed by Charles Bulfinch and completed in 1794, was a monumental structure in the Greek Revival style. It was gutted in 1798 by a fire, which left only the shell of the building standing. The theater was quickly rebuilt in the same general style, and it reopened in Oct. of that same year and continued to function until 1852, when it too was demolished.

The itinerary continues along Franklin St, passing on the r. the huge skyscraper that houses the *National Shawmut Bank,* completed by the Architects Collaborative in 1971. The lower section of this building along Franklin St stands on the site of the old Federal Street Theater. Opposite the bank stands the *111 Franklin St Building,* built by Thomas M. James in 1930.

This stands on the site of yet another vanished Bulfinch edifice, the *Roman Catholic Church of the Holy Cross.* Bulfinch gave the design of this church free of charge in 1800 to Bishop Cheverus and his flock, who did not then have a regular house of worship of their own, and when it was consecrated in 1803 it was the first Roman Catholic church in Massachusetts. Bulfinch designed the church in the Italian Renaissance style, and old photographs show that it was very similar to St. Stephen's in the North End, his only surviving church in Boston. The Church of the Holy Cross suffered the same fate as Bulfinch's other buildings in this neighborhood, and it was demolished in 1868, after its congregation had moved elsewhere in Boston.

At the next corner Franklin St is crossed by Devonshire St, which opens up on the l. into a triangular area known as Winthrop Sq. The large Victorian structure that forms the base of the triangle is the *One Winthrop Square Building*, erected by W. R. Emerson and Carl Fehmer in 1873. In front of the building there is a small park with a bronze statue of the poet *Robert Burns*, who is shown with a book in his l. hand and a collie dog by his r. side. The statue was created by the sculptor Henry Hudson Kitson and was presented to the city of Boston by the Robert Burns Memorial Assoc. It originally stood in a remote location in the Fenway, and was moved to its present location in recent years.

The stretch of Franklin St between Devonshire St and Hawley St, the second turning to the l., marks the site of Charles Bulfinch's most original and ambitious real-estate development project, his ill-fated *Tontine Crescent*. Bulfinch first presented this idea to the General Court in 1793, proposing that a crescent of contiguous town houses be built along what was then known as Vincent's Alley, a pathway through undeveloped marsh lands. The name of the crescent that Bulfinch envisioned came from the type of plan by which he hoped to finance it, a Tontine; this was a scheme, popular in England at the time, by which a group of shareholders agreed to a compact in which the last surviving member would inherit the shares of all of the original participants. However, the General Court refused to grant permission for the Tontine to be formed, probably because the members felt that the ethics of such a scheme were questionable. Nevertheless, Bulfinch decided to go ahead on his own with financial backing from his brother-in-law, Charles Vaughan, and William Scollay. The area that Bulfinch and his associates developed was called Franklin Pl (later to be called Franklin St), with an arc of 16 connected houses on the S. side, the Tontine Crescent; on the N. side a straight line of eight houses in four blocks; and between the line of houses there was a fenced-in semioval park in the center of which there was a commemorative urn to honor the memory of Benjamin Franklin. The Tontine Crescent, which swept in a graceful concave arc 480ft long, had in its center a Greek Revival structure with an arched opening through which a passageway named Arch St led S. to Summer St. Bulfinch generously gave over the upper rooms of the arch building to the Massachusetts Historical Society, founded in 1791, and the Boston Library Society (which later merged with the Boston Athenaeum, established in 1794). The project was a tremendous artistic success, for when the Tontine Crescent was completed in 1796 there was nothing of its type in the U.S. to compare to it in grandeur and in beauty. But at the same time the project was an economic disaster for Bulfinch; adverse economic conditions forced his two associates to withdraw and he himself could not meet his bills, so that later in 1796 he was forced into bankruptcy. This completely changed the economic circumstances of Bulfinch's life, for instead of being a gentleman-architect he was forced to seek paid commissions and to work as a salaried civil servant, becoming Boston's commissioner of police in 1811. But even that latter position did not save him from his creditors, for in July 1811 he spent a month in debtors' prison for nonpayment of debts. Tontine Crescent ruined Bulfinch, but did not long survive him, for it was completely demolished in 1858. Today only the name of Arch St survives to recall Bulfinch's Tontine Crescent.

After one has passed Hawley St, Franklin St becomes a pedestrian mall, the *Lincoln Filene Park*, extending to Washington St. This is one of the most pleasant and lively spots in the downtown commercial area, a welcome breathing space among the crowded streets, and at midday in good weather there are always musicians and other performers to entertain the passing crowds of shoppers.

The Lincoln Filene Park brings one into the center of the *Washington Street Arcade,* a partially glassed-in pedestrian mall that extends along that street between Milk St and the intersection of Winter and Summer Sts, with open pedestrian walkways extending for a block up both of the latter streets. This is a very attractive mall, relieving shoppers from the annoyance of the heavy traffic in the downtown area, and bringing a renewed sense of vitality and more business to a shopping district that was beginning to show increasing signs of decline.

Turn r. from Franklin St into the Washington Street Arcade. On the l. is the venerable *Filene's Department Store,* with the newer building on the Franklin St corner and the older one on the next corner at Summer St.

William Filene, founder of the business, immigrated to the U.S. from Germany after the Revolution of 1848. Starting out as a cap-maker and tailor, he opened shops in Boston, the North Shore, and on Fifth Ave in New York, before finally opening a department store on Winter St just off Washington St in 1881. The business prospered so much that his successors erected the much larger building on the corner of Washington and Summer in 1912, with Daniel H. Burnham as the architect. Even this huge structure eventually proved too small for Filene's business, and in 1972–73 the new annex was added at the corner of Washington and Franklin, along with the pedestrian mall on the latter street. Filene's is renowned throughout New England for its price-reduction policy: the price of goods is reduced a set number of times, and then, if they are not sold by a certain date, they are given away to charitable organizations.

On the l. side of the next block of the Arcade, between Summer and Avon Sts, is another long-established Boston department store, *Jordan Marsh.*

This business was founded by Eben Jordan, who came from Maine to Boston at the age of 14 with a dollar and some change in his pocket, working his way up from a shop clerk to become the owner of one of the biggest commercial enterprises in the city. Jordan, with a fellow clerk named Marsh, founded the Jordan Marsh Co. in 1851, and a decade later the business included a large wholesale store on Winthrop Sq and a retail shop at the present location. Jordan had the good fortune to give up the store on Winthrop Sq just a year before it was destroyed in the great fire of 1872, and from that time on the business was concentrated at the site of Washington St, with the present building there remodeled in 1977–78.

The itinerary now turns r. from Washington onto Winter St, where the pedestrian mall extends to Tremont St, at the next corner. About halfway along Winter St a narrow passage, Winter Pl, leads off to the l., constricting to an even narrower alleyway that cuts through to Temple Place, one of the most picturesque byways in downtown Boston.

The left-hand corner at Winter St and Winter Pl is the site of the house where Samuel Adams and his family lived in his latter years, from after the Revolution until his death, which came on Sun. Oct. 2, 1803. On the day of his funeral the remains of Samuel Adams were taken from this house in a plain coffin, and carried through the streets of Boston in a procession that included all of the dignitaries of the town and a great crowd of its ordinary citizens, stopping at the places where he had played such a vital role in the struggle for American independence, at the Old South Meeting-Place, at Faneuil Hall, at the Old State House, and then finally proceeding to the Old Granary Burying-Ground, where he was at last laid to rest.

At 3–4 Winter Pl, on the l. side of the street just before it narrows down into an alley, is the *Locke-Ober Café,* one of the oldest and most renowned restaurants in Boston.

The restaurant was founded in 1875 by Louis Ober, but before that a cafe had been operating for some twenty years in the cellar of the building, which itself dates to c. 1832. In 1891 a retired Maine sea captain named Frank Locke opened up a wine bar next door at 1–2 Winter Pl, and for the next three years Ober's customers often stopped to drink at Locke's place before coming to dinner. But in 1894 two wine merchants bought both places, and since then it has been Locke-Ober's.

Aside from its virtues as a restaurant, Locke-Ober's is worth visiting to see its vintage Victorian and Edwardian decor, particularly in the Men's Café, the bar-room on the first floor. The star attraction there is the portrait of the rosy nude known to generations of appreciative male diners as Mademoiselle Yvonne, of whom Lawrence Dame wrote: "Demure despite her nudity / She gazes quite sans crudity / Upon the skulls both thatched and bald / Of patrons who are often called—Great Gourmets / . . . The Lady of Locke-Ober's!"

After leaving Locke-Ober's, turn l. and continue through Winter Pl, emerging on Temple Place. Just to the r. of the alleyway, at 37 Temple Pl, there is a handsome Greek Revival house with a bow front. A plaque on the facade of the house records that it was built in 1833 for Thomas Handasyd Perkins, a wealthy merchant and one of the founders of the Boston Athenaeum, who lived there until his death in 1854 at the age of 90. Prior to building this house on Temple Pl, Perkins had lived in a mansion at 17 Pearl St; in 1833 he gave this to Dr. Samuel Gridley Howe to be used as the New England Asylum for the Blind, which was later called the Perkins Institute for the Blind in his honor. In 1856 the Perkins mansion on Temple Pl was acquired by the Provident Institute for Savings, which was founded in 1816 as the first mutual savings bank in the U.S. In the years since then the mansion has been modified and linked to later structures, so that the building now extends from Temple Pl through to Winter St, the most recent addition on the latter side having been done in 1973 by Shepley, Bulfinch, Richardson & Abbott. The plaque also states that the front drawing room of the Perkins mansion has been preserved and is now the office of the bank president, and that within that chamber one of the 23 original fireplaces of the house has been preserved, along with its mantel of Italian marble.

The itinerary now goes back along Temple Pl to Washington St. Turn l. onto the shopping mall. Halfway along the block on the r. is the site of an estate which in the early years of Boston belonged to Robert Hull.

This was inherited by his son, John Hull, the first mintmaster of Boston, and was passed on by him to his daughter Hannah and her husband, Judge Samuel Sewall. Sewall was born in England in 1652 and died in Boston in 1730. He graduated from Harvard in 1671, and soon thereafter became a town counselor, then judge of the Supreme Court, and finally chief justice of the Supreme Court (1718–28). Sewall is best known for his *Diary*, which he kept faithfully through his long career, recording all of the public and private events that took place in Boston, making his memoirs an invaluable source for the political and social history of his times.

At the next corner turn r. onto Summer St, where the shopping mall goes on for most of the block. At the next corner Hawley St leads off to the l. The corner to the l., as one faces Hawley St, is the site of two buildings of colonial Boston. The earliest of these was an inn called *The Seven Stars*, and sometimes *The Pleiades*, which first appears in town records in the late 17C.

This inn was so popular that the main road on which it stood was called Seven Stars Lane, a name that was changed to Summer St in 1708. In 1728 the site on which the inn stood was bought by the vestry of King's Chapel, who wanted to build a new church to accommodate the Anglicans who lived in the S. part of town. The cornerstone was not laid until 1734, and the building was finally opened on Aug. 15 of the following year, when it was dedicated as *Trinity Church*. The original Trinity Church was a large wooden structure, and from descriptions at the time it apparently had the most handsome interior of any church in Boston, adorned with paintings and works of sculpture. When George Washington made his presidential visit to Boston in 1789 he attended services at Trinity Church, sitting in Governor Bowdoin's pew. In 1828 the original wooden building was torn down to make way for a much larger granite edifice, completed in 1829 by Arthur Brimmer; but completely destroyed in the great fire of 1872.

At the next corner Chauncy St leads off to the r., and a little way farther on, Arch St goes off to the l. A short way down the r. side of Chauncy St was the site of a meetinghouse built in 1808 by the First Church of Boston, with Asher Benjamin acting as the architect. Before that time the First Church had been housed in the Old Brick Meeting-House in Cornhill (see above), which was demolished after the move to Chauncy St. Prior to the move the First Church had already built a parsonage on Chauncy St, and it was there that Ralph Waldo Emerson, son of the Rev. William Emerson, was born in 1803.

The First Church continued to use the meetinghouse on Chauncy St until 1868. Then the congregation moved into a new meetinghouse in Back Bay, at the corner of Marlborough and Berkeley Sts, at which time the church and parsonage on Chauncy St were razed.

At the next corner Otis St leads off to the l. from Summer St and Kingston St goes off to the r. The near corner of Summer and Otis Sts is the site of a famous mansion owned by Thomas Russell, a wealthy merchant and shipowner who in 1792 became the first president of the Boston branch of the U.S. bank.

When General Heath became commander of the Continental forces of Boston in 1777 he established his headquarters in the Russell mansion. While in residence there, General Heath entertained Count D'Estaing, Silas Deane, General Count Pulaski, General Baron Riedesel, and General John Burgoyne. After Russell's death his mansion was converted into a luxurious rooming house by Leon Chappotin. One of those who stayed in Chappotin's lodgings was Jerome Bonaparte, brother of the Emperor Napoleon, who visited Boston in 1804, after his marriage in Baltimore to Miss Patterson. Gilbert Stuart also lodged there, in 1805, while he looked for a house in which to install his family, and while there he worked on his monumental painting of *Washington at Dorchester Heights,* now in the Boston Museum of Fine Arts.

At the next corner Devonshire St leads off to the l. from Summer St, and after that Milton Pl runs off in the same direction, while on the r. Bedford and Lincoln Sts join just as they intersect Summer St, together forming a triangular intersection known as Church Green. The intersection took its name from the *New South Meeting-House;* this church stood on land granted to its congregation by the town on Sept. 20, 1715, on what is now the triangular lot at the intersection of Summer and Bedford Sts. The original church was made of wood and dedicated on Jan. 8, 1717; one of its founders was Captain Samuel Adams, father of Governor Samuel Adams. In 1818 this structure was replaced by one designed by Charles Bulfinch, a granite edifice with a neoclassical portico of four Doric columns projecting from the front, and with a steeple tapering to a spire 190ft above the ground. This fine church suffered the same fate as all the other Bulfinch buildings in the S. part of old Boston, for it was demolished in 1868.

Before leaving Church Green, glance at the handsome Victorian structure that forms the S.W. corner of Bedford and Lincoln Sts; this is the *Bedford Block,* built by Cummings and Sears in 1875–76. Facing it across the square, just beyond the intersection of Summer and Devonshire Sts, is the *100 Summer Street Building,* erected by Skidmore, Owings & Merrill in 1970.

Continuing along the l. side of Summer St, cross High St to come to the *Fiduciary Trust Building,* built in 1975 by the Architects Collaborative. Now cross Dewey Sq, the busy intersection of Summer St, the Central Artery, and Atlantic Ave, looking across to the great rounded facade of *South Station* and finally making one's way over to the piazza in front of the *Federal Reserve Bank,* which occupies a vast site of 5.7 acres between Summer and Congress Sts. The Federal Reserve Bank Building, completed in 1977 by Hugh Stubbins and Assocs, is one of the most spectacular skyscrapers in the commercial district, its silvery aluminum surface shining as bright as a sword on sunny days, looming through the spectral fog when foul weather blows in from the sea. This modern Colossus stands on two huge pylon legs, which between them seem to clasp together the 33-story office tower and its blank upper and lower margins, the latter hovering high above the ground, and nestling below it the squarish four-story lower annex. The ground floor of this lower building has an attractive art gallery that is open to the public, with changing exhibitions.

The piazza in front of the Federal Reserve Bank provides an open vista of the massed forms of the buildings across the way. Of those that have not yet been identified the nearest is the *Keystone Building,* which is just beyond the Central Artery, at the intersection of High and Congress Sts. This is a 31-story skyscraper faced with white travertine marble, built by Pietro Belluschi and Emery Roth in 1968. It is a severely regular rectangular parallelopiped in form, with identical rows of tinted bow windows, which with its undulating concave corners give it the appearance of a giant and very neat beehive. To the l. of that is the *United Shoe Machinery Building,* easily identified by its pyramidal roof sheathed in gleaming gold tiles; this was built by Parker, Thomas, and Childs in 1925, and its cascading form of stepped blocks descending in units of decreasing size is recognizable as a product of the zoning laws of the period in which it was built. And on the l. side of Dewey Sq is the 48-story *Dewey Square Tower.*

There is one last site to be identified on this itinerary, and this is located on Purchase St, which runs parallel to the Central Artery on its western side. About 60ft along Purchase St from the point where it intersects Congress St stood the house of Captain Samuel Adams, and this was the birthplace of his son, Samuel Adams, one of the leaders in the American independence movement.

When the younger Samuel Adams was born in 1726, Purchase St was known as Belcher's Lane, just a pathway running along the shore parallel to the docks. The Adams House faced the sea, and on its roof there was a walkway from which all of the harbor and its shipping, with a forest of masts along the wharves, could be seen, Samuel Adams' first view of the world. When Captain Adams died the house passed to Samuel, who lived there with his own family until the Revolution, when they had to leave Boston. When Adams returned to Boston after the British evacuation, he found that the redcoats had so badly damaged the house on Purchase St that it was uninhabitable. He then bought the house on Winter St, where he lived for the rest of his days. The old Adams house on Purchase St is known to have survived until 1800, but after that there is no record of its existence—vanished, along with almost everything else of colonial Boston, its site buried beneath the towers of the modern city.

7   The Waterfront

The present itinerary takes one along the waterfront from the Congress St Bridge to Lincoln Wharf, and from there back through the eastern fringe of the North End, finishing in Quincy Market. There are no historic monuments along this route, but there are two very popular museums: the Boston Tea Party Ship and Museum, and the Children's Museum, as well as the New England Aquarium. Aside from these sights, the main feature of the route is the walk itself, for there are few more enjoyable strolls in Boston than along the waterfront, particularly on a sunny day when there is a cool onshore breeze, with the exciting seascape of Boston Harbor opened up to view. Also, this stretch of waterfront has many historical associations, for this is where Boston had its beginnings and where much of its character was formed.

Approaches. Those who are beginning this Rte immediately after finishing the last one can simply continue along Atlantic Ave past the Federal Reserve Bank to the corner of Congress St, and there turn r. to reach the Congress St Bridge. Those starting out from Boston center can walk to this point along Congress St, or take the free Tea Party shuttle from the vicinity of Quincy Market.

History and Topography of the Waterfront. The area that developed into Boston's waterfront was originally the shore of the Great Cove, which later came to be called Town Cove, the broad indentation on the western side of the Shawmut Peninsula. Town Dock, the first landing stage to be built in Boston, was at the center of this indentation, and it was on the foreshore between this and the Great Spring that the first settlers built their houses.

During the first years of its existence Boston turned to the sea for its sustenance, for the settlers simply could not survive on the food that they grew on the Shawmut Peninsula. So from the very beginning of its history Boston engaged in maritime commerce, which enabled it not only to survive but in time to prosper. William Wood, writing in 1634, described Boston as "fittest for such as can trade into England, for such commodities as the Countrey wants, being the chiefe place for shipping and merchandize."

During the first decades of its history Boston was much concerned about the threat of seaborne marauders, and the town government early on took measures for self-defense. In 1636 a fortress was built on *Castle Island* to guard the approaches to the harbor, and ten years later another defense work was constructed in the North End at Merry's Point, on the northern extremity of Town Cove. This latter fortress, *North Battery,* was designed to command the entrance to the inner harbor and the Charles River. In 1666 still another fortress was built by General (later Governor) John Leverett on the shore beneath Fort Hill at the extremity of Town Cove; this was called the *South Battery,* or sometimes the *Sconce.* But even this was not deemed to be sufficient, for in 1681 a seawall called the *Barricado* was built across the mouth of Town Cove, with openings at the two ends for shipping to pass.

The most important step in the development of Boston's port in the colonial period was the construction in 1710 of *Long Wharf,* which extended for nearly 2000ft out into Town Cove. It extended far out beyond the Barricado, using part of that seawall to form an extension at right angles to the N., the T-Wharf, about halfway along its length. A long row of shops and warehouses lined the N. side of the pier and a thoroughfare ran out along the S. side, thereby extending King St right out into Town Cove and doubling its length. Not only did this vastly increase the docking space in the port but it also made it far more efficient, for even the largest vessels could berth at the pier next to the warehouses. Even before the construction of Long Wharf, Boston was the busiest port in America and had the third-largest shipping tonnage among English seaports, surpassed only by London and Bristol, but after 1710 its volume of trade greatly increased.

Boston's maritime commerce suffered severely during the Revolution, both during the British occupation and in the years of war that followed. Its foreign trade was largely cut off by the British blockade, its merchant and fishing fleets had for the most part been converted into privateers, and its shipbuilding industry had virtually come to a halt, along

Boston Harbor in the second half of the 19C, a period of decline

with all of the subsidiary trades that depended on it. After the war Boston and the other seaports of Massachusetts experienced an extremely serious economic depression, and prosperity began to return only toward the end of the 1780s. But when recovery began it proceeded very rapidly, and in the last decade of the 18C Boston was once again a thriving seaport. In the last years of the 18C ships from Boston, Salem, and other seaports in Massachusetts began to sail to the farthest reaches of the globe in search of profitable trade. On Aug. 9, 1700, the ship *Columbia*, under Captain Robert Gray, returned to Boston after an absence of three years, completing the first voyage around the world by an American vessel. This pioneering journey opened up the N.W. fur trade to Boston's merchant bankers, the first step toward developing what soon became an extremely profitable commerce with China and other countries in the Far East.

The increased volume of trade in Boston at the beginning of the 19C led Uriah Cotting and others to form the Broad Street Assoc. in 1805, their purpose being to develop the waterfront area in the vicinity of Long Wharf. This completely changed the face of the dockside area around Central Wharf, which had been a run-down quarter of old buildings and narrow lanes, transforming it into a new commercial district with broad streets lined with impressive brick and granite warehouses. Within the following decade Cotting and his associates built two huge piers just S. of Long Wharf, calling them Central Wharf and India Wharf, with the former rivalling the old colonial pier in length and in the number of commercial buildings that it supported.

Boston's maritime commerce received a setback with the passage on Dec. 22, 1807, of Jefferson's Embargo Act, which prohibited American ships from clearing for foreign ports. Another act, which went into effect at the same time, forbade the importation of many British goods, further limiting Boston's trade. The Embargo Act was repealed on March 15, 1809, but by that time severe damage had been done to Boston's commerce and its shipping industry, and the war with Britain that began in 1812 delayed the onset of recovery until after the Treaty of Ghent ended hostilities on Dec. 24, 1814.

During the years 1815–45 Boston's economy underwent a transformation, as maritime trade, shipbuilding, and fishing began to be supplanted by manufacturing as the principal source of income. In 1843 Boston was for the first time surpassed by New York as the leading shipowning city in the U.S., a primacy that it would never regain. Boston made a dramatic resurgence in 1850–55, when Donald McKay and other naval architects in the city turned out fleets of clipper ships in local shipyards, producing the fastest and most beautiful sailing vessels ever to fly the U.S. flag. But this boom faded after the mid-1850s, when the changing economic situation no longer made it profitable to build clipper ships. The American Civil War hastened a process that had already begun in world shipping, the supplanting of sail by steam, and Boston's shipowners and merchants failed to keep up with the times.

In 1868 the old port of Boston was completely altered in appearance when Atlantic Ave was laid out across Town Cove on the line of the old Barricado, cutting through India and Central Wharves and destroying many of the handsome warehouses that stood upon them. During the next four years that part of Town Cove between Atlantic Ave and the inner ends of the docks was filled in with earth taken from Fort Hill, which was completely leveled by 1872. Thenceforth the wharves along Atlantic Ave were used principally by the fishing fleet and vessels involved in the coasting trade, with most of the ships engaged in foreign commerce docking in South and East Boston. When Fish Pier in South Boston opened in 1914 the fishing fleet was based there, deserting the old port, and before long the vessels in the coasting trade began docking elsewhere too. Construction of the Central Artery did further violence to the waterfront of Boston, cutting it off from the rest of the city and accelerating its decay. The first steps toward recovery were taken in 1960, when the Boston Redevelopment Authority (BRA) began the Waterfront Project. In the years since then a large stretch of the waterfront has been rejuvenated, with many of the old warehouses restored as condominiums, offices, and for other uses. The climax of this project came in 1976, with the completion of Christopher Columbus Waterfront Park, which once again linked the city to its old port quarter and gave it a splendid promenade along the sea, where the history of Boston had its beginnings.

Begin on the Boston side of the *Congress Street Bridge,* which crosses the Fort Point Channel to South Boston. Fort Point Channel is the last remnant of the waterway that led from Boston Harbor into South Boston Bay, now completely filled in. The present channel was created in the 1870s by the Boston Wharf Co., which also built the brick warehouses on the South Boston side. The three large buildings on the l. side of Congress St on the way toward the bridge were erected in 1908 by the architectural firm of Peabody and Stearns; they stand on the site of the old *Russia Wharf,* built in 1816 for the Russia trade.

Near the center of the Congress Street Bridge on the l. side is the ***Boston Tea Party Ship and Museum.** The museum, which has a number of exhibits connected with the Boston Tea Party, is housed on a small wharf attached to the bridge; moored to the l. side of the wharf is the *Beaver II,* a replica of one of the vessels involved in that historic event.

Admission. The museum is open daily from 9 a.m. till dusk; fee (tel. 338-1773).

History. The climax of the drama known to history as the Boston Tea Party took place on Griffin's Wharf, which was located on the Boston shore at the foot of Pearl St; this would have been about midway along the present course of Atlantic Ave between Congress St and Northern Ave, which crosses Fort Point Channel on the bridge at its northern end. The three tea ships, the *Dartmouth,* the *Eleanor,* and the *Beaver,* which between them carried 340 chests containing 90,000 pounds of tea worth £9000, were moored here. On the evening of Dec. 16, 1773, a band of patriots disguised as Mohawk Indians boarded the ships and dumped all of the tea into the harbor, an act of defiance against the Crown for having imposed the hated tea tax. All of this was done without any violence, and the only damage done was to a lock on one of the tea chests, which was promptly replaced.

When all of the tea had been dumped overboard the "Indians" disembarked from the ships, whereupon they and the silent crowd of spectators headed for their homes.

Interior. Inside the entrance to the museum on the r. there is a model of the American brig *Topaz;* this was built in Newbury, Mass., in 1807, and was similar in dimensions and appearance to the *Beaver,* one of the three ships involved in the Boston Tea Party. On the l. there is a striking photo of the *Beaver II* on her way across the Atlantic in 1973 (see below).

At the front of the main room an audiovisual presentation is based on a children's book published in 1882 by Dodd, Mead & Co., with text by Josephine Pollard and cartoon drawings by H. W. McVicker, while the background music is a colonial quintet by the German American composer Johann Friedrich Peter. In the center of the room are panels with enlarged reproductions of old prints concerning the Boston Tea Party. To the r. of these there are models of the *Beaver II*, the *Fair America*, and the *Flying Cloud*, the latter of which was the most famous of the clipper ships built in Boston by Donald McKay. In the center of the rear area of the room there is an old *tea chest* that is believed to have been one of those used in the Boston Tea Party. On the wall to the r. of this there is a display on the *cultivation of tea*, and beyond that there are *shipbuilding* tools, replicas of those used in Boston in the colonial period. In the rear of the room to the l. a slide presentation shows the building of the *Beaver II* and its voyage across the Atlantic. Behind the panels illustrating the Boston Tea Party there is a plaster *model of Boston* as it was in 1773.

A door leads out to the side of the wharf where the *Beaver II* is moored. This vessel was originally a Danish brig, launched in 1908 and used in the coasting trade. In 1972 the old vessel was chosen to play a part in the forthcoming re-enactment of the Boston Tea Party, because it had the same lines and dimensions as one the three tea ships, which thereafter became known as the *Beaver I*.

The *Beaver I*, smallest of the three tea ships at Griffin's Wharf, was a brigantine of c. 130 tons, and was made in Rhode Island for the Rotche family of Nantucket. On her historic voyage she was commanded by Captain Hezekiah Coffin and had a crew of about ten. On that voyage the *Beaver I* left London in the spring of 1773, carrying a cargo of 112 chests of tea for Boston and assorted merchandise for Nantucket, which was delivered after the Boston Tea Party. The *Beaver I* continued to sail for about a quarter-century after her brief hour of fame, until she was finally lost at sea with all hands in the last years of the 19C.

After its reconstruction and launching, the *Beaver II* was sailed from Denmark by her captain and a crew of ten, docking at Weymouth to pick up a cargo of Chinese black tea. The *Beaver II* was then sailed across the Atlantic in the summer and early autumn of 1973, stopping in the Azores, Bermuda, and Nantucket, before finally entering Boston Harbor on Nov. 11, of that year. There she was finally tied up at her present berth, where on Dec. 16, 1973, there was a re-enactment of the Boston Tea Party, the first event in the celebration of the Bicentennial of American Independence.

After leaving the Boston Tea Party Ship and Museum, turn l. and continue across the bridge to the South Boston side. At the end of the bridge to the l. is moored a former tugboat, the *John Wanamaker*, which has been converted into a restaurant, and on the dock facing it there is a snack bar in the shape of a large milk bottle. At the rear of the dock a large building, formerly a wool warehouse, now houses the ***Boston Children's Museum.**

Admission. From July 1 till Labor Day the Boston Children's Museum is open daily 10–5, Fri. until 9. During the rest of the year it is open Tues.–Sun. 10–5, Fri. until 9; closed on Mon. except for Boston school holidays and vacations (tel. 426-5466).

Interior. The first floor of the building houses the Museum Shop, with children's books, games, gifts, antiques, and reproductions that reflect museum themes.

A stairway leads up to the second floor, where the ticket booth is located. Opposite is the museum's *Resource Center.*

The first room beyond the entrance lobby has on the l. an area known as the *Giant's Desktop*, where children can play with objects 12 times normal size, including a telephone, paper clips, coffee cup, ruler, and spectacles, all scattered about as if a giant had just left them on his desk. Beyond that is an area called *Water Play*, in which small children can splash about with toys floating in tanks and troughs of water.

At the far end of the second floor, are five separate exhibition areas, each with its own theme. One of these is *Small Science*, a rotating series of exhibits demonstrating basic principles of technology using everyday materials; one of the most popular of these is a large frame on which children can create a large sheet of soap bubble before blowing it away. A second area is called *Factory*, in which children can work on a real assembly line to produce "Spree Spinner" tops, which they can then keep. The third exhibition is entitled *Living Things*, which is a natural-history corner of very little interest. The fourth exhibit is *City Slice*, a three-story cross-section of a city street, including a mansard house with exposed construction showing pipes and cables, a sewer catch-basin, a manhole cover into which children can crawl, a cutaway car, and a working traffic light. The fifth exhibit is called *Grandparents' House*, which begins here and extends up into the fourth floor; the area here is known as *Grandfather's Cellar*, exhibiting his workshop and tools.

A stairway here leads to the third floor, with the working kitchen and parlor of Grandparents' House. Next to this is an exhibit called *Work*, in which children can experience something of the working world through role-playing in a make-believe shop called the *Congress St Superette*, and also in a simulated *Health Care Clinic*. Associated with this there is a changing exhibit called *Kids Look at Work*, created by Boston schoolchildren.

A stairway leads to the fourth floor to see the attic of Grandparents' House, where there are Victorian memorabilia and trunks of old clothes that children can try on. On this floor there are also two exhibits that introduce children to the modern world of computer science as well as a closed-circuit television news station with the call letters WKID.

Return to the third floor and walk back along that level of the museum, passing the play clinic and the play store. The first area has a traditional American Indian tepee, and for contrast an apartment which a modern Native American family might live in today. In the next room an exhibition of dollhouses includes some marvelously detailed examples more than a century old. Also in this room are old games that were created and marketed by the firm of Parker Brothers, whose Monopoly is still one of their best-sellers today.

In the next area there is an activity called *Raceway*, in which children can roll balls down inclined planes and around loop-the-loops, illustrating how the velocity of a rolling ball depends on the height from which it starts its motion. Beyond this is an area in which there are exhibited a number of devices and instruments involving mirrors. This is followed by an area called *Play Space*, a castlelike structure in which toddlers can play, slide, and climb about.

The last room at this end of the third floor is given over to an exhibition of objects used in everyday life in modern Japan. Among the objects displayed here are a collection of things that would be in the possession of a typical eight-year-old Japanese schoolboy, including his clothing and school gear, as well as photos of the day-to-day life of such a boy. At the end of the room there is a reconstructed Japanese house called *Kyo-machiya,* a 14th-generation dwelling belonging to a silk merchant in Kyoto, including a traditional Japanese rock garden.

The above is just a summary description of the exhibitions in the museum. In addition to these there are frequent changing exhibits, as well as shows and activities of all sorts; information is posted near the ticket desk and is also given in the museum's monthly newsletter.

Next to the Children's Museum, on the same wharf, is the ***Computer Museum,** which has recently reopened after being closed for a time.

Admission. Winter: open Tues.–Sun. 10–5. Summer: open daily 10–6, Fri. 10–9. Open Mon. on holidays (exc. Dec. 25, Jan. 1, and Thanksgiving) and during Boston school-vacation weeks; fee (tel. 426-2800).
   The Museum Store is on the first floor, beside the Admissions Desk, beyond which is the elevator that ascends to the fifth and sixth floors of the building, which house the museum's exhibit galleries.

The principal exhibit in the museum is the *Walk-Through Computer,* a giant two-story working model of a desktop computer, about 50 times actual size. Using the 25-foot-long keyboard and a five-foot-high trackball, you can run the program *World Traveler* and simulate travel to over 300 cities around the world. Inside, you can see how the different parts of the computer—such as the seven-foot-square microprocessor and giant disk drive—work behind the scenes, as pulsing lights simulate the flow of data through the machine. The *Software Theater* explains how software drives the hardware. Nearby, learning stations let you pursue topics such as how computers are manufactured and how a computer program is created.

Another exhibit is *The Computer and the Image,* which is devoted to the rapidly expanding field of image processing and computer graphics. The computer's ability to create and enhance images is demonstrated through hands-on exhibits, artifacts, film, video, and slide shows. The *Learning Center* is a resource for anyone interested in trying out the latest educational software. The *Smart Machines* gallery is an introduction to the world of computers that talk, compose music, play games, and create original art.

After leaving the Computer Museum, turn r. and walk along the South Boston side of Fort Point Channel, from where there is a marvelous view of the southern stretch of the Boston waterfront, with the massed towers of the downtown skyscrapers in the background. One of the new skyscrapers that dominates the view here, as one crosses Fort Point Channel on the Northern Ave Bridge, is *International Place* on Fort Hill Sq. This complex, recently completed by Philip Johnson & John Burgee Assocs, comprises a cluster of five buildings of various heights and forms, the tallest being a pair of cylindrical towers, 46 and 35 stories, the other three being rectangular structures of 27, 19, and 11 stories, all surrounding a glass-covered court. The square on which International Place stands is named for a fort used by the early settlers to guard against maritime invaders.

On the other side of the bridge turn r. and begin walking along either Atlantic Ave or the new waterfront promenade that leads along Forsters Wharf and Rowes Wharf. This was where the South Battery, or Sconce, was built in 1666; it was also the site of the southern end of the Barricado, the seawall across Town Cove that was completed in 1681. Rowes Wharf is now occupied by a new complex completed in 1987 by Skidmore, Owings & Merrill. The complex includes a luxury hotel, the Boston Harbor, surmounted by an observation tower, with a domed pavilion on the quay by the marina and dock for the airport water shuttle.

Continue along Atlantic Ave to *India Wharf,* where it is possible to walk out to the water's edge along East India Row, passing between the twin skyscraper apartment dwelling known as *Harbor Towers,* built by I. M. Pei & Assocs in 1971. These buildings stand on the site of some of the warehouses built on India Wharf by Uriah Cotting and his associates in 1806, with Charles Bulfinch acting as the architect. On the wharf next to the waterfront tower there is a large abstract sculpture in the form of two pairs of polished stainless steel planes intersecting at an obtuse angle; this is a work of David Schlegell, completed in 1972 and entitled simply *India Wharf Project.*

Next is *Central Wharf,* originally built by Uriah Cotting and his associates in 1816–17, with Charles Bulfinch once again acting as the architect. What remained of the Bulfinch structure was razed to make way for the **New England Aquarium,* built by the Cambridge Seven, opening in 1969. In front of the building is Aquarium Plaza, a cheerful and attractive park with a large cascade fountain in the center. The bronze sculpture at the bottom of the fountain is entitled *Dolphins of the Sea,* a work of Katherine Lane Weems. To the l. of the entrance there is a fenced-in pool in which harbor seals frolic. To the r. of the main building is the *Discovery,* a vessel that houses the Aquarium's sea mammals. Inside the *Discovery* there is a huge theater where dolphins and sea lions perform their astonishing acrobatics. Schedules for these performances are available at the ticket booth.

Admission. The Aquarium is open Mon.–Thur. 9–5; Fri. 9–8; Sat., Sun., & Hol. 9–6; fee (tel. 973-5200).

Interior. The core of the interior is the *Giant Ocean Tank,* which occupies the center of the Aquarium throughout its four levels. This is the largest enclosed tank of circular cross-section in the world; its glass wall is 3.5 inches thick, and it has a diameter of 40ft and a depth of 23ft and contains more than 200,000 gallons of Boston Harbor seawater. The base of the Giant Ocean Tank is surrounded by a huge rock-studded pool called the *Salt Water Tray* containing 150,000 gallons of seawater, with provisions for providing a freshwater environment for some of the exhibits. In addition to the Giant Ocean Tank and the Salt Water Tray, there are more than 70 exhibit tanks lining the gallery walls at the various levels. These tanks are grouped according to saltwater and freshwater communities of fish, and are further subdivided according to the ambient temperature of their environment. More than 2000 different kinds of fish, including the bizarre and the exotic, are on display.

It is recommended that visitors start on the l. side of the ground floor, and from there follow a one-way path along the series of ramps and bridges to the top level, descend along the spiral ramp around the Giant Ocean Tank, and then finally look at the exhibits on the r. side of the ground floor.

On the ground floor of the Aquarium there is an *auditorium;* this is to the r. of the lobby as one leaves. Lectures and multimedia presentations are given here in connection with Aquarium exhibits or about other topics concerning marine life. The Aquarium also has a *whale-watch program,* with a ship sailing from the pier outside to spend a whole day observing whales in the waters between Boston Harbor and Cape Cod. Schedules for this and the program in the auditorium are available at the *Information Desk.*

After leaving the Aquarium, visitors might want to walk out along the N. side of the building as far as the end of the pier, from where there is an excellent view of Boston Harbor, as well as of Long Wharf, the next pier to the N. beyond Central Wharf.

After leaving Central Wharf, walk along the dock to *Long Wharf,* on the head of which now stands the *Marriott Long Wharf Hotel,* completed in 1982. The hotel and the other buildings on the pier stand on the site of the original Long Wharf, constructed in 1710. Beyond the hotel on the wharf is the *Gardiner Building,* a three-story brick structure erected as a warehouse c. 1830 and reconstructed in 1973 by Anderson, Notter Assocs to house the *Chart House Restaurant.* Beyond this is the *Custom House Block,* a line of granite-faced warehouses built on the seaward end of Long Wharf in 1837 by Isaiah Rogers; these were also reconstructed in 1973 by Anderson, Notter Assocs, with the lower floor mostly used as shops and offices and the upper floors converted to condominiums.

The stretch between Long Wharf and Commercial Wharf is the most pleasant on the whole itinerary, with *Christopher Columbus Waterfront Park* connecting the Quincy Market area with the restored dockside, which is paved with large cobblestones and with huge bollards lining the margin of the sea. In the center of the park there is a *statue of Christopher Columbus* designed by Andrew Mazzola.

This brings one to *Commercial Wharf,* which, together with the shops and warehouses that stood upon it, was built by Isaiah Rogers in 1832–33. The warehouses that survived the building of Atlantic Ave and the Central Artery were restored in 1968–69 by the firm of Halasz and Halasz for use as shops, offices, and condominiums, and now give a most impressive appearance to what remains of the old wharf. (Other buildings that were once part of Commercial Wharf are still standing on the other side of Atlantic Ave and will be visited on the return leg of this itinerary.) The dock between Commercial Wharf and Lewis Wharf, the next pier to the N., is now used as a yacht marina, making this the most visually exciting part of the old waterfront.

The itinerary now continues along the waterfront highway, which here changes its name from Atlantic Ave to Commercial Ave. After one has passed the end of the yacht marina, this avenue brings one to the southern side of *Lewis Wharf.*

Lewis Wharf was originally known as *Clark's Wharf,* named after Thomas Clark, a wealthy merchant who built a pier there in the mid-17C. Up until the construction of Long Wharf in 1710, this was the largest and busiest wharf in Boston. In 1761 the pier became the property of Thomas Hancock, John Hancock's uncle, and thenceforth it was called the Hancock Wharf. In 1764 John Hancock bought a warehouse and store on this wharf, advertising in the *Boston Evening Post* that he was offering for sale "a general Assortment of English and India Goods, also Newcastle Coals and Irish Butter, cheap for Cash." That same year John Hancock inherited the wharf from his uncle.

The present Lewis Wharf was built in 1836–40, as were the handsome granite structures that still stand upon it; these are attributed to Richard Bond. During the period 1850–55 Lewis Wharf became a center for the clipper-ship trade with China, Australia, Hawaii, and Europe. As with the other old piers along this stretch of the waterfront, much of Lewis Wharf was destroyed by the construction of Atlantic Ave and the Central Artery, and what remained was restored for commercial use in 1965–69 by Carl Koch Assocs. A very pretty park has been laid out in front of these buildings, beside the marina, with a croquet lawn at its center and a Japanese garden near the seaward end, making this one of the most attractive areas on the waterfront.

On the northern side of Lewis Wharf there is a handsome brick building called the *Pilot House*. This was built c. 1863 by the Union Railroad Co., which originally had its terminal at East Boston, whence ferries carried its passengers to Lewis Wharf. A historical marker on the building states that it was used as a gathering-place for railroad engineers, though its present name suggests that it was later used by ships' pilots, perhaps after the present railroad terminal was built at North Station. The Pilot House stands on the site of a pier that in colonial times was known as *Scarlett's Wharf*, the foot of which formed the northern end of the Barricado. This was the tip of the northern arm of Town Cove, and beyond this point the shoreline ran straight N. for about 300yds before curving around to the W. below the promontory formed by Copp's Hill, just as Commercial Ave does today.

Continue along Commercial Ave, passing *Sargent's Wharf*, which occupies the site of the northern side of the old *Scarlett's Wharf*. Beyond this is *Union Wharf*, on the northern side of which there is a splendid line of old granite warehouses dating from 1846; these were reconstructed and converted into condominiums in 1979 by Moritz Bergmeyer. On the southern side of the wharf there is a line of modern brick townhouses, which suffer by comparison with the much more distinguished old warehouses behind them.

After passing Union Wharf one comes to *Lincoln Wharf*. The wharf is now occupied by the enormous abandoned building that was once the main Boston powerhouse, built in 1907.

The N. side of Lincoln Wharf is bounded by Battery St. This street took its name from the fact that it led to the North Battery, the fortress that was built on Merry's Point in 1646. On June 17, 1775, the day on which the Battle of Bunker Hill was fought, the North Battery was one of the principal embarkation points for the British forces that were being ferried over to Charlestown. After the Revolutionary War the North Battery was abandoned as a fortress, and in 1789 it was converted to commercial use and renamed Jeffrey's Wharf; later still it was called Battery Wharf.

The area on the waterfront a short way beyond Battery St was once the site of the renowned *Hartt's Naval Yard*. This shipyard was founded after the Revolutionary War by Edmund Hartt, one of the charter members of the Mechanics Charitable Association, whose first president was Paul Revere. The most famous of the many ships that were built here was the U.S. frigate *Constitution* ("Old Ironsides"), which was launched at Hartt's Naval Yard on Oct. 21, 1797 (see below).

Battery St is the northernmost limit of the present itinerary, for the waterfront beyond that point has little of interest to offer. But there are a number of interesting buildings and historic sites to be seen on the other side of Commercial St, and so the last stretch of the itinerary will return along the eastern fringe of the North End, going as far as Quincy Market.

Cross Commercial St and turn l. Nearby is the intersection of Salutation St and North St, whose northern end is at this point. The near corner on the r. is the site of a famous tavern of colonial times, the *Salutation Inn*, from which the side street took its name.

This tavern, which was founded no later than 1731, was also called the *Two Palaverers*, from the sign over its door showing two old gentlemen in cocked hats engaged in conversation with one another. The Salutation Inn owes its place in history to the fact that it was here that the political club named the *North End Caucus* was founded in 1774 (see above). This club, which held its meetings secretly at both the Salutation Inn and the *Green Dragon*, was the focal point of American opposition to British rule in Boston, numbering among its members Samuel Adams, John Hancock, Joseph Warren, and Paul Revere. In the period 1774–75 the Caucus held frequent and heated meetings in the Salutation concerning means that might be used to oust the hated redcoats. At one of these meetings John Hancock suggested that, as a last resort, Boston should be burned down to drive out the British, exclaiming, "Burn Boston and make John Hancock a beggar, if the public good requires it!"

The itinerary continues along the r. side of North St. In colonial times this stretch of the road was known as Ship St, for it ran along the head of the wharves, and the bowsprits of some of the vessels must have projected almost as far as the roadway. At the first corner Hanover Ave leads off to the r., leading to Hanover St at the next corner. Hanover Ave was originally known as Methodist Alley, for the first Methodist church in Boston was located there from 1796 to 1828.

At the next corner a tiny byway named Murphy Court leads off l. to Commercial St, and at the corner following Harriss St goes off to the r. The original name of the latter street was Whitbread Alley, for the first bakery in the North End was located there in early colonial times. At the next corner after that North St is crossed by Clark St, so called because in the colonial period it led to *Clark's Shipyard.* This is shown on the Bonner Map of 1722, and was one of a dozen or so shipyards appearing on that earliest extant map of the town.

The far corner at the r., at the intersection of North and Clark Sts, is the site of another well-known tavern in colonial Boston; this was *Noah's Ark,* also known as the *Ship Tavern.* Noah's Ark was functioning as a tavern here as early as 1663, when John Vyal is on record as being its owner, but it seems to have been a well-established institution even before then. Vyal also operated a brewery on the premises, apparently the first to be set up in British America, and his ale was famous not only in the colonies but also in England. The tavern continued to operate until the early years of the 19C, and the building in which it was housed was still known as Noah's Ark until the time of its demolition in 1866.

At the next corner North St is crossed by Fleet St, where on the near corner to the r. there stood still another old tavern of colonial days, the *King's Head.* This inn is believed to have been founded in the mid-17C; it was burned down in 1691 and soon afterward rebuilt. The King's Head is known to have functioned as a tavern as late as 1758, and the building itself survived as a bakehouse till well into the 19C.

During colonial times the head of the Clark-Hancock Wharf extended right up to the present intersection of Fleet and North Sts. This is where Paul Revere lived during his youth and early manhood, above his father's goldsmith shop, which young Paul took over when his father died.

Opposite the head of the Hancock Wharf was the *North End Coffee House,* another famous gathering-place in old Boston. This establishment was opened in 1783 by David Porter, who advertised that his Coffee House was a place where "gentlemen shall be entertained in a genteel manner." His son was Commodore David Porter, one of the most renowned figures in the history of the U.S. Navy, who won fame as the commander of the frigate *Essex* in the War of 1812. Porter was afterward admiral of the Mexican navy and later still was American plenipotentiary in Constantinople (modern Istanbul), then capital of the Ottoman Empire.

The itinerary continues for one more block along North St, then turns l. for one short block on Lewis St before turning r. on Fulton St. Halfway down this block on the r. is the *McLauthlin Building,* one of the gems of 19C commercial architecture in Boston.

This is one of the few surviving buildings in Boston with a cast-iron front, much of it in the form of colonettes framing its numerous round-arched windows, looking more like a Venetian palace than the factory building that it once was. The building was erected in the 1850s as a factory for William Adams & Co., safe-makers. In 1861 the building was acquired by the McLauthlin Co., makers of elevators and other types of machinery. The McLauthlin Co. operated here until 1979, when they moved to Cambridge, after which the building was converted into shops and offices by Moritz Bergmayer. (The building still bears the name of the McLauthlin Co.)

Returning now to Lewis St, turn r. and after a few steps turn r. again onto Commercial St. The block ahead is perhaps the handsomest block in the whole of the waterfront area, lined with splendid old granite warehouses and brick commercial buildings of the mid-19C, all of which have been superbly restored for business use and housing. A short way down Commercial St on the l. is a street named Commercial Wharf N., lined with a row of handsome old brick structures that extend down the length of the block, ending at Atlantic Ave. If one walks to the next street on the l., Commercial Wharf S., the granite fronts of these buildings may be seen. These are warehouses that originally stood on the inner end of Commercial Wharf; they are part of the original project completed by Isaiah Rogers in 1832–33, and were reconverted in 1971 by Anderson, Notter & Assocs.

Continue along Commercial St. On the r. is another reconstructed old warehouse, the *Commercial Block.* Cross Richmond St. On the l. is a huge granite building occupying the entire block, with its front on Cross St and its other side on Atlantic Ave. This is the *Mercantile Wharf Building,* built by Gridley J. F. Bryant in 1857 for the Long and Central Wharf Corporations. The Mercantile Wharf was originally more than twice as long as it is at present, and consisted of 16 contiguous granite warehouses stretching down to the sea. The rest of the wharf was demolished when the Central Artery was built, and what survived was reconstructed for commercial use in 1976 by John Sharatt & Assocs. The main entrance is on Cross St, where one passes into a great atrium that has been converted into a very pleasant garden surrounded by shops and offices.

After leaving the Mercantile Wharf Building, go back along Cross St to Commercial Ave, where the Central Artery can be crossed safely. This leads to Quincy Market, itself once part of the old waterfront of Boston.

8 Charlestown

The present itinerary will take one through Charlestown, principally to see the Charlestown Navy Yard, USS *Constitution,* and the Bunker Hill Monument, but also to stroll through some of the old streets of the town, which is today part of Boston. Those wishing to use public transport to reach Charlestown can take the Orange Line to reach the Community College stop, and from there walk back to the Charlestown Bridge, where the itinerary begins. Those wishing to walk there from downtown Boston can stroll through the North End and cross over the Charlestown Bridge, from the r. side of which there is a fine view of Charlestown and its principal monuments.

History. The site on which Charlestown stands was originally a peninsula; known to the Indians as Mishawum, it was bounded by the Charles and Mystic Rivers and was joined to the mainland by a very narrow isthmus later known as Charlestown Neck. The first European known to have settled there was Thomas Walford, who was probably a former member of the abortive colony that Robert Gorges tried to establish in 1623. In Jan. 1629 a party of settlers from John Endicott's group at Salem settled on the Mishawum Peninsula, which they renamed Charlestown. During their first winter the settlers suffered as terribly as had the Pilgrims at Plymouth nine years before. When Governor John Winthrop and his people arrived in Charlestown in the summer of 1630, according to his account, "they found three score of their people dead, the rest sick, nothing done. . . . The corn and bread amongst them all hardly sufficed to feed them for a fortnight." Nevertheless, Winthrop and his group stayed on for a time in Charlestown, "where the multitudes set up cottages, booths and tents on Town Hill, upon which many perished and died and were buried." Despite their suffering, the settlers in Charlestown gathered in a congregation on July 30, 1630, with the Rev. John Wilson as their pastor, beginning the history of what soon became the First Church of Boston. The suffering continued through the second winter in Charlestown, 1630–31, when some 200 died, by which time Governor Winthrop and many of the settlers had moved over to the Shawmut Peninsula, now called Boston, while others had settled elsewhere. But conditions improved as the settlers built permanent houses, planted farms and orchards, and supplemented their food supplies by hunting, fishing, and trading with the Indians. By 1635 the town government was fully organized under a group of selectmen, a teacher had been hired to educate the children, and a fort had been built to defend the settlement. By the end of its second decade Charlestown was a small but thriving town.

The history of Charlestown in later colonial times is coupled with that of Boston, with whose patriots its people were united in opposition to British rule. Charlestown differed from Boston politically in only one respect, in that its citizens were virtually unanimous in their opposition to the Crown. The sole Tory in Charlestown was Thomas Danford, the town's only lawyer. During the years just prior to the Revolution, the people of Charlestown followed the lead of the patriots in Boston in their rebellious activities, setting up a Committee of Correspondence, burning their own tea after the Boston Tea Party, and cooperating with Paul Revere and his group in keeping watch on the movements of the British troops. The climax of these activities occurred on the evening of April 18, 1775, when British troops began crossing the Charles from Boston to Cambridge. As reported by Richard Devens, of the Charlestown Committee of Safety: "I soon received intelligence from Boston, that the enemy were all in motion, and were certainly preparing to come out into the country. Soon afterwards the signal agreed upon was given; this was a lanthorn hung out in the upper window of the tower of the North Church. . . . I kept watch at the ferry to look for the boats till about eleven o'clock, when Paul Revere came over and informed that the Troops were actually in their Boats. I then took a horse from Mr. Larkin's barn and sent off P. Revere to give the intelligence at Menetomy and Lexington."

After the Battles of Lexington and Concord, on April 19, 1775, most of the populace of Charlestown fled on hearing that the British were retreating in their direction, and took refuge elsewhere. When the battered British forces reached Charlestown that evening only about 100 townspeople remained out of a population of some 2000. A redcoat shot and killed a young boy while crossing the Neck, but otherwise there was no violence during the night, as the British soldiers waited to be ferried over to Boston. Thereafter Charlestown was in a state of siege, along with Boston, as the Continental Army drew a tight cordon around the two towns. Then, on the evening of June 16, a force of some 1200 Continental troops under Colonel William Prescott marched across Charlestown Neck and fortified Breed's Hill. This was the prelude to the Battle of Bunker Hill (see below), which was fought the following day, during which Charlestown was utterly destroyed by a British bombardment.

Charlestown was a ghost town during the British occupation of Boston in 1775–76, with only a handful of townspeople huddling among the ruins. Few of its former residents returned to Charlestown after the British evacuation of Boston on March 17, 1776, for it was feared that the British fleet might return to bombard the town. Only after the British surrender at Yorktown, on Oct. 17, 1781, did the people of Charlestown begin returning in large numbers to begin the slow work of reconstruction. By 1786 the population of Charlestown was over 1000, about half the prewar number, by which time the townspeople had built a new church, schoolhouse, and meeting hall. The climax of this first five-year period of slow recovery came on June 17, 1786, the 11th anniversary of the Battle of Bunker Hill, when the first bridge between Boston and Charlestown was officially opened. The opening of the Charles River Bridge linked Charlestown more closely with Boston, making available greater economic opportunities for its townspeople. This led to a slow but steady increase in the town's population, which was numbered as 2751 at the time of the first U.S. census in 1789, reaching 3500 in 1800, and 4736 in 1810, more than double the prewar figure. The population of Charlestown continued to increase throughout the first half of the 19C, reaching 15,933 in 1850. During the next two decades the population of Charlestown doubled, due to the large influx of Irish immigrants, who in the subsequent half-century were followed by waves of immigrants from other countries. This caused the same kinds of social and civic problems that it did in Boston, some of which still trouble Charlestown today. These common problems, along with the increasingly close linkage of Charlestown and Boston by public transportation and other municipal services, led to a movement to amalgamate the two places under a common city government. A referendum on this proposed union was held and approved in the autumn of 1873, and on Jan. 1, 1874, Charlestown was annexed to the city of Boston.

During the middle half of the 19C the principal employer in Charlestown was its Navy Yard. The decline in Boston's shipping and shipbuilding industries after the Civil War sharply reduced employment at the Charlestown Navy Yard, producing an economic depression there that lasted until the eve of World War II. During that conflict there was a tremendous revival of activity at the Yard, lifting Charlestown temporarily from its doldrums. But when the war ended in 1945 the depression resumed for a time. By the 1950s much of Charlestown was in a state of urban decay, with many of its old houses swept away by scabrous expressways and elevated railways. Revival began in the 1960s, with the establishment of urban renewal programs similar to those instituted in downtown Boston by the BRA. This led many private citizens to acquire dilapidated old houses in Charlestown and restore them to their original condition, so that now in much of the area that was once the colonial town there are pleasant streets lined with venerable houses in excellent repair, with a serene atmosphere reminiscent of old Charlestown.

The itinerary begins at the Charlestown end of the bridge on its downstream side. The area in front of the bridge, now an unpleasant tangle of highways, is known as City Square. This was the marketplace of the colonial town, established here at least as early as 1640. The original area occupied by the town in its earliest years is just inland from City Square and somewhat to the l.; this was where the first crude dwellings were erected by the settlers on the slopes of Town Hill in 1629–30, and where many of them were soon buried. There are several old houses and historic sites to be visited in that quarter (see below).

The first stage of this itinerary follows the red line marking the *Freedom Trail*. This turns r. at the end of the bridge and follows the first street running parallel to the river. A short way along on the r. is a pavilion housing the Battle of Bunker Hill exhibition.

Admission. In summer the pavilion is open daily 9:30–6; in winter daily 9:30–4.

The exhibition features a multimedia presentation concerned with the Battle of Bunker Hill, which includes slides illustrating the history and topography of colonial Boston.

The red line of the Freedom Trail continues along to the main gate of the ****Charlestown Navy Yard.** (One can also go directly to the Yard from the Bunker Hill Pavilion.)

Admission. The main gate to the Yard is open 24 hours a day throughout the year (tel. 242-5670).

History. The Charlestown Navy Yard was established by an act of the Massachusetts Legislature on June 17, 1800, and the following year the present site was purchased. For its first decade the Yard was used primarily as a storage facility, but on the eve of the War of 1812 the secretary of the navy took measures that would make it a shipyard as well. The commandant of the Yard at that time was Commodore William Bainbridge, who in 1813 supervised the construction of both a long wharf and ship-house, a huge structure in which ships could be built under cover. The U.S. Navy's first ship-of-the-line, the *Independence*, was built in this ship-house and launched in 1814. In 1827 work was begun on a huge drydock, completed in 1833. The first ship to be received in this new drydock was the USS *Constitution*, which put in there for repairs on June 24, 1833, attracting crowds of spectators daily. The next large structure to be erected in the Yard was the rope-walk, built by Alexander Parris (1834–37). This is an enormous structure, a quarter-mile long, which produced most of the cordage used in the U.S. Navy from 1837 until the rope-walk ceased operation in 1971. (The rope-walk is still in existence, but it is not open to the public.) As a result of these and other large constructions the Charlestown Navy Yard became one of the most important installations in the U.S. Navy. In addition to being a major repair facility and source of naval supplies, the Charlestown Yard built 23 warships between the War of 1812 and the end of the Civil War, a total that included some of the most renowned vessels in the history of the U.S. Navy during that period.

At the end of the Civil War the U.S. had a large and powerful navy. But the government found itself unable to maintain such an expensive force and decided to retrench, as a result of which the Charlestown Yard was reduced primarily to the status of a repair facility. For the next 60 years most of the vessels built there were derricks, tugs, and oilers. But the threat of World War II changed all of that, and in 1934 the Yard launched its first warship in the 20C, a destroyer named the *Mugford*. The launch of the *Mugford* was the beginning of a tremendous revival at the Yard, and in the 11 years that followed, 150 warships were built or reconstructed there, far more than in all of the previous history of the installation. This brought about a great revival in the fortunes of Charlestown, for at the peak of its activity during World War II some 50,000 workers were employed at the Yard, most of them laboring seven days a week. This boom ended with the war, for the U.S. once again retrenched its shipbuilding activity, and in the postwar years the Yard was used mainly for the modernization of older warships. Finally, in 1974, the Yard was closed altogether. This evoked a heated protest from the people of Boston, not only from those who lost their employment but also from public-spirited citizens who recognized the great historic importance of the installation. The Congress of the U.S. was inspired to pass a law that same year setting aside 30 acres of the Yard as one of the sites in the newly created *Boston National Historical Park*. The principal attraction in the Yard is the USS *Constitution*, which was dry-docked there in 1974 for the complete overhaul she underwent in preparation for the Bicentennial. Since then the *Constitution* has been moored at a dock in the Yard, just across the Charles from where she was launched in 1797.

After entering the Yard, proceed to the *Information Center*, which is at the far end of the long building to the r. inside the gate. (A plaque on the wall at the corner of the building records that this was where the British reinforcements landed during the Battle of Bunker Hill.) The Center provides a free brochure with an excellent map of the Navy Yard. There are regularly scheduled tours of the Yard starting from the Center, and the starting times are posted inside the door.

After leaving the Information Center, turn r. and walk over to the end of the dock, to see the **USS *Constitution*, the oldest commissioned vessel in the U.S. Navy and one of the most historic sites in Boston. The vessel is approached by the little wharf to the r. where a member of the crew escorts visitors aboard for a guided tour of "Old Ironsides." (The crew members are dressed in the style of uniform worn on leave by sailors in the U.S. Navy in the period of the War of 1812.)

Admission. During the summer visitors may board the *Constitution* daily 9–6; spring & fall daily 9–5; winter Mon.–Fri. 10–4, Sat. & Sun. 9–5 (tel. 426-1812).

History. The *Constitution* was built at Hartt's Shipyard in Boston, her keel laid there in Nov. 1794. Construction was delayed because of a shortage of funds, and the ship was not launched until Oct. 21, 1797, with Captain Samuel Nicholson of Boston serving as her first commander. Continued shortage of funds delayed outfitting and she did not begin her maiden voyage until July 2, 1798, when she sailed out of Boston on a shakedown cruise. Her first exploit occurred on May 10, 1800, during the so-called Pseudo-War with France, when the crew captured a French privateer in a Spanish port in the Caribbean. However, they were forced to return their prize when the Spanish government protested that its neutrality had been violated.

The *Constitution* saw her first real combat in the conflict with the Barbary pirates, which began on June 10, 1801, when the Pasha of Tripoli declared war on the U.S. In 1803 President Jefferson sent Commodore Edward Preble to the Mediterranean in command of a squadron of seven warships, with the *Constitution* serving as his flagship. The squadron reached the Mediterranean at the end of Sept. 1803, and on Nov. 20 the Americans block-aded the harbor at Tripoli, beginning a 19-month siege. During that time the *Constitution* was almost constantly at sea, either on patrol or bombarding the harbor and town of Tripoli, as the Pasha's forces put up a spirited resistance. The war finally ended on June 3, 1805, when the Pasha of Tripoli was forced to give up, signing a peace treaty with the U.S. in the wardroom of the *Constitution*. She remained on station in the Mediterranean until 1807, to ensure that the terms of the peace treaty were being honored by the Barbary States, after which she returned to the U.S. for repairs.

The greatest period in the career of the *Constitution* came during the conflict between the U.S. and Great Britain, which began with a declaration of war by Congress on June 18, 1812. Three days later the *Constitution* left Washington Navy Yard to go on patrol in the Atlantic, with Captain Isaac Hull in command. She saw her first action in that war on July 27 of the same year, when she unexpectedly encountered a squadron of five British war-ships, from which she just barely managed to escape after a cat-and-mouse chase that lasted three days. The first sea battle in which the *Constitution* emerged victorious occurred on Aug. 2, 1812, with Captain Hull still in command, when she sank the British frigate *Guerriére* some 600 miles E. of Boston. During the engagement the enemy cannonballs seemed to bounce off the hull without doing damage, whereupon one of her crew exclaimed: "Her sides are made of iron!," from which came the nickname "Old Ironsides" by which she was subsequently known. The next victory of "Old Ironsides" came while she was under the command of Commodore William Bainbridge; on Dec. 29, 1812, she sank HMS *Java* off the coast of Brazil. Her third triumph took place under the command of Captain Charles Stewart; this occurred on Feb. 20, 1815, off the coast of Africa, when she defeated two British warships, the *Cyane* and the *Levant*, both of which she took captive and manned with prize crews. However, the war was already over at that point, although the combatants did not know it, for a peace treaty had been signed in Ghent on Dec. 24, 1814, ending hostilities between the U.S. and Great Britain.

The engagement with the *Cyane* and the *Levant* was the last battle in which the *Consti-tution* engaged, and only 13 years later it looked as if her career was coming to an end when, on July 19, 1828, she was decommissioned. For the next two years the *Constitution* remained moored and rotting at her dock in the Charlestown Navy Yard, and then a struc-tural survey was made of the vessels which showed that she would have to be completely rebuilt before she could ever sail again. The Navy Department decided that she was not worth the expense, after which they announced that the old ship would either be sold or scrapped. This decision aroused a storm of protest throughout the U.S., particularly in Boston, where the *Constitution* was an object of veneration. Then, in Sept. 1830, a young law student named Oliver Wendell Holmes wrote a poem entitled "Old Ironsides" which was published in the *Boston Daily Advertiser*. The poem, which began with the lines "Ay! tear her tattered ensign down, / Long has it waved on high . . . ," aroused an emotional response throughout Boston the day it appeared, and by the following day it was reprinted in newspapers all over the U.S., producing a similar effect. The national response was so overwhelming that the Navy Department was forced to change its decision, and soon funds were appropriated to rebuild the *Constitution*, and to restore her exactly to the appearance that she had when first launched in 1797. The *Constitution* was recommissioned in 1833, and Captain Isaac Hull was once again appointed to be her commander.

Thus began the second career of the *Constitution,* during which she sailed all over the world on various missions, on several occasions being decommissioned for a few years before returning to service. The ship was restored to her original condition by 1930, in preparation for what turned out to be her last extended sailing. "Old Ironsides" began her last and longest voyage on July 2, 1931, when she was toured around the seaboard of the

U.S., stopping in 90 ports along the way, so that the people who had contributed to her most recent reconstruction could have an opportunity to come aboard and see her; 4,614,792 visitors did so. After this voyage of 22,060 miles the *Constitution* returned to what would become her permanent home at the Charlestown Navy Yard, where in 1973 she once again underwent extensive restoration to prepare her for her role in the celebration of the Bicentennial of American Independence. The reconstruction was complete in June 1976, restoring her to the same state she was in when she began her first voyage. Now the only time the *Constitution* goes to sea is on July 4 each year, when she is towed out into the harbor and then brought back into her moorings on the opposite side, so that she will weather evenly, a slow and stately movement that is one of the highlights of the celebration of Independence Day in Boston, with all of the vessels in sight sounding their horns in honor of "Old Ironsides."

The gangway goes up to the spar deck of the *Constitution,* where guided tours of the ship begin. Free pamphlets, available at the booth at the head of the other gangway, give information on the structure and armament of the ship as well as the living conditions aboard her during the War of 1812. Below is the gun deck, where the most interesting objects are the old cannon themselves. One then goes below to the berth deck, where the crew slept and ate and whiled away their off-duty time; this is outfitted exactly as it was in the War of 1812. From there one can look down the ladder wells to the orlop deck, which is not open to the public. The orlop deck was used principally for the storage of supplies, a purpose it still serves today, as well as housing those of the present ship's company who are on duty.

Visitors leave "Old Ironsides" by the gangway opposite the one by which they came aboard. On the opposite side of the dock is the USS *Cassin Young,* a decommissioned World War II destroyer. The destroyer may be boarded any day of the year from 9:30 to 5. There are also ranger-guided tours daily at hours posted by the gangway; these show not only the main deck, but also the bridge, the control rooms of the three five-inch guns, the mess halls, and the former sleeping quarters of the crew. In touring the main deck, notice the plaque amidships on the starboard side; this was placed there by the survivors of the USS *Princeton,* who were saved by the *Cassin Young* after their ship was sunk in the Philippines on Oct. 24, 1944.

After leaving the *Cassin Young,* walk back along the wharf past Drydock No. 1. At the end of the Drydock turn r. and walk to the entrance of the granite building straight ahead; this is Building 22, formerly the pumphouse of Drydock No. 1. The building has been restored in recent years, and now houses the **USS *Constitution* Museum.

Admission. The museum is open daily 9–5; fee.

Interior. The entrance to the museum is to the l. of the ticket desk, while the gift shop is to the r. The ground floor of the museum has a number of exhibits illustrating the structure and armament of the *Constitution,* as well as memorabilia connected with the officers and men who manned her in her prime. A stairway at the rear leads to the second floor, where the first section is given over to an exhibit entitled "Life at Sea," as it would have been lived aboard the *Constitution* during the War of 1812. A feature is an audiovisual program in which the voice of Amos Evans, ship's surgeon, describes the action that took place when "Old Ironsides" encountered HMS *Java* off the coast of Brazil on Dec. 28–29, 1812. Elsewhere on this floor there are a number of prints and paintings depicting "Old Ironsides," as well as a large model of the ship complete with miniature figures of the crew members.

Guided tours of the Navy Yard are given regularly from the Information Center. The most notable site on these tours is the *Commandant's House*, the handsome mansion on the mound directly above the little park in which the flagpole stands. This was built c. 1809; its architect is unknown, but he seems to have been strongly influenced by the style of Charles Bulfinch.

After leaving the Navy Yard, go back along the l. side of the street almost as far as the Bunker Hill Pavilion, and there turn r. to go through the pedestrian underpass to the other side of the highway. After crossing the street, turn r. and follow the red line marking the Freedom Trail, which comes to the foot of Chestnut St. There the red line turns r. onto Adams St; however, the present itinerary goes up Chestnut St to Lexington St, one of the streets bordering the park around the ****Bunker Hill Monument.** One of the entrances to the park is directly across the way, and from there a path goes up to the monument, at the foot of which there is a small museum operated by the National Park Service.

Admission. The museum and the interior of the monument are open daily 9–5 (tel. 241-8220).

History. The first monument to commemorate the Battle of Bunker Hill was built in 1794, erected by King Solomon's Masonic Lodge, of which General Joseph Warren had been grand master. This monument, 28ft high, consisted of a brick pedestal 8ft square on which stood a wooden Tuscan column surmounted by a funerary urn. This monument stood for nearly 30 years, by which time it was in a ruinous state, and as the 50th anniversary of the battle approached there was a general feeling that a new and grander memorial should be built. This led to the formation of the Bunker Hill Monument Association, incorporated on June 7, 1823. The Association's national fund-raising drive raised sufficient money to begin the project, which was inaugurated when Lafayette assisted in laying the cornerstone of the monument on June 17, 1825, the 50th anniversary of the battle. The architect chosen to design and build the new monument was Solomon Willard. Willard's design called for a huge obelisk in the style of those erected in ancient Egypt, to be constructed of massive blocks of Quincy granite. A major problem immediately arose, and that was how to bring the granite from Quincy to Charlestown, for the blocks were far too large to be moved by the means available. A solution was found by Gridley J. F. Bryant, who acquired financial backing to build a horse-drawn railway to haul the granite blocks from Quincy to the Neponset River, from where barges could transport them to the site. Willard was then able to begin building the monument, but chronic shortages of funds halted construction on several occasions, and it was not completed until July 24, 1842. The monument was dedicated on July 17, 1843, with John Tyler, President of the U.S., among the honored guests, who included 11 veterans of the battle. The principal speaker was Daniel Webster, then secretary of state of the U.S., who addressed an audience of some 100,000 people, in what was generally considered to be the greatest oration of his illustrious career. What is remarkable is that Webster had also been a speaker at the laying of the cornerstone in 1825.

In the years since then much work has been done on the site itself, including grading the ground and converting the area around the monument into a pleasant park. A more recent addition was the small granite building attached to the obelisk, which serves as an entryway to the interior and also as a museum, with a few exhibits connected with the Battle of Bunker Hill.

Exterior. The obelisk is 221ft high, with a width of 30ft at the base and 15ft just below its peak. Below the ground there is a foundation made up of 12 courses of uncut stone 12ft deep, while that part of the obelisk that is above ground has 84 courses of smooth-cut granite blocks, capped by a single pyramidal piece of granite weighing 2½ tons. The obelisk stands on an area which would have been close to the S.E. corner of the redoubt that Colonel Prescott had his men construct on the peak of the hill on the night of June 16–17, 1775. Examination of the diorama inside the museum provides a better understanding of the battlefield and how it relates to the present site and monument.

Interior. The interior of the obelisk is in the form of a hollow conical segment, 10ft in diameter at the base and 6¼ft at the top. A spiral staircase of 294 steps goes to the top of the interior, an arched chamber 11ft in diameter and with a maximum height of 11ft. On the sides of the chamber four small windows afford a panoramic view of all of Boston and its environs.

The most interesting exhibit in the small museum next to the obelisk is the large diorama to the r. of the entrance, which shows the whole of the Battle of Bunker Hill, with captions showing how the conflict proceeded during the day of the conflict. Directly opposite the entrance there is a white marble statute of General Joseph Warren (1741–75); this is a work of Henry Dexter (1806–76), a Cambridge sculptor. The Bunker Hill Monument Assoc. commissioned this statue in 1850, and it was unveiled on the site on June 17, 1857. To the l. of the statue two small dioramas show scenes from the battle, and on the l. wall there is a portrait of Major General Henry Clinton, one of the British commanders. In an alcove on that side a watercolor depicts the quarry in Quincy and the horse-drawn railway that transported the granite to the Neponset River.

A few of the main topographical features of the battlefield are identified by markers. An exciting time to visit the site is on June 17 each year, when the Battle of Bunker Hill is re-enacted by Bostonians dressed as redcoats and Continental troops, who fire away at one another harmlessly with their muskets and cannon, a colorful and enjoyable spectacle.

After leaving the museum and obelisk, walk down toward the main entry-way of the site, the Massachusetts Gate. On the mall at the head of the stairway is a dramatic bronze statue of Colonel William Prescott (1726–95), who commanded the American forces at the Battle of Bunker Hill; this was done in Rome by the Boston sculptor William Wetmore Story, and it was dedicated on the site on June 17, 1881.

Story used as his model Arthur Dexter, a great-grandson of Prescott who was living in Rome at the time. Colonel Prescott is shown in the banyan coat he had put on in place of his uniform jacket because of the heat of the day, and he has on a broad-brimmed hat which protected him from the sun as he strode about on the walls of the redoubt during the British bombardment, encouraging his men by his fearless example.

Continue down the steps and leave the site by the Massachusetts Gate. Directly across the way there is an old house bearing the sign *Bunker Hill Museum,* an establishment run by the local women of Charlestown. Exhibits of some minor interest include old prints and drawings of plans and models of the Bunker Hill Monument, some tools used in the Charlestown Navy Yard, prints and photos of Old Charlestown and the Navy Yard, and a few examples of Charlestown crafts.

After leaving the museum, turn r. and walk over to the corner of Monument Sq. Looking to the l. there along Lexington St, notice the last three joined houses just before the corner of Chestnut St. These are the three oldest houses on Monument Sq; with No. 6 built by Peter Hubbel in 1847; No. 7 by George Washington Warren the same year; and No. 8 by Lynde A. Huntington in 1848.

From the corner of the square a short street named Monument Court leads down to Winthrop Sq, an old common-ground converted into a park. In times past this was called the *Old Training Field,* for in the colonial

Marblehead

1. Abbot Hall
Town Hall

2. Jeremiah Lee
Mansion
161 West. St

3. King Hooper
Mansion
8 Hooper St.

1. Salem Maritime
Nat. Hist. Site
Derby Wharf
Pickering Wharf
House of 7 Gab-
Essex Inst Mus
Peabody Mus
Witch Mus.

Stephen Phillips Mem. Trust House 34 Chestnut
Samuel McIntire
N. Hawthorne

Gloucester

1. C.A. Hist mus
   27 Pleas. St

2 Beauport
   75 Eastern Pt Blvd

3 Sargent House
   Museum
   49 Middle St.

_____

Rock

period this was where the town militia of Charlestown mustered and trained. In the middle of the park stands the *Soldiers' Monument;* this is a work of Martin Milmore and was erected in 1876 as a memorial to the men of Charlestown who died in the Civil War.

There are a number of old and interesting houses around the square. The buildings that form the l. side of the square, looking down from the upper corner, are the *Adams Row Houses,* built in 1860. At the far corner of the square on the l. the house at 26 Common St dates to the late 18C. The very handsome house in mid-block at 16 Common St is the *Old Salem Turnpike Hotel,* built in 1781; the elegant dwelling at 14 Common St, the *Arnold House,* dates to 1805. Common St continues around the lower end of the square; the large brick building at No. 3, the second from the corner on the l., is the *Old Training Field School,* founded in 1827.

Continuing along the lower stretch of Common St, turn l. on Winthrop St to leave the square. On the r. there is a row of mid-19C houses and just beyond them stands an elegant Victorian firehouse. The last house before the firehouse (No. 34, but at the time of writing that has disappeared from the door) was once the home of John Boyle O'Reilly (1844—90), the Irish writer, editor, and crusader for civil rights. At the far end of this block on the r. there looms the impressive Gothic edifice of *St. Mary's Church,* a Roman Catholic church erected in 1887.

Continue past St. Mary's and cross Main St.

Down the block, just beyond the church, is the site of the first house ever built in Charlestown, a thatched hut put up c. 1824 by Thomas Walford, the first European settler on the Mishawum Peninsula. Walford came into conflict with the colonists in John Endicott's group soon after they founded Charlestown, and in 1631 he and his family were forced to leave Charlestown. Walford then resettled his family in Piscataqua, now Portsmouth, New Hampshire, where he became a prominent member of the community, and died in 1667.

At the end of the next block, on the r., at the corner of Winthrop and Main Sts, is a large old wooden house of three stories built soon after 1783 by Deacon Larkin, probably on or near the site of an earlier house of his, destroyed by the British bombardment in 1775. It was from Deacon Larkin that Paul Revere obtained the horse which he rode on his famous midnight ride, and he probably set out on his journey from somewhere close to the present corner.

Turning r. onto Main St, one passes a mansion similar in appearance to the Larkin House. This house was built c. 1790 by John Hurd, whose family name still appears on the facade.

At the next corner Main St crosses Monument Ave, which was laid out in 1805. To the r. here there is a striking view of the Bunker Hill Monument, framed by the rising line of houses on either side of the street.

At the next corner Main St crosses Pleasant St, and on the far corner to the r. is the venerable **Warren Tavern.* This is the oldest tavern in continuous operation in the city of Boston, and it is also, probably, the oldest extant building in Charlestown.

History. The Warren Tavern is thought to date c. 1780. A 19C Charlestown scholar described it as one of the first buildings in the town to be "erected after the conflagration. . . . Its large sign, which swung from a high post, bore on either side a likeness of General Joseph Warren in his Masonic insignia as Grand Master. Attached to the house was a large chamber that was afterwards called Warren Hall." King Solomon's Lodge, the first Masonic organization in Charlestown, was founded in the Warren Tavern in March 1786, when Dr. Bartlett delivered the opening address, which would be the first work ever to be printed in

Charlestown. Paul Revere, who had been a close friend of General Warren, stated more than once that the Warren Tavern was one of his favorite watering places, and as grand master he presided over meetings of the Masonic Lodge there. In the autumn of 1789, when President George Washington was visiting Boston, he came over to Charlestown to see his old friend Major Benjamin Frothingham, and while there the two of them stopped at the Warren Tavern for "refreshments." After Washington's death, on Dec. 14, 1799, a procession of mourners came to the Warren Tavern to hear a funeral oration given by the Rev. Jedidiah Morse, minister of the First Church of Charlestown. (Rev. Morse was the father of Samuel F. B. Morse, the painter and inventor of wireless telegraphy.)

Interior. The structure of the Warren Tavern has been completely restored in recent years, and it is now in excellent condition. It has reopened as a tavern, and it is once again a gathering-place for the people of the local neighborhood, just as it was two centuries ago.

Across the avenue from the Warren Tavern, where Main and Harvard Sts join, there is an old three-story building with massive walls of split rocks and quoins of black stone. This building, which is known as the *Austin Block,* was erected in 1822 by General Nathaniel Austin, a state senator of Massachusetts and sheriff of Middlesex County. The stone used to build the house came from Great Brewster Island, which General Austin acquired in 1799. The ground floor of the Austin Block was originally used as a store selling goods from the West Indies trade. In 1827 an office on the second floor housed the *Bunker Hill Aurora,* the first regularly published newspaper to appear in Charlestown.

Continuing past the Warren Tavern, on the same side of the street, one block farther along one sees a cluster of four houses flanking a cobbled alley named Thompson St. If one is standing on Thompson St facing the houses, the nearest one on the r. is the house of Timothy Thompson, Sr., built c. 1794; the one behind that on the r. is the house of his son, Timothy Thompson, Jr., erected in 1805; the first house on the l., with an attractive bow on the alley, is called the *Round-Corner House,* dated 1815; and the one to the l. of that is the *Armstrong House,* built in 1808.

Timothy Thompson, Sr., and his wife, Mary, were one of the first families to return to Charlestown and set up house after the British occupation. Their son was the first boy to be born in Charlestown after the return of the townspeople, seeing the light of day on Feb. 24, 1777. (Susanna Hooper, who was born in Nov. 1776, was the first girl to be born after the return.) All four houses have recently been attractively restored, and their setting on this picturesque cobbled lane gives one some idea of what Old Charlestown must have looked like.

One can now cut through Thompson St to cross Warren St, on the other side of which Cordis St leads uphill. While crossing Warren St, look l. to see the impressive facade of the *Charlestown Savings Bank;* built in 1854, this is one of the most impressive Victorian buildings in the city.

On Cordis St are a number of very attractive houses of the 18C and early 19C; these can be distinguished easily, for their main entryways all face to the side, toward what were once their gardens. The house midway up the street on the l., at No. 16, was built in 1799; the one on the r. at 81B, just across the side street, is thought to have been built in the 1790s, and No. 32, at the end of the block on the l., is the *Francis Hyde House,* dating from 1801. Directly across the street from this on the r., at No. 33, is the *Swallow Mansion,* a Greek Revival edifice (1864), with a huge and very grand entrance portico.

At the top of the hill turn l. into High St. At the first corner on the l., at

Green St, is the *Samuel Dexter Mansion,* erected in 1791. While crossing Green St, look down the way and to the l. to see a large church. This was built as a Methodist church in 1856, and today it is used by the United Church of Christ.

Continue on now until Salem St, the third crossing on the l. The house on the corner, at 100 High St, dates to 1790. As one walks down Salem St, at mid-block on the r. the house at No. 8 dates to c. 1800. The house at the end of the street, to the r., at the corner of Salem and Main St, stands on the site of the *old stagecoach depot,* established in 1790.

After crossing Main St, turn l. and then take the first r. At the end of this short street one finds the entrance to the ***Phipps Street Burying-Ground,** known in colonial times as the Old Burying-Ground.

History. Victims of the terrible first winter of 1629–30 were buried on Town Hill itself, but within a few years a burying ground was set aside at the site here, which was then a little green knoll, around two sides of which flowed the clear waters of a bay on the left bank of the Charles River. All of the original settlers who survived those first years are buried here, along with the townspeople who passed away during the subsequent two centuries. James F. Hunnewell, who wrote a history of Charlestown in 1888, recorded more than 100 tombstone inscriptions dated before 1700, the oldest upright slab bearing the name of John Fownell and the date 1654.

Interior. The pathway from the entryway leads up to the top of the knoll, where the most prominent funerary monument is an obelisk marking the grave of *John Harvard,* after whom Harvard College (now Harvard University) was named. (At the moment of writing, the plaque bearing John Harvard's name has vanished.) The obelisk, a granite monolith 4ft sq. at the base and 2ft sq. at the top, was erected in 1828 at the expense of a group of Harvard alumni, honoring the man whose generosity was so important in the founding of the first institution of higher learning in what is now the U.S.

John Harvard, a Cambridge graduate, arrived in Charlestown in 1637 with his wife, Ann, and assisted the Rev. Zechariah Symmes as a minister of the church. He died of consumption on Sept. 14, 1638, when he was about 27 years of age (the fate of his wife is unknown), bequeathing half of his estate and his library of 320 books to the college that had been founded two years before at Newtown (later to be called Cambridge).

After leaving the graveyard, turn r., then l. at the corner, and then r. again on Main St. A walk of some 200yds brings one to the first turning on the r., Austin St, where Main St and Warren St divide at Thompson Sq. Continue along Main St as it veers slightly to the r., crossing on the r. Union St and then Devens St. Here, at the Austin Block, follow Harvard St as it diverges to the r. from Main St. A short way up this street on the l. is *John Harvard Mall,* a piazza created on what was once Town Hill. Within the mall a number of plaques commemorate some of the events that took place on this historic site, where the first settlers of Charlestown endured their cruel founding years.

Continue along Harvard St. On the r. at No. 16 is a house dating to 1812, once the residence of Edward Everett (1794–1865).

Everett was one of the most distinguished figures of his day, a teacher, clergyman, orator, and statesman. He served in the U.S. Congress from 1825 to 1835; as governor of Massachusetts 1836–39; as minister to the Court of St. James 1846–49; as president of Harvard 1846–49; as U.S. secretary of state 1852; as U.S. senator 1854–60; and candidate for Vice-President on the ticket of the Constitution Union Party in 1860.

After passing the Edward Everett House, continue along Harvard St to City Sq. Those who wish to take the subway back to downtown Boston can walk back to the Community College T station; those who want to return on foot can walk back over the Charlestown Bridge, with a view back to "Old Ironsides" and the Bunker Hill Monument.

9 The West End and the North Slope of Beacon Hill

This itinerary begins in City Hall Plaza, leads from there through what little remains of the West End, goes westward along Cambridge St almost as far as the Charles, then returns along the North Slope of Beacon Hill.

History and Topography. The term West End meant something quite different in the past. In *The Crooked and Narrow Streets of Boston,* by Annie Haven Thwing (1920), the West End is defined as the "section . . . west of Sudbury and Tremont streets and north of Boylston." Today the term applies to a much smaller area: that which is N. of Beacon Hill and E. of the North End, with Cambridge St forming its southern boundary. In the colonial period this part of Boston was sparsely settled and was used chiefly for pasturage, with only a single meetinghouse, the West Church, and just one tavern, the White Horse. The West End was first developed residentially in the third decade of the 19C, after the leveling of Beacon Hill and the filling in of Mill Pond. During the second half of the 19C the West End, along with the North End, was inundated by waves of immigrants, first by the Irish, then by Russian and Polish Jews, and then by Italians. From that time until the middle of the 20C the West End was one of the most vital and colorful quarters of Boston, much as the North End is still today, but then it was totally transformed by the Boston Redevelopment Agency. As Walter Muir Whitehill described this sorry metamorphosis in *Boston: A Topographical History,* a "project, initiated early in 1958, brutally displaced people, disrupted neighborhoods, and destroyed buildings, only to create a vast approximation of a battlefield in the center of the city."

The stretch of Cambridge St that runs between City Hall Plaza and the Center Plaza Building is a modern thoroughfare, laid out during the building of Government Center; this was originally the northern end of Court St, whereas Cambridge St began where the present Center Plaza Building has its northern end. Consequently, the first part of the itinerary goes behind the Center Plaza Building and other modern structures, where a few scattered traces of the Old West End remain. The itinerary begins at the apex of Sear's Crescent. Cross the street to approach the entrance to Three Center Plaza, passing the site of the old Scollay Sq. From the arcade, stairs lead up to the piazza behind the Center Plaza Building. On the l. the piazza is bounded by the skyscraper at No. 1 Beacon St, while at the back it is walled in by the two massive buildings that form the *Suffolk County Courthouse;* the older part of the courthouse, on the l., was designed by George A. Clough and erected in 1895; the taller annex on the r. was built by Desmond and Lord in 1936.

That part of the piazza between the old Suffolk County Courthouse and the Center Plaza Building occupies the site of Pemberton Sq, which was obliterated in the development of Government Center.

This was one of the very oldest squares in colonial Boston; it took its name from Mount Pemberton, the southernmost of the three peaks that constituted Trimountaine, which rose up steeply from its northern side. Mount Pemberton was also called Mount Cotton, for the first to build a house on its lower slopes was the Rev. John Cotton, minister of the First Church of Boston 1633–52. A plaque on one of the benches behind Three Center Plaza identifies the approximate site of Cotton's house. Another plaque records that Sir Henry Vane lived here as well, probably in an annex to Cotton's house. Vane was made governor of the Bay Colony in 1636, when he was just 24, but held that post only until the following year. He then returned to England, where in 1662 he was executed by Charles II as a regicide. There is another historic marker on a bench behind Two Center Plaza; this records that Governor John Endicott lived in a house on that site from 1645 to 1655. The plaque also records that Elihu Yale, after whom Yale University is named, was born in a house on this site on April 5, 1648. Other notables of the colonial period who lived on or near Pemberton Sq or who owned land there were Judge Samuel Sewall, Governor Richard Bellingham, and Peter Faneuil. During the Federal period one of the greatest mansions in Boston stood on the slope of the hill above the square; this was the home of Gardiner Greene, brother-in-law of the painter John Singleton Copley.

There is still another plaque on a bench behind One Center Plaza, with an inscription recording that "on this site once stood the stage of the *Howard Athenaeum,* known the world over as the *Old Howard.* Always something doing from 9 a.m.–10 p.m." The original theater on this site, founded in 1845, took its first name from the fact that it stood on Howard St, and its second name was appended to give the impression that it was a cultural institution, like the nearby Boston Athenaeum. During the 19C the Howard presented performances of drama and opera, but then, in the early years of the present century, it declined, along with the rest of the Scollay Sq area, and it became a house for burlesque and vaudeville. The Old Howard was ruined in a fire in 1961, and soon afterward it was razed to make way for Government Center.

Behind One Center Plaza, and to the r. of the new Suffolk County Courthouse, a passageway leads out to Somerset St. Starting across that street, a pedestrian mall continues in the same direction to Bowdoin St. The skyscraper that borders the mall to the l. is the *John W. McCormack Office Building,* designed by Hoyle, Doran & Berry; built by Voppi & Co.; and dedicated on Dec. 13, 1975. The mall is bordered on the r. by the *Leverett Saltonstall State Office Building,* designed by Emery Roth & Sons and completed in 1965.

As one approaches Bowdoin St, directly across the way is the *Church of St. John the Evangelist,* a brooding edifice that looks more like a medieval fortress than a Christian meetinghouse, with its crenellated tower and walls.

History. The church, a well-built structure of rough-hewn granite, was erected in 1831, and the architect is thought to have been Solomon Willard. It was built for the Bowdoin Street Congregational Society, replacing an earlier meetinghouse that they had built in the West End in 1826, destroyed by fire. During the years 1825–32 the pastor of the congregation was the Rev. Dr Lyman Beecher. Dr Beecher was one of the most celebrated evangelical preachers in New England before he departed for Ohio in 1832, and was an ardent advocate of the abolition of slavery. The Society continued to occupy the church until 1862, when they disbanded, after which the Bowdoin Street Meeting House was taken over by the Church of the Advent, which remained there 1864–83. In 1883 the meetinghouse became the Mission Church of the Society of St. John the Evangelist, which it is still today.

Bowdoin St intersects Cambridge St at the next corner. Cambridge St has been the main thoroughfare of the West End since colonial times. According to the early town records of Boston, the street was first laid down in 1647 as "a highway of twelve feet width through Mr. Stoughton's ground and Thomas Buttolph's to the end of the lots." In early colonial times it was known by various names: "the highway leading . . . among the pastures," the "common way leading to the Bowling Green," and "the way running up to the windmill," and it was not until 1708 that it received its present name.

In times past Bowdoin St opened up into the S.W. corner of Bowdoin Sq, the most important intersection in the old West End, but that vanished during the construction of Government Center. The site of old Bowdoin Sq is the area between the Saltonstall Building and the art-deco structure on the other side of Cambridge St, the *New England Telephone and Telegraph Building.*

At mid-block on the Cambridge St side of the Saltonstall Building is the site of the once-renowned *Revere House,* which in the mid-19C was Boston's most prestigious hotel, unsurpassed by any other hostel in the U.S. The hotel was named after Paul Revere, first president of the Mechanics Charitable Assoc., by whom it was built. Three Presidents of the U.S. stayed as guests at the Revere House during their term in office—Millard Fillmore, Franklin Pierce, and Ulysses S. Grant—and there were a number of royal guests as well, including the future King Edward VII of England. Daniel Webster often used the portico of the hotel as a platform when addressing political rallies held in Bowdoin Sq.

Now cross Cambridge St and walk over to the *New England Telephone and Telegraph Building.* On its facade are two historic markers. Near the center of the facade on the Cambridge St side a plaque honors Charles Bulfinch, the great architect who transformed the face of Boston during the Federal period. The plaque has a portrait of Bulfinch in low relief, copied from a painting done in 1786 by Mather Brown, and below that an inscription stating that the architect was born in a house on this site on Aug. 8, 1763. The first house that Bulfinch designed in Boston was built in 1792 for his cousin, Joseph Coolidge; this was also on the site now occupied by the New England Telephone and Telegraph Building. The second plaque is farther along the Cambridge St side, near the corner. This has a scene in low relief of men in colonial costume playing lawn bowls, and an inscription states that in 1700 there was a bowling green on this site.

This bowling green was apparently a stretch of greensward that sloped gently down from Cambridge St to the Mill Pond, the body of water that separated the North End and the West End. The name of this green for long survived in that of Green St, a road that led off from the N.W. corner of Bowdoin Sq, but this too disappeared in the renovation of the West End. Two prominent men who had houses on Green St in early times were John Welch, who carved the historic codfish that hangs in the State House, and Major Thomas Melvill, one of the patriots who took part in the Boston Tea Party. A painting of the Melvill house and Green St is on show in the Old State House Museum, showing the neighborhood as it was at the time of the major's death in 1832. The only tavern in the West End in colonial times, the White Horse, is thought to have been at the corner of Green and Cambridge Sts.

In a small piazza in front of the New England Telephone and Telegraph Co. there is a commemorative bronze bust of Richard Cardinal Cushing, who served as the Roman Catholic archbishop of Boston from 1944 to 1970; this is a work of James Rosati and was dedicated in 1981.

The itinerary continues along the N. side of Cambridge St, crossing New Chardon St and then Staniford St. The low and very long modern structure on the block between these streets houses the Health, Education, and Welfare Services for the Commonwealth of Massachusetts. This attractive structure was completed in 1970; the coordinating architect was Paul Rudolph, the architectural firm was Shepley, Bulfinch, Richardson & Abbott; with Pederson & Tilney, M. A. Dyer, and Desmond & Lord.

Cross Staniford St. On the r. is the ***Old West Church,** the only Congregational meetinghouse erected in West Boston in colonial times, and still one of the principal adornments of the West End.

Admission. The church is open Mon.–Fri. 9–4:30; Sunday service at 11 a.m.

History. The first congregation to gather on the site of the West Church was organized in 1737. The first pastor was the Rev. William Hooper, father of a signer of the Declaration of Independence, who in 1746 suddenly left the West Church to become minister of Trinity Church. Hooper was succeeded by Jonathan Mayhew, who while minister of the West Church was an outspoken defender of civil and religious liberty. John Adams said of Mayhew's writing that "It spread the alarm against the authority of Parliament and excited a general and just apprehension that bishops and dioceses and churches and priests were to be imposed upon us. If Parliament could tax us they could impose an Episcopal church upon us." John Adams also stated that "Mayhew practically fired the opening gun of the Revolution." Mayhew has also been called "the Father of American Unitarianism," though the Rev. William Ellery Channing was the actual founder of the American Association of Unitarian Churches.

During the British occupation of Boston, Old West Church was used as a barracks by the British troops, who tore down the steeple to prevent the American patriots from using it as a signal post to send information to the Continental Army that was besieging the town. The steeple was replaced after the end of the Revolutionary War, but in 1806 the church was demolished to make way for a new and larger structure designed by Asher Benjamin. From 1806 to 1861 the pastor of Old West was the Rev. Charles Lowell, son of Judge John Lowell and father of James Russell Lowell, the poet and editor of the *Atlantic Monthly*. Toward the end of the 19C the congregation dwindled as the members moved off to new homes in more fashionable neighborhoods of Boston, and in 1892 Old West was finally closed. Two years later the church was bought by the city and converted into the West End branch of the Boston Public Library, a purpose that it served from 1896 to 1960. The building was then acquired by a Methodist church group, and after extensive restoration Old West reopened as a place of worship in 1964.

Exterior. Old West was designed by Asher Benjamin in much the same mode as Bulfinch's St. Stephen's Church in the North End, a structure that had been completed only two years earlier. Like St. Stephen's, Old West consists of a peak-roofed meetinghouse preceded by a towerlike structure with the vestibule below and the clock tower and belfry above, surmounted by a cupola. However, in detail and decoration Old West is simpler in style than St. Stephen's. The only decorative elements in the facade of the tower are rectangular panels of white stone above the lower and upper tiers of windows, the latter framed by pairs of white wooden pilasters, with the cupola carried by pairs of engaged columns.

Interior. The interior of Old West is described by Asher Benjamin himself in his *American Builder's Companion,* first published in 1806: "The size of the house is seventy-five feet square; porch twenty by forty-six feet; to contain one hundred and twelve pews on the lower floor. The gallery is supported by columns of the composite order. The ceiling has a low dome in the center, of forty-two feet in diameter, which rises six feet: the level parts of the ceiling are ornamented with sunk panels." On the rear wall of the meetinghouse are portraits of four distinguished pastors of Old West, each inscribed with his name and the date of his ministry: (to the l. of the entry) Charles Lowell (1806–61); (in the corner to the l.) Cyrus Augustus Bartol (1837–88); (to the r. of the entry) Simeon Howard (1767–1804); (in the corner to the r.) Jonathan Mayhew (1747–66).

Just beyond Old West Church on Cambridge St stands the ****First Harrison Gray Otis House,** the most distinguished and interesting old mansion still standing in Boston. Those wishing to have a guided tour should enter by the side door on Lynde St, the cul-de-sac between the house and Old West Church.

Admission. Open year round Mon.–Fri.; guided tours only, given at 10, 11, 1, 2, 3; groups by reservation only; fee (tel. 227-3956).

History. The mansion on Cambridge St, which was built in 1797, was the first of three town houses designed by Charles Bulfinch for Harrison Gray Otis, one of Boston's most distinguished politicians during the Federal period. (Both of these mansions are still standing on Beacon Hill: the second at 85 Mount Vernon St and the third at 45 Beacon St.) Harrison Gray Otis was born in Boston on Oct. 8, 1765, the son of a wealthy merchant. He graduated from Boston Latin in 1780 and then in 1783 from Harvard, where he was first in his class. He then studied law under the tutelage of old Judge John Lowell, and in 1783 he was accredited as an attorney and counselor of law. Otis saw brief and uneventful service in the Massachusetts militia, in Shays' Rebellion, ending as a major in the Light Infantry. On May 31, 1790, Harry Otis married Sally Foster, daughter of an affluent Boston merchant; a contemporary described her as "remarkable for beauty and wit, as well as for an intellectual vivacity, tempered always by an indescribable grace." By the time they moved into the mansion on Cambridge St, in 1797, Sally Otis had given birth to five children, one of whom died in infancy. Harry Otis had already embarked on his political career, becoming a member of the U.S. House of Representatives in 1796. He remained in Congress until 1801, and then from 1802 to 1817 he was in the Massachusetts Legislature, for six years serving in turn as Speaker of the House and president of the Senate. Then, in 1817, he became a member of the U.S. Senate, a position he held until 1822, and finally, in the years 1829–31, he served as mayor of Boston, the third to hold that office. During that time Harry Otis amassed a considerable fortune in his real-estate and business ventures, becoming one of the richest men in Boston, and he and his wife, Sally, became renowned for their gala dinner parties.

Harry and Sally Otis lived here until 1802, when they moved into a new mansion that Charles Bulfinch had built for them on Beacon Hill, at what is now 85 Mount Vernon St. By then Sally Otis had given birth to four more children, three of whom survived.

The next owner of the mansion on Cambridge St was John Osborn, a paint merchant, who lived there 1802–24. After that the next owner converted it into a multiple dwelling, and in 1834 it was acquired by a Dr. Mott and three associates, who founded there what they described in their prospectus as a "Select Establishment for invalid ladies and gentlemen with their wives." The mansion later became a rooming house, sheltering the poor immigrants who began pouring into the West End in the mid-19C. The mansion was still being used as a rooming house in 1916, when it was purchased by the Society for the Preservation of New England Antiquities (SPNEA), to serve as their headquarters. The Society soon thereafter began extensive work to restore the mansion to its original condition, in its structure as well as in its interior decorations and furnishings. In 1926 the house was moved back about 40ft to make way for a widening of Cambridge St, at which time it was joined to two buildings behind it on Lynde St. In recent years an extension to these buildings has been constructed; this now serves as the headquarters and office space for SPNEA.

Exterior. The exterior of the mansion is a completely symmetrical rectangular block of red brick, with two white marble string courses emphasizing the division into three stories, and with a simple cornice below the shallow hip roof. The entryway is flanked by a pair of engaged columns between pilasters, with an elliptical fanlight above the door and sidelights between the columns and pilasters. Above the entryway there is an elegant Palladian window and above that a semicircular fanlight, all of the same width. These central openings are flanked by three tiers of sash windows, the lower two tiers high rectangles with two sets of three small panes in each of the two halves, while the uppermost windows are squarish and about half the height of those below, with one set of three panes each in the two parts.

Interior. The house is entered through a small courtyard on the Lynde St side, from where a door leads into the small lobby. After purchasing a ticket at the desk, visitors are taken on a guided tour of the house. The rooms on the ground floor on this tour are as follows: first the small room off the hallway which Harry Otis used as a library and home office, then the parlor, and after that the dining room, which are on either side of the broad central hallway. All of these areas, as well as those on the second floor that are open to the public, are furnished and decorated as they were when the house was first built, and the objects either belonged to the Otis family or are typical of those in a Boston mansion of the Federal period. The dining room is particularly elegant and superbly furnished and decorated.

The huge oval table is set for ten places, with wine ready in decanters and bottles of port as well, bowls of fruit down the center of the groaning board, and more refreshments waiting on the sideboard, the last course of a festive dinner, lacking only the jovial presence of the host, whose portrait done in 1809 by Gilbert Stuart hangs above the sideboard. The sumptuous scene recalls the lines that John Quincy Adams wrote to his father, John Adams, in 1816, describing such a dinner party: "It has not fallen to my lot to meet a man more skilled in the useful art of entertaining his friends than Otis."

Stairs lead up to the central hallway on the second floor, approaching the doorway of the front room to the r. On the wall to the r. of the doorway is a portrait of Sally Otis, a work attributed by some authorities to Chester Harding. Also notice the blue-and-white bowl on the table beneath the portrait. This is the famous Lowestoft punchbowl, which sat every afternoon on a table on the landing halfway up the stairway, filled with punch to refresh guests on their way up to the Withdrawing Room.

The Withdrawing Room is so called because the Otises and their guests would withdraw here after dinner to drink tea or brandy, and to amuse themselves with talk as well as with music and games, as evidenced by the spinet, harp, and backgammon board at the end of the room. It was undoubtedly in this elegant room that Harry Otis hung his 17–18C Flemish paintings that Washington Allston acquired for him in Europe, as well as the portraits of his family by John Singelton Copley and Gilbert Stuart.

The mahogany doors at the far corner to the l. lead to the second-floor bedrooms, which are in the ell on that side of the house. The first of these is a small and sparsely furnished chamber, perhaps the bedroom of the nursemaid. The large chamber at the rear was undoubtedly the bedroom of Mrs. Otis and the nursery, since it was situated over the kitchen and was thus the warmest room in the house. The cradle dates to c. 1800, and is probably much the same as the one which Sally Otis used. She gave birth to four of her children in this room during the time the Otis family lived on Cambridge St, and she saw one of her infants die here as well.

The guided tour now returns to the Withdrawing Room, leaving by the door in the opposite corner that leads to the back stairs. Those stairs lead up to the third floor, where the bedrooms of the older children and the servants were located; these are now used for office and storage space and are not open to the public. The back stairway returns to the ground floor, where the guided tour of the house comes to an end. An *Architectural Museum* in the basement can be visited unaccompanied by a guide. It is approached by the stairway to the rear.

The Architectural Museum is housed in *Appleton Hall,* named in honor of the late William Sumner Appleton, founder and corresponding secretary of SPNEA. One notable object here is the pulpit to the r. of the door; this is from the Brattle Street Church and was carved in 1722–23 by either William Crafts or Thomas Crafts, Jr. The pulpit is made of mahogany and is superbly carved and finished; an article in *Boston* magazine on May 4, 1784, called it "the most elegantly finished work in town." The most unusual exhibits in the room are the painted panels on the rear wall near the left-

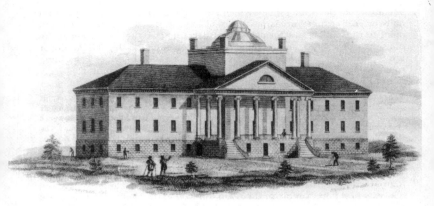

The Bulfinch Pavilion of the Massachusetts General Hospital

hand corner. These are panels from the Clark-Frankland House (see above), and are decorated with painted landscapes. Panels 41 and 43 are possibly works of John Gibbs (d. 1725), and are the earliest known examples in New England of the school of architectural landscape painting that developed in England in the last quarter of the 17C. Also exhibited here is a painting of the Clark-Frankland House itself. Just to the l. of these panels is a finely carved pilaster capital from Charles Bulfinch's State House; this was done in 1795–97 by John and Simeon Skillin.

After leaving the Otis House, return along Lynde St to Cambridge St and turn r.

Until the 1958 renovation of the West End, there was a street just to the W. of the Otis House called Chambers St. In her work on the topography of colonial Boston, Annie Haven Thwing records that in 1733–34 a certain Michael Asher and a tobacconist named Isaac Solomon bought a plot of land on the E. side of Chambers St, which would have included the area just to the W. of where Otis later built his house. Miss Thwing goes on to write that in 1735 Isaac Solomon deeded to Michael Asher the plot on Chambers St, "with all the privileges except the use of the Burying-Ground as it is now fenced in to the Jewish nation." This is the only known reference to a Jewish burial ground on the Shawmut Peninsula in colonial times, but it is not known when or why the graveyard vanished.

The itinerary continues along Cambridge St, taking the second turning to the r. onto Anderson St. Straight ahead at the end of the street is the main entrance to the *White Building,* the central unit of *Massachusetts General Hospital,* and in an inner courtyard to the r. of this is the neoclassical form of the ***Bulfinch Pavilion,** one of the principal public buildings of the Federal period still standing in Boston.

Admission. The Bulfinch Pavilion is approached through the main lobby of the White Building. The hospital and its Ether Dome may be visited any day of the year during daylight hours, except when the latter chamber is being used.

History. The edifice that is today known as the Bulfinch Pavilion was the first part of the hospital to be erected. The first step in the creation of this institution came on Aug. 20,

1810, when a committee of physicians headed by Dr. James Jackson and Dr. John Collins Warren circulated a petition calling for the construction of a hospital to serve the needs of the people of Massachusetts. The petition gave rise to a fund-raising drive that brought in enough money to go ahead with the project, and in 1811 the state issued a charter to the Massachusetts General Hospital. The building committee purchased a four-acre site on what was then the bank of the Charles River, a place known as Prince's Pasture. Charles Bulfinch drew the plans for the new hospital in 1816–17, just before he left for Washington to begin work on the design of the U.S. Capitol. Since Bulfinch could not be present to supervise the building of the new hospital, he arranged for his friend Alexander Parris to be appointed superintendent of the project. The cornerstone of the building was laid in 1818, and Parris carried the project through to completion in 1821. Since then the hospital has been considerably enlarged and has undergone several major alterations. In 1844–46 an octagonal structure was built at the rear of the Bulfinch Pavilion, the original building, and at the same time two wings were added, so doubling the length of the structure. In the past half-century the Bulfinch Pavilion was virtually hemmed in by the White Building and the other modern annexes of the hospital, so that it is no longer a prominent feature of the Boston skyline, as it was in times past.

Exterior. To see the front of the Bulfinch Pavilion at close range, proceed as follows: after entering the lobby of the White Building, take the corridor leading past the l. side of the reception desk; then, after passing the hospital gift shop, take the first corridor leading to the r., which leads into the courtyard in front of the Bulfinch Pavilion.

The Bulfinch Pavilion is made of Chelmsford granite, and it was one of the first large structures in Boston to be constructed of that stone. The hospital is raised on a high basement, and the main entrance is approached by two stairways that lead up to the sides of the portico. The portico is formed by ten unfluted Ionic columns, six in front and three on either side, counting corner columns twice, and above this is the pediment, with a lunette window in the center. Behind that rises the central block of the building, with chimneys at each corner and at the center a huge dome surmounted by a lantern. This dome covers the operating room of the original hospital, the famous *Ether Dome* (see below). The original Bulfinch Pavilion consists of the central section and out past the first six windows on either side, with the wings beyond them dating from the enlargement of 1844–46.

Interior. The Bulfinch Pavilion is entered by the central door in the basement beneath the portico; once inside, climb the stairway up to the top level, where the Ether Dome is entered.

The dome can also be reached from within the hospital, by turning r. on the next corridor past the gift shop and then taking the stairs or elevator to the top level.

The Ether Dome is so called because the first operation in which ether was used as an anesthetic was performed in this operating room. A marker in the room commemorates this historic event: "On 16 Oct. 1846 in this room, then the operating room of the Hospital, was given the first public demonstration of anesthesia. Sulphuric ether was administered by William T. G. Morton, a Boston dentist; the patient was Gilbert Abbot. The operation was the removal of a tumor under the jaw. The surgeon was John Collins Warren. The patient declared he felt no pain and was discharged fully recovered on 7 Dec. News spread from here around the world."

At the side of the operating room one is confronted by a surprising object: an Egyptian mummy in its case! A plaque identifies the mummy as being a male of the 26th dynasty (663–525 B.C.) The mummy belonged to Jacob van Lenep, a Dutch merchant who settled in Boston early in the 19C. In May 1823 Lenep gave the mummy to the hospital so that it could be sent on tour in a fund-raising drive, which netted the institution some $1500.

After leaving the hospital, turn r. at the corner onto Fruit St. At the end of the block and to the l., at the corner of Fruit and Charles Sts, is the *Charles Street Jail,* officially known as the Suffolk County Jail. This fine building of Quincy granite was designed by Gridley J. F. Bryant and constructed in 1850–51. The core of the building is an irregular octagonal structure, from the four large sides of which extend wings, forming a Greek cross. The building is still used as a prison and is not open to the public.

Now turn l. on Charles St, passing the jail, and cross Cambridge St on the pedestrian overpass. Once on the other side, walk over to the S.W. corner of Charles and Cambridge Sts.

The second half of the itinerary returns to the center of town along the North Slope of Beacon Hill.

History and Topography. The point at the corner of the present Charles and Cambridge Sts would have been in shallow water at the river's side in early colonial times, for all of the area W. of Charles St between here and Beacon St is the result of later landfilling operations, producing what is called the level part of Beacon Hill.

In early colonial times Beacon Hill was mostly pastureland, divided by split-rail fences into about a score of fields. The first attempt at real-estate development came in 1725, when several owners of fields on the North Slope of Beacon Hill laid out streets and house plots on their land, which they offered for sale, beginning what came to be called the North Slope village. This development seems to have taken place without careful civic planning, for the North Slope village soon developed into a slum with an unsavoury reputation, and the sailors from the port who frequented its taverns and brothels referred to it as Mount Whoredom. However, after Boston was incorporated as a city in 1822, Josiah Quincy, the second mayor, cleaned up the North Slope village and it became a respectable working-class quarter. Many of those who owned and rented homes on the North Slope were free blacks who worked for the wealthy families elsewhere on Beacon Hill. A number of their houses are still extant, as is the black school and meetinghouse, and these have been organized by the National Parks Service into a *Black Heritage Trail.* The Black Heritage Trail is a walking tour that explores the history of Boston's 19C black community. The tour starts from the Museum of Afro American History, Abiel Smith School, 46 Joy St (tel. 742-1854). A number of sites on the Black Heritage Trail will be visited on this and the next itineraries. Aside from these there are a few other sites of interest that survive on the North Slope of Beacon Hill, and all of those will be seen on the present itinerary.

The itinerary goes E. from Charles St along Cambridge St, passing on the r. a once-charming alleyway named Lindall Pl, now cut through by the MBTA elevated line. Turn r. onto Grove St, beginning a meandering stroll along the North Slope of Beacon Hill. It is immediately apparent that the North Slope is different in character from the other side of Beacon Hill, with its grand mansions along Beacon St; here the houses are humbler and there is less evidence of affluence, with a greater number of commercial enterprises and an appearance of some shabbiness, evidence that this quarter is really part of the West End.

At the next corner turn r. onto Phillips St, which in colonial times was known as Southback St. This and the adjacent streets are among the oldest on Beacon Hill, laid down in 1725 as part of the first real-estate development effort there. The fourth house from the corner on the l. side of the street, at No. 66, is one of the sites on the Black Heritage Trail. The house was built in 1833, and from 1849 until his death in 1889 it was the home of Louis Hayden, an ex-slave who became one of the leaders in the Abolitionist movement in Boston.

After the passage in 1850 of the Fugitive Slave Act, which gave Southern plantation owners legal sanction to retrieve their runaway slaves, Boston ceased to be a refuge for fugitive blacks. Thereupon Hayden and his wife, Harriet, used their home as a station on the Underground Railroad, the chain of safe houses through which fleeing slaves were passed so that they could escape to freedom in Canada. The Haydens reputedly kept two kegs of gunpowder in their basement, saying that they would blow up their home around them rather than surrender the fugitives they were hiding. Harriet Beecher Stowe paid a visit to the Haydens in their house on Phillips St in 1853, while doing research for her *Keys to Uncle Tom's Cabin*, and she was amazed when they brought before her thirteen newly escaped slaves to whom they were currently giving refuge on their way to freedom.

Continue along Phillips St. Toward the end of the block is one of the most picturesque sights in Boston, two narrow alleyways opening off on either side of the street, both of them passing through a series of terraced gardens shaded by trees and vines. The alley to the l. is called Primus Place; the one to the r. has no official name, but it is known locally as Flower Alley. The first of these alleys is named after Primus Hall, a prominent black Bostonian of the Federal period, who in 1798 helped organize the first black community school in town.

At the next corner turn l. on West Cedar St and then l. again at the next corner onto Revere St. The latter corner on the l. is the site of Primus Hall's home, where the first black community school was housed after its foundation. The next house beyond that, at No. 91, was once the residence of Robert Lowell, who, in his *Life Studies*, wrote sadly of how he lived here on "the rim of decency."

On the l. side of the first block on Revere St three extremely picturesque alleyways lined with fine old houses are passed in turn; these are: Bellingham Pl, Sentry Hill Pl, and Goodwin Pl, all of them paved with old cobblestones and lighted with gas lamps, giving them a particularly romantic appearance in early evening.

Cross Grove St. At the next corner on the l. is Anderson St, down which there is a good view of the Bulfinch Pavilion.

A short detour down the l. side of Anderson St may be made to look into Champney Pl, another of the charming alleys in this quarter.

Return to Revere St. A short way along on the l. is another bewitching passage, Rollins Place. At the end of this romantic cobbled lane is a handsome classical facade with a two-tiered portico of wooden Ionic pillars. This is, in fact, *just* a facade, for there is no house behind it, and the portico simply shelters the entryways to the two end houses on either side of the alley.

At the next corner Garden St is crossed, and at the following intersection Revere St reaches its eastern end at Irving St. At the end of the street, in a house that once stood at No. 4 Irving St, Senator Charles Sumner was born in 1811. Turn r. here and then, after a few steps, turn l. onto Myrtle St for two blocks, crossing on the l. Hancock St. Then, at the next corner, turn l. on Joy St; this is the oldest street on Beacon Hill, laid out in 1661 as a narrow lane to connect a hillside pasturage to the Common. A short way down this street on the l. is a delightful little lane named Joy Pl, with old houses on its northern side, and just beyond this, at No. 40–42, are old stables of the 1830s that have been converted into houses. Then, at the first corner on the l. turn into ****Smith Court,** the most interesting byway on the North Slope of Beacon Hill, as well as the most important site for black history in Boston.

The structures on both sides of this short street are all historic sites in the Black Heritage Trail. The house at 46 Joy St, at the l. corner of Smith

Court, is the former *Abiel Smith School;* the impressive edifice with the tall arched windows is the *African Meeting House;* and the five houses on the r. side of the street, Nos. 2–6, were dwellings of black Bostonians throughout much of the 19C. The staff of the Museum of Afro American History offers guided tours of the Trail, which includes 14 sites on Beacon Hill. For information, call 742-1854 or write The Museum of Afro American History, Abiel Smith School, 46 Joy St, Boston, MA 02114.

History. The first African slaves in Boston arrived in 1638, and by 1705 there were 400 blacks in Boston, some of whom had already obtained their freedom. During the colonial period the free black community lived in the North End, but after the Revolution they began moving to the North Slope of Beacon Hill. By that time they were no longer in bondage, for when the first U.S. census was taken in 1790 there were no slaves recorded in Massachusetts, the only state in the Union with a clean slate. Nevertheless, black Bostonians were still an oppressed and despised minority, with virtually no civil rights, and the history of the African Meeting House and the Abiel Smith School on Smith Court records their long struggle to achieve equality under the law.

The African Meeting House, dedicated on Dec. 6, 1806, is the oldest black house of worship still standing in the U.S. It was constructed almost entirely by black laborers and craftsmen, with funds contributed by both the white and black communities. Prior to its opening, blacks could attend other churches in Boston, but they faced discrimination, forced to sit separately in the galleries and denied voting rights in the congregation. Nevertheless, on the day that the African Meeting House was dedicated the general public were invited to attend, with the seats on the main floor reserved for those "benevolently disposed to the Africans," while the black congregation sat in the gallery on that day out of deference to their honored guests.

Two years after the opening of the African Meeting House the black community school was transferred from the home of Primus Hall to the church basement. This was a grammar school and served only the children of the congregation, who along with all of the other black children of Boston were denied entrance to the public school system, though their parents had petitioned the Massachusetts Legislature to permit them entry since as far back as 1787. The city finally established two primary schools for black children in the 1820s. However, the public resources appropriated for them were so inadequate that a white businessman named Abiel Smith left a legacy to the city of Boston to provide for the education of black children. This led to the construction of the Abiel Smith School in 1834 and its dedication the following year, after which the community school in the Meeting House closed. The Abiel Smith School provided education on both the elementary and secondary levels, and it was open to blacks from all over Boston. Nevertheless, a number of black Bostonians, most notably the historian William C. Neill, felt that the Smith School was only institutionalizing their segregation. As a result, Neill in 1839 led a boycott of the Smith School, beginning a controversy that did not end until the Massachusetts Legislature outlawed racial segregation in Boston's public schools, after which the black school on Smith Court was forced to close.

Meanwhile, the struggle for civil rights had politicized the congregation of the African Meeting House, which became known throughout Boston as the Abolition Church and the Black Faneuil Hall. The high point of this political activity in the African Meeting House came on Jan. 6, 1832, when William Lloyd Garrison founded the Anti-Slavery Society there. The black congregation continued to meet in the African Meeting House until the end of the 19C, by which time their numbers had so diminished by the movement of their members to the South End and Roxbury that they decided to close the old church on Smith Court. The Meeting House was then sold to the Jewish community for use as a synagogue, and as such it remained until it was acquired by the National Parks Service as one of the sites on the Black Heritage Trail.

The oldest of the houses on Smith Court is at No. 3; this was built in 1799 by two white bricklayers, and black families began renting it in 1825–30. From 1851 to 1856 this was the residence of William C. Neill, the first published black historian in the U.S. and a leader in the struggle to end racial segregation in Boston's public schools. The other houses on the Court were built at various times in the first half of the 19C, and from then until quite recent times all of them were owned or rented by black families.

The itinerary now follows Holmes Alley, a labyrinthine pathway that leads off to the l. from the end of Smith Court, then turns r. and goes through a tunnel beneath the second floor of a house, and finally emerges on South Russell St. The finest house on this street is the three-story mansion to the r. on the opposite side, at No. 43. This is the *Ditson House*, firmly documented as having been built in 1797, making it the second-oldest house on Beacon Hill.

After looking at the Ditson House, go back up South Russell St and turn l. on Myrtle St, retracing the way to the corner of Joy St. From there continue on to the corner of Hancock, a fine street down which there is a view of the First Harrison Gray Otis House. The oldest house on Hancock St is at No. 20, a little more than halfway down on the r. side; this was built in 1805 and was for a time the residence of Senator Charles Sumner. After it has crossed Hancock the name of the street changes to Derne, passing on the r. behind the N. wing of the State House. On the l. a narrow passage called Ridgeway Lane is crossed, and then, after passing Suffolk University, one comes to Temple St, which has been converted into a pedestrian mall leading down to the West End. Turn r. here and walk up the steps beside the State House, which lead to a large terrace that now serves as a parking lot. In the center of the terrace stands an enormous commemorative column surmounted by the large figure of an eagle.

History. The monument here is a replica of a column designed by Charles Bulfinch, which was erected in 1790 to replace the old wooden signal tower that had stood on the peak of Beacon Hill since the earliest days of Boston. Bulfinch's column, erected to commemorate the winning of American independence, was designed in the Doric order and had a height of 60ft, including the base and pedestal, and it was surmounted by the figure of an American eagle perched on a globe. On the four sides of the pedestal, tablets bore inscriptions describing "the train of events which led to the American Revolution and finally secured liberty and independence for the U.S." The monument originally stood in the center of a park that had been laid out atop Beacon Hill, whose peak was just at about the same level as the top of the State House dome. But in 1810 John Hancock's heirs, who had title to much of the land on which the park was laid out, cut away a large part of the hill so that the earth could be used for landfilling operations. This left Bulfinch's column perched precariously on the half-demolished peak, and in 1811 the city was forced to sell the rest of the park, whereupon the monument was demolished. In 1865 legislation was passed authorizing the rebuilding of the column on the original site, which had been reclaimed for public use. But it was 1898 before the present column was erected, with the four original historic tablets affixed to its pedestal.

After seeing the column, one can continue along the terrace to Mount Vernon St, turning l. there and then r. at the next corner onto Bowdoin St. This goes past the East Wing of the State House to Beacon St.

10 Beacon Hill: Between Beacon and Pinckney Streets

This itinerary begins in front of the East Wing of the State House, near the corner of Beacon and Bowdoin Sts. From there it goes down Beacon St and then meanders along the southern slope of Beacon Hill, including the level area W. of Charles St.

History and Topography. During the colonial period the term Beacon Hill referred to a very limited region around the principal peak of Trimountaine, an area now included within the bounds of the State House. This peak, originally known as Sentry Hill, rose as a steep cone to an altitude about equal to that of the commemorative column behind the State House. From the peak of Beacon Hill, as it came to be called later in colonial times, a ridge extended off to the E., just behind the present Beacon St, terminating in a slightly lower peak, Mount Pemberton, whose site is now occupied by the Suffolk County Courthouse. From the western shoulder of Beacon Hill another ridge ran westerly toward the Charles, rising to a third peak, whose site is just above the present Louisburg Sq. During the colonial period this peak, the lowest of the three summits of Trimountaine, was known by several names, but eventually it came to be called Mount Vernon.

The topography of Trimountaine remained virtually unchanged throughout the colonial period, except for the laying out of the streets and house plots for the North Slope village in 1725. But the situation changed dramatically after work began on the new State House on Beacon St in 1795, when Harrison Gray Otis and his associates in the Mount Vernon Proprietors began planning the development of the large tract of land on Beacon Hill that they had purchased from John Singleton Copley. This was the first step in a series of projects that led to the truncating of the three peaks of Trimountaine, the laying out of streets and house plots, and the erection of mansions by Charles Bulfinch and other architects and builders. In the years since then the quarter now known as Beacon Hill was increased in several stages, the most recent being the filling in of the area W. of Charles St, a gradual process that began in the mid-19C.

On the fence in front of the West Wing of the State House on Beacon St a marker records that the *Hancock Mansion* once stood on this site.

This was one of the most splendid mansions in Boston from the late colonial period until the Civil War. It was built in 1737 by Thomas Hancock, uncle of the future Governor John Hancock, and it stood on an estate that occupied the entire present site of the State House and its grounds. After Thomas Hancock died in 1764 the house was passed on to John Hancock in 1777 by his aunt Lydia Hancock. This was where John Hancock received all of the illustrious figures who visited Boston after the Revolution, most notably the Marquis de Lafayette and President George Washington. Governor Hancock died in this house in 1793, and afterward he lay in state in the great hall of the mansion for eight days before he was buried. The Hancock Mansion remained standing until 1863, when it was demolished by Gardner Brewer and J. M. Beebe to make town houses for themselves.

The itinerary continues down Beacon St. The first buildings seen after passing the State House grounds are the three standing just before the corner of Beacon and Joy Sts. The first of these, at 25 Beacon St, was built in 1925–27 and houses the Unitarian Universalist Association. The next two, at Nos 33 and 34, were erected in 1825 by Cornelius Coolidge, the architect who designed and built many other fine edifices still standing on Beacon Hill. A plaque on the facade of No. 33 honors George Francis Parkman (1823–1908), the public-spirited Bostonian who once lived there. Parkman bequeathed this house to the city of Boston, along with $5 million for the upkeep and beautification of the Common and the other public parks of the metropolitan area. The house also has an interesting literary association; it figured in George Santayana's novel, *The Last Puritan,* in which it was the residence of one of the principal characters, Nathaniel Alden. The building at No. 34 houses the distinguished publishing house of Little, Brown and Co., founded in 1837.

Before crossing Joy St, look up to the row of houses on the l. side in midblock, Nos 1–5. These fine houses, with their undulating facades, are also the work of Cornelius Coolidge, who built them c. 1825–30. Cross Joy St. On the corner at 34½ Beacon is an eight-story apartment called the Tudor, a rather charming Victorian edifice built by S. J. F. Thayer c. 1896. The apartment house is named after Frederic Tudor, whose early-19C mansion stood on this site before the present building. Tudor made his fortune in a most ingenious manner, shipping ice from Boston to the Far East and trading it for goods.

At the next corner cross Walnut St, where on the opposite corner, at No. 1, a squarish mansion with a mansard roof at first appears to date from the Victorian period. However, the Victorian features are from a later restoration, and the house was actually erected in 1804. It was originally built for John Phillips, who in 1822 became the first mayor of Boston after it was incorporated as a city. John Phillips was the father of Wendell Phillips, the renowned Abolitionist orator, who was born in this house in 1811.

Continue along Beacon St. The handsome twin houses at Nos 39 and 40 are entered through the doorway at No. 39. These are the ***Appleton-Parker Houses,** which now belong to the Women's City Club of Boston.

Admission. The Appleton-Parker Houses are open to the public on Wed. 10–4, when guided tours are given; (tel. 227-3550).

History. The houses were built in 1819, both of them designed by Alexander Parris. No. 39 was built for Nathan Appleton, and No. 40 for Daniel Pinckney Parker. Both were men of humble origins who made fortunes before they reached middle age: Appleton as a merchant and as an early investor in the textile industry in Lowell, Mass., Parker in the China trade. They briefly went into partnership, but though this was short-lived their friendship lasted throughout their lives. The Parker house remained in their family until 1863, whereas the Appletons retained theirs until 1886, and both of them had other owners before they were acquired by the Women's City Club, No. 40 in 1914 and No. 39 in 1940. A number of alterations have been made to the buildings since they were first erected, most notably the addition of a fourth floor to both in 1888 by the firm of Hartwell and Richardson. In addition, the Club has amalgamated the buildings by cutting openings in the party wall, as well as making other changes and additions to accommodate the activities of the members.

Exterior. The two houses are mirror images of one another, both internally and externally. They are four-story structures with gracefully curving bows on either side and a flat facade in the center where they are joined, with recessed entryways preceded by neoclassical porticoes.

Interior. Visitors are asked to sign in at the desk in the reception room to the r. of the entryway; while waiting for the guided tour to begin, one can sit in the room just across the hallway, a pleasant oval chamber looking out over the Common. Noteworthy features in this room are: the mahogany doors curved to fit the convexity of the walls, the twin mirrors, and the fine chandeliers, which in their time provided illumination by burning whale oil, then gas, and were finally fitted with electric bulbs. Also notice the few panes of purple glass in the windows; this dates them to 1818–25, when imported glass from Europe contained manganese oxide that caused them to take on this purple hue when exposed to sunlight. Only four other houses in Boston still have genuine purple panes, three of them on Beacon St and one on Chestnut St.

The guided tour begins in the central hallway, which is still paved with its original black-and-white checkuerboard stone flooring. To the r. is the superb spiral staircase, the most beautiful on Beacon Hill. Notice the "peace button" in the navel of the banister at the ground floor; this is put in place only after the mortgage of a house has been paid. At the end of the hallway to the l. is the kitchen, equipped with its original fireplace and a Rumford oven.

On the second floor are the elegant drawing rooms of the twin houses, with superb views out over the Common. Noteworthy features of these rooms are the curved wooden sliding doors, the panes of purple glass in the front windows, and the handsome fireplaces. In the drawing room at 39 Beacon St on July 13, 1843, Henry Wadsworth Longfellow married Frances (Fanny) Appleton, with the bride and groom standing before the fireplace as they took their vows.

As one continues down Beacon St, the next house of note is the *Sears Mansion*, a double building whose main entrance is presently at No. 42. The original mansion, a free-standing structure of two stories with a domed roof, was built in 1819–22 for Colonel David Sears by Alexander Parris. Originally the mansion only had one bay at the center of its facade. In 1832 the house was rebuilt in its present form, with a third story added, and with two semicircular bays built to flank the flat central section of the facade. Today the Sears Mansion houses the *Somerset Club*, which also occupies the two houses on either side, at Nos 41 and 43. The Somerset is the oldest club in Boston; it began as the Tremont Club in the 1840s, and was incorporated under its present name in 1851. On the l. side of the wall in front of the main mansion an inscription records that on this site stood the house of John Singleton Copley, the painter.

Farther along the block is No. 45 Beacon St, another of the great mansions of Beacon Hill. This is the *Third Harrison Gray Otis House,* now occupied by the American Meteorological Society; unfortunately it is not open to the public.

History. The house was built for Harrison Gray Otis in 1805–6 by Charles Bulfinch, the third of the three mansions that the architect designed for him. Otis moved into this mansion with his family in 1806, and he lived there until his death in 1848. During that period Otis served in the State Legislature (1802–16), in the U.S. Senate (1816–22), and finally as mayor of Boston (1829–31). While they lived here Otis and his wife, Sally, gave some of the grandest dinner parties and balls in the social history of Boston, one of the most notable being a reception for President James Monroe in 1817. After Otis died the house passed on to a succession of owners before the American Meteorological Society acquired it in 1951, after which it was extensively restored.

Exterior. The mansion was originally a free-standing house, with a large garden to the r. Then, in 1831, Otis erected an annex in the garden, the present house at No. 44. The mansion at No. 45 has the least elaborate facade of the three houses that Bulfinch built for Otis, the most prominent feature being the neoclassical portico before the front door, flanked by two pairs of Ionic columns. At the l. of the house a cobbled driveway leads to what was once the carriage entrance, and beyond that to the stables at the rear.

After crossing Spruce St, one sees on the facade of No. 50 the following inscription: "Rev. William Blaxton, born Horncastle parish, Lincolnshire, England, 5 March 1596; graduate of Emanuel College, England, 1621, first settler of Shawmut, 1625. Near here stood his dwelling. He removed to Rhode Island 1635, where he died May 29, 1675. 'The Place of his Seclusion became a Great City.' "

The next notable mansion is No. 55, the ***Prescott House,** now the headquarters of the Colonial Dames of America.

Admission. The Prescott House is open Wed. 10–4 or by appointment; fee.

History. The house at No. 55 was one of a pair of twin mansions (the other being No. 54), built in 1807–8 by Asher Benjamin for James Smith Colburn, a wealthy entrepreneur who lived here only until 1819. Over the next quarter-century the mansion passed on to two other owners in succession, and then, in 1845, it was acquired by William Hickling Prescott, the historian, after whom the house is named.

Prescott was born in Salem, Mass. on May 4, 1796, and graduated from Harvard in 1814. While an undergraduate at Harvard, he lost the sight of his left eye during a fracas in the college dining hall, an injury which soon affected his other eye as well, leaving him nearly blind for the rest of his life. Despite this handicap, Prescott was determined to become a writer, and his friend George Ticknor influenced him to pursue a career in Spanish and Latin American studies. The first fruits of his researches in this field came in 1837, with the publication of his three-volume opus, *The Reign of Ferdinand and Isabella*. This was followed by *The Conquest of Mexico* (1843), *A History of the Conquest of Peru* (1847), and finally the first two volumes of his unfinished work, *A History of the Reign of Philip the Second* (1855–58). Prescott died in his house on Beacon St on Jan. 29, 1859, and he was buried in the family vault under St. Paul's Cathedral on Tremont St. After his death the mansion passed on to a succession of owners before it was purchased by the Colonial Dames of America in 1944. Since then that organization has restored it to its original external appearance, as well as renewing the interior and furnishing with objects of the early 19C.

Exterior. The Prescott House and its mirror image at No. 54 are elegant examples of the Beacon Hill mansions of the early 19C, with two symmetrical curving bays flanking a flat central section in which the two entryways are placed, side by side. A wrought-iron balcony carried on slender columns extends along the facade at the second story, and above that four pilasters rise to the cornice, framing the three sections of the twin mansion. Mounted on the facade to the l. of the entryway to No. 55 are three bronze plaques. The uppermost plaque was presented to the Colonial Dames in May 1964, when the house was registered as a national landmark; the one in the middle is a bas-relief portrait of Prescott, done by the sculptor Joseph A. Colletti; and the lower one was presented by the government of Peru, honoring Prescott for his great history of the early days of their country. The two lower plaques were dedicated on Jan. 28, 1959, the centennial of Prescott's birth.

Interior. To the l. of the entrance hall is a lovely oval room, a chamber created by Asher Benjamin to take advantage of the rounded bay of the facade; this originally served as the dining room, but after the Colonial Dames acquired the house it was converted into a library. Another change made by the Colonial Dames is the circular staircase that takes one to the upper floors; this is a modern replacement of the one built by Asher Benjamin, which was somewhat narrower. (The twin of the original staircase survives in No. 54.)

At the front of the house on the second floor is the handsome drawing room, which extends the full width of the mansion, with a marvelous view of the Common. The only surviving elements of the original structure are the long sash windows and the marble chimneypiece, which is carved in the Adam style. The portrait of George Washington is by Rembrandt Peale, a copy made by the artist of his own original work.

Behind the drawing room is the chamber that originally served as the dining room. During the years that Prescott occupied the house, this was used as a sitting room and library, which the historian described as being "big enough to hold all my literary treasures."

Take the stairs to the third floor. At the front of the house is the "Best Chamber," another elegant room with a sweeping view of the Common. The middle room on this floor was the rear chamber of the original house, and beyond this is a wing added by Prescott in 1845–46. The first room entered in this wing was the anteroom to Prescott's study. On display here is a marble bust of Prescott done in 1844 by Richard A. Greenough, along with first editions of the historian's works. There is also a photograph of the Prescott Swords, which originally hung above the door to the study.

One of these was a sword that Prescott inherited from his grandfather Colonel William Prescott, who wore it when he commanded the American forces at the Battle of Bunker Hill; the other one had been passed on to his wife by her grandfather Captain John Linzee, who had it on when he commanded the British sloop *Falcon,* which bombarded the American redoubt in that same battle. William Makepeace Thackeray saw these swords when he called on Prescott during his visit to Boston in 1852, and they inspired him to write *The Virginians,* his novel about two brothers who fought on opposite sides during the American Revolution. The swords are now in the Massachusetts Historical Society.

The Prescott Study was faithfully restored and refurbished in 1968, and now looks exactly as it did when the historian worked here. The restoration was documented largely from a woodcut illustration in George Ticknor's biography, *The Life of Prescott;* a copy of this print is on display in the study.

Prescott himself describes this room in these lines: "Over my present library is my study, which I reach by a private staircase that I enter through a secret door contrived in the bookcase. This study is where I do my work . . . and to this little sanctuary I transfer the books only in immediate use and which I am daily examining."

Also in the study is a Noctograph, a device that Prescott used to aid him in writing his manuscripts, which in final draft were transcribed by his secretary.

The twin of the Prescott House, at No. 54, is not open to the public. As noted above, this was built in 1807–8 by Asher Benjamin for James Colburn. After the house was built Colburn sold it to Nathan Appleton; the Appletons lived there until 1819, when they moved to their new home at 39 Beacon St. The house at 54 Beacon St then became the property of William Appleton, Nathan Appleton's cousin. The house next door, at 53 Beacon St, was built in 1855 by still another Appleton.

The pair of mansions just beyond the Prescott House, at Nos 56 and 57, were built in 1819 by Ephraim Marsh, two of seven houses that he erected on Beacon Hill within five years. The next house of interest after this is No. 61; attributed to Peter Banner, architect of the Park Street Church, it was built c. 1817.

As one continues along, the next two houses of interest are Nos. 63 and 64. These were also built by Ephraim Marsh, erected in 1824. The two buildings now serve as the Rectory and Church House of King's Chapel. Note the panes of purple glass in the windows of No. 63, whose color dates them to the original construction in 1824.

At the near corner of Beacon and Charles Sts there is a large and stately building with entrances at Nos 61 and 62; this was completed in 1890 by the New York architectural firm of McKim, Mead & White, who designed the original structure of the Boston Public Library at Copley Sq.

Cross Charles St, entering the so-called level part of Beacon Hill, all of which is filled-in land. A few steps farther along, cross River St, where one might pause to look at a block of six distinguished mansions, Nos 70—75. These were erected by the Mount Vernon Proprietors in 1828 on what was then the eastern end of Mill Dam, which had been completed seven years earlier, blocking off Back Bay from the waters of the Charles River estuary. All of these houses were designed and built by Asher Benjamin. Notice the lovely oriel window on the r. side of the second floor at No. 70; this is a later addition, but it adds considerably to the charm of the building.

Continue down Beacon St and take the next r. onto Brimmer St, the main N.-S. street in the level part of Beacon Hill. There are many charming recycled stables and coach houses in the level part of the Hill, especially on lower Chestnut St, which is known locally as "Horse Chestnut Street"; there are also early frame houses on Beaver Pl, along with chic London mews there and on Byron St, all of which give this quarter a charming atmosphere. First on the r. is Byron St, then on the l. Beaver Pl, after which Brimmer intersects Chestnut St. Lime St then opens off to the r., and on the l. is an L-shaped byway known as Otis Pl. This brings one to the intersection of Brimmer and Mount Vernon Sts, where on the far corner to the r. stands the ***Church of the Advent,** one of the two distinguished houses of worship on the level part of Beacon Hill.

History: The present building is the fifth home of the Church of the Advent, which was founded in 1844 by a group of High Church Episcopalians influenced by the Oxford movement, and which occupied the Bowdoin Street Meeting-House in 1864—83. The design of the present church began in 1878 and was finished in all its essentials by 1883, though work on details continued for nearly a decade afterward.

Architecture: The Church of the Advent is a High Victorian version of Early English Gothic; it was designed by John Hubbard Sturgis, who was a devoted parishioner and a friend of Street and Pearson, and knew well the works of Butterfield and other Victorian Gothicists. When Sturgis died in 1888 his nephew, Clipston Sturgis, finished certain parts that remained undone: the W. porch, the baptistry, and the Sunday-school chapel. Right from the beginning, Sturgis commissioned the finest artificers of the day to decorate and furnish the church. Charles Kemble, Clayton and Bell, and later Christopher Whall, all English, did the stained glass. Ralph Adams Cram and his partner Bertram Grosvenor Goodhue later did the decorative woodwork in the Lady Chapel, the reredos screen of the two chapels, the great Rood, etc. Frank Wills, architect of the cathedral at Fredericton, New Brunswick, had designed an altar and font for the chapel in early years for a building on Green St. These are now all in the All Saints Chapel and baptistry of the Brimmer St. building. Henry Vaughan, designer of many American churches and the National Cathedral in Washington, D.C., designed the pulpit, a chalice-shaped structure of carved oak. Clipston Sturgis designed an elaborate stone lectern. He preferred a later period of Gothic than his uncle did, and the parts of the church done by Clipston Sturgis are all in the decorated English Gothic style. Isabella Stewart Gardner gave the reredos of French Caen stone behind the high altar, which was designed and carved in England by Harold Peto and Sir Ernest George. The belfry contains one of only two real rings of bells in Boston. The Changes are rung on Sundays and for special observances of the church calendar.

The house at 44 Brimmer St, directly across the street from the church, was the lifelong residence of Admiral Samuel Eliot Morison (1887—1976), the historian.

Admiral Morison was a prolific scholar and writer, the author of more than 50 books, the majority of them on maritime history. Two of his biographical works, one on Christopher Columbus (1943) and the other on John Paul Jones (1960), won Pulitzer Prizes in history. In 1962 Admiral Morison published an autographical work called *One Boy's Boston,* in which he gives a pleasant picture of what life was like in this neighborhood at the turn of the century.

Just across the street, at 6 Otis Pl, is a house where Justice Louis D. Brandeis lived early in his career. Brandeis was appointed to the U.S. Supreme Court in 1916 by President Woodrow Wilson, the first person of the Jewish faith ever to become a member of that tribunal. Brandeis served as an associate justice of the Court until his retirement in 1939, when he was hailed for his outstanding record for defending the civil rights of citizens against big business and big government.

A short way down the street from the Church of the Advent, at 131 Mount Vernon, is a house where Henry James lived for a time in the 1870s; it was here that he finished his novel *Daisy Miller.*

The itinerary continues along the last stretch of Brimmer St, a long and pleasant block that ends at Pinckney St. A number of distinguished figures also lived on this block. The Whitney Hale Parish House of the Church of the Advent covers the site of a house that was once No. 26 Brimmer St, which was for long the residence of Mark Antony DeWolfe Howe (1864–1960), editor and author.

In his remarkably long life Mark Howe wrote some 50 books, including works on history, biography, and the topography of Boston, as well as collections of verse. One of his books, a biography of Barrett Wendell, won a Pulitzer Prize in 1924. His daughter, the novelist Helen Howe, wrote a biography of her father entitled *The Gentle Americans,* in which she gives an evocative description of her father and the brilliant circle of writers and scholars that gathered around him in their house on Brimmer St, and in later years in their subsequent residence on Louisburg Sqe.

Continuing along Brimmer St: at Nos 7–9, on the l., near the end of the block, is the former residence of Admiral Richard Evelyn Byrd (1888–1957), explorer, scientist, author, and aviator, the first person to fly over both the North and South Poles of the planet.

After one has reached the corner of Brimmer and Pinckney, a brief detour of some interest, to the northern end of this narrowing neighborhood between Charles St and Embankment Rd, may be made. To do so, turn l. at Pinckney and then r. on the corner, following Embankment Rd as it crosses Revere St. A few steps past that corner is Charles River Sq, a pretty ring of houses shielded from the city around it, with a covered passage leading out to Revere St. Farther along Embankment Rd is West Hill Pl, an equally secluded and very quaint ring of houses at the end of a passage. A covered passageway at the rear of West Hill Pl leads through a garage and out to Charles St. Just to the N. of the garage the forlorn little garden once belonged to the house at 148 Charles St, now long vanished. This was the residence of Jamie Fields and his wife, Annie, which in the mid-19C was the meeting place for all of the leading writers and intellectuals in Boston, as well as British guests such as Dickens, Thackeray, and Matthew Arnold. One notes with some nostalgia that the flowers in the garden of 148 Charles St were planted for Annie Fields by Henry Wadsworth Longfellow.

A number of members of the Fieldses' literary salon lived close by on Charles St, although most or all of their former residences have either vanished or been replaced by more modern structures. Oliver Wendell Holmes, Sr., lived at No. 164 for a time; Thomas Bailey Aldrich resided at No. 131 in 1871–81; and No. 127 was the home of Lucretia Hale (1820–1900), sister of Edward Everett Hale and the author of humorous books for children, the best known of which is *The Peterkin Papers.*

The itinerary now resumes, going S. along Charles St. Charles St is the main N.-S. thoroughfare of Beacon Hill and the center of its fashionable commercial life, lined with luxury shops, eating places, and bars.

Strolling along the avenue, passing Revere and then Pinckney Sts, one crosses to the S.W. corner of Charles and Mount Vernon, where stands the ***Charles River Meeting House,** the other distinguished old church in the level part of Beacon Hill.

History. The Charles Street Meeting House was built in 1807 by Asher Benjamin for the congregation of the Third Baptist Church. This congregation was formed by dissidents from the First and Second Baptist Churches, and it was formally established on Aug. 25, 1807, the day on which the meetinghouse was dedicated. Charles St at that time was right on the Charles, and those being baptized could be immersed directly in the river. Soon after the Third Baptist Church founded its congregation was involved in a dispute with that of the African Meeting House. The latter congregation claimed that they were in fact the Third Baptist Church of Boston, and so the other group changed their name to the Charles Street Baptist Church. The Charles Street Church early on became deeply involved in the Abolitionist movement, and dissident members of the congregation broke away to form the First Baptist Free Church, which became Tremont Temple, the first racially integrated church in the U.S. Meanwhile, the Charles Street Church had become a forum for leaders in the Abolitionist movement, and from its pulpit spoke such renowned orators as William Lloyd Garrison, Wendell Phillips, Frederick Douglass, and Sojourner Truth. After the Civil War the black population of Beacon Hill had increased to the point where their community needed another place of worship, and in 1876 the Charles Street Meeting House was purchased by the African Methodist Episcopal Society (AME), a black church founded in 1782. The meetinghouse was slated for demolition in 1920, because it stood in the way of a planned widening of Charles St, but members of the congregation and other public-spirited residents of Beacon Hill raised funds to have it moved out of the way. The AME abandoned the Charles Street Meeting House in 1939 to move to a new church in Roxbury. At that time the church was purchased by the Charles Street Meeting House Society, which was formed to preserve the edifice. Later the meetinghouse was occupied in turn by the Albanian Orthodox Church of St. John the Evangelist, and then by the Unitarian Universalists. After the latter group moved on, the church was closed for conversion to commercial use, which was completed in 1982 by the firm of John Sharratt Assocs.

Exterior. Asher Benjamin designed the Charles Street Meeting House on the same general plan as the West Church, which he had completed just a year earlier—i.e., a meetinghouse with a peaked roof and a towerlike structure in front topped by the belfry and spire. The structure that one sees today differs only slightly from the original. What changes there are took place during a reconstruction in the 1850s, when new rooms were created partly below street level. This necessitated raising the main floor by several feet, slightly increasing the pitch of the roof, and redesigning the windows, so that the upper panes were made taller and the lower ones shorter.

Interior. During the recent conversion the interior of the meetinghouse was gutted, and today it houses shops and offices. Although one regrets the loss of this historic interior, the restoration was skillfully and tastefully done, and many of the architectural elements of the church are still visible, incorporated into the modern structure.

After leaving the meetinghouse, continue along Charles St and turn l. at the next corner onto Chestnut St. This is one of the most attractive streets in the city, and many of the houses date to the original period of the development of Beacon Hill by the Mount Vernon Proprietors in the early 19C. The first of the original houses are on the l., at Nos 61 and 59; these were both built in 1824 by the housewright Bela Stoddard, perhaps to plans drawn by Jesse Shaw. The first four houses on the r. side of the street after the corner, Nos 76–70, were all erected in 1828 by Cornelius Coolidge.

On the l. one crosses Cedar Lane Way. This is a very picturesque narrow lane that passes between the backs of the buildings on Charles St and West Cedar St, with smaller houses of its own erected on what were once the back gardens of those dwellings.

After one has crossed Cedar Lane Way, on the l. at No. 57A is a double building dating to 1827–28. Since 1892 this has been the home of the ***Harvard Musical Assoc.** founded in 1837 by several graduates of Harvard University who had taken part in the musical activities there.

One of the first things the members did was to collect musical scores and books on music, establishing the first music library in the U.S., an institution which today is one of the finest in the country. When the Association settled into their present quarters on Beacon Hill in 1892 they celebrated with a gala reception graced by the presence of the Czech composer Antonín Dvořák. The building was renovated in 1907, and in 1913 the beautiful Marsh Room was created by a legacy from Julia M. Marsh, widow of one of the founders of Jordan-Marsh Co. Visitors are welcome to browse in the library, and they are invited to attend the free concerts of the Harvard Musical Assoc.; for information call 523-2897.

On the r. side of the street, the four houses at Nos 68–62 were originally built by the housewrights Lincoln and Hezekiah Stoddard in the period 1811–17; those at Nos 64 and 62 were burned down in 1824, but the Stoddards rebuilt them within two years.

The houses on the l. side of Chestnut between West Cedar and Willow were all built in 1827–30. The building at No. 51 was for eight years the residence of the Rev. Charles Lowell, minister of Old West Church; his son, the poet James Russell Lowell, spent part of his childhood here. The house at No. 43 was for many years the home of Richard Henry Dana, author of *Two Years Before the Mast*.

On the r. side of Chestnut St, the six houses at Nos 60–50 were built in 1824 by Cornelius Coolidge for John Hubbard. The house at No. 52 was purchased early this century by Ralph Adams Cram, the architect and writer. A plaque at No. 50 commemorates the fact that from 1863 to 1895 this was the residence of Francis Parkman, the historian. Parkman's major works, all of them written while he lived here, are: *The Jesuits in North America in the Seventeenth Century* (1867); *The Discovery of the Great West* (1869); *Montcalm and Wolfe* (1884); and *A Half-Century of Conflict* (1892).

The house at No. 48, which may have been erected by the housewright Ephraim Marsh, was built c. 1822 for Mrs Hepzibah Swan. Mrs Swan was the only woman to become a member of the Mount Vernon Proprietors, buying into the syndicate about a decade after it was formed. This is one of eight houses that Mrs. Swan erected on Chestnut St, some of them given as presents to her daughters. The next of the original houses on this side are Nos 44, built by Jeremiah Marsh in 1810, and 42, erected in 1808 for John Howe.

After one has crossed Willow St, the first noteworthy house on the l. side of Chestnut is at No. 29A. This house and the others between it and Willow St stand on the site of a mansion erected in 1799 by Benjamin Joy, one of the original Mount Vernon Proprietors. This mansion burned down soon after completion, and the present house at 29A was erected sometime during the period 1800–2, with Charles Bulfinch thought to have been the architect. The bow front was added c. 1817, as evidenced by the different style of its brickwork and the purple panes of glass in the windows on that

The intersection of Chestnut and Walnut Sts

side. The house and its neighbor at No. 29B share a particularly pretty garden, one of the few on Beacon Hill that can be seen from the street. In 1883 the house at 29A became the residence of Edwin Booth, the tragedian, whose brother John Wilkes Booth had assassinated President Abraham Lincoln in 1865.

On the other side of the garden the neo-Gothic structure once served as the chapel of the Boston University School of Theology, housed in the mansion at 70–72 Mount Vernon St. The chapel was built in 1917–18 by the architectural firm of Aldrich and Holt, and in 1965 it was converted into condominiums by Bulljahn Assocs.

On the r. side of the block at this point is a group of six houses, at Nos 24–12, all of them built in 1822–23; the four at Nos 18–12 were designed by Cornelius Coolidge for Mrs. Swan, with No. 16 serving as her own mansion.

Continuing along the l. side of the street: Nos 25 and 23 were erected in 1809 for Jeremiah Gardner. The next two, at Nos 21 and 19, are also part of the original development by the Mount Vernon Proprietors, but their dates are undocumented.

On the l. are the three most distinguished houses on Chestnut St, those at Nos 17, 15, and 13. The mansions were built in 1816–18 by Mrs. Swan, who gave them to three of her daughters; the architect was Charles Bulfinch, his only row of houses to survive. The house at No. 13 was, in 1863–65, the residence of Dr. Samuel Gridley Howe and his wife, Julia Ward Howe.

Dr. Howe was a physician, reformer, and pioneer teacher of the blind. He was the founder of the Perkins Institute for the Blind, named after Thomas Handasyd Perkins, who in 1833 gave his mansion on Pearl St to Dr. Howe to house his school, the first of its kind in the

U.S. Dr. Howe and his wife were both leaders in the Abolitionist movement, and together they edited *The Commonwealth*, a Boston magazine dedicated to ending slavery. Julia Ward Howe was also a leader in the crusade to gain equal civil rights for women, including suffrage. She wrote many volumes of verse, travel sketches, and essays, but she is best known for having composed the words to "The Battle Hymn of the Republic," which became the rallying song for the Union forces and their supporters during the Civil War. After the Howes left the house it was occupied by Mrs. John T. Sargent. Mrs. Sargent was one of the founders of the *Radical Club*, a group of liberal Unitarians that met regularly at her house for discussions, including such notables as Ralph Waldo Emerson, William Lloyd Garrison, John Greenleaf Whittier, Margaret Fuller, and Julia Ward Howe.

Two other houses believed to be by Bulfinch are the pair at Nos 8–6, with a common portico approached by two winding flights of steps. The houses were built in 1803–4 for Charles Paine, a son of Robert Treat Paine, a patriot leader and signer of the Declaration of Independence. In 1820 the two buildings were acquired by Cornelius Coolidge, who built in the yards to either side of them the houses now at Nos 10 and 4. The buildings at Nos 8–6 are now a Friends' meetinghouse. The last house on the r. side of the block, No. 2, at the corner of Walnut St, dates from 1803.

On the l. side of Chestnut the last six houses are also part of the original development by the Mount Vernon Proprietors. The first three of these, at Nos 11–7, were built in 1824 by Cornelius Coolidge for John Hubbard, while those at Nos 5–1 were erected in 1822 by Ephraim Marsh.

In 1848–51 the house at No. 1 was the residence of John Lothrop Motley (1814–77), novelist, historian, and diplomat, who served as U.S. minister to Spain, Austria, and Great Britain. Motley is best known for his pioneering histories of the Netherlands: *The Rise of the Dutch Republic* (1856), and the four-volume *History of the United Netherlands* (1860, 1867).

Chestnut St comes to its eastern end at Walnut St. Around the corner on the r., 8 Walnut St was the residence of Dr. George Parkman at the time of his murder at the hands of Dr. John Webster on Nov. 23, 1849, the most sensational crime in the history of 19C Boston.

Dr. Parkman left his house early that morning to walk to the West End office of Dr. Webster, a physician on the faculty of Harvard, intending to collect an overdue debt. When Parkman arrived in Webster's office and demanded his money an argument ensued, whereupon the physician struck his creditor with his cane in a fit of rage, killing him instantly. Webster then dissected Parkman's remains and buried them in the dank dungeons beneath Massachusetts General Hospital, and while the long search for the missing man went on he maintained his innocence. After Parkman's remains were finally discovered, evidence indicated Webster's guilt and he was put on trial and convicted of murder; he confessed his crime only shortly before his execution.

The itinerary continues N. on Walnut to Mount Vernon, and there turns r. At the S.E. corner of Mount Vernon and Walnut is an impressive old mansion of 3½ stories, erected in 1803. As one walks eastward along Mount Vernon, the first four houses passed, Nos 34–28, are all part of the original development of Beacon Hill, dating to 1822. This house at No. 32 was in 1870–72 the home of Dr. Samuel Gridley Howe and his wife, Julia Ward Howe. The last of the original houses on this side of the block is No. 26, built in 1838 for Thomas Handasyd Perkins, who gave it as a wedding present to one of his daughters. Perkins himself lived for a time just next door, at the corner of Mount Vernon and Joy Sts. The Perkins Mansion was a five-story edifice that Charles Bulfinch built for him in 1805, but this was demolished in 1853, to be replaced by the Victorian structure that now stands on the corner. The distinguished mansion just across from that, on the S.E. corner of Mount Vernon and Joy, was built in 1824 by Alexander Parris for George William Lyman. Lyman later acquired the adjoining house, around the corner on Mount Vernon St, and the two buildings were joined structurally to form a single dwelling, as they remain today.

Now cross the N.W. corner to begin walking westward along Mount Vernon St. The first four houses passed on the r., Nos 43–49, are for the most part later replacements of mansions built in 1803 for Stephen Higginson, Jr. The house at No. 49 is the only one that still embodies part of its original structure; this is thought to have been built by Charles Bulfinch. In 1851 this house was acquired by Lemuel Shaw, chief justice of the Massachusetts Supreme Court, who built an annex to the E. into what had been the garden. Justice Shaw was the father-in-law of Herman Melville, and it may be presumed that the novelist was frequently a guest in this house.

The next four houses on the r. side of the street, at Nos 51–57, were built in 1804 by Charles Bulfinch for Jonathan Mason, who with Harrison Gray Otis had been one of the leading spirits in the Mount Vernon Proprietors. Mason ranked with Otis as one of the most prominent men in Boston during the Federal period, serving in turn in the Massachusetts Legislature, the U.S. House of Representatives, and the U.S. Senate. Mason's estate, which fronted on Mount Vernon St, included his own huge mansion, built by Charles Bulfinch, which occupied the area taken up by the present Nos 59–67, as well as the four mansions now standing at Nos 51–57, which he gave as wedding presents to his daughters. The Mason house at No. 55, which has its entrance to the side at the end of the garden, is open to the public as the ***Nichols House Museum,** one of the most interesting sites on Beacon Hill.

Admission. Open to the public on Mon., Wed., & Sat. 1–5 p.m., when guided tours are given; fee (tel. 227-6993).

History. The house-museum is named after Rose Standish Nichols, the distinguished woman who lived here for three-quarters of a century. Miss Nichols was born in Roxbury in 1872, and she moved into this house when her parents acquired it in 1885, living here until her death in 1960. Miss Nichols was America's first woman landscape architect, studying under distinguished practitioners in Europe and the U.S., including a course of study at the Massachusetts Institute of Technology. She wrote three outstanding books in that field: *English Pleasure Gardens, Italian Pleasure Gardens,* and *Spanish and Portuguese Gardens.* In addition, she was a skilled wood-carver, furniture-maker, and embroiderer, and examples of these crafts can be seen in the house-museum. Miss Nichols had a wide range of intellectual interests. While still in her teens she organized the Beacon Hill Reading Club, which met here and in other houses on Beacon Hill for more than 60 years. She was also one of the organizers of a pacifist group that met regularly at Cornish, New Hampshire, other notable members being Mrs. Woodrow Wilson and Mrs. Winston Churchill; this later developed into the Foreign Policy Assoc., an organization that now has chapters all over the U.S. Miss Nichols was one of the founders of the Women's International League for Peace and Freedom, remaining an active member until shortly before her death in 1960. By the terms of her will, her residence at 55 Mount Vernon was to be converted into a house-museum open to the public. Furthermore, in keeping with her wishes to promote understanding among the various peoples of the world, the library on the first floor became the headquarters of the Boston Council for International Visitors. Founded in 1961, the Council acts as a clearinghouse for foreign visitors who come to Boston under the sponsorship of the State Department and other agencies of the U.S. government.

Exterior. The four-story brick mansion is the only one of the four Mason houses that has remained unaltered since its original construction by Charles

Bulfinch in 1804. The house faces W. into a very pretty garden, with the entrance at the far right-hand corner, preceded by a classical portico. The facade has features characteristic of Beacon Hill houses of the early 19C: note the arched recesses into which are set the two windows on the ground floor; the stone courses between and above the arches; and the keystone lintels above these and the other windows.

Interior. The house, filled with furnishings, works of art, and other objects collected by Miss Nichols in her widespread travels, remains exactly as it was at the time of her death in 1960. Guided tours begin in the anteroom, the only room on the ground floor open to the public. The fine door leading into the kitchen to the l. is a noteworthy feature, as is the lovely winding staircase.

On reaching the second floor, one sees two original works by Augustus Saint-Gaudens, who was Miss Nichols' uncle by marriage; straight ahead, at the top of the stairs, is a bronze statue of *Diana at the Tower,* and on the wall to the r. is a bronze relief representing Robert Louis Stevenson, with an inscription by the sculptor presenting it to Miss Nichols. The room to the l. is the parlor, which takes up the whole of the front of the house on that level. Over the fireplace is a portrait of Miss Nichols in her middle years, by Polly Thayer. On the wall facing the window is a large Flemish tapestry dated 1555. Copies of Miss Nichols' books on gardening and other works from her library are exhibited on a table to the r., and visitors are free to examine them.

Leaving the parlor and walking back along the corridor to the rear, one comes to the dining room. Over the fireplace there is a portrait of Thomas Johnston, an ancestor of Miss Nichols; this is a copy of the original by Robert Feke. Other noteworthy objects in the room are the tall clock, c. 1700; an 18C chest-on-chest; and a chair that once belonged to Governor John Winthrop. Off to the l. is the charming pantry. The bedrooms are all on the third floor. The master bedroom is at the front of the house, furnished with a four-poster bed with a fine old wooden chest at its foot. The Queen Anne embroidery on the canopy of the bed was made by Miss Nichols herself.

The house at 57 Mount Vernon St, next door to the Nichols House, was in the years 1817–19 the residence of Daniel Webster, who had then just finished his term as U.S. congressman from New Hampshire, and had begun to practice law in Boston as a prelude to his national political career as a representative of Massachusetts. In 1842 the house was bought by Charles Francis Adams (1807–86), son of President John Quincy Adams and grandson of President John Adams, and who himself had a distinguished political career, serving as the U.S. minister to England during the Civil War. His son, the author Henry Adams (1838–1918), describes the house on Mount Vernon St in his autobiographical work, *The Education of Henry Adams* (1907).

The itinerary continues down the r. side of Mount Vernon St, with a fine view of the Charles Street Meeting House and beyond that the Church of the Advent, with the Charles River gleaming in the background. The next houses on the r. are the three at Nos 59–63; these were all erected in 1837, after the Mason Mansion had been demolished to make way for them. The house at No. 59 was designed by Edward Shaw, author of the widely used *Civil Architecture and Rural Architecture.* The Greek Revival portico of this house is one of the most admired on Beacon Hill. In 1885 the house was acquired by Thomas Bailey Aldrich, author and editor of the *Atlantic Monthly,* who lived here until his death in 1907. The house at No. 65 is a replace-

Portico at 59 Mount Vernon Street (Amor Towles)

ment of the one built on the Mason estate in 1838, once the residence of Henry Cabot Lodge.

On the l. side of the street, at the S.W. corner of Mount Vernon and Walnut, the two houses at Nos 40 and 42 were built in 1850 by the house-wright George M. Dexter for Alfred Hemenway, replacing a mansion built in 1822. The three houses beyond these, at Nos 44–48, date to the 1820s. The long, single-story line of apartments at Nos 50–56 are the former stables of the Swan mansions on Chestnut St, built by Charles Bulfinch in 1806. They were converted into apartments in the 1920s, and the painters Maurice and Charles Prendergast lived and worked in one of them for a time.

Continue along the r. side of Mount Vernon St, passing a row of mansions all dating to before 1836. The mansion at No. 77 houses the *Club of Odd*

Volumes, founded by a group of Boston literati in 1887. (The word Odd in the title of the club originally referred to the self-styled eccentricities of the members.) A plaque at No. 83 records that the Rev. William Ellery Channing lived there during 1835—42.

A line of four houses on the l. side of the street, at Nos 62—68, were all erected in 1809—10.

On the r. side of the street at this point, at No. 85, is the grandest mansion on Beacon Hill, the ***Second Harrison Gray Otis House.**

History. This mansion was designed and built by Charles Bulfinch in 1800—2, one of three splendid edifices that he erected for Harrison Gray Otis. The Otis family moved into this mansion in 1802, after leaving the residence that Bulfinch had built for them on Cambridge St. In 1805 Otis sold the mansion on Mount Vernon St and commissioned Bulfinch to build the mansion that now stands at 45 Beacon St. When that residence was completed in the following year Otis and his family moved in, and he and his wife lived there for the rest of their lives. After the Otis family moved out, 85 Mount Vernon St had a succession of wealthy owners, all of whom maintained it as an elegant private residence. It is presently the residence of the Coolidge family, and is not open to the public.

Exterior. The mansion stands on an eminence high above street level; in front, iron pilings stand atop a granite wall; and to the r. of the house, a cobbled driveway leads to the former stables. The most prominent features of the facade are the arched recesses into which the tall windows of the ground floor are set, and the two pairs of tall wooden pilasters of the Corinthian order that rise from the string course between the first and second stories. These pilasters frame the side windows, and each pair is surmounted by a short stretch of entablature, which does not continue across the central section of the facade. Above the cornice a white wooden balustrade borders the hip roof, in the center of which there is an octagonal turret with windows in each of its faces. The original entrance was at the center of the eastern side, but in the 1850s the main entryway was moved to the back corner of that side and a neoclassical portico raised in front of it. In 1882 the bow in the center of the western side was enlarged to create a more commodious dining room within. And early in the 20C the carriage house in the ell to the E. of the mansion to the rear was converted into living quarters.

After passing the Second Harrison Gray Otis House, one comes to the pair of joined houses beyond it, at Nos 87 and 89. Both houses were originally built in 1805 by Charles Bulfinch, who intended to make No. 87 his residence, and to sell the other. However, even before the two houses were completed, his financial condition had declined to the point where he was forced to sell both of them, with No. 87 going to Stephen Higginson, Jr., and No. 89 to David Humphries. No. 87 is still essentially as Bulfinch erected it, but No. 89 has been reconstructed twice, most recently in 1925 by the architect William Dinsmoor.

Now look across to the l. side of the street to see the imposing double mansion of granite at Nos 70—72; this was erected in 1847 for the brothers John E. and Nathaniel Thayer, designed by the English architect Richard Upjohn, who built Trinity Church in New York City. Later it became the theological school of Boston University, and later still the New England College of Pharmacy, both of which institutions extended through to Chestnut St; in recent years the building has been converted for use as condominiums. The only other original buildings remaining on that side of the block are Nos 76 and 78, both built in 1811, and Nos 82 and 84, both dating from 1826.

**Louisburg Sq is the loveliest area on Beacon Hill.

History. When Charles Bulfinch originally drew up a proposed street and lot plan for Beacon Hill in 1796, his design called for a large square in the center of the area to be developed by the Mount Vernon Proprietors. However, the idea did not materialize until 1826, when the Proprietors laid out the present square, designed by Mather Withington on somewhat different lines from those envisioned by Bulfinch. Then a pending lawsuit over title to the land discouraged prospective buyers, and the first house lot was not sold until 1834, with the last one going in 1847. By the end of 1847 the square was completely built up with houses and a park laid out in its center, surrounded by an iron fence. The residents of the square then organized themselves into a group called the Louisburg Square Proprietors, after which they obtained legal possession of the square and the park, a title that they continue to hold today. The name that the Proprietors gave the square came from the successful siege of the great French fortress of Louisburg in Nova Scotia, a victory achieved in 1745 by the Massachusetts Militia led by Sir William Pepperell. From 1847 to the present day the appearance of the square has changed little in its essentials, except for the intrusion of the automobile.

The itinerary proceeds up the W. side of Louisburg Sqe and returns down the E. side. Before beginning, pause at the S. end of the square to look at one of the most characteristic monuments on Beacon Hill, the statue of Aristides the Just. (Aristides the Just was an Athenian statesman who flourished in the first half of the 5C B.C.) This and the statue of Christopher Columbus at the N. end of the park were presented to the Louisburg Square Proprietors in 1850 by Joseph Iasigi, a Greek-Armenian merchant from Smyrna in Turkey, who lived in the house at No. 3 at the time. Both statues are inferior Italian works of the first half of the 19C, but despite their lack of artistic merit they are so much a part of the scene that they have become objects of some affection.

The first house passed, at No. 2, was built in 1847, and was one of the last to be erected on the square. The next two houses, Nos 4 and 6, were erected as a pair in 1842 by Jesse Shaw, the housewright who built a total of ten homes on Beacon Hill over the course of two decades. The house at No. 4 was rented for a year in 1883–84 by William Dean Howells, author and editor of the *Atlantic Monthly*. While he was living in this house, Howells began work on the greatest of his novels, *The Rise of Silas Latham,* which he finished after he left Louisburg Sq to live in Back Bay.

No. 8 is the first of a line of houses that extends from here to the end of the block at Pinckney St, the last one being No. 22. These mansions, all built in 1835–36, are the most beautiful on the square, and many authorities consider them to be the finest row of houses in Boston, perhaps unsurpassed anywhere in the U.S.

Carl J. Reinhardt, Jr., in his monograph on the architecture of Beacon Hill, describes them thus: "The lower side of the square with its row of swelled fronts is particularly fine (numbers 8–24). In these the usual four-story elevation of the time is discarded in favor of a rather novel three-story, areaway and basement scheme, perhaps in deference to the essentially small scale of the square. In these the piano nobile is moved to the first story, which thus becomes the tallest. The areaway and returning wall made it possible to have a large well-lighted room in the front of the basement and in some cases this served as the family dining-room. Number 14 is probably closest to its original form."

Several of the houses in this group have interesting associations. No. 10 was the last residence of Louisa May Alcott and her father, Bronson Alcott, who rented it in 1885. Bronson Alcott died here in the spring of 1888, within two days of the death of Louisa in a nursing home. No. 16 was the last home of Mark Antony DeWolfe Howe, who gave up his house on Brimmer St after his wife's death in 1933 and moved in here, where he lived until his death in 1960. In the mid-19C, No. 20 was the town house of the banker Samuel Gray Ward, who in 1850 became Jenny Lind's financial manager on her American tour. In 1852 Ward's house on Louisburg Sq was the scene of the Swedish Nightingale's wedding to her accompanist, Otto Goldschmidt, a ceremony that took place in his drawing room. Eleven years later Ward won renown by raising the $7.2 million with which Secretary of State William H. Seward purchased Alaska from Russia and annexed it to the U.S.

Crossing over to the E. side of the square, one passes the statue of Christopher Columbus, a childlike figure who bears no discernible resemblance to the great explorer.

The first seven houses on the E. side of Louisburg Sq were built in 1835–39. During the mid-19C the house at No. 9 was the residence of Frederick Walker Lincoln, who served as mayor of Boston during the Civil War. One of the most celebrated events in the social history of Boston in that period took place in this house in 1860, when Mayor Lincoln gave a gala reception for the 19-year-old Prince of Wales, later King Edward VII. This building and the next two now house the Anglican *Convent of St. Margaret,* the large chapel of this community, whose apse can be seen around the corner on Pinckney St; this was built in 1882 by the architect Henry Vaughan.

The houses at Nos 9 and 7, both built in 1835, have associations with the origins of the Swedenborgian movement in Boston. No. 9 was built for the Rev. Thomas Worcester, the first minister in Boston of the Swedenborgian faith. No. 7 was erected for Sampson Reed, one of the early expounders in the U.S. of the doctrines of Swedenborg; he was the father of the Rev. James Reed, who was for many years pastor of the Swedenborgian Church of the New Jerusalem. The Rev. Reed's daughter Elizabeth was born in No. 7 and lived there until her death in 1918, the last of the original families in Louisburg Sq to pass away.

The house beyond that, No. 5, was built c. 1842. Its most distinguished occupant was John Gorham Palfrey, editor of *The North American Review* and author of the *History of New England,* among other works. The last two houses on this side, Nos 3 and 1, were both erected in 1847, the last two to be built on Louisburg Sq. The house at No. 3 was acquired in 1849 by Joseph Iasigi, who adorned Louisburg Sq with the statues of Christopher Columbus and Aristides the Just.

After walking around Louisburg Sq, pause near the statue of Aristides the Just to look down at the block of houses on the S. side of Mount Vernon between Willow and W. Cedar Sts. The first of the original buildings on that block is No. 90, the second from the corner of Willow. This was erected in 1826 and was one of a pair of houses; its twin on the E. was torn down to make way for the apartment building that now stands on the corner of Willow. The house at No. 92 dates to 1834, while those at Nos 96 and 98 were erected in 1835 by Jesse Shaw, housewright, and Alanson Rice, master mason.

At the end of the block, at the near corner of Mount Vernon and W. Cedar Sts, is No. 104, a quaint dwelling in the Greek Revival style erected in 1832.

At the turn of the century this became the Boston town house of Percival Lowell (1855–1916), world traveler, author, and astronomer, the man who in 1894 founded the Lowell

Observatory. Percival Lowell is renowned in the history of science as the person principally responsible for the discovery of Pluto, the most remote planet in the solar system, which was first observed by an astronomer at the Lowell Observatory in 1930. Though Lowell had died 14 years before, after having spent the last two decades in a fruitless search for what he called Planet X, it was his observatory alone that carried on the quest, and when it was found it was almost exactly at the point in the heavens where his calculations had predicted it would be located. Astronomers honored this extraordinary achievement when they called the new planet Pluto, after the Greek god of the Underworld, for the first two letters of its name are the initials of Percival Lowell.

The itinerary now takes a short detour, crossing Mount Vernon St and continuing a short way down Willow St, stopping halfway down the block at the corner of Acorn St. The house on the l. side of Willow at this point, No. 9, was in the late 1950s the residence of Sylvia Plath, the novelist and poetess. Miss Plath was born in Boston on Oct. 27, 1932, and took her own life in London on Feb. 11, 1963. Eight months after her death some of her poems were published in *Encounter* and caused a sensation; this was followed by a volume of her poetry entitled *Ariel* (1965), her autobiographical novel, *The Bell Jar* (1963), and by her *Collected Poems* (1981), for the last of which she was posthumously awarded the Pulitzer Prize for poetry in 1982.

Turn r. and begin walking down Acorn St, a narrow cobbled lane which is the most picturesque byway on Beacon Hill. The nine houses on the street, all on the l. side, were built in 1828–29, most if not all of them designed by Cornelius Coolidge.

At the lower end of Acorn turn r. onto W. Cedar. In colonial times this was known as George St, and was just a country lane until 1826, when it was developed by the Mount Vernon Proprietors. All of the houses on the l. side of the street were built in 1826–27 by the housewright John Hubbard; those on the r. side were erected in 1834–35 by a number of architects and builders. The houses on the r. at Nos 7 and 9 were designed by Asher Benjamin, who made the latter building his residence. The house on the r. corner, at No. 11A, was built around the turn of the century for Percival Lowell, and was used as an annex for the adjacent house that he had bought around the corner at 104 Mount Vernon.

At the corner pause to look down at some of the original houses that have survived on the lower end of Mount Vernon St; these are all located between Cedar Lane Way and Charles St and were built in 1826–27. On the l. side of the street the houses at Nos 12 and 16 were built by the housewright Jesse Shaw; the one on the l. at No. 14 was put up by Meshack Tibbets, a bricklayer, who also constructed the four houses on the r., Nos 103–109.

Continue along W. Cedar past Mount Vernon, where a number of houses date from the period 1826–35. The house on the l. at No. 22 was erected in 1831 by the housewright Melzar Dunbar as his own residence. The house beyond that, No. 24, was owned by Wendell Phillips, the renowned Abolitionist orator. On the r. side of the street at mid-block Nos 23 and 25 date from 1835–36, designed by Asher Benjamin and built by Melzar Dunbar. The next two buildings on the r. side, Nos 27 and 29, were erected in 1834 by the housewrights Bela Stoddard and Micah Cutler. On the l. side of the street, near the end of the block, No. 36 was built in 1828 by Cornelius Coolidge for Dr. George Parkman. Dr. Parkman later moved to 8 Walnut St, where he resided until his murder by Dr. John Webster in 1849.

At the next corner turn r. off W. Cedar onto Pinckney, to begin the last leg of the itinerary. Pinckney St, which was laid out in 1802 by the Mount Vernon Proprietors, has always been a boundary between the two Beacon

Hills, the elite South Slope and the plebeian North Slope, and the street itself reflects this social and economic bifurcation, for while most of the western end is elegant, most of the eastern end is more humble, yet interesting.

The first building passed on the r. after the corner is No. 86; this is the *John J. Smith House,* one of the sites on the Black Heritage Trail. The house is named after a free black from Virginia who moved to Boston in 1848 and established himself as a barber and hairdresser.

Smith's barbershop, at the corner of Howard and Bulfinch Sts in the West End, became a center for black Abolitionists, and among its white visitors the most notable was Senator Charles Sumner. During the Civil War, Smith joined the all-black Fifth Cavalry Regiment, serving in Washington, D.C., as a recruiting officer. After the war he was elected to the Massachusetts House of Representatives in 1868, 1869, and 1872. In 1878, the year that Smith moved to 86 Pinckney St, he was appointed to the Boston Common Council, the first black to hold that post. Smith lived at 86 Pinckney St until 1893, when he moved elsewhere in Boston.

The next house on the r. is No. 84. In 1865–70 this was the residence of Thomas Bailey Aldrich, who was then a young editor working for Jamie Fields. On Thanksgiving Day, 1867, Fields dropped in here with Charles Dickens, who was then making his last tour of the U.S., after which they went on to have dinner in Cambridge with Henry Wadsworth Longfellow. Dickens was so taken by his brief visit with Aldrich and his young bride that he wrote back to England saying how charmed he was by them and by the hospitality that they had accorded him. While living here, Aldrich wrote *The Story of a Bad Boy.*

Farther along on the r. is the head of Louisburg Sq. The house at 87 Pinckney, at the N.W. corner of the square, was for a time the residence of the literary critic F. O. Matthiessen (1902–50), whose books include studies of many of the major figures in the flowering of literature in Boston and its environs in the 19C. The second house beyond that at, No. 83, was in 1883 acquired by the Rev. William Ellery Channing. At the N.E. corner of the square, at 81 Pinckney, is the house where Louisa May Alcott lived in the early 1880s, before she and her father, Bronson Alcott, moved into their last residence, at 10 Louisburg Sq. After one has passed the square, on the r. is the apse of the chapel of St. Margaret's Convent, the entrance to which is on Louisburg Sq. Beyond that, at Nos 78 and 76, are two homes erected in 1838 by the housewrights Loring Dunbar and Samuel Mitchell. Just beyond No. 76 a long covered passage leads to a dwelling known as the "Hidden House of Beacon Hill," since it is completely invisible from the street; you are asked not to enter so as to preserve the peace of those living there. Beyond the passage is No. 74, built in 1829 and still completely in its original condition. This has been for long the residence of Marjorie Drake Ross, whose delightful three-volume work, *The Book of Boston,* is a classic on the history, topography, and monuments of the city.

On the near corner of the first turning on the l., where Anderson St leads down to Cambridge St, a large building has recently been abandoned. This was erected in 1824 to house the English High School, founded by the town of Boston in 1820, which began functioning the following year in a building at the corner of Temple and Derne Sts. This was a school devoted to the education of "lads intending to become merchants or mechanics," an admirable institution that continues to operate today in its present home in the Back Bay Fens. Later the building here at Pinckney and Anderson Sts became the Phillips School, which in the early 1850s became the first racially integrated public school in Boston; this later moved to other quarters on the corner of Anderson and Phillips Sts.

On the r. side of Pinckney, the five houses at Nos 66–58 were built in 1846 by Gridley J. F. Bryant, standing on land that until the previous year had been part of the stables of the Second Harrison Gray Otis House on Mount Vernon St. The first resident of No. 58 was James Freeman Clarke, minister of the Church of the New Disciples, who was a leader in the Abolitionist movement and a central figure in the group of writers and intellectuals who brought about the Transcendentalist movement in Boston and its environs.

The five houses at Nos 56–48 were erected in the early 1880s; No. 54 still retains its original form, but the others have been altered by adding upper floors and bay windows.

During the 1840s No. 54 was for a time the residence of George Stillman Hillard (1808–79), a law partner of Senator Charles Sumner who was prominent in literary circles and much admired for his philanthropy. Hillard was a close friend and adviser of Nathaniel Hawthorne, who stayed as a guest in the house on Pinckney St when he first came to Boston. In his introduction to *The Scarlet Letter*, Hawthorne writes of how he there grew "fastidious by sympathy with the classic refinement of Hillard's culture. . . ." Hawthorne was living in Hillard's house on July 9, 1842, the day that he and Sophia Peabody were married by the Rev. James Freeman Clarke.

On the l. side of Pinckney, the first structure seen after crossing Anderson is No. 65, a four-story building topped by a cupola. This was built sometime before 1807 by merchants in the China trade, to house their sailors in the intervals between voyages. The next two houses beyond this, Nos 63 and 61, were built at about the same time, and they probably also used to house mariners.

As one continues along the l. side of Pinckney, the next original buildings passed are Nos 55–51, all dating from the first decade of the 19C. The pair of houses at Nos 49–47 were built in 1804 by Jeremiah Gardner, a carpenter, and Peter Osgood, a bricklayer.

On the r. side of the street, the house at No. 46 dates to sometime before 1832, and beyond that those at Nos 44 and 40 were also built in the 1830s. The next 11 houses beyond that, Nos 38–12, are built on what was originally the backyard of the Mason estate, the main mansion of which was built in 1802. Jonathan Mason divided up the Pinckney St side of his estate into 11 small building lots in 1827, and within the next decade houses were built on all of them. The house at No. 24 stands on what was originally the stable of the Mason mansion; this was rebuilt in 1884 by William Ralph Emerson, a cousin of Ralph Waldo Emerson, and because of its unusual fenestration it is known as "The House of Odd Windows." The house at No. 20 was in the years 1852–55 the residence of the Alcott family, the first of their several homes on Beacon Hill. No. 14 was the residence of William D. Ticknor, who, together with Jamie Fields, founded the distinguished publishing firm of Ticknor and Fields. Another house with literary associations stands farther along Pinckney St on the same side; this is No. 4, which was for a time the home of Henry David Thoreau. On the l. side of street, the house at No. 15 was the site of Elizabeth Peabody's kindergarten, the first in the U.S.; she established it here in 1862, the year after she founded this institution elsewhere in Boston.

Continuing along: No. 5 is a quaint and venerable house, the *Middleton-*

Glapion House, which some historians of architecture believe to be the oldest dwelling on Beacon Hill. The house is named after George Middleton and Louis Glapion, two free black men who bought a plot of land on this site in 1786. The actual date of construction is not recorded, but it is mentioned as early as 1791, so there is no doubt that it is in fact the oldest on the Hill.

After looking at the Middleton-Glapion House, continue to the end of Pinckney and turn r. onto Joy St. One can then walk back along Joy to Beacon St, ending this long stroll around Beacon Hill.

11   Boston Common and the Public Garden

The itinerary starts at the N.W. corner of Park and Beacon Sts, and goes through Boston Common and the Public Garden.

History and Topography. The Common that is seen today, 48.4 acres in extent, is all laid out on land originally obtained from the Rev. William Blaxton, the first English settler of the Shawmut Peninsula. Even after Governor John Winthrop and his company settled in Boston in 1630, Blaxton was still considered to be the owner of the entire peninsula. However, in 1633 Blaxton signed over to the General Court all of the peninsula except for 50 acres, which he retained as his estate. The following year Blaxton sold all but six acres of his estate to the town of Boston, which paid him £30, raised by imposing a tax of 6 shillings and upward on each householder. Then, in 1635, Blaxton sold his house and estate to Richard Pepys, after which he went off to settle in Rhode Island. Blaxton returned briefly to Boston in 1659 to marry Governor Endicott's widow, Mary; the two of them then returned to his estate in Rhode Island, where he died in 1675.

At first there was some talk about dividing Blaxton's estate among the householders whose tax had paid for it. But by 1640 it had been generally agreed that the land should be set aside for common use, as indicated in this entry in the town records for March 30 of that year: "Also agreed that henceforth there shalbe noe land granted eyther for housplott or garden to any person out of the open ground or Comon Field. . . ." In the early days of Boston the Common was used principally as a pasture. In the town records for 1646 it is recorded "that there shalbe kept on the Common by the Inhabitants of the Town but 70 milch kine; . . . that there shalbe no dry cattell, yonge cattell, or horse shalbe free to goe on the Common this year; but on horse for Elder Oliver; that if any desire to kep sheep, hee may kep foure sheep in lieuw of a Cowe." Also, the use of the Common was restricted to "those who are admitted by the townesmen to be inhabitants," and none who came after 1646 could have the right of commonage, "unless he hier it of them that are Comoners." The town also hired a herdsman, who was paid "two shillings a Cowe," and a shepherd was appointed to look after the flocks of those who chose to keep sheep "in lieuw" of cows.

The Common was also used from the earliest days as a training ground for the town militia units, most notably the Ancient and Honorable Artillery Company. During the various conflicts of the colonial period, principally King Philip's War and the French and Indian Wars, the Massachusetts Militia encamped and drilled on the Common before going off to fight. In 1745, 3000 men of the Massachusetts Militia camped on the Common before embarking on their successful siege of Louisburg under Sir William Pepperell, and in 1758 General Jeffrey Amherst encamped an army of 6400 provincial troops there before his campaign in Canada.

The Common was apparently one of the places where public executions were carried out, although there was also a gallows out beyond the Neck. The place of execution was the Great Elm, a venerable tree standing in the Common when the first settlers arrived in Boston, and which lived on until it was destroyed in a gale in 1876. One of the dark chapters in the history of Boston concerns the execution of four Quakers on the Common in the years

1659–61, including the heroic Mary Dyer, who was hanged from the Great Elm on June 1, 1660. Public executions continued to be held on the Common until 1812.

During the colonial period the Common was on several occasions the scene of duels, some of them fatal. The most celebrated took place in 1728, when Benjamin Woodbridge and Henry Phillips, two young men of good family and reputation, dueled on the Common with swords one night after quarreling over cards in a tavern. Phillips ran Woodbridge through the body with his sword and left him to die on the Common, after which he was smuggled aboard a British warship and fled the country. Woodbridge was carried off for burial in the Old Granary Burying-Ground, where his grave may still be seen.

But, whatever its other uses, the Common was primarily a place where the people of Boston could gather on holidays and promenade in the evening in good weather. John Josselyn, in a description of Boston published in London in 1675, writes thus: "On the South there is a small but pleasant Common where the Gallants a little before Sun-set walk with their Marmalet-Madams, as we do in Morefields, etc., till the nine a clock Bell brings them home to their respective habitations, when presently the Constables walk their rounds to see good orders kept, and to take up loose people."

Throughout the history of Boston, the Common has always been the place where large-scale celebrations and demonstrations have taken place, an outdoor stage on which many dramatic and historic dramas have occurred. During the colonial period the Common was a place of tumult each year on Nov. 5, when Pope Day was celebrated. On that day all of the rough youths and rowdies of the town divided up into two factions, the North End against the South End, and if the latter group were victorious they would burn their captured effigy of the Pope in a huge bonfire on the Common, along with figures of the Devil and the Pretender, usually after a wild melee, an annual fracas that continued until 1774.

In the autumn of 1740, when the young English preacher George Whitefield first came to Boston, his sermons attracted such huge crowds that they could not be accommodated at any of the meetinghouses in town, and so they were forced to congregate in the Common. A contemporary newspaper account estimated that the crowd that listened to Whitefield the first time he spoke in the Common numbered 5000, and that there were 23,000 in attendance when he gave his final sermon there, and this at a time when the population of the town was only 18,000.

The Common was the natural place for the townspeople to gather for the celebration of happy tidings. On July 8, 1745, when news arrived in Boston that the French fortress at Louisburg had fallen to the Massachusetts Militia under Sir William Pepperell, the whole town turned out to celebrate on the Common. In the evening of May 19, 1766, when news was received that the Stamp Act had been repealed, the Sons of Liberty put on a spectacular fireworks display in the Common, while John Hancock put on a pyrotechnics demonstration of his own from his mansion on Beacon St, followed by a huge banquet in which he provided free Madeira wine for the crowd. As one spectator wrote gratefully afterwards "Mr. Hancock behaved very well on this occasion and treated every person with cheerfulness. . . . The whole was much admired and the day crowned with Glory and Honour."

Two years later, on June 20, 1768, the Common was the scene of a riot after one of John Hancock's vessels was seized by the royal custom officers on a charge of smuggling. The conduct of the mob was thus described in an article in the *Boston Gazette* for June 20, 1768: "About 10 o'clock they went to the Docks, and dragged out a large Pleasure Boat belonging to the Collector, this they drew along the street with loud huzzaing all the way into the Common, where they set fire to it and burned it to Ashes: they also broke several windows of the Collector and Inspector-General, which were nigh the Common."

This was one of the disturbances that led to the sending of British troops to Boston to strengthen the hand of the Crown. On Sept. 30, 1768, two regiments of British troops landed in Boston and marched to the Common, where one regiment encamped, the other going on to quarters in Faneuil Hall. From that day until the evacuation of Boston on March 17, 1776, the Common was a British camp, with as many as four regiments living in squalid conditions along with their camp followers, horses, artillery, and supplies. On Aug. 21, 1774, Lord Percy wrote home to England that "I have under my command the fourth, fifth, thirty-eighth and forty-third Regts, together with 22 pieces of cannon and 3 Cos. of artillery encamped in the Common." It was from Boston Common, between 10 and 11 p.m. on April 18, 1775, that "all the Grenadiers and Light Infantry of the Army"—to quote from Lieutenant Barker's diary—"making about 600 Men (under the command of Lieutenant-Colonel Smith of the Tenth and Major Pitcairn of the Marines) embarked and were landed upon the

Boston Common, looking toward the State House

opposite shore of Cambridge Marsh." This was the prelude to the Revolutionary War, and within 48 hours the surviving troops of Percy's force were encamped back on the Common, after the battles of Lexington and Concord and the running fight on their retreat to Charlestown. And many of those killed were buried at the bottom of the Common after those engagements, as well as after the Battle of Bunker Hill two months later. The redcoats remained encamped on the Common throughout the British occupation, some 1750 in number, until they were all evacuated on March 17, 1776. But traces of the British occupation remained to be seen on the Common long afterward, with the ground scarred by trenches, ditches and the remnants of fortifications, the area littered with rubble and debris, and many of the trees cut down for firewood.

Nevertheless, the people of Boston resumed their use of the Common as they slowly returned to town after the British evacuation. In 1778, when Count D'Estaing and his officers were entertained by John Hancock at his mansion on Beacon St, Mrs. Hancock had all of the cows on the Common milked to provide milk for her guests. When news of the surrender of the British forces under Cornwallis at Yorktown reached Boston in late Oct. 1783, virtually the entire populace gathered in the Common and celebrated around a huge bonfire. The last echo of the Revolution, so far as the Common was concerned, was heard in 1824, when thousands gathered there to honor Lafayette on his return to Boston. The New England Guards put on a spirited display of cavalry exercises and artillery practice, and at the climax of the show Lafayette was invited to fire a cannon that had been sighted on a target floating in Back Bay, and the enormous crowd cheered wildly when his shot made a direct hit. Lafayette returned to Boston again the following year, when he was the principal guest of honor at the laying of the cornerstone of the Bunker Hill Monument. On June 17, 1825, Lafayette and all of the others who would take part in the great procession assembled in Boston Common and formed their line of march, starting for Charlestown just

50 years to the day after the British forces left from the Common before the Battle of Bunker Hill.

During the generation prior to the Civil War a number of public occasions of unusual interest took place in the Common. In 1833 President Andrew Jackson was honored at a public gathering on the Common, in which the New England Guards once again put on an equestrian show. At the height of the celebration the Guards saluted the President with an artillery barrage, and the noise so startled his horse and those of his Cabinet that they bolted and fled, and Vice-President Martin Van Buren was very nearly unseated. Perhaps the most extraordinary spectacle that ever took place on the Common occurred in 1837, when Chief Black Hawk visited Boston with a company of his Sacs and Foxes braves. The Chief had led an Indian insurrection against the U.S. government in 1832, the Black Hawk War, and after his defeat he had been imprisoned for a year before being sent on a goodwill tour of the U.S., which now brought him to Boston. On Oct. 30, 1837, Chief Black Hawk and his braves were officially received at the State House, after which, according to the *Advertiser*, "the Governor and suite, with the Indian delegation, and the public officers were escorted to an open square in the Common, where for a considerable length of time, the warriors performed a great variety of war dances, to the great amusement of an immense concourse of spectators." One eyewitness gave this startled account of the dances: "Their dresses of the skins of wild animals with the horns upon them, their weapons decorated with everything in savage use that could make a clatter and a frightful show, their hideous and grotesque manoeuvres, their wild onsets, their uncouth motions in the dance, and their unearthly yell, made them a most impressive spectacle." Ralph Waldo Emerson wrote of these Indians in his *Journal* as "Our Picts, looking as if the bears and catamounts had sent a deputation."

A great moment in Boston's civic development took place in 1848, when the first city water system was completed, with its source at Lake Cochituate. This was marked by a joyous festival in the Common on Oct. 25 of that year, the "Water Celebration," which had its climax when the water from Lake Cochituate spurted forth for the first time from a fountain in Frog Pond. At that point a massed choir of schoolchildren sang an ode written for the occasion by James Russell Lowell, and when their song was finished all the city's church bells were pealed joyously and there was a rolling thunder of artillery fire by the New England Militia. Three years later a festival called the "Railroad Jubilee" marked the opening of railways connecting Boston with the Western U.S. and Canada, with President Millard Fillmore the principal guest of honor. Another celebrated event of the era was the arrival in Boston in 1860 of the Prince of Wales, the future King Edward VII. This was marked by an official civic welcome in the Common, in which the Prince, dressed in the uniform of a colonel in the British cavalry, and mounted on Colonel T. Bigelow Lawrence's horse, Black Prince, reviewed the militia companies of Boston and the surrounding towns—the last such exercise before the outbreak of the Civil War.

During the Civil War the Common was once again used as a mustering field for Massachusetts soldiers going off to war. The state was quick to respond to President Lincoln's initial call for troops, and on April 17, 1861, the Sixth Massachusetts Regiment marched off to war, as Governor Andrews and other dignitaries bade farewell to them from the State House steps. This was the first of many such departures, as the newly formed regiments mustered on the Common, forming their line of march and then listening to messages of farewell before parading down Beacon St. On one of these farewells, on July 18, the men of the 12th Regiment, commanded by Daniel Webster's son Fletcher, began singing "John Brown's Body," a marching song that some of the volunteers had composed while training at Fort Warren. This was the first known instance at which this song was sung in public, and it soon swept across the country and become one of the rallying hymns for the Union cause.

In summer 1862 Boston Common became an important headquarters for recruiting, after President Lincoln had called for 300,000 men to enlist for three years. For the remainder of the Civil War the Common was the center for this and other patriotic activities in Boston, and it was here that the survivors of the Massachusetts regiments were emotionally welcomed back when they returned from the fighting. The last of these events took place on Dec. 22, 1865, more than eight months after General Robert E. Lee's surrender at Appomattox, when the banners of all the Massachusetts regiments that had fought in the war were delivered over to the Commonwealth, in a moving ceremony held on the Park Street Mall of the Common.

In the past century the principal public events held in the Common have been in connection with the celebration of the Centennial of American Independence in 1876 and of the Bicentennial in 1976. The most recent historic event in the Common took place on Oct. 1, 1979, when Pope John Paul II celebrated a public Mass there, a ceremony attended by more than 100,000 people, a reminder that this has been the central gathering-place for Bostonians since the founding of the town.

Although the topography of the Common is much the same as it was in early colonial days, its character and appearance have changed in many significant ways. Cows were no longer permitted to graze on the Common after 1830. The principal change in the appearance of the Common was brought about by the planting of trees, for through most of Boston's first century the Great Elm and two or three other trees were the only ones growing there. The first systematic forestry program was carried out in 1723–29, when a row of elms was planted on the Tremont St side, and then in 1734 a second row was put in parallel to this, creating the first of the malls on the Common. A British visitor to Boston in 1740, one Joseph Bennett, gives this description of the Common and its first mall of trees: "For their domestic amusement every afternoon, after drinking tea, the gentlemen and ladies walk the Mall. . . . What they call the Mall is a walk on a fine green common adjoining the south-west side of the town. It is half a mile over, with two rows of trees planted opposite to each other, with a fine footway between, in imitation of St. James's Park; and part of the bay of the sea which encircles the town, taking its course along the north-west side of the Common—by which it is bounded on one side, and by country on the other—forms a beautiful canal, in view of the walk."

A third row of trees was added to the Tremont Street Mall after the Revolution, and in 1780 John Hancock planted the first of the elms on the Beacon St side of the Common. In 1823–24 Mayor Josiah Quincy planted the trees that make up the Charles Street Mall, and in 1826 he replaced the poplars along the Charles St side with elms. In 1836 Mayor Samuel T. Armstrong completed a mall of trees along the Boylston St side, annexing part of the Central Burying-Ground in the process, and for the first time the Common was surrounded by broad walks and tall shade trees, as it is for the most part today. In 1876 the Common became part of the Municipal Park System founded by an act of the Massachusetts Legislature earlier that year. This eventually brought the paving of the main malls and paths, the installation of benches and public toilets, the construction of a bandstand for public concerts, and the laying out of playgrounds and playing fields. These and other intrusions of the modern world make the Common appear less bucolic and tranquil than it does in the old prints; nevertheless, it is still the focus of Boston life, the scene of political demonstrations, rallies, concerts, art exhibitions, and public events. But, more important, it is a place where Bostonians can find a green breathing-space in the middle of their crowded city, an area where they can walk or picnic or just take their ease on the greensward, as people have been pleasurably doing here now for more than 250 years.

At the N.W. corner of the Common, just across Beacon St from the State House, we see what many believe to be the finest work of public art in Boston: the *monument* honoring Colonel Robert Gould Shaw and his men of the 54th Massachusetts Regiment.

The enlisted men of this regiment were all free blacks from Massachusetts who volunteered for service, the first of their race permitted to the join the Union forces in the Civil War, while Colonel Shaw and all of the other officers were white men. The relief, a fine work of Augustus Saint-Gaudens (1848–1907), shows Shaw and his men at the moment when they passed the State House on May 28, 1863, after receiving their regimental colors from Governor Andrew. As Governor Andrew said to Colonel Shaw at the time: "I know not, Mr Commander, where in all human history to any given thousand men in arms there has been committed a work at once so proud, so precious, so full of hope and glory, as the work committed to you." The regiment fought valiantly in the assault on Fort Wagner, South Carolina on July 18, 1863, a battle in which Shaw and many of his men were killed. One who particularly distinguished himself that day was Sergeant William Carney, whose bravery won him the Congressional Medal of Honor, the first time that it had ever been awarded to a black American. The monument, whose architectural setting was designed by McKim, Mead & White, was dedicated on May 13, 1897, and among the guests of honour that day were Sergeant Carney and other survivors of the 54th. The back of the monument is inscribed with the names of the officers and men of the 54th who were decorated for bravery, as well as the tribute paid to the regiment by President Charles W. Eliot of Harvard at the dedication ceremony.

The steps leading down into the Common on either side of the Shaw Monument are part of Liberty Mall, an area which extends for a short distance to the E. along the walk in that direction; on the top step there is an inscription that this memorial was "dedicated on 27 Oct. 1917 to our Soldiers and Sailors in the Great War." After descending the steps, turn r. and begin walking down the mall that parallels Beacon St. The first two old trees to the l. of the path, behind the Shaw Monument, are about 200 years old, and it is believed that the second one along was planted by John Hancock in 1780. One might pause at this point to look downhill over the northern end of the Common. The paths seen here used to be the tracks taken by the boys of Boston when they coasted down the hill on their sleds and toboggans, a scene frequently depicted in old prints of the Common.

Continuing along: at the foot of Joy St a short flight of steps leads down from a gate opening off Beacon St. These are known as the *Guild Steps*, named after Curtis Guild (1860–1915), who was governor of Massachusetts from 1906 to 1908. On the gateway to the W. at the top of the steps there is a relief bust of Governor Guild, and on the opposite post there is a relief with the emblem of Massachusetts, the figure of an Indian brave.

The top of the Guild Steps is a good spot to survey the area of the Common just to the W. Below and to the r. is the elongated body of water known as Frog Pond (at the moment dry), and beyond that and farther to the r. is Telegraph Hill, on top of which is the Soldiers and Sailors Monument. These landmarks may be used to locate the site of the Great Elm; this would have stood where the main path from the Guild Steps to Tremont St intersects the path between Frog Pond and Telegraph Hill heading N.E. to the Information Center on Tremont St, with the exact site just to the r. of where the paths join. As mentioned earlier, this historic tree fell in a storm in 1876, and today there is nothing to mark the site where it stood.

The itinerary continues along the path parallel to Beacon St past Frog Pond, an old watering place for cattle that has now been cemented in and even denied water. Memoirs of prominent Bostonians of the 19C tell of their joy in fishing for minnows in Frog Pond in summer and ice-skating there in winter, activities that continued up until quite recent times. One hopes that Frog Pond will be filled with water again as soon as possible, and throughout the year, for the scene in the Common is simply not the same without it.

Continue along the path parallel to Beacon St. At the foot of Spruce St on the r. is *Founder's Memorial*. The monument is thought to stand on the site of the spring of clear water near which the Rev. William Blaxton built his house, the first to be erected on the Shawmut Peninsula, which would have stood approximately at the present corner of Beacon and Spruce Sts.

The memorial consists of a bas-relief in bronze by the sculptor John F. Paramino in a stone setting designed by the architect Charles A. Coolidge; it was dedicated in 1930 by Mayor James Michael Curley. The relief shows Blaxton welcoming Winthrop and his party, who have come across to the Shawmut Peninsula from Charlestown, represented by a few houses on the other shore, while the *Arbella* (sometimes spelled Arabella) is shown anchored in the Charles. Beside Winthrop is the Rev. John Wilson, and behind him is Ann Pollard, the girl who was the first of the new settlers to set foot on the soil of Boston, according to tradition; and at the background to the l. there is a group of friendly Indians, and a female figure, symbolizing the Motherhood of Boston, protected by a Puritan soldier. At the rear of the monument inscriptions record the dedication of the memorial and quote two of the founders, John Winthrop and William Bradford.

Winthrop's statement, made aboard the *Arbella* before they landed in Charlestown, reads thus: "For Wee must consider that Wee shall be as a City upon a Hill. The Eies of all People are uppon Us, soe that if Wee shall Deale falsely with our God in this Worke Wee have undertaken . . . Wee shall be made a Story and a By-Word through the World." And below these are Bradford's words, written in Charlestown that same year: "Thus out of smalle Beginnings Greater Things have been produced by his hand that made all things out of nothing. . . . And as one small candle may light a thousand, so the light here kindled hath shone to many yea in som sorte to our whole nation."

Take the path from the Beacon Street Mall toward the southern end of Frog Pond, to approach Telegraph Hill. About halfway along this path on the r. is an upright commemorative stone known as the *Football Tablet*. At the top of the tablet there is a football in low relief, and below it the following inscription: "On this field the Oneida Football Club of Boston, the first organized football club in the United States, played against all comers from 1862 to 1865. The Oneida goal was never crossed." Below this another inscription notes that "This monument is placed on Boston Common November 1925 by the seven surviving members of the team." On the reverse are inscribed the names of the 16 members of the team, the men who began the game that is now one of the national sports of the U.S.

Continue along the path, past the southern end of Frog Pond and up the slope of Telegraph Hill, with a view of the entire Common. The hill received its name from a semaphore station set up there in colonial times to signal ships entering Boston Harbor. In 1774 the British forces built a powder house on the summit of the hill, a massive structure of Quincy granite with walls 7ft thick and capable of holding up to 1000 pounds of gunpowder. The following year the British built a fort on the summit of the hill as well, and this would have been their strongest position if the Continental Army had ever attacked them in Boston, which very nearly happened in the spring of 1776.

Telegraph Hill is now surmounted by the *Soldiers and Sailors Monument,* the most prominent landmark on the Common. This is a work of the sculptor Martin Milmore (1844–83); the cornerstone of the monument was laid in 1871 and it was dedicated in 1877, in a ceremony in which 25,000 Civil War veterans marched six miles in a procession that ended on the summit of Telegraph Hill. The four granite statues standing on pedestals projecting from the four corners of the monument represent Peace, the Sailor, the Muse of History, and the Soldier. Between the projections on which the statues stand there are four bronze bas-reliefs; these depict the Departure of the Forces for the War; the Battle of Fort Sumter; the Work of the Boston Sanitary Commission; and the Return from the War. On the main pedestal of the statue there is an inscription from a speech by Charles W. Eliot, president of Harvard, honoring those who died serving the Union during the war; above this is the massive granite column, with the figures of four maidens encircling its lower drum, and surmounting it a statue of Liberty, the Genius of America.

Directly to the E. of the Soldiers and Sailors Monument, on the l. at the beginning of the path leading down from that side of the summit, there is a very unusual military memento, which on close inspection proves to be a U.S. Navy mine from World War I. An inscription on the side of the mine casing states that "this is a type of one of the 56,571 mines laid and swept in the mine barrage placed in the North Sea during World War I, 1917–1919. Presented to Boston by the North Sea Mine Force Association, 26 Oct. 1921."

Now descend from Telegraph Hill and take the path that leads S. toward the central gate at that end of the Common. A baseball field and tennis courts are on the l. and an open area is to the r. The latter is identified by a marker on a path to the r. as the *Carty Parade Ground;* this is named after Colonel Thomas J. Carty (1904–62), member of the Board of Parks and Recreation 1954–62, and captain of the Ancient and Honorable Artillery Company, which has its annual muster and parade on this field on the first Mon. in June.

Continue toward the central gate on the W. side of the Common. A short distance before one comes to the gate a stone tablet on the r. honors Pope John Paul II, who said Mass here on Oct. 1, 1979, while 100,000 people stood in the pouring rain to participate with him in the ritual. At the top of the tablet there is a portrait bust of the Pope, and below this is inscribed the blessing that he conferred on Boston and its people at that time: "May God's blessing descend on this city of Boston, and bring joy to every conscience and joy to every heart!"

Cross MacArthur Mall, named in honor of General Douglas MacArthur, to the central gate on the W. side of the Common. In colonial times the area around the present gate was a low mound named Fox Hill, which was nearly surrounded by the waters of Back Bay. During their occupation of Boston the British had a redoubt here, defended by a company of troops. Until recently there was a marker on one of the gateposts recording that the British had a fortification here during the Revolution. However, this has been removed, to be replaced by another marker, outside the gatepost to the r. as one leaves the Common, commemorating a time of happier relations between Britain and the U.S. The present marker reads: "Erected by the Royal Navy in gratitude to the people of Boston for hospitality and friendship to many thousands of British sailors from H.M. ships building and refitting during World War II; 1945."

At this point the itinerary crosses Charles St for a stroll through the *Public Garden,* after it leads back along the southern and eastern sides of the Common.

History and Topography. Like the present Back Bay area, the Public Garden is laid out entirely on filled-in land. The Mill Dam was completed in 1821, and three years later the present site of the Public Garden was appropriated by the city. At that time there was considerable pressure to sell the land to private developers, but Mayor Quincy had the foresight to deny the City Council the right to dispose of the land. In 1837 a group of amateur horticulturists, led by Horace Gray, petitioned the City Council for the right to use the site for a public botanical garden. The request was granted in 1839, whereupon Gray and his associates engaged an English garden designer, John Cadness, to take charge of the project. Although the land was only partially filled in, the proprietors built a greenhouse and imported rare plants. They also approached A. J. Downing, a landscape architect, to prepare a design for laying out the grounds as a public garden. However, the project came to a halt in 1847 when Gray went bankrupt. For the next decade the project was held in abeyance, and not until 1856 did the city acquire clear title to all the land; then, in 1859, an act of the Massachusetts Legislature finally ensured that it would be set aside forever as a public garden. In the year 1859–60, a local landscape architect, George F. Meacham, laid out the grounds essentially as they are today, except for some modifications made by the city civil engineer, James Slade. Construction proceeded rapidly, and by 1900 the Public Gardens took on their present form, a major adornment to the city of Boston.

The entryway to the Public Garden on the E. side has an ornate wrought-iron gate, at the top of which there is a bronze plaque with the date 1630 and a relief depicting the colonial town of Boston. On the gatepost beside the entrance to the r. an inscription identifies the mall inside as the "Haffenreffer Walk, named in honor of Theodore C. Haffenreffer (1880–1956); Member of the Board of Park Commissioners 1930–56."

Just inside the gate and to the r. there is a bronze statue of Dr. Edward Everett Hale (1822–1909), by Bela Pratt (1867–1917).

Dr. Hale, Unitarian minister and author, is best known for his story "The Man Without a Country," a patriotic tale that did much to gain support for the Union cause during the Civil War. This statue was unveiled in 1913 by his grandson, also named Edward Everett Hale, while Hale's widow watched from a carriage on Charles St. At the dedication ceremony ex-President Howard Taft described Dr. Hale as a man of "irresistable personality," adding that "his culture, his nobility, his oratory and his disposition all helped to gain him a just reputation which made every individual in this country who knew him, whether of New England or not, proud that Edward Everett Hale was an American."

A short distance off to the r. there is a pool with a bronze statue group at its center; this is entitled *Triton Babies,* and was done in 1922 by the sculptress Anna Coleman Ladd.

Continuing along the central path, one soon crosses over the Public Garden pond on the pretty suspension bridge that spans its narrow waist. To the l. of the bridge is the dock used by the swanboats that sail on the pond in summer months, a concession that has been operated by the same family, the Pagets, since 1877. After reaching the other side of the bridge, turn off immediately onto the first path to the r. This leads to the N.W. corner of the Public Garden, passing on the way an unusual memorial known as the Ether Monument (see below). In the corner of the Garden, near the intersection of Beacon and Arlington Sts, is the *George Robert White Memorial.*

This fine monument is named after George Robert White (1847–1922), a philanthropist who during his lifetime gave considerable sums of money to worthy causes, and who in his will bequeathed $5 million to set up a charitable trust fund in his name, whose "net income was to be used for creating works of public utility and beauty for the use and enjoyment of the inhabitants of the City of Boston." One of the benefactions that derived from the George Robert White Fund was the Paul Revere Mall, or Prado, behind Old North, and another was the memorial in White's name in the Public Garden, completed in 1924. The central element in the memorial is the bronze figure of a winged maiden, standing on a pedestal, shown in the allegorical act of throwing bread into the water of the fountain, which is supplied by two spouts in the form of ram heads with tails like cornucopias. Inscribed on the pedestal are the words "Cast thy bread upon the water and thou shalt find it after many days," and on the outer parapet of the pool is inscribed the name of the donor and his dates. The bronze statue of the maiden is by Daniel Chester French (1850–1931), best known for his statue of Abraham Lincoln in the Lincoln Memorial in Washington, D.C.; the rest of the monument was designed by Henry Bacon.

After seeing the White Memorial, walk back to look at the *Ether Monument,* a work completed in 1867 by the sculptor John Quincy Adams Ward (1830–1910). This monument was erected to commemorate the first use of ether as an anesthetic in an operation, which took place in the Ether Dome of the Massachusetts General Hospital on Oct. 16, 1846. The monument is a fine example of High Victorian sculpture in granite and red marble. It is surrounded by a pool, with water supplied through spouts in the form of lion heads on the four sides of the base of the monument. Above the base on each side arches springing from columns form niches, in each of which there are reliefs and inscriptions related to the first use of ether as an anesthetic. (Dr Charles T. Jackson, who administered the ether in that operation, is not mentioned in the inscriptions, nor is Dr J. C. Warren, who performed the surgery, since at the time there was a heated controversy about who should get credit for the discovery; as Oliver Wendell Holmes put it, "This is a monument to ether or either.") Above this four coupled columns support a capital on which a turbaned figure representing the Good Samaritan supports and comforts a stricken youth.

Now continue along the W. side of the Public Garden to the plaza that precedes the gate leading out to Arlington St; there stands the splendid equestrian statue of George Washington, the most impressive honorific sculpture in the city. This is a work of Thomas Ball (1819–1911), a sculptor who studied art in Boston before going off to Florence in 1854. Funds to build the monument were raised by a Washington Statue Fair in the Music Hall, Nov. 16–24, 1859, after which Ball was commissioned to do the work. He first made the small plaster study that is now on show in the Boston Athenaeum, but his absence in Italy long delayed completion of the monument itself, a bronze sculpture of George Washington mounted on his horse, standing on a granite pedestal, and it was not dedicated until 1869. The model for Washington's mount was Black Prince, Colonel T. Bigelow Lawrence's favorite horse.

On the plaza in front of the Washington statue are two quite simple fountains, in the center of each of which there are small bronze sculptures, both of them representing young boys in an aquatic setting. The one on the l., as one faces the Washington statue, is by Mary E. Moore (1881–1967), and is entitled *Small Child;* the one to the r., entitled *Boy with a Bird,* is a work of Baska Paeff (1893–1979), which she originally sculpted in 1934 and recast in 1977, since the original was stolen.

Continue along the W. side of the Garden to its S.W. corner, where one must walk outside to see the monument there which faces onto Arlington St. This is a bronze statue of William Ellery Channing (1780–1842), the renowned Unitarian minister, a work of the New York sculptor Herbert Adams (1858–1945).

Channing was minister of the Federal Street Church from 1803 until his death. In 1859 the congregation abandoned the church on Federal St and moved into the present church at the N.W. corner of Arlington and Boylston Sts. The monument to Channing was funded by a bequest from a member of the congregation, John Foster, who specified that it should be erected opposite the church. Adams finished the statue in 1903, and it was dedicated on June 1 of that year, the centenary of Channing's ministry. Channing's epitaph could be no better expressed than in the stanza that Longfellow wrote as an encomium to him: "Well done! thy words are great and bold; / At times they seem to me / Like Luther's in the days of old / Half battles for the free!"

Re-entering the Public Garden, one can now walk back eastward along the path paralleling Boylston St, a mall of fine Belgian elms that cast their shade over a line of four commemorative statues. The first of these is a bronze statue of Senator Charles Sumner (1811–74), another work of Thomas Ball. Ball received the commission for this statue in Boston in 1876, and began work on it when he returned to his studio in Florence. When he finished the model he sent it to Paris to be cast by the renowned bronze-founder Barbedienne, and then had it shipped to Boston. The statue was unveiled on Dec. 23, 1878, without formal ceremonies other than the reading of a historical sketch of Sumner's career by Alexander H. Rice, then governor of Massachusetts.

In this sketch Governor Rice recalled the highlights of Sumner's political life, in which he was a leader in the crusades for the emancipation of slaves and for the preservation of the Union. The most dramatic moment in his career occurred in 1856, when Representative Preston Brooks of South Carolina attacked Sumner at his desk in the Senate, striking him on the head with his cane and rendering him unconscious. Sumner was so badly injured by this savage beating that it was nearly four years before he could return to the Senate, and in the interim his empty chair in the Senate chamber became a national symbol among Northerners of Southern viciousness.

Next is a bronze statue of Tadeusz Andrzei Bonawentura Kościuszko (1746–1817), the Polish patriot who fought so valiantly on the American side in the Revolutionary War, rising to the rank of brigadier general and serving as Washington's adjutant. In 1926, on the 150th anniversary of Kościuszko's enlistment in the Continental Army, Polish American groups in Boston sponsored a competition to design a memorial to their hero. The winning design was by the sculptress Theo Ruggles Kitson, who completed this fine and dramatic work in 1927.

The third monument on the mall is a bronze statue of Colonel Thomas Cass, a work of the sculptor Richard E. Brooks. Cass was born in Ireland and immigrated to the U.S., settling in Boston. He became captain of the Columbian Artillery Company, a Massachusetts Militia unit, and when the Civil War broke out he organized a regiment made up entirely of Irish immigrants. This was formed into the Ninth Massachusetts Infantry, the "Fighting Ninth," and Cass was placed in command, with the rank of colonel. Colonel Cass led the Fighting Ninth at the Battle of Malvern Hill in Virginia, where on July 1, 1862, he was killed in action while fighting valiantly at the head of his men. A granite statue of Colonel Cass was erected in the Public Garden in the early 1890s, but this monument was so unsatisfactory that it was removed, and a commission to create the present bronze statue was given to Richard E. Brooks. The present statue was dedicated in 1899 in the presence of a son and daughter of Colonel Cass and surviving members of the Fighting Ninth.

The fourth monument on the mall is a statue of Wendell Phillips (1811–84), the renowned Abolitionist orator, another work of Daniel Chester French, dedicated on July 4, 1915. On the pedestal beneath the statue are inscribed the subject's name and dates, and beneath that this list of his attributes: "Prophet of Liberty, Champion of the Slave," and on the facade of the monument behind him is inscribed a ringing phrase from the climax of one of his speeches: "Whether in chains or in laurels, Liberty knows nothing except victories." On the back of the monument another inscription quotes a speech by Phillips, one that reveals his deepest feelings about the town of his birth and the cause for which he fought throughout his life.

After walking along the last stretch of the mall, leave the Public Garden and cross Charles St to the S.W. corner of the Common. As one bears r. to round the corner of Charles and Boylston Sts, on the l. is a commemorative tablet honoring Edward A. Filene (1860–1937), founder of Filene's Department Store. An inscription below Filene's portrait bust describes him as "Author, scholar, outstanding citizen and public benefactor; acknowledged as founder of the Credit Union movement in the U.S."

After rounding the corner, turn l. on the first pathway leading into the Common. On the r. is the *Central Burying-Ground,* the fourth-oldest graveyard in Boston, established in 1756. One of the few notables known to be buried here is Gilbert Stuart, the painter, but the location of his grave is not known. Also interred here is William Billings (1746–1806), one of America's earliest native composers, whose gravesite is also unknown. Buried here in unmarked graves are British soldiers who died in the Battle of Concord, in the retreat from Concord to Charlestown, and in the Battle of Bunker Hill.

Continue past the graveyard on the same path, pausing at the first cross-path. If one looks to the r. here, a fenced-in triangular area lies just beyond the graveyard, at the corner of Tremont and Boylston Sts. In the 19C this was known as Deer Park, so called because of the tame deer that were kept there, along with peacocks. Ahead and to the l. is the *Parkman Bandstand,* an enclosure consisting of an elevated circular platform covered by a cupola carried by a circlet of 12 Ionic columns. This was built in 1897 by the architectural firm of Derby, Robinson and Shepard. The bandstand is named after George Francis Parkman, whose bequest financed its construction.

Continue walking along the same path, passing the bandstand. The next cross-path is known as the Oliver Wendell Holmes Walk. At this point turn r., and after a short way the *Boston Massacre Monument* is reached.

This is a singularly unattractive work by Robert Kraus (1850–1902), dedicated in 1888. The monument consists of the bronze statue of an allegorical female figure standing in front of a tapering granite column; she is holding in her r. hand a sundered chain, and with her l. hand she is about to unfurl a banner, while beside her an eagle is about to take flight. The top of the column is ringed by 13 stars, and on the shaft below these are the names of the five victims of the Boston Massacre of March 5, 1770: Crispus Attucks, Samuel Maverick, James Caldwell (this is incorrect: his first name is really Jonas), Samuel Gray, and Patrick Carr. On the front of the base a bronze bas-relief depicts the Massacre on King St (now State St), with the Old State House in the background. There are also inscriptions quoting John Adams and Daniel Webster on the historical significance of thi*s* tragic event.

Go out to Tremont St, and turn l. to walk up the mall on that side of the Common. A short way along on the l. is the *Declaration of Independence Monument.* This is a tablet with a bronze relief showing the signing of the Declaration of Independence in Philadelphia on July 4, 1776; below is the complete text of that historic document.

Farther along is the *Parkman Plaza,* at the front of which is the *Boston Common Information Center.* The Plaza is another work coming from the bequest of George Francis Parkman; at its center there is a fountain, unadorned and presently dry, and arrayed around the periphery of the area there are three atrocious bronze sculptures; these are allegorical figures representing Industry (l.), Religion (center), and Learning (r.).

Just beyond the Information Center a tablet honors Commodore John Barry, with a portrait bust of the naval hero above, and below this an inscription summarizing his distinguished career in the U.S. Navy.

A short way farther along is *Lafayette Mall,* at the beginning of which there is a tablet with a portrait bust of the Marquis de Lafayette. From the Lafayette Mall one can walk into the Common a few steps to see the *Brewer Fountain.* This is named after Gardner Brewer, a wealthy Bostonian who purchased it at the Paris Exhibition of 1867; it was one of two copies of the original bronze fountain made by the French sculptor Paul Lienard (1849–1900), which had caused a sensation at the Paris Exhibition of 1855. When Brewer shipped the fountain back from France he had it installed outside his house on Beacon St, just north of the Common; then, in the 1870s, he donated it to the city and it was installed in its present location, with a granite basin. Around the base of the fountain there are bronze statues of four reclining mythological figures—Poseidon (in Latin, Neptune), Amphitrite, Acis, and Galatea, all of whom are water deities; other decorative features are also connected with water and the sea: an anchor, a hawser, an oar, and a rudder, as well as naked nymphs and dolphins. The fountain and its surroundings have recently been restored, making this one of the more pleasant areas in the Common.

After seeing the Brewer Fountain, walk up to the plaza at the N.E. corner of the Common, at the corner of Park and Tremont Sts. As noted earlier, this once-attractive area is marred by the kiosk of the Park St subway station, as well as by the undesirable types that congregate here. On the facade of the kiosk a historic marker records the following information about the subway below, the first to be built in the U.S.: "The first subway in America was designed to solve the city-center problem of traffic-jams caused by street-cars. The new subway opened 1 September 1897. It had only two stops: Park Street and Boylston–Public Garden. To the surprise of critics, the buildings along Tremont Street did not fall down." Although the subway did not harm the buildings on the east side of Tremont St, its construction did result in the destruction of the venerable colonnade of elms on the W. side of the street, the first mall to be planted on the Common.

To the l. of the exit from the park at the corner of Park and Tremont Sts a historic marker commemorates the establishment of the Common in the first years of Boston.

The marker records a deposition made to the town authorities by John Odlin and three other old men in 1684, testifying as to the arrangements made with the Rev. Blaxton in acquiring his estate, which would then become Boston Common: "In or about the year of our Lord 1634, the then present inhabitants of the town of Boston, of whom the Hon. John Winthrop Esq. Gov. of the Colony was chiefe, did treat and agree with Mr. William Blackstone for the purchase of his estate and rights in any lands lying within said neck of land called Boston, after which purchase the Town laid out a plan for a trayning field which ever since and now is used for that purpose and for the feeding of cattell."

The itinerary ends with a stroll up the Park St mall to Beacon St. At noon the bells of the Park Street Church ring out a carillon of melodious old tunes, a reminder of the Common in times past.

12 Through the Old and the New South Ends to Copley Square

The itinerary begins at the S.E. corner of Boston Common, inside the park at the intersection of Park and Tremont Sts, and ends at Copley Sq. This will, in effect, take one through the old South End, as that term was understood in colonial times, and then through the northern fringe of the area that is today known as the South End. This long walk goes through neighborhoods which have, in the most part, decayed considerably in the present century, though parts of the new South End have experienced a remarkable revival in recent years. Nevertheless, decadent though most of it is, the part of town seen on this tour is an integral and important part of Boston, with its own shifting and changing mosaic of characteristics, and no overview of the city would be complete without it.

A. The Old South End

History and Topography. In colonial times the term South End was used in contradistinction to the terms North End and West End in delineating Boston topographically. At that time the South End comprised that part of the Shawmut Peninsula E. of the Common between Boston Neck and the isthmus joining the North End to the main peninsula. The North End and the South End included almost all the population of the colonial town, for the West End was used mainly as pastureland. The old South End reached its peak in the first half of the 19C, when many of the wealthiest families in Boston had splendid mansions there. But in the second half of the 19C the area became more and more given over to commercial enterprises, and the affluent residents moved to better parts of town, principally to the newly filled and developed Back Bay. By that time the topography of this part of Boston had been totally transformed by filling in the shallow waters along its shores: 86 acres of South Cove in 1806–43; 138 acres of South Bay beginning in 1850; and 500 acres of Back Bay starting in 1821. As a result, Boston was no longer a peninsula; the Neck had disappeared; the old South End had lost its identity and had been absorbed in the downtown commercial area; and the new South End came into being, comprising roughly the southern part of the filled-in Back Bay, as well as what had been the Neck and the widening stretch of mainland just to its W. Beginning in 1850, the city instituted measures to improve the public lands in the new South End, and a varied street plan was developed which stimulated the sale of building lots in the area. Throughout the third quarter of the 19C there was almost continual building activity in the new South End, as the population of Boston rose from 136,881 in 1850 to 341,919 in 1875. In 1856 the Metropolitan Railroad began to operate a horse-car service between Scollay Sq and Roxbury, bringing the new South End into convenient communication with the downtown area and making it a more desirable place to live. However, the new South End never developed into the elegant neighborhood that the old South End had been in the first half of the 19C, for most of the people who settled there were of modest means. Perhaps for that reason the quality of the South End began to decline nearly as soon as it was fully developed, as many of the original owners sold out and most of their dwellings were converted into rooming houses to provide shelter for the hordes of poor immigrants pouring into Boston. By 1900, 85 percent of the homes in the Union Park area had been converted into rooming houses, and in other parts of the new South End the percentage of conversions was nearly as high. Thus, by the early years of the present century, the new South End had degenerated into a slum, as was already the condition of the old South End. A vivid picture of what life was like in this part of Boston in the first decade of the 20C is given by Mary Antin in her autobiographical work, *The Promised Land* (1912). The authoress was a young girl at that time, the daughter of Polish Jews who had recently arrived in the U.S. They lived in a slum tenement on Dover St, which ran across what had once been Boston Neck, and was thus on the borderline of what had been the old and new South Ends. But by then the adjectives "old" and "new" were no longer used in describing the area, all of which was simply called *the* South End, and this is how Mary Antin describes that part of it she knew as a young girl: "Dover Street is a noisy thoroughfare cut through a South End slum. . . . Dover Street is intersected, near its eastern end, where we lived, by Harrison Avenue. That street is to the South End what Salem Street is to the North End. It is the heart of the South End ghetto, for the greater part of its length; although its northern end belongs to the realm of Chinatown. Its multifarious business bursts through the narrow shop doors, and overruns the basements, the sidewalk, the street itself, in pushcarts and open-air stands. Its multitudinous population bursts through the greasy tenement doors, and floods the corridors, the doorsteps, the gutters, the side streets, pushing in and out among the pushcarts, all day long and half the night beside. Rarely as Harrison Avenue is caught asleep, even more rarely is it found clean. Nothing less than a fire or flood would cleanse this street." Much of the South End is still a slum, though without the color and vitality that the newly arrived immigrants brought with them, for all of them except the Chinese have long since moved elsewhere. However, in certain parts of the South End the tide has turned in recent years, most notably in Bay Village, as ambitious working people have moved into the area, attracted by its low real-estate prices, and have bought run-down and shabby houses and largely through their own labor refurbished them to create comfortable and attractive homes. Today the South End is a mosaic of depressed slum and decent residential neighborhood, its character changing from block to block and sometimes from house to house.

Begin the itinerary by leaving the park and turning r. outside to walk a short distance down Tremont St, which can be crossed safely at the pedestrian walkway near the subway kiosk. This comes out at the head of Winter St, which is now part of the pedestrian mall called Downtown Crossing, of which the Washington Street Arcade (see above) is the central artery. Both corners of the intersection of Tremont and Winter Sts mark the sites of historic houses of the colonial period.

The plot on the corner to the l., as one faces Winter St, was in 1711 bought by Samuel Vetch, the first British governor of Nova Scotia. William Burnett, royal governor of Massachusetts in 1728–29, lived here during his term of office. Later a house on this site became the property of Francis Bernard, who was royal governor of Massachusetts in 1760–69, the last civilian to hold that post under British rule. During the British occupation of Boston this was one of several houses used as residences by Lord Percy, who led the force that was sent to Lexington on April 19, 1775. When General George Washington was in Boston after the British evacuation, he was entertained at dinner by John Andrews, who then owned the house. The plot on the r. corner was the site of a house that belonged to the Dudley family in 1706–25. The house was owned by Paul Dudley, whose father, Joseph Dudley, resided here and in the family estate in Roxbury after his term as governor, 1702–15. His successor as governor, Samuel Shute, also stayed in this house as a guest of Paul Dudley during his tenure, 1716–23.

The itinerary continues down the l. side of Tremont St, and in the middle of the next block is **St. Paul's Cathedral,** whose neoclassical form will have been noticed on the last leg of the previous itinerary, when walking up the Tremont St mall of the Common.

St. Paul's Cathedral was built by Alexander Parris in 1819–20, with Solomon Willard in charge of the stonework. The facade of the building is in the form of a Greek temple, the second example (after the facade of Bulfinch's New South Church, erected in 1814, now long demolished) of this type of church to be built in Boston; it has a portico of six unfluted sandstone columns with Ionic capitals, carved by Willard. The plans originally called for Willard to decorate the pediment with a scene in low relief showing "Paul before Agrippa," but lack of funds prevented its execution. When the church and its subterranean funerary crypt were completed in 1820, the remains of General Joseph Warren were disinterred from the crypt in King's Chapel and reburied in St. Paul's; then, in 1855, they were excavated once again and finally laid to rest in the Warren family plot in Forest Hill's Cemetery. The most notable of those whose remains are still interred in the crypt is William Hickling Prescott, the historian, who was laid to rest there in the family vault after his death on Jan. 29, 1859. (It is interesting to note that in 1666–67 the land on which St. Paul's stands is known to have belonged to an Indian named John Wampas, the latest date on record that land in Boston was owned by a Native American.)

Continue past St. Paul's, pausing at the corner of Temple Pl. The old *Masonic Temple* was built on this site in 1830–32; this was a large Gothic structure with two fortresslike towers, giving its name to Temple Pl. Ralph Waldo Emerson lectured here in 1832 and again in 1835–37, and it was the latter series of talks, on English literature, religion, and politics, that began his rise to fame. Bronson Alcott opened the *Temple School for Children* here in 1837, assisted by Elizabeth Peabody. The school lasted for only three years, largely because of opposition to Alcott's unconventional ideas on education.

The old Masonic Temple was built on the northern end of *Washington Gardens,* which extended from there to the corner of West St, at the next turning. This was a walled enclosure with trees and flower beds, where as early as 1815 a public concert was given to a paying audience. In 1819 an amphitheater was constructed within the grounds, a place of entertainment that was called *Vauxhall.* Vauxhall was used both as a theater and as a circus, with equestrian performances given there on occasion, the first such establishment in Boston. During the British occupation a battalion of redcoats was encamped within the grounds, at that time known as *Greenleaf's Garden.*

Continue along Tremont to the corner of West St. At the far corner of Tremont and West there was in colonial times a *gun house;* this was a small arsenal that housed the arms and ammunition of the Boston Regiment, a crack militia unit. A short distance down the way to the l., at the near corner of West and Mason Sts, stood the *South Writing School,* founded no later than 1722.

The school and the gun house stood on the same block and were separated only by a garden, a contiguity that coupled the two quite different institutions in a celebrated incident during the British occupation. The commander of artillery in the Boston Regiment at that time was Major Aldino Paddock, and his total armament was two brass three-pounders, which were kept in the gun house at the corner of Tremont and West Sts. These pieces had been recast from two old guns sent by the town to London for that purpose, and while they were in the foundry there the coat-of-arms of the royal Province of Massachusetts was engraved upon their barrels. The two cannon arrived in Boston in 1768 and were first used at the celebration of the King's birthday on June 4 of that year, when a salute was fired in King St. At the outbreak of the Revolution, General Gage ordered that all weapons in the hands of private citizens be turned in to the British forces, and that the armaments of the Boston Regiment and other militia units should be handed over as well. Major Paddock informed the members of his artillery company, all of whom were patriotic mechanics, that he intended to hand over to the British the two cannon in his charge. The mechanics thereupon held a secret nocturnal meeting in the schoolhouse on West and Mason Sts, where they formulated a plan to keep the guns from falling into the hands of the British. That same evening, when the sentinel at the gun house was temporarily absent for roll call, a group of mechanics gained entrance to the arsenal and removed the cannon, which they hid in a large box in the schoolroom used to store firewood. When the loss of the cannon was discovered a frantic search was made for them, which included a thorough examination of the schoolroom while class was in session, but the old schoolmaster, who along with several of his pupils knew that the guns were there, prevented their discovery by resting his gouty leg on the box where they were hidden. The mechanics left the guns in their hiding place for two weeks, until the search was finally called off. The guns were then taken from the schoolhouse and transported in a wheelbarrow to a blacksmith's shop near the docks in the South End, where they were hidden in a coal pile. From there they were soon taken in a boat to Cambridge and carried to the headquarters of the Continental Army, where they were received with joy, for the total armament of the American artillery there at the time was two other three-pounders, which had been smuggled out of Boston only a short time before. The two cannon of the Boston Regiment were in constant combat use throughout the war, and when peace came the Congress restored them to the state of Massachusetts. General Knox, secretary of war, was directed to place suitable inscriptions upon them, which he had done, officially naming them the "Hancock" and the "Adams." After their return the two guns were put in the charge of the Ancient and Honorable Artillery Company, who kept them in their armory in Faneuil Hall. In 1825, the "Hancock" and the "Adams" were presented by the state to the Bunker Hill Monument Assoc. When the monument was completed, the two guns were placed in the chamber at the top of the obelisk, where they can still be seen.

The far side of the intersection of Tremont and West Sts was until 1800 the West Gate to the Common. The *Whipping-Post* and *Pillory*, which were movable instruments, were situated for a time outside the West Gate after being removed from their usual location in the vicinity of the Old State House. Public whipping was inflicted in Boston as late as 1803, and the last recorded use of the Pillory took place that same year. The latter occurred when two men named Pierpont and Storey, the owner and master, respectively, of the brig *Hannah*, were convicted of scuttling their ship in Boston Harbor to collect the insurance. The two men were sentenced to be displayed publicly in the Pillory on two successive days for one hour each time, so that the public could observe and revile them, after which they would pay the costs of their prosecution and then be imprisoned for a year.

The block on Tremont St between West and Avery Sts was once the finest in all of Boston, for it was the site of *Colonnade Row*, a block of 19 brick mansions that stretched down to Avery St, with another five around the corner of the latter street. These were designed by Charles Bulfinch and completed in 1811; they were four-story structures with joined wrought-iron balconies on the second floor that were supported by a continuous row of Doric columns; hence the name Colonnade. Some of the wealthiest and most powerful Boston families lived here during the first half of the 19C, most notably the Lawrences and the Lowells.

One of the most touching incidents in the history of Boston concerns Colonnade Row, and this occurred at the time of Lafayette's visit to Boston in Aug. 1824, after an absence of 40 years. When Lafayette entered the city, in a barouche carriage drawn by four white horses, he was welcomed by Mayor Josiah Quincy, who joined him for the ride into town. During the ride Lafayette told Quincy that he would like to see John Hancock's widow, Dolly, during his stay, for she had been his hostess at the Hancock mansion on Beacon St when he first came to Boston in 1778 as a volunteer officer in the Continental Army. When their carriage reached Colonnade Row, Mayor Quincy pointed out to Lafayette where Dolly Hancock was seated on a friend's balcony, waving down to them. At this, Lafayette had the coachman stop, and then, rising to his feet, "hand over heart, made a graceful obeisance," after which Dolly Hancock rose too, making a graceful curtsy, while the crowd cheered wildly. That evening, after his official welcoming banquet, Lafayette visited Dolly Hancock at her residence on Federal St, where they could quietly reminisce together.

In the second half of the 19C the wealthy residents of Tremont St opposite the Common sold their mansions and moved elsewhere, because of the increasing commercialization of the area. By the end of the 19C all the mansions on Colonnade Row had been demolished and replaced by commercial structures, a few of which are still standing. Of these, the only one of interest, and even that is in debased form, is the building now known as the *Savoy Theater.* This was originally *Keith's Theater,* a structure built in 1893 for Benjamin F. Keith by the New York architect J. B. McElfatrick, best known for his successful remodeling of the old Metropolitan Opera House of New York.

Keith's Theater later became known as "the mother house of American vaudeville," as Keith revolutionized popular entertainment with his concept of "continuous performances" of high-quality variety acts that were kept clean to attract a family clientele, rather than the Scollay Sq types that frequented the Old Howard. This proved to be highly profitable, so much so that Keith eventually built up a nationwide chain of 400 such theaters, one of the most famous being the *Palace* in New York. Unfortunately, the original Keith's Theater on Tremont St, which had a charming facade, was totally ruined architecturally by a brutal remodeling early in the present century.

Starting at the corner of Tremont and West Sts, the itinerary now makes a detour, going around the block via West, Washington, and Avery Sts, where the stroll down Tremont St is resumed for one more block.

Starting down West St, one finds on the l. at No. 9 the *Brattle Book Shop,* an emporium of secondhand and antiquarian books without equal in the U.S.

This establishment advertises itself, quite correctly, as the "successor to America's oldest antiquarian bookshop," being in the direct line of succession to a bookseller named Burnham who set up shop in Cornhill in 1825. The shop is owned by Mr. George Gloss, who was himself a Cornhill bookseller earlier in his career, and who in 1947 purchased this shop when it was on Brattle St, hence the present name. The shop later moved to 5 West St, where it was ravaged in a fire on Feb. 1, 1980, after which Mr. Gloss picked up the pieces and began again here later that same year. Mr. Gloss estimates that he has in stock 350,000 hardbacks and nearly 100,000 paperbacks, and if the book for which you are looking is not there, he will be glad to find it for you.

Continuing down West St: at No. 13 is the site of a bookshop established in 1840 by Elizabeth Peabody, the brilliant young educator and sister of Sophia, the wife of Nathaniel Hawthorne. Miss Peabody's establishment was the first bookshop in the U.S. that catered primarily to women. It was also one of the intellectual centers in Boston in the mid-19C, frequented by people such as Nathaniel Hawthorne, Ralph Waldo Emerson, William Ellery Channing, Margaret Fuller, and Horace Mann, who frequently lectured there to Miss Peabody and her circle.

Mason St opens off to the r. at this point, and at the N. corner is the site of the South Writing School, where the two purloined cannon, the "Hancock" and the "Adams," were hidden from the British in 1775. The S. corner was the site of a pub which in the years just prior to the Revolution was known as *Hatch's Tavern.* In the early years of the 20C the *Massachusetts Medical College* was situated halfway down Mason St, directly behind Colonnade Row. The faculty and the students of the College had a somewhat ghoulish reputation among the local residents, who suspected that the institution had been established on Mason St because of its proximity to the Central Burying Ground, giving them a convenient source of cadavers for the dissecting room. And so there were sighs of relief when the College moved to the West End to become part of Massachusetts General Hospital.

As one continues down West St, the next corner is Washington St. Turn right. In colonial times the *South End Haymarket* was located here, to the r., at the lower end of West St. If one walks along Washington, on the l. is the huge *Lafayette Plaza,* and on the r. at mid-block is the *Savoy Theater,* which now houses Sarah Caldwell's *Opera Company of Boston.* This was originally the *B. F. Keith Memorial Theater,* built by the architect Thomas Lamb in 1928 to honor the memory of the man who made respectable vaudeville a tremendously popular form of public entertainment throughout the U.S., thus establishing the chain of theaters that would become the first "picture palaces" when motion pictures became popular in the 1920s.

The Savoy Theater is constructed partly on the foundations of the famous *Boston Theater of 1854,* and largely follows the plan of that structure. The Boston Theater on Washington St was a direct successor to Bulfinch's original Federal Street Theater of 1794, which was rebuilt in 1798 after a fire and continued to function until 1852, with the new Boston Theater replacing it two years later. Virtually every theatrical star in the second half of the 19C played at the Boston Theater, including Sarah Bernhardt, Lillie Langtry, James O'Neill (Eugene O'Neill's father), and Edwin Booth. Booth was playing the lead in a tragedy at the Boston Theater on the night of April 14, 1865, the same night that his brother John Wilkes Booth shot Lincoln. Booth heard the news the next morning and went into seclusion, whereupon the Boston Theater closed temporarily and canceled the remaining performances of the tragedy. But it was for opera that the Boston Theater is chiefly remembered. All of the legendary divas sang at the Boston, including Calve, Melba, Gadski, and Lehmann; Mahler conducted *Don Giovanni* at the Boston; and Caruso here made his local debut. Concerts were held here as well, and in one of the most memorable of such programs Paderewski performed on the piano. The Boston Theater was also the scene of important civic events, the most notable of which was the Grand Ball given for the Prince of Wales, the future King Edward VII, during his visit to Boston in 1860.

Benjamin Keith began his remarkable career in a small storefront "museum of curiosities" next to the Boston Theater on Washington St; this later developed into a small variety show, the predecessor of the program that he later made so popular in his first regular theater on Tremont St. George Upham, a contemporary of Keith's, recalled in later years that "Keith himself introduced the acts and Mrs Keith kept it clean."

Continue along Washington to the next corner to turn r. on Avery, and at the next corner turn l. to resume walking down Tremont St. The first few buildings on this block stand on the site of the old *Haymarket Theater.* This huge theater, the second to open in Boston, was reputed to be one of the finest in the U.S.; however, it could not compete successfully with the Boston Theater and was closed just two years later, after which it was demolished.

Boylston St is reached at the next corner. The massive structure on the corner is the *Masonic Building,* designed by Loring and Phipps and dedicated on Dec. 28, 1899. The building just across from this on the opposite side of Boylston St is the former *Hotel Tourain,* built in 1897–98 by the architectural firm of Winslow and Wetherell. On this site was the mansion house of John Quincy Adams, sixth President of the U.S., and it was here that his son Charles Francis Adams was born in 1807. The unusual and rather charming building to the l. of this, at 48 Boylston St, houses the *Young Men's Christian Union.* The YMCU is a recreation center for young Christian men, founded in 1851. Its headquarters building here was erected in 1875–76 by the architects Nathaniel J. Bradlee and W. T. Winslow, who designed it in the Italian Gothic style. There was once a tower above the loggia on the projecting l. side of the building, but this was removed in 1912.

Turn l. to walk down Boylston St, which in early colonial times was known as Frog Lane. At the end of the block one should pause for a moment to look up at the facade of the building diagonally across the intersection, at the S.E. corner of Boylston St and Washington St. There in low relief is the model of a tree with wide-spreading branches. The inscription on the relief is difficult to discern because of the grime that has accumulated upon it, but it reads as follows, in four lines: "Liberty 1776 / Law and Order / Sons of Liberty 1776 / Independence 1776." This marks the exact site of the *Liberty Tree,* the rallying point for the Sons of Liberty in the years just prior to the Revolution.

History. The open area at the streets now known as Washington, Boylston, Essex, the latter being the continuation of Boylston St, was in colonial times known as Hanover Sq, from the royal House of Hanover. At that time the present Washington St was known as Orange St, after the royal House of Orange. Orange St was the main thoroughfare from Boston out to the mainland across the Neck, and once out of town it was called the High Road. In the colonial period the area around Hanover Sq was also known as the Elm Neighborhood, from the splendid elms that grew there. It was the oldest and grandest of these elms that came to be called the Liberty Tree; this came about when the Sons of Liberty first began meeting under its wide-spreading branches, whereupon the ground around it took on the name of Liberty Hall. The Liberty Tree first appears prominently in the history of the era just prior to the Revolution in connection with popular opposition to the Stamp Act. At dawn on Aug. 14, 1765, an effigy of Andrew Oliver, the stamp master, was found hanging from the Liberty Tree, along with a boot with a devil's head peering from it—an allusion to Lord Bute, the prime minister who signed the Stamp Act. News of this spread fast, and soon crowds came flocking to the Liberty Tree from town and from the surrounding countryside, causing such a sensation that everyday affairs virtually came to a halt. When Lieutenant Governor Hutchinson heard of this he ordered the sheriff to remove the effigies; however, the sheriff told him he was unable to do so in the face of the powerful opposition he would face. And so the effigies remained hanging from the Liberty Tree all day, as crowds continued to make their way out to Hanover Sq to see the bizarre sight. At sunset the effigies were taken down by the Sons of Liberty, placed upon a bier, and a veritable funeral procession of several thousand people formed up to follow behind Oliver's gibbeted figure as it was carried into town. The procession went first to the Town House, where Governor Bernard and his Council were discussing the affair, and the mob passed right through the open lower floor as the Sons of Liberty led the way to Fort Hill. There the two effigies were burned in a huge bonfire in full view of Oliver's house, after which the mob sacked the houses of Hutchinson and other officials of the government and the Crown, destroying the records of the court of the vice-admiralty in the process.

This violence so frightened Oliver that he announced he was going to resign the post, and when the stamps arrived he consigned them to storage in Castle William. The Sons of Liberty continued to put pressure on Oliver, demanding that he publicly denounce the Stamp Act. Oliver finally agreed, saying that he would state this at a public meeting in the Town House. However, the Sons of Liberty insisted that he make his denunciation before them at the Liberty Tree, which he finally did later that autumn, a great victory for the opponents of the Crown.

These events enshrined the Liberty Tree as an almost sacred symbol of the American cause, and as such the Sons of Liberty looked after it and tried to maintain it in the best possible condition, hiring men to prune it carefully. This action was recorded in a large copper plaque that was affixed to the tree with this inscription: "This tree was planted in the year 1646, and pruned by orders of the Sons of Liberty, Feb. 14 1766."

In May 1766 news arrived in Boston that the Stamp Act had been repealed, and the patriots in Boston were exultant. Early that evening the Sons of Liberty gathered around the Liberty Tree and decked it with banners and lighted lanterns, after which they proceeded to the Common for the great celebration and fireworks display that they had prepared there, the most joyous evening that the town experienced in the decade before the Revolution.

Another dramatic event associated with the Liberty Tree occurred in 1773, in connection with popular opposition to the hated tea tax. In mid-Dec. of that year, while the tea ships were moored at Griffin's Wharf waiting to unload, the consignees of the tea were summoned by the Sons of Liberty to the Liberty Tree, where they would have to state publicly why they could not refuse to accept the tea and have it shipped back to England. When the consignees failed to appear, the Sons of Liberty led a mob that rioted in the vicinity of the

Town House, adding further tension to the already explosive situation, all of which was resolved within a few days by the Boston Tea Party.

After the Revolution began, it was inevitable that the British troops and their Tory sympathizers would wreak their vengeance on an object that had become the symbol of American resistance to the Crown. One day in Aug. 1775 a mob of redcoats and Tories marched out to Hanover Sq with the intention of destroying the Liberty Tree. The following day the *Essex Gazette* reported: "Armed with axes, they made a furious attack upon it. After a long spell of laughing and grinning, sweating, swearing, and foaming, with malice diabolical, they cut down a tree because it bore the name of Liberty." The mob then began to cut up the tree for firewood (some idea of its great size can be gained from the fact that it amounted to 14 cords), and in the course of doing so, one of the soldiers, who was trying to hack off a high branch, fell to the ground and was killed instantly. When news of the incident arrived in the Continental lines, this gave some small comfort to the Sons of Liberty.

After the Revolution a liberty pole was erected on the stump of the severed tree, which for long afterward served as a landmark under the name of Liberty Stump. At the time of Lafayette's visit to Boston in 1824, a handsome arch was constructed at the site of the Liberty Tree, whose stump still remained in place. When Lafayette's carriage passed through the arch he paused to look down on the forlorn stump, saying to Mayor Quincy that "the world should never forget the spot where once stood Liberty Tree, so famous in your annals." In 1833 the stump was enclosed within the *Liberty Tree Tavern,* which became a popular watering place in the South End. The tavern continued to operate until the late 19C, at which point it is no longer mentioned in descriptions of the city, undoubtedly demolished to make way for a commercial building, and with it disappeared the last vestige of the historic Liberty Tree.

Hanover Sq was only half a mile from the Neck, and it was a favorite stopping place for farmers coming into town on their ox carts to sell produce in the market. While there they took their refreshments in a tavern in the square that had been founded by a lively lady named Peggy Moore. Many of the farmers sold or traded their goods at Hanover Sq rather than make the trip into town. The volume of trade at Hanover Sq was such that when the Town Council in 1734 appropriated funds for three market buildings it placed one of them on Hanover Sq, the others being at North Sq and Dock Sq. This market hall stood on the same site as the present buildings at the S.W. corner of Boylston and Washington Sts, directly opposite the building whose facade bears the relief of the Liberty Tree. The market hall functioned there until 1809, when it was demolished to make way for a much larger one, to be called the *Boylston Market.* The architect was Charles Bulfinch, who just three years before had designed and built the larger version of Faneuil Hall. Thus it is no surprise that Bulfinch designed the Boylston Market in the same general style as Faneuil Hall, and of comparable dimensions. John Quincy Adams laid the cornerstone on May 23, 1809, and on Nov. 14 of that same year it opened for business. The Boylston Market remained in operation until 1889, when it was demolished to make way for another building. Its cupola and its clock survive in the structure of the Calvary Methodist Church on Massachusetts Ave in Arlington.

The itinerary now turns r. on Washington St. The long structure on the r., at 2–22 Boylston St, at the S.W. corner of Washington St, is the *Boylston Building,* built in 1889 by the architect Carl Fehmer. It replaced Bulfinch's Boylston Market; it is a distinguished old structure, with its masonry face hung from a cast-iron skeleton.

At the next corner Lagrange St leads off to the l. and Allen's Alley to the r. At the far corner of the latter street, at 681–683 Washington, stands the *Hayden Building.* This is a perfectly ordinary building in all respects, and one would pass it by without notice were it not for the fact that this is the first commercial structure designed by H. H. Richardson (1875).

At the next corner turn l. onto Kneeland St, then at the next corner l. again on to Harrison Ave; this brings one into the heart of Boston's ***China-town,** the most colorful, picturesque, and dramatic neighborhood in the city.

Boston's Chinatown is much smaller than those in New York and San

Francisco. Its core is essentially two square blocks, bounded by Harrison on the W., Hudson on the E., Kneeland on the S., and Beach on the N., with Tyler cutting through the middle from S. to N. Almost all of the Chinese restaurants and shops are concentrated in this two-block area, which is teeming with Oriental life and redolent with heady Oriental aromas. However, a number of Chinese enterprises have expanded into the surrounding neighborhood, particularly to the S., where many former residents of Chinatown have moved to find better housing. The simplest route for a tour of the heart of Chinatown would be as follows: walk along Harrison from Kneeland to Beach; turn r. on Beach and then r. again on Tyler; then turn r. on Kneeland and r. again on Hudson. The building on the S.E. corner of Kneeland and Hudson with the pagoda on its roof is the *Chinese Merchants Association.* At the next corner Hudson returns to Beach St. Looking to the r. here, one sees a large *ceremonial gate.* This is the official entryway to Chinatown, with a pair of guardian lions on either side. It was erected in 1982, and part of the funds for its construction were provided by Taiwan. The inscriptions on the top of the gate contain maxims for the Chinese in their dealings with one another; that in front advises one to deal with others justly, humbly, and with a sense of shame if one does not deal morally; the inscription on the back stresses the need for peace and justice.

After seeing the ceremonial gate, go back along Beach and turn r. on Harrison to return to Kneeland, where the tour of Chinatown ends.

The most sensational time to come here is Chinese New Year, when fire-breathing dragons are paraded through the streets, accompanied by musicians playing traditional Oriental instruments, strutting groups from martial-arts academies, schoolchildren in Chinese costume, the air heavy with burning incense and the acrid smell of exploding firecrackers. And one should come again after New Year for the traditional Blessing of the Shops, when a benevolent dragon, accompanied by a corps of formidable young men from a martial-arts academy, dressed in the medieval garb of one of the militant brotherhoods, goes from shop to shop to give his blessing, which is as prolonged and spirited as the merchant's donation is generous, while a small band of Chinese musicians play atonal, discordant melodies evoking ancient Cathay.

After leaving Chinatown, return up Kneeland to Washington, which, after the crossing, becomes Stuart St. Before continuing up Stuart, pause for a moment and check on the topography of the area through which you have been walking. The detour from Washington down Kneeland into Chinatown left the old South End at Harrison Ave, which formed the shoreline in the colonial period, and went into what was once part of South Cove, land filled in during the period 1806–43. The route is now back on the original Shawmut Peninsula, but on the narrowing part of the Old South End approaching the Neck.

Continue up Stuart St, and on the r. at Nos 31–37 is *Jacob Wirth's.* This is the oldest bar in continuous operation (except during Prohibition) in Boston, founded in 1866, and is still the very best in its class, with its own draft beer, good food at low prices, its original decor intact and even enhanced by the general atmosphere of seediness that is so in keeping with the neighborhood, its generally shabby but loyal clientele fitting in perfectly with the surroundings. No visit to Boston would be complete without a visit to this the last authentic old-fashioned saloon in Boston. The two buildings that house Jacob Wirth's are older than the saloon itself; they were built in 1844–45 by the architect Greenleaf C. Sanborn, and are the only bow-front Greek Revival houses left in this neighborhood, where that type was once very popular.

At the next corner is Tremont St, the center of Boston's historic ***Theater District**. If one looks down Tremont St, to the r. on the far side of the street at mid-block is the *Saxon Theater;* beyond that, with its entrance around the corner on Boylston St, is the *Colonial Theater.* Now look to the l.; on the near side of the street is the *Wilbur Theater;* next to that is *Metropolitan Center;* on the far side of the street and a bit farther on is the *Shubert Theater;* and out of sight behind that is the *Charles Playhouse,* with its entrance on Warrenton St. These are just six of the 24 major theaters and concert halls erected in downtown Boston in 1900–35, not counting dozens of smaller playhouses and music halls. (The Charles Playhouse was actually built much earlier.) Thirteen of these were clustered in the new Theater District that developed during this period on lower Tremont and Washington Sts, of which the half-dozen mentioned above are among the finest extant.

To have a brief look at the exteriors of these theaters, in the order given above, begin by turning r. on Tremont and cross over to the *Saxon Theater.* This was originally known as the *Majestic Theater,* and it was built in 1903 by the architects John Galen Howard and J. M. Wood. The funds for its construction were a gift from Eben Jordan, one of the founders of Jordan-Marsh. The facade is neo-Roman rather than Greek Revival, with four massive engaged fluted columns with capitals of a composite order flanking three high-arched windows, above the keystones of which are affixed theatrical masks. Historians of architecture have characterized its interior as "a theater of artifice and exaggeration" with a "lavish rococo auditorium unmatched in Boston."

Continue down Tremont and turn l. at the corner onto Boylston St, where the *Colonial Theater* stands. The Colonial Theater and the Colonial Building in which it stands were built in 1899–1900 by Clarence H. Blackall. There is nothing exceptional about the theater or the building in which it is housed, except for the handsome two-story loggia that extends across the top of the structure. But the interior, designed by H. B. Pennell, is the richest and most elegant of any of the theaters in the area, with a splendid rococo lobby finished in Pompeian marble and a marble staircase with a burnished bronze banister. The Colonial Theater is renowned for its associations with Irving Berlin and Sigmund Romberg; it was where Ziegfeld launched his Follies, and where Rodgers and Hammerstein opened so many of their musical comedies.

Return to the corner of Tremont and Stuart and cross over to look at the *Wilbur Theater,* one of the most popular playhouses in present day Boston. The facade is revetted in red Harvard brick and there are three neoclassical entryways, each with two engaged columns framed by the pilasters and pediment. Above the doorway there are three large round-arched windows, with theatrical masks framed in the arches, and a wrought-iron balcony over the first floor. When the Wilbur was first opened in 1914 its management proudly announced that it was "the first of the new intimate theaters in Boston."

A plaque beside the entrance gives this information: "Ye Wilbur Theater opened in 1914. It was designed by the architect Clarence Blackall and is renowned for its architecture, individuality, grace and refinement. Ye Wilbur has hosted many world premiers, among them *Our Town, A Streetcar Named Desire, The Miracle Worker, Long Day's Journey into Night.* International stars who have appeared on its stage include Marlon Brando, Anne Bancroft, Kirk Douglas, Patricia Neal, Charlton Heston, Julie Harris, Montgomery Clift, Henry Fonda, Joan Bennett, Carol Channing and Jason Robards."

Next to the Wilbur is *Metropolitan Center,* formerly the *Music Hall* and before that the *Metropolitan Theater,* its original name. This was built in 1925 by Clarence H. Blackall, assisted by several associate architects, and it was the last theater he designed in Boston. Actually, the Met was not intended for the staging of plays or opera, but was designed to be a "picture palace," the greatest of all times. Adolf Zukor, the Hollywood magnate, was one of many notables who came to Boston for the operning of the Met, and he described it as a theater of "mountainous splendour, a movie palace of fabulous grandeure and stupendous stage presentations." Then, as now, it was one of the largest theaters in the world, with 4407 seats, and at the gala opening 20,000 people were present. After entering, one passes through a series of three lobbies before coming to the Grand Lobby, a full city block long and five stories high, encircled by three tiers of promenades. The auditorium is one of the largest in the world, a vast enclosed space of grandiose proportions that one observer described as being a "cathedral of the movies." One can understand the typical reaction of the guests at opening night, whom the *"Boston Advertiser"* described as "rubbing their eyes and wondering if were all a dream." The Met has recently been restored, and it is now called the Wang Center for the Performing Arts.

Now cross the street to visit the *Shubert Theater,* which rivals the Wilbur as one of the most popular playhouses in Boston. The Shubert has a handsome white facade designed in the neoclassical style, with a monumental Palladian window over the entryway framed by a pair of Ionic columns, and with the approach to the entrance covered by a gently curving wrought-iron canopy.

A plaque beside the entrance gives this information about the Shubert and its theatrical history: "The Shubert Theater was designed by the architects Charles Bond and Thomas James. It opened on January 24, 1910 and has enjoyed a rich history of world premiers and memorable performances. International stars who have appeared on its stage include Sarah Bernhardt, W. C. Fields, Mae West, Humphrey Bogart, Ingrid Bergman, Henry Ford, Rex Harrison, Zero Mostel, Helen Hayes, and Cary Grant."

The last theater in the group, the *Charles Playhouse,* is most easily approached by going through the parking lot at the l. of the Shubert, but, if that is blocked, one can go around the block past the Shubert, turning l. on Stuart and l. again on Warrenton, coming to the theater at the end of the block on the r.

As was noted earlier, the Charles Playhouse, or, rather, the structure in which it is housed, is much older than the other theaters in the area. It was originally designed as a church by Asher Benjamin and built in the years 1839—43. It first housed the Fifth Universalist Church; then it was taken over by the Temple Ohabei Shalom, the first Jewish congregation in Boston; still later it was acquired by the Scotch Church, Presbyterian rite; afterward it was for a long time a nightclub until, in 1957—66, it was renovated by the Cambridge Seven for use as a theater. The building is quite handsome and distinctive, with its Greek-temple front formed by two wooden Ionic columns between brick pilasters, which support a wooden architrave and raking cornices that frame the brick pediment. It is a unique and fitting home for a theater.

Continue in the same direction along Warrenton, which curves to the r. after passing the Playhouse and heads out to the highway, Charles St S. Just before reaching the highway on the l. is a little byway named Lyndeboro Place, an exceptionally pretty bricked courtyard closed by an ornate wrought-iron gate and with an old oil lamp in the center. Around the courtyard there are four Federal-style houses dating c. 1838. They are of the same style as the houses across the highway in Bay Village: built of red brick, two stories high, with ridge roofs, dormer windows, recessed door-ways, and plain lintels. This is one of the most charming enclaves in Boston, in the midst of a harsh and ugly urban wasteland.

Until a decade or so ago, Carver St intersected Broadway at this point, just at the foot of Warrenton and next to Lyndeboro Place, but the creation of the highway along Charles St S. wiped out all of that. Along the stretch of Carver St near this intersection there were two houses with literary asso-ciations. Edgar Allan Poe was born in a lodging house at 62 Carver St on Jan. 19, 1809, when his parents were working as actors in a stock company that was playing at the Federal Street Theater. The house that once stood at 77 Carver St was in 1845 the home of Horace Mann, who was then married to Mary Peabody. The following year Nathaniel Hawthorne and his wife, Sophia, Mary's sister, came for an extended stay as guests of the Manns at 77 Carver. Both of these houses had disappeared long before the street on which they stood was itself swept away.

The itinerary now crosses the highway to the foot of Fayette St. This is ***Bay Village,** a small and compact neighborhood whose streets are lined with brick row houses of the 1820s and 1830s. The itinerary has here crossed over from the old South End to the new South End.

History and Topography. The neighborhood now known as Bay Village was in colonial times part of the shallows of Back Bay, an area of mud flats created by tidal flow, and was just offshore from the western side of the Neck near its narrowest part. (The name Bay Village is not found in old maps; it is a modern invention by real-estate developers.) The land was made habitable in a series of projects that began with the completion of Mill Dam in 1821, shutting off Back Bay from the tidal action of the Charles River estuary. A dike was then built in the N.-S. direction from the Mill Dam to the mainland just beyond the Neck, following approximately the line of the present Arlington St as if it were extended to Washington St. Then, in 1825, the Boston City Council passed orders to build another dike on the mud flats from the N.-S. dike to the Shawmut Peninsula along the present line of Fayette St. This enclosed an area in Back Bay between the N.-S. dike and the western shore of the Shawmut Peninsula, and as the waters drained off from the mud flats the land could be laid out in streets and house lots. The streets were laid out in the following order: Fayette and Piedmont Sts, in 1824, even before the completion of the E.-W. dam; Melrose (originally Marion) and Winchester (originally S. Cedar) Sts in 1825; Knox St in 1830; Bay St in 1833; and Church St in 1835. In 1827 a Presbyterian church was erected on what would later be Church St, between Piedmont and Winchester (then S. Cedar) Sts, and from this came the name of the street that today forms the N.-S. axis of Bay Village. Some years later this became the Third Methodist Episcopal Church, with some 20–30 members. The church has since been demolished and its site is occupied by a commercial building, one of the few in Bay Village. This church gave its name to the neighborhood now known as Bay Village, which up until the late 1950s was known as the Church Street District.

The man most active in the development of the Church Street District was Ephraim Marsh (1767–1847), a native of Hingham, Mass., who came to Boston as a young man to earn his living as a housewright. Marsh was made a member of the Common Council, and during Josiah Quincy's term of office in 1823–29 he became the Mayor's "right-hand man," according to the testimony of one of his contemporaries. During his long and useful life Marsh erected some 300 structures in Boston, including several on Beacon Hill, and a number in Bay Village that are still standing. Marsh himself owned ten houses in the Church Street District, including his own residence at 1 Fayette St. Many of the other houses in the area were built by owner-artisans, including housewrights, stair-builders, bricklayers, and carpenters, most of whom had earned their capital by working for the Mount Vernon Pro-prietors in the development of Beacon Hill. Besides these, virtually all of the original hou-seowners in the Church Street District were artisans, skilled workers, or small shopkeepers who had earned the money necessary to buy their plot of land and to build or to have built their house. This undoubtedly gave rise to a sense of "house pride" that gave the Church

Street District far greater stability than the rest of new South End, which is why it has survived virtually intact today, while so much of the surrounding area has decayed or been destroyed. But even the Church Street District declined, though not as seriously as the rest of the South End, part of the general urban blight that Boston experienced from the mid-19C to the mid-20C. The revival of Bay Village, as the area was by then known, started in the late 1950s, when the demand for small houses on Beacon Hill and elsewhere in downtown Boston exceeded the supply. The new residents were generally young or retired couples in the professions or middle-level management who had the time and financial resources necessary to restore those houses that had fallen into disrepair. These new householders quickly banded together to take common action to preserve the quality of life in Bay Village, and to protect it from the decadent and destructive forces present in the depressed areas around it. The residents of Bay Village have succeeded admirably, and their neighborhood is a model of what a downtown residential area could be like in a modern American city like Boston, but rarely is.

There are no monuments in Bay Village, other than the neighborhood itself, and the best approach is just to walk along its quiet streets and look at its fine old houses, appreciating the serene atmosphere of this picturesque quarter. Begin at Fayette St, where the modern building to the r. at the head of the street is the Boston headquarters of Oxfam.

A plaque on the wall of this building gives the following information about the neighborhood: "The character and charm of Bay Village owe much to Ephraim Marsh, its foremost developer. Marsh owned much of the area and laid out the streets in the 1820s. He also built some of the area's finest houses, particularly on Fayette St, where he lived (at No. 1). His house resembled those at Nos 33–39 Fayette St, three-story simple brick structures." (Marsh's house at 1 Fayette St is no longer standing.)

Walk down Fayette St as far as No. 15, where until a few years ago a plaque claimed that the house was the birthplace of Edgar Allan Poe. However, there is firm evidence, as noted above, that Poe was actually born at 62 Carver St, and, in any event, Fayette St did not exist in 1809, the year of Poe's birth, when the area was still part of the mud flats of Back Bay. Continue along Fayette St, crossing Church St. At its eastern end is Bay St, thought to be the shortest street in Boston, though it has a possible rival in Murphy Court in the North End. This picturesque lane has but a single extant house, No. 1, the others having been demolished in 1908 to make way for the Abraham Lincoln School, but this is one of the prettiest structures in Bay Village, with its elegant recessed doorway at the rear of an arched passage reached by a flight of steps, its high-pitched roof, and its ivy-covered walls.

Return to Church St and begin walking N., going off l. and r. to look at the side streets: Melrose, Winchester, and Piedmont. When looking at the l. side of Piedmont, take a l. turn into Edgerly Pl, a picturesque street that runs parallel to Church St for one block; this is the most isolated part of Bay Village, and it is so quiet and peaceful that it is difficult to believe that this is really in the midst of downtown Boston. On Piedmont St do not fail to notice the little building at No. 52; this used to be a livery stable, and it is the only example of its type in Bay Village.

The stroll through Bay Village ends at the W. end of Piedmont St, which emerges at Arlington St. Across the way and to the r. is a very striking structure, the *Armory of the First Corps of Cadets,* looking like a Renaissance Italian fortress, with its turrets, battlements, lancet windows, and crenellated walls, a total anachronism in downtown Boston. To take a closer look at the Armory, cross the street and walk to the corner of Arlington St and Columbus Ave. There are entrances on both streets, and beside the one on Columbus Ave there is a plaque with the following inscription: "The cornerstone was laid on Oct. 19, 1891, marking the 150th anniversary of the First Corps of Cadets. Designed by William Gibbon Preston, F.A.I.A., and constructed by L. D. Willcutt & Sons, the Armory was financed by various military orders, historical societies, and the city of Boston. During the police strike of 1919, the First Corps acted as Boston's sole force to uphold law and order. In recognition of its unique place in Boston's history, the Armory was placed in the National Register of Historic Places in 1973 and was designated a landmark by the Boston Landmarks Commission in 1977." The Armory is now used to house exhibitions.

At this point those taking this itinerary have two options. From here the route continues through the northern part of the new South End, finishing in Copley Sq. This second part of the itinerary can be picked up again at the corner of Arlington St and Columbus Ave, and the center of town can be reached along Arlington St.

B. The New South End

The itinerary resumes, heading away from the center of town along Columbus Ave. On the first block notice the fine old Victorian building on the l. at No. 162; this was built by the architect T. M. C. Clark in 1886; in 1979 it was acquired by the Back Bay Racquet Club and renovated for their use by Pagett Assocs & Graham-Meus. At the corner on the l. there is a modern firehouse (one of the few in downtown Boston) built in 1970 by Carlin & Pozzi. This brings one to Isabella St on the l., where two of the old residential hotels that proliferated in the new South End in the second half of the 19C survive; at No. 34 is the *Hotel Isabella,* built in 1885 by A. S. Drisco; and at No. 40 is the former *Hotel Clifford,* renovated in 1976 by Pagett Assocs and now used as their offices.

Columbus Ave crosses Berkeley St, and at the far corner to the r., at No. 209, is a large commercial building with a marquee; this interesting structure was built in 1890–92 by H. W. Hartwell and W. C. Richardson. Columbus Ave then crosses a dull and featureless stretch cut through by railway tracks and the highway, and reaches Clarendon St. Turn right. The corner to the r., where Columbus Ave and Clarendon St meet at an acute angle, was the site of a house which was for a time the residence of Childe Hassam (1859–1935), one of America's leading Impressionist painters. Clarendon St then crosses in turn Chandler, Lawrence, and Appleton Sts, all of them quiet streets lined with fine old houses of the mid- to late 19C, making this one of the most pleasant areas of the new South End. Clarendon crosses Warren and comes to a common intersection with Montgomery and Tremont Sts.

The whole block to the l. here on Tremont St is taken up by the immense *Cyclorama Building,* now the *Boston Center for the Arts.* This extraordinary building was erected in 1884 by Cummings and Sears, originally with turrets and crenellated walls, which must have made it look like a Disneyland fortress.

The building was designed to hold the Battle of Gettysburg Cyclorama, a multimedia recreation of that historic event by the French artist Paul Philippoteaux. When that panorama finished its run the Cyclorama was used for similar presentations, such as the Battle of Big Horn. Later the building served in turn as a skating rink, a track for bicycle races, a gymnasium and work out ring for professional boxers, a garage, and an exhibition hall, before becoming the Boston Center for the Arts in 1970.

Walking back to the corner of Tremont and Clarendon and crossing the latter street, one comes to the *St. Cloud Hotel.* This was built in 1869–70 by the architect Nathaniel J. Bradlee, who designed it in the French Academic style. This was one of the earliest examples in Boston of an apartment hotel, in which the residents rented "French flats" on a single floor, the predecessors of the apartment houses that proliferated in American cities. This fine old building is undergoing renovation, and when it is completed it will be used by the Boston Center for the Arts for office space and other purposes.

Directly across the street is *Union Park,* which was developed and laid out in 1851 by Ellis S. Chesbrough, the city engineer. Chesbrough and William Parrott were responsible for laying out the streets of the new South End, and the inclusion of green areas like Union Park is one of the most attractive features of their design, and one which continues to enhance the new South End today. Union Park is one of the smallest of the parks and garden squares that dot the South End, the largest being Franklin Sq. The lots around Union Sq were auctioned off in Nov. 1851, and the houses that stand there today all date from the 1850s. A number of very prominent people bought houses in Union Sq at that time, most notably Alexander Rice, mayor of Boston in 1856–57, who lived in No. 34.

The itinerary continues on Montgomery St, heading eastward, away from the Cyclorama Building, passing Dartmouth St on the r. at the next corner. Turn r. at the next corner onto West Canton, then l. at the next corner again onto Warren Ave, passing the *Concord Baptist Church,* and then crossing on the l. in succession West Brookline and Pembroke Sts. After passing on the r. Harriet Tubman Park, Warren Ave reaches the common intersection with West Newton St and Columbus Ave. Cross the avenue diagonally. On the opposite corner is the *Union United Methodist Church,* built in 1877 by the architect A. R. Estey.

From here the itinerary goes northward past the church on Newton St, which crosses the highway on an overpass. On the far side is St. Botolph St, named after the patron saint of Boston. This street and those that intersect it were developed in the 1880s, forming a quiet and pleasant neighborhood just a short block away from the center of town at its closest. At the N.W. corner of the second block to the l., at Cumberland St, is the building that formerly housed the Charles E. Perkins Elementary School; this was erected in 1891 by the architect Henry W. Atwood, and in 1980 it was reconverted for condominiums by Graham Gund.

Crossing St. Botolph St, one now passes on the r. side of the *Colonnade Hotel,* designed by Irving Salsberg & Assocs and completed in 1971. After passing the hotel, one comes to Huntington Ave, with across the way the looming towers of *Prudential Center* and to the l. the church and administration buildings of the *Christian Science complex.* Turn r. here and walk up Huntington Ave to Copley Square.

13 Back Bay I: From the Corner of Beacon and Arlington Streets to Copley Square

This itinerary begins at the N.W. corner of the Public Garden, where Beacon and Arlington Sts intersect, crossing back and forth along the streets of Back Bay from Beacon St to Boylston St, ending in Copley Sq. This is a very long walk, but it is rich in architectural interest, both religious and secular.

History and Topology. As has been noted, the filling in of Back Bay began with the completion of the Mill Dam, closing off the area from the Charles River estuary. But this filling proceeded very slowly at first, and by 1857 the shore of Boston had advanced from Charles St only as far as Arlington St, with the filling in of the land on which the Public Garden would be created, and on Beacon St some 15 houses had been built W. of Charles St on the abutment of Mill Dam. Besides that there were just the two causeways that brought the railroads into Boston, crisscrossing in the middle of Back Bay, and the rest of the area was mud flats into which drains and sewers from all over the city were pouring their effluents, which the tides could no longer sweep out to sea because of the Mill Dam and the causeways. In 1849 the Boston Board of Health had declared the condition of Back Bay to be "one of nuisance, offensive and injurious to the large and increasing population residing upon it." There was much discussion as to what should be done with Back Bay, and in 1856 a tripartite agreement between the Commonwealth, the city, and various private proprietors opened the way for the filling of the area. The Legislature confirmed this agreement in May 1857, and at the same time they approved a plan that provided for the present layout of streets in the Back Bay. Since there were no public funds available the commissioners of the Back Bay either sold plots of land to pay for expenses incurred, or they awarded them to contractors for agreeing to fill in certain areas. Thus in 1857 began the real filling in of the Back Bay, with gravel carried in from Needham, nine miles away, in a railroad built for that purpose.

Once the filling began, building activity proceeded apace. At the beginning of the 1860s virtually nothing had been built in the Back Bay district, other than that indicated above, while by 1869 one-third of the entire area had been built up. Practically all of Beacon St E. of Dartmouth St was built in this period. Marlborough St and Commonwealth Ave were substantially complete out to Clarendon St; Newbury St and Boylston St were lined with houses as far as Berkeley St, while the Museum of Natural History and the first building of the Massachusetts Institute of Technology carried the construction farther W. Building continued at a somewhat slower pace in the period 1870–90, and at a still lower rate in the 1890s, as the builders moved in on the heels of the contractors who were filling Back Bay, so that by the time the area was completely filled in at the end of the century it was also virtually completely built over.

But the filling in and building up of Back Bay was not just another moneymaking real-estate scheme, for from the beginning there was a general feeling among public-spirited Bostonians that the project formed the basis for a significant improvement as manifested in the creation of new municipal institutions, in the erection of numerous public buildings, and in commercial construction on an unprecedented scale. A significant indication of the public ambition for the district is that the Commonwealth was willing to devote more than 43 percent of its total land holdings in the Back Bay for streets and parks. Other evidence of how widespread was the idea that new horizons had been opened for the people of the city is the fact that in the years 1860–90 13 of the city's churches relocated there, as well as 19 schools, public buildings, and clubs. The general feeling was that Back Bay really was a new Boston opening out from the cramped confines of the Shawmut Peninsula, where it had been cooped up for 250 years.

Although filling in and building were virtually complete in the Back Bay by 1900, it took a while for the area to settle in and mellow, for the evidence of recent construction to be cleared away and rough edges smoothed, for trees to grow and for gardens to come into flower, for the intricate network of social relations in a city quarter to be formed. When this came about Back Bay rivaled Beacon Hill in its elegance and sophistication, with the added advantage that its residents had more freedom of movement, both socially and topographically, than did the old-time residents of the Hill. However, in recent years Back Bay has lost some of its elegance, with the intrusion of commercial enterprises on Boylston St and Newbury St, and the proliferation of schools, offices, condominiums, and university residence halls on several of the other once-exclusive streets, not to mention the increased crime that has lowered the quality of life in all American cities. Nevertheless, Back Bay is still one of the premier residential areas in the U.S., and few places can compare with it in terms of architectural interest. Bainbridge Bunting, author of the magisterial work on the architecture of this district, *Houses of Boston's Back Bay,* points out that "there is no example of nineteenth century building and urban planning in America that is comparable to Back Bay."

The itinerary begins at the N.W. corner of the Public Garden, at the corner of Arlington and Beacon Sts. The houses across the way on Beacon St, between Brimmer St and Embankment Rd, are generally considered to be included in the level part of Beacon Hill, but, strictly speaking, they are part of Back Bay. These houses all stand on the eastern end of Mill Dam, and were the first to be built on what was called the "water side" of Beacon St. The original houses that remain on the block between Brimmer St and Beaver St, Nos 88—91, were all built by Wheelwright and Haven in 1852, five years before the filling in of Back Bay even began on a large scale. Only two of the original houses remain on the block between Beaver St and Embankment Rd; these are Nos 93 and 94, both built in 1849 by the architect George M. Dexter.

Cross Arlington St and begin walking along the S. side of Beacon St. The houses on this block are among the oldest in Back Bay proper, since the filling operations started on the Arlington St side and proceeded westward. The houses on the N. side of the street date from 1856—61, and those on the S. side from 1860—65. Toward the end of the block on the l. side is No. 137, the ***Gibson House Museum.** This is the only historic house in Back Bay open to the public.

Admission. There are guided tours of the Gibson House on weekends at 2, 3, & 4 P.M.; fee (tel. 267-6338).

History. The house at 137 Beacon St was built in 1860 for Catherine Gibson by the architect Edward Cabot; it was one of a pair with the house to its l. at No. 135, which was built for Mrs. Gibson's relative Samuel Hammond Russell. Mrs. Gibson was the widow of John Gardiner Gibson (1799—1838), a merchant who made his fortune in Cuba before returning to his native Boston, where he married Catherine Hammond, who built this house some two decades after his death. Their son, Charles Hammond Gibson (1836—1916), married Rosamund Warren, the daughter of Dr. Jonathan Mason Warren and Annie (Crowninshield) Warren in 1871. The bride was a direct descendant of General Joseph Warren, the hero of the Revolution. After their honeymoon in New York, the bride and groom moved into 137 Beacon St with Catherine Gibson, and they lived there for the rest of their lives. Their son, Charles Hammond Gibson, a bachelor, bequeathed the house as a Victorian museum, one that reflects the lives of those who lived in Back Bay during that period.

Exterior. The houses at Nos 135—137 have almost identical facades of brick with brownstone trimmings, each with a recessed door at the top of a short flight of steps, and with an oriel window above on the second floor. The houses are both five-story, with dormer windows on the top story, and the only difference between them is that the Gibson house has three windows on the fourth floor while No. 135 has only two.

Interior. Guided tours begin in the entry hall on the first floor. This floor and the other parts of the house open to the public are furnished and decorated in the style of the Victorian period, with objects which either belonged to the Gibson House or are of the same type and date as those that were used there at that time.

One goes first to the *basement,* which was used for the kitchen, laundry, furnace, and storage. The most interesting feature of the kitchen is the hooded coal range, with a tea-kettle, coffeepot, waffleiron, and flatiron on the stove and a bean pot in the oven.

On the *first floor* the room at the rear is the Dining Room, with large-paned Victorian windows hung with needlework curtains. The dining-room table is set with a Rockingham dinner service with claret-red border, a long white damask tablecloth, English Regency dining chairs inherited by the family, and on the sideboard a ruby Bohemian glass decanter and wine-glasses.

Return to the entry hall to take the stairway to the upper floors. In approaching the stairs, notice the fine, heavily molded woodwork of the newel and the arches that spring from the column above it; this is in its original condition and is typical of the best Back Bay homes of the Victorian period. Notice also the embossed and gilt wallpaper, of the same design and type as was put in Castle Howard during a renovation in 1859 in prep-aration for a visit by Queen Victoria; the bronze statue beside the stairs with its velvet-covered pedestal; and the portrait of Abraham Gibson, grandfather of John Gardiner Gibson.

On the *second floor* the chamber at the rear was used as the Music Room. At the center of the ceiling hangs an elegant chandelier with glass shades and ball drops, and with matching wall lights flanking the white marble fireplace on the r. side of the room. On either side of the fireplace there are Sheraton pole screens, as well as matching pairs of Chinese vases made of export-ware porcelain, and on the mantelpiece there is a classical bisque flanked by a pair of French porcelain vases and a pair of bronze obelisks. On one wall hangs a prized family heirloom, an oil painting by Guido Reni of Bologna, *Cleopatra Dissolving the Pearl.*

The room at the front on the second floor is the Library. This is furnished with built-in bookcases; a library desk-table and desk-chair; green velvet chairs with fringes and carved cresting, two of which are pulled up next to a mid-Victorian stand with a fine chess set; a Turkish tufted sofa; and a fireplace with a carved mantelpiece of rich, dark wood, beside which there is a splendid needlework pole screen. Displayed around the room are paint-ings, drawings, and family photos, and scattered here and there are books, albums of picture postcards, invitations, etc.

On the *third floor* the rooms at both front and rear were used as bed-chambers. The chamber at the rear is furnished with a bedroom set of bird's-eye maple in a bamboo motif. The dressing table is flanked by gas wall lights (now electrified) and on it are scattered a porcelain-covered loose powder jar, a hair-receiver, a ring-tree (on which rings were put at night), a cologne bottle, and a candlestick with matching snuffer.

The upper two floors of the house are not open to the public. The fourth floor had two bedrooms, used by members of the family and guests, while the fifth floor had five bed-rooms for servants.

After leaving the Gibson House we cross Beacon St to No. 152, the former mansion of Governor Fuller, now the library of Emerson College. Nearly all of the original houses on the N. side of the street were built in 1860–63; those on the S. side were erected between 1861 and 1872. The house at No. 152 was built in 1860 for David Stewart, a wealthy New Yorker, who gave it as a present to his daughter Isabella when she was married that year to John Lowell ("Jack") Gardner.

On June 18, 1863, Isabella Stewart Gardner gave birth to a son, but the pregnancy left her semi-invalid and she was warned by her doctor not to have any more children. Then, on March 15, 1865, her son died suddenly and Mrs. Gardner was prostrate with grief, and for two years she remained in a state of profound depression. In spring 1867 her doctor sug-gested to Jack Gardner that a trip to Europe might lift his wife out of her depressed state, and such proved to be the case. When Isabella returned to Boston with her husband that autumn it was to make a fresh start, and high society in Back Bay was soon to notice the difference. As a Boston journalist wrote of her in 1875: "Mrs Jack Gardner is one of the seven wonders of Boston. There is nobody like her in any city in this country. She is a millionaire Bohemienne. She is eccentric, and she has the courage of eccentricity. She is the leader of the smart set, but she often leads where none dare follow. . . . All Boston is divided into two parts, one of which follows science, and the other Mrs Jack Gardner."

In 1880, being in need of a music room, the Gardners bought the adjacent building at No. 150 and added it to their own. While living there over the next two decades, Isabella Stewart Gardner formed the greatest private collection of works of art ever assembled in Boston, a collection that was eventually housed in the museum on the Fenway that bears her name. Jack Gardner died in 1898, and within three years Mrs. Gardner abandoned their home on Beacon St to take up residence in her new museum. The houses at 150–152 Beacon St were demolished in 1904, and the building presently on the site was constructed; this bears the number 150, and No. 152 is skipped in the emuneration of houses on the block, since it was Mrs. Gardner's wish that the number of her original home on Beacon St should never again be used.

Continuing along, one now crosses Clarendon St. All the original houses on the N. side of this block were built in 1862–66, and those on the S. side in 1866–72. The house at No. 241, toward the end of the block on the l., was the last residence of Julia Ward Howe. Mrs. Howe moved here in 1876, after the death that year of her husband, Samuel Gridley Howe, and she remained here until her own death in 1910.

Cross Dartmouth St, where the original houses on the N. side date from 1862–66, and those on the S. side from 1866–72. In comparing these dates with those of the blocks already passed, one can follow the slow process of filling in and building as it proceeds from E. to W. The houses on the N. side are generally built earlier than those to the S.; this is because the houses to the N., the "water side," were highly prized because of their view of the Charles River, which then came right up to their back yards. This trend continues to be evident on the next block, between Exeter and Fairfield Sts, where all but four of the original houses on the N. side were built in the period 1869–72, and those on the S. side were erected in 1870–74. Two of the houses at mid-block on the N. side have literary associations of some interest. The house that originally stood at No. 296 was the last residence of Oliver Wendell Holmes, Sr., who lived there from 1881 until his death in 1894. The house in which Holmes lived is gone, replaced by the present building on the site, but the house at No. 294, which he purchased for use as his library, is still standing. This is the house in which Holmes wrote *Over the Teacups* (1891), his last work, and where he was host to such old friends as Ralph Waldo Emerson, James Russell Lowell, and John Greenleaf Whittier. The original house at No. 302, torn down in 1933 to make way for the present structure, was from 1872–81 the home of George Santayana (1863–1952), the philosopher, critic, poet, and novelist.

During the period when he lived at 302 Beacon St the young Santayana attended the Boston Latin School. Santayana lived in Cambridge during the years he taught at Harvard, 1889–1912, after which he moved to Europe. Among the books that Santayana wrote while he was living in Boston and Cambridge were *The Sense of Beauty* (1896) and the five-volume work *The Life of Reason* (1905–6). Santayana's only novel, *The Last Puritan* (1935), used Boston's Back Bay as one of its settings. In 1885 the house at 302 Beacon St became the home of William Dean Howells (1837–1920), who was editor of the *Atlantic Monthly* in 1871–81. During the first year of his residence in this house Howells finished his best-known novel, *The Rise of Silas Lapham* (1885). Another house on Beacon St that Howells knew well, No. 130, served as the model for the mansion that the fictional Silas Lapham built in Back Bay, on the popular "water side" of Beacon St. As Howells has Silas Lapham say: "Yes, sir, it's about the sightliest view I know of. I always did like the water side of

Beacon. Long before I ever owned property here, or ever expected to, m'wife and I used to ride down this way, and stop the buggy to get the view over the water. When people talk to me about the Hill, I can understand 'em. It's snug, and it's old-fashioned, and it's where they've always lived. But when they talk about Commonwealth Avenue, I don't know what they mean. It don't hold a candle to the water side of Beacon. . . . No, sir! When you come to the Back Bay at all, give me the water side of Beacon."

Continue along Beacon St, crossing in turn Fairfield, Gloucester, and Hereford Sts, before finally coming to Massachusetts Ave. There are no exceptional buildings along this stretch of Beacon St, which has lost much of its exclusivity because of the conversion of many of its old houses into university residence halls; but, on the other hand, the students make this end of the street one of the liveliest parts of Back Bay. The oldest of the original houses along this stretch of the street date to 1871, but most date to the late 1880s and the 1890s, with a number erected in the early years of the present century, one as late as 1904, evidence that this was the last stretch of Beacon St to be filled in and built up. At the corner of Beacon St and Massachusetts Ave is the shell of the *Mount Vernon Church,* built in 1891 by the architects Walker and Kimball. The church was destroyed by a fire in the late 1970s, and for a time its fire-blackened ruins stood forlorn beside the approach to the Boston Bridge. But in recent years the shell of the church has been cleared of debris and its fabric restored, and it is presently being reconstructed for use as condominiums.

The itinerary now turns l. on Massachusetts Ave and l. again at the next corner, to proceed eastward on Marlborough St. The dates of the houses along Marlborough St follow the same general pattern as those along Beacon St, with the most recent structures at the western end, which was filled last, with houses on the block between Massachusetts Ave and Hereford St dated as late as 1895, with some of those at the eastern end, between Berkeley and Arlington Sts, dating to as early as 1863. The houses of the Late Victorian period on Marlborough St are not nearly so distinguished as those from earlier in that period. Cross Fairfield St. On the far corner to the l., at 12 Fairfield St, is a charming little house in the Queen Anne style. This was built in 1879 for Georgianna Lowell by the architects Cabot and Chandler, who successfully designed a number of other Back Bay houses in this mode.

Cross Fairfield St. On the next block are three houses by Cabot and Chandler in the Queen Anne style: just past the corner on the r. at No. 276, and on the l. at Nos 257 and 245; the first of these was built in 1884, and the other two in 1883. The house at No. 249 was for a time the home of Robert Lowell, the poet, one of two places on Marlborough that he rented in turn. The house at No. 239 is the last in a row of eight extending to the corner of Essex St, all erected in 1873–74 for the speculative builder George Wheatland.

Coming to Exeter St, one sees on the far corner to the r. a romantic old house at Nos 196–198; this was built in 1886 by the architect W. Whitney Lewis for E. P. Bradbury, and historians of architecture see in it a combination of concepts of H. H. Richardson with features of the Queen Anne style. On the far corner to the l., at No. 199, there is a seven-story building erected in 1890 by E. N. Boyden, and to the l. of that on the same side there is another seven-story structure, at 295–297 Beacon St, built in 1885 by S. D. Kelley. These were among the first apartment houses erected in Back Bay, designed for those who wanted to live in this fashionable district without the expense and bother of building a free-standing house there.

On the block between Exeter and Dartmouth one might pause to look at three houses. The first of these is on the l. at No. 195, a house in the Queen Anne style built in 1879 by Cabot and Chandler, which Chandler himself owned and occupied, and the second, at No. 170, another house of similar design by the same architects. At No. 170 is the second of the two houses on Marlborough St in which Robert Lowell lived.

At the end of the block between Exeter and Dartmouth there are two distinguished mansions. On the corner to the l., at 163–165 Marlborough, is the *Cushing-Endicott Mansion,* which Bainbridge Bunting, in his *Houses of Boston's Back Bay,* described as "perhaps the handsomest house in the whole Back Bay." Designed by the architectural firm of Snell and Gregerson, the mansion was built in 1871–73 for Thomas Forbes Cushing. In 1898 the mansion passed on to the Endicott family, who retained it until 1958. After that it served as a residence hall for young women, and now it is used as an office building. The two buildings around the corner, Nos 326–328, were also built by Snell and Gregerson in 1871–73. On the corner to the r., at 164 Marlborough, is the Benjamin Crowninshield House, built in 1870 by H. H. Richardson. This is one of only three houses that Richardson was commissioned to build in Back Bay, of which two are still standing, and it shows little of the creative genius that this extraordinary architect would exhibit in his work on Trinity Church and his other masterpieces. (Richardson admitted that he was so busy with his larger projects that he relegated his more minor commissions, such as the design of houses, to assistants in his office.) On the far corner to the r., at 315 Dartmouth St, is a mansion built in 1870 for Hollis Hunnewell, one of the most splendid dwellings in Back Bay.

At the next corner Marlborough St crosses Clarendon St, and at the end of the next block on the r. is the *First and Second Church of Boston.*

The First Church of Boston, founded in 1630, had its first two meetinghouses near the Old State House. In 1808 it moved to Chauncy Pl in the South End, and finally, in 1868, the congregation moved to the corner of Marlborough and Berkeley Sts, into a church built by the architects Ware and Van Brunt. By that time the congregation had become Unitarians, and so their house of worship was called the First Unitarian Church of Boston. The Second Church had been founded in the North End in 1649, and eventually its congregation, who had also become Unitarians, moved into a church in Back Bay, a spireless Gothic structure built in 1872–74 by N. J. Bradlee. The congregation abandoned this church in the second decade of the present century, when they moved out to Audubon Circle. When the meeting house of the First Church was destroyed by fire in 1968, the First and Second Church of Boston combined to create the present house of worship.

The new church, designed by Paul Rudolph, was dedicated in 1972. The original tower and the Berkeley St facade of Ware and Van Brunt's design survived the fire and are incorporated into the new structure, making this an extremely original and attractive house of worship. Three sides of the church site now define a semipublic sunken amphitheater on the Marlborough St side, which is the major external feature. Paul Rudolph describes his unusual and effective design as follows: "The negative space of the amphitheater juxtaposed to the thrust of the tower punctuates the corner of the gridiron of Boston's Back Bay area. The roof slopes away from the sunken plaza, thereby expanding the space of the plaza. The roof is formed to catch the ever-changing light in multiple ways in the fluid interior space, rendering the whole as a special kind of kaleidoscope." At the far corner of the church on the Marlborough St side, beyond the sunken amphitheater, there is a statue of Governor John Winthrop, one of the founders of the Bay Colony and of the First Church of Boston.

This fine work is a bronze replica of the marble statue of Governor Winthrop by Richard S. Greenough that was placed in Statuary Hall in the Capitol in Washington, D.C., in 1876. The bronze statue was originally placed in the center of Scollay Sq in 1880, but in 1903 traffic congestion there caused it to be removed to the courtyard of the First Church. During the fire that ravaged the church in 1968, falling masonry damaged the statue, knocking off Governor Winthrop's head, but since then the sculpture has been perfectly restored. (In the aftermath of the fire a man was apprehended making his way from the church with the head of the statue tucked underneath his arm.) Governor Winthrop's statue represents him dressed in the picturesque flowing clothes of the period, stepping from the gangplank of the *Arbella* holding in his r. hand the charter of the Colony and in his l. hand a Bible.

Directly across the street, on the S.E. corner of Marlborough and Berkeley Sts, is the *First Lutheran Church.* This very original structure was designed by Pietro Belluschi and completed in 1959. One enters through a courtyard and a porch, which imperceptibly make the transition to the serenity of the church. The brick walls of the nave are exposed in the interior, save for a wood-slat screen around the lower altar area, an acoustical aid in the generally hard-surfaced hall.

Now continue along the last block of Marlborough St before the Public Garden. All of the original houses on this block were built around 1863, although some have either been replaced or renovated. Turning the corner to the r. onto Arlington St, facing the Public Garden, one sees a group of four houses from the period 1860—70. The first of these, No. 8, houses the *Atlantic Monthly,* Boston's leading magazine since it was first published in 1859. After passing Public Alley No. 422, one comes to a distinguished building that takes up the whole block between that passage and Commonwealth Ave. This mansion was erected in 1860 by Arthur Gilman, architect of the Arlington Street Church, and one of those principally responsible for designing the street plan for Back Bay when filling operations began on a large scale in 1857. Gilman designed the mansion in the French Academic style that characterizes many of the earlier houses erected in Back Bay, with a facade of Nova Scotia sandstone, the most notable feature being the delicate-looking enclosed balcony above the neoclassical portico.

Late in the 19C the house was acquired by J. Montgomery Sears, who in 1893 also bought the adjoining house on Commonwealth Ave and incorporated it into his mansion. Sears and his wife, Sarah Choate Sears, were among the leading patrons of culture in Boston in the late 19C. Paderewski played the piano at a party held here by the Sears, and John Singer Sargent here painted portraits of Mrs. Sears and her daughter Helen. In the early 1920s the mansion was taken over by the Ursuline Order and for a time it was used as a convent school. Since 1967 the mansion has been known as Harbridge House, the name of the firm of research consultants that has its headquarters there.

Commonwealth Ave is the grandest boulevard in Boston. The avenue consists of a pair of streets flanking a central mall shaded by colonnades of stately trees, with a total width of 220ft between the houses on either side. All of the original houses on this first block of Commonwealth Ave date from the period 1861—70, and their owners included some of the wealthiest men in Boston in the Victorian era, most notably Abbot Lawrence, who lived in No. 5, and Thomas Gold Appleton (No. 10), two self-made millionaires who started their careers as small shopowners on Dock Sq. Appleton was one of the foremost patrons of culture in Victorian Boston, and one of the leading figures in the creation of the Boston Museum of Fine Arts; his mansion on Commonwealth Ave was the most prestigious literary salon of the epoch, with his guests including Henry Wadsworth Longfellow, William Dean Howells, Oliver Wendell Holmes, and Julia Ward Howe.

On the central axis of the mall between these two mansions is the first of the seven honorific statues along Commonwealth Ave. This is a granite statue of Alexander Hamilton (1755–1804), a work of Dr. William Rimmer (1816–79), commissioned by Thomas Lee and presented to the city of Boston in 1865. Dr. Rimmer, a distinguished physician, was an amateur sculptor, and created this statue without a living model, using only a portrait of Hamilton and his own expert knowledge of anatomy. On the base of the statue an inscription summarizes Hamilton's career.

Born on the island of Nevis in the West Indies, Hamilton moved to America and performed brilliantly in the Continental Army during the Revolutionary War, during part of which he served as secretary and confidential aide to General Washington. He was one of the signers of the Constitution, and when the new government was established he organized the Treasury Department, serving as the first secretary of the treasury in Washington's Cabinet. Hamilton resigned from the Cabinet in 1795 to return to the practice of law in New York. His brilliant career came to a premature end in 1804, when he died from a wound suffered during a duel with Aaron Burr, Jefferson's Vice-President.

On the l. side of the avenue at mid-block there is a row of nine houses, Nos 20–36, all built in 1861 by Gridley J. F. Bryant and Arthur Gilman. And at the end of the block on the r., at Nos 25–27, there is a splendid double building with a mansard roof that was also built in 1861; this was originally the property of Samuel Hooper, but the name of the architect is unknown.

Crossing Berkeley St on the r. side of Commonwealth, one comes at the corner to a ten-story building called *Haddon Hall,* erected in 1894. This was another one of the residential hotels that sprang up in Back Bay late in the Victorian period, when there was a great demand for housing in the area but little free space in which to build.

On the axis of the mall, a short way along, there stands a bronze statue of General John Glover, the Revolutionary War hero from Marblehead; this was commissioned by Benjamin Tyler Reed and created in 1875 by the sculptor Martin Millmore.

At the very beginning of the Revolution, Glover's regiment of Marblehead fishermen served on both land and sea, and they were in effect both General Washington's navy and his marines. Glover and his men performed with great valor throughout the Revolutionary War, and it was they who ferried Washington and his army in their crossing of the Delaware River prior to the American victory at the Battle of Trenton. After the Revolution, Glover left the Continental Army and returned to Marblehead. Since he had expended his small fortune in the American cause during the war, Glover was forced to earn his living as a simple shoemaker; nevertheless, he still found the time and energy to serve for several years in the Massachusetts Legislature.

The most distinguished buildings on this block are a group of three mansions toward the end on the l., Nos 76–80; these are brownstone structures in the Gothic style, erected in 1872 for Charles Fox by an unknown architect.

At the S.W. corner of Commonwealth and Clarendon stands one of the most distinguished houses of worship in Back Bay, presently known as the *First Baptist Church.*

History. This meetinghouse was originally known as the New Brattle Square Church. Its congregation had first gathered in 1698 in a meetinghouse on Brattle Sq, where they remained until they moved into the present church. When the congregation decided to build a new meeting hall in Back Bay, they announced that an architectural competition would be held to select the best design for the proposed church. The competition was won by Henry

Hobson Richardson (1838–86), who was just emerging as a creative force in American architecture. Richardson began work on the New Brattle Square Church in 1870 and completed it the following year, winning the young architect wide acclaim in Boston.

The congregation that built the New Brattle Square Church used it for only a very brief time, for dwindling numbers forced them to dissolve their society in 1876. The church then remained unused until acquired in 1882 by the First Baptist Society, who remain in possession. A plaque in the porch of the church records the many peregrinations of the First Baptist Society since it was founded in the North End in colonial times.

Exterior. Mariana Griswold Van Rensaelaer's description of the church in *Henry Hobson Richardson and his Work* (1888) is still entirely accurate today: "It is a cruciform building, not very large, with a lofty tower which stands in the angles between the nave and transept, resting upon four piers connected by great round arches. The carriage-porch which is thus formed opens into a large arcaded portico or vestibule that is built out, flush with the face of the tower, from the end of the transept. This arcade and all the large windows are round-arched, but a range of square-headed lights occurs, beneath a large rose, in the end of the nave. The roof and louvre-boards are covered with red tiles, the frieze and the capitals in the porch are of a light-coloured stone, and the angels' trumpets are gilded. A single kind of stone appears in the rest of the structure—in walls and trimming alike—and the treatment of its surface does not vary. But it is a pudding-stone of a warm yellow tint conspicuously diversified with darker iron-stains, and such good advantage has been taken of its changing tone to avoid monotony in the fields of wall to accent the trimming that the general color effect is both rich and animated."

The most admired feature of the church has always been its tower, which Mrs. Rensaelaer describes as having "magnificent independence—the way it rises in a single spring from its own sturdy feet." Above the arches of the belfry is the frieze, in which the four scenes represented in low relief are Baptism, Communion, Matrimony, and Death. (The trumpets of the angels have led Bostonians to refer to the figures, irreverently, as "The Holy Bean-Blowers.") The scenes in the frieze were originally sketched out by Richardson, after which they were sculpted in Paris by Frédéric-Auguste Bartholdi, who is best known for his Statue of Liberty at the entrance to New York Harbor.

Interior. The interior of the church was never completely finished according to Richardson's original design, because of a shortage of funds and the dispersal of the original congregation. In any event, the interior of this church never aroused anything like the admiration given to its exterior. The only changes in the interior since 1871 have been the addition of the gallery and the construction of a small chapel at the Clarendon St end.

The original houses on Commonwealth between Clarendon and Dartmouth were all built in the period 1869–82, although a number have been remodeled and others replaced by more modern structures. Along the axis of the mall before mid-block is a monument honoring Patrick Andrew Collins (1844–1905), who came to the U.S. as an immigrant from Ireland at the age of four and went on to become mayor of Boston in 1902–5.

Mayor Collins died unexpectedly in office in 1905, and soon after his funeral a public meeting was held to discuss the creating of a suitable monument to honor his memory. The necessary funds were collected in just six days, after which the commission to create the memorial was given to the sculptors Henry Hudson Kitson and his wife, Theo Ruggles Kitson, who completed the monument in three years. The monument originally stood at the western end of the Commonwealth Ave mall, at Charlesgate West, and was moved to its present location in 1908. On the pedestal below the bust of Mayor Collins there is an inscription summarizing his life and career. The monument is flanked by two allegorical female figures symbolizing Erin and Columbia.

A little past mid-block on the l., at Nos 128–130, there are a pair of very unusual houses. These were originally built in 1882 by the architect S. D. Kelley and were remodeled c. 1905. These are delightful and extravagant white stone buildings in the rococo style, looking very much out of place among the sober-sided Bostonian mansions around them. The two buildings have been amalgamated into one structure, which now houses *Chamberlayne Junior College.*

Continuing along Commonwealth Ave and across Dartmouth, one finds on both corners on the far side impressive and interesting buildings. On the corner to the l. is the former *Hotel Vendome,* once the grandest hostelry in the Back Bay district. The hotel was built in 1871 by the architect William G. Preston for Colonel J. W. Wolcott. Among the many famous people who were guests in this hotel in its heyday were four Presidents of the U.S.: Ulysses S. Grant, Benjamin Harrison, Grover Cleveland, and William McKinley. The hotel originally had its long side and main entrance on Dartmouth St, but much of that part of the structure was destroyed in a fire in 1975, after which it was replaced by a modern extension. The much larger wing to the W. was added in 1881 by the architects J. F. Ober and George D. Rand.

The building at the N.W. corner of Commonwealth and Dartmouth is the *Ames-Webster Mansion,* the most elaborate mansion in Back Bay, with a romantic profusion of mansard roofs, turretlike smokestacks, dormer windows, and pavilions, capped off by a two-story glass conservatory on the W. side. The original mansion was built in 1872 for Frederick L. Ames by the firm of Peabody and Stearns, while the pavilion was added in 1882 by the architect John Sturgis. In 1969 the mansion was converted into a suite of offices by Childs, Bertman, Tseckares Assocs.

On the mall in front of the Hotel Vendome there is a seated bronze statue of William Lloyd Garrison (1805–79); this work by Olin Levi Warner (1844–96) was unveiled in 1886. Garrison is renowned as one of the leaders of the Abolitionist movement, which he crusaded for with his many speeches, as well as in articles and editorials in his antislavery newspaper, *The Liberator.*

On the N. side of the avenue facing the Garrison statue there are two buildings, at No. 165 and No. 167, of somewhat original architecture; the first of these was designed by Cummings and Sears in 1879 and the second, built in 1880, is a work of Sturgis and Brigham. On the S. side of the street, just beyond the Hotel Vendome, there are three buildings worthy of notice; these are: No. 172, designed by J. S. Besarick in 1885; and Nos 176–178, a nonmatching pair of houses built in 1883 by the architect Charles Atwood, the former with an extraordinary pediment in the baroque style. At the end of the block on the r. No. 191 is a huge châteaulike building originally known as the *Hotel Agassiz.* This was erected as an apartment hotel in 1872 for Major Henry Lee Higginson, the builders being the architectural firm of Weston and Rand. Higginson named the hotel after his wife Ida Agassiz, whose father was Professor Louis Agassiz, the renowned Harvard naturalist. Major Higginson was very active in philanthropy, and it was he who founded the Boston Symphony Orchestra in 1881.

Cross Exeter St, with interesting-looking buildings on both of the corners on the far side. The building on the l. was erected in 1882 by the firm of Peabody and Stearns; the one on the r. was built in 1881 by the architect J. Pickering Putnam. Next to the latter building, at No. 199, stands an impressive structure that looks more like a Beacon Hill mansion than one in Back Bay, with its facade having a pair of bow fronts flanking the flat central section, in the middle of which is the neoclassical entryway. This was built in 1890 for J. A. Beebe by the New York architectural firm of McKim, Mead & White. The building is presently the home of the *St. Botolph Club*.

St. Botolph's was established in 1879 for Bostonians with intellectual and artistic interests, and among its charter members were such notables as Phillips Brooks, William Dean Howells, Henry Cabot Lodge, Edward Everett Hale, and Francis Parkman. One of the features of the club was an art gallery where a number of important exhibitions were given, including viewings of some of the first Impressionist paintings to be shown in the U.S. It was at one of these exhibitions that Sargent's famous portrait of Isabella Stewart Gardner was shown, depicting her in a very low-cut dress; when one of the members made a scandalous comment about the subject Jack Gardner withdrew the painting, and it was never again seen in public during his lifetime. The painting is now on show in the Gardner Museum.

On the mall directly in front of St. Botolph's stands the newest of Boston's commemorative monuments, a superb bronze statue honoring Admiral Samuel Eliot Morison (1887–1976), whom an inscription below describes as "a sailor-historian." The monument shows the admiral dressed in oilskins and wearing a yachting cap, seated on a rock by the side of the sea. This striking monument is a work of the sculptress Penelope Jencks and was dedicated in 1982; its location is quite appropriate, for Admiral Morison was long a member of St. Botolph's. On either side of the monument there are rocks bearing inscriptions with quotes from Morison's many books on maritime history.

At mid-block on the r. is another distinguished old Boston club, the *Algonquin*, housed at Nos 217–219. This is a palatial mansion in the style of the Italian Renaissance, designed by Stanford White of the firm McKim, Mead and White and completed in 1888, the year that the Algonquin Club was founded. The most prominent features of the building are its massive granite entrance, the two porticoed balconies that stand above the entryway on the second and third stories, and the huge Palladian window at the center of the fourth floor.

Membership of the Algonquin is made up of wealthy bankers, merchants, and businessmen, and it is renowned for its elegant interior as well as for its outstanding food. The club possesses a number of works of art, the most notable of which is a portrait of Daniel Webster by Chester Harding. One of the most prized possession of the club is an authentic cigar-store Indian, 6ft 7 inches in height, with its original gaudy decoration intact.

At the next corner is Fairfield St. Architecturally, the most interesting house on the block between Fairfield and Gloucester is perhaps No. 257, the *Cochran Mansion,* which is near mid-block on the r. This was built in 1886 by McKim, Mead and White, combining elements of the Federal, Georgian, and Renaissance styles. At the end of the block on the r., with its entrance at 17 Gloucester St, there is a splendid old mansion with two bow fronts along the Commonwealth Ave side, and with dormer windows above capped by steep pediments. This is the *Robert Dawson Evans Mansion,* built in 1883 by the firm of Sturgis and Brigham.

After one crosses Gloucester St, on the mall straight ahead is still another commemorative monument. This is a bronze statue of Domingo Faustino

Sarmiento (1811–88), an Argentine writer, educator, legislator, and diplomat, who also served as President of his country.

In the 1860s Sarmiento served as minister to the U.S., and during that time his embassy became a center for educational and cultural exchange programs between the U.S. and Argentina. Sarmiento was an admirer of Horace Mann and his wife, Mary Peabody, and he believed that the Boston public school system was a worthy model for his own country to emulate. Sarmiento's monument was created by the Argentine sculptor Ivette Campagnion; it was shipped from Argentina to Boston in 1973, when it was set up on its present site.

There are three handsome mansions on the r. side of this block, all of them designed in the classical style of architecture that became especially popular in Back Bay in the 1890s. The first of these, No. 287, is just opposite the Sarmiento monument. This white limestone mansion was built in 1892 for Herbert M. Sears by the firm of Rotch and Tilden, who designed it in the Italian Renaissance style. Since 1964 the mansion has housed the *International Institute*, a social-service agency for foreign residents of Boston. The other two houses are a little farther down the street on the same side; these are the pair of buildings at Nos 297 and 303. No. 297 is also made of white limestone and designed in the style of the Italian Renaissance; this was built in 1899 for James Draper by Peabody and Stearns, and since the early 1960s it has served as a Jesuit monastery. The mansion at No. 303, a towerlike structure of light-gray limestone in the extreme classical style, was built in 1895 for G. A. Nickerson by McKim, Mead and White.

At the end of the block on the r. is a handsome mansion with a very pronounced bow on the corner; the entrance is at No. 32 Hereford St, where there is a second bow to the l., with the two corners of the building looking like the turrets of a medieval fortress. This mansion was built in 1883–84 for John F. Andrew by Charles F. McKim of the firm McKim, Mead and White. The entryway is quite elegant, with two pairs of columns of variegated stone capped by Ionic capitals, with a balcony above overlooked by a Palladian window framed by Ionic pilasters. On the third floor directly above is an elegant open balcony with a cast-iron grille from the destroyed Tuileries Palace in Paris.

According to Bainbridge Bunting: "In 1884 the Back Bay's first glimpse of the Italian Renaissance style was provided by the John Andrews House. . . . The importance of this house lies not in the degree of its allegiance to any particular historical style but rather to its historical position as the first indication of the new architectural interest in Boston. . . . This Back Bay house precedes by one year the famous Villard mansions on Madison Ave, and it antedates by three years the celebrated Boston Public Library, a building which is usually considered the spearhead of Classical Reaction in late nineteenth century America."

Cross Hereford St; the building on the far corner to the l., at No. 314 Commonwealth, is the *Albert C. Burrage Mansion*, built in 1899 by the architect Charles E. Brigham. The mansion, made of white limestone, is patterned on the 16C Château de Chenonceaux in the Loire Valley. It is a phantasmagoria of a building, in which no excess of elaboration or ostentation has been spared, with elaborate turrets, towers, spires, and pediments, and with gargoyles perched on the facade. The mansion has served since 1957 as the Boston Evening Medical Center, and so it is possible to walk in and look at the interior, which is as elaborate as the exterior, with gold-leaf ceilings and an enormous marble staircase whose newels are surmounted by bronze statues of cherubs, and with a trio of stained-glass windows in a bow at the first landing.

At the far end of the block on the r., at 355 Commonwealth, stands the *Oliver Ames House.* This was built for Oliver Ames, governor of Massachusetts from 1887 to 1889; H. H. Richardson was originally selected as the architect, but the final design was by Carl Fehmer, who completed the building in 1882. This is the largest private house in Back Bay, an enormous pile of a brownstone mansion, patterned on the French châteaux of the 16C. One of the most striking features of the exterior is the continuous frieze that runs around the facade between the first and second stories, decorated in low relief with floral and vegetable designs. After the Ames family gave up the mansion it was used for a time by the National Casket Co., during which time it must have resembled Dracula's castle in Transylvania. The mansion has recently undergone a thorough renovation for conversion into a suite of offices.

One more block along Commonwealth Ave, at Charlesgate E., is the last of the commemorative statues of the mall, which happens to be a rather odd one in its choice of subject. This is a bronze statue of Leif Eriksson, a work of the sculptress Anne Whitney, unveiled on Oct. 29, 1887.

As Walter Muir Whitehill wrote drolly of this monument in his book *Boston's Statues:* "This was the personal whim of Eben N. Horsford, manufacturer of a patent indigestion cure called Horsford's Acid Phosphate, who by means of the statue sought to reinforce his belief that the Vinland of the Norse discoverers of America was located on the Charles River at Gerry's Landing in Cambridge. His theories were ill received, and the erection of the statue only added fat to fire. Anne Whitney depicted Leif shading his eyes to look west over the Charles River. Now, alas, through recent highway construction, he peers into nothing more poetic than a vast overpass that siphons automobiles from the Fenway to Storrow Drive!"

The statue stands just opposite the *Somerset Apartments* (formerly the Hotel Somerset) on the S. side, at 400 Commonwealth Ave. This enormous structure was built in 1897 by the architect Arthur Bowditch, and at the time of its construction it was considered to be one of the finest places of residence in Back Bay.

Walk back to the corner of Commonwealth and Massachusetts; turn r. there and then l. at the next corner to begin walking up Newbury St. Walking along this block, one sees an astonishing sight, a huge and very life like mural which covers the entire rear side of the large building at the S.W. corner of Newbury and Hereford Sts. The mural is a cross-sectional view in perspective of a huge Renaissance palace or basilica, complete with dome, semidomes, colonnades, and porticoes. This extraordinary work is by the artist Richard Haas, and the building on which it is executed is the *Boston Architectural Center,* whose entrance is at 320 Newbury St. The Center, an architectural school and library, was founded in 1867; its present home, an attractive six-story concrete structure designed by John Meyer and Robert Goodman of the firm of Ashley, Meyer & Assocs, was completed in 1967.

Newbury St is far better known for its art galleries than for its domestic architecture. There are some 30 art galleries along Newbury St at latest count, the largest concentration of which are on the block between Exeter and Dartmouth Sts. (A list of these galleries and their specialties is given in a brochure entitled *Gallery Guide,* which can be obtained in local bookshops and newsagents.) There are also quite a number of restaurants and cafes along this stretch of Newbury St, most of them with tables outside in good weather, making this a pleasant place to pause on a stroll through Back Bay.

On the S.E. corner of Newbury and Exeter Sts formerly stood the *Hollis Street Church,* built in 1883 by the architect George A. Meacham for a congregation that had been gathered at a meeting house at Hollis St in the South End in 1732. In 1887 the Reverend Edward Everett Hale's *South Congregational Church* (which by when had become Unitarian) abandoned their meetinghouse in the South End as well and united with the Hollis Street Church here in Back Bay. These two combined congregations eventually dispersed, after which the church on the corner of Newbury and Exeter Sts was acquired by the Copley Methodist Episcopal Society, and when they in turn abandoned the building it was demolished, in 1966.

The first structure of architectural interest is on the N.E. corner of Newbury and Exeter. This is the extraordinary building known up until fairly recently as the *Exeter Theater,* a structure in the Romanesque style, looking like a fortified medieval monastery, lacking only a drawbridge and keep. This was built in 1884–85 by H. H. Hartwell and W. C. Richardson for a wealthy merchant named Marcellus J. Ayer, who used it to house the First Spiritual Temple of the Working Union of Progressive Spiritualists, of which he was the founder. This was not a church or sect so much as it was a center for those who believed in spiritualism and psychic phenomena, where they could put themselves in touch with "higher intelligences" of the spirit world through the aid of human mediums. The temple was converted into a theater in 1913 by Clarence H. Blackall, who created so many of Boston's playhouses, and it continues to serve that purpose today, though as a cinema. The building now houses a Waterstone's Booksellers, the first branch of that British firm to open in the U.S.

The next two buildings of interest are on the r., on opposite corners of the next intersection, at the S.W. and S.E. corners of Newbury and Dartmouth Sts. The first of these, with its entrance at No. 270 Dartmouth St, is a very unusual-looking building, whose walls are of dark-red brick and sandstone, decorated with elaborate reliefs in floral and vegetable designs; this is a work of the architect William Ralph Emerson, with Edward Clarke Cabot acting as consultant, who in 1881–82 constructed it in the Queen Anne Revival style.

It was designed as the headquarters, meeting place, and gallery for the Boston Art Club. This was an organization founded in 1854 by a score of art-lovers, who, as they stated in their constitution, gathered together in order "to advance the knowledge and love of art through the exhibition of its works of art, the acquisition of books and papers for the purpose of forming an art library, lectures upon subjects pertaining to art, and by other kindred means; and to promote social intercourse between its members." In 1884 the Boston Bicycle Club built a smaller building of almost identical style abutting the Boston Art Club to the W., a work of G. F. Meacham, so that even today the two structures appear virtually as one. In 1970 the two buildings were renovated by the firm of Colleti Brothers, and today they house the Copley Square High School.

Directly across the street, with its entrance at 275 Dartmouth, is the monumental fortresslike building that was originally the *Hotel Victoria.* This was designed by the architect J. Lyman Faxon, and when it opened in 1896 it was one of the largest and best-appointed residential hotels in Back Bay.

The original town houses on Newbury between Dartmouth and Clarendon were built in the period 1871–88 and most of them are still standing, although the appearance of many have been greatly changed by the addition of storefronts.

Crossing Clarendon St, one is now confronted on the r. side by the enormous mass of the *New England Mutual Life Insurance Co.,* built by Cram and Ferguson in 1932–42. This vast building, which takes up two-thirds of the area on the block, stands on the original site of the Massachusetts Institute of Technology. M.I.T.'s first home, which later came to be called the Rogers Building, was completed on this site in 1866. This was a monumental neoclassical structure erected by the architect William G. Preston, comparable in size and architectural style to the former Museum of Natural History, which was completed in 1864 on the eastern end of the block, where it remains today.

In the lobby inside the Newbury St entrance to the Insurance Co. Building there are four dioramas showing the filling in of Back Bay. One of these shows the site in 1863, with the completed Museum of Natural History at r.-center, the foundations of the first M.I.T. building just to its l., and in the background a line of houses along Beacon St and two or three on Commonwealth Ave, with all the rest of Back Bay an empty wasteland.

Return now to look at the building on the N.E. corner of Newbury and Clarendon, with its entrance at No. 233 on the latter street. This is the *Trinity Church Rectory,* built by H. H. Richardson in 1879, three years after he completed Trinity Church itself. As originally constructed, it was a two-story house, with an attic floor above, but in 1893 a full third story was added when a rector with a family succeeded Phillips Brooks, who had been a bachelor. The most prominent feature of the building is its entryway, whose broad Syrian arch dominates the facade. The building still serves as the rectory of Trinity Church.

At 101 Newbury St, the third building on the l. from the corner of Clarendon St, stands the very attractive building housing the ***New England Historic Genealogical Society.**

Admission. The library of the Society is open Tues.–Sat. 9–4:45. Full use of the library is open only to members, but visitors may apply to the librarian for permission to consult materials on the premises; fee (tel. 536-5740).

History. The New England Historic Genealogical Society was incorporated by the General Court of Massachusetts in 1845 for the purpose of collecting, studying, and preserving New England family and local history. Its three key founders were John Wingate Thornton (1818–78), a lawyer and historian; Samuel Gardner Drake (1798–1875), a bookseller, publisher, and author; and Lemuel Shattuck (1793–1859), a statistician, genealogist, local historian, and publisher. The Society's first headquarters was in a room on Court St, and they had several other homes before moving to the present building at 101 Newbury in 1964. Members of the Society have included President John Quincy Adams, President Herbert Hoover, Alexander Graham Bell, Edward Everett Hale, Washington Irving, Henry Cabot Lodge, Samuel Eliot Morison, William Hickling Prescott, Daniel Webster, and Walter Muir Whitehill. The Society is now the oldest and largest institution of its kind in the U.S.

Interior. On the ground floor there is a small museum, where the Society exhibits part of its collection of paintings as well as the *Atkinson-Lancaster Furniture Collection.* The latter collection was inherited through the Atkinson family, who resided in Newbury, Mass., as early as the 1660s, earning their living as small tradesmen and farmers. The two most important pieces in the collection are an armchair and a center table, both made in Bombay c. 1815. The paintings in the Society's collection are of interest primarily because of their historic value, illustrating the looks, the dress, the professions, and the interests of early New Englanders, rather than because of any intrinsic merit. However, there are a number of original works of art of some importance, most notably a portrait of Mrs. Andrew Tyler (1731–83) by John Singleton Copley.

The *library* is on the sixth floor, and contains nearly 300,000 books, pamphlets, and papers relating to the genealogy and local history. It houses a rich collection of town charts, abstracts of local wills, historical studies long out of print, memoirs of early New Englanders, town histories bound or in manuscript, records of naval and military operations and of Indian wars, as well as extensive family records. A number of paintings from the Society's collection are also hung in the library.

On the l. side of the block between Clarendon and Berkeley, two of the town houses in particular have retained something of their former character, though both of them have had storefronts added. The first of these, No. 97, has a distinctly Parisian look about it, with its narrow facade, its small-paned windows, and its mansard roof; this was built in 1872 by Fred Pope for Eban Jordan, one of a block of four houses that the architect made for the department-store owner, the others being at Nos 95–91. The second distinctive house is at mid-block, at No. 77, built in 1874 by Peabody and Stearns, one of a block of eight houses which that firm erected in the period 1869–76 for Charles Freeland, a real-estate speculator, all of them in the line at Nos 69–87.

At the end of the block on the l. stands the **Church of the Covenant,** originally known as the Central Congregational Church.

History. The Central Congregational Church, founded in 1835, originally worshipped at a meetinghouse on Winter St in the South End. This congregation moved to Back Bay in 1866, when the present church was built by Richard M. Upjohn, the son of Richard Upjohn, the architect who designed Trinity Church in New York City in 1839. By the mid-19C the elder Upjohn was the most influential proponent of the Gothic Revival in architecture in the U.S., as well as being one of the leaders in the High Church ecclesiastical movement. Thus it is no wonder that the younger Upjohn, who had learned his profession in his father's architectural office, designed this Back Bay church in the Gothic style.

Exterior. The most remarkable feature of the church exterior is its 236ft steeple. When the church was first built this was the tallest steeple in Boston, and it is still one of the landmarks in Back Bay.

Interior. The Church of the Covenant is renowned for its stained-glass windows, which were created by several designers working for the firm of Louis C. Tiffany c. 1893–1914. The Tiffany project consisted for the most part in filling the Gothic pointed-arch windows with colorful opalescent stained glass representing Biblical scenes. The windows on the N. side are decorated with scenes associated with the Nativity, while those on the S. side are connected with the Resurrection. The most notable object in the interior is the sanctuary lantern, a lamp of bronze filigree and dangling blown glass in the form of a corona on which are standing seven angels, holding in their hands lamps symbolic of seven gifts of the Holy Ghost. This extraordinary lamp was designed by J. A. Holzer and was originally made for the Tiffany Chapel exhibited at the Columbian Exposition in Chicago in 1893, after which it was installed in the Church of the Covenant.

After looking at the Church of the Covenant, cross Newbury St and walk S. on Berkeley St for a half-block to look at the former *Museum of Natural History* (progenitor of Boston's Museum of Science), which occupies the whole block to the W.

History. Boston's Museum of Science traces its ancestry back to the inception of the Boston Society of Natural History, founded in 1830. The first meeting was held on Feb. 9 of that year at the home of Dr. Walter Channing, where there gathered "a few gentlemen of scientific attainments who conceived the design of forming a society in Boston for the promotion of natural history." The Society was at first housed in a room at the Boston Athenaeum, from where it moved in 1833 to "a hall over the Savings Bank on Tremont St," then, in 1848, moving on to new quarters on Mason St. In 1861 the Massachusetts Legislature granted the Society a plot of land on Berkeley St in Back Bay for the purpose of building a proper museum, a splendid edifice that had its grand opening in 1864 as the New England Museum of Natural History. This was designed by William G. Preston (1844–1910), who two years later completed M.I.T.'s first building, just to the W., in much the same style. However, the museum did not develop with the times, and when the Society's centennial came in 1930 one observer described it as: "a grandmother's attic, a hodge-podge of ill-cared-for and often repulsive exhibits which belong by right in a medical school or repository rather than in a public exhibition." A program of reform began after World War II under the directorship of Bradford Washington, who persuaded the trustees to change the name of the institution to the Museum of Science, after which it moved to its present home on Science Park on the Charles River Dam.

Exterior. The *Proceedings of the Boston Society of Natural History* for 1864, the year that the museum was completed, give a summary description of its exterior that is still accurate: "It is built in the classic style of architecture, with Corinthian pilasters and capitals. The foundation of the building is of heavy hammered granite; the first story of freestone, and the second and third of brick, with walls three feet in thickness, having an air space in the interior."

Cross Berkeley St. At mid-block on the l. is the *Emmanuel Episcopal Church.* This is a Gothic structure of Roxbury conglomerate stone designed by the architect A. R. Estey and consecrated on April 24, 1862. Emmanuel was a new Episcopal parish, organized in the Back Bay in 1860 when the Rev. Frederic Dan Huntington left the Unitarian ministry and sought ordination as an Episcopal priest so that he could head the congregation. The church was originally oriented toward the N., but in 1899 a nave designed by Frederick R. Allen was added facing E., parallel to Newbury St, and the original nave was converted into a far-western transept. Adjoining the church to the W. on Newbury St is the *Leslie Lindsey Memorial Chapel,* a Gothic structure designed in 1920 by the architects Allen and Cullen. The chapel was built by the family of Leslie Lindsey, who died on her honeymoon in 1915 in the sinking of the *Lusitania,* her body washed ashore in Ireland, still wearing her father's wedding gift of rubies and diamonds. This gift was recovered and later sold to help pay for the construction and adornment of the memorial chapel. It is sometimes called the Lady Chapel, because it is dedicated to Our Lady, the Blessed Virgin. The ornamental ironwork in the chapel was done by F. Koralewski, and the high altar and stained glass by Sir Ninian Comper.

Continuing along the l. side of the street, at the corner one comes to the S. side of the *Ritz-Carlton Hotel,* whose front takes up the full block on Arlington St as far as Commonwealth Ave. The original Ritz-Carlton was erected in 1931 by the architectural firm of Strickland and Blodgett, with an addition built in 1981 by Skidmore, Owings & Merrill.

Turn r. onto Arlington; at the next corner is the **Arlington Street Church.** This was the first church built in Back Bay, and it is still one of the most handsome landmarks of the area.

History. The congregation that built the Arlington Street Church had been founded in 1729 at Long Lane (later Federal St) in the South End by a group of Scotch-Irish Presbyterians. The church eventually became Congregational in its affiliation, and in 1809 the congregation commissioned Charles Bulfinch to build a fine new meetinghouse for them on Federal St. The congregation remained in the meetinghouse on Federal St until soon after 1859, when they moved to their new church in Back Bay. The architect of this new church was Arthur Gilman, assisted by Gridley J. F. Bryant, who erected the structure in 1859—61. By that time the congregation had become Unitarians, a change in affiliation that had taken place under the leadership of the Rev. William Ellery Channing, who had been minister of the Federal Street Church from 1803—42. The congregation of the church is presently Unitarian-Universalist.

Exterior. The basic plan of the Arlington Street Church has been compared to that of St. Martin-in-the-Fields, London, designed by James Gibbs. The entire structure, which is of brownstone except for the granite base of the belfry tower, rests on 999 piles driven into the soft earth-and-gravel fill of Back Bay. The hip-roofed meetinghouse is preceded by a classical portico, whose four corners are formed by massive pillars, and with the great round-arched entryway framed by two enormous unfluted columns capped by Ionic corner-capitals; these support the architrave and pediment, from which rises the five-tiered architrave and pediment, 170ft from the ground to the tip of the spire.

The design is simpler and more symmetrical than those of the later Back Bay churches, characteristics noted by Arthur Gilman in an article he wrote for the *"Boston Evening Transcript"* in Dec. 1861, after he had finished the Arlington Street Church; as he wrote: "The tower and spire of the church . . . are placed symmetrically in the center of the principal front of the building. This is a wide departure from the practice of tucking them to one corner, so prevalent of later years. . . . The essential ideas should be symmetry, regularity, and a harmonious and even balance of the leading lines and masses of structure."

Interior. Walter H. Kilham, in his *Boston After Bulfinch,* compares the "noble interior" of the Arlington Street Church to that of St. Martin-in-the-Fields, writing that "it is certainly one of the best architectural adornments of the city. Its interior seems Georgian, but Gilman states that its motif was drawn from that of the church of St. Annunziata at Genoa."

The church is also noteworthy for its stained-glass windows, particularly those in the lower tier; these were done by several artists working under the supervision of Louis Tiffany, proceeding according to a plan designed in 1898 and completed soon after 1910. The windows in the upper tier are the work of Frederick Wilson and represent the *Beatitudes.* In the lower tier, the scenes in the four windows to the r., starting with the one closest to the door, are: *The Madonna of the Flowers; The Message of the Angels to the Shepherds, The Annunciation,* and *St. John the Baptist;* those on the l., in the same order, depict: *Jesus and the Children, The Good Shepherd, The Sermon on the Mount,* and *Jesus in the Temple.*

The last part of the itinerary takes one along the N. side of Boylston St to Copley Sq. After one has passed the Arlington Street Church, across the street to the l. is No. 356, now the home of the *Women's Educational and Industrial Union.* This structure was originally erected in 1906 by Parker, Thomas and Rice, and it was restored in 1973 by Shepley, Bulfinch, Richardson and Abbott. The Women's Educational and Industrial Union was founded in 1877 and was originally housed opposite the pond in the Public Garden; hence the gilded swan over the entrance, symbolizing the swan boats that were set in motion there by the Paget family that same year.

At the far corner of the block on the l. side stands the *Berkeley Building,* with its main entrance at 420 Boylston St. This delightful building was designed in 1905 by Codman and Despredelle, the latter a French architect working across the street at the M.I.T. School of Architecture, which remained in the Rogers Building on Boylston St until it was demolished in 1938. The Berkeley Building is constructed of lightweight steel members enclosed in enameled terra-cotta, with wide bay windows in between the vertical sections, making its facade as original as it is charming.

At the S.W. corner of Boylston and Berkeley stands the *Coulton Building*, another structure of some originality, erected by an unknown architect in 1905, reusing the foundations and some of the walls from the YMCA Building built there in 1882 by Sturgis and Brigham. The most interesting features of the design are the five columns of bay windows that rise from the second to the fourth stories, with the one at the corner looking like a glassed-in turret.

Walking along the r. side of Boylston between Berkeley and Clarendon, one passes the mausoleumlike headquarters of the *New England Mutual Life Insurance Co.* The main entrance to this building is at mid-block, and one might enter there and spend a few moments looking at the *Hoffbauer Murals* in the main lobby. Eight large murals by the late Charles Hoffbauer, done in the early 1940s, depict scenes from the early history of New England. Also on display in the lobby is a rotating model of the USS *Constitution.*

The vestibule of the Insurance Co. Building occupies the same site as the entrance hall of the Rogers Building, M.I.T.'s first home. From here broad stairways on either side led up to the second floor, at the rear of which was the great auditorium called Huntington Hall. In his history of the early years of M.I.T. (when it was known as Boston Tech) Samuel S. Prescott gives this description of the auditorium and the important part it played in the civic life of Back Bay: "Huntington Hall was for many years the most dignified and capacious auditorium in the newer residential portion of the city, and it was used for many public purposes as well as for the instruction of Boston Tech students. The great public lectures of the Lowell Institute were held here for two generations, and many men of world-wide reputation spoke from its desk. It is not generally known that for nearly five years while Trinity Church was being built, the Sunday services of that parish were held here, and Phillips Brooks preached regularly from the platform."

After leaving the building, continue on in the same direction along Boylston as far as Clarendon. This brings one to the N.E. corner of Copley Sq, where the next itinerary begins.

14 Back Bay II: From Copley Square to the Back Bay Fens

This itinerary begins where the last one ended, at the intersection of Boylston and Dartmouth Sts, at the N.E. corner of Copley Sq.

History and Topography. The area between Beacon and Boylston Sts was planned from the very beginning as a high-class residential area, and it remained exclusively so until quite recent times. This was possible because the northern part of Back Bay was physically isolated from the poorer areas that developed around it, bounded on the W. by the Back Bay Fens and on the S. by the two railway lines that crossed the shallows on causeways, the Boston & Albany R.R. coming in from the N.W. and the Boston & Providence from the S.W., crossing just S. of what is now Copley Sq. The vast railroad yards of these two lines, which were S. of Boylston St on either side of the present Copley Sq, provided additional protection for the elite residential area to the N., as did the Public Garden to the E. Thus it was evident to the city-planners that the area in the western segment between the two railway lines was not the place to plan an exclusive residential quarter. Instead, they decided that this newly created area, the last part of Back Bay to be filled in as a whole, would be the ideal place to build the new civic institutions for which there was no space in the older, crowded parts of Boston, and for which the burgeoning population of the city was creating a pressing need. The first step in this direction came when a block of vacant land just to the E. of what is now Copley Sq was set aside for public buildings, that bounded by Berkeley, Clarendon, Boylston, and Newbury Sts, with work on the Museum of Natural History starting there in 1862 and the foundations for the first building of what would later be M.I.T. commencing the following year. The next step came in 1870, when the city of Boston awarded a tract of land on what is now the S. side of Copley Sq to the Boston Museum of Fine Arts, founded earlier that year. The first section of the museum opened in 1876, by which time two churches were already standing on the N. side of the square; these were the New Old South Church and the Second Church (now destroyed), both completed in 1874; and with Trinity Church abuilding on the E. side, to open in 1877. The final step was the erection of the Boston Public Library on the W. side, and when that was completed in 1889 the square was fully formed, surrounded by more architecturally distinguished buildings than any other public square in the U.S. Many changes have taken place around the square since then, the two most notable being the demolition of the Museum of Fine Arts to make way for the Copley Plaza Hotel, which opened in 1912, and the erection of the new Hancock Tower at the S.E. corner of the square, completed in 1975. By that time the square itself had been transformed: in 1967 the present plaza in its center was completed by the firm of Sasaki, Dawson, and Demay Assocs, producing today's visually exciting civic center.

**Trinity Church is the principal adornment of Copley Sq and a structure that many believe to be the most beautiful house of worship in Boston, with few if any equals in the U.S.

Admission. The church is open daily from 7:30—5; Sun. services at 8 and 11; free 30-min. guided tour after Sun. service at 11.

History. The original Trinity Church, a simple wooden structure, was built in 1734 on Summer St in the South End, to serve as a house of worship for those Anglicans who were too far removed from King's Chapel. This church was replaced in 1828—29 by a large granite edifice designed by Arthur Brimmer, which was totally destroyed in the great fire of 1872.

Even before the 1872 fire there had been discussions in the congregation about leaving the South End, which was becoming increasingly commercial, and looking for a new house of worship in Back Bay. The Rev. Phillips Brooks, who became rector of Trinity in July 1869, was completely in favor of this, and so in 1871 a plot of land was bought on what became the eastern side of Copley Sq, competitive designs for the proposed church had been invited and received, and Henry Hobson Richardson was chosen to be the chief architect. But before construction of the new church in Back Bay even began, the old one in the South End was totally destroyed, on Nov. 10, 1872, when the Great Boston Fire, in the words of Phillips Brooks, "wrapt its granite walls in glory."

Construction of the new church began on Apr. 21, 1873, when a pile was driven into the soft earth-and-gravel fill of Back Bay, the first of 4500 which would be put in place before the foundations could be laid. Meanwhile, work went ahead on the detailed plans for the design and construction of the superstructure, with Brooks and Richardson conferring closely. In Nov. 1874 work was finished on the chapel building (now the Parish House), by which time the transept, chancel, and aisle walls, as well as the western front, were high above the ground. In the interim the congregation had been using other facilities, with Sunday services being held in Huntington Hall of M.I.T., and with Emmanuel Church opening its doors for weddings, baptisms, and funerals, but with the completion of the chapel the members could once again worship in their own place, while they waited for the main body of Trinity to be finished. Toward the end of 1876, when the church itself was substantially complete, John La Farge was engaged to paint the murals, which he and his six assistants finished just eight days before Trinity was consecrated, on Feb. 9, 1877. The West Porch, though included in Richardson's original design, was not completed until 1897, with the construction carried out by Shepley, Rutan, and Coolidge, who succeeded to Richardson's architectural practice after his premature death in 1886. The present chancel, designed by Charles D. Maginnis, was dedicated on Dec. 18, 1938. In 1952 the West Porch was redecorated under the supervision of Charles Collens, and in 1956 the nave was restored to its original condition by Henry R. Shepley, grandson of H. H. Richardson.

Exterior. Richardson's *Description of the Church,* written in 1877, just after he completed Trinity, still gives a complete and precise picture of the structure as it was at that time. In this account Richardson wrote: "The style of the church may be characterized as a free rendering of the French Romanesque, inclining particularly to that school that flourished in the eleventh century in Central France—the ancient Aquitaine. . . . Among the branches of the Romanesque of Central France, nowhere were the peculiar branches of the style so strongly marked as in the peaceful, enlightened and isolated cities of Auvergne. The central tower, a reminiscence, perhaps, of the domes of Venice and Constantinople, was here fully developed, so that in many cases the tower became, as it were, the Church, and the composition took the outline of a pyramid, the apse, transepts, nave and chapels forming only the base to the obelisk of the tower. In studying the problem presented by a building fronting on three streets, it appeared desirable that the tower should be central, thus belonging equally to each front, rather than putting it on any corner, where, from at least one side, it would be nearly out of sight; and in carrying out this motive, it was plain that with the ordinary proportion of Church and tower, either the tower must be comparatively small, which would bring its supporting piers inconveniently into the midst of the congregation, or the tower being large, the rest of the Church must be magnified to inordinate proportions. For this dilemma the Auvergnine solution seemed perfectly adapted. Instead of the tower being an inconvenient and unnecessary addition to the Church, it was itself made the main feature. The struggle for precedence, which so often takes place between a Church and its spire, was disposed of, by at once and completely subordinating nave, transepts, and apse, and grouping them about the tower as the central mass." The tower is an adaptation of the tower of the Old Cathedral in Salamanca. Its walls are of yellowish-gray Dedham granite, ornamented with reddish-brown Longmeadow freestone. The West Porch, the "Galilee," is based on that of St. Trophime, in Arles.

The sculpture of the West Porch was done by John Evans, Hugh Cairns, and Domingo Mora. The central features of the sculpture are the ten large statues of leading figures in the Judeo-Christian heritage; between some of these and above are smaller statues of other Hebrew and Christian leaders; between and below there is a series of reliefs representing important events in the lives of these people. (In the description that follows, all figures and reliefs are identified from l. to r.) N. side: the two large statues are of Abraham and Moses; the smaller ones are of Samuel, David, Solomon, Daniel, and Elijah; the reliefs represent *The Journey of Abraham* and *The Worship of the Golden Calf.* W. front: large statues: Isaiah, St. Matthew, St. Mark, St. Luke, St. John, and St. Paul; to the r. of Isaiah, on the front and inner side of the arch, respectively, there are two reliefs: *The Lord Sitting upon the Throne among the Seraphim* (Isaiah 6), and *The Peaceable Kingdom* (Isaiah 11); to the l. of St. Matthew, on the inner and front side of the arch, respectively, are two reliefs: *The Nativity,* and *The Visit of the Magi;* between and above St. Matthew and St. Mark are three smaller statues: the Virgin Mary, Elizabeth, and Anna; below the smaller statues is a relief showing *Christ in the Temple with the Doctors;* to the r. of St. Mark, on the front and inner sides of the central arch, respectively, are two reliefs: *The Baptism of Christ* and *Christ Blessing the Little Children;* to the l. of St. Luke, on the inner and front sides of the central arch, respectively, are two reliefs: *The Prodigal Son* and *The Triumphal Entry into Jerusalem;* between and above St. Luke and St. John are three smaller statues: Mary, Martha, and Mary Magdalene; below these there is a relief depicting *The Last Supper;* to the r.

Trinity Church, flanked by the New, and backed by the Old Hancock Towers

of St. John, on the front and inner sides of the arch, respectively, are two reliefs: *Christ Before Pilate* and *The Appearance of Jesus to Thomas;* to the l. of St. Paul, on the inner and front sides of the arch, respectively, are two reliefs *Saul on the Road to Damascus* and *Paul Preaching on the Aereopagus;* S. side: the two large statues are of St. Augustine, early missionary to England, and Phillips Brooks; between them and above are five smaller statues of English Christian leaders: Wycliffe, Hooker, Taylor, Robinson, and Wesley; beneath the five smaller statues are two panels, of which only the one on the l. is carved, and this with a relief depicting the baptism of King Ethelbert by St. Augustine. On the bases of the six piers on the West Front there are carved the following: the symbol of the Trinity, the four emblems of the Evangelists (angel, lion, ox, and eagle), and the XP with Alpha and Omega.

Interior. Richardson's analysis of the interior plan and structure, as given in his *Description of the Church,* is still the most lucid and complete analysis of the building. His description is as follows: "In plan the Church as it stands is a Latin cross, with a semicircular apse added to the eastern arm. [Modern historians of architecture describe Trinity as having the shape of a Greek cross rather than a Latin cross, and they are correct, if one includes the semicircular apse as an addition to the eastern arm, but Richardson is quite clear on that point.] The arms of the cross are short, in proportion to their width. In general, taking the square at the intersection of nave and transepts as a modulus, the total length of the auditorium is three squares, of which the chancel, including the apse, forms one, the square at the intersection another, and the nave a third, the transepts being each half a square. Over the square at the intersection stands the tower. The aisles would be very narrow for a Gothic Church, but are in character for the Romanesque, and are much more serviceable when thus reduced to passage-ways, than when their width compels their being occupied by pews. The clear-story is carried by an arcade of two arches only. Above the aisles a gallery is carried across the arches, which, from its position, was distinguished by the names of the 'triforium' gallery, and serves as a passage to connect the three main galleries, one across either transept, and one across the west-end of the nave, over the vestibule. Both the west gallery and the two triforium galleries connect with the staircases which occupy the western towers, and the transept galleries are also reached by special staircases, ascending, one from a north-easterly vestibule, which serves as entrance both from Huntington Avenue directly and from the cloister connecting from the Chapel, and the other from a south-eastern vestibule entered from St. James Avenue. The robing-room opens from the north-east vestibule, as well as from the chancel. The main vestibule is 52 feet long, the width of the nave, without counting the lower story of the western towers, which virtually forms a part of it, and increases its length to upwards of 86 feet. In the middle of the west front is the main portal, and a secondary door opens into each of the towers, giving thus three entrances in the west front, and five double doors open from the western vestibule into the Church. The upper regions of the Church are reached by a winding stair in the northeastern turret of the great tower, starting from the room over the northeast vestibule. This lands at the bell deck over the flat ceiling which closes the tower in the Church. The whole interior of the Church and Chapel is finished in black walnut, and all the vestibules in ash and oak.

Trinity is renowned for its beautiful frescoes, which were painted by John LaFarge and his assistants, the most notable of whom was Augustus Saint-Gaudens. LaFarge's technical success in this very difficult project is astonishing, in the first large-scale decoration in fresco by an American artist. One inevitably looks first at the fresco decoration in the ceiling of the tower, which hovers more than 103ft above the floor of the nave. The magnificent paneled ceiling is completely covered with intricately designed arabesques of gold in Romanesque style. The paintings in the 12 small lunettes above the high windows of the tower can best be viewed from the side galleries. These can be identified as follows, proceeding again from l. to r.:

over the E. windows: *Journey into Egypt, Mother and Child, The Resurrection;* over the S. windows: *Samson and the Lion, The Good Shepherd, Jonah and the Whale;* over the W. windows: *Morning* (an allegory), *The Jeweled Cross, Evening* (an allegory); over the N. windows: *The Garden of Eden, The Peaceable Kingdom, Abraham and Isaac.*

On either side of each group of three high tower windows the wall is decorated with crosses and the symbols of the four Evangelists. These are, where the identifications are once again from l. to r.: E. wall: ornamental crosses; an angel (symbol of St. Matthew); an eagle (symbol of St. John); W. wall: two illuminated texts: "I will give them an heart to know me, that I am the Lord, and they shall be my people," and "Go ye therefore and teach all nations, baptizing them in the name of the Father, and of the Son, and the Holy Ghost"; N. wall: an ox (symbol of St. Luke), a lion (symbol of St. Mark).

Beneath the high windows, on a gold border around the tower, is a large illuminated text that reads: "Blessing and honour and glory and power be unto him that sitteth upon the throne and unto the lamb forever." Below the border, and over the great arches of the tower, are decorative paintings of angels in blue, violet, and rose. The figures at the sides of the great arches can be identified as follows: E. wall: St. Peter, St. Paul; S. wall: Isaiah, Jeremiah; N. wall: David, Moses.

Elsewhere in the church are the following paintings by John LaFarge: E. wall of the N. transept: *St. James;* N. wall of the nave, between the clerestory windows: *Christ and the Woman of Samaria at the Well;* S. wall of the nave, between the clerestory windows: *Christ and Nicodemus,* which is generally considered to be one of the greatest of all of LaFarge's religious paintings.

Trinity is also celebrated for its beautiful stained-glass windows, which were created by artists and artisans in both the U.S. and Europe. This project was started by John LaFarge, who was overseer of the interior decoration of the church, and who designed and made some of the windows himself.

All seven windows in the chancel were made by Clayton and Bell of London in 1877–78; the subjects are, in the usual order: *The Nativity, The Discussion in the Temple, The Baptism, The Preacher, The Last Supper, The Resurrection,* and *The Commission to the Apostles.* The window in the Baptistery, which is to the r. of the apse, depicts *David's Charge to Solomon;* this was designed by Sir Edward Burne-Jones and was executed in 1882 by William Morris and Co., London. In the S. transept, the three-lancet window over the gallery was designed and executed by A. Oudinot of Paris in 1878; the scenes are: *The Resurrection, The Ascension,* and *The Day of Pentecost.* There are two windows in the W. wall at the gallery level; on the l. is *St. Luke the Physician and Evangelist,* by Heaton, Butler and Bayne of England, done c. 1920; and on the r. is *The Transfiguration,* by Henry Holiday, of London, c. 1878. Below the gallery are four windows, three in the southern wall and one in the western, all by Cottier and Co. of New York and London, c. 1878; those on the S. wall are: *The Sower and the Reaper, The Virgins,* and *The Angel Troubling the Pool;* and on the W. wall the scene is *Peace, Be Still,* whose title comes from Mark 4:39: "And he rose and rebuked the wind and said unto the waves "peace, be still.' " There are two clerestory windows in the S. wall of the nave; the one on the l., designed and executed by John LaFarge in 1888, shows *The Presentation of Mary at the Temple;* and the one on the r., done c. 1878 by Clayton and Bell of London, depicts *David's Removal of the Ark to Jerusalem.* On the S. and N. sides of the nave, immediately above and below the passageways, are eight small windows, all designed c. 1927 by Mary Redmond of Boston. On the S. side, above the passageway, are the *Four Evangelists;* below the passageway they are shown composing their respective gospels. On the N. side of the nave are the *Twelve Apostles;* above: Andrew, Philip, Peter, and Paul; below: James, son of Alpheus, Matthias, Thomas, Bartholomew, James, son of Zebedee, Simon the Canaanite, Thadeus, and Barnabas. There are also two windows by Mary Redmond in the N. wall of the West Porch, at the beginning of the stairway leading up to the galleries, also done c. 1927; the one on the l. contains the scenes *Saul Anointeth David* and *David Plays Before Saul;* and on the r. are the scenes of *The Queen of Sheba Before King Solomon* and *God Save King Solomon.* In the W. wall of the nave is a three-lancet window created by John LaFarge in 1883; in the center is *Christ in the Act of Benediction,* which is said to have inspired Phillips Brooks when he was preaching, and on either side of him are depicted alabaster columns against a blue background. In the N. wall of the nave are two clerestory windows by Henry Holiday of London (1878). The window on the l. has three panels decorated with scenes from the life of St. Paul; above: *Saul at the Feet of Gamaliel;* center: *Saul on the Damascus Road;* below: *Paul Preaching on the Aereopagus in Athens;* the window on the r. shows *Christ Blessing Little Children.* Looking at the windows in the N. transept: on the W. wall, over the gallery, there is a pair by John LaFarge; on the l. is *The New Jerusalem,* done in 1884; and on the r. is *The Resurrection,* dating from 1902. On the N. wall over the gallery is a three-lancet window designed by Sir Edward Burne-Jones and executed by William Morris and Co. in 1880; the one on the l. depicts *The Adoration of the Shepherds;* center: *The Worship of the Magi;* r.: *The Journey into Egypt.* Under the gallery, there are four windows done in 1877–78 by Burlison and Grills of London; the subjects are: *Job and St. Stephen,* symbolizing Patience and Fortitude; *Abraham and Eunice,* exemplifying Faith; two *Angels,* standing for Hope; and *The Good Samaritan, Dorcas,* the personification of Charity.

The furnishings and decorations in the chancel are particularly elegant. The choir rail, designed by Charles A. Coolidge and executed by John Evans, is a white marble parapet with 12 panels carved with designs in low relief, decorated with religious symbols in the Byzantine style. On the l. side is the pulpit, also created by Coolidge and Evans; this is in finely carved white marble, and on its parapet are the figures of five leaders in the history of Christianity: St. Paul, St. John Chrysostom, Martin Luther, Bishop Hugh Latimer, and Phillips Brooks, with the panels between the statues decorated with scenes from the life of Christ. The chorister's stalls, designed by Charles A. Coolidge and made by A. H. Davenport, are of stained quartered oak. To the r., just inside the choir rail, is the rector's chair, with an ornate canopy carried on two pilasters and two columns, the latter resting on the backs of a pair of lions, in the Romanesque style. The altar is a giant block of Montenelle marble, quarried near Trieste, with carved faces and inserted borders of Venetian gold glass and colored glass mosaics; on the front face are the figures of two confronted peacocks, the Byzantine symbol of eternal life, flanked by clusters of grapevines, representing the sacred wine served in Communion. The credence table at the r. side of the altar is supported by columns of red Numidian marble. The altar rests on a base of Galena Siena marble, of which the steps and altar face are also made; the floor has borders of Brocatelle Siena, and the pair of bishop's chairs flanking the altar are of Montenelle marble. The large cross above the altar is made of wood covered with gold leaf and polychrome, with the symbols of the Evangelists at the ends of the four arms. The communion rail is also of Montenelle marble, with panels of Morocco Red Flammé marble. The curving wall of the chancel has a high wainscoting of Green Alps marble framed by panels of Red Levanto marble, with a border above of "Cosmati" work—i.e., marble-gold-and-glass mosaics. Above this there is a frieze with seven Biblical quotations separated by marble reliefs depicting the scenes referred to in the inscriptions. Above this are seven bronze reliefs by Ernest Pellegrini; these represent seven leading figures in the history of Christianity at important moments in their lives; they are, from r. to l.: Paul before Agrippa and Bernice; St. Athanasius with the Emperor Constantine the Great at Nicaea; St. Augustine of Hippo presenting the *City of God* to Marcellinus; St. Francis and the Cured Leper; John Wycliffe translating the Vulgate into English; John Wycliffe and his horse; and Phillips Brooks telling little children about the birth of Jesus. In this last relief the prominent star above indicates that Brooks is reciting to the children the popular Christmas hymn that he composed, "O Little Town of Bethlehem."

In the Baptistery, the font is of Devonshire marble and alabaster, on an octagonal granite base; this was produced by Forsyth of London and installed in 1875. On the r. is a bust of Phillips Brooks by Daniel Chester French, dedicated in 1898, and on the l. there is a bust of Dean Arthur Stanley, done c. 1885 by Mary Grant.

Precincts. After seeing the interior of Trinity, one might leave by the front door and turn r. outside to stroll around the precincts of the church. Outside the N. transept of the church is a statue of Phillips Brooks, designed by Augustus Saint-Gaudens. However, Saint-Gaudens died before the statue was sculpted, and the work was done by his assistants at his studio in Windsor, Vermont. The marble canopy framing the statue was designed and executed by McKim, Mead & White, and the monument was dedicated in 1910.

The *Parish House* is on the N. side of a square in which the cloisters form the other three sides. The Parish House contains a library and conference room on the ground floor, offices and a nursery on the mezzanine and second floor, and St. Andrews Hall on the third floor. The area enclosed by the cloisters has in recent years been transformed into a pretty garden, within which there is a small statue of St. Francis of Assisi. As one walks through the S. side of the cloisters, approaching the rear entrance of the church, one sees on the l. a plaque honoring Henry Hobson Richardson. Embedded in the wall above this is a rosette which was part of the Gothic tower of the present church's predecessor on Summer St, the church that was destroyed in the great fire of 1872. On the r., built into the wall of the cloister, there is a Gothic window tracery from the Church of St. Botolph in Boston, Lincolnshire.

Now cross over to look at the **New Hancock Tower,** in whose gleaming glass facade Trinity Church is spectacularly mirrored, providing one of the most dramatic contrasts in Boston of the old and the new in architecture. The Tower, which is the headquarters building of the John Hancock Mutual Life Insurance Co., was designed by I. M. Pei and Partners, with Harry N. Cobb in charge of the design, and was erected by the Gilbane Building Co. of Providence, Rhode Island, with construction beginning in 1968 and completed in 1976. The skyscraper has 60 stories and is 740ft high, making it the tallest building in New England. Its facade is made up of gray-tinted glass windows framed in black aluminum, which mirror the Boston sky in all of its changing moods. In plan the building is a slightly irregular rhomboid, which makes its form appear different when seen from different vantage points—from some parts of Boston one sees only the broad front and back sides; from others only one side, and from still others it appears as a thin sliver—all of which adds to the dynamism of this extraordinary structure. An *Observatory* on the 60th floor (fee) commands a breathtaking view of Boston and its environs.

Several displays and activities in the Observatory are connected with the history and topography of Boston. *Boston 1775* is a sound-and-light show that describes Boston in the colonial period, including the historical events that led up to the American Revolution. *City Flight* is a seven-min. filmed fly-over of the city in a helicopter. *Skyline Boston* provides a sit-down look at Boston from a grandstand viewing area, with narration by the late Walter Muir Whitehill describing the topographical changes that have occurred in the area since the first settlement of the Shawmut Peninsula. *Photorama* is a display of 110 illuminated photographs of historic landmarks in Boston. There are also high-powered telescopes available on the viewing deck, some of which are already focused on important landmarks.

The New Hancock Tower is the most recent of three buildings in the immediate vicinity that have been used in succession as headquarters by the John Hancock Mutual Life Insurance Co., with the other two occupying the entire block bounded by Clarendon, St. James, Berkeley, and Stuart Sts. The first Hancock building in Back Bay is just across from the New Hancock Tower, with its entrance at 200 Clarendon St. This building was erected in 1922 by Parker, Thomas and Rice, who in 1924 received the Harlestone Parker Award from the Boston Society of Architects for its design. The building was once more elegant and handsome than it is now, for much of its original structure is obscured by later additions. Just beyond is the second Hancock building, also known as the *Old Hancock Tower;* this was completed in 1947, and at that time it was the tallest building in Boston. The architects were Cram and Ferguson, who in 1950 received the Harlestone Parker Award for its design.

The S. side of Copley Sq from Trinity Pl to Dartmouth St. is occupied by the *Copley Plaza Hotel.* This was designed by Clarence H. Blackall and built by Henry Hardenbergh, who completed the structure in 1912. Though the Copley Plaza gives a touch of elegance to Copley Sq, it has little of architectural interest.

The Copley Plaza stands on the site of the old *Boston Museum of Fine Arts,* the first public building to be erected in Back Bay S. of Boylston St. The old museum was designed by Sturgis and Brigham, and its first section, the West Wing, opened on July 4, 1876, while the rest of the building opened on March 18, 1890. The old museum was a splendid Gothic structure revetted with English terra-cotta, one of the first large buildings in the U.S. to use this material for decorative purposes. The Museum of Fine Arts moved into its new home on the Fenway in 1909, whereupon the old museum on Copley Sq was demolished to make way for the Copley Plaza Hotel.

The W. side of Copley Sq is occupied by the old building of the ****Boston Public Library,** one of the most celebrated buildings in the city.

Admission. The main entrance to the old library building is at Dartmouth St on Copley Sq; the entrance to the new building is on Boylston St. The library is open Mon.–Thurs. 9–9, Fri. & Sat. 9–5; Sun. 2–6.

History. The Boston Public Library was founded in 1852 and first opened to the public in 1854 on Mason St. It was the first free municipal library in the U.S. supported by general taxation. The library moved to a new and larger home in 1858; this was a neoclassical structure erected by the architect Charles Kirby on Boylston St just opposite the Common, on the site of the present Colonial Theater. At that time the library had a collection of 70,000 volumes, and by the time it moved to its present site in Copley Sq, in 1895, this had risen to 610,000. The rapid growth in the size of the library's collection made it apparent early on that a larger home was needed, and in 1880 the Commonwealth granted land in Back Bay for that purpose. However, bureaucratic bungling delayed action until 1887, when the trustees of the library were finally able to go ahead with the project. At that time the trustees chose a design for the proposed building submitted by Charles F. McKim, of the New York architectural firm of McKim, Mead & White. The challenges faced by McKim in designing the library were formidable and complex: to create a monumental public building directly across the square from Richardson's much-admired Trinity Church, a Romanesque structure, not to mention its distinguished neighbor on the S. side of the square, the Museum of Fine Arts, a Gothic structure that had won high praise when it opened. McKim's solution was original and brilliant, though the building was not without its detractors. The splendid edifice he created was the first example in the U.S. to be designed in the style of Renaissance Beaux Arts academicism, setting a new standard of taste and elegance, a classically rectilinear structure of gleaming, smooth white granite, contrasting favorably with Richardson's soaring pyramidal mass of rough-hewn ashlar across the way. Original as it was, McKim had three archetypes for the celebrated facade of the library: Labrouste's Bibliothèque Sainte-Geneviève in Paris, Alberti's Tempio Malatestiano in Rimini, and Richardson's Marshall Field Wholesale Store in Chicago. Aside from the design, the library was distinguished by the perfection of the stonework and in the lavish works of art included in its decoration, making it the most magnificent combined creation of architect, builders, artisans, sculptors, and painters produced in the U.S. until that time. When the library was first opened to the public in March 1895 not all of the decorative work had been finished, and not until 1912 were all of its sculptures and works of art complete and in place. Something of the impression that the new library created at the time of its completion may be discovered from a paragraph in Ralph Adam Cram's *My Life in Architecture,* writing of his student days in Cambridge, in a period when enthusiasm for Richardson's work had temporarily declined somewhat: "No greater contrast could be imagined than that between Trinity Church and the new Library across the way. On the one hand an almost brutal, certainly primitive, boldness, arrogance, power; on the other a serene Classicism, reserved, scholarly, delicately conceived in all its parts, beautiful in that sense in which things have always been beautiful in periods of high human culture."

By the beginning of the 1960s the McKim building on Copley Sq, by then known as the Main Library, was no longer adequate to house the enormous collection of books and other scholarly materials that had accumulated. In 1964 the decision was made to build adjacent to it a new general library with open shelves, thus preserving the McKim building as a reference library to house special collections. Philip Johnson was hired to design the new building, which opened on Dec. 12, 1972. The new library building that Johnson created is in complete harmony with the old one, the two of them linked structurally and presenting white granite facades of comparable dimensions along Boylston St, providing an elegant contrast in the distinguished architectural styles of the late Victorian period and the modern epoch.

Exterior of the Old Library. The height of the McKim building is 70ft from sidewalk to cornice, and its length on the side facing Copley Sq is 225ft. The building stands on a stepped granite platform that elevates it above the flat plane of Copley Sq. The massive ground floor, with rusticated stonework, has at its center three great round-arched entryways, with five large rectangular windows on either side. The upper story (as seen from the outside, for in the nonceremonial rooms the building internally has six to seven floors) is faced in smooth blocks of Milford granite, grayish-white with faint pinkish highlights; here the facade is pierced by 13 enormous windows with round arches, the most remarkable feature of the exterior, and one of the principal points of similarity between the library and two of its archetypes: the Bibliothèque Sainte-Geneviève and the Tempio Malatestiano. Above is the pantiled hip roof, surmounted at its corners by metal masts.

At the edge of the platform flanking the Copley Sq entrance there are a pair of heroic-sized bronze statues of seated female figures on massive granite pedestals. These were done by Bela Pratt and are dated 1911; the figure on the l. is the personification of *Science* and the one on the r. represents *Art,* with the names of prominent scientists and artists, respectively, carved on the pedestals.

One might now examine the Copley Sq facade in more detail. Each of the three arched entryways is closed by heavy wrought-iron gates and flanked by ornate wrought iron chandeliers, each with four lamps. On the keystone of the center arch there is carved in high relief a bust of Athena (Roman Minerva), the goddess of wisdom, with her visored helmet pulled back over her forehead, by Augustus Saint-Gaudens and Domingo Mora. Above, on the parapets of the three central windows, are carved in low relief on pink Knoxville marble three seals; on the l. is that of the Commonwealth; in the center the seal of the Boston Public Library, with the legend FREE TO ALL carved below, a work of Saint-Gaudens; and on the r. the seal of Boston. The panels of the other parapets are carved with the names of distinguished figures in the history of human culture—519 in all, of which four were repeated by the carvers by mistake: Aristophanes, Rabelais, Whitney, and Maury. This roll call of the great caused a scandal when a Boston newspaper hostile to the new library discovered that the firm of McKim, Mead & White had wittily worked its own name into the initial letters in three of the panels; this aroused such indignation from certain taxpapers that the architects were forced to eliminate the witty acrostic. In the spandrels of the window arches on all three facades there are granite medallions carved in low relief; these were done by Domingo Mora and contain the trade devices of early printers. Just below the cornice on the Copley Sq facade a deeply cut inscription in Roman capitals runs the entire width of the building; it reads: "THE PUBLIC LIBRARY OF THE CITY OF BOSTON BUILT BY THE PEOPLE AND DEDICATED TO THE ADVANCEMENT OF LEARNING. A.D. MDCCCLXXXVIII." On the Boylston St side a similar inscription reads: "THE COMMONWEALTH REQUIRES THE EDUCATION OF THE PEOPLE AS THE SAFEGUARD OF ORDER AND LIBERTY." And on the Blagden St side the inscription runs: "MDCCCLII. FOUNDED THROUGH THE MUNIFICENCE AND PUBLIC SPIRIT OF CITIZENS." Above is the finely carved classical cornice, the upper portion of which is adorned with a row of lion heads, with the whole topped by an elaborate green copper cresting formed into a series of clam shells (replacing the Greek antefix) and dolphins, symbolizing Boston's ancient connection with the sea.

Exterior of the New Library. McKim's building on Copley Sq and Johnson's annex on Boylston St are unified by their size, shape, and structure, just as they complement one another in their architectural styles. Philip Johnson, in his design of the annex, divided the available building space into nine equal squares, at the corners of which he built 16 towers, connecting them with curtain walls. The front four towers form the dominant features of the facade on Boylston St. These and the other towers support overhead trusses from which the upper floors are hung. In addition to their structural function, these trusses give the upper part of the annex a compatible shape to the sloping roof of the old library. Other prominent features of the facade are the graceful inwardly curving arches in the form of catenaries that frame the three windows on the second level, with the entryway beneath the central arch. There are long and very low windows on the level above, and above these the uppermost level of the facade projects slightly outward in three huge blocks, which seem wedged in between the towers.

Interior of the New Library. The 16 towers that support the structure divide the interior into 16 equal bays. The central square, known as the Great Hall, is hollow, and contains the stairs and mezzanines. Floor plans, displayed prominently throughout the building, show the location of the various collections and library services.

Proceeding now to the old library, turn l. after passing through the turnstiles and continue straight ahead through the stacks. Go as far as possible in that direction until arriving at the end of a hallway, in which there is a display of books about Boston. On the r. there is a diorama with scenes from *The Arabian Nights*, created by Louise Stimson of Concord, Mass. On the l. a door leads into an anteroom, and from there one goes straight across into a small room where there are two more dioramas by Louise Stimson, *The London of Dickens* and *Alice in Wonderland*. The doorway on the r. leads into the inner courtyard of the old library.

**Interior of the Old Library. The inner courtyard of the old library is one of the loveliest spots in Boston, with a Renaissance cloister bordering three sides of a formal garden, a reflecting pool with a fountain in the center, and trees to provide welcome shade during the summer months. On the walls of the arcade there are memorials to benefactors of the library and to its employees who died during World War I; one of these, a medallion portrait of Robert C. Billings, is a work of Augustus Saint-Gaudens.

Continue to the opposite end of the portico to enter the interior of the old library. Once inside, proceed straight ahead and turn r. at the first corner to enter the *Main Entrance Hall.* Before examining the hall in detail, turn l. and go through the great doorway into the *Vestibule* in order to see the various parts of the interior of the old library in the order in which the architect intended that they should be seen. (Since the main entrance to the old library is not presently in use, the Vestibule is closed off from the entrance hall by a chain, but the guard on duty will allow visitors to pass on request.)

The floors, walls, and vaulted ceiling of the Vestibule are of pink Knoxville marble, and the floor is inlaid with veined patterns of brown Knoxville and Levanto marble. The three doorways leading into the entrance hall are smaller-scale replicas of the great entrance portal of the Erechtheion on the Athenian Acropolis. The six bronze leaves of the three doors, which weigh 1500 pounds each, are adorned with female allegorical figures in low relief, the work of Daniel Chester French. These are identified by legends above as: (l.) *Music and Poetry;* (center) *Knowledge and Wisdom;* (r.) *Truth and Romance.* These superb works were cast by the John Williams Foundry and installed in 1905. At the N. end of the Vestibule there is a deep niche with a bronze statue of a dashing figure dressed in the costume of a cavalier. This fine and dramatic work is by the sculptor Frederick MacMonnies (1863–1937), and portrays Sir Henry Vane, one of the first governors of Massachusetts.

Return to the *Main Entrance Hall,* which is designed in the Roman style, divided into three aisles by massive pilasters and piers of Iowa sandstone. The floor is paved in white marble, and in the central aisle there is a mosaic inlaid with brass; represented are the signs of the zodiac and their symbols; inscriptions commemorating the founding of the Boston Public Library in 1852; the commencement of construction of the Copley Square Library in

1888; the library seal; and a laurel wreath with the names of eight men prominent in the founding of the library and in its early history. The ceiling, which is arched in the central aisle and has domical vaults in the side aisles, is adorned with a mosaic in the form of a vine-covered trellis; this is inscribed with the names of six distinguished Bostonians, and in the pendentives of the domical vaults there are the illustrious names of 24 others.

Before ascending the stairs, one might take a moment to look at the large chamber to the r. of the entry, which one passed on entering from the courtyard. This is the *Government Document Room,* originally the Periodicals Room. This is an interesting chamber, with a row of columns on high pedestals supporting a series of vaults whose ceilings are of brick in a herringbone design, with windows in recessed arches looking out onto Copley Sq.

Return to the Main Entrance Hall. The Main Staircase impressed Henry James with "its amplitude of wing and its splendour of tawny marble, a high and luxurious beauty." The walls are revetted in variegated yellow Siena marble veined in black, especially quarried for the library. The steps are of ivory-gray French échaillon marble mottled with fossil shells. The deeply coffered ceiling is of plaster, cream-colored and light-blue, and hanging from it over the stairs there is a spherical chandelier of bronze and cut glass. The landing is paved with geometric patterns of red-streaked Numidian marble. The landing is flanked by a pair of guardian lions in unpolished Siena marble; these were done by Louis Saint-Gaudens, brother of the more famous Augustus; they are memorials to the men of two Massachusetts regiments who died in the Civil War, and the pedestals are inscribed with the names of the battles and campaigns in which these units fought.

Ascend the second stage of the staircase to the vaulted upper hallway at the top, where an extremely attractive loggia overlooks the stairwell. On the wall of the hallway in front of the loggia is the celebrated mural painted in 1895–96 by Puvis de Chavannes (1824–98), the French painter renowned for his murals in the Hotel de Ville in Paris. The mural, which is 20ft high and some 40ft long and painted on canvas which was attached to the wall, is entitled *Les Muses Inspiratrices Acclament Le Génie, Messager de Lumière* (The Muses of Inspiration Welcoming the Harbinger of Light). The painting portrays the Nine Muses of Greek mythology ascending from Mount Parnassus while singing the praises of a naked winged youth above, who represents the Spirit of Enlightenment. In the upper part of the stairwell there are eight more murals by de Chavannes, three under the arches on either side and two flanking the window that looks out over the courtyard.

The themes depicted in these paintings are the great intellectual traditions represented in the library's collections. These are, as viewed from l. to r. and using the artist's own identifications: (l. wall, top of stairs to l.) *Philosophy,* in which Plato sums up in an immortal phrase the eternal conflict between Spirit and Matter: "Man is a plant of heavenly not of earthly growth"; *Astronomy,* in which the Chaldean shepherds observe the stars and discover the law of numbers; *History,* attended by a Spirit bearing a torch calls up the Past; (l. of window) *Chemistry* (mineral, organic, vegetable), in which a process of mysterious change evolves itself under the magic wand of a fairy surrounded by watching spirits; (r. of window) *Physics,* in which, by the wondrous agency of Electricity, speech flashes through space and swift as lightning bears tidings of good and evil; (r., bottom of stairs) *Pastoral Poetry,* Virgil; *Dramatic Poetry,* Aeschylus and the Oceanides; *Epic Poetry,* Homer crowned by the *Iliad* and the *Odyssey.*

The floor of the *Chavannes Gallery,* as this central section of the hallway is called, is paved in a pattern of attractive colored marbles: yellow, Verona, gray Bottichino, dark-gray aldorado, and reddish-grey Chiampo Perlatto.

A large portal opposite the loggia in this gallery leads to the main reading room of the library, *Bates Hall*. The reading room is named after Joshua Bates, a self-made millionaire who became the Boston Public Library's first great benefactor. This grand chamber is by far the largest in the library, a monumental Roman hall, 218ft long, 42.5ft wide, and 50ft from the floor to the top of its barrel-vaulted ceiling, with vaulted apses at either ends, and lighted by 15 arched windows protected by grilles. The articulation of the walls of this room is based on a plan of three squares, each centered on one of the three entrance portals. Each square is three bays wide and as high as the ribs of the barrel-vaulted ceiling, leaving the interval of one bay between each square, with apsidal ends. The walls are made of sandstone from Amherst, Ohio; the floor is paved in terrazzo with a border of yellow Verona marble; the bookcases are of English oak on bases of red Verona marble; and around the room are white marble busts of eminent Bostonians and of great writers and scholars. Over the central doorway there is a finely carved balcony of Indiana limestone. At the two ends of the hall there are doorways carved from black Belgian and Alps green serpentine marble, with columns surmounted by bronze Corinthian capitals, and in the adjacent bays there are two Renaissance mantels of sandstone and red Verona marble.

Leaving Bates Hall by the central door, turn l. and pass through a small but sumptuously decorated anteroom with a domical vault. One then enters the *extraordinary room beyond, which was originally the Delivery Room, but which is now the site of the Circulation Desk for the Research Library. The official handbook of the Boston Public Library, prepared by Peter Arms Week, describes the decor of this room as follows: "Here the treatment is based on Venetian models of the Early Renaissance with a high wainscot panelling of oak, the heavily beamed ceiling decorated in the manner of the library of the Doge's Palace in Venice, the doorways and fireplace mantel with massive projecting entablatures and flanking Corinthian pilasters in a blood-red *rouge antique* (the columns in green and red Levanto). . . . The floor is laid in contrasting squares of gray Istrian and red Verona marble."

The most remarkable feature of the room is the 8ft-high painted frieze that extends around the four walls between the wainscot and the ceiling. This is an Arthurian cycle of murals entitled *The Quest and Achievement of the Holy Grail,* created by Edwin Austin Abbey, R.A., an American artist who lived and worked in England, and it was installed in the library in 1895. The Delivery Room was designed by Abbey as a setting for these murals, which depict episodes from the life of Sir Galahad and the Knights of the Round Table, based principally on Tennyson's *Idylls of the King.*

The most dramatic of the scenes depicted is the large central panel over the book-delivery desk, which Henry James describes as follows in his brief monograph, *An Outline of the Legend:* "The Arthurian Round Table and the curious fable of the Seat Perilous are here dealt with: the Seat Perilous—'perilous for good and ill'—in which no man has sat with safety, not even the fashioner himself, but into which, standing vacant while it awaits only a blameless occupant, the young Sir Galahad, knighted by Arthur, has sworn a vow to be worthy to take his place. The Companions of the Order are seated in Arthur's hall, and every chair, save one, is filled. Suddenly the doors and windows close of themselves, the place becomes suffused with light, and Sir Galahad, robed in red (the color emblematic of purity), is led by an old man clothed in white, Joseph of Arimathea, who, according to one of the most artless features of the romance, has subsisted for centuries by the possession of the supreme relic. The young knight is thus installed in safety in the Seat Perilous, above which becomes visible the legend, " 'This is the seat of Galahad.' "

In the center of the room there is an antique teakwood table ornately carved and with a pink marble top. This originally belonged to Antonio Panizzi, principal librarian of the British Museum in 1856–66; according to tradition, it was on this table that he sketched the plans for the reading room of the museum.

Return now to the loggia of the Chavannes Gallery and continue on to the vaulted anteroom at its far end, where an enclosed stairway of gray sandstone ascends to the upper floor of the library.

At the top of the stairway one emerges into the long vaulted hallway known as the *Sargent Gallery,* whose mural decoration constitutes one of the forgotten masterpieces of American art, hidden away here in this poorly lighted corridor to which few visitors ever come. The theme of the decoration is *Judaism and Christianity,* a conception to which John Singer Sargent devoted 30 years of thought and labor, not only in painting the murals but in the design and decor of the whole hall, for he looked upon this gallery as the supreme artistic achievement of his entire career. The murals were put in place during four different periods: those at the N. end of the hall in 1895; the S. end of the hall in 1903; the niches and vaulting at the S. end and the lunettes along the side wall in 1916; and the two panels over the staircase in 1919.

John Singer Sargent himself wrote a monograph on these murals, describing them thus: "The Sequence begins at the north end of the hall, at the end, that is, farthest from the stairs. This portion has for its theme the confusion which fell upon the children of Israel whenever they turned from the worship of Jehovah to that of the false gods of the heathen nations. . . . The lunette represents the children of Israel under the yoke of their oppressors. . . . In the ceiling are the pagan dieties, the strange gods whom the children of Israel went after when they turned from Jehovah. . . . The third division of this part of the work is the frieze of the Prophets with Moses as the central figure holding the tablets brought down from Sinai. . . . The portion of the decoration in corresponding position at the opposite end of the hall sets forth the Dogma of the Redemption, and to this the three Judaic lunettes on the east wall, above the staircase, lead up. Of these the subjects are: in the center *Law;* flanked on the left by *Gog and Magog;* and on the right by *The Messianic Era;* while the three on the west wall, opposite, set forth the development of the Christian concepts of *The Judgment,* in the center; with *Hell* on the r.; and on the l. *The Passing of Souls into Heaven..* . . . At the south end of the hall is set forth the Dogma of the Redemption with the related theme of the Madonna. Just as the figure of Moses, with the law as the central fact of the religion of the Jews, forms the focal point in the first decoration, so here the Crucified Redeemer, as the central fact of Christianity, through the symbol of the Crucifix fulfils a like function. In the lunette above, seated in state upon a magnificent throne are three colossal figures, the Three Persons of the Blessed Trinity. . . . On the cross is the figure of the dead Christ, with the figures of Adam and Eve, typifying Humanity, kneeling on either side. . . . In the frieze of the Angels which flanks the Crucifix on either side, we have a balance for the frieze of the Prophets opposite. . . . In the niche on the east wall is portrayed the Handmaid of the Lord, Our Lady with her Divine Child. . . . Opposite this on the west wall is Our Lady of Sorrows. . . . Upon the vault of the ceiling between these two niches are represented the fifteen Mysteries of the Rosary. Above the Madonna and Child the panels devoted to the five Joyful Mysteries make the principal feature of the east side of the vault. . . . Opposite, on the west side of the arch, the five Sorrowful Mysteries occupy the corresponding panels. . . . These lead up to the last group, *The Crucifixion and Death of Our Lord.* In the center of the arch are the medallions and surrounding reliefs which represent the Five Glorious Mysteries. . . . The great circle of the medallion is filled by the relief representing *The Coronation of the Virgin.* . . . In the central lunette on the west wall *The Judgment* balances *The Law* opposite. . . . . . . The two companion lunettes on this wall continue the central composition. In the *Hell* is seen a Satanic monster swimming in a sea of flame and devouring the multitude of lost souls. . . . In contrast with this the composition on the left expresses the divine harmony which attends the entrance of the Blessed into the Kingdom."

At the center of the W. side of the Sargent Gallery a short flight of steps leads up to the entrance to the *Cheverus Room,* originally the Treasure Room, for the safekeeping of valuable objects that belonged to the library. The present name of the room honors John Cheverus, the French priest who was the first Roman Catholic Bishop of the Archdiocese of Boston, and who after his return to France became a cardinal. The room is used to display various memorabilia associated with Cardinal Cheverus and a number of works of art, the most notable of which is a painting by John Singleton Copley entitled *Charles I Demanding in the House of Commons the Five Impeached Members* (1782–95).

At the two ends of the Sargent Gallery doors open into domed chambers, with the one to the N. known as the *Charlotte Cushman Room,* and the one to the S. the *Albert H. Wiggin Room.* The latter chamber is used to display the *Albert H. Wiggin Gallery of Prints and Drawings,* and at its far end there is a smaller room with a number of dioramas created by Louise Stimson; these depict 11 different artists at work on their prints, including Rembrandt, Daumier, Toulouse-Lautrec, and Whistler.

Return to the Sargent Gallery and descend the stairs. On the lower landing on the second floor a plaque on the wall to the r. was dedicated on March 3, 1931, by the Boston Society of Architects to honor Charles Follen McKim (1847–1909).

After leaving the Boston Public Library, walk over to the N.W. corner of Copley Sq to visit the **New Old South Church,** which stands at the corner of Boylston and Dartmouth Sts.

History. The congregation here is the third oldest in Boston, originally gathered in 1669 in the Old South Meeting-House on the corner of what is now Washington and Milk Sts. The congregation moved into its present home in 1875, a structure designed by the architectural firm of Cummings and Sears.

Exterior. The church is designed in the North Italian Gothic style, its walls made from Roxbury pudding stone with trimmings of brown Connecticut and light Ohio freestone. The most remarkable feature of the exterior is the campanile, which is a replacement. The original campanile, which was 15ft higher than the present tower, was demolished in 1931, when it seemed in danger of toppling.

Interior. The main adornments of the sanctuary are its stained-glass windows of the 15C English type; these were designed by Clayton and Bell of London and were installed when the church was erected in 1875.

At the l. of the organ the windows depict the Prophets Isaiah, Jeremiah, Ezekiel, and Daniel; at the r. the Evangelists, Matthew, Mark, Luke, and John. In the N. transept there are depicted five miracles: *The Stilling of the Tempest, The Raising to Life of Jairus' Daughter, The Water Changed to Wine at the Cana Wedding Feast, The Raising of Lazarus from the Dead,* and *The Resurrection of Christ.* The windows in the S. transept have scenes showing *The Five Parables of Our Lord: The Sower, The Prodigal Son, The Good Samaritan, The Wise and the Foolish Virgins,* and *The Husbandmen of the Vineyard.* The window behind the pulpit contains a scene portraying *The Announcement by the Angels to the Shepherds of the Birth of Christ.*

The *Gordon Chapel* and the *Children's Chapel* are designed in the 13C Gothic style. The chapel windows, by Wilbur Herbert Burnham of Boston, are decorated with the symbols of the four Evangelists: the *Angel,* for St. Matthew; the *Winged Lion,* for St. Mark; the *Winged Ox,* for St. Luke; and the *Eagle,* for St. John.

The itinerary continues westward along the l. side of Boylston St, passing the Boston Public Library. Cross Exeter St and then Ring Rd to reach the beginning of the **Prudential Center.** This vast and characterless complex was designed by Charles Luckman and Assocs, and its various buildings were constructed in the following order: the 52-story *Prudential Building* (1959–65), which, when it was completed, was the tallest skyscraper in Boston, since surpassed by the New Hancock Tower; the *Hotel Sheraton-Boston* (1962–65); *The Prudential Apartments* (the *Fairfield,* the *Gloucester,* and the *Boylston;* 1964–68); *Lord and Taylor* (1968); *Saks Fifth Avenue* (1971); and the addition to the *Hotel Sheraton-Boston (1977). In front of the Prudential Plaza is an enormous (five-ton) bronze sculpture by Donald Delue entitled Quest Eternal,* which has no known admirers in the city.

This point in the itinerary is where the finish line of the Boston Marathon is located, opposite the plaza of the Prudential Center. On the last leg of the Marathon the runners go eastward on Commonwealth Ave, turn r. on Hereford St, then turn l. on Boylston St for the final sprint to the finish line in front of the plaza of the Prudential Center.

At the far end of the Prudential Center one passes on the l. the *John B. Hynes Veterans Auditorium,* at the S.E. corner of Boylston and Dalton Sts, built by Hoyle, Dalton, and Berry in 1963–65. Across the street to the r., at the N.E. corner of Boylston and Hereford Sts, is the *Tennis and Racquet Club,* a massive edifice erected in 1902–3 by the architectural firm of Parker and Thomas.

At the N.W. corner of Boylston and Hereford Sts there are a joined pair of fascinating buildings in the Romanesque style, erected in 1886–87 by the architect Arthur H. Vinal. The building on the r. was and still is a firehouse, while the somewhat larger structure to the l. was originally a police station, serving as such until 1965. In 1974, the police station was recycled by Graham Gund Assocs; presently it houses the *Institute for Contemporary Art,* and, on a lower floor, the *Hermitage Restaurant.* The Institute is one of the most important noncommercial art galleries in Boston, and the reconversion that created it was extremely effective and original. Just to the l. of the building is the entrance to the *Theater of the Institute for Contemporary Art,* a small playhouse associated with the gallery.

The itinerary continues along the l. side of Boylston St, which here bridges the Massachusetts Turnpike Extension. At the first intersection St. Cecilia St is crossed, named after the Roman Catholic *Church of St. Cecilia* a short way off to the l. At the beginning of the next block on the l. is the *Berklee Center for the Performing Arts,* the performing space for the *Berklee School of Music,* which specializes in popular music. One then crosses in turn Massachusetts Ave and then Hemenway St, passing on the r. the Roman Catholic *Church of St. Clement,* a neo-Gothic structure belonging to the Franciscan Missionaries of St. Mary. To the l. at the end of the block is the handsome edifice at No. 1154, which houses the ***Massachusetts Historical Society.**

Admission. The premises are normally open only to members of the Society, but visitors can apply at the front desk for permission to use the library and to look at the artworks in its collection; open Mon–Fri. 9–4:45.

History. The Massachusetts Historical Society, founded in 1791, is the oldest historical society in the US. The leading spirit in establishing the Society was Dr. Jeremy Belknap, minister of the Federal Street Church in Boston. The organization received its charter as the Massachusetts Historical Society in 1794, naming as its first president James Sullivan, who was then attorney general of Massachusetts. In its constitution, the Society set forth its aims in the following statement: "The preservation of books, pamphlets, manuscripts, and records, containing historical facts, biographical anecdotes, temporary projects, and beneficial speculations, conduces to mark the genius, delineate the manners, and trace the progress of society in the United States, and must always have a useful tendency to rescue the true history of this country from the ravages of time and the effects of ignorance and neglect."

During its early years the Society had a number of homes, the most permanent of which was an upper room in the central pavilion of the Tontine Crescent, which Charles Bulfinch permitted them to use free of charge, and where the organization remained from 1794 to 1833. In 1833 the Society moved to new and larger quarters on Tremont St, where they remained until they moved into their present home at 1154 Boylston St in 1899.

Exterior. The handsome edifice that houses the Society was built in 1899 in the Renaissance Revival style; the architect was Edmund March Wheelwright of the firm of Wheelwright and Haven. The facade, which is of speckled light-brown brick, has two prominent bows flanking the flat central section, with a neoclassical portico below, and above two enormous Ionic pilasters flank the two central windows, the upper one of which is surmounted by a round arch and with a balcony in front.

Interior. The manuscript collection of the Society is its chief attraction to scholars, for it is the finest in New England and one of the most important sources in existence for the study of American history and culture. The importance of the collection was pointed out in 1954 by the National Historical Publication Commission, who reported that, of 112 eminent Americans whose papers deserved publication, almost one-third were represented in the Massachusetts Historical Society by the principal collection of their extant papers or by significant bodies of correspondence.

Among the more than 2000 distinct collections are the papers of three Presidents of the U.S.: John Adams, John Quincy Adams, and Thomas Jefferson, as well as substantial collections of the writings of Presidents Martin Van Buren, James Madison, Theodore Roosevelt, and Dwight D. Eisenhower, along with those of Vice-Presidents Aaron Burr and Eldridge Gerry. The Society's holdings, extending across three centuries in every field of endeavor, represent a truly national resource, relevant not only to Massachusetts but to New England and the nation. The Society's collection of early printed items is very important, and it is truly outstanding in the following categories: Boston and Cambridge imprints; books relating to the New England Indian wars, captivities, and treaties; collections of the early printed laws of the Massachusetts Bay Colony and Plymouth Plantation; and Massachusetts broadsides. The collection also includes such treasures as: the manuscript journal that Governor John Winthrop kept from the time he departed England in 1630 until his death in 1646; the original manuscript of George Washington's Newburgh Address of March 15, 1783; the *Diary* of Judge Samuel Sewall, covering the period 1674–1729, which one historian has described as being "an incomparable picture of the mind and life of a Puritan of the transition period"; a copy by Thomas Jefferson of his original draft of the Declaration of Independence, as well as a copy that John Adams made of that same document; and a first separate edition (1758) of Benjamin Franklin's *Poor Richard's Almanack*.

The Society also has a large and distinguished collection of paintings, including works by John Smibert, John Singleton Copley, Gilbert Stuart, and Chester Harding. Some of these are on display in the two reading rooms on the ground floor; the others are kept in storage and may be seen on request. The most important of the paintings on more-or-less permanent display are in the room to the r. of the entryway, *Ellis Hall*. These are (starting at the l. of the door from the front and proceeding around the room in that direction): *Peter Faneuil* by John Smibert; *Judge Samuel Sewall* by

Nathaniel Ellis; *Margaret Temple* by Joseph Blackburn; *The Old State House, 1801,* by James B. Marston; the *Ship Bethel* by an anonymous English artist; *James Freeman, c. 1794,* by Christian Gullager; and the *Rev. George Edward Ellis, 1880* (a former president of the Society, after whom Ellis Hall is named), by Frederich P. Vinton.

The Society also has a number of interesting objects of historic interest, the most notable of which are the pen with which President Abraham Lincoln signed the Emancipation Proclamation, and the *Prescott Swords,* which are displayed over the door inside the director's office.

After leaving the Massachusetts Historical Society, turn l. and cross the street to look at the monument beside the approach to the bridge over the Back Bay Fens. This is a memorial to John Boyle O'Reilly (1844—90), the Irish patriot who became a naturalized citizen of the U.S. and went on to a distinguished career as a poet, journalist, and crusader for human rights, much of which he did as editor of *The Pilot.* This fine monument was created by Daniel Chester French and was unveiled in 1896. On the front of the monument there is a bronze bust of O'Reilly on a tapering stone pedestal, with a background of carved Celtic interlaces; and behind there is a bronze statue group, in which the central female figure is a personification of *Erin,* flanked by allegorical figures representing her sons, *Courage* and *Poetry.*

The bridge which here carries Boylston St across the Back Bay Fens is a work of Henry Hobson Richardson, built in the years 1880—84. Mariana Griswold Van Rensaelaer, in her book on Richardson's architectural works, describes this bridge as being "simply utilitarian in character. But the fine curve of the single great arch and the charming color of the pudding-stone make it a thing of beauty as well as of very evident strength and serviceableness."

The Fenway (or Back Bay Fen) that one sees today is largely the creation of Frederick Law Olmsted, who in 1878 was officially appointed landscape architect adviser to the newly created Boston Parks Commission. By that time Olmsted was the world's foremost designer of public parks, of which his most famous works are Central Park in Manhattan and Prospect Park in Brooklyn. The Fenway was originally that part of the Back Bay which was left unfilled, a salt marsh through which ran two streams, Stony Brook and Muddy River. Olmsted transformed this into a string of five major parks: Back Bay Fens, Muddy River Improvement (later renamed Olmsted Park), Jamaica Park, the Arnold Arboretum (see below), and Franklin Park (see below), which, together with their connecting parkways, extend for a total distance of five miles, bringing a refreshing touch of nature through the otherwise characterless outer reaches of Boston.

Cross back over to the building that houses the Massachusetts Historical Society, and there turn r. to walk S. along the Fenway, the name of the road that runs along the Back Bay Fens. A short way along on the l. *Boston Conservatory of Music,* founded in 1867, is passed. Follow the Fenway as far as the first turning on the l., the beginning of Westland Ave. Here two white stone pillars that flank the street form the *Johnson Memorial Gate,* an architectural nonentity dedicated to the memory of Jesse C. Johnson. Beyond the "gate" Westland Ave crosses Hemenway St, and at the next corner Massachusetts Ave is crossed. This brings one to the vast complex known as the **Christian Science Center,** the international headquarters for the Church of Christ, Scientist.

The Christian Science Center

Precincts. The focal point of the Christian Science Center is the *Extension of the Mother Church,* a huge domed structure with an enormous curving portico. This edifice, a pretentious jumble of stylistic elements deriving from Byzantium and the Italian Renaissance, was designed by Charles E. Brigham and Solon S. Beman and constructed in 1903–6, with the huge portico added in 1975. Behind this is the original *Mother Church,* known as the *First Church of Christ, Scientist,* an innocuous Romanesque structure designed by Franklin I. Welch and built in 1893–94. The tiered neoclassical structure to the l. of the church is the *Christian Science Publishing Society Building,* designed by Chester Churchill and erected in 1932–35. This edifice houses *The Christian Science Monitor,* a distinguished newspaper begun in 1908 by Mary Baker Eddy, the originator of Christian Science. The remainder of the complex was created in 1968–73 by I. M. Pei and Partners, with Cossutta and Ponte Associated Architects. These newer buildings stand around the periphery of a long reflecting pool, which makes this one of the coolest spots in downtown Boston in the summer. The structure in front of the pool, as observed from the Massachusetts Ave side of the complex, is the *Sunday School Building,* completed in 1971; behind the churches and to the l. of the pool is the long arcaded building known as the *Church Colonnade,* finished in 1973, which houses the communications department of the Christian Science Center; and at the far end of the pool on the r. is the 28-story *Church Administration Building,* completed in 1973.

History. Mary Baker Eddy, the founder of the Christian Science movement, was born near Concord, New Hampshire, in 1821. She was a member of the Congregational Church until 1866, when she had a remarkable religious experience in which she was cured of a serious illness through the spiritual inspiration that came to her in reading some verses in the Bible, the account of how Jesus cured the paralyzed man (Matthew 9:1–8). This led her to the belief that all disease was mental and not physical, and that illness could be cured by faith but not by doctors. For the following three years she studied the Bible intently and gradually formulated the basis for her new religion, Christian Science. In 1875 she published her views in a book entitled *Science and Health with Key to the Scriptures,* which became the denominational text of Christian Science. In 1876 she began expressing her ideas to small classes of instruction, with most of her listeners being members of evangelical churches. In 1879 she and her followers formed their own religious group, with the members resolving to "organize a church designed to commemorate the work and nature of our Master, which should reinstate primitive Christianity and its lost work of healing." By 1892 Christian Science had assumed its present structure, and in 1893–94 the First Church of Christ Scientist was erected here in Back Bay. Mary Baker Eddy died in 1910 in Chestnut Hill, a suburb of Boston, leaving behind her a church with some 100,000 members. Since then Christian Science has spread throughout the world, with some 2200 churches in the U.S. and 1100 elsewhere.

Admission. The Christian Science Center, at 175 Huntington Ave (tel. 450-2000), is open Nov. 1–April 30 Mon.–Sat. 10–3:45, Sun. 11:45–3:45; May 1–Oct. 31 Mon.–Sat. 9:30–4, Sun. 11:15–4:45; services Sun. at 10 a.m. & 7 p.m., Wed. at 7:30 p.m. (tel. 450-3790 for services information) No fee is charged for entry to any of the tours and activities in the Christian Science Center. Schedules of these tours and activities are available in the lobby of the Publishing House. Within the Publishing House one can use the reading room and walk through the *Mapparium,* a crystalline globe of the Earth 30ft in diameter. To see the extension to the Mother Church and the original church enter the lobby under the curving portico; there an attendant will give directions for the elevators to the nave of the new church, where guided tours begin. At the far end of the Church Colonnade there is an audiovisual display entitled "A Light Unto My Path," which is an exploration of the Bible. And in the lobby of the Church Administration Building there is a display entitled "Christian Healing Today."

After visiting the Christian Science Center, walk to the corner of Massachusetts Ave and Huntington Ave to look at *Horticultural Hall,* a distinguished edifice, erected by Wheelwright and Haven in 1900–1, which houses the *Massachusetts Horticultural Society.* The organization was founded in 1829, and is the second-oldest institution of its kind in the U.S. Douglass Shand Tucci, in his *Built in Boston,* describes Horticultural Hall as what "may be the handsomest English baroque building in the city."

The itinerary now takes one S.W. along the r. side of Huntington Ave, crossing Massachusetts Ave. On the other side of the avenue, directly opposite Horticultural Hall, is *Symphony Hall,* designed by Charles F. McKim, and completed in 1900. This is generally considered to be one of McKim's least successful designs, principally because of the top-heavy facade and the overly massive Ionic portico that supports it. The auditorium is much admired because of its superb acoustics.

The itinerary continues along the r. side of Huntington Ave. After the first intersection on the l. is the *New England Conservatory,* housed in a building erected by Wheelwright and Haven in 1901; the auditorium of the conservatory, *Jordan Hall,* is one of the most important performance spaces for classical music in Boston. On the block beyond that one passes between the various buildings of Northeastern University. One block farther along on the r. is Forsyth Way. On the block beyond is the imposing edifice of the *Boston Museum of Fine Arts* (see Rte 15).

Near the end of Forsyth Way, before it intersects the Fenway, there stands a formidable statue of Governor John Endicott (1589–1665); this is a work of the sculptor C. P. Jennewein and was unveiled in 1937.

Walk to the end of Forsyth Way and cross the Fenway, taking the path just opposite that leads into the park. A short way along is what is probably the most unusual and least known of Boston's minor sights: a *Japanese temple bell,* brought back to Boston in 1945 by sailors on the USS *Boston.* Just beyond are the *Kelleher Rose Gardens,* which are resplendent in late spring and early summer.

15 The Boston Museum of Fine Arts

The ****Boston Museum of Fine Arts** (MFA) can be reached from downtown Boston by taking the Arborway E branch of the MBTA Green Line; this becomes a surface tram after it emerges from the tunnel at Northeastern University, and the Ruggles-Museum stop on Huntington Ave is next to the MFA. The No. 39 Arborway bus also provides service to the MFA from Copley Sq.

Admission. The entire MFA, including the new West Wing, is open Tues. 10–5; Wed. 10–10; Thurs.–Sun. 10–5; in addition the West Wing only is open Thurs. and Fri. 5–10 p.m. The entire museum is closed Mon. and Hol.; fee. No admission charged on Sat. 10–12, or for visitors using only the Museum Shop, restaurants, Library, Remis Auditorium, and Mable Louis Riley Seminar Room. The Museum Shop has books, records, reproductions of works from the MFA's collections, jewelry, and other gifts. It also has books published by the MFA on its various collections. The Museum Shop is open Tues. and Sat. 10–4:30; Wed.–Fri. 10–9:30; Sun. noon–4:30.

There are three dining areas in the West Wing. On the First Floor is the *Galleria Café,* open Tues., Sat., & Sun. 10–4; Wed.–Fri. 10–9:30. On the lower level is the *Cafeteria,* open Tues., Sat., & Sun 10–4; Wed.–Fri. 10–8. On the Second Floor is the *Fine Arts Restaurant,* open Tues., Sat., & Sun. 11:30–2:30; Wed.–Fri. 11:30–2:30 & 5:30–8:30.

Library: Tues.–Fri. 1–4:45, Sat. 10–1. Closed weekends Memorial Day–Labor Day.

Slide Library: slides of objects in the Museum may be borrowed or purchased. Open Tues., Thurs., Fri. 10–4; Wed. 10–7.

Musical Instruments Collection: Tues.–Fri. 2–4; Sat. & Sun. 1–5.

Japanese Garden: Open Tues.–Sun. through Nov. 27, 10–4.

Limited paid parking is available in a lot off Museum Rd on the W. side of the museum; parking for disabled visitors is available near both entrances, and there are wheelchairs for the handicapped.

One may enter the museum either from the Huntington Ave side or through the entryway of the West Wing off Museum Rd. For general information call 267-9300, or dial 267-9377 for a recorded message giving weekly events and schedule.

History. The Boston Museum of Fine Arts evolved as an outgrowth of the Boston Athenaeum, which in the latter part of the 19C decided to concentrate on its function as a research

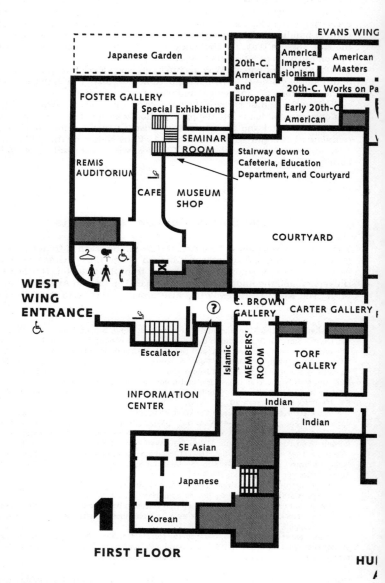

MUSEUM OF FINE ARTS (First floor)

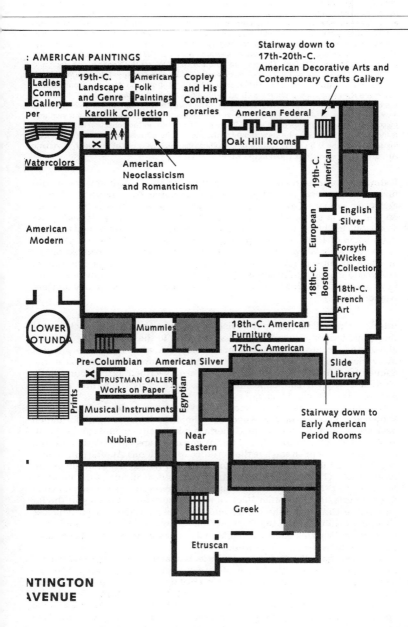

: AMERICAN PAINTINGS

Ladies Comm Gallery per

19th-C. Landscape and Genre

American Folk Paintings

Copley and His Contemporaries

Stairway down to 17th-20th-C. American Decorative Arts and Contemporary Crafts Gallery

Karolik Collection

American Federal

Watercolors

Oak Hill Rooms

American Neoclassicism and Romanticism

19th-C. American

American Modern

European

English Silver

18th-C. Boston

Forsyth Wickes Collection

18th-C. French Art

LOWER ROTUNDA

Mummies

18th-C. American Furniture

17th-C. American

Slide Library

Pre-Columbian

American Silver

Prints

TRUSTMAN GALLERY Works on Paper

Egyptian

Stairway down to Early American Period Rooms

Musical Instruments

Nubian

Near Eastern

Greek

Etruscan

NTINGTON AVENUE

library and scholarly society. The present institution came into being on Feb. 4, 1870, when the Massachusetts Legislature passed an act establishing "a body corporate by the name of the Museum of Fine Arts, for the purpose of erecting a museum for the preservation and exhibition of works of art, of making, maintaining, and establishing collections of such works, and of affording instructions in the Fine Arts." The MFA had its first home on the S. side of Copley Sq, with its West Wing opening on July 4, 1876, and the remainder of the building on March 18, 1890. The present home of the MFA on the Fenway was designed in 1906 by the architect Guy Lowell, assisted by R. Clipston Sturgis, Edmund M. Wheelwright, and Desiré Despradelle. The main building on Huntington Ave was completed in 1909; the Evans Memorial Wing was built behind this on the Fenway side in 1911–15; the Decorative Arts Wing was added to the E., on the Forsyth Way side, in 1924–28; and the new West Wing, designed by I. M. Pei, was completed in 1981. The MFA has a vast and incredibly varied collection of all kinds of works of art. Judging the collection as a whole, it is generally considered to be second only to the Metropolitan Museum in New York among institutions in the U.S.; while certain of its collections, such as those of the Dept. of Asiatic Art, are probably without equal in the world.

Exterior. The most dominant feature of the original building is the monumental neoclassical portico above the Huntington Ave entrance, with an architrave supported by four enormous Ionic columns. In front of the museum on that side is a dramatic bronze equestrian statue entitled *Appeal to the Great Spirit;* this is by Cyrus E. Dallin and received a gold medal at the Paris Salon of 1909; it was installed on its present site in 1913. The handsome new West Wing, which is constructed of smooth and gleaming blocks of white granite, is totally different from the old museum building in its architectural style; nevertheless, the two structures make a harmonious pair. (The granite facing for both buildings came from the same quarry on Deer Island, Maine.)

Interior. One might open a first visit to the MFA by taking a quick tour of the whole building, beginning at the entrance to the West Wing. This will allow one to locate the main sections of the MFA, after which one can visit the various departments in turn, as they are summarily described in the pages that follow. (All works of art that are described in this tour will be identified by their catalogue numbers as well as by their titles and the names of the artists, if known.)

Immediately inside the entrance to the West Wing is the vast outer lobby known as the Hilles Gallery, where the admissions counter and information desk are located. To the l. is the Galleria, a lofty atrium roofed with a barrel-vaulted skylight; on the r. side of this as you enter are the Galleria Café and the Museum Shop; on the l. is the entrance to the Remis Auditorium, a 380-seat hall used for lectures and performances in the MFA's program of cultural events. (The monthly Calendar of Events is available at the information desk.) At the far end of the Galleria a stairway on the r. leads down to the Cafeteria, the Education Dept., and the Courtyard. Opening off the far end of the Galleria is the Henry and Lois Foster Gallery, which houses changing exhibitions by the Dept. of Contemporary Art. Opening off from the north side of this gallery is the Mabel Louise Riley Seminar Room, used for conferences, lectures and workshops.

Return to the Hilles Gallery to take the escalator up to the second floor of the Galleria. Permanently displayed here is an enormous painting, *The Passage of the Delaware* (03.1079), done in 1819 by the American artist Thomas Sully. This was originally commissioned by the state of North Carolina for the State Capitol, but the painting proved to be too large for the allotted space and was thus rejected. Continuing along, we see on our r. the Fine

Arts Restaurant, and on our l. the Graham Gund Gallery, used for special exhibitions. At the far end of upper floor of the Galleria is the North Gallery, used for exhibitions of modern art.

After seeing the upper level of the Galleria, we return to the ground floor and continue on into the inner lobby, which connects with the older part of the MFA. Entering the inner lobby, we pass on our r. one of the entrances to the Dept. of Asiatic Art, whose galleries occupy most of the rooms in the S.W. wing of the MFA on both the first and second floors. The various galleries in this department are devoted to artworks of the following cultures: Islamic, Indian, Southeast Asian, Chinese, Himalayan, and Japanese.

Continuing ahead, we pass in turn through the Brown Gallery, with the Members' Room on the r., and then the Carter Gallery, from whose r. side one enters the Torf Gallery. All three of these rooms are used for changing exhibitions, with the Brown and Carter Galleries devoted mostly to works from the Dept. of American Decorative Arts and Sculpture.

After leaving the Carter Gallery, we enter the Lower Rotunda, which is behind the stairway leading up from the Huntington Ave entrance of the old part of the MFA. The hall leading off to the left is hung with Modern American paintings. At the far end of the hall one enters the Evans Wing, which takes up the northern side of the old museum building. The first floor of the Evans Wing is devoted mostly to American paintings and sculpture, along with some watercolors, prints, and photographs, as well as a number of European works of art. The galleries here are devoted to the following themes and collections: Watercolors, 20C Works on Paper, American Masters, American Impressionism, Early 20C American, 20C American and European Painting and Sculpture, 19C Landscape and Genre, the Karolik Collection, American Folk Paintings, American Neoclassicism and Romanticism, and Copley and His Contemporaries.

The northern end of the first floor of the Evans Wing is devoted to an exhibition of American Art of the Federal period; on the r. side here we pass the Oak Hill Rooms, the first of a number of Period Rooms exhibited by the Dept. of American Decorative Arts and Sculpture. The rest of these rooms are in the basement floor of the MFA, approached by stairways at the two ends of the north wing. The stairway at the northern end of the Evans wing leads down to the 17–20C American Decorative Arts and Contemporary Crafts Gallery; this in turn leads to the Early American Period Rooms.

The galleries on the first floor of the North Wing are devoted to the following themes and collections: 19C American Decorative Arts, European Decorative Arts, English Silver, 18C Boston Decorative Arts and Paintings, and the Forsyth Wickes Collection of 18C French Art. Then, continuing back into the S.E. wing, we pass successively through galleries devoted to 18C American Furniture and Paintings, American Silver and Paintings, and Pre-Columbian Art. On the l. side of the corridor we pass one of the entrances to the galleries belonging to the Department of Egyptian and Ancient Near Eastern Art, which occupies about half the rooms on the first and second floors of the S.E. wing, with most of the other rooms in the two floors of this wing taken up by the Department of Classical Art, which includes works of the ancient Greek, Roman, Etruscan, and Italic civilizations. Other rooms on the first floor of the S.E. wing are devoted to the Department of Prints and Drawings and to the Collection of Musical Instruments, both of whose exhibition galleries are entered from the N. side of the corridor leading from the Lower Rotunda to the Huntington Ave entrance.

We now ascend the main staircase to the second floor, and at the top we

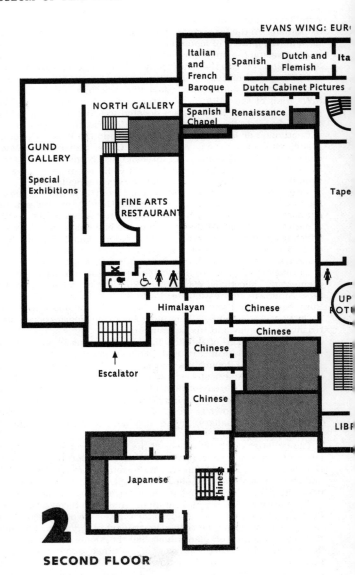

SECOND FLOOR

MUSEUM OF FINE ARTS (Second floor)

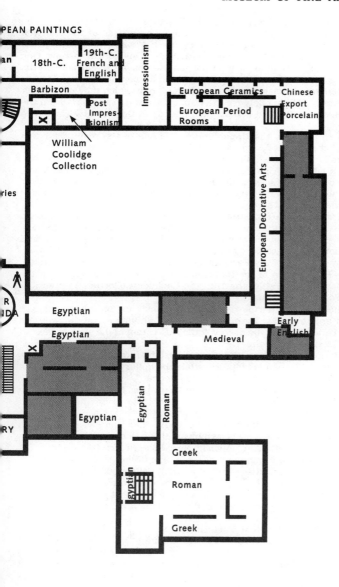

EUROPEAN PAINTINGS

18th-C. | 19th-C. French and English | Impressionism

Barbizon

Post Impressionism

European Ceramics

European Period Rooms

Chinese Export Porcelain

William Coolidge Collection

European Decorative Arts

Egyptian

Egyptian

Medieval

Early English

Egyptian

Egyptian

Roman

Egyptian

Greek

Roman

Greek

pause to examine the decorations on the Upper Rotunda. The reliefs in the Rotunda and the murals there and on the upper surface of the stairwell were done by John Singer Sargent in the years 1917—25. These decorations are all based on scenes from Greek mythology or allegorical themes. One painting of particular interest is in the lunette above the entrance to the Library; this is a scene entitled *The Danaids,* in which these demigoddesses mount a double staircase carrying amphorae, from which they pour water into a fountain. (The models for the Danaids were dancing girls from the chorus line of the Zeigfeld Follies, then playing at the Colonial Theater in Boston.)

Directly to the r. of the Upper Rotunda is one of the main exhibition galleries of the Dept. of Egyptian and Ancient Near Eastern Art, while to the l. there is one of the main exhibition halls of the Dept. of Asiatic Art. Also on the left is the Special Exhibition Gallery of the Dept. of Paintings, where one occasionally sees examples of the MFA's collection of Ship Models. Straight ahead is the Tapestries Gallery, which has changing exhibitions of works in the Dept. of Textiles.

Passing through the Tapestries Gallery, we find ourselves on the second floor of the Evans Wing, most of which is devoted to European Paintings. The various galleries in this wing are devoted to the following periods and areas: Italian and French Baroque, Spanish, Dutch and Flemish, Dutch Cabinet Pictures, Italian of the Early Renaissance, Catalan, Italian and French of the 16—18C, French of the Barbizon School, French and English of the 18C, French and English of the 19C, the Coolidge Collection, Impressionism, and Post-Impressionism.

The galleries at the northern end of the Evans Wing on the second floor on the left are devoted to European Ceramics, while those on the right are European Period Rooms. The gallery at the N.E. corner of the wing is devoted to Chinese Export Porcelain.

The galleries in the North Wing contain exhibits from the Dept. of European Decorative Arts and Sculpture, while the gallery at the S.E. corner of the wing contains an Early English Period Room.

Heading back toward the Upper Rotunda, we pass first through a gallery devoted to European Decorative Arts of the Medieval Era, then through rooms belonging to the Dept. of Egyptian and Ancient Near Eastern Art. This completes our brief first tour of the MFA, whereupon we now begin a more detailed examination of the exhibits in the various departments, starting with that of Egyptian and Ancient Near Eastern Art. (Here and in the other departments, the numbers currently identifying the various exhibition galleries are used; these are occasionally changed, which may well lead to confusion. The various collections here and in the other departments of the MFA are described in detail in a number of books and monographs published by the MFA and on sale in the Museum Shop.)

Egyptian and Ancient Near Eastern Art

In the early years of the MFA many of the antiquities in this department were acquired through gifts and purchases, and by participation in the Egyptian Exploration Fund, beginning in 1885. However, the most fruitful period of acquisition began in 1905, with the establishment of the joint MFA-Harvard Expedition under the direction of Dr. George A. Reisner. Reisner's first excavations for the Expedition began at the Giza pyramid plateau W. of Cairo, and from there he extended his digs up the Nile. In a series of pioneering excavations from 1915 to 1932 Reisner unearthed much of the history of the ancient land of Kush, a culture that flourished in the

Sudan upstream from Egypt, covering the period 2400 B.C.–A.D. 330. Dr. Reisner died at Giza in 1942 and the MFA-Harvard Expedition was officially terminated at the end of World War II, after which the museum was again forced to rely on gifts and purchases. But as a result of Dr. Reisner's work the MFA has a collection of Old Kingdom sculpture that is unrivaled except at the Cairo Museum, which shared in his finds; in addition the museum has a rich collection of antiquities from the Middle Kingdom, the New Kingdom, and the Late Period, and its store of objects from the Kushite culture is incomparable. In 1958 the department assumed charge of the MFA's collection of antiquities from the western regions of Asia, ranging from ancient Iran through Mesopotamia and Anatolia to the Middle East, so that there are few museums that can compare with it in the geographic extent of its exhibits from that part of the ancient world.

The earliest Egyptian antiquities are in ROOM II-15, the narrow hall to the r. of the Upper Rotunda at the head of the stairs. The exhibits here date from the Prehistoric period (before 4000–3000 B.C.), and the Archaic period (3200–2680), which includes the first three dynasties: I (3200–2980), II (2980–2780), and III (2780–2680). The most interesting exhibit here is perhaps (58.324) the limestone head of a pharaoh with a tall conical headdress; this is thought to represent King Khasekhem, Dynasty II, c. 2800, wearing the White Crown of Upper Egypt.

Return to the Rotunda and enter ROOM II-16, the large gallery that opens off to the r. at the head of the stairs. Here are exhibited some of the finest works of sculpture to survive from the Old Egyptian Kingdom, which comprised Dynasties IV (2680–2565), V (2565–2420), and VI (2420–2258). On entering the gallery, one sees straight ahead a colossal alabaster *statue of King Mycerinus* (09.204), builder of the Third Pyramid at Giza, Dynasty IV, who ruled in 2599–71. Mounted on a pedestal to the l. of the entryway is an alabaster head (09.203), which is thought to be another representation of King Mycerinus; it was found in Giza and dates to his reign. Along the l. side of the room, are two more representations of Mycerinus: in one fragmentary *Triad* (09.200) he is shown to the l. of the goddess Hathor, while to her r. is a female figure personifying the Hare Nome, a province of upper Egypt; next to this he is shown with his Queen Kha-Merer-Nebty II in a slate-gray *pair statue* (11.738). The latter work is the oldest-known "pair statue" in Egyptian art, and it set the standard for that type of representation. On a pedestal in the center of the room is another masterpiece of Old Kingdom sculpture, a *painted bust of the Vizier Ankh-Haf* (27.442), 2625–2600 B.C. As one continues along the l. side of the room, the next exhibit of note is the *Head of a Princess* (14.719) in white limestone; this is from the reign of Cheops (Khufu), builder of the Great Pyramid at Giza, dating to 2656–2533 B.C. This is of the type known as a "Reserve Head"; these were realistic portraits of their owners, presumably put in their tombs to replace their mummies if they were destroyed. Beyond this, on the same side, is a *pair statue of Ptah-khenuwy and his wife* (06.1876), found in a tomb in Giza and dating from the second half of Dynasty V, c. 2500 B.C. On the opposite side of the room the most interesting exhibits are: a *pair statue of the Treasurer Nofer and his wife* (31.786), c. 2640 B.C.; a white limestone *"Reserve Head" of Nofer* (06.1886); a relief *portrait of Nofer* from his mastaba, or tomb-sanctuary, at Giza (07.1002); a red granite *head of an official named Seshem-nofer II* (12.1487), 2571–2567 B.C.; and a seated *statue of Prince Khuenre* (13.3140), a son of King Mycerinus, 2599–2571 B.C.

Walk back into ROOM II-15 to see the exhibits at the far end of the hallway—i.e. to the l. Some of these are of much later date and have no association with the culture of ancient Egypt, and so only a few of the older Egyptian objects will be described here. The most interesting objects here are two *wooden statuettes*. One of these is a fragmentary figure of the *Vizier Mehy* (13.3466); this is from Giza in the reign of Unas, Dynasty V, 2450–2420 B.C.; the second is a representation of *Methethy* (47.1455), from Saqqarah, Dynasty V, c. 2500 B.C. In one of the cases on the r. there is a display of seven *statuettes of King Mycerinus* in various stages of completion.

Now turn l. into ROOM II-18, the gallery beyond II-16, which contains more exhibits of the Old Kingdom. The main exhibit in this room is a replica of the canopy in the tomb of Queen Hetep Heres, mother of King Cheops, including her funerary bed, armchair, and curtain box. (The originals are in the Cairo Museum.)

Cross the corridor to enter the extremely long exhibition hall on the other side, ROOM II-2. The entryway is flanked by two *mastabas* unearthed near Saqqarah, Dynasty V, c. 2500 B.C., with the one on the l. belonging to Ptah-Sekhem-Ankh, and that on the r. to Kaemnofret. The two tomb-sanctuaries are open; fascinating paintings decorate their walls. The remainder of the room is used to exhibit large statues, reliefs, and architectural members of all periods in the history of ancient Egypt. The best of these is in the center of the room, a life-sized statue in black granite of the *Lady Sennuwy* (14.720); this fine example of Middle Kingdom sculpture is from Kerma in the Sudan, c. 1950 B.C.

A door on the r. at the end of the gallery leads to ROOM II-1, with a display of Middle Kingdom (2040–1786) Coffins and Decorative Arts. The exhibits of greatest interest here are in the left-hand corner of the room. Against the wall there are the inner and outer coffins of Djehuty-Nekht (20.1822), c. 1860 B.C., decorated with exquisite paintings; and in a case to the r. of this there are four remarkable figurines (21.326) from the same tomb.

Return to ROOM II-2 and turn r. to continue on at the end of the gallery into ROOM II-3, devoted to Sculptures and Decorative Arts of the New Kingdom (1570–1085 B.C.). Objects exhibited here include statues, portrait busts, figurines, wall paintings, reliefs, jewelry, scarabs, and articles of everyday use in the New Kingdom. On a pedestal off to the l. from the entrance is a quartzite *portrait-head* (09.288) of Amenhotep III (1410–1372 B.C.) and a *statue* in green stone (23.734) of the same King. The most prominent exhibit is the red quartzite *sarcophagus* (14.272) in the center of the room; this was made for Queen Hapshepsut, who ruled Egypt from 1504 to 1483.

Continue into ROOM II-6, the little alcove beyond. In a case to the r. of the alcove there is a fragment (60.1472) from the mummy wrappings of Tuthmosis III (1504–1450), inscribed in cursive hieroglyphic script with texts from the *Book of the Dead*. Within the alcove are displayed jewelry, beads, scarabs, pendants, and semiprecious stones. One of the finest of these pieces is a red jasper inlay (69.1944) representing the head of a king, perhaps Seti I (1313–1301 B.C.), in the case facing the alcove door.

Continue through the alcove to ROOM II-6, at the Huntington Ave end of the building, with Egyptian objects of the Late Period. In a case beside the door there is a fine bronze figurine (52.1026) in which a cat sits poised upon a papyrus column, a work dating from the 7–6C B.C. On a pedestal in front of this there is a green schist *portrait-head* (04.1749) of a man of mature years (nose shattered). This is known as the "Boston Green Head," and is generally considered to be one of the finest extant works from the Late Period; some authorities have dated it to the 4C B.C., whereas others hold that it is from the 2C. In the case at the far l. corner of the room are funerary objects from the curious Horse-Burials of the Kushite-Ethiopian Kings of Dynasty XXV (751–656 B.C.). When a king of this dynasty died the horses that had pulled his quadriga were buried with him—beheaded before burial and interred standing up. When the tombs were excavated the horses were found to be splendidly accoutered, draped with bead nets, hung with cowrie shells and ornaments of faience and silver, one of them wearing a silver collar and with a gold plume-holder on its head. Another noteworthy exhibit in this gallery is a black diorite *statue* of a priest of Amon named Khonsu-ir-aa, c. 670–660 (07.494).

Take the stairs down to the first floor to ROOM I-2, where the tour through the Dept. of Egyptian and Ancient Near Eastern Art continues. The exhibits in this gallery reflect all aspects of the many cultures that flourished in the lands around the eastern Mediterranean from the fourth millennium B.C. until the beginning of the Hellenistic age. The most distinguished exhibit here is a superb diorite *portrait-head* of Gudea, governor of Lagash in Sumeria, c. 2200 B.C. (26.289).

ROOM I-20, the Egyptian Orientation Gallery, contains antiquities from the Old Kingdom. At the end of the last of three rows of cases to the r. of the center of the gallery is a painted wooden *statuette* (04.1780) of a male figure dated c. 2100 B.C.

Now cross the hall to enter ROOM I-17, where there is an exhibit of Egyptian Mummies and Funerary Art, ranging in date from 1600 B.C. to A.D. 300. Among the exhibits here are a number of anthropoid sarcophagi, the most notable of which is one of basalt (30.034A-B) found in Giza and dated c. 775 B.C. Also fascinating are the funerary portraits, the finest of which are affixed to two coffins (11.2891–2) near the front of the room, works of the 2C A.D.

This completes the tour through the Dept. of Egyptian and Ancient Near Eastern Art. The next tour covers the Dept. of Classical Art; to get there, walk back through the Egyptian rooms on the last part of the previous tour as far as Room I-5, the large gallery near the Huntington Ave side of the museum.

Classical Art

The collections of the Dept. of Classical Art encompass the entire range of Greek, Roman, and Etruscan art, with its greatest strength in antiquities of the 6–4C B.C. The collection of bronze figurines from the Archaic period has few rivals outside Greece, and the red-figured vases constitute a comprehensive survey of the major painters of Athens in the 5C B.C. From the 4C B.C. to the end of the Hellenistic period the collections contain an unusually large number of original works by some of the greatest Greek artists of that period. Other important objects are in the collections of terra-cotta figurines, jewelry, coins, and in the renowned Warren collection of cameo and intaglio gems.

The objects exhibited in ROOM I-5 are mostly from the classical period, 490–323 B.C., along with a few objects from earlier eras. The first case along the l. wall has a display of objects, mostly bronzes from Magna Graecia (S. Italy and Sicily), dating from the first half of the 5C B.C. Continuing

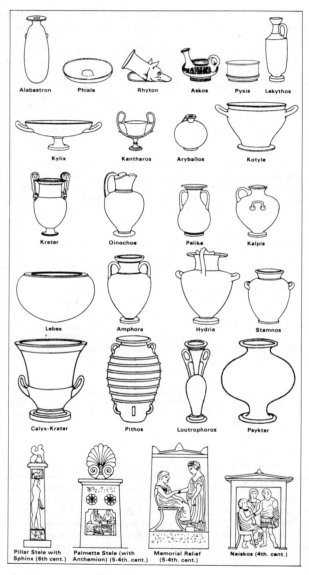

Greek Pottery and Funerary Monuments

along, on the r. is a long case with pottery of the classical period; and on the l. is an Attic red-figured *vase* (26.61) known as the Nolan Amphora, c. 480 B.C., decorated by an Athenian known as the Brysos Painter; beyond that is a case with coins dating from the late 7C B.C. to the first half of the 5C B.C. Beyond this case, on a pedestal, is an Attic *grave stele* (08.288), c. 550 B.C., and then the fragmentary *head of a kouros* (34.169), a youth personifying Apollo.

Among the exhibits at the rear of the gallery, one of the most striking is a *grave stele* (99.339) with the figure in low relief of a warrior on horseback, found near Thebes and dating to c. 500—490 B.C. To the r. is a red-figured Attic *calyx krater* (97.368), c. 475 B.C.; this is decorated with two scenes of combat from the Trojan War, with Achilles fighting Memnon on one side and on the other Diomedes battling Aeneas. In a wall case to the l. there is a display of vases of various types, and on the r. a case with an exhibit of terra-cotta figurines showing people engaged in everyday activities; one of the most interesting of these is (97.349) the figure of a man cooking over an open fire, a Boeotian work of the late 6C B.C. In front of the case on the r. is a large marble statue of a headless *sphinx* (40.756) standing on a volute; this once surmounted a tombstone, c. 530 B.C., and is considered to be one of the finest Attic funerary monuments in existence.

Walking along the S. side of the room, one sees first on the l. a case with a marble *discus* of the 6C B.C., with a fragmentary inscription reading "From the Games. . . ." Farther along on the r. there is a case with a display of pottery, and on the l. a case (shared with Room I-7) with a display of Attic vases; the finest of these is perhaps a red-figured *bell krater* (10.1851), c. 470 B.C.; this is decorated on one side with the Death of Aktaeon, and on the other Pan is shown pursuing a goatherd.

Cross the front of the room. On the l. are three cases with objects excavated at Assos, a site on the Aegean coast of N.W. Asia Minor. In front of these is a red-figured Attic *amphora* (63.1515) of the late 6C B.C., decorated on one side with a scene showing Heracles and Apollo struggling for the Delphic tripod, and on the other a Maenad and two Sileni; then the marble torso of a youth (39.552), an Attic work of 550—540 B.C.; and finally a red-figured Attic *skyphos* (13.186), a superb work of the early 5C B.C.

This is one of the most famous of the Greek vases in the museum; on its handles are inscriptions recording that it was made by Hieron, one of the most renowned potters in ancient Athens, and that it was painted by Makron, among the greatest artists of his time. The vase is decorated with two related themes; on one side Helen is shown being led away by Paris, and on the other side she is discovered by Menelaos after the capture of Troy. The vase here is generally considered to be Makron's masterpiece, and it is his only signed work in the museum.

The corridor to the l. of the main hall is devoted to display of antiquities excavated at Assos in 1880 and 1881 by the Archaeological Institute of America. In addition to antiquities from the site, there are exhibited a number of drawings made there in 1882 by Francis Henry Bacon, including his pictures of the famous sarcophagi of Assos, which were exported all over Asia Minor. Also on display are two reliefs (84.67a&b) from the Temple of Athena at Assos, built c. 530 B.C. The exhibit also extends into the area behind Room I-5, where there is a study case of pottery and figurines from Assos, a map of the Troad, and photographs of the site.

The gallery at the far end of I-5 is ROOM I-8, with art of the Minoan period, and antiquities from the Cypriot, Mycenaean, and Cycladic cultures.

Enter Room I-8 by the door on the l.; on the l. is a case with Cycladic statuettes and pottery of the period 2500–2000 B.C., including a marble *"idol"* (35.60), a highly stylized statue from the Bronze Age. These idols were buried with the dead during the Bronze Age, not only on the Cyclades, but throughout the mainland of Anatolia as well, and they undoubtedly represent the fertility goddess, the Great Earth Mother, who was worshipped in that region in antiquity. In the next case is one of the most famous works of art in the museum, the gold-and-ivory *Snake Goddess* (14.863). This extraordinary statuette, just 6.5 inches tall, is a product of the Late Minoan I period, dating to 1600–1500 B.C. Very few examples of sculpture in the round have survived from the great Minoan civilization in Crete, and this exquisite figure is the finest in existence. In the last case on the l. is another fascinating work of art from Minoan Crete, a gold *votive ax* (58.1009), c. 1600–1500 B.C., with an inscription in Linear A script indicating that it was dedicated to the Great Earth Mother. Another masterpiece of the Bronze Age is to be seen on a pedestal in front of the first window on the l.; this is a superb *"idol"* (67.758) from the early Cycladic period, c. 2400 B.C.

After seeing the objects in Room I-8, walk back through the gallery to enter ROOM I-7, on the Huntington Ave side of the building. Here there is a display of antiquities, principally vases, most of which are from the Geometric and Archaic periods. The finest of the vases are perhaps those in a case that forms part of the partition between Rooms I-7 and I-5. One exceptional work there is an Attic black-figured *amphora,* c. 540 B.C. (63.952); this is a work of the painter and potter Exekias, one of the great masters of the style. Just beyond this case, beside the door, there is a fine black-figured *Panathenaic amphora* (01.8121), c. 525. These amphorae were given as prizes to winners in the Panathenaic Games. Another characteristic Attic vase of early date is to be seen on a pedestal to the rear of the gallery at its center; this is a *Dipylon amphora* of the 8C B.C. (03.782). These amphorae were named after the main gate of ancient Athens; this portal led to the Kerameikos, the great cemetery, where most of the potteries were located. Other exhibits of exceptional interest are to be seen in the wall case behind this on the Huntington Ave side of the room. The most fascinating object here is a terra-cotta *vessel* (28.49) known as a Magic Wheel, an Attic work of the late 8C B.C. In the case beyond this there are two fine bronze figurines; one of them is a stylized *statuette of Apollo* (03.997), a Boeotian work of c. 700 B.C.; and the other is a charming group (98.650) representing a deer nursing her fawn with a bird perched on her back, from Thebes, 8C B.C. Beyond this is a long aisle case with bronze figurines, among which there are three of exceptional interest. The first is a charming *statuette of Artemis* (98.658), found near Olympia and dated c. 525 B.C. The second is a miniature figure (04.6) of *Hermes Kriophorus,* the "Ram Carrier," c. 520–10 B.C., a votive offering to the god in his role as protector of flocks. The third is a figurine of *Athena Promachos* (54.145), "First in Battle," Minorca, c. 500 B.C.; the goddess is represented about to hurl a thunderbolt at the foe, a traditional pose in her role as protectress of the city. The last case on the l. before the door into Room I-6 holds gold and electrum jewelry, disks, and repoussé plaques of the 7–6C B.C., many of them from Kameiros on Rhodes; the most interesting of the last is perhaps (99.383), which has a representation of Artemis in her role as Protectress of Animals.

Now enter ROOM I-6, devoted to Etruscan and Italic Art. Outstanding exhibits here are a pair of *Etruscan sarcophagi* on the r. side of the room, both of which have on their lids the figures in relief of the husband and wife whose remains they once contained. The sarcophagus on the l. (86.145), is of alabaster, c. 330–300 B.C., while the one on the r. (1975.799), which dates to 290–280 B.C., is of a stone called peperino; both are decorated on their sides and ends with sculptured scenes in relief, patterned on Greek sarcophagi. On the wall behind the sarcophagus there are the fragmentary figures of a leopard and a lion, both Etruscan works of c. 570 B.C. Near the corner of the room to the r. there is the lid of a sandstone sarcophagus (10.683), decorated in relief with the reclining figure of an Etruscan, 3–2C B.C. On the wall above this are the charming figures of two leopards, Etruscan works of c. 560 B.C.; these are carved in nenfro, a volcanic stone, and were once affixed to the lintel of a tomb as symbolic guardians.

Ascend the stairs to ROOM II-5, the Graeco-Roman Court. Nearly all of the exhibits in this huge hall are statues or portrait-busts, most of them from the Graeco-Roman period. The description that follows includes only those works of more than ordinary artistic or historic interest. (Roman emperors are listed with the years of their reign in parentheses; in most cases their statues or portrait-busts date from that period.)

At the front of the gallery at its center there is a headless statue (03.749) of a Roman lady, a copy done in the 1C A.D. of a Greek work of the late 5C B.C. Straight ahead, in the very center of the gallery, is a marble bust of the Emperor Augustus (27 B.C.–A.D. 14), a work thought to date from the reign of the Emperor Hadrian (A.D. 117–38). On the l. wall of the gallery are nine sections of the Romano-Campanian wall painting of c. A.D. 60. In the first wall case on that side there is a collection of Roman coins ranging in date from 42 B.C. to A.D. 327. Beyond this there are a pair of Roman sarcophagi of the 3C A.D., decorated with scenes in low relief in the ancient Greek style. Next is a series of sculptures of the Roman period, including the following imperial figures: a head (58.1005) of the Emperor Numerianus (282–84); (88.347) a bust of the Emperor Balbinus (ruled A.D. 238); (1977.337) an elegant bust of the Emperor Elegabalus (218–22); (60.928) a head of the Emperor Septimius Severus (193–211); and a beautiful statue (1979.556) of Vibia Sabina, wife of the Emperor Hadrian.

There are a number of sculptures at the rear of the gallery, but none is of any great interest or artistic merit. Walking toward the other side of the room, one sees the cuirassed *torso* (99.346) from the statue of a Roman emperor, thought to be Domitian (88–96). Now, walking back along the other side of the room toward the front of the gallery, one sees a series of sculptures, of which the most distinguished are these: (99.343) a fine *head* of an old man, 1C B.C., carved from a volcanic stone called palombino; and (01.8008) a superb terra-cotta *portrait-bust* of a Roman, late 1C B.C., found in the ruins of Cumae.

Now go on to ROOM II-7, the gallery that extends along the Huntington Ave side of this wing. If one enters by the portal at the front of the gallery, just to the l. of the door is a headless *statue* of a youth (22.593), a Roman copy of a Greek original by an Attic sculptor, c. 480–460 B.C. Just beyond this is a three-sided relief (08.205), the famous *"Boston Throne,"* a remarkable work dating from c. 470–460 B.C.

On the front of the monument, a naked youth holding a balance stands between two seated women, the one on the l. cheerful and the other sad; on the end piece to the l. a naked youth plays a lyre, and on the other end is the seated figure of an old woman. The scene is thought to represent the mythical contest of beauty between Aphrodite (the winner) and Persephone, which Eros judged for Adonis. This work is the counterpart of a similarly shaped relief in Rome, the "Ludovisi Throne," and the two may once have been the sculptured decoration of the two wings framing the steps of a very large altar of Aphrodite. The two reliefs were excavated at different times in the 19C, during construction work on the Ludovisi estate on the Pincian Hill in Rome, an area which in antiquity was known as the Gardens of Sallust.

Continue past a series of six sculptures, all Roman copies of Greek originals of the classical period. The first outstanding object is in a pedestal case just before a door to Room I-5; this is a red-figured *rhyton* (21.2286) with a base in the form of an Amazon astride a galloping horse, and a vessel decorated with a scene of Greeks battling Persians.

The base is signed by the Athenian potter Sotades, and it was made in the late 5C B.C.; but it was not found in Athens but at Meröe, the remote capital of the Sudanese kingdom of Kush, more than 1200 miles up the Nile; it was discovered there at the base of a small pyramid-tomb of a Meröitic prince of the early 4C B.C.

Another outstanding object is to be seen on a pedestal against the rear wall near its center. This is a fragmentary Attic *grave stele* (04.16) of the late 5C B.C., with a relief showing a woman, the deceased, gazing sadly into a mirror. To the r. of this, in the corner of the room, a case holds seven handsome Attic vases, the finest of which is perhaps a red-figured *stamnos* (95.21), from the third quarter of the 5C B.C. Begin walking back along the Huntington Ave side of the room. In a case facing the rear door into Room II-5 is a red-figured Attic *pelike* (34.79) dating from c. 440 B.C. and decorated by the Lycaon Painter. The scene on the vase is taken from an episode in the *Odyssey*, where Odysseus sacrifices two rams in the Underworld; at the l. the shade of his departed comrade Elpinor rises up from the ground, and at the r. is Hermes.

On the l. is a plaster model of the Athenian Acropolis. In the center of the room is a large marble *statue of Athena Parthenos* (1980.196). This is a smaller-scale Roman replica of the huge chryselephantine (gold-and-ivory) statue of Athena Polias by Pheidias that stood in the Parthenon. The original work by Pheidias, which with its pedestal was 39ft tall, was completed in 432 B.C.; this copy was done c. A.D. 200.

Continuing along: on the l. is a case of red-figured Attic vases, the finest of which is perhaps a *krater* dating to c. 460 B.C., and decorated by the Dokimasia Painter (67.1246). The two scenes on the vase are from the *Oresteia* of Aeschylus; on one side Aigisthos is in the act of murdering Agamemnon, while Klytaimnestra lifts a double ax to hit her husband should her lover miss; and on the other side Orestes kills Aigisthos, encouraged by Elektra.

A wall case behind this has a fascinating collection of cameos and intaglios of the 6-5C B.C. The two finest of these are: a *chalcedony intaglio* (21.1194) with the figure of a kneeling archer, c. 500 B.C., attributed to Epimenes; and a red-and-yellow jasper *intaglio portrait* of a bearded man (23.580); this dates from the third quarter of the 5C B.C. and is signed by Dexamenos, one of the most renowned gem-cutters of that period.

Farther along on the l., on a pedestal near the corner of the room, is a *statuette of Heracles* (14.733), a Roman replica in marble of a large bronze original of the 5C B.C. The original, very famous in antiquity, was probably by the sculptor Myron, and may have been dedicated in the temple of Hera on Samos. A case in the corner of the room contains a collection of Attic *lekythoi,* white-ground oil bottles which were also in frequent use as funerary monuments. The three finest of these are in the center (93.106, 13.201, 13.187); these are dated c. 440 B.C. and are attributed to the Achilles Painter.

On a pedestal to the r. of this is an Attic red-figured *krater,* c. 465 B.C., by the Altamura Painter; the vase is decorated with vivid scenes from the Fall of Troy, probably patterned on famous murals that existed in Athens at the time of the Persian Wars.

Return to Room II-5 and walk through that gallery to enter ROOM II-8. Turning l. at the entryway, one immediately sees one of the museum's masterpieces, the *Bartlett Head* (03.743), a marble representation of Aphrodite named after its donor, Francis Bartlett.

This surpassingly lovely sculpture dates from the late 4C B.C., and is so close to the style of Praxiteles that it is believed to be the work of a contemporary and close follower of the great master. Some art historians have compared the beauty of this head with the most famous of all the works of Praxiteles, his lost Aphrodite of Knidos. The traces of red in the hair are evidence that Greek work in marble continued to be illuminated with color during the 4C B.C.

Along the wall to the l. there are four statues on pedestals. The finest of these is the second in line (04.12), a large marble *head of Zeus,* found near the ancient Carian city of Mylasa, in S.W. Asia Minor.

This was carved by an unknown master sculptor, c. 350 B.C., patterned on a famous statue of Zeus made by Pheidias at Olympia nearly a century earlier. The head here was probably part of a cult image of the god, perhaps that which stood in the great Carian sanctuary of Zeus Stratius. Two holes in the head suggest that the god wore a metal polos crown, part of the unusual native costume of the ancient Carians.

A case facing the entryway has an assortment of bronze mirrors, gold jewelry, and other objects, the most extraordinary of which is a *gold earring* (98.788). This exquisite piece, only two inches high, is in the form of a Nike with outspread wings riding through the heavens in a biga, a chariot pulled by two horses.

It dates from the mid-4C B.C., and it is thought to have been attached to the earlobe of a large cult statue of some female deity, perhaps Athena. (In 1963 the earring was stolen from the museum by an eccentric thief, who confessed that he had buried it nearby on the Fenway; it was unearthed there by an archaeologist from the Classics Dept. of the MFA, and was found to be hidden in a soup can.)

Also noteworthy is a *gold brooch* (99.371) with filigree decoration; this is thought to have been made in Campania in the 4C B.C. To the r. of the case there is a *grave stele* (1971.129) from Attica (c. 390 B.C.) engraved with the name of the deceased, Stratokles, and decorated with a dramatic scene in low relief.

On the r. side of the room, near the middle of the wall on that side, is a marble votive *stele* (96.696), dedicated to Heracles Alexikakos, an Athenian work of c. 375–350 B.C.

The inscription on the stele records that it was presented to Heracles, the Averter of Evil, a title acquired by the god for his mythical role as a healer during the terrible plague that ravaged Athens at the beginning of the Peloponnesian War. Art historians believe the sculptor who carved the relief on this stele was strongly influenced by both Pheidias and Polykleitos.

Return to Room II-5 and turn r. to enter ROOM II-10 by the portal at the rear of the gallery, which contains objects of the Hellenistic and Graeco-Roman periods, some of them from S. Italy. Many of the exhibits in the rear of the gallery are from ancient Greek colonies in S. Italy, most notably a *volute krater* (03.804) from Apulia, 4C B.C., decorated with a painting of the death of Thersites. Farther down the room on the r. a case has a collection of terra-cotta figurines from the Tomb of the Erotes at Eretria, 4–3C B.C. On a pedestal to the l. is another of the museum's masterpieces, the *head of a goddess* from Chios (10.70), a hauntingly beautiful representation of some unknown deity.

Here again, as in the case of the Bartlett Head of Aphrodite, the artistic merit of this work is so exceptional that at one time some authorities attributed it to some great but unknown artist of the early Hellenistic period, strongly influenced by Praxiteles. The goddess is now generally dated to c. 320 B.C.

On the l. is a bronze *portrait-bust* (96.712) of Queen Arsinöe II, who married Lysimachus, King of Thrace, in 299 B.C., and later became the wife of Ptolemy II, ruler of Egypt; this dates to the early 3C B.C. On the l. is a two-sided case, in the rear of which there is a collection of *Tanagra statuettes*. These charming terra-cotta figurines take their name from the Boeotian town of Tanagra, where they were first made in 340–330 B.C. as funerary offerings to the dead.

Farther along on the l. is a *Herm-bust* (97.288) of a handsome man believed to be the comic playwright Menander (341–291). This may be a work by the sons of Praxiteles known to have been set up in the Theater of Dionysos in Athens early in the 3C B.C. Still farther along on the l. is a fragmentary statue of the "Hanging Marsyas," a Roman copy of the original by a sculptor of the Pergamene school, which flourished in the 3–2C B.C. It represents the satyr Marsyas, flayed alive by Apollo and hung from a tree, after having attempted to compete with the god in a contest of music. On the pedestal just beyond this is a huge marble head of the Cyclops Polyphemos (63.120), with his one terrible eye beneath the center of his furrowed forehead; this dates to c. 150 B.C. or later, and reflects the style of the school of Pergamum. The head is thought to have been part of a colossal statue or group.

In the center of the room is an exceptionally fine *portrait-bust of Homer* (14.13), a work of the late Hellenistic period or the Graeco-Roman era. Beyond this, at the r. of the corridor leading to the next gallery, there is a headless statue (99.350) of Aphrodite, a Roman copy of the Capitolene type, after an original done in the Hellenistic period.

At the end of Room II-10, turn r. into ROOM II-20, a long hall devoted to an exhibition of Late Antique and Roman Provincial Art. In a case halfway down the corridor and on the l. is a small *equestrian statuette* (53.63) of Zeus Sabazios, a very Christ-like figure on horseback; this was found in Constantinople and dates to c. A.D. 150–250. Near the end of the hall on the same side is a *mosaic pavement* (60.531) from Tunisia, in which a she-ass is nursing two lion cubs, a very late Roman work of the 4–5C A.D.

This completes the tour through the Dept. of Classical Art. From the Information Desk in the inner lobby on the ground floor within the new West Wing of the museum turn r. into the long and narrow hall, to begin a tour through the Dept. of Asiatic Art.

Asiatic Art

The Department of Asiatic Art has the finest collection of Oriental works of art under one roof in the world, with each of the principal civilizations of the East represented by major pieces. Though none of the department's individual collections surpasses those of the national museums in the countries where the works of art originate, no museum matches the MFA's collection of Asiatic art in size, scope, and quality. The Dept. of Asiatic Art reopened in autumn 1982 after having been closed for several years for rehabilitation and reorganization, and today it is one of the most attractive and interesting areas of the MFA. (The rooms in the Asiatic Dept. are numbered differently from those in the Egyptian and Classical Depts. and these labels will be referred to in the account that follows.)

The first gallery of the Asiatic Dept. entered from the inner lobby of the West Wing is ROOM 1Y11. This is devoted to the art of the Islamic lands of W. Asia, principally Iran and Turkey, as well as works from Egypt in the Mamluk period, which had its cultural roots in the two latter countries. Among the works exhibited here the most fascinating are the Islamic miniatures, ranging from early Moslem scientific manuscripts to the courtly paintings of the Safavid dynasty in Iran, along with some superb imperial albums commissioned by the Ottoman dynasty in Istanbul. Because of the perishable nature of these paintings, they are exhibited only periodically, and so in the account that follows they will not be described individually.

To the l. of the entryway to Room 1Y11 there is a capital from a palace complex built in Spain by the Omayyad Caliph Abd al-Rahman III (963–71). Between the first two windows on the r. there is a superb Iranian *vase* (58.92) with a stamped relief, a work of the 8–9C A.D. The cases on the r. side of the room have changing exhibits of Islamic miniatures; while those on the l. display vases, pottery, metal works, and ceramics, mostly from Iran, but with important objects from Egypt, Turkey, Syria, and Iraq. The most important of the objects in the wall cases to the l. are the following: (65.238) an Iranian *glass flask* of the Abbasid period, 9–10C A.D.; (09.103, 50.3629) two *lusterware bowls* of the Seljuk period, 13C; (34.168) a *candlestick* of hammered brass inlaid with gold and silver, made in Egypt in 1342; and, in the last two cases on the l., a display of *Iznik pottery,* the most beautiful ceramics ever made in the Islamic world. Above the door leading into the next room there is a beautiful *lunette* (06.2437) in superb Iznik tiles; this is from the Istanbul mosque of Piyale Pasha, erected in 1573 by the great Ottoman architect Sinan.

Before continuing on into the gallery directly beyond Room 1Y11, go back a short way and turn r. into ROOM 1Y10, which is given over to exhibits from India (including some works from what is now Pakistan).

The MFA's collection of Indian art is the oldest and one of the most comprehensive in the U.S., with its principal strength in the vast holding of paintings, as well as a particularly fine group of early sculpture. Among the paintings are many fine works of the Mughal school, some of the best-known creations from the various Rajput courts, the earliest-known paintings from the Punjab Hills, and a fine collection of Rajasthani works. All phases of ancient Indian sculpture are represented, as well as numerous works from the early Buddhist period. The MFA is one of the few institutions in the U.S. to possess an extensive collection of Indian terra-cotta sculptures, architectural members, and archaeological objects, ranging in time from ancient sites in the Indus Valley to works from the Gupta period. A large number of these antiquities came to the Museum as a result of an expedition to Chanhu-daro in the Indus Valley, jointly sponsored by the MFA and the University of Pennsylvania. The museum's medieval Indian sculpture includes objects from almost all of the many regions and diverse cultures in India. Particularly noteworthy are the large stone sculptures from the Cola period in S. India. Other significant areas of the collection include Indian jewelry and fine ivory sculptures from Kashmir and Orissa.

Room 1Y10 is used mainly for changing exhibitions of watercolors from India; see the department's handbook, *Asiatic Art in the MFA,* on sale at the Museum Shop. After looking at the paintings currently on display, enter the gallery that opens off to the side of this hall, ROOM 1Y1, where there is a permanent display of sculpture from India.

Enter the gallery by the rear door. In the corner to the l. is a fragmentary sandstone statue (31.435) of an ancient fertility goddess known as a *yaksi.* Yaksis were pagan deities that were early on incorporated into Buddhism; they were local goddesses who were associated with fertility, and they were prayed to by those wanting children. Figures of yaksis were placed at entrances to shrines, acting as guardians; the one here came from the Great Stupa Bahrut in central India, and dates to c. 120 B.C. The fragmentary sandstone figure of another yaksi can be seen across the gallery, between the first two windows at this end. This beautiful and erotic *torso* (29.999) is from the great Stupa Sanchi in central India, and dates from the period 25 B.C.—A.D. 25. The sensuality of the figure and the unabashed representation of the female parts identify this yaksi at once as a fertility goddess.

Walk down the Huntington Ave side of the gallery. On the r. is a fine statue in gray schist of a *bodhisattva* (37.99), from Gandhara in N.W. Pakistan, dating from the late 2C A.D. On the l., between the second and third windows, a sandstone relief represents the *river goddess Ganga* (26.26), from Besnagar in central India, mid-5C A.D. Ganga and her sister deity, Yamuna, are the personifications of the two great rivers that emerge from the Himalayas and run through the heartland of central India; their figures were placed over temple doorways to purify those who entered through the cleansing waters they symbolized. Between the next two windows is a stylized *head of Buddha* (21.2230), from Mathura in N. India, mid-5C A.D.; and beyond this is an elegant image (35.40) in black schist of the *Lotus-Bearing Bodhisattva,* from Bengal, E. India, late 10C A.D. On the r., in the center of the room, is a double row of reliefs from various sites in India. Just beyond the reliefs is a seated figure of *Buddha* (1970.3), a work of gilt bronze with silver inlay, from Nagapattinam in S. India, c. 9C A.D. In front of this is a standing sandstone figure of *Vishnu* (25.438), from Bundelkhand in N.-central India, c. A.D. 1000. In front of this is a four-headed *figure* (42.120) in green schist representing the combined natures of Brahma and his son Siva, from the Tamilnadu region in S. India, late 10C A.D. In the corner to the l. is a gracefully convoluted *relief* (69.1047) in red sandstone depicting Siva as Lord of Dancers, central India, 9C A.D.; and in the middle of the room is the threatening but erotic *figure* (27.171) of the goddess Durga as the Slayer of the Buffalo Demon, S. India, 8C A.D.

Walk along the inner wall of the room, where there are a number of images of Siva; in the corner to the l. he is shown with his wife, Uma, and in two others he is depicted with Vishnu. In the first case on the l. there are examples of ancient Indian glass, and also a gleaming Mughal *dagger* with a jade handle and a sheath studded with rubies. Past that on the l. is a relief (67.2) in reddish-brown sandstone in which the principal figure is the river goddess Yamuna, central India, 9C A.D. In the next case there are bronze votive figurines, the most noteworthy being (69.928) a seated figure thought to be the *tirthankara* Parsvanatha, the 23rd of the teachers of Jainism, W. India, early 11C A.D. On the r., facing the door into the next hall, there is a two-sided relief (29.151) in schistose marble depicting the Sacred Bath of Buddha in the Nairanjana River, a work from the Amaravati region in S. India, c. A.D. 50. In the next case on the l. the most interesting objects are a pair of *ivory throne legs* (66.1138—9) of fantastic form, in the shape of monstrous two-headed lions with small human and animal figures clustering beneath them. One more object of interest to be seen in this gallery is in the penultimate case along the inside wall; this is an *ivory statuette* (63.1495) representing the seated Buddha flanked by the tiny figures of two attendant bodhisattvas, a work done in Kashmir, N. India, 8C A.D.

Now return through ROOM 1Y10 to 1Y11, and turn l. there to go on into the next gallery, ROOM 1Z12A, devoted to the Art of Southeast Asia. This collection is particularly strong in Cambodian art and antiquities, most notably in Khmer works, but there are also fine and interesting objects from Thailand, Burma, Indonesia, and Sri Lanka.

On entering the gallery, one sees on a pedestal to the r. a small sandstone *statue* (24.929), a composite image of Vishnu and Siva (Harihara) from Cambodia, early 7C A.D. Along the rear wall to the l. there are a number of sculptures from Cambodia, including two gigantic heads (24.8, 24.412) found in Angkor Thom, 12–13C A.D. There are also three architectural fragments with reliefs, the finest of which is perhaps (23.445), which is to the l. of the door leading into the next room. This consists of two blocks of sandstone, on each of which there are the charming figures in relief of demigoddesses called apsaras; these were found in the Cambodian temple of Prasat Khna Sen Keo Kompong Thom, and date to the second half of the 11C. To the r. of the door there is a fragmentary limestone *statue of Buddha* (1973.694) from Thailand, 8C A.D. In a case at the front center of the room there are gold and bronze objects from Indonesia, 13C A.D., and from Thailand, 15C A.D.; the most beautiful piece here is a *gold crown* (1982.14) in the form of a lotus pond, E. Java, 13C. Beyond that, in the center of the room, is the most striking sculpture in the gallery, a large and threatening *statue* (1972.251) of a deity carved in andesite, a volcanic stone. This is a 14C work from E. Java, and is believed either to represent the Hindu god Bhairava, who is the destructive aspect of Siva, or to be a figure of the Buddhist deity of death, Mahakala. Another arresting figure is to be seen to the l. of the central door leading into the next room; this is an andesite statue (1971.625) of the demon Mahisa, E. Java, 14C A.D. The area beyond the partition is part of the exhibit area of the Dept. of Japanese Art.

ROOM 1Z6 begins a tour through the Dept. of Japanese Art. The MFA's collection of Japanese art is one of the greatest in the world, not only because of the enormous number of works that it contains, but also because of its extremely high quality and comprehensiveness. The collection of Japanese painting includes representative works of almost every category, religious as well as secular, from the 8C A.D. to modern times, and a substantial number are of unique artistic and historical significance. Among the areas of particular excellence are Buddhist paintings, works in the "monochrome-ink" tradition, paintings by artists of the Kano school, genre and Ukiyo-e work, and paintings by artists of the Edo school. The collection is rich in sculptures, with many exceptional Buddhist icons. Other noteworthy collections include lacquers; swords and sword fittings; ceramics, particularly of the Edo period; miniature personal accessories, most notably netsuke, or sash toggles; No robes, kimonos, and other varieties of traditional clothing, as well as examples of textiles; metalwork, comprising a diverse range of objects such as Buddhist ritual implements and accessories, cast mirrors, vessels, tobacco pipes, and objects from archaeological sites. In the area of Japanese woodblock prints the museum's holdings are unsurpassed anywhere in the world, with more than 50,000 examples, of which a significant number are beautifully preserved and of the greatest historical and artistic importance. Because of the delicate nature of these prints and paintings, and also because of the enormous number in the collections, most of these works are exhibited on a rotating basis. Consequently, descriptions of the paintings will not be given on this tour, other than to mention the places where a few of the masterpieces are exhibited periodically; those wishing a more detailed account of these works should consult the department's handbook, *Asiatic Art.*

At the rear of the gallery, in a case beside the door to the next room, is a complete *suit of Japanese armor*, 18–19C. After seeing this, walk over to the cases in the center of the room. The five cases toward the front of the room contain a superb collection of swords, daggers, sheaths, sword guards, and hilt ornaments. Two of the finest are in the long case in the center of the room; one of these is a superb *dagger* (11.5144), dated by an inscription to 1319; and the other is a *dagger mounting and sheath* (11.11252), made in the mid-19C by Toshiyoshi, one of the outstanding lacquer masters of the late Edo period. Another object of considerable interest is to be seen in the front case to the r., a *sword handle and pommel* (08.161) of bronze and silver; this was found in the tumulus of the Japanese Emperor Nintoku, who ruled c. 395—427. The case in the front of the room to the l. contains pottery ranging in date from the 14C to the 17C, including a 14C vase (19.880). The most noteworthy objects in the front case to the r. are perhaps (31.1) a gold lacquered box of the Kamakura period, 13—14C; and a gilt bronze box (70.46), with engraved and punched design, a work of the Muromachi period, 14—15C; this served as a container for ritual implements used during the ordination ceremonies for priests of the Esoteric Buddhist sect.

The wall cases around the periphery of the room have a splendid collection of *No robes* of the Edo period, most of them dating to the 19C. No is a Japanese art form which is a combination of dance, song, and mime performed in a slow, ritualistic fashion, an entertainment that had its origins in the 11C and which evolved into its present form in the 14C. The colorful robes seen here, worn by the male actors who played both the male and female parts, were an important element in the dramatic effect of these No plays. In the case to the r. of the door to the next room there is a display of *Bugaku masks,* caricature masks worn by performers of Bugaku dances. Bugaku includes native Japanese dances as well as those imported from China and Korea, a tradition that originated in the 9C A.D. In this case there is also an elegant *lacquer writing-box* (08.170), made of paulownia wood with inlay decoration; this is a work of Ogawa Haritsu (1663—1747). In the case to the l. of the door there are also some superb *swords and scabbards.*

To the rear of this gallery is ROOM 1Z7, which is used for changing exhibitions of Japanese paintings. Two masterpieces from the collection are exhibited here periodically, in the long case in the center of the room, both of them hand scrolls with paintings in ink and color on paper. One of these is an *Illustrated Hand Scroll of Minister Kibi's Trip to China* (32.131), a depiction of the legendary adventures of Kibi no Makibi, Japanese ambassador, on his mission to T'ang China in A.D. 753; this work was done in the Heian period, late 12C. The second is a *Scroll with Depictions of the Night Attack on the Sanjo Palace* (11.4000), a representation of a battle that took place during the bloody wars between the Taira and Minamoto clans during the latter half of the 12C; this was done during the Kamakura period, second half of the 13C. The exhibition of Japanese art continues in the next gallery, ROOM 1Z12B, where there are changing displays of woodblock prints.

In the opposite direction is ROOM 1Z3, which is on the Huntington Ave side of this wing, a gallery which exhibits mostly Korean art. The MFA is one of the few museums in the Western world with an important collection of works of art from Korea, with distinguished examples of paintings, pottery, porcelains, metalwork, works in terra-cotta, lacquers, and impressed roof tiles.

On the two outer walls of the gallery are exhibited five examples of Korean paintings in ink and color on silk. The finest of these is (19.265), which is presently hung in the center of the wall on the Huntington Ave side; this is a representation of the *Buddha of Healing and Attendants,* Koryo dynasty, late 14C. To the r. of this, on a pedestal in the center of the room, is a gilt bronze *statuette* (32.436) of the Buddha of Healing, c. 9C. Of the many objects exhibited in this room, one might notice in particular a *ewer and basin* (35.646), in the long case against the inner wall, near its far end. These superb pieces are made of solid silver, parceled gilt and engraved, works of the Koryo dynasty, 11–12C. In the center of the case at the rear of the room is a *ceremonial belt* (68.45), 5C A.D. The belt consists of a buckle and thong and thirty links, to which were attached variously shaped pendants, of which only a few remain. This is a work of the Silla Kingdom in S.E. Korea, whose rulers were descendants of tribesmen from eastern Siberia. The belts were part of the paraphernalia of the shamans (sorcerers and exorcists), who played an important part in the religious life of these nomadic people.

Now return to Room 1Z6 and ascend the stairs to the second floor, emerging there in ROOM 2Z6. This large and attractive gallery is used for changing displays of Japanese paintings on screens, as are the four smaller galleries on the l. side, ROOMS 2Z1–4. In Room 2Z1, at its far end to the r., is a handsome *wooden cabinet* (73.596) of the Ming dynasty, late 16–early 17C. Cabinets such as this were standard pieces of equipment for a scholar's study in the late Ming period, used for holding books, scrolls, and writing materials. Go on through Room 2Z6 to the chamber at its far end; this is ROOM 2Z7, the Japanese Temple Room.

The *Temple Room* is for many visitors the most extraordinary exhibit area in the museum, a dimly lit chamber around the periphery of which are figures of Buddhist deities. These sacred images are all made of wood, painted and gilded, and they range in date from the 9C to the 14C. They are, beginning at the l. of the entryway from Room 2Z6: (05.212) the Bodhisattva of the Earth Matrix, 9C; (08.440) the Eleven-Headed Bodhissatva of Compassion, 9C; (11.12) the Divine Guardian of the North, 10C; (09.73) the Buddha of Infinite Light, 12C; (09.72) the Historical Buddha, late 10C; (09.531) the Buddha of Infinite Illumination, 11C; (09.383) Aizen, the King of Wisdom, 14C; (11.10) another representation of the Buddha of Infinite Illumination, 11C; (11.11) the Guardian of the South, 10C; (12.128) the Bodhisattva of Compassion Bearing a Lotus, 9C; and (11.11409) the Divine Guardian of the North, 11C.

Leave the Temple Room by the door on the r. side, which leads into ROOM 2Z14, the first of three galleries of Japanese art on that side of the wing. Exhibited here are statues of deities and paintings on silk on religious themes. The paintings are rotated frequently and so they will not be described below; those wishing to know more can consult the department's handbook, *Asiatic Art.* The statues described below are, except for one bronze work which will be identified, carved from wood which is then painted and/ or gilded. In Room 2Z14 there are three statues along the wall to the l., all of them of the 12C, and one 14C work against the back wall; these are, starting from the entryway: (09.533) the Buddha of Medicine; (09.532) the Buddha of Infinite Light; (09.530) the Historical Buddha; and (11.15a–c) the Bodhisattva of the Space Matrix. On entering the next gallery, ROOM 2Z13, one sees in the center of the room a statue (12.754) of the Buddha of Infinite Light, 10C. In the corner to the r. is a figure (20.723) of the *Bodhisattva of the Future;* a written statement found inside the statue records that it dates to 1189, and that it was made by the sculptor Kaikei, one of the masters of the Kamakura period. On the wall above is a charming figure (12.334) of a *hiten* (the Japanese version of an apsaras), one of a group of celestial maidens believed to have been created during the churning of the ocean to create ambrosia; this is dated to the second half of the 11C. In the corner to the l. is yet another image (05.227a–d) of the Bodhisattva of the Earth Matrix, mid-12C. Continue into ROOM 2Z12. In the center of the room is a fine bronze statue (11.11447) of the Bodhisattva of Compassion Bearing a Lotus, dated by an inscription to 1269. In the corner to the r. is a figure (05.220) of the god Fudo, one of the Wisdom Kings worshipped in Esoteric Buddhism. Near the corner on the l. is a fragmentary image (05.228) of a monstrous three-headed deity known as Dai-itoku, another of the Wisdom Kings, a work of the 11C. At the far end of the gallery, across the corridor, a superb painted wooden statue (05.212) represents the Bodhisattva Hachiman as a Buddhist priest. Hachiman was originally an agricultural deity in northern Kyushu, but by the 8C his fame had spread throughout Japan and he acquired the title of bodhisattva, thus becoming one of the first Shinto gods to be accepted into the Buddhist pantheon. An inscription inside the head of the statue records that it was made in 1328 by the sculptor Koshun, whose dated works are from the period 1311–66.

Walk around the stairwell to the small chamber at its rear, ROOM 2Z8. Here begins a tour through the MFA's collection of Chinese art, which takes up all but one of the remaining galleries of the Asiatic Dept. on this floor.

The strength of the MFA's Chinese collections lies in the areas of paintings and ceramics, while sculptures, bronzes, and the decorative arts are all well represented. The paintings include some of the earliest extant works in scroll form, most notably those attributed to the 7C artist Yen Li-pen and the Sung Emperor Hui-tsung (1082–1135). The Sung treasures include a group of Buddhist paintings acquired from the Daitoku-ji in Kyoto; among the latter paintings works of the Suchou masters of the middle to late Ming period are especially well represented. Notable in the collection is a group of Taoist paintings and stone images, most of the latter bearing dated inscriptions. In the ceramics section, the Hoyt Collection contains many fine pieces dating from the Six Dynasties to the Sung period, including a large number of "marbled" wares of the T'ang and Sung periods, and some 18C imperial porcelains. The stone sculptures include a number of important Buddhist works, as well as secular objects of the Six Dynasties and T'ang periods. Among these the most impressive are those of the early 8C A.D., most of which were part of elaborate funerary monuments. The collection of early Chinese bronzes is renowned for the relatively large number of Western Chou ritual vessels and a number of Han pieces with painted decoration. Other collections include a sizable group of Chinese lacquer pieces, most of which are decorated with inlaid mother-of-pearl, including a fine group from the Ryuku Islands; glass vessels of the Ch'ing period; and other branches of Chinese decorative arts, such as furniture, articles in everyday use, and carvings in jade and other stones, as well as in rhinoceros horn and bamboo.

ROOM 2Z8 has a small collection of Chinese glass of the 18C and also of Chinese jade of the 18–19C. Additional examples of Chinese glass and jade are exhibited in the other galleries of the department.

The first gallery beyond the stairwell is ROOM 2Z10, where there is a display of Chinese works of the Ch'ing period. The objects exhibited here range in date from the 15C to the 19C and include changing displays of hanging scrolls. There is also a permanent exhibit of works in jade, aquamarine, agate, amber, marble, steatite, bamboo, and lacquers, and samples of earthenware pottery. In the center of the room is a fine lacquered and engraved *table* (50.161), 17C, flanked by two hanging scrolls.

The next gallery is ROOM 2Y6, devoted to Chinese Decorative Arts. On either side of the doorway is a large and elegant pair of *dress-cabinets* (1981.345, 391), c. 1700. On the l. side of the room at the near end, the first two wall cases have porcelains of the 16–17C, and the one beyond that has pages from an album of Chinese fans, after which there is an elegant pair of folding armchairs flanking a scroll table, works of the 17C. In the middle of the room and on its r. side are an *incense burner* (17.1156), dated 1520; a handsome vase (1974.480), 14C; and on the wall an elegant *Coromandel screen* (1975.333) of carved wood with lacquer and colors, on which is depicted a scene of European Hunters in China, c. 1700. In the very center of the room is an earthenware *model* (50.1806) of a house with figures of humans and animals, a work of the Ming dynasty, 1368—1644. To the r. is a case with charming earthenware figurines of the 7—8 C; in the center of the room beyond that are two superb *figurines* in earthenware with three-color glaze representing a pair of horses (27.2, 46.478); these are works of the T'ang dynasty (618—906), and were funerary offerings in the tombs of nobles or high-ranking officers. A case in the right-hand corner has earthenware representations of a soldier and his horse (36.140—1), mid-6C A.D. In a case at the corner of the room on the l. there are five enchanting earthenware *figures* with painted decorations, representing soldiers and court officials, 6C A.D. To the l. of the door into the side corridor is a quaint earthenware *model* (50.1864) of an ox cart and its drivers, early T'ang dynasty, 7C A.D. In the wall case just to the l. of this is the beautiful *headgear* (40.749) of a Khitan envoy. (The Khitans were tribespeople who invaded China from the N. during the Northern Sung dynasty.) This superb work is made of gilded silver, with repoussé decoration, c. A.D. 1000.

Now enter the side corridor, ROOM 2Y8, where there is an exhibit of Chinese Ceramics. These include works ranging in date from earliest antiquity up until the beginning of modern times, the oldest of which is a Hu *ceremonial vessel* (50.1808) of earthenware with painted decor, 2C B.C. Detailed information on the outstanding ceramic works displayed here and in the other galleries of Chinese works is available in the handbook on *Asiatic Art.*

Now return to ROOM 2Y6 and go on into ROOM 2Y19, which is devoted to the art of the Han period, 50 B.C.—A.D. 50. (When dates for objects in this gallery are not given, they are from the Han period.) On either side of the entryway cases contain a collection of ceramic roof tiles with impressed designs, 1C B.C. Against the wall to the l. is a *lintel* (39.228) from a tomb, with a fine relief showing a chariot procession. In the first wall case on the r. there are two works in glazed earthenware: (50.1754) a *model of a watchtower;* and (27.308) *a model of a goat corral and farmhouse.* At the far end of the room, on the l., there are three charming earthenware figures (48.1265,6,7) of the 2—1C B.C. In the short corridor behind the glass wall case at the r. side of the room there are two interesting funerary objects; to the l. is a wall panel (39.731) of a tomb, and at the end is an architectural member of a mausoleum (40.69), both decorated with reliefs.

Turn r. at the r.-hand corner of ROOM 2Y19, where a long corridor has an exhibition of Chinese objects of the Bronze Age. In a pedestal case to the l. at the beginning of the corridor; is a charming bronze and jade *figurine of a youth* (31.976). He holds upright sticks on which are perched a pair of chained birds, 4—3C B.C. In a wall case midway down the corridor on the l. is a drum framed by pairs of birds and tigers, 4—3C B.C. In the last case on the l. there is a marvelous covered *wine vessel* (34.66) known as a *wu,* a bronze work dating to 13—11C B.C. Returning along the other side of the corridor, about halfway along, is another bronze *wu* (34.63), 11—10C B.C.; and in a case beyond that beautiful jade objects of the third and second millennia B.C.

Return to ROOM 2Y19 and turn r. to enter ROOM 2Y37, Buddhist and Taoist art. On the walls there are changing exhibits of hanging scrolls. For information on the Chinese art displayed here periodically, consult the handbook, *Asiatic Art*. In a pedestal case to the l. of the entryway is a white marble *altarpiece* (50.1074) with the figure of Maitreya, the Buddha of the Future, c. A.D. 560. Past the door leading to the next gallery is a painted and gilt *statuette* (50.175), the Bodhisattva of Compassion, 10–11C; and beyond that, in the corner, a lacquer *head* (50.1937) of Lohan (an enlightened sage), 11–12C. As one continues around the room in the same direction, in the corner to the l. is a bronze *altarpiece* (47.1407–12), in which the central figure is the Amitabha Buddha, who is known both as the Buddha of Infinite Light and the Lord of the Western Paradise, dated to A.D. 593. In the corner to the r. is a marvelous *figurine* (50.1073) in dry lacquer, representing a Dvarapala, a Chinese gateway guardian, 10–11C.

Now walk back across the gallery to enter ROOM 2Y38, which has paintings and sculptures from the Himalayan lands of Tibet and Nepal. On the walls of the gallery there is a changing exhibition of religious paintings from Tibet and Nepal done in gouache on cotton. To the l. of the door from Room 2Y37 is the fantastic figure (21.2168) in painted copper of *Vajrabhairava*, the tutelary deity of the Ge-Lug-Pa sect of Lamaism, a Tibetan work of the 17C. Continuing around the room in that direction, one sees in turn the following objects: (62.331) a gilt copper figurine of the Tibetan deity Syamatara, 18C; (67.5) a gilt copper statuette of Vishnu in his Universal Form, Nepal, 9–10C; and (17.2315) a superb copper figurine, gilt and jeweled with jacinth, a representation of the Bodhisattva of Compassion Bearing a Lotus, Nepal, 14C; and in a case to the r. a collection of figurines in brass, bronze, and gilt copper of Tibetan and Nepalese deities.

ROOM 2Y32, entered from Room 2Y37, is a large gallery of Chinese sculpture. To the l. of the entryway is a painted wooden *statue* (20.590) of Kuan Yin, the Bodhisattva of Compassion, represented in the Posture of Royal Relaxation, a superb work of the 12C. On the wall behind a large mural (36.139) in ink and color depicts Mahaprajapati with the Infant Buddha, a work of the Ming dynasty, 1368–1644. In the center of the gallery there is a large marble *statue* (15.254) of Kuan Yin, late 6C. In the center of the room is a black limestone *sarcophagus* (37.340) in the form of a house, c. A.D. 530. Behind that there are an epitaph table and its cover (33.680a&b), with inscriptions recording that they belonged to the Lady Yuan and dated A.D. 522. To the l. is a black limestone *sarcophagus* (16.287) of the early 8C; and flanking the door to the Rotunda a pair of tomb doors in black limestone is decorated with the figures of women bearing funerary offerings, 8C A.D. Here the tour through the Dept. of Asiatic Art ends in the Rotunda.

The next tour will take one through the Dept. of Paintings, whose main exhibit area is in the Evans Wing.

Department of Paintings

The Dept. of Paintings was organized in 1902, by which time the MFA had already acquired an important collection of American and European paintings. The first registered acquisition by the MFA dates to 1870, when it received as a gift *Elijah in the Wilderness,* by Washington Allston; in the following year it acquired two of the finest works of François Boucher: *Halt at the Spring,* and *Return to the Market.* When the first MFA building was opened in Copley Sq in 1876 a distinguished group of American paintings was deposited by the Boston Athenaeum and the city of Boston, initiating a collection of American art that has become one of the finest in the U.S. Particularly significant are the portraits of the colonial and early Federal periods, including over 60 by John Singleton Copley and more than 50 by Gilbert Stuart. Of similar importance is the M. and M. Karolik Collection of American Paintings from 1815 to 1865. The Dept. also has an unusually large and fine group of American paintings by the Romantics and Realists of the latter part of the 19C, most notably Winslow Homer, Thomas Eakins, James A. McNeill Whistler, and Mary Cassatt.

The collection of European paintings is a testimony to the tastes of Boston's collectors, whose donations fill the galleries. Boston collectors were among the first to appreciate the revolutionary developments of 19C French art. Consequently, the MFA's collection of French painting from the second quarter of the 19C to the turn of the century is equaled by no more than six museums in the world. It includes masterpieces by Delacroix, Courbet, Corot, Millet, and other Barbizon artists, whose works appeared initially in the U.S. in Boston collections; these were later donated to the MFA, as were works by the Impressionists, particularly Monet, Manet, Pissarro, Sisley, and Renoir. Today the MFA's collections of paintings and pastels by Millet is the most important in the world, and the group of works by Monet is surpassed only by the collection in Paris. The MFA similarly obtained works by masters of the Post-Impressionist era, most notably Van Gogh, Cézanne, and Gauguin. Other strong points in the European collection are works of the Spanish, Venetian, and Netherlandish schools. The collection also has exceptional paintings by French and English artists of the baroque, rococo, and Romantic periods; although not large in number, these do include masterpieces by Poussin, Claude Lorrain, Bourdon, Boucher, Chardin, Gainsborough, Romney, Reynolds, Lawrence, and Turner. In 1965 the collection of French works of art of the 18C was considerably strengthened by the Forsyth Wickes Collection, which included 37 paintings, pastels, and miniatures. The department also has samples of the major artistic movements of the 20C. American paintings of the earlier part of the century, especially of the school of "The Eight," are well represented. Some of the major developments in Europe are outlined by the works of the Cubists, Picasso, Braque, Gris, and Feininger; as well as by the German Expressionists, Kirchner, Beckmann, and Kokoschka; and also by Munch, Giacometti, Appel, Nicholson, and De Staël. The department also has a collection of miniatures by European and American artists such as Smart, Copley, and Malbone.

The location of all paintings on exhibition is subject to change at any time, and no attempt will be made in this guide to specify the galleries in which the various pictures are on view. The description that follows simply lists the most outstanding European and American paintings in the MFA. (The dates of the various paintings will be given when known; otherwise the artist's dates are given.) The MFA has published a two-volume illustrated catalogue of all the American paintings in its collection. Unfortunately, there is no catalogue of the European paintings; those wanting more information should consult the *Illustrated Handbook of the MFA, Masterpieces from the Boston Museum,* and *Western Art in the MFA.* All of the books mentioned above are on sale in the Museum Shop.

European Paintings. The oldest European painting in the collection is a *Byzantine fresco* (21.1285) from the apse of the Church of Santa Maria de Mura in Catalonia, depicting Christ in Majesty with the Apostles and Scenes from the Nativity, a work dating from the second half of the 12C. The oldest of the Italian paintings in the collection is a *triptych* (45.880) by Duccio di

Buoninsegna, dating from c. 1305–7; the central scene is the Crucifixion, with depictions of St. Nicholas and St. Gregory in the side panels. Some of the other outstanding European paintings in the collection are, in approximate chronological order: Barna da Siena (c. 1320–56), the *Marriage of St. Catherine* (15.1145); Bohemian School, *Death of the Virgin*, c. 1350 (50.2716); Barnaba da Modena (fl. 1364–83), *Virgin and Child* (15.951); Rogier van der Weyden, *St. Luke Painting the Virgin*, shortly after 1435 (93.153); Anon. Alsatian, *Man of Sorrows*, 15C (56.262); Giovanni di Paolo (1403–82), the *Virgin of Humility* (30.772); Fra Angelico, *Virgin and Child with Angels, Saints, and Donor*, c. 1445 (14.416); Gentile Bellini (1452–1507), *Portrait of a Doge* (36.934); Anon. Flemish, *The Martyrdom of St. Hippolytus*, last quarter 15C (63.660); Martin de Soria, *Retable of St. Peter*, last quarter 15C (46.856); Master of the Barberini Panels, *Presentation of the Virgin in the Temple*, late 15C (37.108); Hieronymus Bosch (fl. 1488–1516), *Ecco Homo*, a triptych (53.207); Lucas Cranach the Elder, *The Lamentation*, c. 1515 (1970.348); Lucas Cranach the Younger (1515–86), *Portrait of a Lady* (11.3035); Lorenzo Lotto, *Mother and Child with St. Jerome and St. Anthony of Padua*, c. 1521–22; Titian (c. 1487–1576), *St. Catherine of Alexandria* (48.499); Il Rosso Fiorentino, the *Dead Christ with Angels*, c. 1524–27 (58.527); Lucas van Leyden, *Moses Striking the Rock*, 1527 (54.1432); Tintoretto, *The Nativity*, c. 1550 (46.1430), *Alessandro Farnese*, 1560–65 (27.862), *Adoration of the Magi*, c. 1580; Paolo Veronese, *Diana and Acteon*, c. 1560 (59.260), *Atalanta and Meleager*, c. 1560 (64.2079); Jacopo da Empoli, *Entry of a Cardinal into Rome*, c. 1600 (49.1981); El Greco, *Fray Hortensio Paravicino*, 1604 (04.234); Peter Paul Rubens, *Portrait of Mulay Ahmad*, c. 1610 (40.2), *The Head of Cyrus Brought to Queen Tomyris*, c. 1622 (41.40), *Mercury and Argus*, c. 1630–35 (42.175); Pieter Lastman, *Wedding Night of Tobias and Sara*, 1611 (62.985); Jacob Jordaens, *Double Portrait of a Man and His Wife*, c. 1620 (17.3232), *Bacchus and Ariadne*, c. 1647–49 (54.134).

Rembrandt, *The Artist in His Studio*, c. 1628–29 (38.128), *An Old Man in Prayer*, c. 1628–30 (03.1080), *The Rev. Johannes Elison*, 1634 (56.510), *Mevr Johannes Elison* (Maria Bockenolk), 1634 (56.51), *Man in a Black Hat*, 1634 (19.1475), *Woman with a Golden Chain* (93.1474); Velázquez, *Luis de Gongora y Argote*, 1622 (32.79), *Don Baltasar Carlos and His Dwarf*, 1651 (01.104), *Infanta Maria Theresa*, c. 1653 (21.2593); Francesco del Cairo, *Salome with the Head of John the Baptist*, c. 1635 (26.772); Francisco de Zurburán, *St. Francis*, c. 1645 (38.1617); Nicolas Poussin, *Mars and Venus*, c. 1630 (40.89), *Achilles Among the Daughters of Lycomedes*, c. 1655 (46.463); Jacob van Ruisdael, *Rough Seas*, 1660–70 (57.4); Frans Hals, *Portrait of a Man*, c. 1664–66 (66.1054); Claude Lorrain, *Parnassus*, 1681 (12.1051); Luca Giordano, *Apollo in His Chariot*, 1680 (47.1560); Giuseppi Maria Crespi, *The Lute Player*, 1695–1700 (69.9581); Sebastiano Ricci, *Phineas and the Sons of Boreas*, c. 1695 (1980.275); Antoine Watteau, *La Perspective* (The Vista), 1716–18 (23.753); Giovanni Battista Piazzetta, *Peasant Girl Catching a Flea*, 1720–25 (46.461), *Young Peasant Boy at Market*, 1720–25 (46.262); Canaletto, *Bacino di San Marco*, early 1730s (39.290); Nicolas Lancret, *Le Déjeuner de Jambon* (The Ham Luncheon), c. 1735 (65.2649); Giovanni Battista Tiepolo, *Time Unveiling Truth*, c. 1745 (61.1200); Francesco Guardi, *Reception of a Dignitary*, c. 1763 (11.1451); Jean-Baptiste-Siméon Chardin, *The Tea Pot*, 1764 (83.177); François Boucher, *Halt at the Spring*, 1765 (71.2) (one of the first two European paintings acquired by the MFA); Adolphe Ulrik Wertmüller, *Jean*

Jacques Caffieri, 1784 (63.1082); Thomas Gainsborough, *Captain Matthew,* 1772 (25.134); George Romney, *Anne de la Pole,* 1786 (61.392); Francisco de Goya, *Allegory: Spain, Time and History,* c. 1800 (27.1330); John Constable, *The Stour Valley and Dedham Church,* 1814 (48.266); Jean-Baptiste-Camille Corot, *Island of San Bartolomeo, Rome,* c. 1827 (23.118), *The Girl with a Pink Shawl,* 1868–70 (19.81), *Ophelia,* 1868–70 (23.511); Joseph M. W. Turner, *The Slave Ship,* 1840 (99.42); Eugène Delacroix, *The Entombment,* 1848 (96.21); Jean-François Millet, *The Sower* (17.1485), *Harvesters Resting* (Ruth and Boaz), 1853 (06.2421), *Young Shepherdess,* 1869–71 (77.249); Gustave Courbet, *The Quarry,* 1857 (18.620).

Edouard Manet, *The Street Singer,* 1862 (57.38), *Execution of the Emperor Maximilian,* 1867 (30.444), *The Music Lesson,* 1870 (69.1123); Edgar Degas, *The Duke and Duchess of Morbilli,* 1867 (31.33), *Degas Father Listening to Pagans Playing the Guitar,* c. 1872 (48.533), *Two Young Ladies Visiting a Museum,* c. 1877–80 (69.49), *Carriage at the Races,* c. 1873 (26.7900), *Edmund and Thérèse,* c. 1861–64 (31.33); Claude Monet, *Le Japonais,* 1876 (56.147), *Haystack in Winter,* 1891 (1970.253), *Rouen Cathedral, Sunset,* 1894 (36.371), *Water-Lilies,* 1905 (39.804); Paul Cézanne, *Madame Cézanne in a Red Armchair, Self-Portrait with a Beret,* c. 1898–99 (1972.950), *The Turn in the Road,* c. 1881 (48.525), *Uncle Dominique,* 1865–66 (112.1979); Pierre-Auguste Renoir, *Mixed Flowers in a Vase,* 1869 (48.952), *Rocky Crags at L'Estaque,* 1882 (39.678), *Le Bal à Bougival,* 1883 (37.375); Alfred Sisley, *Early Snow at Louveciennes,* c. 1870; Camille Pissarro, *The Gisors, Pantoise,* 1873 (48.857), *The Road to Ennery,* 1874 (25.114). *Maison de la Folie,* 1885 (25.115), *Market Place, Gisors,* 1885 (48.588); Vincent van Gogh, *The Postman Roulin,* 1888 (35.1982), *La Berceuse,* 1889 (45.548), *The Ravine,* 1889 (52.154); Henri de Toulouse-Lautrec, *"A la Mie,"* 1891 (40.748); Edvard Munch, *The Voice,* 1893 (61.1138); Paul Gauguin, *"D'où venons-nous?—Que sommes-nous?—Où allons-nous?,"* 1897 (36.270); Odilon Redon, *The Large Green Vase,* c. 1910 (48.951); Henri Matisse, *The Vase of Flowers,* c. 1921 (48.577); Pablo Picasso, *Standing Figure,* 1908 (58.976), *Rape of the Sabines,* 1963 (64.709); Ernst Ludwig Kirchner, *Reclining Nude,* 1909 (57.2); Georges Braque, *Still Life with Plums,* 1925 (57.523); Oskar Kokoschka, *Double Portrait of Trudi,* 1931 (61.1138); Nicholas de Staël, *Rue Gauget,* 1949 (57.385).

American Paintings. The two most famous works in the MFA's collection of American paintings are the unfinished portraits of *George Washington* (Ath. 1) and *Martha Washington* (Martha Dandridge Custis) (Ath. 2), both painted from life by Gilbert Stuart in 1796.

The portraits were purchased from Stuart's estate by the Washington Assoc., Boston, and 22 subscribers, who gave them to the Boston Athenaeum in 1831. When the MFA opened in its first home in Copley Sq in 1876, the Boston Athenaeum deposited the two portraits with it. The portraits are currently owned jointly by the MFA and the National Portrait Gallery in Washington, D.C., rotating between them every three years.

Other noteworthy pictures in the collections of American paintings are, in chronological order: Anon., *Robert Gibbs,* 1670 (249.35); John Smibert, *Judge Samuel Sewall,* 1729 (58.358); Joseph Badger, *Mrs. John Edwards* (Abagail Fowle), c. 1750–60 (24.421); Robert Feke, *Isaac Winslow,* c. 1748 (42.424); Joseph Blackburn, *Isaac Winslow and His Family,* 1755 (42.684); John Singleton Copley, *Mary and Elizabeth Royall,* c. 1758 (25.49), *John*

Watson and the Shark, *by John Singleton Copley, c. 1788 (Courtesy, Museum of Fine Arts, Boston)*

Hancock, 1765 (30.76d), *Boy with a Squirrel,* 1765 (1978.297), *Nicholas Boylston,* c. 1767 (23.504), *Paul Revere,* c. 1768–70 (30.76c), *Mrs. Ezekiel Goldthwait* (Elizabeth Lewis), 1771 (41.84), *Watson and the Shark,* 1778 (a replica of the original, now in the National Gallery, Washington, D.C.), *Joseph Warren,* c. 1772–74 (95.1366), *John Quincy Adams,* 1795 (17.1077); Benjamin West, *The Hope Family of Sydenham, Kent,* 1802 (06.2362); Gilbert Stuart, *General Henry Knox,* c. 1805 (30.76b), *Washington at Dorchester Heights,* 1806 (30.76a), *George Washington,* 1810 (29.788) (one of many replicas that Stuart made from his "Athenaeum Head"), *Paul Revere,* 1813 (30.782), *Mrs. Paul Revere* (Rachel Walker), 1813 (76.347), *Mrs. James Smith Colburn* (Sarah Dunn Prince), c. 1817 (10.232), *Bishop Jean-Louis Lefebvre de Cheverus,* 1823 (21.9), *Josiah Quincy,* 1824 (76.347); John Trumbull, *Sortie from Gibraltar,* 1789 (Ath. 10), *Alexander Hamilton,* 1806 (94.167); Henry Sargent, *The Dinner Party,* c. 1821 (19.13), *The Tea Party,* c. 1821–25 (19.12); Samuel F. B. Morse, *Niagara Falls from Table Rock,* 1835 (48.456); John Neagle, *Gilbert Stuart,* 1825 (Ath. 35), *Pat Lyon at the Forge,* 1826–27 (16.40); Thomas Sully, *The Torn Hat,* 1820 (16.104), *The Passage of the Delaware,* 1825 (exhibited in the West Wing) (03.1079); Washington Allston, *Rising of a Thunderstorm at Sea,* 1804 (78.46), *Landscape with a Lake,* 1804 (47.1241), *Self-Portrait,* 1805 (84.301), *William Ellery Channing,* 1809–11 (97.65), *Moonlit Landscape,* 1818 (21.429), *Elijah in the Desert,* 1818 (70.1) (the first painting acquired by the MFA);

Robert Salmon, *South Sea Whale Fishing*, 1831 (27.356); Francis Alexander, *Charles Dickens*, 1843 (24.18); Chester Harding, *Abbot Lawrence*, c. 1840–45 (61.239), *Amos Lawrence*, c. 1844–45 (59.857); Jerome B. Thompson, *A "Pic-Nick", Camden, Maine*, c. 1850 (46.852); Thomas Cole, *Expulsion from the Garden of Eden*, c. 1827–28 (47.1188); Henry F. Darby, *The Rev. John Atwood and His Family*, 1845 (62.269); Fitz Hugh Lane, *Boston-Harbor*, c. 1850–55 (66.339); George Caleb Bingham, *The Squatters*, 1850 (no number); George P. A. Healy, *Daniel Webster*, 1853 (17.106); John LaFarge, *Vase of Flowers*, 1864 (20.1873); Martin Johnson Heade, *Approaching Storm: Beach near Newport*, 1860s (45.889); William Morris Hunt, *Italian Peasant Boy*, 1866 (29.1117), *Ida Mason*, 1878 (32.127); Elihu Vedder, *Lair of the Sea-Serpent*, 1864 (84.283); Albert Bierstadt, *Storm in the Mountains*, c. 1870–80 (47.1257); George Inness, *Italian Landscape*, 1872 (38.1417); Winslow Homer, *Long Branch, New Jersey*, 1869 (41.631), *The Fog Warning—"All's Well,"* 1885 (99.23), *Adirondack Guide*, 1894 (47.268); Thomas Eakins, *Starting Out After Rain*, 1874 (35.1953), *Walt Whitman*, c. 1887 (30.122), *The Dean's Roll Call*, 1899 (43.211); John Frederick Peto, *The Poor Man's Store*, 1892 (62.278); William Michael Harnett, *Old Models*, 1892 (39.761); John Singer Sargent, *Rehearsal of the Pasdeloup Orchestra at the Cirque d'Hiver*, 1876 (22.598), *The Daughters of Edward D. Boit*, 1882 (19.124), *Mrs. Fiske Warren* (Gretchen Osgood) *and Her Daughter*, 1903 (64.693); James A. M. Whistler, *The Last of Old Westminster*, 1862 (39.44), *The Lagoon, Venice: Nocturne in Blue and Silver*, 1879–80 (42.302), *The Little Rose of Lyme Regis*, 1895 (96.950); Mary S. Cassatt, *At the Opera*, 1879 (10.35), *A Cup of Tea*, c. 1880 (42.178); Frederick Childe Hassam, *Boston Common at Twilight*, 1885–86 (31.952), *Grand Prix Day*, 1887 (64.983); Maurice Prendergast, *Race Track*, c. 1900 (62.321); John Sloan, *Pigeons*, 1910 (35.52); William McGregor Paxton, *The New Necklace*, 1910 (22.644); George Bellows, *Emma and Her Children*, 1923 (25.105); Edward Hopper, *Drug Store*, 1927 (48.564); Lyonel Feininger, *Regler Church, Erfurt*, 1930 (57.198); Thomas Hart Benton, *New England Editor*, 1946 (46.1456); John Marin, *Movement—Sea or Mountain as You Will*, 1947 (63.1527); Andrew Wyeth, *Anna Christina*, 1967 (1970.250).

We now return to the Tapestries Gallery, which has changing exhibitions of works in the collections of the Dept. of Textiles.

Department of Textiles
Although the Dept. of Textiles was not established until 1930, the founders of the MFA had from its beginning the idea of assembling a fine and comprehensive collection of textiles. When the MFA opened its first building in 1876, the Boston Athenaeum deposited with the museum a number of handsome textiles, silk weavings, embroideries, and ecclesiastical vestments. Today the museum's collection of textiles ranks among the greatest in the world, both in terms of the high quality and rarity of individual pieces and as a general collection of representative weavings, embroideries, laces, printed fabrics, and costumes from all over the world, ranging in date from the first millennium B.C. to modern times.

The following groups constitute the most outstanding holdings. First, the collection of tapestry weavings, which includes fine examples woven in the eastern Mediterranean world in the first millennium A.D., as well as the collection of European tapestries of the 14–16C, with important examples from weaving centers in France, Flanders, and Germany. The collection of

Peruvian tapestries from the colonial period, ranging from the second half of the 16C to the 18C, stands unrivaled as a single collection, not only in the U.S. but in Peru as well. French, German, and Italian tapestry weaving of the 17–18C is also well represented. Earlier Peruvian weavings and embroideries, dating from the pre-Christian era through the middle of the 16C, were chosen for beauty of design and workmanship; many of the pieces, particularly the collection of embroidered mantles and skirts from the Paracas culture, 500–200 B.C., are also of the greatest rarity and archaeological importance. Other important areas include English and Continental embroideries and laces of the 15–19C, New England embroideries of the late 17C through early 19C, and embroideries from Greece and the Greek islands. Other objects in the collections include Coptic textiles; pre-Columbian embroideries; European, Turkish, Indian, and Persian silk weavings; Indonesian weavings; Middle Eastern rugs; Turkish velvets and embroideries; classical and nomadic carpets; Italian velvets; and various textiles from India. There is also a superior collection of costume material (high fashion, ethnographic, and ecclesiastical), dating from the 16C to the present. Those who wish to see items in storage should apply for permission in the Textile Study Room on Floor 0, on the lower level.

Return to the first floor, to visit the galleries of the Dept. of Prints and Drawings. There are two exhibit areas used by the department on this floor: just to the r. of the stairway as one enters from the Huntington Ave side of the building, and the corridor and galleries to the r. of the rear stairway on the Fenway side of the Evans Wing. The works exhibited there are rotated quite frequently, both because of the enormous number in the collection and also because of their perishable nature.

Department of Prints and Drawings
The department, founded in 1887, estimated in 1975 that it had more than a half-million works in its collections, ranging from the 15C to modern times. The importance of the collection derives from the fact that for many artists there are multiple impressions of a print, along with preparatory drawings, so that students and scholars can observe these works of art in the course of their creation. The Italian 15C engravings are the most outstanding group in the U.S. Among them are a complete set of the broad-manner Prophets in the first state, the only complete impression of the large Judgment Hall of Pilate, as well as a unique impression of a Ferrarese Annunciation. The collection is also strong in northern engravings of the same period, owning the single known impression of the small Garden of Love, by the Master of the Gardens of Love, a "Queen" by the Master of the Playing Cards, and a pair of drypoints (one of them unique) by the Master of the Amsterdam Cabinet. One of the treasures of the department is a hand-colored copy of the first book ever illustrated by engravings, Colard Mansion's 1476 edition of Boccaccio, *De la Ruyne des Nobles Hommes et Femmes,* printed in Bruges. The Dürer collection is extremely rich, not only in fine engravings, drypoints, and woodcuts, but also in its wealth of comparative impressions. Other strengths are a magnificent set of Duvet's Apocalypse, and the collection of chiaroscuro woodcuts by artists such as Ugo da Carpi, Vincentino, Andreani, Goltzius, Baldung, and Weiditz; this area has been expanded to encompass the 17–18C as well, including an extraordinarily complete and rich group of Zanettis. The 17C printmakers are well represented, the most notable being the etchings of the Lorraine mannerist Bellange. The collec-

tion of ornament prints and books includes 16C Italian woodcut lace designs, 17C Spanish calligraphy, as well as a wealth of 18C material, from Pillement etchings to watercolor patterns for embroidery and *mise-en-cartes* for weaving fabrics. There is an especially fine collection of prints by the two Tiepolos and by Canaletto. Among the rare works is a complete set of the "Blot Prints" by Alexander Cozens, together with his explanatory text. The department has long had an interest in acquiring fine Goyas, and it now owns some 120 trial proofs for the various series, a set of the Caprichios bound for the artist, and an impression of the rare Giant, as well as a number of drawings. The department is also known for its trial proofs by Turner and Constable. Another strength is in 19C lithography, with a collection ranging from the early experiments of German professionals and English amateurs through the great prints of Daumier, Delacroix, Géricault, Manet, Degas, Toulouse-Lautrec, Gauguin, Redon, Bonnard, and Vuillard, and includes posters by great designers such as Steinlen, Mucha, and Will Bradley. The department also has a number of fine prints by Matisse, Villon, Munch, Kollwitz, and the German Expressionists, as well as a complete Vollard Suite by Picasso. In recent years the department has been acquiring the work of major contemporary printmakers such as Rauschenberg, Johns, Ruscha, and Dine, along with those of lesser-known artists.

The drawing and watercolor collection of some 25,000 works ranges from the 15C to modern times. The most important large groups are by Blake, the Tiepolos, Millet, Homer, Prendergast, John Singer Sargent, and the great M. and M. Karolik Collection of American Drawings and Watercolors, 1800–75, which comprises some 3000 works. The bequest of Forsyth Wickes, which included 79 French drawings and watercolors of the 18C, has greatly enriched the collection. Also represented in the collection are the drawings of major artists such as Dürer, Rembrandt, Goya, Daumier, and Picasso. Books illustrated by printmakers are an integral part of the print collection. The rare-book collection now comprises about 5000 illustrated volumes, ranging from the 15C to the present.

The department has a small but growing collection of original photographs. The two most important groups are the Southworth and Hawes daguerreographs and the Stieglitz photographs. The collection includes the works of photographers of the 19C and early 20C, such as Gertrude Käsebier, Hill and Adamson, Frederick Evans, and Alvin Langdon Coburn. In addition, the department continues to purchase works by contemporary photographers.

The room next to the print galleries beside the front staircase houses the museum's *Collection of Musical Instruments.* The collection numbers about 1000, and among the outstanding early pieces are 11 keyboard, nine wind, and three string instruments. Many are in playing condition, and the collection offers the best source in the U.S. for the study of the evolution of keyboard instruments. The MFA is one of the first museums in the U.S. to have a major portion of its musical-instruments collection restored to playing condition and made available for study; and the first to employ musicians who perform on a regular basis. Each year, from Oct. to the end of May, the Musical Instruments Collection presents weekly concerts performed on instruments in the collection or similar to those in the museum. In addition, the collection offers courses in the history and playing of early instruments and in the construction of copies of instruments used before 1800, such as clavichords, lutes, recorders, and viols.

The next part of the itinerary covers the Dept. of American Decorative Arts and Sculpture, whose exhibition area begins in the long corridor leading E. from the Lower Rotunda.

Department of American Decorative Arts and Sculpture

Although this department was not founded until 1977, for a century before that the MFA had been acquiring American-made objects of artistic merit and historical significance. One of the great strengths of the department lies in New England products prior to the Civil War, including silver, furniture, glass, pewter, ceramics, metalware, sculpture, and folk art. The silver collection includes over 500 works from the 17–18C and a selection of 19C church silver. Master works by 17C joiners and early 19C cabinetmakers form the nucleus of the museum's outstanding collection. During 1934–65 the M. and M. Karolik Collection greatly added to the holdings of early American folk art and 18C furniture. Recent acquisitions of American sculpture, glass, ceramics, and pewter supplement the museum's important holdings in those areas. Some of the 19C sculptures are exhibited in galleries not belonging to the department, while many American paintings are hung in the exhibit areas of American Decorative Arts. Only a few paintings not listed in the previous tour will be described below. Much of the museum's collection of antique furniture is exhibited in Period Rooms, along with other objects of daily use.

(*Note.* In describing this and the Dept. of European Decorative Arts and Sculpture, the same system of room numbers will be used as in the tours through the Egyptian and Classical collections; area maps using these numbers are posted at several points in the exhibit areas. In the description given below, only the most outstanding and interesting exhibits will be mentioned.)

The first section of the long corridor leading eastward from the Lower Rotunda is ROOM I-15. At the beginning of the corridor on the l. is a huge painting by John Singleton Copley, depicting George IV, when Prince of Wales, c. 1804–9 (25.98). The wall cases have examples of colonial American silver as well as fabrics and gold objects from pre-Columbian Central and South America. At the end of Room I-15 is the pinewood entryway of a house that once stood in Hatfield, Mass.; this was built c. 1722 by Lieutenant Elihu Page and in 1812 became a tavern.

Beyond the entryway the corridor becomes known as ROOM I-19; this is the principal exhibit area for the museum's collection of American silver, and the first of many rooms used to display its very extensive collection of Early American furniture. The exhibits are moved and rotated from time to time, and so no attempt will be made in this guide to locate them in any particular gallery. The following are some of the most outstanding and interesting works in the museum's collections of Early American silver and furniture.

American Silver. The most famous work in the collection is the Liberty Bowl (49.45), a silver punchbowl made in Boston by Paul Revere in 1768 for 15 Sons of Liberty, whose names are engraved around the rim. The bowl was commissioned by them to honor 92 members of the Massachusetts House of Representatives who refused to rescind a circular letter to the colonies protesting the Townshend Acts, and on its side there is an inscription to this effect. Two other works by Paul Revere in the collection are, a gilt-lined silver goblet (35.1769), Boston, 1782, and a silver coffee urn (60.1419), Boston, 1793. There are also two masterpieces by John Coney, the renowned goldsmith; these are: a silver chocolate pot (1976.771), Boston, 1710–22, the only example of its type in Early American silver, and a sugar box (13.421), Boston, 1680–90, one of the most intricate and elaborate works in the collection. Another very important piece of early American silver is a standing-salt (32.371), Boston, 1690–1700, by Jeremiah Dummer, Boston's first native goldsmith. Other outstanding works in silver from the colonial and Early Federal periods are: a tankard (37.263), Boston, c. 1670–80, made by Robert Sanderson, the earliest American silversmith whose work is known; a salver (31.227), Boston, c. 1680, Timothy Dwight; a pair of candlesticks (54.594–5), Boston, c. 1695–1700, John Noyes, rare and handsome examples of 17C American silverwork, engraved with the Bowdoin family crest; a teakettle on stand (1971.347a&b), Boston 1730–40, Jacob Hurd, the only published New England colonial work of its kind, originally owned by the Rev. John Lowell; a teapot (1971.50), Boston, c. 1760, Zachariah Brigden; and a coffeepot (56.589), Philadelphia, c. 1770–80, Richard Humphries, among the most beautiful examples of its kind in existence. Another piece of historic interest is a silver bowl (13.560), worked in Newburyport and Boston, 1811, by Ebenezer Moulton. The bowl is engraved with a scene showing a fire brigade fighting a conflagration in a colonial meetinghouse, an event identified by the following inscription; "To Mr Isaac Harris / For his intrepid and successful exertions / on the roof of the Old South Church / when on fire December 29th 1810 / The Society presents this token of their / GRATITUDE / Boston / January 29, 1811."

American Furniture. The maker of each piece is given, if known.) Joined chest (29.1015) of oak and pine, Ipswich, Mass., 1665–70, attributed to William Searle; chest-on-chest (1973.289), mahogany with white pine, Boston, 1782, John Cogswell; chest-on-chest (41.580), mahogany, ebony, satinwood, and white pine, Salem, Mass., 1796, cabinetwork attributed to William Lemon, carving attributed to Samuel McIntire; Grecian couch (one of a pair) (19.776), rosewood trimming on maple, Boston, 1815–25, originally purchased by Nathan Appleton for his mansion at 39 Beacon St; wainscot armchair (37.316), red oak, Ipswich-Rowley area, 1680–90; press cupboard (32.251), oak and pine, Ipswich, c. 1680–90, attributed to Thomas Dennis; chest (32.216), oak and pine, Enfield, Conn., c. 1714, carved in large letters with the name MARY PEASE, and thus attributed to her father, John Pease, Jr., a joiner, who presumably made it for his daughter's wedding in 1714; high chest on frame (32.227), japanned maple and pine, Boston, c. 1725–40; desk and bookcase (39.176), walnut, Boston, c. 1730; armchair (60.31), walnut, Philadelphia, 1740–50; side chair (1971.280), mahogany, Newport, Rhode Island, c. 1760; bureau table (41.579), mahogany, Newport, Rhode Island, c. 1765–75, Edmund Townsend; tea table (41.592), mahogany, Boston, c. 1760–80; desk and bookcase (56.1194), Boston, c. 1780, George Bright; speaker's desk (63.112), mahogany veneer on pine with satinwood inlay, Annapolis, Maryland, c. 1797, used in the Maryland State House, probably in the House of Representatives, John Shaw; card table (23.16), mahogany and satinwood, Salem, c. 1796, Samuel McIntire; commode (23.19), mahogany and satinwood, Boston, 1809, Thomas Seymour; side chair (61.1074), ash and hickory, Boston, c. 1810–20, Samuel Gragg, considered to be the finest piece of its kind in the U.S.; card table (58.19), mahogany, New York, c. 1810–20, attributed to Duncan Phyfe; pier table (1972.652), mahogany and chestnut with mirror back and marble top, Boston, c. 1813–25, Emmons and Archibald.

In addition to silver and furniture, Room I-22 also has some interesting photographs of early colonial tombstones, from graveyards in Boston and elsewhere in New England.

The exhibition of early American furniture continues in ROOM I-21, the gallery parallel to Room I-21, and extends on into ROOM I-26, the first gallery along the E. side of the Evans Wing. Both of these rooms are also hung with American paintings, most of them portraits of figures prominent in the early history of Boston.

All the galleries beyond Room I-26 on the E. side of the Evans Wing belong to the Dept. of European Decorative Arts and Sculpture; most of the exhibits in this wing, which comprises Rooms I-27 through I-32, are from the collections of English furniture and silver. Most of the objects exhibited here, as in many of the museum's galleries, are rotated and shifted from time to time, and so the account that follows, for the most part, will simply list the more outstanding objects from the collections. Much of the silver collection is in Room I-28.

One of the most distinguished pieces of English furniture in the collection s presently in Room I-27 a *lady's writing table with fire screen* (1974.423), 1800–5. Brilliant satinwood with inlays in rich brown purpleheart have been combined to create this Early Regency masterpiece. Although it was based on a Sheraton design, the unknown craftsman who made this piece added original touches of his own. Another notable example of 18C English decorative arts in this collection is a gilded pine *girandole* (34.1325), or ornamental, branched candleholder, c. 1765. This is one of a pair of rococo girandoles that follow in their major details Plate 178 in Thomas Chippendale's *Gentleman and Cabinet-Maker's Directory* of 1762, though they have been enriched by the addition of the fantastic crowning birds. (Other pieces of English furniture are on display on Floor Two, and are described below along with other works in the Dept. of European Decorative Arts and Sculpture.)

The following are some of the more outstanding pieces of English silver in the collection: jewel casket (53.2375), made of silver and tortoise shell, mid-15C; Charles II tray, London, 1669, one of the few large decorative silver trays of its period that have survived, with a central scene in relief of Nessus and Deianeira, probably from a composition by Rubens or one of his followers; a pedestal salt (51.1618), silver gilt and rock crystal, London, 1587–88, decorated with typical 16C mannerist ornamental caryatids, in the center a group of amorini dancing around Venus, who is holding a wreath, and on top the figure of a bagpiper as the finial and handle for the cover; hourglass (59.533), silver gilt, c. 1525–50; cake basket (65.2307), London, 1744, made by Paul de Lamerie, a Huguenot refugee, decorated in the French rococo style with rich combinations of floral motifs, cherub heads, caryatids, shells, and feet with masks and rococo ornaments, with the arms of the Duke of Montrose in beribboned garlands; a pair of candlesticks (66.436-7), silver gilt, made by Paul Storr (1771–1844); and a ewer and basin (1979.261-2), parcel gilt silver, signed "PM" and dated 1567, inscribed with an ambitious iconographic theme which depicts every English sovereign from William the Conqueror to Elizabeth I, with scenes from the Old Testament. There are also two superb pieces of Irish silver in the collection. One of these is the Emly Shrine, also known as the Monsel of Tervos, (52.1396), a reliquary of silver inlay, gold cloisonné enamel and gilt bronze on yew wood, dating from c. A.D. 800. This is one of the rare surviving works of pre-Carolingian Anglo-irish culture; reliquary shrines of this type were suspended on a strap and worn like a pendant. The second is a silver racing trophy (1973.482), Dublin, 1751, made by William Williamson and engraved by Charles Pomarede. The horse race commemorated by this trophy is shown in a scene that encircles the bowl, and the arms of the competitors embrace the following inscription: "A prospect of the great Match Run on the Curragh Sept. 5th 1751 for 1000 guineas between Black and All Black belonging to the Hon. Sr Ralph Gore and Bajazit the Property of the Rt Hon. the Earl of March won with ease by the former."

Other objects of interest in these galleries are: in Room I-27, a case filled with Wedgwood ware, and two cases with stoneware ornamental pieces made by Josiah Wedgwood; and Room I-29, the reconstructed parlor from Woodcote Park, the manor house of Lord Baltimore, Epsom, Surrey, designed in the rococo style by Isaac Ware, c. 1750.

The galleries at the W. end of the Evans Wing on the Fenway side all belong to the Dept. of American Decorative Arts and Sculpture. The gallery at the corner of the building, ROOM I-33, is principally devoted to a display of American furniture in the Federal and Empire styles. There is also a marble statue entitled *Pandora* (1979.200), a work done in 1863 by the American sculptor Chauncy B. Ives. Room I-33 is also hung with pictures from the collection of American paintings, as are the next four galleries along the Fenway side of the museum, ROOMS I-34 through I-37, with the latter galleries also having a number of pieces from the collection of American furniture. There are also a number of antique American clocks, the finest of which is in ROOM I-35, a timepiece (27.585) of gilt and painted pine made in 1790 by Simon Willard.

Opening off to the l. of Rooms I-35 through I-37 are ROOMS I-38 through I-40. These have been used to reconstruct three rooms from Oak Hill, a mansion that once stood in Danvers, Mass. Oak Hill was built in 1800—1 for Nathaniel West and his wife, Elizabeth, daughter of the Salem shipping magnate Elias Hasket Derby.

The mansion is thought to have been designed and built by Samuel McIntire, to whom also is attributed the interior woodwork. The MFA acquired the interior of the mansion in 1921, when it was slated for demolition, and these three rooms were reconstructed in their present galleries in 1928, undergoing refurbishing in 1980. Room I-38 is the dining room of the mansion, I-39 is the parlor, and I-40 is a bedroom; signs outside each of the rooms identify all of the furnishings, decorations, and other objects within. The silk hangings used for the upholstery and window hangings correspond with the documentary evidence of the "orange damask curtains" listed in Elizabeth Derby West's 1814 inventory.

After seeing the Oak Hill rooms, return to the corner of the building and take the stairs down to the lower level, where the early *American Period Rooms* are located. ROOM 0-34, at the bottom of the stairs, has a number of interesting works of American decorative art. First there are the following sculptures by American artists: a marble statue entitled *Water-Lily Girl,* 1914 (16.96), by Bela Pratt; a bronze statue of the *Young Diana,* 1924 (1979.121), by Anna Hyatt Huntington; and these works by Augustus Saint-Gaudens: seven portrait-busts in low relief, of which the most interesting is one in plaster of *John Singer Sargent,* 1880 (57.41); a bronze *head of Victory,* 1907 (1977.600); and a stained-glass and leaded roundel called *The Fish,* c. 1890 (69.1224). Facing the stairway there is a six-paneled stained-glass window (1974.498a-f) done c. 1878 by John LaFarge; this was made for the William Watts Sherman Mansion in Newport, Rhode Island, designed in 1874 by H. H. Richardson. There is also a display case with samples of New England pottery of the early 20C.

Beyond Room 0-34, along the Fenway side of the museum, there are three galleries. The first of these is ROOM 0-35, devoted to 19C American sculpture; next is ROOM 0-36, in which there has been reconstructed a parlor from the Dodd House, built on Salem St, in the North End of Boston, in 1803, with samples of American neoclassical furniture.

Go on into ROOM 0-30, the first gallery along the E. side of the Evans Wing on the ground floor. The exhibits here are principally samples of Early American furniture and folk art, including some marvelous weathervanes and wooden figurines. To the l. is ROOM 0-31, now temporarily closed, which houses the museum's excellent collection of ship models.

Opening off from the inner corner of Room 0-30, in behind the stairwell, is a series of small galleries, the first of which has a very fine collection of Early American glass and pewter. Beyond this is the reconstructed parlor from the Schumway House in Fiskedale, Mass., c. 1740. Next is the parlor of the Mansfield House in Marblehead, Mass., c. 1743, with a display of 18C American furniture, glass, and ceramics. After this comes the parlor of the George Shepard House, Bath, Maine, c. 1803; and beyond that is a small room with an exhibit of Early American folk art.

Return to Room 0-30, and continue to the series of Period Rooms beyond that on the E. side of the Evans Wing. The first is ROOM 0-29, with the reconstructed parlor of the George Jaffrey House in Portsmouth, New Hampshire, c. 1740, with furniture mostly in the Queen Anne style. Next is ROOM 0-28, the Essex County Room, devoted to Early American furniture and glassware. Opening off to the l. here are two Period Rooms, furnished with objects from several colonial houses in Essex County; the first has Queen Anne furniture of 1725—60, and the second is furnished in William and Mary style, with pieces from 1695 to 1725. ROOM 0-27 has a hall from the Brown-Pearl House, West Boxford, Mass., c. 1704, with 17C furniture; the heavy oak structural framing, the paneling, the leaded-glass windows, and the fireplace are typical of New England houses of this early period. Beyond this is ROOM 0-26, the main hall from the Manning House, Ipswich, Mass., c. 1675, with the architectural framework assembled from the original structure, and with more 17C furniture.

This tour of the Period Rooms finishes at a small anteroom at the foot of the stairs; this belongs to the Dept. of European Decorative Arts and Sculpture, whose office is straight ahead. This room has a small, select display of English decorative arts, including some particularly fine gold and silver ware of the 17C. To the r. is the Textile Study Room; those wishing to inspect some of the works stored here should apply to the Dept. of Textiles.

Some statues in the collection of the Dept. of American Decorative Arts and Sculpture are presently displayed elsewhere in the museum. Two by William Wetmore Story flank the entrance to the Tapestries Gallery from the Upper Rotunda; on the l. is Venus, 1864 (88.329), and on the r. Bacchus, 1863 (88.328). There are more American sculptures at the rear of the Evans Wing on the first floor; to see them take either of the corridors that lead around toward the Fenway entrance to the museum (now closed). At the ends of both of these corridors there are large marble statues of female figures. On the l. is Jochebed, the mother of Moses (10.114), done in Rome in 1873 by Franklin Simmons; and on the r. is Sappho (1977.772), Rome, 1863, W. W. Story. Another group of sculptures is located at the foot of the stairs leading down to the ground floor of the Evans Wing, at its center. At the lower landing there are marble busts in niches on either side; on the l. is an allegorical representation of Faith (1965.70), c. 1873; and on the r. is Eve (1907.714), both works of Hiram Powers. In the corridor at the foot of the stairway are grouped six marble sculptures. These are, starting from the l. and going around in the clockwise direction: Nydia, the Blind Girl of Pompeii (1973.617), Rome, 1856, Randolph Rogers; Orpheus and Cerberus (1975.800), Rome, 1839, Thomas Crawford, a work first exhibited in 1844 in Boston, where its very favorable reception marked the beginning of Crawford's success and the awakening of popular interest in American neoclassical sculpture; a large marble relief cameo of Castor and Pollux (92.2642), Florence, c. 1845—47, by Horatio Greenough (according to mythology, the brothers Castor and Pollux in their afterlife dwelt alternately in Hades and heaven; the relief depicts them on horseback as they pass one another en route); Christ (24.118), Rome, c. 1886, William Wetmore Story; The Sleeping Fawn (12.709), Rome, c. 1865, Harriet Hosmer; and Young Columbus (71.8), Rome, 1871, Giulio Monteverdi.

This completes the tour of the Dept. of American Decorative Arts and Sculpture. But before going on, one might take this opportunity to examine the Hemicycle, the monumental entrance hall at the Fenway side of the Evans Wing. From the first floor a grand double staircase curves upward to the upper floor, where there is a semicircular loggia formed by an impressive colonnade of Ionic columns supporting a semidome. At the center of the balustrade of the loggia a large tablet commemorates Robert Dawson Evans (1843–1909), husband of Marie Antoinette Evans, who contributed the funds to build the Evans Wing in his name.

The final tour of the museum covers the Dept. of European Decorative Arts and Sculpture. Begin by going to the Upper Rotunda, and then walk eastward through Room II-15 to the gallery at its far end; this is Room II-23, the first gallery to be visited on this last tour.

The Department of European Decorative Arts and Sculpture

This department, organized in 1908, is concerned principally with the decorative arts and sculpture of Europe in the broadest sense, ranging from the 6C A.D., the end of antiquity, to the mid-20C. When the department was first formed the bulk of its holdings consisted of the Wales Collection of European Ceramics, significant examples of Italian Renaissance sculpture, and the extraordinary carved gilt panels designed by Ledoux for the Hôtel de Montmorency in Paris. In the years that followed, the department broadened its holdings, strengthening especially its medieval collections along with baroque sculpture and decorative arts. The department has a relatively comprehensive collection of English silver (see above), ranging in date from the 15C to the 19C, as well as a smaller but growing collection of English furniture, 18–19C. There is also a distinguished collection of French decorative arts of the 18C, much of which came from the Swan Collection and the bequest of Forsyth Wickes. Another strength is English porcelain of the 18C, much of it from the Paine and Katz Collections, which have made the MFA a major international source for the study and enjoyment of this field. Besides these, the museum's collection of Chinese export porcelain remains the responsibility of the department, as does the Musical Instruments Collection. At the present new directions are being pursued, particularly as regards 19C sculpture and in strengthening the department's holdings of English furniture of the 18–19C.

ROOM II-23 is devoted to Northern European Decorative Arts and Sculpture. (The gallery to the l. of this, ROOM II-21 is devoted to Southern European Decorative Arts and Sculpture.) Just to the l. of the entryway is a polychromed wood statue of the *Crucified Christ* (51.1405); this masterpiece of the late 11C is thought to be from Reichenhall, near Salzburg. Another outstanding work is on a pedestal a short way along on the l.; this is a pillar carved with the figures of a *Deacon and Acolytes* (47.1290), done in 1264–67 by Nicolo Pisano in collaboration with Arnolfo Cambio and Fra Guglielmo. This pillar, along with its companion piece in the National Museum in Florence, originally supported the tomb of St. Domenic in Bologna. A little farther along on the r. are two statues standing back to back; in front is a polychrome poplar figure of St. John (67.767), 14C; and behind a limestone representation of St. Malo (54.797), Normandy, c. 1250. In a wall case to the r. there are two superbly carved *oliphants* (57.581, 50.3426) from S. Italy, possibly Salerno, dating to the late 11C. During the Middle Ages elephant tusks were imported in great quantity from India and Africa to the ports of Italy, to be fashioned into oliphants (hunting and signal horns) and drinking vessels; the pair here were probably tenure horns, which were blown to symbolize and testify to the legal transfer of land. Across from this, on the l. side of the room, is a splendid *saddle* (69.944), made of polychromed bone with birch-bark binding, from the Italian Tyrol, c. 1450. The saddle is decorated in the Gothic style with figures in low relief, including a scene of St. George slaying the dragon; an inscription in German reads, "Think before you leap." Past the center of the room on the r. is a beautiful statuette of the *Virgin and Child* (57.583), a Lombardo-Emilian work of the late 12C; the Virgin here is of a familiar Byzantine type known in Greek as *glykophilousa*, "The Sweetly Kissing Mother of God." Farther along on the l. is a remarkable bronze *aquamanile* (40.233), or pouring vessel, fashioned as a group of Daniel and the Lion; this dates from c. 1240 and comes from the parish church in Achern, between Strasbourg and Baden-Baden. A wall case just beyond this has a number of liturgical pieces in precious materials, including a small relief representing the *Baptism of Christ* (50.858), a work of champlevé enamel and gilded copper, embossed and engraved; this is from Limoges, first half of the 13C, and originally formed part of an altar frontal or retable. A little farther along to the r. is a lovely statue of the *Virgin and Child on the Crescent Moon* (65.1354), carved from a single piece of poplar wood, polychromed and gilded, lower Austria, c. 1450–60. This is one of the finest extant examples of the Gothic type known as Schoenen Madonnen, here represented as the apocryphal Virgin standing on the sickle moon. Against the wall to the r. is a remarkable relief in polychromed alabaster representing the *Holy Trinity,* an English work, possibly from Nottingham, first half of the 15C. The seated figure of God the Father enfolds in his bosom the naked souls of the righteous, among them a king and a bishop, with the crucified Christ between his knees, while carved on the base are the kneeling figures of two donors; the dove of the Holy Ghost, the third figure of the Trinity, is now missing. At the center of the rear wall is a surpassingly beautiful statue of the *Virgin and Child* (59.701) in polychromed and gilded oak, an early 13C work from the Ile-de-France. It has been suggested that this masterpiece was created by the same sculptor who carved certain figures on the N. transept of Chartres Cathedral.

Leave Room II-23 by the door at the far left-hand corner, and turn r. there to emerge on the landing at the head of the stairs, ROOM II-26, the first of four galleries devoted to Baroque and Renaissance Sculpture and Decorative Arts. (At this corner of the building there are two other small galleries; to the r. is ROOM II-24, Late Medieval Sculpture and Decorative Arts, and opening off from that is the Tudor Room.)

Turn l. on entering Room II-26. On a pedestal to the l. beside the door is a superb bronze statuette of *St. Christopher* (51.412); this is from Florence and is dated to 1407 by an inscription on the sole of the r. foot.

This figure is the earliest dated Renaissance statuette known, and as such it is highly important in the study of the development of Florentine art of the Quattrocento. Rubbed areas on the head and l. shoulder of the figure indicate that he bore a Christ Child, cast as a separate figure, and a piece of bronze in his r. hand is part of a walking staff. The statuette suggests the spirit and style of the first generation of Florentine sculptors of the Renaissance, Brunelleschi, Ghiberti, and Nanni di Banco. Some authorities find the figure to be so closely related to the documented bronzes of Brunelleschi as to suggest that it might be by his hand.

A short way along on the l. on the wall is an icon of ethereal beauty representing the *Madonna of the Clouds* (17.1470), by Donatello, done in Florence c. 1425–28. (This is also called the Shaw Madonna, after its donor, Quincy A. Shaw.) This early masterpiece by Donatello is one of his very few authenticated works in the U.S. In creating this icon, Donatello used an original technique called *rilievo schiacciato*—very low relief with incised forms—which allowed him to create the illusion of space around the Madonna, who is surrounded by angels and putti. A little farther along on the same wall there are two lovely reliefs in tin-glazed earthenware attributed to Luca della Robbia, both done in Florence c. 1460–70. The first depicts the *Madonna and Child* (no number), and the second represents the *Madonna and Child with Angels* (17.1476); the latter is also called the Madonna of the Lilies, because the Virgin is holding out the Child so that he can touch a lily plant. On the r., at the end of the room divider, there is a unique and charming *portrait-bust of a lady* (54.146), who is shown smiling pleasantly, garbed in brightly colored clothes, and wearing a necklace. This is a Tuscan work, from either Florence or Caffagiolo, c. 1500, and it is one of the very rare secular portrait-busts of its time to survive. Against the wall to the r., just beyond the room divider, is a magnificent *bancone* (62.7), a table made in Florence c. 1550. The bancone, which is attributed to Giovanni Angelo Montorsoli, is made of richly carved walnut, adorned with the figures of mermaids at its four corners. It came from a palace in Palermo, and takes its name from the fact that it was used as a money-exchange desk.

Aside from the rotating exhibition of European paintings that hang in this and the other galleries in this wing, the other art works of greatest merit are to be seen toward the far end of the room. On pedestals along the r. wall near the corner there are two superb statuettes. The first is an extraordinary statuette of the *Emperor Hadrian* (1972.354), whose torso is made of calcite crystal, with a base of matching calcite marble, and with his head and hands in gilt bronze. The Emperor's body is a Graeco-Roman work of late antiquity, c. 4C A.D. ; marble base and the gilt bronze head and hands were added when the statuette was repaired in Italy c. 1550. The second statuette is a bronze personification of *Architecture* (40.23), represented as a naked maiden holding a board in her l. hand and in her r. the symbolic tools of the architect, the compass, protractor, and carpenter's square. This graceful figurine, which dates to c. 1570, is signed by Giovanni Bologna. Another outstanding sculpture is to be seen on a pedestal directly across the room to the l.; this is a bronze bust of *Cleopatra* (64.2174), from Mantua, a work of Pier Jacopo Alari Bonacolsi, called "Antico" (c. 1460–1528). This "Boston Cleopatra," as it is called, is believed to be a companion piece for three bronze busts in Vienna: Ariadne, Bacchus, and Antinoüs, all of them made by Antico for the small study of Isabella d'Este in Mantua.

The most prominent exhibit in ROOM II-27 is at the center of the wall to the r. of the entryway. This is a monumental French *chimneypiece* (48.371) of limestone, c. 1560, one of the finest works of its kind that has survived from the mid-16C.

The chimneypiece is from the Château de Bourgen-Vexin, owned by the Marquise de Boury; it is decorated with superb sculptures in relief, of which the most striking is the figure of Judith holding the head of Holofernes, in the panel to the l., while Joshua is depicted to the r. They are represented as victorious heroes of the Old Testament; in the center, Joshua, in the war against Gideon, slays the five kings brought out of the cave (Joshua 1:20–26). During the late Renaissance in Italy and France the chimneypiece of a great house was regarded as a piece of monumental sculpture rather than a work of interior decoration, as is shown by the quality of the example here, which is thought to have been created by a follower of Jean Goujon.

In front of the chimneypiece there are two bronze andirons (57.8), French works of c. 1530, and in the corner to the l. there is an alabaster relief depicting the *Adoration of the King* (41.219), Spanish school of Burgos, c.

1525–30. Against the side wall to the l. of this is a marble statue of *St. Joseph* (48.257), a Florentine work of the 16C, attributed to Giovanni Angelo Montorsoli.

Another prominent exhibit is the sculpture in the center of the room (68.583 a–f); this is a group in cast bronze and beaten copper, with God the Father standing on the Globe of the World supported by the four Evangelists. This was done c. 1591 by Girolamo Campagna, and was a model for the centerpiece of the high altar in the church of San Giorgio Maggiore in Venice.

Aside from the European paintings, the other exhibits of interest are mostly in the wall cases on the l. side of the room. The most noteworthy of these are three objects in the last three cases along that wall. In the first of these three cases there is an *oval platter* (60.8) of lead enameled earthenware, a work of the French artisan Bernard Palissy (c. 1510–90). This is a sample of Palissy's famous platters in the *style rustique,* made up of casts from plants, animals, reptiles, and insects; the objects in the open dish, an undulating snake surrounded by a fish, frog, shells, and leaves, are glazed in imitation of their natural colors, while the earth is mottled in several shades, a process perfected by Palissy. In the next case there is a glittering model of the *Crucifixion* (57.664), made of rock crystal, silver, gilt bronze, and semiprecious stones; this is a late-17C work thought to be from Augsburg. And in the last case there is a remarkable object called the *Nautilus Beaker* (63.1256), a vessel in the form of a lavishly decorated nautilus shell with silver mounts. The beaker was made in the Hague for Admiral Gansneb Tengnagel in 1659, with the present silver stand added in 1700. On the inner shell in ajouré is the admiral's coat-of-arms; on the outer shell are engraved figures from the commedia dell'arte, after prints by Jacques Callot. In the far corner of the gallery to the r. is the marble statue of a knight (44.813) kneeling in prayer, a work of Pompeo Leoni (c. 1530–1609).

In ROOM II-28 the most famous exhibits are the *boiseries* (79.326–9), four carved oak panels nearly 12ft high, painted in watercolors and gilt on gesso. These were taken from a salon in the Hôtel de Montmorency in Paris, where they formed part of the wall decoration designed by Claude-Nicolas Ledoux between 1770 and 1772. Depicted in relief are classical nymphs, cupids, trophies of arms, musical instruments, and shields with the interlaced initials "MO" (for "Montmorency"). The extremely fine modeling, chasing, and gilding, as well as the imposing size and elegant proportions, mark these panels as outstanding examples of French art in the Louis XVI style.

The remarkable ceiling decoration in Room II-28, an oil painting on canvas, is from the Mocenigo Palace in Venice, c. 1755–60. The allegorical scene depicts Dawn, in the person of Aurora, seated in the clouds above, accompanied by a winged female figure and putti, dispersing the Clouds of Night below.

Among the many samples of European decorative arts in the gallery, three in particular seem worthy of notice. In the center of the wall to the r. of the entry there is an exceedingly handsome French *commode* (1925.79) of unusual size and exaggerated serpentine form, made of various woods veneered on oak with gilt-bronze mounts and modern marbleized top. This masterpiece was made c. 1735 and is attributed to Gilles Joubert, who was cabinetmaker to the King in 1763–74. The *lady's writing desk* (65.2506) in the center of the room is an elegant work of veneered red, gold, and black lacquer, its surfaces decorated with gold chinoiserie scenes on a brightly lacquered red background; its interior is of tulipwood, with a gold-tooled writing surface. This piece was made in Paris c. 1760 by Pierre Macret, an important cabinetmaker to Louis XV. The third outstanding exhibit is a very charming terra-cotta group, *Three Dancing Figures* (65.2212), a work done in 1800 by Claude Michel, better known as Clodion.

ROOM II-29 is the last of the four galleries in this wing devoted to Baroque Sculpture and Decorative Arts. Aside from the European paintings, the most outstanding exhibits here are three sculptures, all of which are in the area to the r. of the entryway. On a pedestal just to the r. of the entry is a marble statuette of *Maximillian II Emanuel of Bavaria* (59.177), done after 1714 by Giuseppi Volpini, although some authorities attribute it to Wilhelm de Graff. The second sculpture of note is to the r. of the entry; this a polychromed limewood *statuette of St. John* (1972.46), done by an anon. Austrian sculptor c. 1740. This statuette, which is a most important example of 18C Austrian baroque sculpture, was originally part of a group representing St. John supporting the Virgin fainting under the Cross. The third sculpture is on a pedestal a short way along the side wall to the r. This is a statue of the *Madonna of Victory* (61.1185), made of Schrezheim faience, white-glazed, with contours and certain features purposely left unglazed.

This masterpiece of S. German religious rococo sculpture is signed and dated 1771 by Johann Martin Mutschele. The Madonna was commissioned by the Teutonic Knights to be placed under a canopy in the niche over the main door to their residence in Wolframs-Eschenbachs, the Prinzen Inn. Statues of this type were not merely pious ornaments; their function was to grant heavenly protection from evil both to the house and its inhabitants.

There are three more sculptures of some interest at the other end of the room, two of them flanking the axis of the gallery past its center, the other at the center of the rear wall. These are: (l.) a terra-cotta statue of the Virgin and Child (66.952), c. 1697–1700, attributed to Pietro Stefano Monnot; (center, rear), a statue of the Virgin (69.1283) in polychromed limestone, Munich, first half of the 17C, attributed to Hans Degler; (r.) a terra-cotta statue representing the Sacrifice of Abraham (58.335), a German work of the late 17C. The two cases along the middle of the wall to the l. contain other objects of interest. In the first of these there is a beautiful *crucifix* (1973.40), made of ebony and gilt bronze with ivory corpus, a Flemish work of c. 1625–30. In the case beyond that there is an interesting collection of terra-cotta bozetto figures, which were used as models by sculptors.

After leaving Room II-29, turn r. to enter ROOM II-32, the first of three small galleries on the corner of the building at the Fenway side. Room II-32 is used for changing exhibitions of European Glass and Jewelry, and the gallery beyond that, at the N.E. corner of the museum, houses the Helen Woolworth McCann Collection of Chinese Export Porcelain. The four galleries along the N. side of the Evans Wing on the Fenway side, ROOMS II-34 through II-37, are devoted to English and European Pottery and Porcelain.

Returning to Room II-32, turn r. and go past the stairwell into ROOM II-38, which houses the reconstituted *High Dining Room of Hamilton Palace,* Lanarkshire, Scotland. Construction of the palace began in 1591 and continued on into the next century. The palace was demolished in 1922, and in 1924 the MFA acquired the oak paneling, carved woodwork, and chimneypiece from the High Dining Room, all of them dating from c. 1700. The pieces of English furniture displayed in the room are not from Hamilton Palace but are similar to the originals, as are the other furnishings. The chimneypiece with its magnificent reliefs was carved in 1698–1700 by William Morgan of London. Notice also the delightful painted "Welcoming Figures" before the fireplace.

Room II-39 has been furnished and decorated to simulate a salon in Paris during the reign of Louis XVI (1774–92). The walls are of painted and gilded wood with Beauvais tapestry panels. The furnishing and decorations all date from the period of Louis XVI, except for older objects that one would expect to find in the salon of a wealthy and cultured Parisien, such as the pair of Chinese vases (30.523–4), which are from the K'ang Hsi period (1666–1722). The salon is also adorned with three works of sculpture: (l.) a bronze statuette (30.1974) of Perseus, by Corneille van Cleve (1645–1732); (r.) a bronze statuette (1962.668) of Odysseus Trying the Bow of Hercules, by Jacques Bousseau (1681–1740); and in the corner to the r., a faience bust of a nobleman (60.1397), a French or Danish work of the mid-18C.

A number of European sculptures are exhibited in other areas of the museum, particularly in the galleries belonging to the Dept. of Paintings. The following is a list of some of the most important European sculptures in the MFA that were not described previously.

European Sculptures. The more important works of European sculpture that were not previously described are as follows, in approximate chronological order: *The Virgin* (49.466), gilt-bronze statuette, eastern France, second half of the 12C; *Crowned Head* (47.1447), marble, Pisa, c. 1260–80, manner of Nicolo Pisano; *Plaque Depicting the Resurrection* (1973.690), ivory, Paris, c. 1300; *The Madonna of the Niche* (17.1475), glazed terra-cotta, Florence, c. 1448, Luca della Robbia; *Portrait Bust of a Hafner Master* (64.1), glazed polychromed terra-cotta (Hafner Ware), Salzburg, c. 1500; *Bust of a Prophet* (49.4), lindenwood, Augsburg, c. 1518, attributed to Sebastian Loscher (the only surviving example of a series of busts made for the stalls of the Fugger Chapel in Augsburg, 1512–18); *Death Triumphant* (55.988), fruitwood statuette, Lorraine (?), late 16C (the subject, taken from the Late Gothic "Dance of Death" is intended as a moral allegory); *Sleeping Endymion* (56.141), terra-cotta statuette, 1716, Agostino Cornacchini (this was a model for many bronze, marble, and porcelain versions of the subject); *Bust of Caracella* (1973.103), blue-and-white Delftware, 1718, attributed to David Kam, from the factory "De Paeaw" (The Peacock); two *Statues of Angels* (58.43, 44) (exhibited in the Upper Rotunda, flanking the entrance to the Tapestries Gallery), polychromed and gilt wood, Augsburg, Ehrgott Bernhard Bendl (1660–1738); *Horse Galloping on Right Foot* (1973.82), bronze, 1865–81, Edgar Degas; *The Little Dancer of 14 Years* (38.1756), bronze, 1880–81, Degas; *Man with a Broken Nose* (51.1923), 1863–64, Auguste Rodin; *"Les Premières Funérailles"* (59.92), small bronze group, c. 1900, Rodin; *Le Printemps* (37.1292), white marble bust, Paris, 1874, Jean-Baptiste Carpeaux; *"Soyez Amoureuses Vous Serez Heureuses"* (57.582), relief, in carved, polished, and polychromed lindenwood, c. 1889, Paul Gauguin; *Self-Portrait of a Warrior* (60.958), polychromed plastic, Vienna, 1908, Oskar Kokoschka; *Head of a Woman* (1976.821), bronze, 1904, Pablo Picasso; *The Golden Fish* (57.739), polished brass and steel, 1924, Constantin Brancusi; *Femme Qui Marche* (64.520), 1933–34, Alberto Giacometti; *Seated Figure Against Curved Wall* (54.477), bronze, Henry Moore.

The Forsyth Wickes Collection

One very important part of the Dept. of European Decorative Arts and Sculpture is the Forsyth Wickes Collection of 18C French Art, which is displayed in galleries on the first floor of the North Wing. It is named for Forsyth Wickes (1876–1965), an American of old New York stock who began collecting these works to furnish his home in Paris in 1925; in 1945 he bought a new home in Newport, Rhode Island, Starboard House, where he lived for the last 20 years of his life, adding to his collection all the while. When he died he left his collection of some 800 works of art to the Boston MFA, which kept them together under the aegis of the Dept. of European Decorative Arts and Sculpture. The collection includes Drawings and

Watercolors, Oil Paintings and Pastels, Porcelains, Sculpture, and Furniture, of which the most noteworthy are perhaps the following (the artists are all French, unless otherwise noted):

Drawings and Watercolors: *Four Studies of a Woman* (65.2610), drawing by Jean-Antoine Watteau (1684–1721); *Mascarade* (65.2572), drawing by Claude Gillot (1673–1733); *Young Woman with Two Cherubs* (65.2538), drawing by François Boucher (1703–70); *L'Entretien Galant* (65.2604), watercolor by Gabriel de Saint-Aubin (1724–80); *Petite Fille Endormie* (65.2592–93), drawing by Jean-Michel Moreau (1741–1814); *The Serapeum, Pozzuoli* (65.2601), drawing by Hubert Robert (1733–1808); *Madame Mère* (Mother of Napoleon I) (65.2555), drawing by Jacques-Louis David (1748–1825); *Cavaliers Anglais* (65.2606), watercolor by Carle Vernet (1758–1836); *La Promeneuse* (65.2608), drawing by Adélaide Labille-Guiard Vincent (1749–1803); *La Jolie Visiteuse* (65.2585), drawing by Jean-Baptiste Mallet (1759–1835); *Standing Nude* (65.2598), drawing by Pierre-Paul Prud'hon (1758–1823).

Oil Paintings and Pastels: *Le Déjeuner de Jambon* (65.2649), painting by Nicolas Lancret (1690–1745); *Jeune Femme au Ruban Bleu* (65.2664), pastel by Jean-Marc Nattier (1685–1766); *Le Jeune Ecolier* (65.2663), pastel, c. 1770, by Nicolas-Bernard Lépicié (1735–84); *Louis XV as a Boy* (65.2655), pastel by Rosalba Carriera (Venetian) (1675–1757); *Mademoiselle Hainaut* (65.2655), painting by François Hubery Drouais (1727–75); *L'Escalier des Lavandières*, 1796, painting by Hubert Robert; *The Earl of Huntington* (65.2652), c. 1735, painting by Jean-Baptiste Perronneau (1715–83).

Porcelains: *soup tureen and stand* (65.2026), sceaux faience, c. 1770; *soup tureen and stand from a service ordered by Catherine II of Russia* (65.1885), model by Jean-Claude Duplessis, decorators Dodin and Pierre, Vincennes porcelain, 1756; *pair of snail-shaped incense burners* (65.1859–60), Vincennes porcelain, ormulu mountings. c. 1775; *pair of flower holders and stands*, the so-called *Coventry Vases* (65.1799–1800), Sèvres porcelain, 1759; *ecuelle and tray* (65.1786), decorator Jean-Rene Dubois, "rose marbré de violet" Sèvres porcelain, 1761; *pair of vases, mounted as incense burners, made for Augustus the Strong* (65.2095), Meissen porcelain, decorated in the Chinese manner by Loewenfinck, c. 1728; *soup tureen with boar's-head finial and stand, painted with Turkish battle and camp scenes after Augsburg prints* (65.2072), Meissen porcelain, c. 1740–45; *incense burner in the form of Chinese figures astride an elephant* (65.2028), celadon Meissen porcelain, ormulu base, c. 1730; *Venus and Aeolus* (65.2105–6), models by Domenico Auliczek, Nymphenburg porcelain, mounted in ormulu candelabra, c. 1765.

Sculpture: *mantel clock* (65.2236), on fluted porcelain column, chased gilt-bronze figures of draped nude in the manner of Falconet holding two hearts and a miniature portrait (Marie Antoinette?), cupid and begging dog, marble base, ormulu mounts, dial inscribed "Ageron," Paris, c. 1779; *Louis XV* (65.2014), perhaps after a marble bust by Jean-Baptiste Lemoyne, made for Cardinal de Rohan of Strasbourg, white-glazed Ludwigsburg faience, 1746; *posthumous portrait of François de Lamotte Fenélon* (65.2213), terracotta, 1724, Jean-Louis Lemoyne (attributed) (1665–1755); *Mademoiselle Dangeville* (65.2219), terra-cotta, signed and dated 1752, Jean-Baptiste Defernex (1729–83); *Madame Olivier* (65.2218), terra-cotta, signed and dated 1774, Augustin Pajou (1730–1809); *Pygmaleon and Galatea* (65.1812), after Etienne-Maurice Falconet (1716–91), decorator Louis-Antoine Le Grand, biscuit group on royal-blue base, Sèvres porcelain, c. 1790; *Baigneuse* (65.2206), after Christophe-Gabriel Allegrain (1710–95), marble, c. 1780; *Two Bacchantes Dancing and Cupid* (65.2212), terra-cotta, signed and dated 1800, Claude Michel called Clodion (1738–1814); *Faunesse with Tambourine* (65.2221), terra-cotta, Joseph-Charles Marin (1759–1834); *Charles-François Fontaine de Bire* (65.2203), marble, signed and dated 1786, Jean-Antoine Houdon (1741–1828); *Madame M. Charpentier as a Painter* (65.2208), original plaster, signed, Joseph Chinard (1756–1813); *portrait bust of a man* (65.2216), terra-cotta, signed, Joseph Chinard; *Nereid Riding a Sea Monster* (65.2208), bronze, Florence, c. 1560.

Furniture: *lady's writing desk (bureau de dame)* (65.2506), veneered red, gold, and black lacquer with chinoiserie decoration, ormulu mounts, Pierre Macret, Paris (1727–96); *jewel and writing cabinet (bonheur-du-jour)* (65.2504), veneered kingwood and palisander wood with marquetry, ormulu mounts, Paris, c. 1750, a gift of Marie Antoinette to Princess Isabelle Lubomirsky, Joseph or Bernard van Risen Burgh (attributed); *Commode* (65.2513), veneered black lacquer with chinoiserie decoration, ormulu mounts, c. 1760; *imported Chinese incised lacquer cabinet on Charles II gilt-wood stand* (65.2528), London, late 17C; *commode* (65.2510), manner of Charles Cressent, veneered kingwood, inlaid with ebony and brass, ormulu mounts, Paris, c. 1745; *set of six fauteuils and canapé covered with Beauvais tapestry depicting fables after designs by Jean-Baptiste Oudry* (65.2495), beechwood, Paris, Louis XV period; *commode,* (65.2509), veneered kingwood inlaid with palisander wood, ormulu mounts, Louis XV period; *commode* (65.2515), veneered black lacquer with chinoiserie decoration, ormulu mounts, Paris, c. 1760; *guéridon* (table) (65.2503), veneered kingwood and tulipwood with marquetry decoration, ormulu mounts, Louis XV period; *écritoire* (writing desk), venerered harewood (mahogany), ormulu mounts, attributed to Jean-Henri Riesener, Paris, c. 1780.

Before leaving the museum, one might visit the new ***Japanese Garden,** which is just beyond the N. end of the West Wing. (When the garden is not open it can be viewed from the windows in the North Gallery, on the second floor.)

This is known in Japanese as Tenshin-en, the Garden of the Heart of Heaven; it was designed by Kinsaku Nakane of Kyoto, and it was dedicated on Oct. 24, 1988, in honor of Okakura Kakuzo, who was one of the first curators of the Dept. of Asiatic Art, a post he held from 1906 to 1913. The roofed gate and the wall of the garden were made by Japanese craftsmen according to time-honored traditions. In the garden, the raked gravel represents a vast body of water. Around it there are set more than 150 boulders from Boston's North Shore to create a landscape that has elements of both Japan and New England. The most prominent feature is a large rocky hill with a simulated waterfall of black stones running down its slope; this represents Mount Sumeru, which Japanese mythology holds to be the center of the universe; bridges cross to tiny islets known as Tortoise Island and Crane Island, mythical isles said to bring good fortune and immortality to those who looked upon them. The small mushroom-capped lantern near the water basin and the seven-storied Japanese pagoda are part of the MFA's Asiatic collection, and they were formerly on view in the little court garden in the Asiatic Wing. There are over 70 species of plants in the garden, both

American and Japanese. Cherries, Japanese maples, and pines are all sig-nature plants of a Japanese garden, evoking the changing seasons, while azaleas of many colors and varieties provide continual bloom from spring into summer, combining with haircap moss to form a soft and verdant ground cover. As Kinsaku Nakane said in 1987, the year before he completed this garden: "The idea behind this landscape is the recreation of the essence of mountains, the ocean, and islands in a garden setting, as I have seen them in the beautiful landscape of New England." And as Okakura Kakuzo wrote in *The Book of Tea* in 1906: "One who has trodden this garden path cannot fail to remember how his spirit . . . became uplifted above ordinary thoughts. One may be in the midst of a city, and yet feel as if one were . . . far away from the dust and din of civilization."

16 The Isabella Stewart Gardner Museum

The approach to the ****Isabella Stewart Gardner Museum** by public trans-port is the same as for the Museum of Fine Arts: i.e., take the Arborway branch of the Green Line and get off at the Ruggles-Museum stop. From there walk down Museum Rd, past the West Wing of the MFA; then turn l. on the Fenway, passing the Museum School. Follow the Fenway on its l. side as it curves to the r. after one has crossed the three intervening streets, the Gardner Museum is reached; enter by the door on the l. side of the building.

Admission. Open Tues. 12–6:30 (July & Aug. 12–5), Wed.–Sun. 12–5; fee (exc. Wed.). Guided tours are available. Sept.–June concerts are given Tues. at 6:30 & Sun. at 1:30 (tel. 566-1401, and 734-1359 for recorded information). There is a small but excellent cafeteria at the rear of the museum on the ground floor; in warm weather tables are set out in the garden, making this one of the most pleasant places to dine in Boston. There is also a sales desk at the rear on the ground floor with books on the various collections in the museum. One of these is an excellent, inexpensive, and indispensable guide, with maps of the gal-leries on the three floors.

History. The museum is the personal creation of Isabella Stewart Gardner, who began to acquire works of art as early as 1860, the year after her marriage to Jack Gardner. Her interest in collecting increased through friendships with such artists as James A. McNeill Whistler and John Singer Sargent, who in 1887 painted the portrait of her that now domi-nates the Gothic Room in the museum. With the death of her father in 1891, and an inher-itance of nearly two million dollars, Mrs. Gardner was at last able to embark on a career of serious collecting. In doing so, she relied heavily on the advice and assistance of Bernard Berenson, whom she had met when he was an undergraduate at Harvard, and from 1894 onward he purchased paintings for her in Europe. By that time Jack and Isabella Gardner were talking of building a museum to house their collection, and their first thought was to tear down their two adjoining houses on Beacon St and build it there. But eventually they decided that a location on the newly filled Back Bay Fens would be more suitable, and the present site was chosen late in 1898, shortly before the sudden death of Jack Gardner on Dec. 10 of that year. Mrs. Gardner purchased the plot early in 1899, and shortly afterward ground was broken for Fenway Court, the name she chose for her new museum. Mrs. Gardner then went off to Europe, to search for furniture and architectural elements for Fenway Court, in the meantime continuing to purchase works of art for her collection. She returned to Boston in Dec. 1899 to supervise the construction and design of Fenway Court, every minute detail of which was required to have her specific approval. By the close of

1901 Fenway Court was essentially complete, some of the sculptures were in place, and plants were growing in the courtyard, for Mrs. Gardner's passionate interest in art was only equaled by her love for flowers and music, both of which remain as integral elements of her museum today. Mrs. Gardner took up residence in Fenway Court in Dec. 1901, and on Christmas Eve of that year she and six members of her family attended an Anglican Mass in the chapel there.

During the year that followed, only a select few friends of Mrs. Gardner were admitted to Fenway Court, while she supervised the installation and arrangement of her collection. The formal opening of the museum came on the evening of Jan. 1, 1903, when guests were invited to Fenway Court to hear the Boston Symphony Orchestra play a Bach chorale. The public was admitted to Fenway Court for the first time a month later, and thereafter attendance was limited to 200 visitors a day for about a month each year. Mrs. Gardner continued to collect works of art and to supervise the activities of her museum until Dec. 1919, when she suffered a stroke. She lived on in her beloved Fenway Court until her death on July 17, 1924, after which she was waked for three days in the Chapel and then buried in Mount Auburn Cemetery beside her husband and her child. Her memorial is the museum that bears her name, and her epitaph might well be the phrase she had inscribed on the plaque above the main entrance to Fenway Court, with the symbol of a phoenix rising from its ashes, "C'est Mon Plaisir."

Thieves broke into the museum in the early morning hours of Sun., March 18, 1990, and stole 11 priceless artworks, including paintings by Rembrandt, Vermeer, Degas, and Manet. These works have not been recovered to date; the places where they were formerly exhibited bear the note "Stolen on 18 March 1990."

In view of the large number and great variety of the objects in the museum, the description that follows will mention only the most important and interesting. Those who wish more detailed information on any of the works in the collection can consult the Museum Guide or any of the books on the museum available at the sales desk.

After entering the museum, turn l. into the YELLOW ROOM. In the wall cases here there are memorabilia of famous musicians, singers, composers, and conductors, many of whom were friends of Mrs. Gardner. The most noteworthy paintings displayed here are: *Love's Greeting,* Dante Gabriel Rossetti (1828–82); *Madame Gaujelain,* 1867, Hilaire-Germain-Edgar Degas; *Nocturne, Blue and Silver; Battersea Reach,* James A. McNeill Whistler (1834–1903); *The Terrace, St. Tropez,* 1904, Henri Matisse; *The Round Tower,* c. 1817, James M. W. Turner.

On the r. side of the entrance lobby is the BLUE ROOM. The four cases contain letters to Mrs. Gardner from distinguished friends who were either authors, critics, or connoisseurs of art. The paintings and watercolors are all works of the 19–20C, many of them by artists who were friends or acquaintances of Mrs. Gardner, including four paintings by John LaFarge and four paintings and seven watercolors by John Singer Sargent. The most distinguished painting here is to be seen just to the l. of the doorway from the entrance lobby; this is by Edouard Manet, a portrait of *Madame Auguste Manet,* the artist's mother, painted c. 1863. Another painting by Manet, *Chez Tortoni,* was exhibited below this portrait until it was stolen on March 18, 1990. Other paintings of merit here are *Noonday,* by Corot (1796–1875); *A View Across the River,* Gustave Courbet (1819–77); and *The Crusader,* Delacroix (1798–1863).

After passing through the entrance lobby, on the l. is the SPANISH CHAPEL. On the floor under the window is a marble tomb relief of a knight in armor, c. 1500, believed to represent a member of the Maldonado family of Salamanca. The painting over the altar is *The Virgin of Mercy,* c. 1630–35, from the studio of Francisco de Zurbarán; this was the first old master acquired by Mrs. Gardner, purchased in 1888, when she and her husband

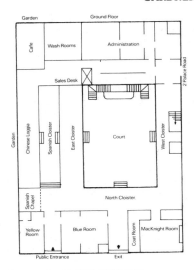

Garden Ground Floor

Cafe | Wash Rooms | Administration

2 Palace Road

Sales Desk

Garden | Chinese Loggia | Spanish Cloister | East Cloister | Court | West Cloister

Spanish Chapel

North Cloister

Yellow Room | Blue Room | Coat Room | MacKnight Room

Public Entrance Exit

THE ISABELLA STEWART GARDNER MUSEUM
(Ground floor)

were on holiday in Seville. The wrought-iron grilles here and elsewhere in
the museum are Italian and Spanish works of the 16–17C, as are all the
gates and railings.

Before going on, look up to the l. to see the limestone reliefs that flank
the door leading into the entrance lobby; on the l. is *The Entry into Jerusalem;* and on the r. is a representation of *Two Kings of the Apocalypse.*
These French Romanesque figures date from the mid-12C (the lower halves
of the Two Kings are modern additions), and are from the church of Notre-
Dame-de-la-Couldre at Parthenay, in Poitou.

THE SPANISH CLOISTER is dominated by the huge and dramatic painting at the far end, *El Jaleo,* 1882, by John Singer Sargent, named after the
spirited Andalusian dance being performed by the beautiful lady who is
the central figure. The Moorish arch and lighting from below evoke the idea
of the stage on which Sargent had seen flamenco dancers performing in
Granada. The Moorish arch is supported by late-medieval Italian columns
with animal bases, a typical example of Mrs. Gardner's ability to combine,
successfully, architectural and artistic elements from different places, cultures, and periods in time. The E. and W. walls of the cloister are revetted
in 17C tiles from a ruined Mexican church. At the center of the wall on the
r. there is a handsome limestone portal of the late 12C, once the entryway
to a private house near Bordeaux; and in the second window beyond this
there is an elaborately carved stone arch, believed to be a French work of
the late 15C.

At the l. side of the Spanish Cloister steps lead up to the CHINESE LOG-
GIA. This hall takes its name from the carved Chinese limestone stele to
the r. on entering. On the front of the stele the large central figure in the
relief is the Buddha Sakyamuni, who is flanked by the figures of two attendant monks and two bodhisattvas. On the upper part of the reverse of the

stele are the carved figures of the Ten Spirit Kings. The main inscription, carved on the front of the base, consists of the dedication and a list of 78 donors, with the date July 2, A.D. 543. In the bay window on the l. side of the hall there is a bronze Japanese temple bell of the 19C. At the rear a corridor leads to the sales desk, the rest rooms, and the cafeteria. Elsewhere in the hall there are a number of fragmentary statues and cinerary urns, all of them of the Graeco-Roman period and none of any great interest. There are also two sculptures of later date at the N. end of the hall; these are a stone *Madonna and Child,* a French work in the style of the early 14C; and above this a relief shows a *Patrician Family at Prayer,* done in Westphalia in the early 17C.

At the center of the Chinese Loggia steps lead down into the MONKS' GARDEN, which is open in favorable weather. If one takes the path to the r., on the l. is a fountain with a fragmentary marble group, showing *Eros Transported on a Dolphin,* a Graeco-Roman copy of a Hellenistic creation of c. 100 B.C. At the end of the path is a marble statue representing a *Dancer with Her Hands on Her Hips;* this is a mid-19C copy of an original done in 1812 by Antonio Canova for the Empress Josephine. At the end of the path leading off to the r. there is a marble statue of *Diana.* This is also a mid-19C copy; the original is a Roman work called the *Diana de Versailles,* now in the Louvre, which once adorned the Grande Galerie at Versailles.

Return to the Chinese Loggia and walk back through the Spanish Cloister, turning l. to enter the North Cloister; pause there to look into the COURTYARD, a sight of enchanting beauty. The quality of this court stems partly from its setting, for one has here the feeling of being in the cloister of a Renaissance palace, and also from the sculpture and architectural fragments that Mrs. Gardner has gathered here from all over Europe and even Egypt; but perhaps its surpassing loveliness comes principally from the garden itself, for, protected by a glass roof four stories above, the Courtyard is in bloom throughout the year with plants and flowers grown in the museum's greenhouses. In the spring there are freesia, jasmine, and azaleas, with lilies and cineraria at Easter; in autumn the chrysanthemums are in bloom, and poinsettias at Christmastime; many varieties of orchids are on exotic display throughout the year.

The window frames, balconies, and balustrades that overlook the garden are all from Venetian buildings of the 14—15C. In the panels of the arched windows of the upper floors, and in the spandrels of the cloister arches, there are 38 decorative roundels. These are reliefs which from the 12C onward were used to decorate the facades of Venetian palaces and great commercial houses, such as the Fondaco dei Turchi; the reliefs here differ widely in date, with the oldest probably of the 12C. The inset reliefs on the facade and the stone arches, columns, and capitals of the portico are variously from the Romanesque, Gothic, and Renaissance periods, with some modern architectural members. On the S. facade, between the second and third stories on either side of the central windows, are lion antefixes, Tuscan works of the 12C. Above the central window on the second story there are two 12C Venetian reliefs; on the l. are the figures of four peacocks around a double column; and on the r. is the figure of a winged ox holding an open book, the symbol of St. Luke.

At the rear of the courtyard, staircases on either side lead up to the balcony of the central window on the second floor. Above the balustrade on the first landing of the staircase on the l. is a marble representation of *Odysseus Creeping Forward During the Theft of the Trojan Palladium,* a

A view of the Courtyard of the Gardner Museum, with its fine Roman mosaic pavement (Courtesy, Isabella Stewart Gardner Museum)

Graeco-Roman copy of 50 B.C. in the style of 490 B.C. The prototype for this work is believed to be a pedimental sculpture on the Temple of Aphaia on the Greek island of Aegina in the Saronic Gulf. Next to the stairway on the r. there is a marble *torso of a goddess,* a fine Roman copy, c. 50 B.C., of a Greek original of the Archaic period. Between the staircases there is a fountain with a friezelike rim, a Venetian work of the 17C. The rim is made up of five horizontal and six vertical panels with reliefs: figures of tritons blowing horns, and dolphins, cornucopias, sea monsters, shells, and masks. At the center of the wall behind the fountain is a fragmentary *relief of a Maenad* or Hora, a Graeco-Roman work of the 1–2C A.D.; this is one of a set of eight dancing maidens that once decorated a funerary monument or perhaps the base of a Dionysiac tripod. The Gardner relief was removed from the monument in late antiquity or the Middle Ages, and the other seven reliefs were excavated in Rome only in 1908, and are now in the Museo delle Terme there. Flanking the relief at the rear of the pool is a pair of dolphins of Istrian stone, once part of the decoration of a 17C Venetian fountain.

In the center of the garden is an almost perfectly preserved Roman *mosaic pavement.* This was unearthed in 1892 just N. of Rome, on the site of a villa erected during the reign of Hadrian, A.D. 117–38. The mosaic, which was apparently the pavement of a small bathing establishment within the villa, has at its center the head of Medusa, with wings and snakes instead of hair. This is surrounded by panels with a convoluted ribbon design, and the rest of the center panel is filled with linked flowered scrolls with a different bird in the center of each side. The border of this panel is a double guilloche with a design of scrolls inside a narrow black line. In the garden behind the pavement is a granite figure of an Egyptian Horus Hawk, a representation of the sun god Horus, personified on earth by the ruling king; this is dated c. 333–23 B.C. Near the corners of the pavement at its rear are a pair of marble shafts standing on rectangular cinerary urns. The shafts, which are of the late 1C A.D. or the early 2C, are thought to have been found on the site of the Gardens of Sallust in Rome; the one on the l. is hexagonal, with garlands hung on the upper half and slender torches in acanthus-bordered frames on the sides of the lower half; the one on the r. is in the form of a twisted vine ending in foliage and surmounted by twin peacocks, with double rosettes on either side. Outside the middle of the pavement on its l. is a fragmentary marble *throne,* said to be from Telesina in S. Italy; this is a Roman work of the late 2C A.D., copied from a famous lost throne of the Late Hellenistic period. On the back of the throne there is the figure of a bearded winged creature in Near Eastern costume, with legs terminating in acanthus scrolls; and at the sides are seated sphinxes, their bodies turning into similar scrolled foliage. On the facade of the portico behind the throne, in the spandrels of two of the arches, are two small reliefs; the one on the l. representing St. John the Baptist, and the one on the r. a deacon saint; both of them N. Italian works of the 16C. On the r. side of the pavement directly opposite the throne is a lovely marble *statue of a female figure,* said to have been found in Tusculum; this is a Graeco-Roman copy of an original believed to have been done c. 375 B.C., a work which some scholars attribute to Kephisodotus, father or uncle of Praxiteles. The statue was originally identified as an Amazon, but more recent opinion holds that it is a figure of Artemis the Huntress. The panther-skin boots that she is wearing are not part of the original statue, but from another Graeco-Roman work of unknown identity. At the front of the pavement there is a limestone sarcophagus that once contained the remains of a child, whose portrait-bust in relief is on the far side. The other reliefs on the sarcophagus depict Medusa, Erotes, Maenads, Nikes, and Sphinxes, with garlands strung between them. The sarcophagus comes from W. Asia Minor and dates to c. A.D. 250. In the near corner of the garden to the l. is a fine marble *statue of a female figure,* missing her r. arm and l. forearm, clothed in a long chiton covered by a draped himation. This is a copy of the period 1C B.C.–1C A.D., from a Greek original of c. 350–20 B.C., and is thought to have been part of a funerary monument. The identity of the figure is uncertain, but it is suggested that she is Persephone. In the near corner of the garden to the r.

there is another fine marble *statue of a female figure,* missing her head and parts of both of her arms, clad in Doric dress. This statue, which was discovered on the site of the Gardens of Sallust, is a Graeco-Roman copy of a Greek original of c. 455–450 B.C.; the figure is called the "Peplophorus" and it is thought that she too is a representation of Persephone.

One might now stroll around the periphery of the courtyard to look at some of the objects in the porticoes, beginning at the far end of the E. portico. The wall fountain was constructed from odd bits and pieces of Italian stone carving. In the center of the portico there is an ornate stone portal from central Italy, with an inscription dating it to the papacy of Julius II, 1503–13. Between the two windows to the l. of the doorway there is a panel made up of reconstructed architectural and sculptural fragments of an ambo from the Church of St. Lucia in Gaeta, S. Italy, dating from the first quarter of the 13C. The larger fragments are four marble panels with reliefs framed by a colored mosaic of Cosmati work in green-and-red porphyry. The upper reliefs represent the winged lion of St. Mark (l.), and the winged ox of St. Luke (r.); while the lower ones depict a stag (l.) and a perched rooster (r.) with a dragonlike tail, the medieval manner of representing a basilisk. At the N. end of the portico, over the passageway to the Spanish Cloister, there is a large stone escutcheon, a Spanish work of the 16C; the arms are those which the Holy Roman Emperor Charles V adopted after his marriage to Isabella of Portugal in 1526. At the junction of the E. and N. porticoes is a limestone *retable* from a church in Lorraine, c. 1425; the carving is divided into nine compartments by a series of arcades, with the Crucifixion in the center; three scenes of Passion on either side; and at the ends the donors with their patron saints, John the Baptist (l.) and St. Catherine (r.). On the court side of the portico, on a column, is an Istrian stone figure of St. Christopher Carrying the Christ Child, N. Italian, early 16C. Beyond that, on a capital resting on the balustrade, is a large marble head of a divinity thought to be Apollo; this is a Graeco-Roman work deriving ultimately from the Apollo Lykeios created by Praxiteles in the 4C B.C. The columns of the central arch of the N. portico are extremely interesting. The pair of *figured capitals* are Roman works of the period c. A.D. 220–85, of a very rare type; from the complex foliage emerge centaurs with amphorae, while the four main figures on either side represent Dionysos and his followers in an orgiastic procession. The *stylobates* on which the columns rest are in the form of lions; the one on the l., N. Italian, late 12C or early 13C, has a small beast in his claws, while beside him an atalante helps to bear his burden; the one on the r., a Tuscan work of the second half of the 12C, has beneath him a struggling male figure, who has just plunged a knife into the beast's flank.

Continue along the North Cloister, passing on the r. the hallway leading to the exit. On the r. a door leads into the MACKNIGHT ROOM, temporarily closed to the public. This was Mrs. Gardner's sitting room during the years she lived at Fenway Court. Displayed here are paintings and watercolors by American artists and work by American sculptors, including a watercolor entitled *Mrs. Gardner in White* (temporarily in the Yellow Room), by John Singer Sargent, done in Sept. 1922 at Fenway Court.

Now turn into the West CLOISTER. On the N. wall is a limestone tabernacle in a triptych, a work of Bartolomeo Giolfino (c. 1410–86). The central figure is Christ as the Man of Sorrows; in the niche to the l. is St. John the Baptist, and on the r. is the figure of a young man in the costume of a knight, perhaps a military saint. Across from this, in the corner of the garden, is a marble Roman sarcophagus whose sides and ends are decorated with a profuse and erotic relief showing a procession of Maenads and Satyrs gathering grapes. This work, which dates to c. 222–35, is one of the most elegant sarcophagi to have survived from the Roman imperial period. Continue along the portico. On the wall to the r. is a series of four fragmentary frescoes on lime plaster transferred to linen, all of the 15C; the subjects are (r. to l.): St. Francis; the Madonna and Child Enthroned; an Angel Catching the Blood of the Redeemer; and Mater Dolorosa. Under the stairway is a Venetian fountain, c. 15C, in which are displayed small fragments of Graeco-Roman statuary. Beneath the stairs is a fragmentary Persian tombstone with superb carvings, a late-15C work from the Timurid capital of Herat. At the S. end of the cloister a relief shows the enthroned Virgin holding a disk with the symbol of the Wheel of Charity. Below in Roman numerals is the date 1522; this was once affixed to the facade of one of the buildings of the Scuola della Carita in Venice, and is a work of Giovanni Maria Mosca (fl. 1515–53).

At the S. end of the West Cloister a passageway leads to the sales room, rest rooms, and cafeteria. Midway along the rear of this corridor, on the l., is a gilded polychrome wooden *statue of Kuan Yin,* the Bodhisattva of Compassion, c. 1050–1150, one of the masterpieces of medieval Chinese sculpture.

The staircase in the West Cloister leads up to the second floor. The stairway is paved in Istrian stone and has a marble balustrade from a 19C Venetian structure. Set into the wall on the l. are medieval Venetian architectural fragments, and above them there are painted Japanese doors and panels of the 18C. The tiled floors in the stair hall and elsewhere in the museum were made for Mrs. Gardner by Henry Mercer of Doylestown, Pennsylvania, and are replicas of 14C tiles at the Castle Acre Priory, Norfolk, England.

At the N. end of the stair hall is the EARLY ITALIAN ROOM, whose principal exhibits are Italian paintings of the period 1320–1540. The paintings exhibited here are, beginning at the r. of the entryway: (on the S. wall) (above) *The Annunciation,* anon. Florentine, c. 1365–95; (below) *Sacra Conversazione,* c. 1495, Andrea Mantegna; *A Prayer Before a Tomb,* Antonio Cicognara (fl. 1480–1500); *The Circumcision,* c. 1470, Cosimo Tura; *The Dormition of a Nun,* from the studio of Giovanni da Rovezzano (c. 1412–59); *A Young Man in a Scarlet Turban,* c. 1425–27, Masaccio; *Hercules,* a fresco, c. 1465–70, Piero della Francesca; two companion panels, the *Triumphs of Fame, Time, and Eternity,* and the *Triumphs of Love, Chastity, and Death,* both by Pesellino (1422–57) (these probably came from the front of two wedding coffers, made c. 1448 for the marriage of Piero de' Medici, father of Lorenzo the Magnificent, and Lucrezia Tornabuoni); *Lady with a Nosegay,* Bacchiacca (1494 / 5–1557); *Boy in a Scarlet Cap,* Lorenzo di Credi (c. 1448–1537); a polyptych, the *Madonna and Child with Four Saints,* Simone Martini; *Bishop Saint,* Michele Giambono (fl. 1420–62); *Madonna and Child Before a Rose Hedge,* in the style of the early 15C, by a follower of Gentile da Fabriano; *Crucifixion,* 15C, by an Umbrian known as Il Meastro Esiquo (The Tiny Master); a triangular tempera panel, *St. Elizabeth of Hungary,* Ambrogio Lorenzetti (fl. 1319–47); *St. Anthony Abbot, with Four Angels,* Nicolò di Pietro Gerini (fl. 1368–1416); *Madonna Enthroned, with Saints and Angels,* Bartolommeo Bulgarini (fl. 1337–78); an altarpiece, *Madonna and Child, Crucifixion,* anon. Venetian, 14C; a triptych, *Crucifixion with Saints,* attributed to Paolo di Giovanni Fei (fl. 1369–1411); *Madonna and Child, SS. Matthew and Francis,* Bicci di Lorenzo (1373–1472); a triptych, *The Madonna of Humility, with Saints,* anon. Venetian, c. 1400; *The Dormition of the Virgin,* c. 1450, Fra Angelico; *Madonna and*

Child, Pintoricchio (c. 1454–1513); *Madonna and Child with a Goldfinch,* Bernardo Daddi (died 1348); *The Child Jesus Disputing in the Temple,* Giovanni di Paolo (died 1482 / 83); and *The Madonna of Humility, with a Donor,* 15C, in the style of Gentile da Fabriano.

On a 17C Italian walnut table there is a drawing in pen and gouache of a *Turkish Artist,* by Gentile Bellini. This was undoubtedly done in 1479–80, when the Doge of Venice sent Bellini to Istanbul at the request of Sultan Mehmet II, the Conqueror; and it was at that time that the artist also painted the miniature portrait of the Conqueror that is now in the British Museum. Also exhibited here, in a case, are various pieces of 15C Italian metalwork; and in a glass cabinet there are a number of antiquities, including an Egyptian alabaster canopic jar of the second half of the second millennium B.C.; and two Chinese bronze statuettes of bears, Han dynasty, 1C B.C.

The splendid RAPHAEL ROOM looks out over the Courtyard from its N. side. This gallery takes its names from two paintings by Raphael exhibited in it. The paintings in this room are, once again starting from the r.: *Woman in Green and Crimson,* Piero del Pollaiuolo (c. 1443–96); *The Annunciation,* c. 1480, attributed to Antoniazzo Romani; *Madonna and Child,* a contemporary copy of a painting by Cima da Conegliano (d. c. 1518); *Madonna and Child,* c. 1465, Giovanni Bellini; *The Tragedy of Lucretia,* c. 1505, Sandro Botticelli; *Virgin and Child, SS. George and Martin,* Francesco Comes (fl. 1380–95); *St. George and the Dragon,* 1470, Carlo Crivelli (when Bernard Berenson acquired this painting for Mrs. Gardner in 1897, he wrote to her, "It is the only one I shall envy you. The others may be greater, but I love this one most"); *Madonna and Child, with a Goldfinch,* attributed to Il Francia (c. 1450–1517); *Count Tommaso Inghirami,* 1511–12, Raphael; on an easel in front of the above, a Pietà, 1503–6, Raphael; *Madonna and Child with the Little St. John,* c. 1480, Francesco Botticini; *Madonna and Child,* 15C, attributed to several N. Italian painters as influenced by Andrea Mantegna; and *Madonna and Child, with a Swallow,* Pesellino (1422–57).

Other objects of interest in the Raphael Room include: (to the l. of the entry) a Venetian commode of walnut, late 17C or early 18C, decorated with figures and scenes inlaid in ivory and stained satinwood; (along the wall to the l.) a 15C N. Italian fireplace, flanked by two large velvet hangings with the embroidered arms of Cardinal Hohenlohe (1823–96); (draped over a lectern to the r.) a 15C Italian velvet chausable, with eight embroidered scenes from the Life of Christ; and (at the far end of the room toward the r.) a Sienese *cassone,* gilt and gesso on wood, 16C. This latter cassone was used as a marriage chest, and is decorated in low relief with a wedding scene; the coat-of-arms, which is part of the decoration on the lid and either end, is that of the Picolominis of Siena, a family that produced Popes Pius II and III.

The SHORT GALLERY is a narrow hall containing most of the museum's collection of prints and drawings, which are exhibited in four cabinets. The collection includes a *Pietà* by Michelangelo, five works by Matisse, five by Degas (all stolen on March 18, 1990), 43 by James A. McNeill Whistler, and 88 by Anders Zorn. There are also two sketches in pencil and watercolor by Leon Bakst (1866–1924) of costumes worn by dancers in Serge Diaghilev's Ballet Russe, including one worn by Anna Pavlova. There are also a number of portraits of Mrs. Gardner and members of her family, the most notable being *Mrs. Gardner in Venice,* by Anders Zorn, painted in the Palazzo Barbaro in 1894, with fireworks over the Grand Canal visible in the background. Other works of interest are: *A Gondolier,* a drawing attributed to Vittore Carpaccio (d. 1526); *The Flax Spinners,* an etching done in 1868–69 by Millet; and *The Casa Loredan, Venice,* 1850, by John Ruskin.

Next is the LITTLE SALON, in the N.E. corner of the building. Most of the furniture and decorative woodwork in this room are Venetian works in the French Louis XV style. The four tapestries with scenes of courtly pleasure are called the Château and Garden series. Those on the S. and W. walls are from the Geubels family workshops in Brussels, late 16C and early 17C; the two on the E. wall were made in Paris at the shop of Raphael de la Planche, a Fleming, in the mid-17C. The tapestries originally belonged to Cardinal Antonio Barberini, nephew of Pope Urban VIII and grand prior of France. The painting to the l. of the fireplace is *The Car of Venus*, by François Boucher (1703—70). Other exhibits in the room include a number of objects of Meissen porcelain and china, along with three antique musical instruments: a single-action pedal harp, made by Georges Blaicher of Paris (fl. 1782—1828); a 19C monochord constructed in the style of the 17C; and an English spinet, school of Stephen Keene, London, c. 1680.

A door in the S. wall leads into the TAPESTRY ROOM. This is the largest gallery in Fenway Court; concerts are given here regularly except in July and Aug. The ten large tapestries that hang on the walls were woven in Brussels in the mid-16C; the set of five with a Latin inscription at the top depicts scenes in the life of Abraham; the other set depicts events in the life of Cyrus the Great as described in the *Histories* of Herodotus.

On the l., on an easel beside the window, is a painting of *St. Engracia*, c. 1474, by Bartolomé Bermejo. On the other side of the easel is a portrait of *Pope Innocent X*, a contemporary copy after the larger portrait done in 1650 by Velázquez, now in the Doria-Pamfili Gallery, Rome. Along the wall to the l. one sees in turn: a lectern, covered in red velvet, bearing the arms of Pope Clement IX (1667—69); an iron pulpit, Spanish or French, 14—15C; under the pulpit, a walnut chest, Spanish, 16C; beyond, a tier of three oak choir stalls, French, 14—15C. The Gothic-arched stone window to the r. and the two windows on either side of the fireplace on the S. wall are probably Spanish, late 14C or early 15C. The French Gothic stone fireplace dates from the reign of François I (1515—47), though it was later restored. In the center of the relief that decorates the fireplace are two angels supporting the symbol of the kings of France, a crowned shield with three fleurs-de-lis, and on either side there is a frieze of animals and mythical beasts. Over the fireplace there is a painting of *St. Michael* by Garcia de Benabarre, 15C. Against the W. wall, to the r. of the doorway, is a black-painted walnut chest, a Spanish work of the 17C. Above the chest is a painting of *La Gitana* (The Gypsy), 1920, done in Seville by Louis Kronenberg; overhead is a large iron bracket with lantern, German, 17C. On the stand is a Russian icon, *The Assumption of the Virgin*, probably Sc. of Novgorod, 15C. In the center of the long table is a carved wooden head of Christ, S. German, 15C. In front of the windows is an oak Jacobean dresser, English, late 17C; on the dresser is a Persian manuscript of the *Divan* by Hafiz, dated 1489—90, with five miniatures. On a pedestal is a polychromed wooden candelabrum of the Madonna della Misericordia, central Italian, 16C. Beyond the windows is a long refectory table, Spanish, 17C; on the table are six Arabic and Persian miniatures, 13—15C. To the r. is an upholstered sofa with gros- and petit-point embroidery, English, early 18C. At the N. end of the room is an oval table, Italian, 17C; in the center near the fireplace is an oak draw table, Dutch, 17C; above, supporting the ceiling beams, are six wooden brackets, Norman works, carved in grotesque forms of human beings and animals. The two full-length ecclesiastical figures are thought to be English works, 17C.

A doorway in the W. wall leads into the SECOND FLOOR PASSAGE,

THE ISABELLA STEWART GARDNER MUSEUM (Second floor)

where a number of Japanese paintings are exhibited. Above the carved oak door is a twofold screen painting, *The Vinegar Tasters,* 17C. To the r. is a set of four sliding doors painted on a gold ground; the scene is entitled *Chrysanthemums and Bamboo,* Kano Sc., 17C; three others of the set are on the opposite wall near the Courtyard window. Opposite, on the W. wall, is a sixfold screen painting on gold ground, *Flowers and Birds,* Kano Sc., 17C. Below is another sixfold screen painting, *Young Pine Trees,* 17C, with a border mounting made from strips of a 14C Buddhist scriptural manuscript.

One now enters the DUTCH ROOM, named after the Dutch old masters that are exhibited there, along with other works. This is the most splendid gallery in the museum, situated at the head of the double flight of stairs that rise from the garden court, hung with green damask and floored with red tiles, furnished with superb antiques, and its walls lined with masterpieces of Northern European art. Flanking the entryway there are a pair of portraits by Hans Holbein the Younger, the Dutch artist who in 1536 became court painter to King Henry VIII. The portrait on the l. is of *Sir William Butts, M.D.,* court physician to Henry VIII, and the one on the r. is of his wife, *Lady Butts;* these were done in 1543, the last year of Holbein's life. The other paintings and works of art in the room are, beginning once again at the r. of the entryway: (on the wall to the r. of the entryway) *A Lady in Black and White,* 16C, in the style of the Florentine painter Bronzino; (between the windows) *A Lady with a Rose,* c. 1635–40, by Antoon Van Dyck, a Fleming who was court painter to Charles I of England and also briefly to the Regent Isabella of Flanders; *A Man in a Fur Coat,* 1521, by Albrecht Dürer; *Self-Portrait,* c. 1629 (stolen on March 18, 1990), Rembrandt (with the arrival of this portrait in Boston in 1896, the first of four Rembrandts that Mrs. Gardner acquired in a five-year span, she and her husband decided to create their own art museum); (below, on a cabinet) an etching by Rembrandt, *Portrait of the Artist as a Young Man,* c. 1633; (over the doorway) a polychromed lindenwood statue of *St. Martin and the Beggar,* Bavarian, c. 1520; (to the l. of the door) a portrait of *Isabella Clara Eugenia, Archduchess of Austria,* done in 1598–1600 by Frans Pourbous II; (on an easel, by the window) *The Concert,* c. 1658–60 (stolen on March 18, 1990), Jan Vermeer; (on the other side of the easel), a landscape, *The*

Obelisk, 1638, by Rembrandt; (beside the window) *Virgin and Child,* an early-16C copy, in reduced size, of a large painting in St. Martin's Church at Colmar, Alsace, done in 1473 by Martin Schongauer; (on the cabinet) a terra-cotta bust, *St. John the Baptist,* workshop of Benedetto da Maiano (1442–97); (on the S. wall to the r.) *A Doctor of Law,* c. 1630–39, Francisco de Zurbarán; *The Storm on the Sea of Galilee,* 1633 (stolen on March 18, 1990), Rembrandt (his only known seascape; the figure closest to the viewer, holding on to his hat, is the artist himself); *The Dauphin of France* (1517–36), oldest son of François I, a contemporary copy of a lost portrait by Corneille de Lyon, 16C; (above) *Madonna and Child,* by an anon. Netherlandish painter influenced by Rogier van der Weyden (c. 1400–64); *Thomas Howard, Earl of Arundel,* c. 1630, by Peter Paul Rubens; *Anna van Bergen, Marquise of Veere* (1492–1541), after Jan Gossaert van Maubeuge, called Mabuse (c. 1478–1532); *Lady and Gentleman in Black,* 1633 (stolen on March 18, 1990), Rembrandt; *A Young Commander,* c. 1650–55, Justus Suttermans (the subject is probably a member of the Medici family, since the artist was their court painter); (on the E. wall) *A Lesson on the Theorbo,* Gerard ter Borch (1617–81); *Queen Mary of England* (1516–58), from the studio of Anthonis Mor (c. 1519–77); (to the r. of the fireplace), a drawing, *The Annunciation,* a copy of a lost original by Rembrandt; (flanking the fireplace) two wood carvings, representing *The Nativity* and *The Resurrection,* N. Italian or S. German, 16C; (l. of the fireplace) a colored pencil sketch, *Three Captives,* by Peter Paul Rubens, after Mantegna's *The Triumph of Caesar.*

The room's painted ceiling is Italian, c. 1500, and is decorated with the coats-of-arms of several prominent Roman families of the period. The red marble fireplace is also Italian, 16C; on its hood there is a marble panel from Venice, dated 1497; and on its mantel there are two stone angels holding candlesticks; the one on the l. is Italian, 15C, as probably is that on the r. Below the fireplace is an oak chest with carved top, N. German, 17C; on the chest is a Dutch linen press, in the style of the 17C. Proceeding around the room in the same direction as before, one sees in turn the following objects: (over the doorway) a large needlepoint embroidery, French, dating from the reign of Henry II, 1547–49; (to the l. of the doorway) one of a set of six Empire chairs, with figured damask, French, 19C; (in the corner) a French bread-cooler of walnut, Arles, 18C; (between the windows) a high-backed walnut bench with inlays, Florentine, early 16C, partly restored; (beyond, on the same side of the room) a carved oak cabinet, a 19C work done in the style of the 17C; (on either side of the cabinet) two chairs, probably Italian, of a set of 14 in the room, all in the French style of Louis XIV; an ivory-inlay chest, decorated in marquetry of burl walnut with satinwood borders; (in the corner, on a black wooden column with gilded capitals) one of four bronze candelabra, French, early 19C; (on a table at the W. side of the room) two rare Chinese tomb figurines: a serpentine pig, c. 3C B.C., and an earthenware dog in an iridescent green glaze, Han dynasty, 206 B.C.–A.D. 220; (farther along on that side) a cabinet with European silver, 17–20C; (starting along the S. wall) a Chinese bronze ceremonial beaker, or ku, 1200–1100 B.C. (stolen on March 18, 1990); a high-backed carved oak throne (the back and seat are modern restorations), Auvergne, 16C; a carved walnut cabinet, Italian, late 16C; (on the cabinet) a stoneware jug, Grenzhausen ware, bearing the arms of the city of Amsterdam, German, 18C (found in excavating the cellar of the old Brattle Street Meeting-House, and probably brought to America by the Hessian soldiers who were housed in the church in 1775–76); (on the E. side of the room) an upholstered walnut sofa, French or Flemish, period of Louis Philippe (1830–48); (in the middle of the room) a large refectory table, Tuscan, dated 1599; the other table there is also Italian, 16C.

A doorway in the N.W. corner of the room leads into the S. side of the SECOND FLOOR STAIR HALL. Beyond the first window overlooking the Courtyard hangs a Flemish tapestry with a scene entitled *Man and Lady,* 18C; (above) an eightfold Japanese screen painting, *The Battle of the River Uji,* 17C; (to the r. of the window) a Flemish tapestry with a scene thought to represent *Sinon Persuading Priam to Accept the Trojan Horse.* The marble door-frame is Venetian, c. 1500, with the arms of the Doge Andrea Gritti; (above) a tapestry with a *Forest Scene,* Dutch or Flemish, late 16C or early 17C. In the corner there are two tapestries; these are (l.) *Spring,* Brussels, mid-16C; and (r.) *The Tower of Babel,* late 16C or early 17C. In front of this is an octagonal table, Florentine, 18C, with pedestal legs in the form of sphinxes; set into the wall of the staircase is a fragment of a Roman sarcophagus, c. A.D. 300; below this is a marble relief escutcheon, Italian, 16C, with the arms of Andrea Valle, who was bishop of Cotrone from 1496 to 1508; to the r., over the courtyard window, there is a fragmentary fresco, *Musicians,* c. 1610–50, thought to be a Neapolitan work.

Stairs ascend to the N. side of the THIRD FLOOR STAIR HALL. On the wall to the l. are three Flemish tapestries; these are, l. to r.: *Flemish Proverbs,* late 15C, a fragment of a larger work depicting nine Flemish folk proverbs; *The Amazon Queens,* c. 1430; and *Esther Before Ahasuerus,* early 16C. To the r., on the E. wall, there is a painting of *A Lady in Black,* by Tintoretto (1518–94). Farther to the r., beyond the window, hangs a Flemish tapestry, with a scene depicting *The Story of Jehu and Jezebel, and the Sons of Ahab,* c. 1470. Beyond the triple window, to the l. of the grille separating the N. and S. parts of the stair hall, there is a polychromed and gilt poplar statue of *The Angel of the Annunciation,* late 16C, a superb work that some scholars attribute to the Sienese sculptor Domenico di Nicolo dei Cori (1363–1453); the companion piece, the Annunciate Virgin, is in the Musée Jacquemart-André, in Paris.

Now walk back through the stair hall to the VERONESE ROOM, whose walls are covered with various pieces of tooled and gilded Spanish leather of the 17–18C. The carved, gilded, and painted ceiling of this gallery was done in Milan in 1901 for Mrs. Gardner, who wanted to create an Early Renaissance setting for *The Coronation of Hebe,* the painting that adorns the center of the ceiling. Mrs. Gardner had acquired it in Paris in 1899, at which time it was attributed to Paolo Veronese (1528–88), after whom she named this room; however, art historians now believe that it was done by an anon. assistant of the master, painted for a ceiling in the Della Torre Palace in Udine. The only work in this room actually by Veronese is exhibited to the l. of the entryway on a carved and gilded lectern, Italian, late 18C; this is a drawing in ink and gouache on paper of *The Marriage of St. Catherine,* c. 1575. The other objects of interest in the Veronese Room are, beginning once again at the r. of the entryway: (to the r. of the door) a walnut armchair with tooled leather back and seat, one of a set of six in the room, Italian, early 17C; (on the wall) a large mirror, engraved with figures of heroes of antiquity, Venetian, 1750–1800; (below) a Venetian commode in the Louis XVI style, 18C or later; (on the commode) a Venetian toilet mirror, mid-18C, and two majolica apothecary jars, 18C; (in the corner, beyond the window overlooking the courtyard) *The Morning Toilet,* 1888, a painting by Anders Zorn; (below) a Venetian armchair in the style of Louis XV, mid-18C; (to the l.) a painted Italian tip-table, mid-18C, with a scene

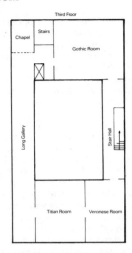

THE ISABELLA STEWART GARDNER MUSEUM
(Third floor)

depicting Diana seated in the clouds with Apollo and Cupid; (facing the courtyard window) a sedan chair with paintings of garden scenes, a composite of 17–18C work; (to the l. of the door) a Venetian sofa in the Louis XVI style, 19C; (above) *The Wedding of Barbarossa,* c. 1749–50, by Giovanni Battista Tiepolo (a sketch for part of the fresco in the Kaisersaal of the Residenz of the Prince Bishop at Würzburg, depicting the marriage of the Holy Roman Emperor Frederick I, known as Barbarossa, or Red Beard, to Beatrice of Burgundy, a ceremony that took place in Würzburg in 1156); (below) four small pictures by Whistler, of which the most interesting is the last on the r., a sketch in pastel on cardboard entitled *Mrs. Gardner in Yellow and Gold,* 1886; (in the corner) a 19C German writing-desk; (above) a painting by Filippo Lauri (1623–94) of *The Vision of St. Anthony of Padua;* (between the windows on the N. wall) a marble-topped Venetian console table, late 18C; (in the small wall-case) a Madonna in black glass, Murano, c. 1600; (above) a portrait thought to be of *Alessandro Contarini,* by an anon. Venetian artist, with an inscription dating it to 1766; (in the corner cabinet) samples of fine European laces, 16–19C; (to the r. of the fireplace) two paintings by Francesco Guardi (1712–93): *The Clock Tower in the Piazza San Marco,* and *Venice Across the Basin of San Marco;* (to the l.) a painting of *The Story of David and Bathsheba,* Herri met de Bles (fl. 1535–75); (below) a painting thought to depict *The Birth of Caterina Cornaro* (1454–1510), who was for a brief period Queen of the vestigial Crusader principality that comprised Cyprus, Cilician Armenia, and the Holy Land, done by an anon. Venetian artist c. 1550–1600.

The TITIAN ROOM overlooks the Courtyard from the center of its N. side. Begin by looking at the exhibits to the l. of the entryway, then continue around the room in that direction. One sees here (to the l., on the W. wall) a painting of *The Child Jesus Disputing in the Temple,* c. 1545, by Paris Bordone; (below) an English settee, 18–19C; (on either side) a pair of armchairs, Italian, 18C, part of a set of four in the room; (to the r.) a portrait of *Juana of Austria* (1535–73), with a child thought to be her niece Margaret, by Alonso Sánchez Coello (c. 1531–88) (Juana was the youngest of three children of the Emperor Charles V and his wife, Isabella of Portugal; at the age of 18 she served as Regent, when her father and her brother, later to reign as Philip II of Spain, were away in the Netherlands); (to the r. of the window) *The Continence of Scipio,* a painting from the studio of Bonifacio Veronese (1487–1553); (below) a red velvet hanging, Italian, 16C; a halberd with etched and inlaid designs, a work of Camillo Borghese (1552–1621), which originally belonged to the household of Pope Paul V; (below) two small Italian cabinets in the style of Louis XVI, late 18C; (between the cabinets) two high-backed side chairs in English Jacobean style with marble inlay, Venetian, 19C; and two Italian mahogany side chairs, of a set of six in the room, early 19C; (below the window, on an easel) a painting of *Christ Bearing the Cross,* from the Palazzo Loschi in Vicenza, attributed to Giorgione (d. 1510); (in the cabinet to the r.) a collection of European decanters, drinking glasses, vases, and glass boxes, 17–19C; (on the cabinet) a marble bust of a Venetian senator or procurator, 17C, wearing an elaborate wig of long curls; (on the E. wall) *The Rape of Europa,* by Titian, painted in Venice in 1561–62 for Philip II of Spain, when the artist was 85 years old; (below) two Italian console tables, mid-18C; (on the table to the l.) a silver chalice, Roman, late 16C, with the arms of the Colonna on the underside; a bronze *Cupid,* attributed to the Flemish sculptor François Duquesnoy (1597–1643); and an enameled Venetian copper plate, 16C; (on the table to the r.) a small bronze plaque representing *The Rape of Europa,* by the American sculptor Paul Manship (1885–1966); (over the doorway) a painting depicting *The Delivery of the Keys to St. Peter,* by Vincenzo Catena (fl. 1500–31) (another version of this, by the same artist, is in the Prado, Madrid); (to the r. of the doorway) a portrait of *King Philip IV of Spain,* by Velázquez (1599–1660) (this is a replica of a virtually identical portrait in the Prado); (on a column to the r.) a bronze bust of *Bindo Altoviti,* dated 1550, by Benvenuto Cellini, one of only two of his surviving portrait-busts; (to the r.) a *Self-Portrait* by Baccio Bandinelli (1493–1560); (on the S. wall, below, beyond the window) *Girl with a Lute,* Bartolomeo Veneto (fl. 1502–46) (there are three other versions of this painting in Milan); (above) *The Magnanimity of Antigonus,* from the studio of Bonifacio Veronese; (in front) an 18C Italian chest covered with 17C Venetian brocade; (to the r.) *Nativity,* a painting by Liberale da Verona (c. 1445–1526); (by the double window) six leather-covered walnut chairs, Italian, 18C; a portrait of *Bearded Man in Black,* 1576, by Giovanni Battista Moroni; (r.) *Girl Taking a Thorn from Her Foot,* 16C, a painting ultimately derived from a work of Raphael; a Venetian commode (undated), on top of which is a Japanese lacquer chest, mid-17C; (above and to the r.) a portrait of *A Lady in a Turban,* by Francesco Torbido (c. 1483–1561); (below) *Sacra Conversazione,* c. 1528, by Bonifacio Veronese; (over the door) a portrait of *Zacharias Vendramin,* a procurator of the church of San Marco in Venice, from the studio of Tintoretto (1518–94). In the center of the room there is an Isfahan carpet, on which stand 17C Italian armchairs, along with a pair of 19C marble-topped console tables from Siena.

The LONG GALLERY extends along the full length of the museum; this is divided into three sections, the first two separated, to the r. of the entryway, by a Moorish archway on double columns; the third section, farthest to the S., is the Chapel. Turning l., one sees first a walnut armchair, Spanish, 16–17C, one of four unmatched but similar pieces in the room; (above) a glazed tabernacle front, from the workshop of Andrea della Robbia (1435–1525); a superb Florentine *sideboard,* late 15C; (on the sideboard) a marble bust of a youth thought to be Raphael Riario, Cardinal Sansoni (1460–1521); (on the wall above) *Madonna and Child of the Eucharist,* 1470, by Botticelli; (near the window) a marble relief *Bust of a Woman,* by Mino da Fiesolo (1429–84); (in the corner) a painted terra-cotta group, *Virgin Adoring the Child,* attributed to Matteo Civitali (1436–1501); (r., on the wall) *Nativity,* thought to be from the studio of Botticelli; (below) an Italian bench, gilt over gesso, 17–18C; (opposite the doorway) a large canopy and a red velvet dossal, Italian, 16C, said to have been made for Francesco Cenci, a prince of the Holy Roman Empire; (in front) a marble relief of *Madonna and Child,* possibly the work of Giovanni Bastianini (1830–68); a polychromed and gilt terra-cotta relief representing the *Madonna and Child,* 1494–97, by Benedetto da Maiano; (in the long case against the wall) letters and autographs of prominent Americans, including those of 13 Presidents of the U.S.; (on a pedestal to the r.) a white enameled terra-cotta bust of a young lady, 19C, in the style of Rossellino; (opposite) a painting of *A Young Lady of Fashion,* attributed to Paolo Uccello (1397–1475); (below) a small Italian chest of drawers veneered in walnut and mahogany, 18C; (to the r.) a glazed polychrome relief, *The Lamentation over the Dead Body of Christ,* by Giovanni della Robbia (1469–1529); (over the cupboard to the r.) a marble torso of a male, 1C B.C.–1C A.D., from the Greek island of Thasos.

In the middle section of the Long Gallery are the following exhibits: (in a bookcase to the r.) a collection of letters and documents bearing the autographs of famous personages, including Ferdinand and Isabella, Sir Francis Bacon, Maria Theresa, Louis XIV, Marie Antoinette, and Bismarck; (above) a marble Herm-bust of a *Greek Man of Affairs or Intellect,* a Graeco-Roman copy of an original work of c. 320–280 B.C.; (high on the wall) a large painted wooden escutcheon, German, 16C, with nine crests and 21 shields of the most prominent German families of that period; (l., in a glass cabinet) a collection of medieval and Early Renaissance religious articles; (beyond the window) a small desk-case, containing miniatures from 15C Books of Hours; (above) a gilt-metal crucifix, French, 13–14C; (below) a painted and carved wooden frieze, Burgundian, early 16C; (between the two bookcases) two carved and inlaid armchairs, N. Italian, early 18C; (l., in the desk-case) three 16C Limoges polychrome enamel plaques: *The Madonna,* a *Pietà,* and *The Entombment;* (above) two small paintings: in the first a depiction of *St. Jerome, Mary Magdalene, and St. Francis,* from the studio of Giovanni Fei (fl. 1369–1411), and in the second a representation of *The Martyrdom of St. Bartholemew,* by an anon. Florentine, c. 1375–1425; (by the triple window, in the bookcase) fine bindings of rare editions of French and Italian literature, including some with the arms of kings, popes, and cardinals; (l. beyond the window) five choir stalls, N. Italian, 15C; (above) a tapestry, probably Flemish, with a scene entitled *The Abduction,* 18C. Returning to the Moorish arch, one sees, against the outer wall, a case with letters and autographs of renowned authors from England and the Continent; (on either side of the case) two carved and inlaid armchairs, 17C, thought to be N. Italian; (to the r.) a case with letters to Mrs. Gardner from contemporary painters and sculptors; (above) a Graeco-Roman marble Herm of *Dionysos.* On the wall, l. to r., are the following paintings: *Battista, Countess of Urbino* (1446–72), a copy after the portrait by Piero della Francesca in the Uffizi, Florence; *Madonna and Child,* after a composition attributed to Bernardino Luini (c. 1475–1532) in the Ambrosiana Gallery, Milan; *A Procurator of San Marco,* after a portrait by Tintoretto, now in Berlin; (on the r.) a case with letters, documents, and manuscripts of renowned European authors and historical figures; (r.) a Roman cinerary urn, upon which rests a marble bust of a Roman, c. A.D. 150; (on the wall) a tapestry with a scene entitled *God Shows Noah the Rainbow as a Pledge,* by Jasper van Brugghen (fl. 1640–55); (below) a high-backed walnut sacristy bench, Italian, in the style of the 17C; (on top of the bench) four small 15C reliefs; (to the r.) a Roman cinerarium, 1–2C A.D., on which rests a marble head of a youthful deity, a Graeco-Roman copy of an original work of c. 465 B.C.; (by the window) a case with objects that once belonged to English rulers; (on the r.) a bookcase with three early editions of Dante's *Divine Comedy,* along with a collection of 18 Venetian manuscripts of the 16–18C; (on the bookcase) half-figures in stone of the *Virgin and the Angel Gabriel,* by Giovanni Antonio Pilacorte (c. 1455–1531); (above) *Madonna and Child, with SS. Francis and Clare and other Saints;* signed and dated 1307 by Giuliano da Rimini; (opposite) a case with letters and photographs of actors and authors, many of whom were friends of Mrs. Gardner; (above the case and to the l.) a sketch entitled *The Spanish Madonna,* by John Singer Sargent; (on the wall above) an oval embroidered cartouche, Italian, 16C; (above, to the r.) a painted terra-cotta representation of the *Madonna and Child,* after Benedetto da Maiano.

At the S. end of the Long Gallery is a small medieval chapel where Mrs. Gardner was waked for three days after her death on July 17, 1924, and each year on her birthday, April 14, by her request, an Anglican High Mass is said here in her memory by clergy of the Society of St. John the Evangelist. The works of art exhibited in the Chapel include the following: (flanking the entrance) two painted copper lanterns, Venetian, 17–18C; and two low stalls, French, 15C, with 16C Italian red velvet cushions; (by the window to the l.) a 19C version of a late 18C *voyeuse,* or spectator's chair; (above the window) a painted wooden *Madonna with a Bishop and King,* Franconian, mid-17C; (opposite) a walnut prie-dieu, with mother-of-pearl inlay, Italian, 17C; (above) a painting of *The Wedding Feast at Cana,* by Tintoretto; (l.) a tall bronze candlestick, one of four in the Chapel, Italian, 15–16C; two walnut choir stalls, Italian, 16–17C; a gilt and painted wooden standing lantern, Italian, c. 15C; (beyond the doorway and around the altar) a set of 15 walnut choir stalls, Italian, 16C; (on the wall, nearest the alcove) a lindenwood figure of *St. Jerome,* German, c. 1500; (in the alcove, high on the wall) a picture of the *Interior of the Abbey Church of St. Denis,* by Paul-César Helleu (1859–1927); (below) a painted wood *Pietà,* Netherlandish, c. 1500; and a pair of stained-glass windows from the Milan Cathedral, c. 1500; (in front) a large iron candelabrum, 15C, thought to be Italian; (over the altar) a stained-glass window, N. France, early 13C; (behind the altar, l.) wooden figures of *St. John* (l.) and a *Female Saint* (r.), Ulm, c. 1500; (on the W. wall, near the corner) *St. Philip Neri,* by an anon. Roman artist, c. 1575–95; (on top of the stalls to the r.) polychromed wooden statuettes of eight saints, Bavarian, c. 1510–20; (over the doorway) a polychromed and gilt pine figure of *St. Margaret,* a Bavarian or Tyrolese work of c. 1520–30.

On the r. side of the Chapel one passes into the THIRD FLOOR PASSAGE, whose principal adornments are the following 17C Japanese screen paintings: (to the l.) *Listening to the Lute;* (on the opposite wall, above) *The Tale of Genji;* (below) *Pheasants and Small Birds.* Hanging on the elevator enclosure are four carved and gilded Chinese doors of the late 19C.

The entryway to the next gallery, the GOTHIC ROOM, leads through a carved oak *tambour,* a work from N. France, c. 1500; (above the tambour) a *Madonna and Child,* by an anon. Venetian, c. 1425–75; (to the r.) a

Madonna and Child with Apple, anon., N. Italian, c. 1430–80; (high up on the walls) a frieze, N. Italian, 15C, with 68 portraits of renowned figures of the Renaissance; (below) an upholstered Italian armchair, 17C; three children's chairs, Italian, early 17C; a late-17C English day bed; the fireplace is a Venetian work in the style of the 15C; the andirons, with ecclesiastical figures in relief, is French, 15C, as is the fireback; (above the fireplace) a painted wooden group of *St. Maurice and the Theban Legion,* Upper Rhenish or Swiss, 1515; (on the fireplace canopy) an iron coat-of-arms of Queen Isabella of Spain (1454–1504); (to the r.) a walnut armchair, Italian, 17C; (on a wall bracket) a life-sized wooden figure representing one of the Magi, French, early 16C; (along the wall) a range of choir stalls, N. Italian, 15C; (on top) a mounted figure, thought to be St. Hubert or St. Eustace, S. German, c. 1470–80; (to the r.) an oak credence, French, in the style of the 15C; (high on the wall) a figure of St. Agnes, Italian, 14C; (on the S. wall, center) a stone wheel-window, probably Italian, 15C; (around the latter) six stained-glass windows, c. 1500, the upper pair from Nuremberg and the four below from Milan Cathedral; (on the shelf to the l.) the figures in gilt and polychromed wood of the *Enthroned Virgin and Child, Flanked by Angels,* Austrian or N. Italian, c. 1425; (in front) two armchairs of carved and inlaid walnut, N. Italian, c. 1600; and a wrought-iron candelabrum with the arms of the bishop of Toledo, Spanish, 16C; (below the wheel window) a carved walnut chest, French, c. 1525; (on the chest) a painted stucco *Madonna and Child,* Florentine, 15C, perhaps from the workshop of Ghiberti; (on the shelf to the r.) a gabled shrine with the figures of the Virgin and Child, from the Veneto, 15C; and four gilt and painted candlesticks in the form of angels, Italian, 17C; (in front) three walnut chairs, Italian, 17C; (r.) an iron torchère, Spanish, c. 1400; an iron lectern, probably French, 15C; and an oak credence, French, c. 1450, though largely restored; (on the credence) a painted gilt stucco bust of a woman, Italian, 19C; high on the walls is a figure of St. Agnes, Aquileis, c. 1315; (in the S.W. corner) an oak chest, Spanish, 15C; (on the chest) a leather-bound choir book, Italian, mid-17C; (behind) a portrait of *Isabella Stewart Gardner,* 1878–88, by John Singer Sargent; (on the wall) a tapestry with a scene entitled *The Message to the Woodcutters,* Franco-Flemish, early 16C; on an easel, by the Gothic-arched windows, a small altarpiece with a representation of the *Madonna and Child,* by Lippo Memmi (died 1357); (standing in front) a peasant chair, provincial N. Italian, 17C; (on the opposite side of the easel) *Presentation of the Infant Jesus in the Temple,* by Giotto (1267–1336/37); (in front) a so-called Dante chair, a folding type common in the time of Dante; (beyond the window) two ends of a stall, French, c. 1400; (above) a lindenwood statue of *St. Elizabeth of Hungary,* Upper Rhenish or Swabian, c. 1490; (in the corner) a tapestry showing *The Education of the Prince of Peace,* Tournai, early 16C; (above the doorway) a polyptych, *St. Thomas Receives the Madonna's Girdle,* anon. Ligurian, c. 1450–1500; (r.) a Spanish *barqueno* in walnut, restored in the style of the 17C; (on it) a painted terra-cotta bust of *St. Bernardino of Siena* (1380–1440), Tuscan, 15C; (on the wall) *Adam and Eve,* by Lucas Cranach the Elder (1472–1553); (by the court windows) four walnut armchairs, probably Sicilian, 17C; (between the windows, on the wall) carved *triptych* of painted lindenwood, with the central panel representing the Holy Kinship, Saxon, c. 1510–20; (below) an oak credence, French, c. 1500; (high on the wall) a limestone statue with modern polychromy of the *Madonna and Child,* Ile-de-France, mid-14C; and fragments of a mille-fleurs tapestry, probably Flemish, early 16C; (by the double window) wrought-iron reading stand, French, c. 1300; five silver plaques, Italian, 14C; (beyond the win-

dows, higher up) *Altar of the Trinity with St. Catherine and a Bishop Saint,*
N. German, 1510–20, attributed to the circle of Bernt Notke, the Lübeck
master; (on the sideboard below) a pair of brass candlesticks, Italian, 16C,
and a brass-bound, leather-covered liqueur chest, Italian, 17C; (out in the
room, near the fireplace) a walnut refectory table, Italian, 16C, around which
are Italian chairs of c. 1600; (on the table) a chained book, Sermons of
Johann Nider, printed by Conrad Fyner at Esslingen in 1476–78, with its
original binding; (near the W. end of the room) a table with a top of *cipol-
lino-rosso* marble, Venetian, 19C; (on the table) a gilt-metal processional
cross, provincial Italian, 14–15C; (between the tables) an iron candlestand,
French, 14C; (hanging from the ceiling) a chandelier, made of two antlers
and a painted wooden figure, Bavarian, 16C.

One now passes through the doorway into the S. end of the Third Floor
Stair Hall; (over the doorway) a wood crucifix, French or Spanish, 16C; (r.)
a painted wood figure in low relief of *St. Peter Martyr,* N. Italian, late 15C;
(on the W. wall) a painted terra-cotta relief of *The Entombment of Christ,*
by Giovanni Minelli (c. 1460–1527) (the kneeling figure at the l. is Cerlota,
illegitimate daughter of James I, King of Cyprus, who died at the age of 12,
and this relief was made for the altar over her tomb, c. 1483, in the church
of Sant' Agostino, Padua); (on the floor, l.) a marble capital, Venetian, 13C;
(against the wall to the l.) an oak credence, French, 15C, with a modern
top; (above) a pair of gilt and polychromed wood doors, Spanish or French,
15C; (across, to the r. of the court window) a tapestry with a scene in which
God Commands Noah to Build the Ark, Brussels, mid-17C; (below, to the r.
of the door) a painted limestone retable, French, with a carved inscription
and the date 1507 (the coat-of-arms is that of the Arnal family of Langue-
doc); (l. of the court window) a wood figure of Christ from a Deposition
Group, Catalonian, 12C.

Now descend the two flights of stairs to the ground floor and pass through
the corridor to the exit. The exit is flanked by a pair of life-sized male figures in gilt and polychromed wood, both of them bearing lances; (l.) St.
George, Bavarian or Tyrolean, c. 1500–10; (r.) St. Florian, S. Bavarian or
Austrian, c. 1520–25 (the lance is modern).

After leaving the museum, turn to examine the fine doorway, a Genoese
work of the 15C; above the lintel is a relief of St. George and the dragon,
while the portal itself is decorated with a grapevine motif. The doorway is
flanked by two stone lions, Italian works of the 19C.

II CAMBRIDGE

History and Topography. Boston and Cambridge have shared a common cultural heritage since their foundation, and today they are linked so intimately in the Greater Boston Metropolitan Area that many visitors are unaware that they are two separate cities, each with its own distinctive character.

The first settler within the present limits of Cambridge was Thomas Graves, who in 1629 built a house for himself and his family in what is now East Cambridge. On Dec. 28, 1630, Governor John Winthrop and the other Puritan leaders selected the site for what would be Old Cambridge, as the original colonial settlement was known in later years. The site was on the left bank of the Charles River five miles upstream from Boston, at the entrance to a small creek that followed much the same course as the present Eliot St. At that time the Massachusetts Bay Colony consisted of just four little settlements: the coastal towns of Boston, Charlestown, and Salem, and the inland village of Watertown. (Watertown was originally on the left bank of the Charles six miles upstream from Boston, at Gerry's Landing, but in 1635 it moved to the present site of Watertown Sq.) The Puritan leaders were apprehensive that the three coastal towns might be subject to naval raids, perhaps by pirates, or by the French, or even by English warships, in case the charter of 1629 were ever revoked, and there was also the fear that the Indians might attack the settlements, particularly Watertown. Thus Winthrop and his assistants decided to establish a fortified capital on this site a mile downstream from Watertown, calling the place Newtowne; they felt that the administrative center of the colony would be more secure here, and they also believed that it was a strategically placed location where the settlers of the other four towns could take refuge in case of attack.

The first houses in Newtowne were built in spring 1630, and the following year work began on the fortifications of the village. The defenses were to consist of a watchtower on a hill within the village and a surrounding "Pallysadoe," a fortification composed of stakes, willows, and an outer trench. The Pallysadoe, which was built in 1631—32, extended in an arc from what is now the foot of Ash St to the intersection of Oxford and Jarvis Sts, and possibly beyond. In 1632 the settlers constructed a second defense-line, the "Common Pales," which was little more than a high rail-fence; this extended from what is now the corner of Mount Auburn and Linden Sts to the Charlestown (now Somerville) line. The watchtower was not completed until a decade after the town was founded, when it seems to have been erected on or near the present site of Harvard Sq. But by that time the need for a fortified capital had passed, for the Indians had proved friendly and the settlement had not been threatened by naval forces. Furthermore, the administrative center of the Bay Colony had been established in Boston, which in 1631 became the seat of the governor and his assistants, and in 1638 the General Court moved there as well.

On Oct. 28, 1636, the General Court agreed to give £400—a quarter of the Bay Colony's tax levy for that year—toward the foundation of a "schoale or colledge." This, the first institution of higher learning in what would later be the U.S., was to have a profound influence on the intellectual life of the country as well as on the character of the town in which it was founded. The spirit that engendered the founding of the college is best expressed in *New England's First Fruits,* written in 1643, describing the early days of the Bay Colony: "After God had carried us safe to New England, and we had builded our houses, provided necessaries for our liveli-hood, rear'd convenient places for God's worship, and setled the Civill Government: one of the next things we longed for was to advance learning and perpetuate it to Posterity, dreading to leave an illiterate Ministery to the Churches, when our present Ministers shall lie in the Dust." By the autumn of 1637 the first Board of Overseers had been formed "to take order" for the new college, and in summer 1638 classes began for the first 12 freshmen. In autumn 1638 the Rev. John Harvard died in Charlestown, leaving half of his estate and all of his books to the college. Shortly thereafter the General Court, as an expression of gratitude, named the school Harvard College in his honor. In that same year the General Court changed the name of the community from Newtowne to Cambridge, after the English alma mater of many of the leading colonists.

In autumn 1638 the first printing press in the British colonies arrived in Cambridge. In 1641 the press was acquired by Henry Dunster, who the year before had become Harvard's first president, and the college was soon using the apparatus. The town acquired a second printing press in 1659 and a third in 1665, whereas the first press in Boston was not set up until 1674, before any others existed in the British colonies. Thus the history of printing in the present U.S. begins in Cambridge, one of many intellectual distinctions that can be claimed by this extraordinary community.

The area of the original settlement enclosed within the Pallysadoe and the Common Pales amounted to about 1000 acres. During the period 1632—36 additional land was granted to the settlement, including the areas that became Brighton, Newton, Arlington, Lexington, Billerica, and parts of Lincoln, Bedford, Belmont, and Winchester. A final grant of land in 1641 carried the boundaries of Cambridge to the Merrimac River. At that time the territory of Cambridge had a maximum length of some 36 miles, from Billerica to Newton, comprising an irregular area that was only a mile wide at what is now Harvard Sq. But thenceforth the area of the township steadily diminished, as outlying settlements broke off to form separate communities, the last major changes coming with the incorporation of the towns of Arlington and Brighton in 1807.

Old Cambridge in its earliest years was the most carefully laid-out settlement in the Bay Colony, undoubtedly because the Puritan leaders had originally planned to establish their capital there. William Wood in his *New England's Prospect,* written in 1633, described the settlement as "one of the neatest and best-completed towns in New England, having many fair structures and handsome contrived streets." The "streets" of the town were "laid out in squares" on a somewhat irregular grid, which was placed across the gentle hill rising above the tidal marsh. Four streets ran parallel to the Charles and three were perpendicular to it, running approximately E.-W. and N.-S. The town was bounded to the N. by the open space that became Harvard Sq, on the W. and S. by the creek that ran along the base of the hill, along which ran streets known as Creek and Marsh Lanes (Eliot and South Sts), and on the E. by two other lanes known as Bow and Arrow Sts, which retain their names. A decree of the General Court in Jan. 1633 ordered that "no houses shall be permitted beyond the pallisade," and that "by joint consent the town shall not be enlarged until all vacant places be filled with houses." Another order that same year decreed that "all houses shall range even and stand just six feet from the street," and also that "all houses within the bounds of the town shall be covered with slate or board, not with thatch."

During the early decades the principal "high street" of the town was Water St, now known as Dunster St. The first meetinghouse, erected in Dec. 1632, stood at what is now the S.W. corner of Dunster and Mount Auburn Sts. At the foot of Dunster St was the landing for the ferry service across the Charles, which began in 1635, making this the main thoroughfare for traffic going to Boston; as a result the town's first tavern was set up on this street, along with a number of shops and homes. The focal point of the town in its earliest years was the marketplace, which was established in 1635 on what is now Winthrop Sq.

During the first five years of its existence the town grew quite rapidly, increasing from ten houses in 1631 to 86 houses in 1635. The growth of the settlement was more gradual during the next generation, and in 1670 there were perhaps 130 houses in the township, with about 75 homes in Old Cambridge itself and most of the others on the high roads leading to the surrounding communities. Among the other structures erected in the first half-century of the town's history were a new meetinghouse in 1650, a schoolhouse in 1669 (the first school in Cambridge had opened in a private house in 1635), a parsonage in 1670, and a new hall for Harvard College in 1672—77. The settlement had been designated as the court town of Middlesex County in 1636, and in 1643 it became the shire town or county seat as well. The date of construction of the first courthouse is unknown, though there is evidence that early trials were held in the first meetinghouse, and there is a record of an early courthouse being destroyed by fire in 1671. The most famous trial to take place in the first meetinghouse in its early years occurred in 1637, when Anne Hutchinson was convicted of sedition and banished from the Bay Colony. The first jail was built before 1655, and among those imprisoned there were Quakers, incarcerated for a time before being driven out of town. Another prisoner of record was a Cambridge woman named Kendall, who was imprisoned here when she was convicted as a witch, after which she was hung from a gibbet on Gallows Hill, N. of the present Linnaean St.

Cambridge's ties with Boston were made more direct when the Great Bridge was built across the Charles River in 1660—62. On the Cambridge side the bridge began at the foot of Wood St (which later became Boylston St and is now known as John F. Kennedy Drive), from where a causeway led out across the marshes to the span itself. This greatly facilitated travel to Boston from Cambridge and communities farther afield, stimulating trade and commercial development in the region.

The area now known as Harvard Sq was originally called Watch House Hill, due to the fortification erected there about 1640. This structure was torn down sometime before 1650, when the second meetinghouse was constructed on its site. This made the area far more of a focus than it had been when it was merely an open space through which townspeople passed to reach the high roads leading to Charlestown and Watertown. The completion of the Great Bridge in 1662 further added to the importance of the area, since it became a crossroads for travelers going to and from Boston and the surrounding towns. The bridge also changed the traffic pattern in the town; since JFK Drive was the principal approach it soon surpassed Dunster St as the main commercial avenue. At that time the shape of the future Harvard Sq was irregular and without definite boundaries; with JFK Drive heading S. from its S.W. corner; and with Braintree St, the present Massachusetts Ave, leading E. from its S.E. corner. On its W. side was the Burying-Ground, one house, and a large field; to the E. and S. were the college and meetinghouse; along Braintree St stood four houses of tradesmen, and a tavern which sold "beer and bread" to Harvard students. By the beginning of the next century the square began to take on a more definite form; this came about through the construction of additional buildings by Harvard College: the erection of the third meetinghouse in 1706, replacing the one built in 1650; and a new courthouse in 1708. In the mid-18C there was a great deal of construction around the square, with still more buildings by Harvard; a fourth meetinghouse built in 1756 to replace the third; and a new courthouse in 1758. By the end of the colonial period the square had a quite definite though irregular shape and well-defined boundaries, though it passed through many more transformations before acquiring its present form.

The Common is another central area of Old Cambridge that formed during the colonial period. The territory in the original settlement was divided into three different categories: house lots within the village; fields for farming outside the village; and land set aside for common use, the latter constituting by far the greatest area in the early years. During those early years the common lands formed a vast reservoir of undivided land that could in the future be granted to new settlers as farms or set aside for other uses. The present Common, which originally extended as far N. as Linnaean St, was primarily a cow pasture, with the area nearest Harvard Sq used as a drill field by the local militia; the territory in North Cambridge between Rindge Ave and Alewife Brook became after 1638 the Ox Pasture; the area from the brook to Pleasant St in Arlington was used in turn for grazing cows and sheep; while the hilly land from Pleasant Ave to Arlington Heights, known as the Cambridge Rocks, was set aside as timberland and to provide wood for fuel and for building material. In 1724 the Common in Old Cambridge had its northern boundary shifted from Linnaean St to Waterhouse St, which delineates it today on that side, thus reducing its area from 86 acres to 16, its present extent. Within the next half-century about a dozen houses and other structures were built along the streets that surround the Common, most notably the Episcopal Christ Church, erected in 1760; these, together with the row of elms planted along the Garden St side in 1700, established the visual boundary of the Common that one sees today. During the first half of the 19C the remaining sites around the Common were taken up by buildings. In 1830 the Common was fenced in; by 1875 a system of paths had been laid out through it; and by 1930 it had been landscaped to its present parklike appearance.

During the last century of the colonial period Cambridge grew quite slowly. According to a provincial census in 1765, the population of the entire township was 1571, only 785 of whom seem to have resided within the present city limits. In the period just prior to the War of Independence, the people of Cambridge had divided into two quite distinct groups. The most numerous of these comprised the descendants of the original Puritan settlers or later arrivals of the same type; these made up more than 90 percent of the populace, and earned their living as farmers, artisans, or small tradesmen, as well as those associated with the college or the church. The people of this group were all members of the Congregational Church and were unanimous in their opposition to British rule, following the lead of their compatriots in Boston. The smaller group, which consisted of little more than a dozen families, many related by marriage, were wealthy members of the Episcopal Church and were loyal supporters of the Crown. A few of these, most notably the Brattles, were descendants of early Cambridge families who had amassed wealth through business and shipping and who had rejected Puritan ways for a more luxurious life-style. Others in this group, such as the Phips and Vassall families, had moved to Cambridge in the second quarter of the 18C and had made fortunes from West Indian plantations, or were living high on stipends received for services to the Crown. These Loyalists had little to do with the main populace of Cambridge, living in great mansions on the present Brattle St, then known as Tory Row, where they entertained one another lavishly. In 1775, after the onset of the War of Independence, the Provincial Congress ordered the Loyalist mansions "to be cleared" for the quartering of General Washington and his staff and for use as hospitals by the Continental Army. Virtually all of the Loyalists in Cambridge left America with the British fleet when Boston was evacuated on March 17, 1776. After the war the Common-wealth appropriated all but one of the Loyalist mansions on Tory Row and sold them to patriots in Cambridge. Today seven of these stately mansions still stand along Brattle St; two are open to the public and are described in Rte 17.

As noted above, the great majority of the townspeople of Cambridge made common cause with the patriots in Boston in the struggle for independence. After the Stamp Act was imposed in 1765, the town meeting in Cambridge ordered its representatives "by no means whatsoever to do any one thing" that might allow the Crown officials to enforce the legislation. After the Boston Massacre on March 5, 1770, the citizens of Cambridge imme-diately sent a message of sympathy and support to their compatriots across the Charles. The Cambridge town meeting sent numerous petitions to the King protesting the injustices of British rule, including the following expression of grievances in 1772: "We have been sighing and groaning under oppression for a number of years; our natural and charter rights are violated in too many instances here to enumerate; our money extorted from us, and appropriated to augment our burdens." In Nov. 1772 Cambridge followed Boston's lead in organizing a Committee of Correspondence. The people of Cambridge joined the Bostonians in their opposition to the tax on tea, and when the port of Boston was closed after the Tea Party they sent aid to them, although they themselves also suffered from the closure of the harbor. Then, on Sept. 1, 1774, Cambridge became directly involved in the struggle, when a pair of related incidents almost sparked the American Revolution before its time. At 4:30 a.m. on that day British troops under orders from General Thomas Gage raided the powder house in what is now Somerville, confiscating the entire store of gun-powder belonging to the local militia, and at the same time another detachment of redcoats seized two cannon in Cambridge, armaments of the militia there. The motive for Gage's move seems to have been his suspicion that the Americans were planning an uprising, but instead of thwarting this his actions almost precipitated a rebellion. The patriots of Boston, Cambridge, and the surrounding towns took up arms and prepared to defend themselves against a British attack. That same evening a mob rioted outside the Tory Row house of Jonathan Sewall, attorney general of Massachusetts, breaking windows and being fired upon by those inside. The following morning a crowd of several thousand angry people gathered in Harvard Sq in front of the courthouse, where there was a meeting of the Man-damus Council, the Crown-appointed body that had been substituted for the Massachusetts Legislature since the revocation of the charter in May 1774. Members of the Council emerged to address the crowd in an attempt to placate them, but in vain. Thereupon two members of the Council resigned to protect themselves, after which the lieutenant governor, Thomas Oliver, rode off to Boston to inform General Gage of the rebellious mood of the mob in Cambridge. When Gage heard the news he decided against sending troops to keep order in Cambridge, undoubtedly because he felt that such a move would only worsen matters. When British troops failed to appear in Cambridge, the crowd of thousands that had gath-ered in the Common eventually dispersed, and the incipient rebellion never materialized.

During Oct. 1774 the Provisional Assembly formed by the Massachusetts patriots con-vened in the Cambridge meetinghouse on Harvard Sq. At their first meeting the delegates appointed a Committee of Safety, which would also plan for the stockpiling of arms, ammu-nition, and supplies; later they formed a second committee to keep watch on the movement of the British troops.

On the evening of April 18, 1775, Paul Revere and William Dawes rode off from Boston to inform the minutemen in the surrounding towns that British troops were on their way to seize the American armaments in Concord. While Revere rode across Charlestown Neck toward Concord, Dawes crossed the Great Bridge and passed through Cambridge Common before dawn on the 19th. As soon as Dawes alerted them, the minutemen of Cambridge armed themselves and prepared to protect the Concord arsenal, while others dismantled the Great Bridge to impede the British. Unfortunately, they left the planking of the bridge on the left bank of the river, so that Lord Percy's troops were able to reassemble the span and cross; nevertheless, the action gained valuable time for the Americans. After the Bat-

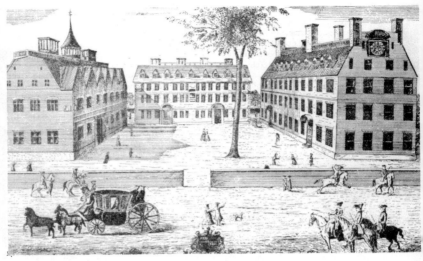

The colleges in Cambridge, drawn in 1726

tles of Lexington and Concord later that day, the minutemen of Cambridge joined the militia of the surrounding towns in attacking the British on their return march to Charlestown, and 14 men of the town died in that running battle. When news of the fighting spread through the countryside, volunteers began marching to Cambridge, and within a week there were nearly 2000 militiamen camped on the Common. General Artemas Ward was appointed commander of the growing volunteer force in Cambridge, which by May was estimated to number 16,000, about ten times the population of the town. The residence halls of Harvard were converted into barracks, and those of the students who did not volunteer moved to temporary quarters in Concord, where classes were held for nearly a year. Christ Church and the abandoned mansions of the Loyalists on Tory Row were converted into barracks, with some of them also fitted out as hospitals, prepared to receive the wounded from the imminent fighting. Soon afterward General Israel Putnam arrived with 3000 militiamen from Connecticut, bringing the American forces in Cambridge to an estimated 20,000. After sunset on June 16, 1775, some 1200 American militiamen under the command of Colonel Prescott marched from Cambridge to Charlestown on the eve of the Battle of Bunker Hill. Late on the following day the survivors of that epic struggle returned to their camp on Cambridge Common, while the wounded were looked after in makeshift hospitals in the town. Among the men of Cambridge who died in the Battle of Bunker Hill was Thomas Gardner, second in command to Colonel Prescott.

General George Washington, who had been appointed commander-in-chief of the Continental Army, arrived in Cambridge on July 2, 1775. Washington assumed command the following day, when he reviewed the American troops on Cambridge Common. Washington was appalled at the condition of the soldiers under his command, whom he found to be an unkempt and undisciplined rabble. While he worked at trying to train this force into a regular army, he also directed his men in hastily constructing a series of fortifications designed to hem in the British troops in Boston in preparation for a siege of the town. However, this siege could not be carried out without artillery; the Continental Army had neither cannon nor ammunition, for the only arms the American troops possessed were the muskets they brought with them when they volunteered. Moreover, the funds at Washington's disposal soon ran out, and on Sept. 21, 1775, he informed the Continental Congress that he could not continue without additional appropriations. As he wrote at that time: "The paymaster has not a single dollar in hand; the commisarry assures me he has strained his credit, for the subsistence of the army, to the utmost. The Quartermaster General is precisely in the same situation, and the greater parts of the troops are in a state not far from mutiny, upon the deduction from their stated allowance." This alarming message prompted the Continental Congress to send Benjamin Franklin and two other delegates to Cambridge. The congressional committee spent nine days in Cambridge in Oct. 1775, conferring with Washington and his staff and inspecting the camp. At the end of their visit Franklin and the other delegates promised Washington that the Congress would send him additional funds. They also agreed with him that the Continental Army was not yet ready to attack the British in Boston, and said that they would so inform the Congress. The Continental Army in Cambridge began to receive small quantities of ammunition during that autumn. Then, in Jan. 1776, Colonel Henry Knox arrived in Cambridge with 59 cannon taken from the British fortress at Fort Ticonderoga, New York, having dragged them 300 miles over the snow with ox-drawn sleds. Washington emplaced most of these cannon in the fortifications that now ringed Boston, but held a number in reserve in Roxbury, to be used in a plan that he and his staff conceived that winter. The first step in this plan was carried out on the evening of March 4, 1776, when American troops stealthily fortified the summit of Dorchester Heights and emplaced there the several cannon that had been held in reserve in Roxbury. The following morning the British found that the approach to Boston Harbor was now under the guns of the Continental Army, a situation that led them to evacuate their forces from the town 12 days later.

Washington's army left Cambridge soon after the British evacuation of Boston, marching off to New York. The 11 months of occupation by the Continental Army left Cambridge in a shambles, and it took several months to restore it to its former condition. But no sooner had Cambridge recovered from its occupation by American troops than a new one began. This occurred in Nov. 1777, when an escort of Continental soldiers led into Cambridge General John Burgoyne and the 5700 British and Hessian troops whom he had surrendered at the Battle of Saratoga the month before. Old Cambridge was spared the brunt of this second occupation, for only the officers were lodged in the town itself, whereas the ordinary soldiers were housed in barracks that the Continental Army had erected at Prospect and Winter Hills (now in Somerville). General William Heath, district commander of the Continental Army, arranged to house the highest-ranking officers in the abandoned mansions on Tory Row, with General Burgoyne assigned to the Apthorp mansion, and the Hessian commander, General Baron von Riedesel, in the former home of Jonathan Sewall. But, despite the fact that only the officers were quartered in the town, there was considerable bad feeling between them and the citizenry and a number of altercations occurred, one of which resulted in the death of a British officer. General Burgoyne and part of his army were escorted out of Cambridge in April 1778 and marched to a new detention center in Rhode Island; the rest of the prisoners were sent south in Nov. of that year. This was to be the last involvement of Cambridge in the Revolutionary War, and life soon returned to normal in the town. During the period Sept. 1779–May 1780 the meetinghouse at Harvard Sq housed the convention empowered to frame a constitution for Massachusetts, a document that was drafted by John Adams. The town meeting in Cambridge approved the document on May 23, 1780, and after it was ratified by Boston and the other towns of the Commonwealth it became the constitution of Massachusetts. This constitution, which remains in effect to this day, served as the archetype for the U.S. Constitution adopted in 1787.

The Federal period in the history of Cambridge began auspiciously with President Washington's visit in 1789, his first return since he and his troops had left in the spring of 1776. Cambridge had changed little since Washington's first visit, for no public buildings had been erected in the town in the interim because of the financial hard times that had occurred during the war and in its aftermath. Stoughton Hall at Harvard had been torn down because of the damage done when it was used as a barracks by Washington's troops, and the mansions on Tory Row had new owners. The population of Cambridge, which then still included within its boundaries Arlington and Brighton, had grown significantly since the beginning of the war, increasing from about 1600 in 1775 to 2115 in 1790. During the following four decades the population of Cambridge increased steadily, even though its boundaries were contracting; so that in 1830, when the town's area had reached essentially its present limit, its population was 6072. Part of this increase was due to the settling of Cambridgeport and East Cambridge. The development of Cambridgeport began in 1793 with the completion of the West Boston Bridge, whose site is now occupied by the Longfellow Bridge. The financiers who built the bridge had in mind the creation of a port in Cambridge, and so the community that developed around the end of the span on the left bank of the Charles was called Cambridgeport. The first settlement in Cambridgeport was in the vicinity of the present Kendall Sq, which was then on the edge of the saltwater marshes fringing the lower reaches of the Charles River. Cambridge received congressional approval as an official port of entry on Jan. 11, 1805, by which time the population of Cambridgeport amounted to about 1000 people. The first schoolhouse was erected in Cambridgeport in 1802; a fire-fighting company was organized there in 1803; and on Jan. 1, 1807, the First Church of Cambridgeport was dedicated. However, hopes for developing a port in Cambridge were dashed by the enactment of the Embargo Act in 1807. This legislation not only stopped all foreign shipping at Cambridgeport, but it brought about a severe financial depression in all the coastal towns of New England, and it ended for all time the dream of having a major port in Cambridge.

The next stage in the development of Cambridge began on Aug. 30, 1809, with the opening of the Canal Bridge between Boston and Lechmere Point, whose site is now occupied by the Charles River Dam. The Canal Bridge was the creation of Andrew Craigie, a speculator who in 1795 began the financial manipulations that led to the building of the bridge and the creation of East Cambridge. Craigie, motivated by a desire for quick profits, was determined to create a viable community in East Cambridge, and so he began maneuvering to have some of the township's public institutions relocated there. Craigie accomplished this by offering to build a new courthouse and jail in East Cambridge at his own expense, to replace the dilapidated and overcrowded facilities in Old Cambridge. At first his offer was refused, because many of the town elders in Old Cambridge were reluctant to admit that the newer settlements in East Cambridge and Cambridgeport were beginning to achieve status comparable to their own community. But Craigie's offer was eventually accepted; the new courthouse was erected in 1814 and the jail in 1816, both structures being designed by either Charles Bulfinch or someone strongly influenced by his style. The jail has vanished, but the courthouse still stands in East Cambridge, though much altered. The relocation of the courthouse and jail were the first steps in the decentralization of Cambridge, the next phase coming with the transfer of the Town Hall to Cambridgeport in 1832.

James Russell Lowell's delightful book, *Cambridge Thirty Years Ago,* written in 1854, gives an evocative picture of what life was like there during his childhood. He writes that "We called it 'The Village' then, and it was essentially an English village—quiet, unspeculative, without enterprise, sufficing to itself, and only showing such differences from the original types as the public school and the system of town government might superinduce. A few houses, chiefly old, stood around the bare common, with ample elbow-room; and old women, capped and spectacled, still peered through the same windows from which they had watched Lord Percy's artillery rumble by to Lexington, or caught a glimpse of the handsome Virginia general who had come to wield our homespun Saxon chivalry. The hooks were to be seen from which had swung the hammocks of Burgoyne's captive redcoats. If memory does not deceive me, women still washed their clothes in the town spring, clear as that of Bandelusia." Lowell also gives a vivid picture of what Cambridgeport was like at the time, writing that most of it was then little more than a "huckleberry pasture." He goes on to say that "Its veins did not draw their blood from the quiet old heart of the village, but it had a distinct being of its own, and was rather a great caravansaray than a suburb. The chief feature of the place was its inns, of which there were five, with vast barns and courtyards. . . . There were, besides the taverns, some huge square stores where groceries were sold, some houses, by whom or why inhabited was to us boys a problem, and, on the edge of the marsh, a currier's shop, where, at high tide, on a floating platform, men were always beating skins in a way to remind one of Don Quixote's fulling mills."

Many of the people in Old Cambridge resented the fact that important public institutions had been transferred from their community to East Cambridge and Cambridgeport. Also, by the middle of the 19C the character of the two new settlements differed markedly from that of Old Cambridge, which was still a serene college town, with Harvard having celebrated its bicentennial in 1836. Cambridgeport and East Cambridge, on the other hand, were hurly-burly commercial communities, peopled largely with recently arrived immigrants who had been attracted by the many industrial firms established there. These differences led a group of citizens from Old Cambridge to submit a petition to the General Court in Dec. 1842, asking that Cambridgeport and East Cambridge be separated from their own community. Their request caused consternation in all three communities, and after lengthy debate the motion was rejected by a large majority at a town meeting in Feb. 1846. The town meeting then decided that Cambridge should follow the example of Boston and other neighboring communities, and the citizenry petitioned the General Court to give them a city charter. The Massachusetts Legislature granted this charter on March 17, 1846, and 13 days later the town meeting in Cambridge ratified the act.

When Cambridge became a city its population was only 12,500, but by the end of the 19C it had increased to nearly 100,000, about the same as it is today. The largest part of this increase took place in Cambridgeport and East Cambridge. This growth was due to the rapid industrialization that took place in Cambridge in the second half of the 19C, with the number of manufacturing firms in the city increasing from 94 in 1845 to 578 in 1885, the vast majority of these enterprises being established in Cambridgeport and East Cambridge, their employees mainly recently arrived immigrants. This tremendous growth and industrialization intensified the centrifugal tendencies that already existed in the city, and in 1855 the citizens in both Old Cambridge and East Cambridge petitioned the Massachusetts Legislature to grant them separate status, but in both cases their requests were denied. While the debate on separation was still under way, the *Cambridge Chronicle* published an editorial on this issue which characterizes the general civic opinion still current in Cambridge, emphasizing that "the importance of cultivating the most friendly relations between different sections of the city is far greater than the pleasure which we could give by the statement of evidence, or arguments of counsel, which, to say the least, would tend to widen the unfortunate differences which seem to exist among us. . . ." Eventually, the growth of Cambridge melded the three communities into one continuous urban group, though even today each of them has its own distinctive character. At the same time all parts of Cambridge became ever more closely linked with Boston; more bridges were built across the Charles; numerous public-transport lines were created between the two cities, first horse-drawn trams, then electric trolleys, and finally, in 1912, a subway was opened between Park St in Boston and Harvard Sq. Harvard participated in this tremendous expansion; during the presidency of A. Lawrence Lowell (1909–33) more buildings were erected than had been built in the prior 273 years of the institution's history. Another important event in the city's history took place in 1916, when the Massachusetts Institute of Technology relocated in Cambridge. The presence of these two great universities has made Cambridge one of the cultural centers of the U.S., attracting to the city many "high-tech" firms and other corporations that have utilized the extraordinary intellectual resources stemming from Harvard and M.I.T. Old Cambridge has in recent years become very trendy, with a proliferation of restaurants, cafes, bars, boutiques, and bookshops, but despite this it has still the ambience of a small college town. One has only to go a short way to leave behind the crowds and traffic of Harvard Sq, to stroll in the dappled shade of Harvard Yard and through the serene byways of Old Cambridge.

17 Old Cambridge I: West of Harvard Square

Approach. The most convenient way to travel from downtown Boston to Old Cambridge by public transport is the Red Line from the Park St T station, getting off at Harvard Sq. Those walking from Boston can cross the Charles by a number of bridges, the most pleasant one being the *Weeks Memorial Bridge* (pedestrians only). From this bridge, turn l. and walk along the pedestrian path beside the river at the end of the *Larz Anderson Bridge,* which occupies the site of the Great Bridge. Turn r. onto John F. Kennedy Drive (formerly known as Boylston St), which soon reaches *Harvard Sq.* This approach comes to the center of Old Cambridge by the same route taken by townspeople returning from Boston in colonial times.

In recent years the center of Old Cambridge has become one of the liveliest, noisiest, and most crowded areas in the Boston Metropolitan District, with a proliferation of restaurants, bars, shops, and boutiques, thronged with students from Harvard and thousands of other young people attracted to the street scene and the night life, along with hordes of tourists. The square has recently been restored, after the completion of the new Harvard Square underground T station and the extension of the subway to Porter Sq. Excavations for the new line during the years 1981–85 revealed some 150,000 artifacts that have been studied by archaeologists, the oldest being stone tools from an Indian hunting camp dating from c. 1500 B.C.

Before starting out on the itinerary, pause for a moment in Harvard Sq to get oriented. The best vantage point is the center of the square itself, one of the most popular meeting places in Cambridge. Massachusetts Ave enters the square from the E. and makes a right-angled bend to the N., forming the S. and W. sides of Harvard Yard; JFK Drive leads off to the S. and Brattle St to the W. This itinerary goes N. along Massachusetts Ave.

Topography and History. Harvard Sq developed soon after the settlement of Newtowne, since when it has been the center of Old Cambridge's life, the site of some of the most important events in the community's history. Roads diverged from here to all of the surrounding settlements, and throughout most of the colonial period the courthouse and meetinghouse stood on the square. Early in the 18C the town's market house was erected in the center of the square, with a fish market on the lower floor, and beside this building were the town pump and the standard scales used to check the balances of the local merchants.

Standing on the traffic island in Harvard Sq and looking to the N. along Massachusetts Ave, one sees to the r. some of the university buildings that form the W. and S. sides of Harvard Yard, while to the l. is the *Harvard Coop,* a large cooperative department store (huge bookshop in an annex to the rear) associated with the university.

At this point one is well situated to identify the sites of some of the historic buildings that once stood in Harvard Sq. The most notable of these were the second, third, and fourth courthouses, which stood successively on or very near the present site of the Coop; to the r. of the traffic island, where Lehman Hall now stands at the S.W. corner of Harvard Yard, was the site, in turn, of the second, third, and fourth meetinghouses. The fourth courthouse, which was built in 1758, was where on Sept. 2, 1774, an angry mob of patriots forced the resignation of two members of the King's Mandamus Council, Judges Danforth and Lee. The fourth meetinghouse, erected in 1756, served as the first convention hall for the Provincial Assembly of Massachusetts, which met there in Oct. 1774 to form Committees of Safety and Correspondence and to take over the civil and military government from the Crown. During the period Sept. 1779–May 1780 the church also housed the popularly elected convention that framed the constitution of Massachusetts, the document forming the basis for the government of the Bay State to the present day. The fourth meetinghouse was demolished in 1833, but the fourth courthouse survived until 1930.

Cross over to the Coop and turn r. to begin walking up that side of Massachusetts Ave. After passing the Harvard Trust Co., one comes to a long building with a mansard roof, its facade making a bend as it extends to the end of the block. This is the *College House,* erected in 1845–59 and considerably altered since; it was originally built by private investors as a dormitory for Harvard students, with shops on the ground floor. This structure replaced an earlier dormitory of the same name, also called Wiswall's Den, erected in 1769. Many of General John Burgoyne's captive British and Hessian officers were quartered here in 1777–78, following their surrender at the Battle of Saratoga.

At the next intersection Church St is crossed, and at the far corner is the **First Church Unitarian,** also called the First Parish Church. This was built in 1833 by the architect Isaiah Rogers in the Gothic Revival style; the structure standing today is essentially the same as the original. The stone parish house at the rear was added in 1901 by the architect J. W. Richards.

The congregation of the church originally worshipped at the fourth meetinghouse, but in 1829 a dispute split the members into two factions, the Trinitarians and the Unitarians. The Trinitarians left to form their own church, while the Unitarians remained in possession of the fourth meetinghouse. In 1833 the Unitarians decided to build the present church; when this was finished the fourth meetinghouse was sold to Harvard, which demolished the building to make way for a new college hall.

Continuing along, on the l. is the *Old Burying-Ground* (described later on in this itinerary). Just inside the graveyard fence, near the intersection of Massachusetts Ave and Garden St, is a milestone that originally stood in Harvard Sq.

On the front of the stone is the inscription "8 MILES / 1734 / A I"; this gives the distance from Harvard Sq to Boston, by a route which took one over the Boylston St Bridge and on through Brighton, Brookline, and Roxbury. The reverse side of the stone reads "CAMBRIDGE / NEW BRIDGE / 2¼ MILES / 1793," which was the distance for the new and much more direct route over the West Boston Bridge, opened in 1793. The letters "A I" on the front are the initials of Abraham Ireland, who carved the original inscription.

Outside the Old Burying Ground, Garden St diverges to the l. from Massachusetts Ave, the two thoroughfares bounding Cambridge Common on the W. and E., respectively, with Waterhouse St forming the northern limit of the park. In 1975 a traffic island at the intersection of Garden St and Massachusetts Ave was dedicated as a memorial to William Dawes, who in the early morning of April 19, 1775, rode this way to alert the patriots that the British were marching on Concord. On the sidewalk that passes through the traffic island an inscription commemorates this event, and bronze hoofmarks mark the course of Dawes' ride through this southern corner of Cambridge Common.

Cross over to the southern entrance to the ****Common.**

History. As mentioned before, in the early days of the settlement the Common was used primarily as a place to fence in cattle and to protect them from wolves and marauding Indians. It was also used as a training ground and muster field for the Cambridge Militia, and Harvard students thronged the Common when celebrating their commencement exercises. In the early days of the settlement it was also a place where outdoor forums were held, particularly at election time. On such occasions the townspeople gathered around an ancient tree known as the Election Oak that stood on the eastern side of the Common, and discussed the issues and candidates. The most exciting of these outdoor meetings took place in 1636, when Sir Henry Vane and John Winthrop were contending for election as governor of the Bay Colony. The adherents of Vane and Winthrop gathered in great numbers around the Election Oak, and their discussions grew so heated that there were fears that violence would break out. This led the Rev. John Wilson, pastor of the First Church in Boston, to climb up into the tree, from which vantage point he addressed the crowd and persuaded them to calm down. Another historic landmark on the Common was the Whitefield Tree, which stood just beyond the N.W. corner of the present park, on Garden St just past its intersection with Mason St. This tree was named for the Rev. George Whitefield, the Wesleyan evangelist, who in 1740 stood beneath it when he preached to multitudes of his followers, denouncing the New England clergy for being deficient in piety, and severely criticizing Harvard College for its lax moral code.

Cambridge Common was the scene of several events connected with the American Revolution. Here in Sept. 1774 a crowd of some 2000 men from all over Middlesex County angrily called for the dissolution of the King's Mandamus Council, forcing two of the three members to resign. On the morning of April 19, 1775, the minutemen of Cambridge, alerted by William Dawes, mustered on the Common before going off to fight the British. In the weeks afterward thousands of volunteers arrived in Cambridge and camped on the Common, as General Ward took command and began to organize them into an effective fighting force. After sunset on June 16, 1775, Colonel William Prescott mustered his band of 1200 men on the Common before marching off to Charlestown, and before they left, President Samuel Langdon of Harvard College offered prayers to God that the cause of liberty and right should overcome. After the Battle of Bunker Hill the next day, Prescott led the survivors back to their encampment on the Common, as the wounded were taken off to the several hospitals that had been set up in town.

The most dramatic event in the history of the Common occurred on July 3, 1775, when General George Washington rode there to assume command of the Continental Army, which officially came into being on that day. According to tradition, this ceremony took place in the shade of an ancient elm that stood near the N.W. corner of the Common, at what is now the intersection of Garden and Mason Sts; however, some modern historians are of the opinion that Washington took command in the Wadsworth House, which still stands today in Harvard Yard (see below). In any event, the ancient tree on Cambridge Common was thereafter known as the Washington Elm, an object of veneration throughout the U.S. The Washington Elm remained standing until 1923, when it was finally removed to make way for traffic. At the time of removal several cuttings were taken from the old tree and raised in a nursery, and in 1946 the scion was replanted in Cambridge Common, where it still grows. Other cuttings from the Washington Elm were similarly raised and replanted to replace the Election Oak and the Whitefield Tree, the first of these scions standing at the N.W. corner of the park and the second midway along the eastern side.

Entering the Common at its S.E. corner, one passes through the *George Washington Memorial Gateway*. This monument, of pink Milford granite, was commissioned by the General Society of the Daughters of the American Revolution, and was dedicated on Oct. 19, 1906. To the l. of the entry there is a medallion portrait of George Washington, along with the following inscription: "Near this spot on July 3d, 1775, George Washington took command of the American Army."

From the gateway a path leads to a central area from which paths lead off to all parts of the park. In the center of the clearing stands the *Soldiers' Monument*, a memorial to the 30 officers and 310 noncommissioned officers and men from Cambridge who died in the Union Army during the Civil War. The structure was designed by the brothers Cyrus and Darius Cobb, themselves Civil War veterans, and it was built by the architect Thomas W. Silloway. The cornerstone was laid in 1867 and the monument was dedicated in 1870, with James Russell Lowell reading a poem he had written for the occasion.

Now take the path that leads to the l. from the monument, heading toward the exit at the corner of Garden and Mason Sts. Near the end of this path is a mall around which there are several objects of historic interest.

A stele commemorates the events that took place here on July 3–4, 1775; on the front a bronze relief shows General Washington on his horse beneath the elm that came to bear his name, his sword extended as he reviews his troops on the day he assumed command of the American forces in Cambridge. On the reverse side an inscription gives the text of Washington's General Orders given at Cambridge on July 4, 1775, the congressional document that officially formed the colonial militias into a unified Continental Army.

On the r. side of the mall, protected by a railing, is the scion of the Washington Elm that was planted there in 1946, with a sign recording its historic significance. (The Washington Elm, which was planted c. 1700, actually stood in the center of Garden St, near its intersection with Mason St.) On the l. side of the mall are arrayed three old cannon, with a historic marker recording that they were left behind by the British when they abandoned Fort Independence (Castle William) at the time of the evacuation of Boston on March 17, 1776. At the border of the park a marker honors General Tadeusz Kościusko, the Polish patriot who fought so valiantly in the Continental Army.

The path continues past the mall toward the exit at the corner of Garden and Mason Sts. Just before the exit the path is flanked by two bronze historic markers. The one on the l. is a map showing the course of the old Charlestown-Watertown path. This was laid down in 1630, the first road in the British colonies, and it was the way taken by the Rev. Thomas Hooker and his followers in 1634, when they left Newtowne to move on to Hartford, Connecticut. The marker on the r. has a relief showing the corner of Garden and Mason Sts c. 1860. The relief shows the Washington Elm; the Fay House, which is still standing across the way (see below); and the Abraham Hill House, which has since been demolished.

After leaving the Common, cross over to the N. corner of Garden and Mason Sts, where the **First Church Congregational** stands.

History. The First Church Congregational is a descendant of the original church founded at the time of the settlement of Newtowne in 1630. As noted earlier, this congregation, then housed in the fourth meetinghouse, broke into two factions in 1829, the Unitarians and the Trinitarians, whose views were orthodox congregational. The latter group, led by the old minister, the Rev. Abiel Holmes, father of Oliver Wendell Holmes, Sr., incorporated themselves as the Shepard Congregational Society, and the group eventually moved into a new meetinghouse they erected on the N.W. corner of Holyoke and Mount Auburn Sts. They remained there until 1872, when they moved into the present edifice, designed by Abel C. Martin. The old church on Holyoke and Mount Auburn Sts was then sold to the Roman Catholic diocese and became the first home of St. Paul's parish. The first St. Paul's Church was demolished in 1915, when the congregation moved into a new house of worship.

Exterior. The church designed by Abel C. Martin is built of traprock trimmed with brownstone and red granite. The handsome stone spire of the church originally rose to a height of 170ft, but in 1938 this was rebuilt with a lower slate roof by the architects Allen, Collens, and Willis. The superb weathervane in the form of a gilded rooster is much older than the church itself. It was made in 1721 by Shem Drowne, who also made the gilded grasshopper on Faneuil Hall. The vane originally belonged to the New Brick Meeting-House on Hanover St in the North End, which took its name of "Cockerel Church" from the gilded rooster on its spire. At the rear of the church there was originally a small parish hall built in 1873; in 1926 this was replaced by a new parish house and office wing designed by William H. McLean.

Interior. The nave of the church is in the form of a T, with the pulpit standing on the central axis in the front of a spacious apse. Other departures from the sparseness and simplicity of the traditional Puritan meetinghouse are evidenced in the sumptuous interior fittings and decoration, particularly the fine stained glass in the traceried windows of the S. transept. The polygonal vaulted ceiling is part of a double roof; the space between it and the exterior roof conceals a system of ventilation ducts, an innovation in air conditioning created when the church was built.

Just to the S. of the First Church Congregational, on the block bounded by Garden, Mason, Brattle, and Appian Way, is the building complex that surrounds *Radcliffe Yard,* the center of the distinguished women's college that is now an integral part of Harvard University.

History. The institution that became Radcliffe College had its beginnings in Dec. 1878, when Arthur Gilman, the Cambridge historian, proposed to President Eliot of Harvard the foundation of a college for women. The college that he proposed would be completely separate from Harvard, the only link being that instruction would be provided on a private basis by members of the university faculty. President Eliot accepted Gilman's proposal, and a committee of seven Cambridge ladies was appointed to make plans for the new institution. After several Harvard faculty members agreed to teach at the new institution, a public announcement was made in Feb. 1879 of the opening of the "Private Collegiate Institute for Women." Entrance exams were given in Sept. of that year, and shortly afterward 27 young women began classes in rooms leased for the school at 6 Appian Way. As enrollment increased additional rooms were rented in nearby houses for classrooms, laboratories, and a library. In Oct. 1882 the managers became a corporation under Massachusetts law as "The Society for the Collegiate Instruction for Women," though the school was popularly known as the "Harvard Annex." In 1885 the school moved into its first permanent home, the Fay House, a handsome mansion that still stands at 10 Garden St, near the corner of Mason St. In 1894, with the consent of Harvard, the school was incorporated as Radcliffe College; the name derived from Anne Radcliffe (Lady Moulson), a wealthy Puritan who in 1643 had presented Harvard with its first scholarship fund.

During the first half-century of its existence Radcliffe grew rapidly, as it became one of the leading women's colleges in the U.S., adding a library, gymnasium, student center, and two teaching buildings, developing a residential quadrangle on upper Garden St, and acquiring Greenleaf House on Brattle St as the presidential residence. In 1943 Radcliffe and Harvard reached an agreement to begin combining men and women students from the two institutions in the same classes, a gradual process that was not completed until the 1970s.

If one starts at the corner of Mason and Garden and walks back along the latter street, the first Radcliffe building seen is the *Fay House*. This Federal brick mansion was erected in 1807 for Nathaniel Ireland, a Boston iron merchant, and in 1870 it was modified by the addition of a mansard roof. The mansion was acquired by Radcliffe in 1885 as the first permanent home of the college; in 1890 it was almost entirely rebuilt by the architectural firm of Longfellow, Alden, and Harlow. At that time the facade was faced with new brick, a third story was added, and the original house was almost entirely obscured by two new wings. The Fay House today serves as the administrative center for Radcliffe.

After passing the Fay House, turn r. to enter ***Radcliffe Yard,** a tranquil haven in the heart of busy Cambridge. On the l. is *Byerly Hall;* this multichimneyed structure was built in 1931 by Coolidge and Carson to house Radcliffe's science departments; today it contains the Harvard and Radcliffe admissions offices. At the entrance to the Yard a map identifies the various buildings that form its periphery. At the W. end of the Yard a trio of buildings is connected by a curving portico; these are, from r. to l.: the *Hemenway Gymnasium,* 1898 (McKim, Mead & White); *Agassiz House,* 1904 (A. W. Longfellow, Jr., the poet's nephew); and the edifice that houses the *Schlesinger Library* and the *Bunting Institute,* 1907 (Winslow and Bigelow; remodeled in 1966). The Schlesinger Library is renowned for its collection of books and manuscripts on the history of women in America. On the E. side of the Yard, which is bounded by Appian Way, is the largest and most impressive structure in the precincts; this is *Longfellow Hall,* a brick neo-Georgian edifice inspired by Bulfinch's University Hall in Harvard Yard, erected in 1929 by Perry, Shaw, and Hepburn, the architectural firm that was in charge of restoring the colonial town of Williamsburg, Virginia. *Massachusetts Hall,* originally built as a student dormitory, is now part of the Harvard Graduate School of Education.

A gateway beside Massachusetts Hall leads out of Radcliffe Yard to Appian Way. Across the street to the r. is the *Monroe C. Gutman Library* of the

Harvard Graduate School of Education, built in 1969 by Benjamin Thompson and Assocs. To the l. of the library a picturesque passageway leads from Appian Way to Farwell Pl. Near the end of this passageway on the l. is a small square with two old houses. The first of these is the *Read House,* dating to c. 1772, which originally stood at 55 Brattle St. The house is named after its first owner, a tanner named James Read, who marched off with the Cambridge Militia on April 19 to do battle with the British on their return from Lexington and Concord. The elaborate entryway is copied from Batty Langley's *The City and Country Builder's and Workmen's Treasury of Design,* a pattern book published in London in 1756. Just beyond, at the corner of Farwell Pl, is the *Nichol House,* a dwelling that once stood at 63 Brattle St. This was erected in 1827 by the builder Oliver Hastings for John Nichols, a renowned surgeon who served in the Union Army during the Civil War. The charming Federal house has two bow-fronted bays projecting under a front porch whose roof is supported by six Tuscan columns.

Now turn l. into Farwell Pl, a picturesque byway with four quaint old houses on the r. and another on the l., dating to various times in the period 1834–73. At the end of the street is the apse of ****Christ Church,** the next stop on this itinerary, the finest and most historic house of worship in Cambridge. This is approached by a narrow path to the r., between the church and the Old Burying-Ground.

History. Those who built Christ Church were originally members of the congregation at the fourth meetinghouse. But shortly after that church was built, in 1756, a group of prosperous Tory members broke away to form their own Anglican congregation. The congregation chose as their architect Peter Harrison, who had so successfully designed King's Chapel in Boston. Harrison did not finish his design until 1760, and another year passed before the building was completed. The first rector of Christ Church was the Rev. East Apthorp, who left Boston in 1764 to take up permanent residence in England. At the outbreak of the American Revolution, Christ Church was abandoned by its Tory congregation, most of whom left with the British fleet when Boston was evacuated. After the Battles of Lexington and Concord, Christ Church was used as a barracks by General Israel Putnam's Connecticut Militia, whose rough usage soon reduced the building to a shambles. The church was summarily repaired and reopened for services on New Year's Eve, 1775, when General George Washington and his wife, Martha, worshipped there, after which the building reverted to use as a barracks. Additional damage was done to the building in 1777, when General John Burgoyne's British and Hessian troops were quartered in Cambridge. As noted earlier, one of the British officers was killed in an altercation with some townspeople, who resented the presence of the enemy troops quartered in their homes. The officer's funeral was held in Christ Church, with General John Burgoyne and all of his British and Hessian staff in attendance, and afterward the young man was laid to rest in the Vassall family crypt. This pompous ceremony greatly offended many of the townspeople in Cambridge, and afterward some of them vandalized the church. As one of the British officers described it, the mob used the occasion as an opportunity "to plunder, ransack, and deface every thing they could lay their hands on, destroying the pulpit, reading desk, and communion table, and ascending the organ loft, destroyed the bellows and broke all the pipes of a very handsome instrument."

After the war Christ Church was in a sorry state, with no congregation to restore it. Dr. Hoppin, in his monograph on the history of the church, writes: "Christ Church was left for many years in a melancholy and desecrated condition, the doors shattered and all the windows broken out, exposed to rain and storms and every sort of depredation, its beauty gone, its sanctuary defiled, and the wind howling through its deserted aisles, and about its stained and decaying walls; the whole building being a disgrace instead of an ornament to the town." No effort seems to have been made for the restoration of the church and the renewal of divine worship until the beginning of 1790. At that time a subscription was made to pay for the restoration of the church, which was reconsecrated at a service on July 14, 1790. For the next 30 years there was no permanent clergyman attached to Christ Church, and services were conducted by lay readers, many of them students or faculty members at

Harvard, or occasionally by visiting ministers. In 1824 the condition of the church was so wretched that another subscription fund was raised, with contributions coming from Harvard and from other churches all over Massachusetts, a drive that made possible a thorough restoration of the building in 1825–26. During the next generation the fortunes of the church began to improve, and by 1857 the congregation has increased to the point where it became necessary to enlarge the building. In 1860 a chime of 13 bells was procured through another subscription fund. Subsequently the church underwent additional minor alterations and repairs; in 1868 a parish hall was added in the form of a side wing, to be replaced in 1897 by the present porticoed structure; and in 1948 a brick wing was added facing Farwell Place.

Exterior. The design drawn by Peter Harrison for Christ Church was a much-simplified version of the plans he used for King's Chapel in Boston. The original building was a wooden structure 60ft long and 45ft wide, in front of which was the present entrance tower, with the belfry being added in 1766. In 1857 the church was enlarged in an ingenious manner; this was done by cutting through the building, moving back the apse and the first bay by 23ft, and then inserting two new bays into the intervening space. During the course of this alteration the external design of the church was not altered, and except for changes in paint color and trim it remains the same to this day. The exterior walls are plain, the only decoration being the Doric frieze and cornice that extend around the building, pierced by a single course of round-arched windows.

A sign to the l. of the entrance notes that President Theodore Roosevelt, while a student at Harvard, served as a Sunday-school instructor at Christ Church. In passing through the vestibule, notice the small area of damaged woodwork high on the wall just to the r. of the central door; a bronze plaque identifies this as a bullet hole made by a stray shot fired by a redcoat on April 19, 1775, when the British marched across Cambridge Common on their way to Lexington and Concord.

Interior. The interior consists of a nave roofed with a coved ceiling, with side aisles separated from the central area by colonnades of wooden monoliths on high pedestals; these columns were originally surmounted by Tuscan capitals with their entablatures, whereas the present Ionic capitals were put in place in 1826. The nave ends in a shallow apse, in the center of which is the simple altar, with the pulpit off to the l. In 1853 the original 44 box pews were replaced by the present ones. Then, in the 1880s, the church was redecorated in the Victorian style; the chancel was enlarged at that time to accommodate the choir. A cherished treasure of the church is its silver communion service, whose vessels are inscribed with the names of William and Mary and the date 1694. This service had been originally presented to King's Chapel by the King and Queen in 1696, along with the library that is now exhibited at the Boston Athenaeum. But in 1772 Governor Hutchinson brought to King's Chapel a new communion service as a present from George III, whereupon the old service was divided between Christ Church in Cambridge and the Anglican church in Newburyport, Mass.

Just to the E. of Christ Church is the ****Old Burying-Ground,** also known as God's Acre. Those who wish to enter the graveyard should apply to the sexton of Christ Church, who will open the gate at the end of the path beside the church.

History. This very picturesque graveyard was originally part of the Common, but sometime before 1635 it was set aside for burials, superseding the older burying ground "without the Common Pales." The Old Burying-Ground originally consisted of only about an acre, but additions were made from time to time by enclosing more of the Common. In 1735 the town built a stone wall on the side of the graveyard facing the road at a cost of £150, with Harvard paying £25, as it stands in the records, "Because the College has used and expects to make use of the Burying-Place, as Providence gives occasion for it." The cemetery reached its present limits in the latter part of the 19C, with the cast-iron fence that now surrounds it being erected in 1891, but by that time burials had long since ceased there.

Among those interred in the Old Burying-Ground are most of the early settlers of Cambridge, the first ministers who served them, the early presidents of Harvard, a number of students of the college in its early years, and some of the leading figures in the history of colonial Massachusetts. The oldest stone now standing is that of *Ann Erinton,* one of the early settlers, who died on Christmas Eve, 1653. Known to be buried here, although his tombstone had not been located, is the *Rev. Thomas Shepard.*

Shepard succeeded the Rev. Thomas Hooker as minister of the first meetinghouse after the latter left Newtowne in 1634 with many of his congregation, migrating to Hartford, Connecticut, in search of religious freedom and more abundant farmland. The Rev. Shepard served until the time of his death on Aug. 25, 1649, and thus was minister of the first meetinghouse throughout most of its history.

The graves of the early presidents of Harvard are for the most part to be found behind the First Parish Church. The oldest of these tombs is that of *Henry Dunster,* Harvard's first president, who died in 1659. Among the early Harvard students whose tombstones have been identified is *Winslow Warren* of Plymouth, who died on March 9, 1747, aged 15; his epitaph describes him as "A Young Gentleman of Considerable Hopes." In the graveyard lie 14 veterans of the Continental Army whose graves are known and marked, decorated annually on Memorial Day by the Washington Elm Chapter of the Daughters of the American Revolution. Also buried here, although the locations of their graves are unknown, are 14 Cambridge minutemen who died on April 19, 1775, killed in the running battle that took place as the British marched back to Charlestown after the Battles of Lexington and Concord; in 1870 the city erected a simple shaft inscribed with the names of these heroes. Another monument in the graveyard commemorates the soldiers of the Continental Army who were wounded at the Battle of Bunker Hill and who died at Elmwood, the Tory mansion that was converted into a hospital, with their remains then being interred here. Two black minutemen of Cambridge who survived the battle of April 19, 1775, are buried here as well; these are *Neptune Frost* and *Cato Stedman,* slaves who were interred in the tombs of their masters.

Near the front gate is the tomb of *Governor Jonathan Belcher* and those of *Judges Remington* and *Trowbridge.* Belcher, who was born in 1681 and graduated from Harvard in 1699, served as royal governor of Massachusetts and New Hampshire from 1730 to 1741 and of New Jersey from 1747 to 1757; he died in Elizabethtown, New Jersey, on Aug. 1, 1757.

A touching story about Belcher and the two judges who are buried beside him is told by William Thaddeus Harris in his *Epitaphs from the Old Burying-Ground in Cambridge;* as he writes: "It appears that Governor Belcher and his cousin, Judge Remington, were ardent friends, so much so as to desire to be buried in one grave. Judge Remington dying first, his body was committed to the earth. The Governor's remains, having been brought here from New Jersey, were deposited in a tomb, constructed a short time before, agreeably to his orders, contiguous to that of Judge Trowbridge; the body of Judge Remington was disinterred, and placed by his side."

The grave of Judge Trowbridge is now known as the Dana tomb, for buried there as well are *Chief Justice Francis Dana* and *Richard Henry Dana,* author of *Two Years Before the Mast.* Another distinguished person interred in this tomb is the painter *Washington Allston.*

The tombstones in the Old Burying-Ground make it a museum of Early American funerary art. The oldest monuments are slate stones with scalloped shoulders, most of them decorated with death's heads and other traditional funerary symbols of medieval origin. The finest of these early tombstones is that of William Dickson, dated 1692; this was done by Joseph Lamston, a Charlestown stonecutter, and is one of six monuments in the graveyard carved by him. The most impressive of the later funerary monuments is the Vassall tomb, a reddish freestone slab resting on five fluted columns. This was erected to Colonel John Vassall, who died in 1747; buried here with him are his wife and other members of that distinguished Tory family.

After leaving the graveyard, walk out to Garden St and turn l. On the short stretch between Christ Church and Appian Way are three venerable houses, the first two of which belong to the church and the third to Harvard. The long building at 2 Garden St, just beside the church, is a late Federal house of three stories with a hip roof, erected in 1820 by the master builder William Saunders for his own use. The house next to this, at No. 2, which dates to 1835, was also built by Saunders, who sold it to another party. The house on the corner, No. 3, also dates to 1835, but the identity of the architect is unknown.

Now turn l. and begin walking down Appian Way, passing on the l. *Larsen Hall,* built for the Harvard Graduate School of Education in 1965 by Caudill, Rowlett & Scott. After passing Larsen Hall, turn l. into the passageway that runs beside it, with the backs of the Read and Nichols Houses on the r. This returns to Farwell Pl, where one turns r. and walks out to Brattle St. At the corner turn l. and begin walking toward Brattle Sq, crossing Church St, and a short way along cross over to look at the handsome mansion at 42 Brattle, which presently houses the *Cambridge Center for Adult Education.* This is the first of the Tory mansions to be seen on this next stretch of the itinerary, which goes E. along Brattle St for more than a mile.

Brattle St was originally part of the path that led from Charlestown to Watertown, the oldest thoroughfare in the U.S., later to be called the King's Highway. The street took its present name from the Brattles, the most prominent of the Tory families who built their stately mansions by its side in the last half-century of British rule. The heads of these families were either wealthy merchants, high Crown officials, or persons of note, who were Loyalist in politics and Anglican in religion, all of them members of the congregation of Christ Church. Most of them already possessed residences in Boston, the metropolis; attracted by Harvard College and the fertile countryside, they bought lots along the King's Highway and developed them as country estates and retreats from business affairs in the summer, where they entertained one another lavishly. The best picture of what life was like on Tory Row at the end of the colonial period is found in the letters and memoirs of Madame Riedesel, wife of General Burgoyne's Hessian commander. She and her husband, General Baron von Riedesel, were quartered in Richard Lechmere's mansion on Tory Row after Burgoyne's surrender at Saratoga. As she wrote, "Never had I chanced upon any such agreeable situation. Seven families, who were connected with one another partly by the ties of relationship and partly by affection, had here farms, gardens and magnificent houses, and not far off plantations of fruit." By the time Madame Riedesel wrote those lines the sybaritic life on Tory Row had ended, for virtually all of the Loyalists in Cambridge left with the British fleet on March 17, 1776, never to return. Now only their mansions on Brattle St remain as reminders of an elegant age.

The mansion at 42 Brattle St is the *William Brattle House,* built in 1727. The house is of two stories, with a gambrel roof and dormer windows in the attic. Expect for the projecting entrance porch, added in 1891, the front part of the house is from the original structure.

The house was built for General William Brattle, son of the Rev. William Brattle, who had been minister of the First Church in Cambridge from 1696 until his death in 1717, and who had also served very effectively as treasurer of Harvard College. The younger Brattle married Katherine, daughter of Governor Gordon Saltonstall, in 1727, and that same year they moved into their new home on Tory Row. Brattle was not only the richest man of his time in Cambridge, but also the most versatile, and one contemporary chronicler wrote of him that "A man of more eminent talents and of greater eccentricities has seldom lived." In his time he was a preacher, physician, soldier, lawyer, and public official, holding several positions of great responsibility; he rose to be captain and then adjutant general of the Ancient and Honorable Artillery Company, and in 1771 he was appointed by the Crown as major general of all the colonial militias in the royal Province of Massachusetts. But the rising tide of patriotism in Massachusetts brought his career to an end just before the Revolution, and General Brattle and his family were forced to abandon their mansion and leave with the British fleet when Boston was evacuated. During 1775—76 the Brattle House was given over to Major Thomas Mifflin, Washington's commissary general, who was soon joined by his wife. John Adams writes of having dined in the Brattle House twice as guest of the Mifflins, the second time when he was on his way to sign the Declaration of Independence. After the Mifflins left, the house passed on to a series of owners and tenants. Thomas Gold Appleton and the historian John Lothrop Motley, both of the class of 1831, roomed here while students at Harvard, and Margaret Fuller lived here in 1833.

The itinerary now goes W. along Brattle St, beginning on the l. side of the avenue. After crossing Story St and walking halfway down the next block, one sees at No. 54 an old house, now serving as a restaurant, set back between an apartment house and an office building. This is a simple two-story Federal house with a hip roof, dating to 1808.

It was originally the house of Dexter Pratt, a blacksmith, whom Henry Wadsworth Longfellow immortalized in his poem "The Village Blacksmith": "Under a spreading chestnut tree / The village smithy stands, / The smith a mighty man is he,/With large and sinewy hands; / And the muscles of his brawny arms / Are strong as iron bands." The chestnut tree in front of 54 Brattle was cut down in 1876, despite Longfellow's strong protest, on the grounds that its spreading branches endangered the drivers of passing wagons. A chair was made from its wood, and the children of Cambridge presented it to Longfellow on his 72nd birthday, Feb. 27, 1879. Longfellow was so moved by this that he was inspired to write a poem that very day, entitled "From My Easy Chair" in appreciation of the gift. He made copies of the poem and presented one to any child who visited him, seating all of them in the chestnut chair.

At the next intersection Hilliard St leads off to the l. and Appian Way to the r. At the far corner of Hilliard and Brattle is the *Loeb Drama Center,* Harvard's undergraduate theater; this attractive building was erected in 1959 by Hugh Stubbins and Assocs. Directly across from this, at 69 Brattle, is the *Putnam House,* dating from 1839, now used as office space by Radcliffe. Farther along on the r., at 77 Brattle, another old house, dated 1821, has also been converted into a Radcliffe office building. Opposite this, at No. 76, is the *Greenleaf House,* an old mansion with a huge lawn, almost obscured by shrubbery. This house was built in 1859 for James Greenleaf, who married Mary Longfellow, the poet's sister; it was acquired by Radcliffe in 1913 and since then it has served as the presidential residence. Just beyond this is Radcliffe's *Cronkhite Graduate Center,* which extends to the corner of Ash St and down around the latter block. Those with time to spare might want to stroll down Ash St and along the streets that lead off from it in the immediate vicinity, for they are lined with a number of fine 19C houses. Opposite the Cronkhite Center, at 85 Brattle, which is on the short block between James and Mason Sts, there is a charming neo-Tudor house built in 1847 by Michael Norton.

At the N.E. corner of Brattle and Mason Sts, on a large plot of verdant land, stand the buildings of the *Episcopal Divinity School*. The most prominent building on the campus is *St. Paul's Chapel,* a handsome Victorian Gothic structure completed in 1868 by the architects Ware and Van Brunt. Other structures on the campus erected by Ware and Van Brunt form three sides of a rectangle; these are: the first dormitories (1872 and 1880); a library and commons building (1875); and a refectory (1879). In the years since then other structures have been erected on and around the campus; these include: the Winthrop Hall dormitory (1893); the Wright Hall library (1911); a dining hall (1961); and the Sherill Library (1965).

Directly across the street from the seminary, at 90 Brattle, is the *Stoughton House,* erected in 1883 by the renowned H. H. Richardson.

The house was built for Mrs. Edwin Stoughton, mother of the historian John Fiske. Fiske took up residence here himself in 1900, at which time he had the house enlarged to accommodate himself and his large library; the renovations were done by Shepley, Rutan, and Coolidge, Richardson's successor firm, and so the additions are done in the same style as the original house. Authorities consider the Stoughton House to be one of the earliest and finest examples of the Shingle Style of American architecture.

At the next intersection Hawthorne St leads off to the l. On the near corner, 94 Brattle, is the *Henry Vassall House*. The first dwelling on this site is believed to have been erected c. 1637; the present house was erected in 1746, apparently making some use of the original 17C structure, and alterations were made c. 1825.

The house was built for Colonel Henry Vassall, whose family were West Indian planters; he was a prominent figure in Cambridge life and represented the town in the General Court in 1752 and again in 1756. After his death in 1769 his widow continued to live on here until Cambridge became the headquarters of the Continental Army, after which she moved to Boston and then to her family estates in Antigua. Unlike the other mansions on Tory Row, her house was not confiscated, since Mrs. Vassall was a widow and neither she nor her late husband had sided with the Crown, and so she was able to reclaim her estate after the war. During 1775–76 her house was converted into a military hospital, and it became the first headquarters for the medical corps of the American army. The physician in charge at the headquarters was Dr. Benjamin Church, Jr., surgeon general of the Continental Army. On Oct. 2, 1775, it was discovered that Dr. Church was engaged in traitorous correspondence with the enemy, whereupon he was confined to a room in the Vassall House to await trial. While there, Dr. Church carved his name on the door of his room, an inscription that is still legible today. Church was subsequently found guilty of treason. After a term of imprisonment he was banished from America, but the ship upon which he sailed disappeared.

Farther along on the r. side of Brattle St, at No. 101, there is a fine mansion set far back from the street behind a granite-and-iron fence. This was erected in 1844 by the architect-builder Oliver Hastings, who used it as his own residence. Later it became the home of the distinguished Episcopal Bishop William Lawrence, and today it belongs to the Episcopal Theological School.

Continue along on the r. side of Brattle St to the next estate, and the **Longfellow National Historic Site.**

Admission. The Longfellow National Historic Site is open daily 10—5 for guided tours; fee.

History. The estate on which the house stands originally belonged to Colonel John Vassall, brother of the Henry Vassall whose mansion stands across the street. In 1759 Colonel Vassall's son, John Vassall, Jr., inherited the estate and built this house upon it. Vassall's wife, Elizabeth, was the sister of Thomas Oliver, the last royal lieutenant governor of massachusetts, who was married to Vassall's sister Elizabeth, an example of how intimately interrelated were these Tory families of Cambridge. During the 15 years that they lived in this house the Vassalls had seven children, and by all accounts their life was a happy one. However, in Sept. 1774 the Vassalls and all of the other Loyalists on Tory Row found their mansions surrounded by angry mobs of patriots. They were forced to take refuge in Boston and were then evacuated by the British fleet. Their mansion in Cambridge was requisitioned by the Continental Army, and after the Battles of Lexington, Concord, and Bunker Hill it was used as a hospital. When American volunteers began streaming into Cambridge in the spring of 1775, the house was used to quarter Colonel John Glover and his Marblehead Regiment of marines. When General Washington arrived in Cambridge on July 2, 1775, he first moved into Wadsworth House, residence of the president of Harvard; however, he soon found this to be unsatisfactory and on July 15 he moved into the Vassall mansion. The date of his initial occupancy is established by the following note in his account book: "July 15, 1775, paid for cleaning the house which was provided for my occupation and which was occupied by the Marblehead regiment, two pounds ten shillings and ninepence." During the next nine months this was not only Washington's residence, but also served as his headquarters as commander-in-chief of the Continental Army, where he and his staff planned the operation that eventually resulted in the evacuation of the British from Boston. Martha Washington joined him here on Dec. 5, and on Jan. 6 they celebrated their 17th wedding anniversary here with a Twelfth Night Party. Washington continued in residence here until April 4, 1776, when he left Cambridge to direct operations farther to the S.

After the war the first owner of the mansion was Nathaniel Tracy, a wealthy shipowner from Newburyport, who bought the house in 1781. Tracy entertained lavishly, and among the many gala parties he gave here was a reception for Admiral D'Estaing and his officers when the French fleet visited Boston. Tracy wanted to serve his guests what he thought to be their favorite dishes, and when the French officers sat down for the first course they were amazed to find a full-grown frog in each bowl of soup. In 1786 Tracy suffered severe financial reverses, and as a result he was forced to sell his mansion in Cambridge to Thomas Russell, a wealthy Boston merchant. Russell continued the tradition of the house and gave festive dinner parties and balls, in one of which the guest of honor was the Duke of Kent, father of Queen Victoria. Then, in 1791, the house passed to Andrew Craigie, who had fought at Bunker Hill and who had been the first apothecary general of the American army. While living here, Craigie engineered the financial speculations and real-estate maneuvers that led to the building of the West Boston Bridge and the subsequent development of East Cambridge. Craigie put much of his profits back into his beloved mansion, enlarging it by the addition of a pair of piazzas at the sides and a large ell at the rear, as well as purchasing contiguous lands, increasing the estate to 140 acres, so that it extended all the way from Observatory Hill (near the present Garden St) down as far as the Charles. Craigie built on his estate an ice house and a greenhouse, both of them the first in Cambridge; he also placed statues on an islet on the pond behind the mansion, and erected a summer house on the top of Observatory Hill, near an artesian well whose water was conducted through hollow logs down to the mansion. In Jan. 1793 Craigie married the young and beautiful Elizabeth Shaw of Nantucket. Craigie was eventually ruined financially, partly because of Jefferson's Embargo Act, but also because of the collapse of some of his grandiose schemes. He died in 1819, a bankrupt, leaving his vast estate tied up with huge debts. The widow Craigie was forced to dismiss ten of their 12 servants and to sell off all but five acres of the estate in order to retain the mansion, and then, in order to meet her current expenses, she was forced to take in lodgers, many of whom were Harvard students. Among those who roomed with Mrs. Craigie were Jared Sparks, Edward Everett, and Josiah Quincy, all of whom in turn later became president of Harvard, with Quincy assuming that post after he had served two terms as mayor of Boston.

In summer 1837 Henry Wadsworth Longfellow rented a suite of two rooms on the top floor of Mrs. Craigie's house, a bedroom and a sitting room, thus beginning a residence that would last for the rest of his life. At that time he was a professor of modern languages at Harvard, a position that he had taken just the year before. Mrs. Craigie died in 1841, but Longfellow continued to live on in the house, renting from her heirs. In 1843 Longfellow married Frances (Fanny) Appleton, daughter of the very wealthy Nathan Appleton of Beacon Hill, who purchased the mansion on Brattle St and presented it to the couple as a wedding present. (Fanny Appleton was Longfellow's second wife; his first, Mary Storer Potter, whom he married in 1831, died in childbirth in 1835.) They lived here together happily for nearly two decades, as Fanny bore six children, while Longfellow established an international reputation as a poet and a man of letters. But then, in July 1861, Fanny was severely burned in a freak accident in the library of the mansion and died the following day, leaving Longfellow bereft. Longfellow continued to live on here until his own death on March 24, 1882, leaving two sons and three daughters. After Longfellow's death some of his children remained in residence; his daughter Alice, in particular, devoted herself to maintaining the house as it was during her father's lifetime, preserving his books, manuscripts, correspondence, works of art, antiquities, and mementos. In 1913 the Longfellow House Trust was formed, in order to preserve the mansion "as a specimen of the best colonial architecture of the middle of the eighteenth century, as an historical monument of the occupation of the house by General Washington during the siege of Boston in the Revolutionary War, and as a memorial to Henry Wadsworth Longfellow." The house and grounds now constitute the Longfellow National Historic Site; this is administered by the National Park Service of the U.S. Department of the Interior, who have done a superb job of restoring the house and exhibiting it to the public.

Exterior. Except for the pair of side piazzas and the ell to the rear added by Andrew Craigie in 1793, the exterior of the house is virtually the same as when it was first erected in 1759. Constructed of wood with clapboard siding, it is a characteristic horizontal block with a symmetrical facade and a low hip roof crowned with a balustrade, above which rise two tall chimneys. The facade typifies High Georgian attempts to add distinction to the familiar five-bay, two-story elevation by adding ornamental features, in this case the device of bringing the central bay slightly forward (nine inches) to carry a pediment that interrupts the cornice of the projecting pavilion and the main block. The central pavilion is framed by two giant pilasters with Ionic capitals, with similar pilasters at the ends of the facade, all of which gives the house a decided Gibbsian appearance. The frame of the front door derives from Plate 32 of Batty Langley's 1756 pattern book for builder-architects.

Interior. The first room entered in the house is the *Laundry,* which is at the back of the ell added by Andrew Craigie in 1793. From there one is guided through the long *Kitchen Hall* into the *Blue Entry,* a narthexlike hall which was added to the main house by Andrew Craigie when he put on the ell to the rear. The hall is in two sections, with a door to the r. opening onto the garden, and one to the l. leading into the Library. To the r. of the door to the Library there is a bust of Mrs. Longfellow's father, Nathan Appleton, and to the l. there is one of her uncle, Samuel Appleton. Midway along the r. wall in this part of the Blue Entry there is a large mahogany bookcase filled with French books, including the 75-volume set of Voltaire's works which Longfellow bought at the sale of Mrs. Craigie's effects in 1841. To the l. of this bookcase is a watercolor sketch of the Longfellow House from the rear, made by the French painter Vautin in 1845. Beneath this there is a bust of Longfellow by Kitson. On top of the bookcase opposite there are earlier busts of Longfellow, one representing him at the age of 40 and the other at 50. In the section of the Blue Entry that leads to the garden there is a marble bust of Longfellow by Henry Dexter, as well as a bust of Sandalphon, the Angel of Prayer, the subject of Longfellow's poem "Sandalphon" along with a bust of Olympian Zeus and a figurine of the Venus de Medici. Midway along the wall to the l. there is a large table dating from the reign of Louis XVI, one of many antiquities in the house that Longfellow brought back from trips to Europe. Above the table there is a large portrait by the American artist Rose Lamb of two of Longfellow's grandsons, Richard H. Dana, the elder of the two, and Henry Wadsworth Longfellow Dana, the younger boy with blond hair, who in the last years of his life wrote the monograph which is the principal source of information for the present description of the Longfellow House. Elsewhere in the Blue Entry there are two paintings by Longfellow's son Ernest. One of these depicts the village of Cadenabbia on Lake Como, about which Longfellow wrote his "Birds of Passage," beginning with this stanza: "No sound of wheels or hoof-beat breaks / The silence of the summer day / As by the loveliest of all lakes / I while the idle hours away. . . ."

From the Blue Entry one passes into the *Dining Room*. This room was originally the kitchen and had a large open fireplace. But when Andrew Craigie enlarged the house in 1793 he built a new kitchen in the ell which he added at the rear, and at that time this chamber was converted into a dining room. Midway along the wall opposite the two windows there is a red lacquer altar table, partly Chinese in its workmanship and partly Japanese. On the table there is a large Japanese Imari plate and two bowls, as well as two jars from Canton, all of which were brought home by Longfellow's son Charles after his trip to the Orient in 1869. Above the table there is a large oil painting done by Thomas Buchanan Read in 1859, depicting the Longfellows' three daughters, Alice, Edith, and Annie Allegra. His beloved daughters were the subjects of one of Longfellow's best-known poems, "The Children's Hour" in the third stanza of which he describes them as "Grave Alice, and laughing Allegra, and Edith with golden hair." To the r. of this is a picture by George P. A. Healy of Mrs. Longfellow's sister, Mary Appleton, and to the l. there is a portrait by Healy of Fanny Appleton done a few years before her marriage to Longfellow. Below this there is a small painting by Albert Bierstadt depicting the departure of Hiawatha into the sunset, which the artist presented to Longfellow at a dinner given in the poet's honor in London in 1868, a scene from the 22nd canto of his epic, *The Song of Hiawatha*. Midway along the wall, to the l. of the door from the Blue Entry, there is a black-walnut sideboard, and on the wall behind this there are a number of Longfellow family portraits. On either side of the sideboard there are large portraits of Mrs. Longfellow's parents, both painted by Gilbert Stuart c. 1812; on the l. is her mother, Maria Theresa Gold Appleton, and on the r. is her father, Nathan Appleton. Below Mrs. Appleton's portrait is a miniature painted in 1835 by the French artist Isabey (who, to judge from his name, was probably a Turk in exile); this depicts Fanny Appleton, who is dressed in white, and her sister, Mary, in black. Over the sideboard is a portrait of Mrs. Longfellow's brother, Thomas Gold Appleton, painted in Rome by the French artist R. S. Lauder. Farther to the r. is a portrait of Alice Longfellow painted by Charles Sidney Hopkinson. To the l. of the door from the Blue Entry is a portrait of Longfellow's daughter Edith, painted by her brother Ernest in 1867, when she was 13 years old. Over the doors to the l. and r. of the fireplace there are crayon portraits of Longfellow's sisters, Mary Longfellow Greenleaf and Anne Longfellow Pierce; these were done in 1846 by the American artist Eastman Johnson, many of whose portraits are exhibited in the house. In the center of the room is the round mahogany table where the Longfellows entertained their many distinguished guests, and against the walls are two

Sheraton folding card-tables with inlaid satinwood panels and borders; upon them are two antique Chinese vases.

Between the Dining Room and the Parlor there is an anteroom in which there are exhibited a number of interesting objects. In a cabinet to the r. of the entryway there is old Longfellow and Appleton china, as well as a silver tankard made in 1760 from the silver coins earned by Longfellow's great-great-grandfather Stephen Longfellow, who worked as a blacksmith in Newbury, Mass. On the wall are pictures of the frigate *Constitution,* of the American fleet before Tripoli, and of the explosion of the fireship *Intrepid* in the harbor of Tripoli in 1804, when Henry Wadsworth sacrificed his life. It was for him that Henry Wadsworth Longfellow was named. Below these prints are silhouette portraits of Longfellow's maternal grandparents, General Peleg Wadsworth and Elizabeth Bartlett Wadsworth; between them is a silhouette of their daughter Zilpah, Longfellow's mother. To the l. of the entryway there is an oval portrait of Longfellow's first wife, Mary Storer Potter. Longfellow refers to her in the "Footsteps of Angels," one of the first poems he wrote in this house, calling her "the Being Beauteous / Who unto my youth was given / More than all things else to love me, / And is now a saint in heaven. . . ."

The *Parlor* served as a drawing room throughout the history of the mansion. The room is preserved almost exactly as it was in 1846, when Mrs. Longfellow redecorated it, with the same types of wallpaper, window curtains, upholstery, and rug. The eight Louis XVI armchairs of carved walnut, upholstered in flowered silk-and-wool tapestry, originally belonged to Mrs. Craigie, and were bought by Longfellow when her effects were sold in 1841. The fireplace side of this room is more elaborately carved than in any of the other rooms in the house, with an arched niche on either side, a paneled marble chimneypiece in the center, and a pediment above supported by two Corinthian pilasters. On the hearth are Japanese vases and on the mantel Japanese bronzes brought back by Charles Longfellow in 1869. Above the fireplace is a seascape painted by Isabey. In a niche to the r. of the fireplace, on a tall pedestal, is a bust of Mrs. Longfellow. On the wall to the r. there is a large portrait of Sir William Pepperell's grandchildren, who were related to John Vassall, the original owner of the house; this was originally attributed to John Singleton Copley, but art historians now believe that it was done by Mather Brown. On the wall opposite this picture there is an oval portrait in pastel by Eastman Johnson depicting two of the Longfellows' sons, Charles and Ernest, done c. 1850. On the wall beside the window to the r. of the door from the Blue Entry there are three portraits; below is an engraving of Baroness Riedesel, above this is a miniature portrait of Elizabeth Craigie, and also a portrait of Mrs. Longfellow, painted by her brother, Thomas Gold Appleton.

From the Parlor one passes into the *Front Hall,* once the main entryway to the mansion. The three-run stairway to the second floor is remarkable for its elaborately carved newel post and its balustrade, designed in three different styles. Beside the staircase there is a bust of George Washington, a copy of the original by Houdon. Halfway up the first run of the stairs there is a portrait of Washington thought to be by Jane Stuart, a copy of the original done by her father, Gilbert Stuart. At the top of the first run of the staircase there is an ornate Dutch clock of the 17C, one of the antiquities that Longfellow brought back after his European journey.

Passing through the Front Hall, one enters the *Study,* the large room to the r. of the front door. This is a room rich in historical and literary associations, and here more than anywhere else in the house one feels the presence of the illustrious figures who once dwelt here. During the period July 1775–April 1776 Washington conferred in this room with his general staff, which included Generals Israel Putnam, Artemas Ward, Charles Lee, and Nathaniel Greene. In Oct. 1775 Washington met in this room with the congressional delegation headed by Benjamin Franklin, who assured him that he would have the funds necessary to form the American troops into an army that could take Boston from the British. At the nearer side of the table is the Chippendale chair which Washington used when this was his office, and across from this is the Hepplewhite armchair used by Longfellow, whose study this was from 1846 until his death in 1882. The old-fashioned folding desk on which Longfellow wrote is opened up on the table in front of this chair. There too is the quill pen which he used and three of his inkstands. One is a green French china well, in which the height of the ink can be adjusted. Another bears the inscription "Saml. Taylor Coleridge; his inkstand," and beside it is a letter from Longfellow thanking his English friends for having presented him with this inkstand, which Coleridge had used when writing "The Rime of the Ancient Mariner." The third inkwell belonged in succession to three poets: George Crabbe, Thomas Moore, and Longfellow. On the table behind Longfellow's chair is a copy of Severn's portrait of Keats. On the walls of the room is a series of crayon portraits of Longfellow's friends, drawn in 1846 by Eastman Johnson. To the l. of the fireplace is Johnson's portrait of Charles Sumner, later to become a U.S. senator renowned for his vehement opposition to slavery. Below his portrait is a bookcase containing Sumner's speeches in 15 volumes, and the chair in which he sat when visiting Longfellow. Behind the glass door in the bookcase is a pencil sketch done by Longfellow in 1847, showing himself in this same chair where he sat beside the fire writing his epic *Evangeline.* The other Eastman Johnson portraits are these: Ralph Waldo Emerson, the Sage of Concord; Nathaniel Hawthorne, who had been Longfellow's classmate at Bowdoin College in Maine, and who had suggested to him the subject for *Evangeline;* Cornelius Conway Fenton, Longfellow's first friend in Cambridge and his roommate during their first year at Harvard, the two of them collaborating in the editing of *The Poets and Poetry of Europe,* a man who later became president of Harvard; and beyond that a portrait of Longfellow himself, shown at the age of 38, still clean-shaven and youthful. In another corner of the room is a later portrait of Longfellow, done in pastels by Francis Alexander in 1852, showing the poet with muttonchop side whiskers. A still later portrait of Longfellow, depicting him with a full beard, stands on an easel behind his Hepplewhite armchair; this was painted by his son Ernest in 1876. Elsewhere in the room are to be seen photographs of the poet at various periods. Other friends of Longfellow are also represented in the study. A bust of George Washington Greene, done in 1841 by Thomas Crawford, stands on the Queen Anne table to the r. of the easel. On the wall opposite is a photograph of Oliver Wendell Holmes, the Autocrat of the Breakfast Table, and nearby is a portrait of Louis Agassiz, the renowned Swiss scientist who came to teach at Harvard, and to whom Longfellow wrote poems in both French and English. On a round table in the corner of the room is a standing-desk, at which Longfellow occasionally wrote during the day, with a sweeping view across the meadows toward the Charles River. Beyond this table stands an old Aaron Willard clock in a tall mahogany case, with fluted round corner columns. Over the fireplace is an old girandole convex mirror, surmounted by two dolphins and an eagle holding festoons of chains and balls. To the r. of the fireplace stands the armchair made from the wood of the "spreading chestnut tree," of which

Longfellow wrote his poem "The Village Blacksmith." In a drawer of the bookcase beside the chair there is a book containing the names of the Cambridge schoolchildren who contributed their coins toward the making of this chair, presented to Longfellow on his 72nd birthday, Feb. 27, 1879. It was in gratitude for this gift that Longfellow wrote his poem "From My Arm-Chair," copies of which he gave to the children who visited him, seating them in the chair. The ornately carved bookcases in the study contain part of Longfellow's vast collection of European literature. Displayed on these bookcases are busts and statuettes of writers representing these national literatures: Virgil, Molière, Goethe, Shakespeare, and Dante. Above the statuette of Dante is an early-18C mirror, below which is a carved Italian casket in which Longfellow kept some fragments of Dante's coffin and other mementos.

From the Study one passes into the *Library*. Originally this was the dining room of the Vassall mansion. During 1775–76 it was used as the Ward Room and Officers' Mess for Washington's staff. When the house was enlarged by Andrew Craigie in 1793 the room was lengthened and two fluted columns with Corinthian capitals supporting a heavy entablature were added in the middle of the long wall. The old molding was kept on the fireplace end, but a more elaborate wainscoting was put up on the other three walls. This enlarged room was then used by the Craigies as a ballroom, and occasionally as a banquet hall. When Longfellow took over the house he converted the room into a library and music room, and it was here that he had his piano. Placed along the walls are French and Italian bookcases elaborately carved in brown oak; a 17C English high-backed chair surmounted with unicorns; an old carved-leather chair from a Spanish convent; and an armchair that belonged to Longfellow's maternal grandfather, General Peleg Wadsworth. Above the bookcases are busts of the Greek poets: Homer, at the far end of the room, and the Greek dramatists Sophocles and Euripides against the side wall. The bookcases hold part of Longfellow's collection of European literature, the 19C French poets in elaborate gold-tooled bindings, the Italian poets in white vellum, and the German poets in green leather. Near the bookcase containing the Italian works there is a marble bust of Longfellow done by the English sculptor Sir Thomas Brock in 1884, two years after the poet's death. The bust is a duplicate of the one which at that time was placed in the Poets' Corner in Westminster Abbey in London, a photograph of which is displayed nearby in the library. On the side wall to the l. of the columns is a portrait of Franz Liszt, painted by George P. A. Healy at Rome in 1880. Longfellow and Healy had gone to visit the Abbé Liszt, as he was then called, who was living in the former Convent of San Francesco Romano. Liszt came to the convent door, holding up a candle to light his guests on their way. Longfellow was so impressed by the inspired expression on the composer's face, as it was illuminated by the light of the candle, that he asked Healy to paint Liszt just as they saw him at that moment. In the corner to the l. there are two representations of the Falls of Minnehaha, described by Longfellow in his *Song of Hiawatha;* one of these is a watercolor sketch by the English artist Lord Dufferin, and the other is an oil painting by the American artist John F. Kensett. The fireplace mantel is of Italian marble, carved with a frieze of griffins and flaming urns and a lion in bas-relief. This was brought here in 1847 from the Kirk Boott house in Bowdoin Sq, Boston. To the l. of the mantel is a watercolor sketch done by Longfellow's niece, Mary King Longfellow, representing this end of the library as it appeared in 1876. In the corner beyond is a reproduction of the crayon drawing of Longfellow's wife by Rowse;

along with a photograph of her brother, Thomas Gold Appleton; a sketch of her niece, Eva Macintosh; and a sketch of the French scholar, Xavier Marmier, who translated Longfellow's poems into French. On the table by the central window, which has now been converted into a door, is a Japanese writing-case and inkwell, with a lamp supported by a statue of the German prince, Henry the Fowler. On the bookcase beyond is a statuette of the Greek poetess Sappho, by the American sculptor Crawford. Hanging from the ceiling in the center of the room is an old bronze chandelier, and on the table beneath is a bronze copy of the Flying Mercury by Giovanni Da Bologna. The table itself is a 19C Italian work with carved spiral legs and a green baize top.

After leaving the house, visitors may stroll through the lovely garden at the rear of the estate. When the Craigies were in residence there was a barn to the l. of the mansion at the rear and the gardener's house stood to the r. These buildings were both destroyed by a fire in 1840. In 1845, when Longfellow had come into possession of the estate, he built a new barn on the site of the old one and laid out a garden on the site of the gardener's house. Later he enlarged the plot to its present size, following a design made for a garden that he had seen on a visit to Italy. The flower beds with their borders of box make up a symmetrical pattern, resembling the design of an Oriental carpet. In the center of the garden four pear-shaped beds make up a circle; this in turn is enlarged by triangular beds in the corners to create a square, on the sides of which are large oblongs, broken up into quatrefoils and triangles. Later a sundial was added in the center of the garden, inscribed with one of Longfellow's favorite mottoes, a line from Dante's "Purgatorio," xii, 84: *Pensa che questo di mai non raggiorna;* which Longfellow translated as "Think that this day will never dawn again."

Across the street from the Longfellow National Historic Site is *Longfellow Park.* This was originally laid out by landscape artist Charles Eliot in 1883, and in 1914 the sculptor Daniel Chester French created a memorial to Longfellow. In one corner of the park, at 108 Brattle, there is a house built in 1870 for the poet's son Ernest Longfellow; at the other corner is the *Church of Jesus Christ of the Latter Day Saints,* erected in 1955. At 5 Longfellow Park there is a *Friends Meeting House,* which in 1937 was added by the architects Duguid and Martin to a house that already existed on the site.

Continuing along the r. side of Brattle St: at Nos 113 and 115 are the houses that were built in 1887 for Longfellow's daughters, the first for Edith Longfellow Dana and the second for Annie Longfellow Thorp. Across the way, on either side of Willard St, there are two fine houses; the one at 112 Brattle is a Greek Revival structure dating to 1846; and the one at No. 114 is in the Colonial Revival style, built in 1903. Farther along on the r. No. 121 is a house built in 1843 for lexicographer Joseph Worcester. Opposite this on the l. side of Brattle, at Nos 126 and 128, is a pair of houses built in 1892 by Ralph Adams Cram and his partners, Wentworth and Goodhue. In the middle of the next block on the l. side, at Nos 134–136, is a double Italianate mansion dating to 1857.

At the next intersection on the r. Sparks St leads off to the N. and Craigie St heads off at an angle to the E. At 27 Craigie is another Italianate mansion, this one built in 1853 by the architect Henry Greenough. On the W. corner of Sparks and Brattle Sts stands the *Armenian Church of the Holy Trinity,* built in 1960 (architect John S. Bilzerian). Just beyond that, at 145 Brattle, is a Colonial Revival house built in 1887; this stands on the site of the Lechmere mansion, one of the original Loyalist dwellings on Tory Row, which has been moved up the street to No. 149, in the middle of the next block on the r. side. The house at No. 149 is just a shadow of its former self, the original of which was built in 1761 by Richard Lechmere and which later became the residence of Judge Jonathan Sewall. In 1869 the house was jacked up a story and a lower floor and veranda were added; then, in 1886, the original top floor was removed. Such as it is, the house does have some historical interest, for in 1777—78 Baron and Baroness von Riedesel were quartered here. It is said that Madame Riedesel's initials can still be seen carved in one of the windowpanes. A short way along on the same side of the street, at No. 153, is a house built in 1803 for Thomas Lee, nephew of Judge Joseph Lee, one of the members of the Crown's Mandamus Council, who resigned his office after a popular demonstration on Sept. 2, 1774.

Judge Lee's own home is a block farther along on the same side of Brattle St, at No. 159. This is known as the ***Hooper-Lee-Nichols House,** and is the headquarters of the Cambridge Historical Society.

Admission. The Hooper-Lee-Nichols House is open Mon. and Thur. 3—5; fee.

History. Between 1657 and 1660 John Holmes of Salem, Mass. bought a tract of land on this site, extending about three-quarters of a mile between the marshes of the Charles River and the shores of Fresh Pond. Holmes may have constructed here a saltbox house, but there is no definite record of this. In 1685 Holmes sold the property to Dr. Richard Hooper of Watertown, who died in 1691, leaving mention of a house in his estate, which his widow two years later was licensed to keep as an inn. The house then passed on her son, Dr. Henry Hooper, who is known to have been at one time personal physician to John Leverett, president of Harvard College in 1708—24. Dr. Hooper repaired and enlarged the house in 1717, moving another house frame to the site in order to replace the original timbers of the E. side, which had been ravaged by "ye worms." In 1733 the house was acquired by Cornelius Waldo, a Boston merchant, who is believed to have added the third floor c. 1740—45. Then, in 1758, the house passed on to Joseph Lee, who served as judge in the Court of Common Pleas of Middlesex County, 1769—74, and who was one of the founders of Christ Church, Cambridge. Judge Lee was forced by public pressure to resign from the Mandamus Council on Sept. 2, 1774, after which he took refuge with Tory friends in Boston. But since he had not strongly aligned himself with the Crown his mansion was not confiscated after the Revolution, and he returned to it and lived on there until his death in 1802. Lee's descendants remained in residence until 1850, when the house was rented to Mr. and Mrs. George Nichols, who purchased it ten years later. Early in the present century the house passed on to the Nichols' grandson, Austin T. White, who commissioned the architect Joseph E. Chandler to renovate the structure, at which time the present library was added. The house was completely renovated in 1980—81, under the direction of the Cambridge Historical Society and the Society for the Preservation of New England Antiquities.

On the block beyond the Hooper-Lee-Nichols House there are five 19C mansions of interest. On the r. side, at No. 163, is a mansion built in 1810 for John Appleton on a portion of Judge Lee's estate; beyond that, at No. 165, is a house erected in 1873 for John Bartlett, a Harvard Sq bookseller renowned for his *Familiar Quotations;* and at No. 167 is a rambling mansion built in 1883 by the architect Henry Van Brunt, who lived there himself. On the l. side, at No. 168, is an unusual house in the Colonial Revival style erected in 1888 by Arthur Little; and beyond that, at No. 170, is a mansion put up in 1880 by Oliver Hastings; the latter structure originally stood on the site of the Episcopal Theological School, and was moved to its present location in 1965.

At the beginning of the next block on the r., at 175 Brattle, one sees still another of the Loyalist mansions of Tory Row, the *Ruggles-Fayerweather House.* This was originally built c. 1764 for George Ruggles, a Jamaican planter; and during the Revolution it was owned by Thomas Fayerweather, who allowed it to be used as a hospital after the Battle of Bunker Hill. During the first part of the 19C the mansion served as a boys' school, and among those who studied here were the sculptor William Wetmore Story and the author and editor James Russell Lowell.

At the next corner the itinerary turns l. from Brattle St onto Elmwood Ave, following the ancient course of the King's Highway. The short street ends just a block farther along, at Mount Auburn St, after crossing on the l. a byway called Trall St. Just before the end of Elmwood Ave, on either side of the street, are two of the oldest houses in Cambridge. On the l., at No. 30, is the *Watson House,* a gambrel-roofed structure dating to c. 1750, moved here in 1965 from Russell St in North Cambridge. Across the street, at No. 33, stands one of the finest of all the old Loyalist mansions on Tory Row; this is *Elmwood,* a three-story Georgian edifice built in 1767 for Thomas Oliver, the last lieutenant governor of the royal Province of Massachusetts, today used as the residence of the president of Harvard University.

After the Revolution the house was the residence of Eldridge Gerry, a signatory of the Declaration of Independence who was Vice-President of the U.S. during the administration of President James Madison. In 1818 the house was acquired by the Lowell family. James Russell Lowell was born in Elmwood on Feb. 22, 1819, and lived here until his death in 1891. Longfellow wrote of Lowell's home in one of the poems in *Birds of Passage,* a work entitled "The Herons of Elmwood," whose second stanza is an evocative picture of what this place was like in 1878, when the Charles River flowed by the lower reaches of the estate: "Silent are all the sounds of the day; / Nothing I hear but the chirp of crickets, / And the cry of the herons winging their way / O'er the poet's house in the Elmwood thickets. . . ."

This point is the end of the long stroll along Tory Row. On Mount Auburn St one can catch a bus back to Harvard Sq. But for those who have enough stamina to return to foot, the following is an interesting itinerary back to the center of Old Cambridge by a circuitous route to the N. of Brattle St. Walk back along Elmwood to Brattle and cross over to continue N. along Fayerweather St as far as the first turning on the r., which is Reservoir St. Follow that street as it bends around to the l. and take the first turning to the r. onto Highland, following that street as far as Craigie. Then turn l. on Craigie and follow that to the first major intersection, turning to the r. there onto Huron, and following that until turning r. onto Garden St, which goes back to Cambridge Common and then to Harvard Sq. Those who follow this extension of the itinerary will be rewarded by the sight of some serene old Cambridge neighborhoods not usually seen by visitors to the city. There are also a number of historic houses to be seen along the way, the two oldest of which are summarily described below.

The *Cooper-Frost-Austin House* (open to the public by appointment only; call 227-3956) at 21 Linnean St is one of the two oldest dwellings in Cambridge, sharing that distinction with the Hooper-Lee-Nichols House on Brattle St. It was restored by the Society for the Preservation of New England Antiquities. The oldest part of the house was built c. 1691 by Samuel Cooper, at a time when Cambridge Common extended as far as Linnean St. Originally only half its present size, the house was enlarged c. 1720 by Walter Cooper, who added the section to the l., with further changes being made in 1810 and again in 1830 by Thomas Austin. In 1912, after the house was acquired by the SPNEA, the house was carefully restored by the architect Joseph Chandler.

Another interesting old house is to be seen at the very end of this extension of the itinerary, where Garden St returns to Cambridge Common. If one turns l. there onto Waterhouse St, on the l., at No. 7, is the *Waterhouse House,* the only pre-Revolutionary dwelling still standing on the periphery of the Common. This old mansion was built in 1753 and is named after Dr. Benjamin Waterhouse, who resided there for many years in the late 18C and the early 19C.

Dr. Waterhouse, who was long a member of the Harvard Medical School faculty, introduced the practice of smallpox vaccine inoculation to the U.S. in 1800, and he was one of the first physicians in the country to publish a treatise warning against the smoking of tobacco. James Russell Lowell, in his description of the Old Cambridge of his youth, writes that Dr. Waterhouse was one of the most familiar figures in the village. As he describes the renowned old physician: "I remember he used to turn his whole person in order to bring the foci of his great spectacles to bear upon any object. One can fancy that terrified Nature would have yielded up her secrets at once, without cross-examination, at their first glare."

In completing the itinerary, one might take the opportunity to walk back along the northern and eastern margins of the Common. At the N.W. corner of the park a marker records that barracks stood there in 1775–76, where the troops of the Continental Army berthed during the siege of Boston. Near the N.E. corner of the park there is a fine statue of a Puritan, done in 1912 by Daniel Chester French.

This is a representation of John Bridge, one of the first colonists in Newtowne. Bridge left his native Braintree in Essex County, England in 1631 as a member of the Rev. Thomas Hooker's company, arriving in Newtowne early in 1632. Bridge remained behind when the Rev. Hooker and his followers moved on to Hartford, Connecticut in 1634, and became one of the leading citizens in Cambridge, serving as a Selectman and also a Representative to the General Court.

Continuing along the eastern side of the Common, midway along is another historical marker, this one indicating the course of the ancient path between Charlestown and Watertown. The marker also records that Colonel Prescott and his men marched that way before and after the Battle of Bunker Hill.

After walking around the eastern side of the Common one comes again to the intersection of Massachusetts Ave and Garden St. From there it is just a short stroll to Harvard Square.

18 Old Cambridge II: Around Harvard Yard

The present itinerary goes around Harvard Yard and other parts of the university campus to the N. of that venerable enclosure. The following itinerary will be a short stroll through that part of Old Cambridge which lies between Harvard Yard and the Charles River, where many of the university buildings were erected in the past half-century.

History. As mentioned earlier, Harvard was founded on Oct. 28, 1636, just six years after the first settlers landed in Newtowne. As the Rev. Thomas Shepard, one of the first overseers of the college, wrote in his autobiography: "Thus the Lord was pleased to direct the harts of the magistrates (then keeping court ordinarily in our town because of their stirs at Boston) to thinke of erecting a Schoole or Colledge, and that speedily be a nursery of knowledge in these deserts and supply for posterity." After John Harvard, who died on Sept. 14, 1638, bequeathed to the new institution half of his estate (some £375) and his library of 400 books, the college was named for him. Harvard's first president was Henry Dunster, who took office in 1640, and after his appointment the college began to flourish. Dunster organized the curriculum after the English model, with courses in "the Liberal Arts, the Learned Tongues, and the Three Philosophies." He also erected a building that served both as a residence for the students and their place of study, in keeping with the plan of the founders to have a truly residential college, and to establish a "collegiate way of living." The first commencement of the college was held in 1642, with nine graduates, orations in Greek and Latin, and a banquet for 50 guests. On Dunster's petition in 1650, the royal governor of Massachusetts granted Harvard the charter by which it is still governed today, making it the oldest corporation in the Western Hemisphere. Though many early graduates became ministers, Harvard was never a seminary as such. As Samuel Eliot Morison wrote in his history of the founding of the college: "Harvard was founded, and in the seventeenth century supported, as a college of English university standards for the liberal education of the young men of New England, under strict religious discipline." By 1654, when Dunster's presidency came to an end, to quote Professor Morison, "there were about fifty or sixty students in College, including graduates studying for the Master's degree; boys had been sent to Harvard from Bermuda, Virginia, and New Amsterdam as well as from England, where Harvard degrees had been accepted by Oxford and Cambridge as equivalent to their own." By 1736, 1248 young men had received their degrees from the college, laying the foundations for the intellectual development of New England. A turning point in the history of Harvard came in 1707, with the election of John Leverett as president, an office he held until 1724. All presidents of Harvard prior to that time had been clergymen, and Leverett was the first layman to be given the position, an important step in establishing the intellectual independence of Harvard. Massachusetts Hall, which is Harvard's oldest surviving building, is the only structure surviving from Leverett's presidency, having been erected in 1720. However, four other buildings at Harvard survive from the last half-century of the colonial period; these are: Wadsworth House, erected in 1726; Holden Chapel, in 1744; Hollis Hall, in 1763; and Harvard Hall, in 1766—all evidence of the considerablerable expansion of Harvard during that time. However, the college suffered a considerable setback in 1764, when a disastrous fire destroyed the science laboratory, with all of its equipment, and also the Library with 5000 books, which had been the largest collection of works in America at that time.

When William Dawes alerted the patriots in Cambridge on April 19, 1775, that the British were coming, six students from the college marched off with the minutemen; all of them survived, but two Harvard graduates were among those killed that day. Farmers from the surrounding countryside barricaded themselves in the college buildings, prepared to fight the redcoats if they returned to Boston via Cambridge, but the battle was avoided when the British marched to Charlestown instead. During the year 1775–76 the college moved to temporary quarters in Concord, as some 1500 Continental soldiers were housed in Harvard buildings. The college returned to Cambridge in June 1776, after Washington had moved his army S. Classes continued in Cambridge throughout the remainder of the war, but suffered from lowered attendance and an acute shortage of funds.

Harvard's fortunes revived quickly after the war, and in 1780 the new Massachusetts constitution officially referred to the institution as the "University." Two years later the Medical School was founded, as Harvard's curriculum grew broader and placed more emphasis on less traditional areas of human knowledge, particularly on science. This tendency has already been evident at Harvard even in colonial days, beginning with the establishment in 1721 of the Hollis Professorship of Mathematics and Natural Philosophy. In 1816 the Divinity School was founded, with a constitution stating that "no assent to the peculiarities of any denomination shall be required," and the following year the Law School opened. In 1840 the Harvard Observatory was established and then, in 1847, the Lawrence Scientific School was founded, numbering on its faculty such distinguished scientists as the Swiss naturalist Louis Agassiz, the botanaist Asa Gray, the chemist Wolcott Gibbs, and the mathematician and astronomer Benjamin Peirce. Other famous scholars who lectured or did research in Harvard during the 19C were Oliver Wendell Holmes, Sr., George Ticknor, Henry Wadsworth Longfellow, James Russell Lowell, Edward Everett, and William James, who began there his pioneering researches in human psychology, not to mention John Quincy Adams, who for three years held the new Boylston Professorship of Rhetoric and Oratory. Meanwhile, new residences and other buildings were being erected to accommodate the expanding student body and faculty, with Stoughton Hall being erected in 1805, as well as a library building in 1841, a chemistry laboratory in 1857, and a natural-history museum in 1860. The library in Harvard Hall held nearly 20,000 volumes in 1815; a quarter-century later 41,000 volumes were moved into the new Gore Hall, constituting the largest and most valuable collection of books and maps in the U.S. at the time. (By 1915, when the Widener Library replaced Gore Hall, the collection was approaching a million volumes, and by 1970 it was in excess of eight million.)

A new era in Harvard's history began in 1869, when Charles William Eliot, a chemist, became president of the university, a position he would hold for nearly four decades. At the time that he took office Eliot declared that "We mean to build here, securely and slowly, a university in the largest sense." And as Samuel Eliot Morison wrote in his history of the university, evaluating the Eliot administration, it "set new standards for higher education in the U.S." Eliot began by reorganizing the Schools of Law and Medicine, putting them on a more professional level and eventually housing them in new buildings, as well as founding a new College of Dentistry. But Eliot's most important innovation was his founding of the Graduate School of Arts and Sciences, which was begun in 1872. The creation of this school meant that American students could now complete their higher studies and obtain their doctorates in the U.S. rather than go off to European universities, providing a great stimulus for scholarship and research in the U.S., a development that Eliot continued in founding the Graduate School of Business Administration in 1908. The creation of the graduate school gave rise to a great renaissance at Harvard in European and American history, literary scholarship, and philosophy, with the latter department boasting a quartet of Olympians known as "The Philosophical Four," namely Josiah Royce, George Herbert Palmer, William James, and George Santayana, with several other departments having their own distinguished faculties. Another innovation made by Eliot during his administration was the introduction of the elective system, which gave Harvard students a freer and much wider choice of subjects, a philosophy of education that was eventually adopted throughout the U.S. Harvard underwent an unprecedented expansion during Eliot's administration, with the enrollment increasing from 1000 to 3000, the faculty from 49 to 278, and the endowment from $2.3 million to $22.5 million. This expansion and development continued under Eliot's successor, A. Lawrence Lowell, who was president from 1909 to 1933. As mentioned earlier, more university buildings were built during Lowell's presidency than during the 273 years of Harvard's history prior to his accession, including residence halls, laboratories, lecture halls, museums, and the huge Widener Library, completed in 1915. One important development during Lowell's administration was the institution of the House System, begun in 1930 through a gift of $13 million from Edward S. Harkness. This enabled the university to erect seven Georgian residence halls between Harvard Yard and the Charles River, each housing 350–450 undergraduates, with three more houses being added after World War II. Though most formal courses are given elsewhere, the houses are in all other ways the center of the undergraduates' life at Harvard after the first year. Each house has members of the faculty associated with it, and its own dormitories, dinging hall, library, athletic teams, and social events, all of which is designed to provide a more intimate small-college atmosphere within a large university.

Harvard really hit its stride intellectually during the presidencies of Eliot and Lowell, who between them held that office in turn for 64 years. When Lowell retired in 1933, to be succeeded by the distinguished chemist James Bryant Conant, Harvard was considered to be the finest institution of higher learning in the U.S., ranking with the greatest universities in the world. These developments have continued apace in the years since then, under the presidencies of Dr Conant (1933–53); Nathan Marsh Pusey (1953–71); Derek Curtis Bok (1971–91); and Neil Rudenstine, who became president in 1991.

As mentioned earlier, another important development that has taken place in the university during the past century has been the integration of men and women students in its classes, a program that continues under Radcliffe's current presudent, Linda Wilson, who is also dean of Radcliffe in Harvard University.

Today, as the university describes itself in its brief pamphlet on the history of the institution: "Harvard is a highly decentralized institution comprising an undergraduate College (Harvard and Radcliffe), a graduate school of arts and sciences, and nine other major departments of enrollment: business administration, design, divinity, education, government, law, medicine and dental medicine, and public health. Occupying an area of more than 450 acres, concentrated mainly in Cambridge and Boston, including Allston, the University has a regular enrollment of 15,500 students, plus some 10,000 in the summer school and other continuing education programs. The faculty and full-time supporting staff number 16,000, and so the University community includes more than 40,000 individuals. . . . The student body represents every state and territory of the United States and more than one hundred nations of the world. There are now some 215,000 alumni, and more than 150,000 have received degrees since Harvard's founding." Harvard takes pardonable pride in the fact that six of its graduates have gone on to become President of the United States; these are, with the year of their class: John Adams (1755), John Quincy Adams (1787), Rutherford B. Hayes (1845), Theodore Roosevelt (1880), Franklin Roosevelt (1904), and John Fitzgerald Kennedy (1940).

The present itinerary starts where the last one began and ended, at Harvard Sq. This time the tour will at first take one just a single block to the E. along the r. side of Massachusetts Ave, where, after crossing Dunster St, one comes to Harvard's Holyoke Center. On the l. side of the arcade leading into the Holyoke Center is the Harvard Information Center, where there is available, without charge, an excellent and very detailed map of the area to be covered on this itinerary, with all of the major buildings of the university clearly identified. The Information Center also gives free guided tours of Harvard at regular intervals.

On the opposite side of Massachusetts Ave from the Information Center stands the first site to be seen on the present tour; this is ***Wadsworth House,** Harvard's second-oldest surviving building and one of the most picturesque structures on the campus.

History. This yellow frame house was erected in 1726 by the Massachusetts Legislature; it was designed to be the residence of the president of Harvard, and served that purpose until 1849. The house is named for its first resident, the Rev. Benjamin Wadsworth, who served as president of Harvard from 1725 to 1736, after having been minister of the First Church in Boston for 30 years. When General George Washington first came to Cambridge to take command of the Continental Army, on July 2, 1775, he was quartered in the Wadsworth House, but moved out on July 15 to take up residence in the more commodious mansion of John Vassall on Tory Row. Many modern historians believe that, when Washington officially assumed command of the Continental Army, on July 3, 1775, the ceremony did not take place under the Washington Elm, as popularly believed, but in the Wadsworth House. During the siege of Boston the Wadsworth House was used as the headquarters for Washington's commissary department. The last president of Harvard to live here was Edward Everett, who was housed here in 1847—49. Wadsworth House now contains alumni offices.

Exterior. The Wadsworth House is a good Cambridge example of Early Georgian design. The most distinctive feature of the five-bay facade is the gambrel roof with hip dormers. The windows are arranged symmetrically and are substantially larger than usual in colonial houses, but the 12-by-12 glass panes are smaller than those used a half-century later. The shutters date from just prior to the Revolution, when they were first introduced in American architecture; those in the first floor are examples of the earliest form, with heavy, widely spaced louvers. Also characteristic of the period is the manner in which the window frames project out strongly from the facade; and the fact that the clapboards are narrower than those presently used, hand-planed to a beaded edge. The house was enlarged in 1783 to add the bays at the ends of the facade and probably the entrance porch as well; the brick-ended kitchen wing at the rear was done in 1810.

Wadsworth House stands on the site of Harvard's first home. This was a simple dwelling, built by William Peyntree c. 1633; it was sold to the overseers of the college in 1637 or 1638, when its owner followed the Rev. Hooker on his migration to Connecticut. The first freshmen at the college, 12 in number, began their classes in this house in the summer of 1638; they were taught by a single master, Nathaniel Eaton, a graduate of Trinity College, Cambridge, and also of the University of Franeker in the Netherlands. However, Eaton did not prove to be successful; he flogged his students for the most minor transgressions, beating one of them with a cudgel "big enough to have killed a horse," after which he was charged with assault and dismissed from his post; eventually he died in debtors' prison in Southbank. The college remained closed for the entire academic year after his dismissal, and it did not reopen until Henry Dunster was appointed president on Aug. 27, 1640. In the meantime, the overseers had erected the college's first permanent home, known today as Harvard Hall I; this was situated behind the present site of Wadsworth House, and it was completed in time for the first commencement in 1642. This building faced Braintree St (Massachusetts Ave), and was screened from that road by the Peyntree House and the Goffe House, a dwelling purchased by the overseers from William Goffe in 1651 to provide additional housing for the "scholars." Harvard Hall I was a long and narrow structure with wings to the rear that created a courtyard facing onto a pasture to the N. and with cow yards on either side; thus it became common practice to refer to the campus of the college as the "Yard," the ancestor of today's Harvard Yard. The main hall of this building was used for prayers, dining, lectures, and college ceremonies and celebrations, with a library on the upper floor; all other space, including the attic, was used to house the tutors and students. Harvard Hall I remained in use until 1679, when it collapsed for the second time (the first was two years earlier) and was demolished.

There were two other structures on this first Harvard campus, both of which stood between Harvard Hall I and the present site of Harvard Sq. The structure at the S.W. corner of the Yard, by Harvard Sq, was the college brewhouse, for apparently beer was an important part of their diet for scholars and tutors alike. The building between that and Harvard Hall I was the Indian College, which grew out of a desire by President Dunster and others to educate the Native Americans in Massachusetts. Dunster received financial support for the project from the English Society for the Propagation of the Gospel in New England, and c. 1655 the Indian College was completed, with living quarters and lecture rooms ready to accommodate about a score of native students. A dozen or so likely-looking Indian students were sent to Master Corlet of the Cambridge Latin School, where they were to be prepared for entrance to the college. However, only four or five of the Indians ever managed to qualify for entrance to Harvard, and only one of these eventually took his degree; this was Caleb Cheeshahteaumuch, who died of tuberculosis a year after his graduation. The concept of the Indian College was thenceforth abandoned, but the English Society for the Propagation of the Gospel in New England persisted in its efforts to bring the Word of God to the Native Americans. The printing press that President Dunster had acquired for Harvard was installed on the lower floor of the defunct Indian College, where it was used to print the Rev. John Eliot's Indian translation of the Bible. This gave rise to the first college press in America, the ancestor of the present Harvard University Press; in its early years, in addition to Eliot's Bible, it also turned out a considerable Indian library, as well as almanacs, lawbooks, broadsides, catechisms, psalm books, sermons, an occasional reprint of an English work, and a few volumes of verse of New Englanders, most notably those of Anne Bradstreet, America's first poetess.

After this somewhat lengthy introduction to the earliest days of Harvard, it is possible to make a real start on the tour, which now goes into **Harvard Yard**. The best approach, beginning at the Wadsworth House, is to follow

Massachusetts Ave as it rounds the S.W. corner of Harvard Yard. In so doing one passes in turn *Lehman Hall* and *Strauss Hall*, two Harvard Houses built in 1924 by the firm of Coolidge, Shepley, Bulfinch, and Abbott. This brings one to *Johnson Gate,* the principal entryway to the Yard. This elaborate neo-Georgian gateway was built in 1889 by McKim, Mead & White, and it was the first part of the brick-and-iron fencing that they erected around the Yard at that time; the entryway is named for Samuel Johnson (B.A., 1855), one of the first Western graduates to remember Harvard in his will.

Through the Johnson Gate is a large open area flanked by two of Harvard's most ancient and historic structures, with ***Massachusetts Hall** on the r. and ***Harvard Hall** on the l. The former building is the older of the two, and so should be looked at first.

History. Massachusetts Hall is the oldest of Harvard's surviving buildings, erected in 1718–20. It was designed to provide quarters for 60 students and one or two tutors, and was divided into 32 chambers, each with two smaller studies. It also included an early "Apparatus Chamber" for the study of science. During the Revolutionary War troops of the Continental Army were quartered here. In 1870 the building was completely gutted to create four large spaces, each two stories high, to be used for lectures, laboratories, and examination rooms. After a fire in 1924 the interior was rebuilt as a dormitory. However, in 1939 the first two floors were again remodeled to house administrative offices, including those of the president, while the upper floors continue to fulfill their original function as dormitories.

Massachusetts Hall retains its original external form, a three-story building with an attic floor with dormer windows, and a pair of tall paneled chimneys at the gable ends, between which runs a balustrade. The painted clockface at the W. end marks the site of the former college clock and bell.

Now walk across to look at Harvard Hall, the somewhat smaller but equally impressive building that faces Massachusetts Hall.

History. Harvard Hall is the third building of that name to stand in the Yard. Mention has already been made of Harvard Hall I, the first permanent college building, which was demolished in 1679. Harvard Hall II was erected on the present site in 1672–82; when complete, it was the most impressive building in New England, two stories high to the main cornice, and with two more stories under the gambrel roof. (The illustration on p. 352 shows Harvard Hall II standing across from the present Massachusetts Hall, while between them to the rear is Old Stoughton Hall, now demolished.) Harvard Hall II contained a library of 5000 books, the largest in America at that time, including the collection that had been bequeathed to the college by John Harvard; it also housed the chapel, lecture rooms, dormitories, a scientific laboratory, and a kitchen and buttery. On the night of Jan. 26, 1764, Harvard Hall II was completely destroyed in a fire; this conflagration also consumed the laboratory and its scientific apparatus, along with the library and all but one of John Harvard's books.

The present Harvard Hall was erected on the same site in 1764, designed by Governor Francis Bernard and erected by the master builder Thomas Dawes. The building originally served the same purpose as its predecessor, though the library and science laboratory had to be built up again from scratch. During the year 1775–76 Harvard Hall was occupied by troops of the Continental Army, and during that time about 1000 pounds of lead were stripped from the roof and melted down to make bullets. Additions to the building were made in 1842 and again in 1870; the interior was extensively remodeled in 1968, and now is used exclusively for classrooms.

Harvard Hall remains as an important example of Georgian architecture, although the two 19C additions have somewhat obscured its original form.

The two-story central pavilion of three bays was added to the front of the building in 1842 by Richard Bond. Then, in 1872, a pair of single-story wings were added on the sides of this pavilion, filling the corners of the T-shaped structure, a project carried out by Ware and Van Brunt. The last addition was made with great care in order to maintain the original style of the building; the new brickwork as well as the brownstone trim matched exactly the colonial masonry; the new fenestration repeated the pattern of the old round-arched windows; and even the granite blocks from the foundation of the old facade were reused so carefully that it is impossible to detect a break between the new and old structures.

After seeing Massachusetts Hall and Harvard Hall, continue straight ahead to enter the main area of the *Old Yard*, a vast quadrangle with its principal axis oriented N.-S., its periphery formed by eight venerable halls, which include some of the finest of Harvard's buildings. The most impressive of these is the one standing straight across to the E. on the minor axis of the quadrangle; this is ***University Hall**, which many historians of architecture consider to be Harvard's most splendid structure.

History. University Hall was erected in 1813 by Charles Bulfinch, one of two buildings that the architect designed for Harvard. Bulfinch conceived of University Hall as a core about which to organize a new academic precinct, and in fact it has fulfilled that function, though not in quite the way the architect had intended. Nevertheless, the erection of University Hall was the first step in defining the great quadrangle of the Old Yard, whose periphery was eventually defined in the inward-facing buildings that one sees there today; Bulfinch's building also initiated the development of a second quadrangle to the E., in what is now the central area of Harvard Yard. University Hall was originally designed as a commons, including dining halls, six classrooms, a chapel, and the president's office; however, it now houses the administrative offices of the dean of the Faculty of Arts and Science as well as those of the deans of Harvard College.

Bulfinch chose to construct University Hall of Chelmsford granite, a material that had become available to Boston builders and architects through the construction of the Middlesex Canal, completed by 1803 by the engineer Loammi Baldwin. Baldwin had made use of Chelmsford granite two years before in the construction of Harvard's first stone building, Holworthy Hall, which stands at the N. end of the quadrangle (see below). Both Baldwin and Bulfinch were criticized for having deviated from the style of the traditional red-brick edifices that already stood in the Yard, but the favorable opinions of modern historians of architecture have vindicated their choice of building material. The facade of University Hall is in three parts: a central section of six bays in two stories, with the upper windows round-headed; this is flanked by a pair of entrance bays, each of which is framed by a pair of giant wooden Ionic pilasters; above these eight bays is a full entablature and a roof balustrade; and at the two ends of the building there are three-story wings of three bays each. A single-story porch that originally extended across the front of the building was removed in 1842, at which time the two flights of steps were erected; similar stairs in the identical E. facade were not added until 1917.

In front of University Hall, between the two stairways, there is a bronze statute by Daniel Chester French, dedicated in 1884 as a memorial to John Harvard, and installed in its present location in 1924. Engraved statements on the base of the monument contain three errors. First, the subject is identified as John Harvard, whereas the figure is an idealized representation, modeled by a young Harvard graduate whom French thought to typify his subject; second, John Harvard is identified as the founder of the college, when in fact he was merely its first benefactor; and third, the date 1638 is carved on one side, implying that this was when the college was founded, but the true date of founding is 1636, and 1638 is the year in which John Harvard died and made his bequest to the college. In any event, this statute is the most photographed object in Harvard Yard, a favorite with out-of-town visitors and parents on Commencement Day.

After seeing University Hall, one might walk down toward the southern end of the quadrangle to look at the three Victorian buildings which define that boundary of the Old Yard. In the center, at the S. end of the quadrangle, is *Grays Hall,* on the l. is *Weld Hall,* and on the r. is *Matthews Hall;* all three of these were built as dormitories within a single decade during and after the Civil War, evidence of the rapid expansion that Harvard underwent at that time. Grays Hall was built by N. J. Bradlee in 1862; Weld Hall by Ware and Van Brunt in 1870; and Matthews Hall by Peabody and Stearns in 1871. Off in the background beyond the S.E. corner of the quadrangle, seen between Grays Hall and Weld Hall, is *Boylston Hall.* This distinctive edifice was originally built in 1857 by Paul Schultze; its upper floor with mansard roof was added in 1871, and in 1959 its interior was completely renovated by Architects Collaborative. Boylston Hall was originally designed as a science building, with a chemistry laboratory that was one of the first in the U.S.; and it also had an anatomical museum, as well as rooms housing an extensive collection of mineralogical specimens. In the course of time it has served many other purposes, and after the 1959 restoration it was converted into a language laboratory, a function it continues to fulfill today.

One can now walk back toward the northern side of the quadrangle to identify the venerable dormitories which defined that end of the Old Yard. On the r., just beyond University Hall, is *Thayer Hall;* straight ahead, at the N. end of the quadrangle, is *Holworthy Hall;* to the l. of this, at the N. end of the W. side of the Yard, is *Stoughton Hall;* and to the S. of this on the same side is *Hollis Hall,* which abuts Harvard Hall. The description that follows begins with Thayer Hall, and then continues from there around that end of the Yard.

Thayer Hall was built in 1896 by Edward D. Harris, junior member of the architectural firm of Ryder and Harris. The building is named for Nathaniel Thayer, a Harvard alumnus, of whose generosity in erecting this dormitory President Eliot gives the following account: "The main object which Mr. Thayer had in view was to secure a solid and durable building (almost all the interior partitions are brick) with a considerable rental and accommodations for a large number of students. He deliberately preferred a plain building to an ornate but smaller one. . . . At the start the Corporation expected to pay part of the cost of the Hall, but before the plans and specifications were complete it became perfectly understood that Mr. Thayer meant to pay the whole cost. He made all the contracts and paid all the bills himself. . . . I never knew the exact cost of the whole work." The building, which is made of brown Nova Scotia sandstone, is four stories high with a central pavilion that juts out slightly from the main facade. It was designed to house 117 students and three proctors.

Holworthy Hall was erected in 1811 by the engineer-architect Loammi Baldwin; as mentioned earlier, this was built of Chelmsford granite and was the first stone building put up in Harvard Yard. It was also the first

Harvard dormitory to abandon the medieval tradition of closet-sized studies opening off from a central sitting room; instead, Baldwin provided each suite with a sitting room looking S. toward the Yard and two bedrooms on the N., an arrangement that gave better lighting and cross-ventilation. Holworthy Hall has undergone very little alteration since it was first erected; the only significant change was made in 1871, when the cornice was raised by 2ft to increase the height of the rooms on the top floor.

Stoughton Hall is the second building of that name to stand on this site. Its predecessor, Old Stoughton Hall, was erected in 1699, partly constructed with bricks salvaged from the old Indian College. During 1775–76 Old Stoughton was used as a barracks to house 2000 troops of the Continental Army, and it was so badly damaged during that time that the college authorities decided to demolish it in 1781. The present Stoughton Hall was designed by Charles Bulfinch and was erected in 1804 by the master builder Thomas Dawes. Stoughton Hall was damaged by a fire in 1876, at which time the cornice was replaced; otherwise the building has exactly the same appearance as when it was first built.

Hollis Hall is Harvard's third-oldest extant structure, erected in 1762 by the master builder Thomas Dawes. Hollis Hall differs from the older Massachusetts Hall in just the ways in which one would expect a building of the Middle Georgian style to deviate from one dating from the early part of that architectural era: with a hip roof of lower pitch rather than a gambrel roof; windows in the top floor shorter than those in the lower story; and the designs of entryways elaborated with pilasters and a dentil course rather than simply framed by an architrave. Only one original door-frame is preserved in Hollis Hall, that of the false center door on the W. side, and this now lacks its original segmented pediment. The dormitory originally had its front entrances facing onto the roadway outside, and the rear doorways opening into the Yard were used to gain access to the college privies and the pump. But early in the 19C, after the erection of Holworthy and University Halls in 1811 and 1813, the center of gravity of the campus shifted eastward as the present quadrangle took form; then the doors on the E. side became the main entrances to the dormitory. Today, the doorways on the side of the building facing Massachusetts Ave are no longer used.

Outside Hollis Hall there is a replica of the Old College pump. This was built in 1936 to replace the original pump, which was blown up by some students in a mad prank late in the 19C. The pump was fed by a spring which was the source of water for those living in and around the Yard in colonial times. Professor Wigglesworth, the first occupant of the Hollis Chair of Divinity, whose house was just to the E. of the Wadsworth House, used to water his cow here in the years just prior to the American Revolution.

Notice some of the cracks in the old pavement outside Hollis Hall, for they tell a rather interesting story. It seems that when the college students returned from Concord in June 1776, after the Continental Army had departed from Cambridge, they found a large number of iron cannonballs lying around in the Yard. The students living in Hollis Hall put these to good use in warming their rooms during the very cold winter of 1776–77, placing the balls in the dormitory fireplaces until they were red-hot, and then carrying them in braziers into their chambers, to give off heat during the early hours of the night. Then, in the spring of 1777, when heat was no longer needed, the students dropped the cannonballs from their windows, producing the cracks in the pavement that one sees today.

Now walk between Hollis and Stoughton Halls into the small quadrangle

John Hancock.

OFFICIAL LIFE INSURANCE SPONSOR
1994/1996 U.S. OLYMPIC TEAMS

U S A

36 USC 380

behind those dormitories and Harvard Hall; straight ahead is ***Holden Chapel,** the most charming building in Harvard Yard.

History. This gem of Georgian architecture was built in 1742, probably according to plans brought from England along with the funds to build the chapel; this was a gift from the widow and daughters of Samuel Holden, a prominent Dissenter who had been a Member of Parliament and governor of the Bank of England. The building served as the college chapel in 1744–66 and again in 1769–72, when the students gathered there for morning and evening prayers. Just prior to the Revolution the Provincial House of Representatives of Massachusetts convened in Holden Chapel for a time, and here James Otis delivered one of his historic orations. During the years 1775–76 troops of the Continental Army were also quartered here. In 1783 the newly founded Harvard Medical School used the building as a demonstration hall for human dissections; subsequently it served successively as a carpentry shop, fire station, clubhouse, chemistry laboratory, theater, lecture hall, auditorium for classes in public speaking, and as a hall for choir rehearsals; presently it is the headquarters and office space of the Harvard Glee Club.

Exterior. The identical E. and W. facades of the building are framed by paired black pilasters surmounted by Tuscan entablatures, which are merely wooden boards attached to the brick walls. The chapel originally faced toward the W., and the pediment on the side is adorned with a florid wood carving done when the building was first erected in 1742, a very elaborate design in the center of which is the coat-of-arms of the Holden family. (The baroque enframement of the coat-of-arms was a source of inspiration for Cambridge architects in the present century, who used it as an archetype for similar pedimental decoration on the new Harvard Houses constructed between the Yard and the Charles River.) The identical carving on the E. pediment is a replica done in the present century. In the mid-19C the main entrance to the building was shifted to the E. side; the elaborate roundheaded entryway that one sees today on that end, framed by pilasters and a classic entablature, was created in 1850 by Gridley J. F. Bryant. The former main entrance on the Massachusetts Ave side was sealed in 1880. The side walls are pierced by three tall roundheaded windows, lengthened by 2ft in 1814, which are separated by pilasters with elegantly profiled brownstone caps.

Interior. The interior of Holden Chapel is a sorry disappointment, just an open and unadorned area used as office space by the Harvard Glee Club, whose cluttered desks, filing cabinets, and bulletin boards are desecrations in a place designed to be a house of worship; one would think that some more appropriate use could be made of this exceedingly elegant and unique building.

The two neo-Georgian dormitories flanking Holden Chapel are *Lionel Hall* (l.) and *Mower Hall* (r.), both completed in 1924 by the firm of Coolidge, Shepley, Bulfinch, and Abbott. The N. end of this little quadrangle is formed by *Phillips Brooks House*. This was built in 1898 by Alexander Wadsworth Longfellow, Jr., the poet's nephew, and is obviously inspired by Harvard Hall, the back of which forms the S. side of the quadrangle. Brooks House contains offices and meeting rooms for Harvard's religious and social-service organizations.

Now return to the main quadrangle and walk straight across it through the other side, passing between Thayer and University Halls; this brings one into a second quadrangle, which forms the central area of Harvard Yard. The W. side of this quadrangle, which is known as the New Yard, is

formed by the backs of Thayer University, and Weld Halls; to the S. is the
monumental Widener Library; hidden away in the S.E. corner are the
Houghton and Pusey Libraries; to the E. one sees on the r. a side of Emerson Hall and to the l. of that the front of Sever Hall; and on the N. side is
the imposing Memorial Church, whose splendid spire is one of the landmarks of Harvard Yard. The next part of the itinerary will take one around
the New Yard to see the buildings that define its periphery, proceeding in
the order indicated above.

The first building is the ***Widener Memorial Library,** the huge edifice
that dominates the New Yard from its S. side.

History. The Library is named after Harry Elkins Widener of the Harvard Class of 1907,
who died at sea in 1912 when the steamship *Titanic* sank after colliding with an iceberg;
funds for the construction of the building were given to the university by his mother, Eleanor
Elkins Widener. The architect in charge was Horace Trumbauer, who erected the building
in 1913–15, and the Library was dedicated on June 24, 1915, Commencement Day. The
building replaced an older and smaller library that was housed in Gore Hall, a Gothic
Revival structure erected in 1883. The Widener is the chief depository of the Harvard College Library and the administrative center of the university's network of 92 libraries; together
these contain the third-largest collection of books in the U.S., surpassed only by the Library
of Congress and the New York City Public Library.

Exterior. The most impressive feature of the Widener Library is its enormous portico, formed by 12 huge columns surmounted by Corinthian capitals, from which a broad flight of steps leads down to the campus.

Interior. At the end of the long lobby a flight of marble steps leads up to
the Widener Memorial Room, and from there the stairway goes on up to
the anteroom of the Main Reading Room. The walls flanking the entrance
to the anteroom of the Widener Memorial Room are decorated with murals
by John Singer Sargent; these are patriotic scenes depicting the entry of
the U.S. forces into France in World War I, and are probably the very worst
works of public art ever done by a major American painter. After passing
through the monumental anteroom, one comes to the *Widener Memorial
Room,* where on the wall facing the entryway is a portrait of Harry Elkins
Widener. In a case to the r. of the entryway there are displayed two of the
most extraordinary books in the Widener's vast collection, a *First Folio of
Shakespeare's plays and a *Gutenberg Bible.

The 1623 Folio was the first attempt to bring together a collected edition of Shakespeare's
dramatic works. Had it never been published, there would have been no text at all of at
least 17 of his plays, and only extremely corrupt versions of at least four more of his works.
John Heminge and Henry Condell, actors in Shakespeare's company, produced this edition
"without ambition either of selfe-profit or fame: onely to keep the memory of so worthy a
Friend, and Fellow, alive, as was our wish." The Gutenberg Bible, the first major book in
the world printed from movable type, was planned and printed under the direction of Johannes
Gutenberg and his associates in Mainz between 1450 and 1456. About 200 copies were
printed, 165–70 on paper and 30–35 on vellum, of which 47 copies survive, but only 22 of
them complete. The first known owner of the Harvard copy was Johann Vlyegher, a priest
of Utrecht, who in 1471 bequeathed the Bible to the monastery at Soest near Amersfoort,
in the diocese of Utrecht. The Widener family obtained the Bible in 1912, and in 1944 they
presented it to the Harvard Library.

Before leaving the Widener Library, examine the three dioramas in the two
passageways beneath the staircase. One of these depicts Old Cambridge

as it was in 1677, the second as it was in 1775, and the third in 1936, Harvard's Tercentenary.

After leaving the Widener Library, one might walk over to look at the extraordinary monument that stands midway along the W. side of the building, near Boylston Hall; this is an ancient Chinese stele presented to Harvard by its alumni in China at the time of the University's Tercentenerary in 1936. The stele was placed here because at that time Boylston House housed the Yenching Institute, Harvard's library and research center for the study of Chinese and other Far Eastern cultures.

Beside the Widener Library, in the S.W. corner of the New Yard, are the semisubterranean *Pusey Library* and also the *Houghton Library*. Among other works, the Pusey Library houses Harvard's archives, its Theater Collection, and its Map Collection. The Houghton Library contains the university's collection of rare books, some of which are on display in the oval room at the entrance to the building. In the bookcases that line this room there are displayed works from the personal libraries of John Masefield, Samuel Taylor Coleridge, Edwin Arlington Robinson, Michel de Montaigne, Thomas Hollis, John Harvard, and Cotton Mather. The John Harvard Collection consists of works known to have been part of his original bequest to the college, all but one of which were destroyed in the fire of 1764. On display in this case is the title page of the single surviving book from John Harvard's collection, a work by John Downame entitled *The Christian Warfare Against the Devil, World, and Flesh,* and on the opposing page is a description of the fire that destroyed the library in Harvard Hall.

Near the S. end of the E. side of the New Yard is *Emerson Hall,* erected in 1904 by Guy Lowell, the architect who designed the Boston Museum of Fine Arts on the Fenway. To the l. of this, defining most of the E. side of the New Yard, is ***Sever Hall,** an enormous structure built in 1880 by Henry Hobson Richardson. The most striking features of this very distinctive Romansque building are the turreted towers that flank its main entrance, which is framed by a huge Syrio-Roman arch, and the very elaborate decorative brickwork. Douglass Shand Tucci, in his *Built in Boston,* ranks Sever Hall with Richardson's greatest works, writing that: "Sever is more than a masterpiece. Like Trinity it is both old and new, but in Sever's case Richardson's inspiration was not only Medieval but closely related to the Old Georgian buildings of the Yard, with which Sever is, in fact, very sympathetic: Sever's distinction lies chiefly in the fact that its almost Classical serenity of mass catches perfectly the spirit of the dormitories of the old Yard even as its discreet cut-brick detail and low towers and broad-arched entrances establishes its modernity in its own time." Sever Hall was originally designed to hold lecture halls and large and small classrooms, a function it continues to fulfill today.

The northern end of the New Yard is dominated by **Memorial Church,** which was completed in 1931 by Coolidge, Shepley, Bulfinch, and Abbott. The church stands on the site of Appleton Chapel, which was built in 1856–58, and which served as Harvard's house of worship until the erection of the present building. The facade of Memorial Church is a very unusual, with two monumental Doric porticoes, one of them facing S. into the New Yard and the other facing W. toward Thayer Hall. The main entrance to the church is through the W. portico, whereas the S. portico counterbalances the huge portico of the Widener Library, which it faces across the New Yard. Another distinctive feature of the church is its handsome steeple, one of the landmarks of Harvard Yard; this was patterned on the famous steeple of Christ Church in the North End, the historic Old North. The church was a memorial to the men of Harvard who died in World War I, and their names are inscribed on the walls of the nave. The transept of the church is known as Appleton Chapel, perpetuating the name of the older house of worship that originally stood on this site. A memorial wall in the chapel commemorates the men of Harvard who died in World War II.

At the N.E. corner of the New Yard is *Robinson Hall,* tucked in the angle between Memorial Church and Sever Hall. This was erected in 1900 by McKim, Mead & White, and was intended for use by the School of Architecture. As such, it was designed with a huge "Hall of Casts" in the space behind the central facade. However, the architectural school, which is now part of the Graduate School of Design, is now housed mainly in a new building outside the N.E. corner of the Yard (see below).

At this point the itinerary takes one on a brief tour of some of the university buildings N. of Harvard Yard. In the past, this more modern part of the campus was separated from the Old Yard by the busy highways that radiated off from Massachusetts Ave at the southern end of the Common, particularly Cambridge St. But in 1967 work was completed on the Cambridge St Underpass, engineered by Charles A. Maguire and Assocs; and above it an attractive parklike pedestrian overpass was created by Sasaki, Dayson DeMay Assocs, landscape artists. Two gates behind Holworthy Hall lead to this overpass, and from there one can cross to the northern part of the campus.

The vast futuristic complex of buildings that one sees straight ahead while crossing the overpass is the *Undergraduate Science Center,* completed in 1970 by Sert, Jackson, and Gourley. Immediately to the l. of this is the huge neoclassical facade of *Littauer Center,* completed in 1938 by Coolidge, Shepley, Bulfinch, and Abbott. This edifice, which houses the Department of Government, is built of Chelmsford granite, and it is quite obviously patterned on Bulfinch's original structure of Massachusetts General Hospital.

After crossing the overpass, take one of the paths that lead l. in front of Littauer Center, skirting the tangled knot of highways that winds around this corner of the campus. Once past Littauer, one approaches a quaint little Greek Revival structure with a neoclassical portico; this is the **Gannett House,** now used as office space by the Harvard Law School.

The Gannett House has been dated to 1838, but it is only the most recent in a series of dwellings erected on this site since the earliest days of Cambridge, the first being a cottage put up by John Meane in 1635. The house is named in honor of the Rev. Caleb Gannett, who was steward of Harvard from 1779 to 1818, and who himself lived next door for many years. Gannett House originally faced S., but was rotated by 90 degrees when Littauer Center was built, so as to face inward onto the newly formed campus. The house originally stood on a little L-shaped byway called Holmes Place, which cut in from the Common past the present site of Littauer, where in colonial times the King's Highway from Charlestown to Watertown crossed the turnpike to Lexington. In late-colonial times just four houses stood on this lane, the present Gannett House being closest to the Common. Three of these stood in a row along the very short W.-E. stretch of Holmes Place, and the fourth was just around the bend of the L-shaped lane, about where is now the S.W. corner of Littauer. At the beginning of the Revolution the third house belonged to Moses Richardson, the college carpenter, who was killed at the Battle of Lexington, on April 19, 1775. In later years one of his daughters said: "I well remember the night my father was called up. He slept in the eastern front bedroom facing the colleges. It was about one o'clock when he marched to Lexington, and he was killed about five o'clock." His two sons identified their father's body the following morning, and later he and the other local victims were laid to rest in the Old Burying-Ground in Cambridge, where a century later the town erected a monument in their honor.

The fourth house on the little street, the one just past the turn, was in the early years of the 19C the home of the Rev. Abiel Holmes, who was for nearly four decades minister of the First Parish Church. His son, Oliver Wendell Holmes, Sr., was born in this house on Aug. 29, 1809. As Oliver Wendell Holmes wrote later in his life: "It was a great happiness to have been born in an old house, haunted by such recollections, with harmless ghosts walking its corridors, and that vast territory of four or five acres around it, to give a child the sense that he was born to an old principality. I should hardly be happy if I could not recall at will, the old house with the long entry and the white chamber, where I wrote the first verses that made me known ["Old Ironsides"] and the little parlor, and the study and the old books . . . and the dear faces to be seen no more there or anywhere on this earthly place of farewells."

Beside one of the paths leading to the Gannett House there is a plaque commemorating an event that took place there on June 16, 1775, on the eve of the Battle of Bunker Hill. Shortly after sunset that day Colonel Prescott and his men began their march toward Charlestown, but they paused here for a few moments to receive the blessing of the Rev. Samuel Langdon, president of Harvard, who wished them good fortune in their fight for freedom.

Just to the W. of Gannett House stands *Austin Hall, the most splendid building in this part of the campus and one of the finest structures in the university. This was completed in 1881 by Henry Hobson Richardson, and was designed to house lecture halls, offices, and a large library; historians of architecture consider this to be one of the architect's greatest works of this type, comparable to his Sever Hall. Austin Hall has several distinctive features that can be recognized as Richardson's trademarks: three superb round-arched entryways supported on groups of colonettes, a conical-capped turret placed asymmetrically to the r.; polychromatic masonry, combining pink granite and two shades of sandstone (unfortunately obscured by grime); and elaborately decorative brickwork—altogether a handsome edifice.

On the W. side of the campus, beyond the Gannett House, there is first the *Hemenway Gymnasium* (1938), then *Walter Hastings Hall,* a fine dormitory erected in 1888 by Cabot and Chandler, and past that, opposite the N.E. corner of the Common, is the *Harvard-Epworth Methodist Church,* completed in 1891 by A. P. Cutting, who was here strongly influenced by the style of H. H. Richardson. Standing just to the E. of these and other university buildings in this part of the campus is *Langdell Hall,* which is the administrative center of the Law School and houses the Law Library. The southern half of this enormous neoclassical edifice was completed in 1906 by Shepley, Rutan and Coolidge; the northern half and the W. wing were finished in 1928 by Shepley, Bulfinch, and Abbott. A separate building for the *International Legal Studies Center* was erected to the N.W. of Langdell Hall in 1957, bordering on Massachusetts Ave, by Shepley, Bulfinch, Richardson, and Abbot. Langdell Hall defines the W. side of the large quadrangle that gives cohesion to this part of the campus. The N. side of the quadrangle is formed by the Harvard Graduate Center, all the buildings of which are dormitories except the *Harkness Commons,* which contains dining areas and meeting rooms; this attractive complex was completed in 1949 by the Architects Collaborative, a project initiated by Walter Gropius. Inside the Harkness Commons there are a number of works of art by renowned modern artists, most notably Joan Miró. To the E. of the Graduate Center, outside the main area of the quadrangle, is an enormous Victorian dormitory called *Perkins Hall,* erected in 1893 by Shepley, Rutan, and Coolidge.

The S. side of the quadrangle is defined by still another huge Victorian building; this is the *Jefferson Physical Laboratory,* completed in 1884 by Shaw and Hunnewell. The same architects erected the large building that takes up most of the E. side of the quadrangle; this is *Pierce Hall,* a laboratory for physics and applied science finished in 1900. Between these two structures, in the S.E. corner of the quadrangle, there are two smaller and more modern science buildings, the *Cruft Laboratory* and the *Lyman Laboratory.* Behind these, aligned with the E. end of the Science Center, is the *Gordon McKay Laboratory,* erected in 1951 by Coolidge, Shepley, Bulfinch, and Abbott.

The eastern half of this northern campus is a labyrinth of laboratories, museums, and libraries. The best approach is to walk over from the middle of the western side of the campus along its central axis, crossing Oxford St and continuing along as far as Divinity Ave. On the r. is the complex of laboratories recently grouped together as the *Cabot Science Center.* The largest and most impressive of these is the *Mallinckrodt Chemistry Laboratory,* distinguished by its massive neoclassical portico; this was erected in 1927 by Coolidge, Shepley, Bulfinch, and Abbott. On the l. one sees first the modern building that houses the Hoffman Laboratory of Experimental Biology, built in 1962 by the Architects Collaborative. Beyond that on the l. is the enormous U-shaped building that houses the University Museum, which was built by a number of architects in several stages during the period 1859–1915. This and the other Harvard museums are described in Rte 20.

One now comes to Divinity Ave, where across the street on the l. stands another enormous U-shaped building, which faces the U of the University Museum across the way; this houses the Biological Laboratories and was erected in 1930 by Coolidge, Shepley, Bulfinch, and Abbott. The N.W. corner of this vast edifice is a Gothic structure that now houses the *Farlow Herbarium.* This building was erected in 1886 by Peabody and Stearns to house the library of the Divinity School, whose buildings are behind the Biological Laboratories to the N.E. However, after the completion of the biology building the library was transferred to one of the buildings of the Divinity School and the structure here was then used to house the herbarium. Just to the N. of the University Museum and the biology buildings are laboratories for engineering science, biomedicine and nuclear physics, and also a structure that houses the Harvard Cyclotron and Linear Accelerator.

Now turn r. on Divinity Ave. To the r. is the Biochemistry Laboratory of the Cabot Science Center, and on the l. are first the Semitic Museum (visited on the next itinerary), and then the *Yenching Institute.* The latter institution houses the university's collection of books, periodicals, and manuscripts on the Far East. At the end of the block is Kirkland Ave, where on the l. stands the 15-story white concrete skyscraper called *William James Hall,* erected in 1963 by Minoru Yamasaki and Assocs. James Hall brings under one roof Harvard's extensive teaching and research in such fields as sociology, social anthropology, social psychology, clinical psychology, and behavioral psychology. Guided tours of the university given by the Harvard Information Office include a visit to the terrace at the top of James Hall, from which there is a panoramic view of old Cambridge and its environs.

At the N.W. corner of Divinity Ave and Kirkland St is Adolphus Busch Hall, which will also be visited in Rte 20. Directly across the way, on the

S.E. corner, is the *Church of the New Jerusalem*. This stone Gothic structure was erected in 1903 by Warren, Smith, and Biscoe, and originally served as the chapel of the New Church Theological School, a Swedenborgian institution.

Now turn r. and begin walking down Kirkland St; in times past this was known as Professors' Row, because of the large number of Harvard faculty who lived along it. Just past Adolphus Busch Hall there is a small courtyard which has recently been dedicated as the entrance mall of the Cabot Science Center. At the back of the mall a bronze relief map identifies all of the various laboratories in the Center, along whose periphery one has been walking.

Just beyond the entrance mall of the Cabot Science Center is a handsome old house with its side to the street, facing E., with an old barn, now used as a garage, at the inner end of the courtyard to the r. This house was built in 1838 in a combination of Greek Revival and Regency styles, and its most remarkable features are the wide pilasters that frame the bays of its facade. The house was erected by Daniel Treadwell, inventor and Harvard professor. In 1847 it was acquired by Jared Sparks, a professor of history at Harvard, who had previously been a prominent minister and editor. Sparks lived in this house while he was president of Harvard, 1849–53, and in his honor the building was named after him. The house originally stood at 48 Quincy St, at the corner of Kneeland, and c. 1903 it was acquired by the New Church Theological School. In 1966 the property on which the building stood was purchased by Harvard for the construction of Gund Hall (see below), after which the old house and its barn were moved to their present site. The present placement of the house, with its side facing the street, is the same as on the original lot; many old Cambridge and Boston houses looked out onto a side garden.

Just beyond the Sparks House is a single-story neoclassical building known today as the *Lowell Lecture Hall*. The building is now named after its donor, Harvard President A. Lawrence Lowell, who anonymously donated the funds necessary to erect the building. Only when President Lowell was identified as the unknown benefactor, years later, did the building receive its present name. The architect was Guy Lowell, President Lowell's nephew, who completed the building in 1902. Lowell Hall has a large lecture hall on its main floor, and a series of tutorial rooms in its basement.

Now cross Kneeland St to visit ***Memorial Hall**, the vast Gothic structure that has been looming in the background throughout most of this itinerary.

History. Though many visitors mistake it for a cathedral, Memorial Hall was erected to commemorate the Harvard men who died in the Civil War, and it has never been consecrated as a house of worship. The idea of a war memorial was first discussed among the alumni in 1863, by which time a large number of Harvard men had already given their lives for the Union cause, and many more would die in the remaining two years of the conflict. By 1865 a Committee of Fifty was formed to carry out the project, and an architectural competition was held to find a design for the proposed memorial. The design chosen was by William Ware and Henry Van Brunt, two Harvard graduates who had studied architecture there under Richard Morris Hunt. Ware and Van Brunt had their plans for the memorial complete by 1866, though they made significant changes in the details of their design in 1868 and again in 1871. Their basic plan called for a cathedrallike building surmounted by a huge tower at the end of the nave, and terminating in a large apse. The nave of the building would serve as a banquet hall, the transept would be the memorial hall, and the apse would contain a combination auditorium and theater. This would be the largest and most elaborate structure that the university had attempted; it stands as a milestone in American architectural history, and presents the first large-scale cooperative fund-raising program undertaken by Harvard alumni. By the time the building was completed, the committee had raised $368,980.90, a figure representing one-twelfth of the total endowment of Harvard at that time. One of the contributions was a bequest of $50,000 received in 1863 from Charles Sanders, a citizen of Cambridge, for "the erection of a large and substantial hall of simple architecture"; consequently, when the auditorium in the apse was completed it was called the Sanders Theater. Work began on the building in the autumn of 1870; the banquet hall in the nave and the memorial hall in the transept were finished in time for commencement in June 1874; Sanders Theater was substantially complete by May 1875, but it was not used for commencement exercises until June of the following year. The tower was finished in 1877, and in 1878 the Committee of Fifty finally adjudged Memorial Hall complete and formally turned it over to the university. The great clock in the tower was added in 1897, a gift of the class of 1872, dedicated at the time of their 25th reunion. During World War II the iron casting on the tower was removed, and the building fell into a state of some disrepair; it was being restored in Sept. 1956 when the wooden substructure in the tower roof was consumed in a fire. This tall, pinnacled roof, elaborately decorated with polychrome brickwork, has never been replaced, so that the tower today has a somewhat truncated appearance and is less impressive without its crowning glory.

Exterior. Memorial Hall is 310ft long and up to 115ft wide, and its tower with the original pinnacled roof was 195ft high, rivaling in size such great medieval cathedrals as Lichfield. The style of the building has been called Ruskinian Gothic, from the version of Italian Gothic made popular in the mid-19C by the English architectural critic John Ruskin, particularly in his very influential work, *The Stones of Venice* (1851–53). The three parts of the exterior structure reflect the tripartite function of Memorial Hall as it was originally designed: the nave with its steeply pitched roof revetted with decorative polychrome bricks, covering what was once the banquet hall, the front facade and side walls pierced by traceried stained-glass windows with ogive arches; the transept with its pair of elaborate pedimented entryways to the memorial hall flanked by pairs of towers with pyramidal roofs, also sheathed in decorative polychrome brickwork, with the great tower rising from its center, missing its tall, pinnacled roof; and at the W. the great apse housing the Sanders Theater, a five-sided structure inscribed in a circular arc, whose diameter equals the length of the transept. In addition, there is a very attractive narthexlike structure that serves as a vestibule at the W. end, with pedimented porticoes on its N. and S. sides, and in the center an elegant loggia of arches supported on double colonettes and capped with ogive arches. Historians of architecture generally agree with the evaluation that Douglass Shand Tucci wrote in his *Made in Boston,* when he described Harvard's Memorial Hall as "one of the great Ruskinian landmarks in America today."

Interior. Entering from the N. end of the "narthex," one passes into what was originally the great banquet hall, a vast area now used for student registration, final examinations, and other such activities. The inspirations for the open-trussed ceiling of this great room were the dining halls of Cambridge and Oxford colleges. The 59ft width of the room here is not much less than the 68ft of Westminster Hall, the largest wood-trussed interior surviving from the Middle Ages. A dado of walnut paneling along with the stained-glass windows and the painted design on the ceiling further enhances the interior. Around the walls of the hall there is an array of paintings, portrait-busts, and a statue, portraying some of the great men of Harvard and of the towns of Cambridge and Boston. None of the paintings has the least artistic merit, but some of the statuary is by well-known

American sculptors, including *William Wetmore Story, Hiram Powers, Shubal Vail Clevenger, Bela Pratt, Richard S. Greenough,* and *Daniel Chester French.* Particularly noteworthy are a bust of Ralph Waldo Emerson by French; a bust of William Wetmore Story by the sculptor himself, in which he is depicted wearing a Rembrandt-like beret; and, to the l. of the door at the far end of the hall, a large seated statue of Governor John Winthrop, done by Richard S. Greenough in Paris in 1856. Nevertheless, despite these works of art and the other decorations, most notably the stained-glass windows, the great hall is ultimately a disappointment, its grandiose dimensions notwithstanding. The stained-glass windows are covered with soot, permitting only a dim light to filter in from outside; there are always tables and chairs lying about after some student activity, along with the usual academic debris; and there is a general air of neglect about the place. At first one has the feeling that one is in a deserted and deconsecrated cathedral; but then one remembers that this cathedrallike place was never consecrated as house of worship, and that is perhaps what ultimately detracts from its grandeur.

The memorial hall in the transept is grand but equally disappointing. Nevertheless, the long roll roll of the inscribed names of the Harvard men who died in the Civil War is evocative.

Doors at either side of the transept give entry to *Sanders Theater,* and stairways on either side lead to the upper level of the auditorium. There is no feeling of disappointment here, for this superb chamber is still performing the function for which it was originally designed, and as such it is well cared for and in constant use for plays and public functions. There is an excellent description of the auditorium in the report published by the Cambridge Historical Commission in 1973, in preparation for the American Bicentennial; there one reads: "The greatest achievement of Memorial Hall is Sanders Theater. Its woodwork is lustrous, carving and colors sympathetic, acoustics and visibility excellent; the spatial configuration is so good that the auditorium, although seating 1200 spectators, nevertheless conveys a feeling of intimacy." The report goes on to say of the founder, Charles Sanders, that, "although he did not specify the Sheldonian Theatre in Oxford, that building seems early to have been in the minds of university officials and architects. The five-sided structure of Sanders transforms Wren's Baroque theatre into Gothic Revival terms without sacrifice of function. The west balcony over the stage—designed to accommodate overflow crowds—is an acoustical aid whose covered surface projects sound toward the audience, while the many different surfaces of the roof, walls and trusses break up the pattern of reflected sound to make the acustics excellent. Roof trusses of wood conceal iron tension rods, a subterfuge for which the architects were much criticized by their contemporaries. Concerts as well as Commencement exercises were first held here in 1876."

After leaving Memorial Hall, cross to the E. side of Quincy St, where the whole block to the S. of the Church of the New Jerusalem is taken up by *Gund Hall.* This modernistic structure of mirrored glass and concrete was erected in 1969–72 by the firm of John Andrews, Anderson, and Baldwin. The building is named after George Gund, a Cleveland banker who graduated from Harvard in 1908 and who later studied at the Harvard Business School. Gund Hall houses all the departments of the Harvard Graduate School of Design: Architecture, City and Regional Planning, Landscape Architecture, Urban Design, the Program in Advanced Environmental Studies, and the Laboratory for Computer Graphics and Spatial Analysis.

Now walk S. along Quincy St, crossing Cambridge St at the next corner. On the r. is a modern Cambridge firehouse with a neo-Georgian appearance, designed to make it compatible with the many Harvard buildings built in that style. On the l. side of the street is the Arthur M. Sackler Museum. Continue along on the l. side of Quincy, crossing Broadway at the next intersection; on the r. is Robinson Hall, described earlier in this itinerary. One then passes on the l. the Fogg Museum, along with its new wing to the N. Beyond the Fogg is Harvard's *Carpenter Center for the Visual Arts,* erected in 1961 to a design by *Le Corbusier,* in collaboration with Sert, Jackson, and Gourley. This is Le Corbusier's only building in the U.S., and it contrasts dramatically with the more traditional Harvard buildings in its immediate vicinity. The most distinctive feature of this unique structure is the open pedestrian ramp that takes one up from street level into the center of the buildings on an upper level, where there is an exhibition hall open to the public. The tall supporting *"piloti"* (pillars) and concrete *"brise soleil"* (sun breakers) are Le Corbusier trademarks.

A little farther along to the r. and set back from the street is a handsome three-story brick mansion with an elegant neoclassical portico formed by a circlet of columns. This was built in 1911 by Guy Lowell to house the president of Harvard, who at that time was his uncle, A. Lawrence Lowell. The mansion here replaced an older presidential residence of 1861 that stood next door, and which was subsequently demolished. The mansion here on Quincy St served as the presidential residence until 1971, when it was supplanted by Elmwood. Farther down Quincy St on the l. is a hip-roof Federal house with a front porch formed by a colonnade of six wooden columns. This is the *Dana-Palmer House,* built in 1822; it originally stood across the street on the N.W. corner of Quincy and Harvard Sts, on the present site of the Lamont Library, and it was moved to its present site in 1946. Behind the Dana-Palmer House, fronting on Prescott St, is the *Warren House,* dating to 1833; this originally stood on Quincy St, but it was moved back in 1900 to make way for the Harvard Union. The latter building, which faces to the side near the N.E. corner of Quincy St, is a Georgian Revival structure erected in 1900 by McKim, Mead & White; its most noteworthy features are its pilasters of alternating red brick and white stone.

Now turn r. and begin walking toward Harvard Sq, passing the *Lamont Library,* built in 1947 by Coolidge, Shepley, Bulfinch, and Abbott. Halfway along toward the square one passes a long building known as *Wigglesworth House.* This is named after the Wigglesworth estate, which Harvard acquired in 1793.

Wigglesworth House stands on the site of the Old Parsonage, which was built here in the first years after the settlement of Newtowne; this is recorded on a plaque at the rear of Boylston Hall, which is directly behind Wigglesworth. The Old Parsonage was built by the Rev. Thomas Hooker in 1633, when he and his followers first arrived in Newtowne. When Hooker and his people left for Connecticut in 1636, the townspeople organized the First Church in Cambridge, and installed the Rev. Thomas Shepard as their minister. The Rev. Shepard lived on here in the parsonage until his death in 1649.

Now continue along Massachusetts Ave, noticing on the wall of Harvard Yard beyond Wadsworth House a plaque commemorating the Rev. Thomas Shepard, who is here honored as one of the first overseers of the college. A short way beyond this is Harvard Sq, where the itinerary comes to an end.

19 Old Cambridge III: Between Harvard Yard and the Charles River

This itinerary goes through the very oldest part of Cambridge, that part of the city which lies between Harvard Yard and the Charles River. This was the extent of the original settlement of Newtowne, and the streets of this part of Cambridge coincide almost exactly with those of the colonial village. (To review the topography of this part of the city, refer to the introductory section that precedes the Cambridge itineraries.)

This itinerary begins at the S.E. corner of Harvard Sq. The land here was originally allocated to Simon Bradstreet, who in 1630 was secretary of the Court of Assistants in the administration of Governor John Winthrop and Deputy Governor Thomas Dudley. While Winthrop and most of the other Puritan leaders soon left Newtowne to settle in Boston, Dudley and Bradstreet remained behind, and were the political leaders of the settlement during its first years Bradstreet later became governor of the Bay Colony. Bradstreet's wife was Dudley's daughter Anne, whom he had married in England in 1628, when he was 25 and she 16. Anne Bradstreet became America's first poetess, writing her first verses in 1632, while living in their house on what is now the S.E. corner of Harvard Sq. Her first volume of poetry, entitled *The Tenth Muse, Lately Sprung Up in America,* was published in 1650 by the press at Harvard College, one of its earliest publications. She was also renowned in early-colonial Massachusetts for her prose works, particularly her *Meditations, Divine and Morall,* dated March 20, 1664. Anne Bradstreet, an invalid throughout most of her adult life, died of tuberculosis on Sept. 16, 1672; her place of interment is not known, but it is probable that she was buried in her father's tomb in Roxbury. Her epitaph could well be the elegiac verse she wrote for her mother, Dorothy Dudley, who died in 1643: "Religious in all her words and wayes / Preparing still for death at end of dayes; / Of all her Children, Children lived to see / Then dying, left a blessed memory."

One of the landmarks in the Harvard Sq area is the Wursthaus, a restaurant and bar at 4 JFK Drive, housed in the second building from the S.E. corner of the intersection. The Wursthaus is the oldest eating place in Cambridge, having served continuously on this site since 1917. This building and the one next to it on the S.E. corner of Harvard Sq have the appearance of modern edifices; however, the Cambridge Historical Commission's architectural survey dates the core of both structures to the late 18C. Like the site on the S.E. corner, the plot at 4 JFK Drive has a history dating back to the first years of the settlement at Newtowne. The first person to erect a house on this site was the Rev. Samuel Stone, who came from England with the Rev. Thomas Hooker and settled here in 1633. The Rev. Stone was born in Hartford, England, and was educated at Emmanuel College, Cambridge. According to the early records in Newtowne, "After solemn fasting and prayer," the Rev. Stone was appointed "teacher" to the First Church in the settlement and remained there until 1636, when he joined the Rev. Hooker's migration to Connecticut. Another historian of the early years of Newtowne records that the Rev. Stone "was Chaplain to the little army of ninety brave men under Major Mason, who by their valorous deeds exterminated the Pequot Nation of Indians."

The itinerary goes down the l. side of JFK Drive, which in the early-colonial period was known as Wood Lane. At the first intersection is Mount Auburn St, originally called Spring Lane.

This street took its name from the fact that it led to the town spring, whose site is now occupied by Brattle Sq, one block W. The building on the N.W. corner of JFK and Mount Auburn stands on the site of one of the most famous public house in colonial Cambridge, the *Blue Anchor Tavern.* This inn opened its doors for the first time on Dec. 27, 1652, when the Town Council granted to Andrew Belcher a license to there "sell bread and beer" for the entertainment of strangers and the good of the town. The innkeeper's grandson, Jonathan

Belcher, became the royal governor of the combined territories of Massachusetts and New Hampshire, and afterward he was appointed governor of New Jersey.

On the S.E. corner of the same intersection, at 44 JFK Drive, there is a fine mansion that houses the Fox Club, a Harvard clubhouse erected in 1906 by the architect Guy Lowell. As one walks down the next block, on the r. is Winthrop Sq, the site of the first marketplace in the colonial settlement of Newtowne. Cross Winthrop Sq and continue for another block to the next intersection, where JFK Drive crosses South St. On the far corner, to the l., is one of the very few colonial dwellings extant in this part of Cambridge, the *John Hicks House, erected in 1762. This house originally stood on the S.E. corner of Dunster and Winthrop Sts, and was moved to its present location in 1928. The house is named after John Hicks, a minuteman who was killed on April 19, 1775, fighting against the British on their retreat from Concord to Charlestown. The Hicks House is a gambrel-roofed structure that retains its colonial center-chimney; however, the kitchen ell to the rear is a later addition. The building now serves as the library of *Kirkland House*, the huge Harvard dormitory that occupies the remainder of the block, an edifice erected in 1913 by the firm of Shepley, Rutan, and Coolidge. Directly across from Kirkland House on JFK Drive is the John F. Kennedy School of Government, one of Harvard's new institutions.

Now turn l. off JFK Drive onto South St, which in colonial times was known as Marsh Lane. Midway along the block, on the l., at No. 17, there is a fine old Federal house dating to 1826. At the next corner turn l. onto Dunster St, which was originally called Water Lane. The near corner to the l. is the site of the first house built in Old Cambridge, erected in 1630 by Thomas Dudley. Dudley, originally deputy governor under John Winthrop, later served as governor on a number of occasions. Dudley was also one of those principally responsible for the founding of Harvard College.

Now walk N. along Dunster, passing on the r. Harvard's Indoor Athletic Building, erected in 1929 by Coolidge, Shepley, Bulfinch, and Abbott. Theodore Roosevelt (1855–1919), 26th President of the U.S., lived in a house on this site when he was a student at Harvard. Midway along the l. side of the block, at No. 69, one sees another fine old house of the Federal period, built in 1829 by the housewright Oliver Hastings. On the near corner to the l. is the *University Lutheran Church*, erected in 1950 by Arland Dirlam; despite its name, this edifice has no affiliation with Harvard.

Now cross Winthrop St for the second time, and on the far corner to the l., at 53 Dunster, one sees a three-story house in the Greek Revival style. This stately building was erected in 1841 by the housewrights William Saunders and Stephen S. Bunker; it now serves as the master's residence for Harvard's Dudley House.

Continuing N. on Dunster, one passes at mid-block on the l. the site of the first tavern in Old Cambridge. The tavern was opened by Deacon Thomas Chesholme, who in 1636 was licensed by the General Court to "keep a house of entertainment." The tavern stood close to the First Meeting-House, which was on the next lot to the N. (see below). This close proximity of church and alehouse led one 19C historian to remark that "the first tavern was next to the first meeting-house, and the first inn-keeper was deacon of the church." Deacon Chesholme was also the first steward of Harvard College. His inn remained standing until 1839, when it was destroyed in a fire.

Continue up Dunster to Mount Auburn St. On the near corner to the l. is a neo-Georgian structure erected in 1930 by Perry, Shaw, and Hepburn. This building stands on the site of the First Meeting-House, erected in 1632.

This first meetinghouse was a plain and simple structure, apparently quite small. As one reads in the records: "There was no altar, no choir, nothing even that in older countries would be called a pulpit; only a desk, with seats before it for deacons and elders and rows of benches beyond for men on one side and for women on the other. . . . It may have been bare, not because its builders loved to have it so, but because they had not the wealth or the skill to give it beauty." The first synod of the churches of the Bay Colony met in this little building in 1637, a group that included virtually all of the teaching elders and learned divines of New England. Anne Hutchinson's trial that same year was probably also held in this meetinghouse, when she was banished from the colony because of her heretical beliefs. And the first Harvard College commencement was held here as well, in 1642. As mentioned earlier, the minister of the First Meeting-House throughout most of its history was the Rev. Thomas Shepard, who served here until his death in 1649. By that time Cambridge had outgrown this little church, and in 1652 a new and larger meetinghouse was erected on what is now the S.E. corner of Harvard Sq. As soon as that building was complete, the old meetinghouse here on Dunster St was demolished and the lot sold.

There are buildings of some interest standing on the other three corners of Dunster and Mount Auburn Sts. On the N.W. corner is the *Garage,* which was originally erected in 1860 as a stable and car barn for the Union Railway Company, whose horse-drawn trolley service was the predecessor of the MBTA. In 1917 the building was converted into a parking garage and garage. Then, in 1973, the structure was rebuilt by ADD, Inc., who added an extra floor and converted the Garage into an attractive retail complex, with shops, cafes, and restaurants.

The huge building that occupies the whole block beginning at the N.E. corner of Dunster and Mount Auburn is Harvard's *Holyoke Center,* built in 1961–66 by Sert, Jackson, and Gourley. The ten-story main building contains university offices and meeting rooms, along with the University Health Services, with doctors' offices and laboratories, as well as the Stillman and Radcliffe Infirmaries. The building has open plazas and a central arcade that allows one to pass easily from Massachusetts Ave to Mount Auburn St; there is also a huge parking garage beneath the building, with entrances on both Dunster and Holyoke Sts. Holyoke Center stands on the site of a colonial mansion that was used as a hospital by the Continental Army after the Battle of Bunker Hill. General Baron von Riedesel and his family lived in this house briefly in 1777, when General Burgoyne's British and Hessian troops were quartered in the town after their surrender at the Battle of Saratoga; however, the Riedesels later moved to the Lechmere mansion on Tory Row.

On the S.E. corner, at 46 Dunster is an elegant Federal mansion erected in 1820 by the housewright Daniel Dascomb. In 1902 the building was taken over by the Signet Society, a Harvard literary club. The Society commissioned Bertram Goodhue and Pierre LaRose to reconstruct the building in a number of ways, at which time the glittering Georgian Revival ornament was added to the facade over the portico. The clubhouse stands on the site of a dwelling built in the very first years of Old Cambridge by Samuel Dudley, son of Governor Thomas Dudley. The younger Dudley married Governor John Winthrop's daughter, Mary, and the two of them lived here with their children before moving on from Cambridge c. 1642.

Now turn r. onto Mount Auburn St. At No. 78 is an unpretentious old house in the Greek Revival style, dated to 1839. This is one of the few houses of its period remaining in an area that was once almost totally residential, but which has been overwhelmed by institutional buildings in Harvard's expansion S. to the Charles River. Even the building here has been absorbed by Harvard, and now houses university offices.

This part of Mount Auburn St was in times past known as the Gold Coast. The quarter took its name from the dormitories and clubhouses on this and adjacent streets that catered to the sumptuous life-style of wealthy students at Harvard. Four of these clubs are still housed in elegant mansions along the r. side of Mount Auburn on the next two blocks: At 76 Mount Auburn is the Spee Club, in a mansion erected in 1931 by William T. Aldrich; at No. 74 is the Adamesque Iroquois clubhouse, built in 1916 by Warren and Wetmore; at No. 72 is the neo-Georgian Phoenix-S.K. Club, put up in 1915 by Coolidge and Shattuck; and at 2 Holyoke Pl, with its gable end at Mount Auburn, is the Fly Club, a work of H.D. Hale dating to 1899–1902, with a very impressive neoclassical portico. On the l. side of Mount Auburn St are two enormous Victorian piles that were also part of the Gold Coast, serving as dormitories. The first one, at the N.W. corner of Mount Auburn and Linden, is *Claverly Hall,* erected in 1892 by George Fogarty; and the second, which stands on the N.E. corner of the same intersection, was completed in 1897 by Coolidge and Wright. Both of these dormitories are part of Harvard's **Adams House,** which extends for 2½ blocks along Mount Auburn, and more than halfway up the streets to the N.

Contained within the Adams House complex is one of the grandest colonial mansions surviving in Cambridge; one can approach this by going up Lindon and turning r. through the gateway midway along the block, following the path within the grounds. This brings one to the ***Apthorp Mansion,** now the master's residence for Adams House.

History. The mansion is named after the Rev. East Apthorp, first minister of Christ Church in Cambridge. East Apthorp was one of 18 children of Charles Apthorp, a wealthy businessman, whose daughter Susan married Thomas Bulfinch, and one of their children was the architect Charles Bulfinch. Charles Apthorp was probably the wealthiest man in Boston in his day, and was also the paymaster and commissary of the British forces stationed in the town. East Apthorp went from the Boston Latin School to Jesus College, Oxford, where he received his B.A. and in 1753 his M.A. In 1759 the Society for the Propagation of the Gospel in Foreign Parts appointed the Rev. Apthorp to serve as minister to the Episcopalians in Cambridge, Mass. At about that time he married Elizabeth Hutchinson, sister of Thomas Hutchinson, then chief justice of the Supreme Court and later governor of the royal Province of Massachusetts. Soon after his return to Cambridge, the Rev. Apthorp began to erect this mansion, which was completed in 1760; it is possible that his architect was Peter Harrison, who finished his design for Christ Church in Cambridge that year. The mansion was so grand and luxuriously furnished that the Congregationalists in Cambridge referred to it sarcastically as The Bishop's Palace. Nevertheless, the Rev. Apthorp himself seems to have been well thought of by most of the townspeople, particularly the members of the Episcopal Church and the authorities at the college. Christ Church records a number of generous donations by the Rev. Apthorp, and in 1764, after the fire that destroyed Harvard's library, he contributed £300 for the purchase of new books. The Rev. Andrew Barnaby, archbishop of Leicester, England, in his *Travels Through the Middle Settlements of North America* (1760), wrote that "The Rev. East Apthorp is a very amiable young man, of stirring parts, great learning, and pure and engaging manners." However, the rising tide of patriotic opposition to British rule made life increasingly difficult for the Tories in Cambridge and Boston, and in 1764 the Rev. Apthorp left for England with his family, never to return.

The year after his departure the Apthorp Mansion was sold to John Borland, a wealthy Boston Tory. Borland died of an accidental fall in the mansion early in 1775, just before the outbreak of the Revolution. In the spring of 1775 troops of the Continental Army were quartered in the Apthorp Mansion, and there are references to the rough soldiers looting the well-stocked wine cellar. On May 15, 1775, the Cambridge Committee of Safety found other quarters for the troops, and after cleaning the mansion they appropriated it for their own use, and so one may presume that patriot leaders such as John and Samuel Adams, Dr. Joseph Warren, and John Hancock were visitors to the house at that time. A little later on it was used as a residence by General Israel Putnam and other high-ranking officers of the Continental Army. Then, in 1777, General Burgoyne was quartered in the mansion after his surrender at Saratoga. After the war the mansion passed on to a succession of owners, and at some time early in the Federal period a third story was added to the structure. One of these owners, Jonathan Simpson, decided c. 1793 to divide up the estate, which at that time extended all the way down to the Charles River. He retained the plot on which the mansion now stands and sold the rest as house lots, after which the present Linden and Plympton Sts were laid out. Late in the 19C the mansion was acquired by Harvard, appearing in the university catalogue as a dormitory named *Apthorp House.* Then, in 1930, the university restored the house inside and out for use as the master's residence for *Adams House,* producing the stately mansion seen today.

The mansion is built in the Georgian style, and the facade of the original two lower stories is virtually identical to that of the Tory Row mansion of John Vassall, Jr. (now known as the Longfellow House), which was built just one year earlier. The most noteworthy architectural elements on the facade are the great pilasters that rise to the height of the original cornice; a pair of these frame the central bay, which is surmounted by a pediment; another two form the corners of the building; while four much shorter pilasters rise from these to the cornice of the added upper floor.

After seeing the Apthorp Mansion, continue along the pathway that passes through the Adams House, to emerge at the gateway on Plympton St. Across the street, at No. 14, is a neo-Georgian mansion erected in 1914 by Jardine, Hill, and Murdock; this houses the offices of the *Harvard Crimson,* the university's renowned undergraduate newspaper.

Turn r. on Plympton and walk to the end of the block, where Bow St diverges slightly to the l. from Mount Auburn. In the narrow wedge between Bow and Mount Vernon Sts, a virtual sliver of real estate, is the most unusual and interesting structure in Cambridge, the ***Lampoon Building,** often called the *Castle.* This extraordinary building, which was erected in 1909 by Wheelwright and Haven, makes extremely imaginative use of its difficult wedge-shaped site, having a castlelike turret at the corner and broadening out into two identical facades that could easily be part of a medieval manor or monastery.

William Germain Dooley, in a jocular but affectionate description of the Castle, wrote: "The building smiles at you like the caricature of a face—circular windows for eyes, hanging lantern for a nose, a domed roof for a hat with a birdcage tassel, Gothic windows for ears, classical pilasters, gargoyles and what have you." The Castle houses the clubrooms and officers of the *Harvard Lampoon,* the university's famous undergraduate humor magazine; the club's emblem is an ibex, who perches atop the tower at the corner of the building, from where it is occasionally stolen by members of the *Crimson.* The interior of the building is as idiosyncratic as its exterior; it is open only to members and their guests, which is a pity, since it has to be seen to be believed.

After seeing the Lampoon Building, walk E. along Bow St, which after the first block begins to curve around to the l., eventually meeting Massachusetts Ave near the N. end of Plympton St. At the point where Bow St begins to bend N. it intersects Arrow St, a short byway that cuts E. to Massachusetts Ave. Both of these streets have retained their names and courses since the earliest days of Old Cambridge, when they were at the western extremity of the village. (Their names may not be as whimsical as they seem, since on a detailed map they do appear to form an arrow about to be fired from a well-stretched bow.) At the intersection of Bow and Arrow Sts stands *St. Paul's Roman Catholic Church.* This edifice was built in the Italian Romanesque style in 1915 by T. P. Graham; its most striking feature is its tall campanile, which was apparently inspired by the Torre del Commune in Verona.

Walk back to the intersection of Mount Auburn and Plympton; then turn l. on the latter street to look at some of the *Harvard Houses* in that quarter.

Most of these Harvard Houses were built by the group of architects who erected so many of the university's buildings in the present century; Shepley, Bulfinch, Richardson, Rutan, Coolidge, and Abbott. These prolific architects combined in one grouping or another to build most of the older houses to be seen on this last brief stretch of the itinerary; to save space, their individual names will not be given, only the date of construction.

Start down Plympton. On the l. is *Quincy House,* the modern parts of which were erected in 1958; the older building at the S.W. corner of the complex is *Mather Hall,* which dates to 1930. On the r. is *Lowell House,* an immense neo-Georgian structure erected in 1929 around two enclosed quadrangles. The blue-domed belfry of Lowell House, which has a chime of old Russian monastery bells, is one of the landmarks of Cambridge as seen from the Charles River. After crossing Mill St, one comes to Riverview Ave, passing on the l. *McKinlock Hall* (1925), now part of Leverett House (see below).

At this point one might best cross Riverview Ave and Memorial Drive; then turn l. and walk along the embankment to the *Weeks Memorial Bridge..* This graceful footbridge was erected in 1926 by McKim, Mead & White, and it is the most convenient way to pass from Cambridge to the other side of the Charles, where a vast complex of buildings houses the Harvard Graduate School of Business Administration.

Standing on the Weeks Bridge, one can easily identify the major Harvard buildings on the N. shore of the Charles, proceeding from r. to l. A little more than a half-mile off to the r. is *Peabody Terrace,* a group of three 22-story skyscrapers connected by buildings three to seven floors in height, with intervening plazas. This huge complex was completed in 1964 by Sert, Jackson, and Gourley, and serves as a residential center for some 500 families of married Harvard students. About a quarter-mile to the l. of the bridge is *Mather House;* erected in 1968, this is Harvard's newest undergraduate house. Just to the r. of the bridge is *Dunster House,* a huge neo-Georgian edifice erected in 1929, its brick-red domed belfry contrasting with the blue dome atop the bell tower of Lowell, which is set back behind it to the r. Directly opposite the bridge are the two high-rise buildings that form the newer part of *Leverett House,* erected in 1959 along with the lower building in front with the parasol roof, which houses the library. Just to the l. of the bridge is *McKinlock Hall,* the 1925 building passed a little earlier, and which became part of Leverett House in 1930. Farther to the l. are the two neo-Georgian buildings that constitute *Winthrop House,* both erected in 1913, the one nearest to the Weeks Bridge being *Gore Hall* and the farther *Standish Hall.* The courtyard facade of Gore Hall is said to have been inspired by that of Hampton Court Palace, as rebuilt by Christopher Wren late in the 17C. Beyond them, at the foot of the Larz Anderson Bridge, is *Eliot House,* erected in 1930, its green dome distinguishing it from Lowell and Dunster. Behind and between Eliot and Winthrop is *Kirkland House,* erected in 1913, and across the avenue from that is the huge complex that makes up the *John F. Kennedy School of Government,* completed in the late 1980s.

At this point the itinerary comes to an end. But before moving on, one might want to take a last scan from the Weeks Bridge, for the domes and spires of the Harvard Houses along the river give old Cambridge one of the prettiest skylines in the U.S. Then one might want to take a last stroll along Riverview Ave, to look more closely at the architecture of the neo-Georgian dormitories, and perhaps to wander into their shady, sun-dappled quadrangles, where one senses more intimately the spirit of this oldest and most distinguished of American universities.

20 The Museums of Harvard University

This itinerary describes the museums of Harvard University, most of which we passed on Rte 18.

Starting in Harvard Sq, walk east along Massachusetts Ave and make the first l. onto Quincy St; toward the end of the block on the right, beyond the Carpenter Center, is the ****William Hayes Fogg Art Museum,** and at the beginning of the block beyond that is the ****Arthur M. Sackler Museum.** These are two of the three Harvard University Art Museums. The third, the ****Busch-Reisinger Museum,** was formerly housed in Busch Hall, at the northwest corner of Kirkland St and Divinity Ave, which we will pass after visiting the Fogg and Sackler Museums. The Busch-Reisinger is now housed in a new building on Prescott St, Werner Otto Hall, which is behind the Fogg. An outstanding guide to the artworks in these three institutions was published in 1985: *Harvard University Art Museums,* by Kristin A. Mortimer, with contributions by William G. Klingelhofer, is the principal source for the descriptions of the Fogg, Sackler, and Busch-Reisinger collections that follow.

The Harvard Art Museums: History and Collections

As Dr. Mortimer writes in the preface to her book: "Harvard's art collections, like those of the much older universities of Oxford and Cambridge in England, have been a natural product of the institution's long intellectual and social history." The oldest of the Harvard Art Museums is the Fogg; this is named after William Hayes Fogg, whose widow, Elizabeth Perkins Fogg, endowed the institution with a bequest in memory of her husband shortly after his death in 1891. The museum opened in 1895 in its first home on Cambridge St, a neoclassical building designed by Richard Morris Hunt, professor of architecture at Harvard. The original museum building was from the beginning criticized on both aesthetic and practical grounds. This eventually led to a decision to erect the present building at 32 Quincy St, which was completed in 1927 by Coolidge, Shepley, Bulfinch, and Abbott.

In the meantime, the second of Harvard's art museums had come into being, the present Busch-Reisinger. Originally known as the Germanic Museum, this was founded in 1903 by Prof. Kuno Francke of Harvard's Department of Germanic Literature and Language. As Francke wrote in the introduction to the first edition of the museum's guide in 1906, the institution's purpose was "to illustrate by reproductions of typical works of the

fine arts and crafts the development of Germanic culture from the first contact of Germanic tribes with the civilization of the Roman Empire to the
present day." In 1910 it became the Busch Museum, renamed for Adolphus
Busch, a German American brewer from St. Louis, who provided a quarter
of a million dollars to build a more suitable home for the collection. This
was Busch Hall, designed by Prof. German Bestelmeyer of Dresden, with
modifications by Prof. Warren of the Harvard School of Architecture. The
new Busch Museum opened in 1921, its completion having been delayed
for four years by reaction against the idea of a Germanic museum when the
U.S. was fighting Germany in World War I. The same reaction surfaced in
World War II, as a result of which the Busch Museum was closed in 1942–
48. Its reopening was largely due to a new endowment by the Reisinger
family of St. Louis, which led to its being renamed the Busch-Reisinger
Museum. By that time the director of the museum was Prof. Charles L.
Kuhn, who succeeded Prof. Francke in 1930 and directed the institution
until 1968, during which time he acquired many of the paintings which are
today widely regarded as the greatest treasures of the Busch-Reisinger's
collection. The museum closed temporarily in 1987 so that its collection
could be moved to its new home on Prescott St; designed by the New York
architectural firm of Gwathmey Siegel and Assoc., the new building also
houses part of Harvard's Fine Arts Library.

The third of Harvard's art museums, which opened in 1985, is named for
its principal benefactor, Arthur M. Sackler, a philanthropist, physician, and
art collector. The building in which it is housed, on the N.E. corner of Quincy
St and Broadway, was designed and built by the London architectural firm
of James Sterling, Michael Wilford and Assoc., in collaboration with the
Boston architects Perry, Dean, Rogers and Partners.

The principal reason for the creation of this new institution was the enormous growth in the size of the collections of the Harvard Art Museums,
which in the previous half-century had increased in number from 6000 to
100,000, so that more than 95 percent of the artworks were not on permanent display. Although the percentage is now larger, the number on permanent display is still small, though during the course of the year a much
larger number are exhibited for a time, particularly in the Fogg, most of
them as part of Harvard's courses in art history. As Dr. Mortimer writes of
the size and scope of the resources of the Harvard Art Museums: "Included
among its vast treasures are portraits of local dignitaries by John Singleton
Copley; European master prints collected before the Civil War by Francis
Calley Gray; the Pre-Raphaelite drawings and paintings acquired under the
influence of Charles Eliot Norton, Harvard's first art historian; and the rich
holdings of modern German material which accompanied the architect Walter Gropius when he left Germany to become dean of the Graduate School
of Design in 1937." Some of the collections are unrivaled by any other
museum in this country—early Chinese jade carvings, for example, or French
drawings from the 15C through the 19C; others are exceedingly strong—
Greek vases and coins, Romanesque sculptures from France and Spain, and
Japanese prints. Even those parts of the collections which are not unusually
rich play a meaningful role in teaching and research, the primary mission
of both the museums and the university.

Admission. The Harvard Art Museums are open Tues.—Sun. 10–5; the fee admits the visitor to all three museums. There are free guided tours on weekdays. Lectures and seminars
are scheduled regularly, and performances of chamber music are given in the courtyard of
the Fogg (tel. 495-9400).

The Fogg Museum
Interior. After passing through the lobby, we enter the Central Court. This splendid area, constructed of travertine marble and surrounded by a portico, rises up through two stories of the building, surrounded by a colonnaded balcony on the upper level. The courtyard was adapted (⅘ scale) from the facade of the presbytery of the 16C Church of the Madonna de San Biagio at Montepulciano in Italy. Another grand chamber is Warburg Hall, in the first floor of the S.E. wing (to the r., as you enter). This magnificent room is distinguished by its beautiful carved-oak ceiling, a French work of the 16C from Dijon.

Collections. The Fogg's collections include nine works by Picasso, 27 by Rodin, 54 watercolors by William Blake, the finest collection of the paintings of Ingres outside of France, some 300 prints by Dürer, and 200 by Rembrandt, as well as works by Fra Angelico, Rubens, Géricault, Van Gogh, Renoir, Monet, Degas, Whistler, Rosetti, Homer, Beardsley, Pollock, and Morris Louis, among others, along with outstanding collections of photographs, prints, and drawings. The Fogg also houses the Center for Conservation and Technical Studies, the nation's first research center for the scientific study of works of art, and the Fine Arts Library, a branch of the Harvard College Library, which contains an outstanding research collection and more than a million photographs and slides of artworks.

The works of art in the Fogg's collections are displayed in the following categories, with the exhibition areas identified on the museum plan:
First Floor Galleries: Corridor: Romanesque and Gothic Sculpture; I (Warburg Hall): temporary offices, subsequently to be used for temporary exhibitions; II, III: Italian Renaissance; IV, V, VI (Hammer Galleries): French and Italian Baroque and Rococo; VII (Hammer Galleries): Dutch Baroque; VIII (Hammer Galleries): American and English 18C, Archibald Hutchinson Silver Collections.
Second Floor Galleries: Corridor A: British 19C; Corridor B: French 19C; Corridor C: American 20C; Corridor D: British 19C; X (Lehman Gallery); Corridor E: temporary exhibitions; XI (Lee Gallery): temporary exhibitions; XII, XIII: French 19C; XIV: American 19C; XV: Decorative Arts in England and America, 1640–1810; XVIa: European 20C; XVIb, XVII: Maurice Wertheim Collection of Impressionistic and Post-Impressionistic Art; XVIII, XIX (de Menil Galleries): American 20C.

Western Painting. (Artists listed alphabetically. Date of painting given if known; otherwise painter's dates given.)

American. Washington Allston (1779–1843), *The Sisters* (1957.1); *Diana in the Chase,* 1805 (1956.2). Albert Bierstadt, *Rocky Mountains, Lander's Peak,* 1863 (1895.698). John Singleton Copley (1738–1815), *Portrait of Benjamin West* (1943.128); *Portraits of Colonels Hugo and Schlepegrell,* 1787 (1942.180); *Portrait of Major General de la Motte* (1942.179); *Mrs. Thomas Boylston,* 1766 (1828, H 16) Thomas Eakins, *Portrait of Miss Alice Kurtz,* 1903 (1969.1). Hans Hofmann, *Blue Rhapsody,* 1963 (1970.56). Winslow Homer (1836–1910), *Pitching Horseshoes* (1940.292). Franz Kline, *Composition,* 1952 (1959.17). Morris Louis (1912–62), *Color Barrier* (1963-105); *Blue Veil,* 1958–59 (1965.28). Robert Motherwell, *Elegy,* 1948 (1949.49). Kenneth Noland, *Karma,* 1964 (1965.22). Jackson Pollock, *No. 2, 1950,* 1950 (1965.554). Mark Rothko, *The Black and the White,* 1956 (1981.122). John Singer Sargent (1856–1925), *The Breakfast Table* (1943.150). Charles Sheeler, *Upper Deck,* 1929 (1933.97). Frank Stella (1936–), *Red River Valley* (1973.135). James A. M. Whistler (1834–1903), *The White Woman* (1943.165); *Nocturne in Grey and Gold: Chelsea Snow,* 1876 (1943.172).

404 FOGG MUSEUM

Fogg First Floor Galleries

Corridor—Romanesque and
Gothic Sculpture

Straus Gallery—*Painterly Reproductions: The Difficult Art of
Expressing Paint in the Mono-
chrome Print* (Through April
12); *Barnett Newman Prints*
(May 2–July 5)

I (Warburg Hall)—Temporary
offices

II, III—Italian Renaissance

IV, V, VI (Hammer Galleries)—
French and Italian Baroque and
Rococo

VII (Hammer Galleries)—Dutch
Baroque

VIII (Hammer Galleries)—Ameri-
can and English 18th century;
Archibald Hutchinson Silver
Collection

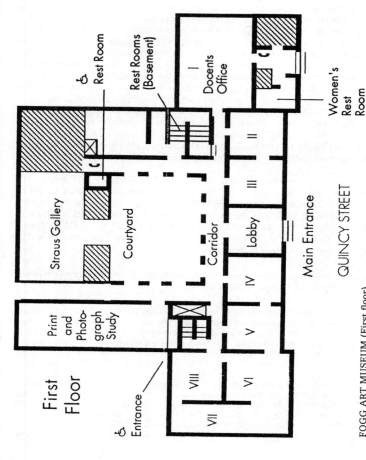

FOGG ART MUSEUM (First floor)

Fogg Second Floor Galleries

Corridor A—British 19th century
Corridor B—French 19th century
Corridor C—American 20th century
Corridor D—British 19th century
X (Lehman Gallery), Corridor E—
  Michelangelo (Through May
  24); *Tiepolo in Madrid: The
  Fogg* Aneas *Sketch Investigated*
  (June 6—August 30)
XI (Lee Gallery), XII, XIII, XIV—
  19th-century European and
  American painting and sculp-
  ture
XV—Decorative Arts in England
  and America, 1640–1810
XVIa—European 20th century
XVIb, XVII—Maurice Wertheim
  Collection of Impressionist and
  Post-Impressionist Art
XVIII, XIX (de Menil Galleries)—
  The Social Context of Greek Art
  (Through May 31)

Entrance to Busch-Reisinger Museum
in Werner Otto Hall

Second
Floor

FOGG ART MUSEUM (Second floor)

406   FOGG MUSEUM

British. William Blake (1757–1827), *Christ Bleeding* (1943.180). Edward Burne-Jones, *Perseus and Andromeda,* 1875 (1943.679). Thomas Gainsborough (1827–88), *Portrait of Benjamin Thompson, Count Rumford* (1922.1). William Holman Hunt, *The Triumph of the Innocents,* 1870–76 (1943.195). Albert Moore (1841–93), *Blossoms* (1943.199). Dante Gabriel Rossetti (1828–82), *The Blessed Damozel* (1943.202). George Frederick Watts, *Sir Galahad,* 1862 (1943.209); *The Survival of Greek Poetry,* 1878 (1943.207).

Flemish and Dutch. Gerrit Adriaenz Berckhyde (1638–98), *View of a City* (1968.65). Vincent van Gogh (1853–1900), *Self Portrait* (1951.65); *Self Portrait Dedicated to Paul Gauguin,* 1888 (1951.65). Frans Hals, *Portrait of a Preacher,* c. 1625 (1930.186). Rembrandt van Rijn, *Self Portrait,* 1629 (1969.56); *Portrait of a Man,* 1629 (1969.57); *Portrait of an Old Man,* 1632 (1930.191); *Head of Christ,* c. 1648–52 (1964.172). Peter Paul Rubens, *"Ques Ego" (Neptune Calming the Tempest),* c. 1635 (1942.174). Jacob van Ruisdael, *A Waterfall,* c. 1665 (1953.2). Salomon van Ruysdael, *A Seacoast Scene,* 1663 (1935.29).

French. Pierre Bonnard (1867–1947), *Nature Morte au Panier de Fruits* (1951.69). Georges Braque (1882–1963), *The Mandolin* (1960.246). Paul Cézanne (1839–1906), *Auvers, Small Houses* (1934.28); *Still Life with Commode,* c. 1885 (1951.46); *Cupid in Plaster* (1964.72). Jean-Baptiste Corot (1796–1871), *Honfleur—A Fishing Boat* (1962.88). Honoré Daumier, *Scapin and Géronte,* 1858–62 (1943.225). Jacques-Louis David, *Portrait of Emmanuel Joseph Sieyès,* 1817 (1943.229). Edgar Degas (1834–1917), *At the Races—They're Off!* (1934.30); *Portrait of Mme Olivier Villette* (1925.7); *Young Spartans Exercising* (1931.51); *The Rehearsal,* 1873–74 (1951.47). Eugène Delacroix, *Combat of the Giaour and the Pasha Hassan,* 1856 (1943.233). Jean-Honoré Fragonard (1732–1806), *La Jeune Fille Brune* (1975.73). Paul Gauguin, *Poèmes Barbares,* 1896 (1951.49). Théodore Géricault (1791–1824), *English Horse Guard* (1943.365); *The White Horse Tavern,* 1821–22 (1943.244); *The Bull Market,* 1817 (1943.242). Jean-Baptiste Greuze (1725–1805), *La Savonneuse* (1957.181). Jean-Auguste-Dominique Ingres (1780–1867), *The Golden Age* (1943.247); *Odalisque with a Slave,* 1840 (1839.251); *Raphael and the Fornarina,* 1814 (1943.252); *Studies for the Martyrdom of St. Symphorien,* 1833 (1943.245); *Portrait of Madame Frédéric Reiset,* 1846 (1943.249) Edouard Manet (1832–83), *Le Skating* (1951.56). Henri Matisse (1869–1954), *Geraniums* (1951.52). Claude Monet (1840–1926), *Cliff at Etretat* (1957.163); *Fish* (1925.16); *Road Toward the Farm, St. Simeon, Honfleur,* c. 1867 (1943.260); *Red Boats, Argenteuil,* 1875 (1951.54); *The Gare St.-Lazare, Paris: Arrival of a Train,* 1877 (1951.53). Camille Pissarro (1831–1903), *La Mi-Carème sur les Boulevards* (1951.58). Nicolas Poussin, *The Infant Bacchus Entrusted to the Nymphs,* 1657 (1942.167); *Holy Family in a Landscape,* 1650–51 (1942–168). Pierre Renoir (1841–1919), *Spring Bouquet* (1943.277); *Seated Bather,* c. 1883–84. Georges Seurat (1819–91), *Vase of Flowers* (1974.100). Alfred Sisley (1839–99), *Le Pont de Conflans à Moret* (1942.206). Jacques Stella (1596–1657), *Liberality of Louis XIII and Cardinal Richelieu* (1972.362). Henri de Toulouse-Lautrec (1864–1901), *Augusta* (1934.33); *Gueule de bois* (1951.63); *The Hangover of the Drinker,* c. 1887–89 (1951.63).

Italian. Fra Angelico, *Crucifixion,* c. 1446 (1921.34). Spinello Aretino, *The Madonna Enthroned with Angels,* c. 1380 (1905.1). Michelle Bonelli, *Portrait of a Cardinal,* 1586 (2905.12). Paris Bordone, *Adoration of the Magi,* c. 1550 (1953.104). Sandro Botticelli, *Magdalene at the Foot of the Cross,* c. 1500 (1924.27). Canaletto (1697–1768), *View of the Piazzo San Marco, Facing the Basilica* (1943.106). Giovanni Battista Caracciolo (called "Il Battistello"), *Martyrdom of St. Sebastian,* c. 1610 (1924.31). Simone dei Crocifissi, *Tabernacle of the Virgin, Annunciation and Saints,* c. 1360 (1962.283). Bernardo Daddi: *Crucifixion, Agony in the Garden and Six Saints,* 1334 (1918.33). Dorso Dossi, *A Condittiere,* c. 1530 (1966.74). Defendente Ferrari (c. 1511—after 1535), *Adoration of the Child* (1941.134). Attributed to Paolo Finoglia (1590–1645), *Joseph and Potiphar's Wife* (1962.163). Orazio Gentileschi, *Madonna with the Sleeping Christ Child,* c. 1610 (1976.10). Domenico Ghirlandaio (1449–94), *Virgin of the Annunciation* (1969.36). Attributed to the workshop of Giotto, *The Stigmatization of St. Francis,* c. 1320 (1929.234). Matteo di Giovanni, *St. Jerome in His Study,* 1492 (1966.3). Francesco Guardi (1712–93), *Venice: Fondamenta della Zattere* (1943.113). Pietro Lorenzetti, *Crucifixion, with SS. Clare and Francis,* c. 1320 (1943.119). Lorenzo Lotto, *Portrait of a Domenican Friar as St. Peter Martyr,* 1549 (1964.9). Simone Martini, *Christ on the Cross,* c. 1320 (1919.51). Master of Camerino, *Madonna and Child Enthroned,* c. 1330 (1927.306). Master of the Fogg's Pietà, *The Lamentation Over the Dead Christ,* c.

1330 (1927.306). Girolamo Mazzalo-Bedoli, *Madonna with the Christ Child in a Landscape,* c. 1540 (1972.22). Roberto d'Odorisio, *Man of Sorrows,* c. 1345 (1937.49). Giovanni di Paolo (1403?—after 1482), *St. Catherine of Siena* (1921.13); *The Nativity* (1943.112). Francesco Pasellino, *Construction of the Temple of Jerusalem,* c. 1445 (1916.495). Bartolomeo Passarotti, *A Man Holding a Letter,* c. 1580 (1932.68). Jusepe de Ribera, *St. Jerome,* 1640 (1920.7). Sienese school, *St. Domenic,* mid-13C (1920.20) (this is the oldest European painting in the Fogg). Giovanni Battista Tiepolo, *The Apotheosis of Aeneas,* c. 1765 (1949.76). Luca di Tomme, *Processional Crucifix,* c. 1365 (1970.59).

Spanish. Juan Gris, *Violin and Glass,* 1915 (1963.117). Joan Miró, *Untitled Painting,* 1953 (1972.361). Bartolomé Estéban Murillo, *Holy Family,* c. 1670 (1934.189) Pablo Picasso (1881–1973), *Woman in Blue* (1959.151); *Verre d'Absinthe et Cigarette* (1975.3); *Mother and Child,* 1901 (1951.57); *Plaster Head and Bowl of Fruit,* 1933 (1966.138).

Western Sculpture.

The Fogg's small but superb collection is focused on works in the Romanesque style, done in the late 11C and the 12C.

Most of the Romanesque sculptures are done on capitals of churches, richly decorated with reliefs either depicting narrative scenes or in foliate design. One group consists of 13 capitals from the abbey-church of Moûtier St. Jean, the oldest Benedictine foundation in Burgundy, c. 1125–30, done by a sculptor called the Moûtier Master. A second group comprises four capitals from the cloister of St.-Pons-de-Thomières, c. 1140, in the S. of France near Narbonne. A third group is a pair of capitals from the abbey-church of Santa Maria de Labanza, in the N. Spanish region of Palencia, 1185–90. The Fogg also has another piece of sculpture from this church; this (1933.100) is a columnar support with the figures of three Apostles: SS. Matthew, Jude, and Simon. The support is one of a group of four pieces; the others are in the National Archaeological Museum in Madrid.

The outstanding single piece in the collection is a small capital (1922.22) from the cloister of the Cathedral of Notre-Dame-des-Domes in Avignon; this dates from the third quarter of the 12C, and its four sides are decorated with episodes from the life of Samson, as told in Judges, chapters 14–16. Another piece of Romanesque sculpture (1925.11) is a statue in wood with traces of polychrome, depicting the Mourning Virgin. This dates from c. 1125 and is from the Church of Santa de Tahull, Catalonia, where it was part of a group representing the Deposition from the Cross. Another superb piece of Romanesque sculpture, presently in Warburg Hall, is (1936.11); this is a sepulchral monument of Don Diego Garcia, from Villamayor de los Montes, Burgos Province, Spain, late 12C.

An extremely important group is the series of clay preparatory sketches *(bozzeti)* by the great Roman baroque sculptor Gianlorenzo Bernini (1598–1680). Bernini must have made many hundreds of these small and fragile terra-cottas in his long and prolific career, of which only 40 survive. The Fogg has by far the largest and most important collection, with 15 pieces, one of the richest treasures of the museum. Since they cover nearly the whole of Bernini's creative life, and include instances of multiple studies for the same project, they provide a unique opportunity to follow the generative process that produced his famous sculptures in marble and bronze.

Among the earliest and most important of the Fogg's *bozzeti* is a model (1631) for the over-life-sized marble statue of St. Longinus which Bernini made in the 1630s and 1640s for one of the niches in the piers that support the dome of St. Peter's in Rome (1937.51). Another very significant *bozzeto* is a life-sized head, done in 1661, a study for the marble figure of St. Jerome, which Bernini sculpted during 1661–63 for the chapel of Pope Alexander VII in the Cathedral of Siena (1937.77). Also extremely important are the two series of studies for angels, one standing, the other kneeling. The four standing figures form part of Bernini's contribution to a project carried out in the late 1660s under his general supervision, in which the balustrades of the Ponte Sant'Angelo were decorated with ten over-life-sized marble statues of angels carrying the instruments of the Passion. The first two of these statues that Bernini created, the angels carrying the Crown of Thorns and the Inscription on the Cross, were regarded as too fine to be placed on the bridge, and are now in the Church of Sant'Andrea della Fratte in Rome. An assistant's copy of the first of these was installed on the bridge, along with another version of the second one by Bernini himself. The Fogg possesses two *bozzeti* (1937.67 and 1937.69) for the first version of the angel with the Inscription, and two (1937.57–58) for the initial version of the angel with the

Crown. The Fogg's series of five kneeling angels preserve successive steps in the development of one of Bernini's last major projects, done in 1673–74, an altar for St. Peter's in Rome, surmounted by bronze figures with a container for the Holy Eucharist. The finest of this group (1937.63) is of particular interest because of the incised calibration marks at equal intervals along the base, which allowed the sculptor to scale up accurately from the *bozzeto* to the statue modeled upon it. Bernini was apparently the first sculptor to use this technique of proportional enlargement; through it he succeeded in virtually eliminating the difference between the small-scale model and the large final work, another evidence of his genius.

The Fogg's outstanding works of Western Sculpture, besides those identified by catalogue number above, include the following:

The Offering of Cain and Abel, c. 1125–39, marble capital from the abbey-church of Moûtier-St-Jean, Burgundy (1922.18). *Marble columnar support with Three Apostles: Matthew, Jude, and Simon*, c. 1125–50, found in San Pelayo Anteatlares, Santiago de Compostela (1933.100). *The Supper at Emmaus*, c. 1140, marble capital from St.-Pons-de-Thomières, near Narbonne (1922.67). *Samson Destroying the House of the Philistines*, third quarter of the 12C, marble capital from Notre-Dame-des-Doms, Avignon (1922.132). *Censing Angel*, marble, c. 1295, attributed to Arnolfo di Cambio (1957.57). *Pair of Portrait Busts* (man and woman), c. 1515, terra-cotta, Northern European (1981.188, 189). *St. Longinus*, 1630–31, terra-cotta with later gesso and gilding, Giovanni Lorenzo Bernini (1937.51). *St. John the Baptist*, 1878, bronze (1943.1147). *Ballet Dancer, Dressed*, 1880, bronze, Edgar Degas (1943.1128). *Young Cyclist*, 1907, bronze, Aristide Maillol (1962.199). *The Pianiste*, c. 1917, painted wood, Elie Nadelman (1956.200). *Caryatid II*, 1915, red oak, Constantin Brancusi (1968.2). *Acrobat (Upside-Down Figure)*, 1927, bronze, Gaston Lachaise (1962.78). *Branch R*, c. 1951, bronze, Fernand Léger (1962.183). *Upright Motive, No. 8*, 1955–56, bronze, Henry Moore (1959.42). *Books and Apple*, 1957, silver, David Smith (1979.408).

The following are selective lists of some of the outstanding Western Decorative Arts, Western Drawings, Western Prints, and Photographs in the Fogg's collections:

Western Decorative Arts. *"Great Salt,"* London, c. 1630, silver (881.1927). *Two-Handled Covered Cup, "The Stoughton Cup,"* Boston, 1701 (877.1927). *Secretary Desk*, Boston, 1755–95, mahogany (205.1972). *Traveling Alarm Clock*, London, c. 1710, John Paulet (1943.1067). *Portland Vase*, 1790–95, Wedgwood (1943.1181).

Western Drawings. *The Visitation (Verso)*, 14C, anon. Italian (1935.65). *Eight Apostles Watching the Ascension of Christ*, c. 1464, Andrea Mantegna (1926.42.1). *Funeral Procession of the Virgin*, 1449–50, Jacopo Bellini (1932.275). *Fighting Nudes*, c. 1460–65, Antonio Pollaiuolo (1940.9). *Four Standing Nudes*, 1495–96, Pietro Vannucci, called Perugino (1926.42.2). *Study for a Frieze with Siren and Acanthus*, c. 1481, Tullio Lombardo (?) (1979.63). *The Adoration of the Magi*, c. 1506, Vittore Carpaccio (1932.281). *The Madonna and Child with a Kneeling Angel*, c. 1500–4, Fra Bartolommeo (1965.356). *Pietà with Saints and Angels* (Recto), after 1495, Filippino Lippi (1932.129). *Ganymede*, c. 1533, Michelangelo (1955.75). *The Rest on the Flight into Egypt*, Paolo Caliari, called Veronese (1528–88) (1965.430). *Two Sketches of a Nude Youth (Recto)*, c. 1519 (?), Jacopo da Pontormo (1932.342). *Heads of the Annunciate Angel and Virgin*, early 15C, Bohemian (1947.79, 80). *Pietà*, Simon Marmion (c. 1420 / 25–89) (1941.343). *St. Agatha*, c. 1496–97, Bernhard Strigel (1959.158). *The Lamentation*, 1521, Albrecht Dürer (1965.39). *Head of a Young Man*, 1523, Hans Holbein the Younger (1949.2). *An Alpine Landscape*, Peter Brueghel the Elder (c. 1525–69) (1932.369). *An Allegorical Group Representing Astronomy*, Francesco Primaticcio (1504–70) (1959.160). *Portrait of Claude Gouffier De Boisy*, c. 1555, François Clouet (1949.5). *Head of a Wind God (Recto)*, Agostino Caracci (1557–1602) (1975.91). *Man Reading at a Table*, c. 1630s, Giovanni Francesco Barbieri, called "Il Guercino" (1932.233). *A Crossbowman Assisted by a Milkmaid*, c. 1600, Jacques de Gheyn II (1953.86). *A Study for the Figure of Christ*, c. 1609–10, Peter Paul Rubens (1949.3). *Portrait of Don*

Carlos Coloma, 1628, Anthony van Dyck (1961.150). *A Winter Landscape*, c. 1648–52, Rembrandt van Rijn (1932.368). *View of Rhenen*, c. 1645–48, Aelbert Cuyp (1949.33). *Six Studies of Heads*, c. 1717–18, Jean-Antoine Watteau (1965.336). *Portrait of the Painter, Bachelier*, 1773, Jean-Baptiste-Siméon Chardin (1939.89). *The Infant Bacchus Entrusted to the Nymphs*, 1657, Nicolas Poussin (1958.290). *Reclining Female Nude*, c. 1738, François Boucher (1965.235). *The Young Girl Abandoned (L'Abandonée)*, Jean-Honoré Fragonard (1732–86). *The Rest on the Flight into Egypt*, Giovanni Battista Tiepolo (1699–1770) (1965.418). *A Circular Church*, c. 1750, Antonio Canal, called Canaletto (1932.327). *Portrait of the Family of Lucien Bonaparte*, 1815, Jean-Auguste-Dominique Ingres (1943.837). *The Mutiny on the Raft of the Medusa*, c. 1818, Théodore Géricault (1943.824). *Portrait of Frédéric Villot*, c. 1838, Eugène Delacroix (1949.6). *Religious Procession, Study for "Los Disparates,"* Francisco José Goya y Lucientes (1979.55). *Agnolo Brunelleschi Being Transformed into a Serpent*, c. 1824, William Blake (1943.432). *Simplon Pass*, after 1841, Joseph Mallord William Turner (1954.133). *View of Mount Soracte from Città Castellana*, 1827, Jean-Baptiste-Camille Corot (1965.247). *Race Course at Longchamps (Recto)*, 1864, Edouard Manet (1943.387). *A Young Woman in Street Costume*, c. 1867–72, Edgar Degas (1965.260). *Study for Portrait of Julie Burtey*, c. 1863–66, Edgar Degas (1965.254). *Café-Concert*, c. 1887–88, Georges Seurat (1943.918). *Portrait of a Man*, 1867, Wilhelm Leibl (1943.530). *Portrait of a Young Girl*, 1881, William Michael Harnett (1965.120). *Mink Pond*, 1891, Winslow Homer (1943.304). *The Days of Creation (The First)*, 1875–76, Edward Burne-Jones (1943.354-59). *The Peacock Skirt*, 1894, Aubrey Beardsley (1943.649). *Peasant of the Camargue*, c. 1888, Vincent van Gogh (1943.515). *Mont Ste-Victoire (Recto)*, 1889–90, Paul Cézanne (1977.173). *Mother and Child and Four Studies of Her Right Hand*, 1904, Pablo Picasso (1965.318). *Head of a Man With a Hat*, 1912, Pablo Picasso (1979.18). *Landscape*, c. 1907–8, Piet Mondrian (1963.122). *A Lady with a Necklace*, 1936, Henri Matisse (1965.307). *The Parade*, 1954, Fernand Léger (1964.61). *Highland Light (North Truro)*, 1930, Edward Hopper (1930.462). *Fruit and Sunflowers*, c. 1924, Charles Demuth (1925.5.3). *Study for the Northampton Madonna and Child*, 1943, Henry Moore (1958.24). *Study for "The Calendars,"* c. 1946, Arshile Gorky (1976.78). *The Yellow Ear*, 1946, Alexander Calder (1981.120). *Untitled Study for Sculpture "Agricola I,"* 1951, David Smith (1974.148). *Untitled*, 1874, Richard Diebenkorn (1978.94). *Untitled*, 1981, Katherine Porter (1981.84).

Western Prints. *Emperor Augustus and the Tiburtine Sibyl*, c. 1466, Master E.S. (G2610). *St. John on Patmos*, c. 1475–80, Martin Schongauer (M13646). *The Madonna on a Grassy Bank*, 1503, Albrecht Dürer (M12972). *David Playing Before Saul*, Lucas Van Leyden (1494–1533) (M12150). *Jan Six*, 1647, Rembrandt van Rijn (G3284). *Youth and Girl Each Offering the Other an Apple*, c. 1470–80, Baccio Baldini (?) (G2936). *The Descent from the Cross* (after Raphael), c. 1521–22, Ugo da Carpi (M657). *Battle of the Ten Nudes*, c. 1470–75, Antonio Pollaiuolo (M377). *Imaginary View of Padua (also called Murano)*, Antonio Canal, called Canaletto (1697–1768) (R2968). *The Blacksmith's Shop* (after Joseph Wright of Derby), 1771, Richard Earlom (G1162). *Junction of the Severn and the Wye*, 1811, J. M. W. Turner (G5044). *Rue Transonian, Le 15 Avril 1834*, Honoré Daumier (M13712). *The Balloon*, 1862, Edouard Manet (M13710). *Church and Farm at Eragny*, 1894–95, Camille Pissaro (M19867). *Misères Humaines (Souvenir de Bretagne)*, Paul Gauguin (1848–1903) (M12945). *La Clownesse Assise (from "Elles")*, 1896, Henri Toulouse-Lautrec (M13499). *Night in the Park*, 1921, Edward Hopper (M10100). *Rue des Rats*, 1928, Stuart Davis (M15568). *Satyr Dévoillant une Femme (Vollard Suite 27)*, 1926, Pablo Picasso (M13164). *Etching, No. 1*, 1969, Barnett Newman (OM20186). *Barcelona Series (Proof of No. 6)*, 1944, Joan Miró (M15233). *Flag I*, 1960, Jasper Johns (M20192).

Photographs. *Bridge of Sighs, St. John's College, Cambridge*, 1844, W. H. Fox Talbot (P1981.7). *Coal Miners, Pa.*, c. 1908, Lewis M. Hine (P1975.38). *Woman, New York*, 1916, Paul Strand (P1972.175). *Black and White*, c. 1930, Gertrude Käsebier (P1978.1). *Wooden Houses, South Boston*, 1930, Walker Evans (P1971.30). *Sheriff During Strike, Morgantown, W. Va.*, 1935, Ben Shahn (P1970.1225). *Ritual Branch*, 1958, Minor White (P1972.181). *Feet, 133*, 1958, Aaron Siskind (P1972.50). *Portrait of Alexander Liberman, Tatiana Liberman, and Francine Du Plessix Gray*, 1954, Irving Penn (P1981.22.6). *Roots, Foster Garden, Honolulu*, 1948, Ansel Adams (P1980.154). *Cal, Wisconsin*, 1965, Danny Lyon (P1972.204). *Untitled*, 1983, Lorie Novak (P1983.15).

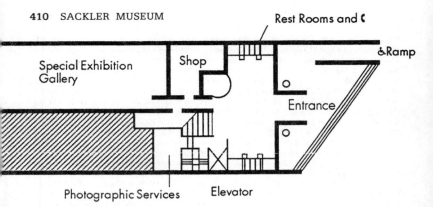

Rest Rooms and (

Special Exhibition
Gallery

Shop

&Ramp

Entrance

Photographic Services   Elevator

ARTHUR M. SACKLER MUSEUM (First floor)

Arthur M. Sackler Museum

The galleries at the Sackler Museum are devoted to the following exhibitions:

First Floor: Special Exhibition Gallery.
Second Floor: 1—Islamic Art; 2, 3, 4—Asian Painting, Ceramics, Prints, and Textiles.
Fourth Floor: 5—Ancient Chinese Jades, Bronzes, and Ceramics; 6—Chinese Buddhist Stone Sculpture; 7—Chinese Sculpture; 8—Indian and Southeast Asian Art; 9—Ancient Roman Art; 10—Ancient Greek Art; 11—Egyptian and Ancient Near Eastern Gallery.

The following is a selective list of the most notable artworks in the various collections of the Sackler Museum.

Pre-Columbian. *Yoke,* c. A.D. 300–900, Mexican, Classic Vera Cruz (1943.246); this horseshoe-shaped stone of dark-green basalt and some 50 pounds in weight, intricately carved in low relief, was evidently connected with the ancient Mexican ball-court game and had some religious-ceremonial significance. *Life-sized head,* c. 14C A.D., Mexican, Aztec, dark-gray lava stone (1943.1041). *Pair of hammered ear-plugs,* c. 14–15C A.D., gold, carved in low relief (1943.1072a–b).

Chinese. *Fang-I (ritual wine container),* 12C B.C., China, Shang dynasty (Anyang period), bronze (1943.52.109). *Kuang (ritual wine server),* c. late 13—early 12C B.C., China, Shang dynasty (Anyang period), bronze (1943.52.103). *Yu (ritual wine bucket),* 10C B.C., China, early Western Chou dynasty, bronze (1943.52.107). *Fang-I (ritual wine container),* late 11C B.C., China, early Western Chou dynasty, bronze (1944.57.37). *Chung (ritual bell),* China, late Eastern Chou dynasty (475–221 B.C.), bronze (1943.52.178). *Tui (ritual food vessel),* first half of 4C B.C., China, late Eastern Chou dynasty, bronze (1943.52.115). *Mirror,* China, late Eastern Chou dynasty (475–221 B.C.), bronze (1943.52.147). *Mirror,* China, Sui dynasty, bronze (1943.52.164). *Heavy ax,* China, Neolithic period (3rd millennium B.C.), grayish-green stone (1943.50.112). *Disk-ax,* China, Shang dynasty (c. 1500–c. 1030 B.C.), jade (1943.50.527). *Notched tablet with incised bird figure,* 10C B.C., China, Western Chou dynasty, jade (1943.50.232). *Configuration of dragon, bird, and snake,* China, late Eastern Chou dynasty (475–221 B.C.), jade (1943.50.468). *Scabbard buckle,* 2–1C B.C., China, Western Han dynasty, jade (1943.50.398). *Seated Buddha with Flaming Shoulders,* c. late 4C—early 5C A.D., China, Northern Wei dynasty, gilt bronze (1943.53.80). *Buddha,* dated A.D. 484, China, Northern Wei dynasty, gilt bronze (1943.53.59). *Bhikṣu (Monk),* 560–70, Ting-chou school, China, Northern Chi dynasty, white marble with polychrome (1943.53.31). *Avalokiteśvara,* China, Sui dynasty (581–618), limestone (1943.53.43). *Avalokiteśvara,* early 8C A.D., China, T'ang dynasty, gilt bronze (1943.53.61). *Śàkyamuni Buddha,* c, 715, China,

T'ien-lung-shan, Shansi, T'ang dynasty, sandstone (1943.53.22). *Avalokiteśvara*, China, Sung or Chin dynasty (960–1279), wood with gilt and polychrome (1928.110). *Eleven-headed Kuan-Yin*, dated A.D. 985, China, Tun-huang, Northern Sung dynasty, hanging scroll, ink and colors on silk (1943.57.14). *Attendant Bodhisattva*, early to mid-8C, China, Cave 320, Tun-huang T'ang dynasty, fragmentary wall painting (1924.43). *Attendant Bodhisattva*, c. 700, China, Cave 328, Tan-huang T'ang dynasty, polychromed unbaked clay (1924.70). *Ladies of the Palace*, datable to 1140, after Chou Wen-chu, China, Southern Sung dynasty, handscreen, ink and slight color on silk (1945.28). *Winter Birds*, signed Liang K'ai (fl. early 13C), China, Southern Sung dynasty, ink and slight colors on silk (1924.88). *Guardian of the Valley*, Li Shih-hsing (1282–1328), China, Yuan dynasty, ink and color on silk (1923.211). *Plum Blossoms*, 16C, Liuh Shih-ju, China, Ming dynasty, ink on silk (1923.191). *Saluki Dogs*, dated 1427, Emperor Hsuan-tsung, China, Ming dynasty, ink and slight color on paper (1931.20). *Autumn Landscape*, dated 1627, Chang Hung, China, Ming dynasty, folding fan mounted as album leaf, ink and slight color on gold-treated paper (1984.1). *T'ai-P'ing Shan-Shui T'u*, dated 1648, Hsiao Yun-ts'ung, China, Ch'ing dynasty, printed book, ink on paper (1981.36). *Small Bridge over Flowing Stream*, dated 1733, Fang Shih-shu, China, Ch'ing dynasty, folded fan mounted as album leaf, ink and light color on mica-coated paper (1978.89). *Prancing horse (tomb figurine)*, China T'ang dynasty (618–907), earthenware (1950.86). *Jar*, China, T'ang dynasty (618–907), stoneware (1951.15). *Shallow dish*, China, T'ang dynasty (618–907), earthenware (1954.122). *Dish* (Ting Ware), early 12C, stoneware (1956.1156). *Pillow* (Tz'u-Chou Ware), 13C, China, Chin dynasty, stoneware (1950.156). *Large plate with Arabic inscription*, mid-14C, China, Yuan dynasty, porcelain (1961.112). *Flower pot and stand*, China, Chin dynasty (1115–1234), Chun ware (1942.185.56 a–b). *Bottle-shaped vase*, late 14C, China, Ming dynasty, porcelain (1961.113). *Double-gourd vase*, Chia-ching reign (1522–66), China, Ming dynasty, porcelain (1944.254).

Korean. *Buddha*, c. late 8C–early 9C, Korea, Unified Silla dynasty, gilt bronze (1943.53.72). *Buddhist shrine with bodhisattvas*, c. 11–12C, Korea, Koryŏ dynasty, silver alloy, gilt bronze (1943.53.71).

Japanese. *Gigaku mask*, c. 754, Japan, Tempyō period, wood with traces of polychrome and hair (1943.56.11). *Zōchō-Ten, Guardian of the South*, late 13C–early 14C, Japan, Kamakura period, wood with polychrome (1951.108). *Shrine doors with Bonten and Tais-hakuten*, 14C, Japan, Muromachi period, color on black lacquer panels (1928.184). *Wooden core of hand drum*, Japan, Momoyama period (1568–1603), lacquered wood with gold powder (1983.39). *Section of the Hokke-Kyō (Lotus Sutra)*, c. 1150, Japan, Late Heian period, section of a hand scroll, mounted as a hanging scroll, ink on paper, decorated with gold and silver leaf (1977.202). *Diary of the Bright Moon*, dated 1226, Fujiwara Teika, Japan, Kamakura period, mounted as a hand scroll, ink on paper (1977.203). *Earthquake Scene (fragment from the Illustrated Legend of Jin'o-Ji)*, c. 1350–1400), Japan, Namboku-cho period, section of a hand scroll, mounted as a hanging scroll, ink, color, and gold on paper (1973.64). *An Illustrated History of the Yūzū Nembutsu Sect*, dated 1471, painted by the monk Musashi Hogen, Japan, Muromachi period, two hand scrolls, ink and color on paper (1973.68). *Section from a Buddhist cosmology*, dated 1402, illustrated by the monk Ryūyu, text copied by the monk Ryūi, Japan, Muromachi period, hand scroll, ink and color on paper (1973.66). *Twofold screen: magnolia blossoms on gold ground*, early to mid-17C, attributed to the school of Tawaraya Sōtatsu (?–1643?), Japan, Edo period, color and gold on paper (1962.89). *Twofold screen: scene in a geisha house*, early 17C, attributed to the school of Matabei (1603–1868), color on paper (1921.14). *Poem on Meditation*, mid-18C, Hakuin Ekaku, Japan, Edo period, hanging scroll, ink on paper (1964.165). *Woman Running to Escape a Sudden Shower*, Suzuki Harunobu (c. 1725?–70), Japan, Edo period, poly-chrome woodblock print (1923.24). *The Actor Matsumoto Koshiro*, c. 1795, Tabūsai Shar-aku, Japan, Edo period, polychrome woodblock print with mica-dust background (1933.4.510). *A Concubine and Her Child at Noon, from the Series Fūzoku Bijin Tokei*, 1801(?), Kitagawa Utamaro, Japan, Edo period, polychrome woodblock print (1933.4.589). *Fuji from Kajika-zawa, from the Series Thirty-six Views of Mount Fuji*, Katsushiki Hokusai (1780–1849), Japan, Edo period, polychrome woodblock print (1933.4.2693). *Eggplants*, Totaya Hokkei (1780–1851), Japan, Edo period, polychrome woodblock print (1933.4.1884). *Sprout D*, Shinoda Toko (1913–), Japan, lithograph (1971.154).

South and Southeast Asian. *Head of a Serpent Queen,* 1C A.D., India, Mathura, sandstone (1982.61). *Male and Female Devotees,* 3–4C A.D., said to come from Hadda, Afghanistan, stucco (1981.23.24). *Turbaned Head of a Royal Figure or Bodhisattva,* 3–5C A.D., stucco (1947.23). *Avalokiteśvara with Yama,* 10C, India, Bihar, gray-brown schist (1965.48). *Gaṇeṣa,* c. 900, India Rajasthan, carbonaceous matasiltstone (1974.55). *Seated Viṣnu,* early 13C, India, Tamil Nadu, bronze (1982.32). *Greater Sutra of the Perfect Wisdom (Astasahasrika Prajñāpāramitā),* c. 1100, Nepal or Eastern India, polychromed wood and palm leaves (1973.90). *Sutra Cover,* c. 15C, Nepal or Tibet, wood with traces of polychrome and gilding (1978.515). *Plaque with Scenes from the Life of the Buddha,* 12–13C, Burma, alabaster (1979.328). *Head of Buddha,* early 13C, Cambodia, stone (1928.165).

Islamic and Later Indian: *Bahram Gur and the Monster Wolf (Karg), Miniature from the "Demotte" Shahnama ("Book of Kings"),* c. 1330–40, Iran, Tabriz, Mongol, Ilkhanid period, opaque watercolor on paper (1960.190). *Nomadic Encampment, from Shah Tahmasp's Khamsa ("Quintet") of Nizami,* dated 1539–43, Mir Sayyid'Ali, Iran, Safavid period, opaque watercolor on paper (1958.75). *Youth with a Golden Pillow,* c. 1560, attributed to Mirza-'Ali, Iran, Mashad, Safavid period, opaque watercolor on paper (1958.61). *Daydreaming Youth,* c. 1590, signed by Riza, Iran, Qazvin, Safavid period, black ink on paper (1952.7). *Mystical Journey,* c. 1650, probably Iran, Safavid period, black ink and watercolor on paper, with gold rulings (1950.135). *Dragon Cavorting,* 16C, Turkish, Ottoman period, ink heightened with color, gold, and silver, on paper (1974.101). *Folio from a Blue Vellum Kuran,* c. 9C, Tunisia, Qairawan, Aghlabid period, gold ink on blue vellum (1967.23). *Folio from a Kuran,* late 11C–early 12C, Iran, Seljuk period, ink and color on paper (1982.40). *Tughra of Mahmud I (1730–54) with an Iris,* Turkey, Ottoman period, ink and watercolor on paper (1982.40). *Bowl,* late 10C–early 11C, Iran, Samanid period, ceramic (1960.28). *Bowl,* c. 14C, Iran, "Sultanabad Ware," Ilkhanid period (1962.154). *Pen box,* late 14C–early 15C, Iran, Timurid period, bronze inlaid with silver and gold (1979.352). *Binding of a Manuscript: The Divan of Hafiz,* c. 1530, Iran, Safavid period, lacquer (1964.149). *Ivory-hilted dagger,* blade 1800–1, handle 1834–38, Iran, Qajar period (1958.1.31). *Helmet with chain mail,* 17C, Iran, Isfahan, Safavid period (1960.39). *Pilgrims' banner,* 1683, North Africa, silk (1958.20). *Medallion and hunting carpet,* 16C, Iran, Safavid period, wool (1974.57). *Marasali prayer rug,* 19C, Caucasus (U.S.S.R.), wool with silk (1977.166). *The Poet's Visit to an Indian Temple, from a Bustan of Sa'di Manuscript,* c. 1540, Bukhara, repainting attributed to the Mughal artist Bishandas, c. 1620, opaque watercolor and gold on paper (1979.20). *Slaughter on the Ramparts, folio from the Dastan-I Amir Hamza ("Tales of Amir Hamza"),* c. 1570, India, Mughal period, opaque watercolor on cotton (1941.292). *Anvari Entertains in a Summer House, folio from a Divan of Anvari,* 1588, attributed to Basawan, India, Mughal period, opaque watercolor on paper (1960.117.2). *Prince Dara Shikoh Conversing with Sages,* c. 1630, India, Mughal period, opaque watercolor on paper (1968.47). *An Encounter at a Well,* c. 1740–50, attributed to Nihal Chand, India, Kishangarh, opaque watercolor on paper (1972.350). *A Lady Yearning for Her Lover,* c. 1775, India, Bundi, opaque watercolor on paper (1972.352). *Chritini Nayika, from a Rasikapriya Series (Classification of Heroines and Heroes),* c. 1780, opaque watercolor on paper (1971.126). *A Nayika and Her Lover, from a Rasamanjari Series,* c. 1670–80, gouache and opaque watercolor on paper (1972.74).

Egyptian, Near Eastern, Bronze Age Aegean, Etruscan. *Lion-headed God and Goddess (Sekhmet),* Egypt, late period (712–525 B.C., bronze (1943.1121a–b). *Charioteers with Ladies-in-Waiting in a Royal Procession,* c. 1352–1333 B.C., Egypt, Dynasty XVIII, limestone (1960.170). *Head of a Man,* 2300–2000 B.C., Akkadian, dark stone (1929.228). *Pair of Lions,* from the Temple of Ishtar, Nuzi, Mesopotamia, Hurrian, glazed terra-cotta (1931.162). *Bull Protome, from a Cauldron,* 8–7C B.C., East Anatolia, Urartian, bronze (1943.1321). *Winged Being Protecting the King,* c. 485–60 B.C., Persian, Achaemenid, dark limestone (1943.1062). *Female Statuette,* c. 1600–1450 B.C., Crete, Minoan, bronze (1975.60). *Figure of a Woman with a Pomegranate (probably the goddess Turan),* c. 400 B.C., Etruscan, bronze (1956.43).

Greek Vases. *Funerary jug (pitcher-olpe),* c. 700 B.C., Greek (Attic), The Lion Painter, ceramic (1950.64). *Black-figure column krater,* c. 565 B.C., Greek (Attic), attributed to Lydos, ceramic (1925.30.125). *Red-figure calyx krater,* c. 500 B.C., Greek (Attic), Kleophrades Painter, ceramic

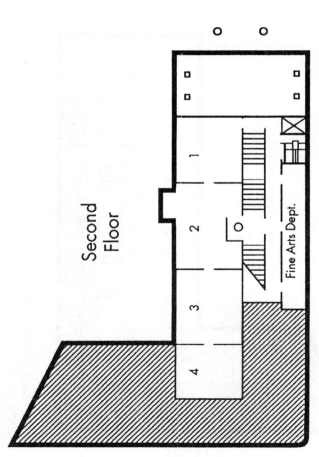

ARTHUR M. SACKLER MUSEUM (Second floor)

Second Floor Galleries

1— Islamic and Later Indian Art: *Miniatures from the Courts of the Ottomans and Their Contemporaries* (Through May 17); *Precisely to the Point: Daggers and Drawings from India and Persia* (May 30–July 26)

2, 3, 4—Asian Painting, Ceramics, Prints, and Textiles

Fourth Floor Galleries

5— Ancient Chinese Jades, Bronzes, and Ceramics.
6— Chinese Buddhist Stone Sculpture
7— Chinese Sculpture
8— Indian and Southeast Asian Art
9— Ancient Roman Art
10— Ancient Greek Art
11— Egyptian and Ancient Near Eastern Gallery

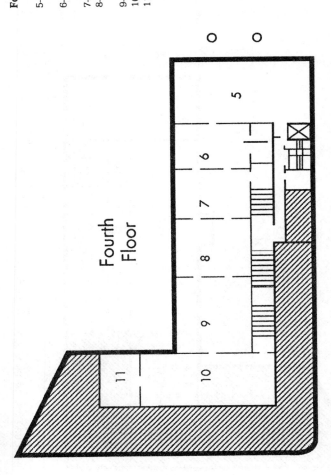

Fourth Floor

ARTHUR M. SACKLER MUSEUM (Fourth floor)

(1960.236). *Red-figure hydria (kalpis),* c. 510–500 B.C., Greek (Attic), ceramic (1972.40). *Red-figure kylix,* c. 490–480 B.C., Greek (Attic), Foundry Painter, ceramic (1927.149). *Red-figure kylix,* c. 490–480 B.C., Greek (Attic), Onesimos, ceramic (1972.39). *Black-figure Panathenaic Prize amphora,* 340–339 B.C., Greek (Attic), ceramic (1925.30.124).

Greek and Roman. *Bust of a Youth (Attis or Orpheus?),* c. 335–300 B.C., Greek, Tarentine, terra-cotta (1943.1085). *Portrait Bust of Antonia Minor,* c. A.D. 50 or later, Roman, marble (1972.306). *Statue of Meleager,* c. A.D. 100, Roman copy after a Greek original of c. 340 B.C., attributed to Skopas, Parian marble (1926.48). *Statue of Trajan,* c. A.D. 120, Roman, Pentelic marble (1954.71). *Amazon Sarcophagus,* late 2C A.D., Roman (made at Athens), marble (1932.49a–b) and (1899.9a–c). *Bearded Male Head,* mid-3C A.D., Roman, Luna marble (1949.47.138). *Man Leading a Ram by the Horn,* 8–7C B.C., Greek, bronze (1970.26). *Bearded Man with a Staff,* c. 525–500 B.C., Greek (Arcadian), bronze (965.533). *Hydria,* c. 425–400 B.C., Greek, bronze (1949.89). *Aphrodite Holding a Ram,* c. 450 B.C., Greek, bronze (1960.666). *Statuette of Hephaistos,* 2C A.D., Greek (Athens?), bronze (1982.35). *Plaque with a Bust of Victory,* 2C A.D., Roman, bronze (1962.12). *Portrait-Head of Julia Domna,* A.D. 193–217 or later, Roman (Syrian), bronze (1956.19).

Provincial Roman and Coptic. *Portrait of a Lady with Earrings,* c. A.D. 130–40, Egypt (Fayum), encaustic on wood (1923.60). *Funerary Relief of a Woman,* c. A.D. 200, Roman, Syria (Palmyra), limestone (1975.41.116). *St. Theodore,* 5–6C, Coptic, textile fragment, wool and linen (1939.112.1).

Ancient Coins. *Silver tetradrachm,* c. 405 B.C., Greek, Sicily (Katane) (1972.143). *Silver denarius,* 43–42 B.C., Roman (1972.244). *Silver denarius,* c. 37 B.C., Roman (Gaul) (1979.267).

The Busch-Reisinger Museum

The most notable works in the collections of the Busch-Reisinger Museum are the following:

Sculpture. *The Madonna and Child,* c. 1430, Austrian, Tyrolean, polychromed poplar (BR 1963.2). *St. John the Evangelist,* c. 1490–1500, German, Lower Swabian, lindenwood (BR 1964.5). *St. Anthony Abbot,* c. 1510, attributed to Tilman Riemanschneider, lindenwood (1969.214). *Reclining Nymph,* c. 1739, George Raphael Donner, lead statuette on marble base (BR1964.7). *Triumph of a Sea-Goddess,* 1530s, Peter Flotner, steatite (BR 1951.213). *The Return of the Holy Family from Egypt,* c. 1690, Meinrad Guggenbichler, polychromed lindenwood (BR 1956.275). *The Four Seasons,* c. 1760–65, workshop of Johann Joachim Günther, sandstone (1952.11a–d). *Large Daphne,* 1930, Renée Sintenis, bronze (BR 1959.49). *Dancer,* 1914, Georg Kolbe, bronze (BR 1932.64). *Construction in Space with Balance on Two Points,* 1925, Naum Gabo, black, white, and transparent plastics (1958.46). *Light-Space Modulator,* 1923–30, Laszlo Moholy-Nagy, mobile construction of steel, plastics, wood, and other materials with an electric motor (BR 1956.5). *Adam and Eve,* 1936, Max Beckmann, bronze (BR 1976.5). *Crippled Beggar,* 1930, Ernst Barlach, terra-cotta (BR 1931.5). *Cup, Saucer and Tray,* 1904, Otto Eduard Gottfried Voight, porcelain, Meissen (BR 1970.10a–c).

Paintings. *The Madonna and Child,* c. 1460s, Dirck Bouts, Flemish School (1959.186). *The Madonna and Child* (follower of Rogier Van Der Weyden) and *Portrait of Joos Van Der Burch Presented by a Bishop* (follower of Gerard David), c. 1475–1525, Flemish school (BR 1965.22). *The Visitation,* c. 1495, Rueland Fruehauf the Elder, German school (BR 1965.52). *St. Jerome in His Study,* c. 1521, attributed to Joos van Cleve the Elder, Flemish school (BR 1965.17). *Angel,* c. 1530, follower of Lucas van Leyden, Dutch school (BR 1965.24). *Portrait of a Bearded Man and Portrait of a Lady Holding a Flower,* c. 1535–40, Barthel Bruyn the Elder, German school (BR 1966.36,37). *Forest Idyll,* c. 1870, Hans van Marees (BR 1960.31). *Rue de Rivoli,* 1891, Edvard Munch (1963.153). *Pear Tree,* 1903, Gustav Klimt (BR 1966.4). *Head of a Woman,* c. 1911, Alexei van Jawlensky (BR 1951.267). *Harbor Scene,* 1911, Karl Schmidt-Rottluff (BR 1954.115). *Triptych: To the Convalescent Woman,* 1912–13, Erich Heckel (BR 1950.415a–c). *The Mulatto,* 1913, Emil Nolde (BR 1954.117). *Suprematist Painting, Rectangle and Circle,* c. 1915, Kasimir Malevich (BR 1957.128). *Self-*

Busch-Reisinger Galleries
in Werner Otto Hall

Corridor Gallery—Introduction to
*Art & Design from Central &
Northern Europe Since 1880*
1—Turn of the Century
2—Early Expressionism
3—The Bauhaus
4—Realist Art
5—The 1930s and 40s
6—Varieties of Post-War
    Abstraction

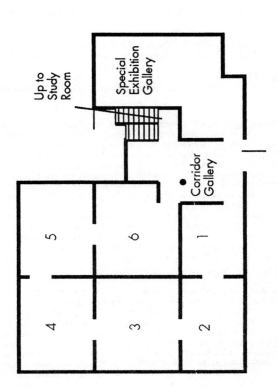

BUSCH-REISINGER MUSEUM

Portrait with a Cat, 1920, Ernst Ludwig Kirchner (BR 1950.12). *Portrait of Dr. Heinrich Von Neumann,* 1916, Oskar Kokoschka (BR 1952.21). *Proun 12E,* c. 1920–22, El (Lasar Markovitch) Lissitzky (BR 1949.303). *Bird Cloud,* 1926, Lyonel Feininger (BR 1950.414). *Jocular Sounds,* 1929, Wassily Kandinsky (BR 1956.54). *Hot Pursuit,* 1939, Paul Klee (1955.66). *Self-Portrait in Tuxedo,* 1927, Max Beckmann (BR 1941.37). *The Actors,* 1941–42, Max Beckmann (BR 1941.37).

Drawings. *Portrait of Herwarth Walden,* 1910, Oskar Kokoschka (1949.137). *Brother and Sister,* 1910, Erich Heckel (BR 1978.5). *Café,* c. 1919, George Grosz (BR 1934.195). *Costume Designs for the "Triadic Ballet,"* c. 1922, Oskar Schlemmer, ink, gouache, metallic powder, graphite, and collage (BR 1950.428). *Landscape Wagon No. 14,* 1930, Paul Klee, watercolor on gray silk mounted on white card (BR 1951.46). *Design for a Children's Book, of Two Squares,* c. 1920–22, El (Lasar Markovitch) Lissitzky, pen and ink over graphite on cream machine-made laid paper (BR 1961.38). *Design for the Chicago Tribune Competition,* 1922, Walter Gropius, ink rendering (BR 1969.59b).

Prints. *Madonna,* 1895, Edvard Munch, lithograph (M20227). *Bauhaus Proclamation (Cathedral of Socialism),* 1919, Lyonel Feininger, woodcut (BR 1949.198). *Self-Portrait With Hat,* 1921, Max Beckmann, drypoint (M12208). *Composition with Head in Profile,* 1921, Kurt Schwitters, lithograph (BR 1974.17). *Opus 1,* 1950, Naum Gabo, wood engraving (1961.37).

After leaving the Busch-Reisinger Museum, we return to Quincy St and continue in the same direction, crossing Cambridge St and then Kirkland St. We continue north along Divinity Ave, passing on the corner to the l. the building at 27 Kirkland St that formerly housed the Busch-Reisinger Museum. This is now called the Adolphus Busch Hall and houses the Center for European Studies at Harvard University. Then, at the end of the block, on the right, we come to the ***Semitic Museum,** the next stop on our itinerary.

Admission. Open Sun. 1–5, Mon.–Fri. 11–5; fee (tel. 495-3123).

History. The Harvard Semitic Museum was founded in 1889, at which time its charter called for it to perform a variety of functions, namely to be "the home of the Department of Near Eastern Languages and Civilizations, a library for the department, a public educational institute, and a center for archaeological exploration." According to a brochure recently published by the institution: "Early Museum achievements included participation in the first U.S. expedition to the Near East in 1889, the first scientific excavations in the Holy Land (at Samaria in 1907–12) and important explorations at Nuzi and the Sinai, where the earliest alphabet was found. During World War II the Museum was taken over by the Navy. After the War the building was used by the University for other-than-Museum purposes. The collections were stored in the basement, and the Museum continued its work from underground.' "

The Semitic Museum has in recent years undergone a renaissance, largely through the efforts of Father Carney E. S. Gavin, a Roman Catholic priest who became curator in 1980. The museum's activities are now focused on an area that Father Gavin opened up in 1970, when he discovered on the top floor of the building an extraordinary collection of some 28,000 prints, lantern slides, and negatives, "sumptuous nineteenth-century views of Middle Eastern scenes, architecture, and figures," which now constitute the world's largest collection of early photographs of the Levant. This discovery led, several years later, to the foundation of FOCUS, Father Gavin's acronym for a worldwide campaign which he initiated to find, organize, copy, utilize, and share old photographs. Since 1978 FOCUS has held at the Semitic Museum two symposia for curators and photo-historians from the U.S., Europe, and several Middle Eastern countries, including Israel. In addition, the Semitic Museum continues its archaeological excavations, which include a dig at Numeira, E. of the Dead Sea, and another at Carthage.

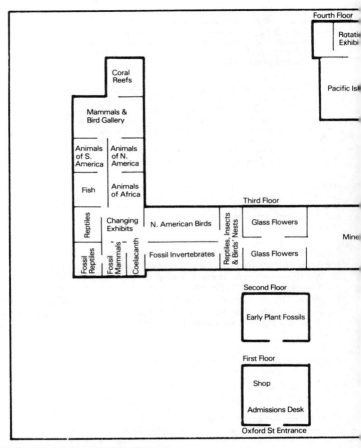

THE HARVARD UNIVERSITY MUSEUMS

Interior. The Semitic Museum has little to offer in the way of permanent exhibits, other than a very small but fascinating collection of Levantine costumes and artifacts, mostly early 19C. The museum's attractions are its changing exhibitions, particularly those based upon its incomparable collection of old photographs of the Middle East.

After leaving the Semitic Museum, cross Divinity Ave and go W. along Converse St, which goes past the S. side of the enormous building that houses the ****Harvard University Museum.** After passing that side of the building, turn r. and walk to the main entrance, which is at the middle of the W. side of the structure.

Admission. The Harvard University Museum is open Mon.–Sat. 9–4:30; Sun. 1–4:30; fee (tel. 495-1910, recorded message; 495-3045 general information).

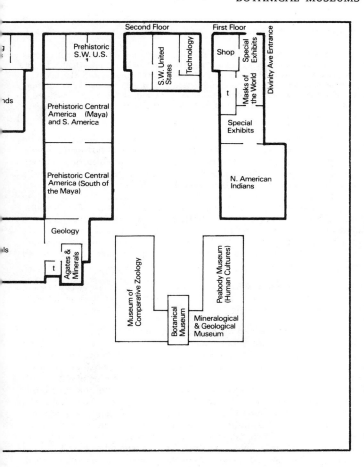

Second Floor

Prehistoric
S.W. U.S.

Prehistoric Central
America (Maya)
and S. America

Prehistoric Central
America (South of
the Maya)

Geology

Agates &
Minerals

t

S.W. United
States

Technology

First Floor

Shop

Special
Exhibits

Divinity Ave Entrance

t

Masks of
the World

Special
Exhibits

N. American
Indians

Museum of
Comparative Zoology

Botanical
Museum

Mineralogical
& Geological
Museum

Peabody Museum
(Human Cultures)

History. The Harvard University Museum, whose construction extended from 1859 to 1913, was conceived by Prof. Louis Agassiz as a center dedicated to nothing less than "the study of Earth and life on Earth." Constructed in 11 different stages by a number of different architects and builders, the University Museum is actually made up of four separate but linked institutions. The N. wing and the N.W. corner of this immense building house the *Museum of Comparative Zoology;* the center of the W. wing is occupied by the *Botanical Museum;* the S.W. corner is devoted to the *Mineralogical and Geological Museum;* the S. wing is the home of the *Peabody Museum of Archaeology.*

Interior. The **Botanical Museum** is located on the second and third floors at the center of the W. wing. The second floor of this central bay, which is numbered Botany 1 in the labyrinthlike map of the Harvard Museum, is devoted to an exhibit of Early Plant Fossils. The third floor of this central bay, which is divided into two sections identified on the map as Botany 2 and 3, houses the **Ware Collection of Glass Flowers*.

The Ware Collection of glass models of plants represents the artistic and scientific efforts of just two men, Leopold Blaschka (1822–95) and his son Rudolph (1857–1939). The collection was brought to Harvard through the efforts of Prof. George Lincoln Goodale, who first visited the Blaschkas in 1886. The entire collection of models is a gift to Harvard from Mrs Elizabeth C. Ware and her daughter Miss Mary Lee Ward, of Boston, as a memorial to Dr. Charles Eliot Ware of the Class of 1834, and it was officially presented to the university on April 17, 1893.

According to the monograph by Oakes Ames: "The Ware Collection now on exhibition contains specimens illustrating 164 families of flowering plants, a selected group of cytograms illustrating complicated life-histories, a group of models illustrating the relation of insects to the transfer of pollen and a group of rosaceous fruits illustrating the effect of fungus diseases."

Also on display in the Botanical Museum is an extraordinary work on the *Plant Lore of Shakespeare*. This was done in the 1890s by Miss Rosalba Towne, a Philadelphia artist who painted representations of all of the plants and flowers mentioned in Shakespeare's writings. This collection of 73 plates depicting 175 different plants and flowers was lost until the 1930s, when it turned up in a Paris antique shop, where it was purchased and presented to Harvard's Botanical Museum.

All of the plates have recently been exquisitely published in bound form—an exact copy of the original—by the Frame House Gallery of Louisville, Kentucky; this work, or individual prints from it, may be purchased at the bookshop of the Botanical Museum.

The western side and W. wing of the building house the **Museum of Comparative Zoology** (MCZ), also known as the *Agassiz Museum*. As described in the brochure published by the University Museum Council: "The exhibits range from the earliest fossil invertebrates and reptiles to fish and reptiles alive today, as well as special exhibits on the latest theories about inheritance, distribution, and evolution. Among the rare and unique specimens to be found are whale skeletons, the largest turtle shell ever found, the Harvard mastadon, the lobe-finned coelancanth, the giant sea-serpent, Kronosaurus, George Washington's pheasants, extinct birds such as the great auk and the passenger pigeon, and the world's oldest reptile egg."

The **Mineralogical and Geological Museums** are housed in the W. side of the building. According to the brochure of the University Museum Council: "The Mineralogical Museum, the oldest University mineral collection in the United States, contains a large systematic exhibit of minerals, gemstones, and polished agates. Over 6000 mineral specimens are exhibited in the systematic collection. A giant group of gypsum crystals from Naica, Mexico and a 3040 carat topaz gem are of special interest. Rubellite crystals from the pegmatites in California and a suite of copper minerals from Bisbee, Arizona are also displayed. New England minerals are featured in another gallery. Babingtonite from Massachusetts, amethyst from Rhode Island and tourmaline from Maine are a few examples of the hundreds of mineral specimens from the six-state region on exhibit. The recently-renovated Geological Museum features exhibits on meteorites, cave formations, and volcanoes. Two eighteen-foot panoramic photomurals depicting Mt St. Helen's before and after its volcanic eruption are the focal point."

The S. wing of the museum is the home of Harvard's **Peabody Museum of Archaeology and Ethnology,** one of the country's outstanding anthropological museums. Collections include treasures from prehistoric and historic cultures found all over the world. They include North American Indian artifacts, pre-Columbian remains from Middle America (particularly the Maya), pottery collections from North and South America, materials from the Palaeolithic and Iron Age cultures of Europe, and ethnographic specimens from Siberia to Tierra del Fuego.

21   Central and East Cambridge

The most important places visited on this itinerary through Central and East Cambridge are the *Massachusetts Institute of Technology* (M.I.T.) and the *Science Museum.* This is a very long itinerary, and for those with limited stamina it is divided into two connected parts, the first going through Central Cambridge to M.I.T., and the second going on from there to the Science Museum and East Cambridge. Those with more persistence can do the route all in one go.

A.   Harvard Square to M.I.T.

Beginning again at Harvard Sq, walk E. along Massachusetts Ave past Harvard Yard, then continue straight ahead on the r. side of Harvard St. At the intersection of Harvard and Prescott Sts is the **Old Cambridge Baptist Church,** one of the landmarks in this part of the city. This handsome Gothic-Romanesque edifice was erected in 1867 by Alexander R. Esty.

The itinerary now continues E. along Harvard St for nearly a half-mile as far as Bigelow St, the eighth turning on the r. after the Old Cambridge Baptist Church.

This part of Cambridge is called *Dana Hill,* for much of it is on land that was originally part of the Dana estate. The estate originated with Richard Dana, who came from England to Cambridge c. 1640. His great-grandson was Francis Dana (1743–1811), one of the leading patriots in Cambridge during the Revolution, who rendered distinguished service in Europe after the war as a diplomat, during the administrations of President George Washington and John Adams. Richard Henry Dana, author of *Two Years Before the Mast,* was a member of this family, and the artist Washington Allston was related to them by marriage.

The area now known as Dana Hill was first divided into streets and house lots in the 1830s and 1840s, and in the mid-19C it became a fashionable residential district. A number of homes and apartment houses from that era are still extant along this part of the itinerary, and the following is a list of those structures on this stretch of Harvard St and the streets that lead off from it. (As one heads E. along Harvard St, odd numbers are on the l. and even numbers are on the r.; streets leading off from Harvard St are identified in order, l. or r., after Prescott St.)

On the near corner at the first turning to the r., Remington St, one sees at 382–392 Harvard St a rambling multifamily dwelling erected in 1889 by Ricards and Co. Down Remington St on the r. side, at Nos 11–13, is a double cottage in the Greek Revival style put up in 1846 by the builders Nathaniel U. Stickney and Sumner P. Shepard. At the N.W. corner of Harvard and Trowbridge, the second turning on the l., there is a Georgian Revival apartment house at 371 Harvard St, erected in 1899 by Wheelwright and Haven. On the l. side of Harvard St on the next block, at Nos 369, 367, and 359–357, there are three handsome apartment buildings erected in 1877, 1895, and 1867, respectively. Down the next turning to the r., Ellery St, one finds on the l. side two simple dwellings in the Greek Revival style, the one at No. 20 erected in 1846 and that at No. 8 put up c. 1840. At the N.W. corner of Harvard and Dana Sts, at 343–341 Harvard St, there is a fine double house in brick erected in 1855, and at the N.E. corner, at 337 Harvard, there is a home erected in 1887 by the architect James P. Kelley, moved to its present site in 1898. On the S.E. corner there is another double house, this one with a mansard roof, erected in 1857.

Those with time to spare might want to turn r. for a short walk along Dana St, for there are a number of interesting dwellings to be seen on the block to the S. of Harvard St. These are (odd numbers to the r. and even numbers to the l.) No. 11 (1870), No. 7 (1841), No. 8 (1848), and No. 5 (1840); these are among the most charming houses to survive on Dana Hill.

Continuing along Harvard St, one passes, on the long block between Dana and Hancock Sts, the following 19C houses: No. 335 (1850), No. 338 (1859), and No. 325 (1853), after which one comes to the *Harvard Street Lutheran Church,* erected in 1911 by Newhall and Blevins. There are two more buildings of some interest on the next block along Harvard St, between Hancock and Lee Sts; at mid-block on the l., at 307 Harvard, is a mansard-roofed home built in 1865; and on the r. at the far end of the block, at Nos 302–304, is a group of row houses put up in 1857. At the near right-hand corner of the next block, the S.W. corner of Harvard and Bigelow Sts, there is a rambling old Victorian mansion built in 1887 by Hartwell and Richardson.

The itinerary now turns r. onto Bigelow St, where on the single block between Harvard St and Massachusetts Ave there are three picturesque old houses with mansard roofs: No. 22 (l., 1870); No. 17 (r., 1873); and No. 6 (l., 1872).

Turning l. off Bigelow St onto Massachusetts Ave, one is confronted with the most important civic building in Cambridge, the ***City Hall.** This imposing edifice in the Romanesque style was completed in 1888 by Longfellow, Arden, and Harlow; its most striking feature is the campanilelike tower that rises from the center of its facade on Massachusetts Ave. Across Massachusetts Ave to the S.W. is *St. Peter's Episcopal Church,* a Gothic Revival structure designed by Alexander R. Esty and originally built in wood by Woodcock and Meacham in 1864–67; the present brick facade is the result of a reconstruction in 1932 by Allen and Collens. At the S.E. corner of the same intersection is the *Cambridge YMCA;* the oldest part of this edifice was erected in 1896 by Hartwell, Richardson, and Driver, with an addition in 1910 by Newhall and Blevins. The S.W. corner of the next intersection to the E., where Pleasant St leads S. from Massachusetts Ave, is occupied by the *Post Office,* a granite edifice in the Classic Revival style erected in 1932 by Charles R. Greco. Facing that building across the avenue, on the N.W. corner of Massachusetts Ave and Inman St, is an enormous Victorian pile erected in 1888 to house the Cambridge Fire Insurance Co. Up Inman St on the same side is *St. Mary's Syrian Church.* This was originally erected in 1822 on Lafayette Square in East Cambridge for a Universalist congregation; it was moved to its present site in 1888, minus its steeple, which was removed in 1858.

The itinerary continues E. along Masachusetts Ave, and at the next inter-section one comes to Central Sq. At the N.E. corner of this scruffy intersec-tion, which is at the center of Cambridge's administrative activities, there is a three-story structure that is one of the oldest commercial buildings in this part of the city, put up in 1814. Now walk E. along the r. side of Mas-sachusetts Ave, crossing Pearl St. At the middle of the next block on the r. is *Odd Fellows Hall,* an elegant structure erected in 1884 by Hartwell and Richardson. On the r. side of the following block, at 458–452 Massachu-setts Ave, is a pair of attached buildings erected in 1806–7 by the Dana family, which are probably the oldest surviving structures in what was once the center of Cambridgeport.

This now brings one to Lafayette Sq. Continue straight ahead along Mas-sachusetts Ave to approach the vast campus of the **Massachusetts Institute of Technology** (M.I.T.), one of the two major sites on this itinerary. The first element of the university complex reached is a very short way along on the l., at 265 Massachusetts Ave, where one finds the **M.I.T. Museum.** The entrance to the Museum is a short distance down the street to the l., and the collection is housed on the second floor of the building.

Admission. The M.I.T. Museum is open Tues.–Fri. 9–5, Sat. & Sun. 1–5.

History. As mentioned earlier, M.I.T. was first housed in Back Bay in a structure later to be known as the Rogers Building, erected in 1866. (The site of this structure, one of the first public institutions to be erected in Back Bay, is now occupied by the New England Mutual Life Insurance Co., on the block bounded by Newbury, Boylston, Berkeley, and Clarendon Sts.) The building was named after William Barton Rogers, the founder of M.I.T.

Rogers was born in Philadelphia on Dec. 7, 1804, one of four remarkable brothers, all of whom became distinguished scientists. He attended the College of William and Mary, in Virginia, where his father, Dr. Patrick Kerr Rogers, an immigrant from County Tyrone in Ireland, was professor of natural history and chemistry. Upon his father's death in 1828, William Rogers succeeded him in that chair, when he was just 23. In 1835 Rogers was elected to the professorship of natural philosphy at the University of Virginia, founded in Charlottesville just 16 years earlier by Thomas Jefferson. Though Rogers remained on the faculty of the University of Virginia for 18 years, he was much distressed by the religious and racial intolerance, bigotry, and violence that he detected in Charlottesville, and after a vacation in New England with his brother Henry he first thought of moving to that area. As he wrote to another of his brothers, Robert, "Since my summer's rambles with Henry, I have been unable to shut out the contrast between the region in which I live and the highly-cultivated nature and society of glorious New England." These ties with New England became even deeper in 1849, when William Rogers married Emma Savage, the eldest daughter of James Savage, a wealthy and scholarly Bostonian. But even before that time Rogers had begun dreaming of founding a polytechnical school in Boston, an innovative institution that he believed would "overtop the universities of the land." As Rogers wrote at that time to his brother Henry, describing the kind of graduate such a school would turn out: "When thus instructed in science, the mechanician, chemist, manufacturer or engineer clearly comprehends the agencies of the materials and instruments with which he works, and is, therefore, saved from the dangers of blind experiment, is guided securely because understandingly in a profitable routine, and is directed in the contrivance of new and more combinations."

In 1853 Rogers resigned from the University of Virginia, whereupon he and his wife moved to Boston. During the six years that followed, Rogers became a prestigious figure in the intellectual world of Boston, and his lectures on science and its role in education were very well attended. Rogers' golden opportunity to put his theories into practice came in 1859, when Governor Banks, in his message to the Massachusetts Legislature, pointed out that the recently begun filling in of Back Bay presented the opportunity for creating "such educational improvements as will keep the name of the Commonwealth forever green in the memory of her children." Dr. Rogers and a number of like-minded individuals there-upon organized themselves into a group called the Massachusetts Conservatory of Arts and

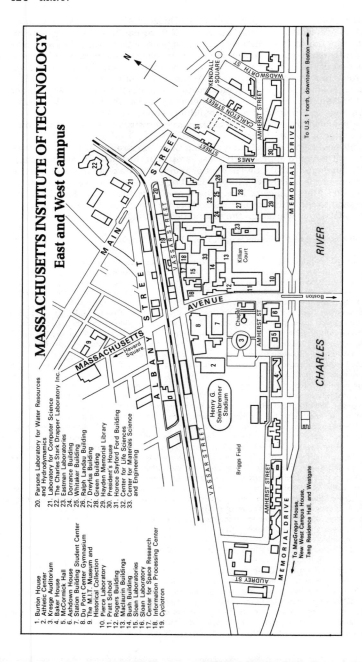

MASSACHUSETTS INSTITUTE OF TECHNOLOGY
East and West Campus

1. Burton House
2. Athletic Center
3. Kresge Auditorium
4. McCormick Hall
5. Baker House
6. Ashdown House
7. Station Building Student Center
8. Du Pont Center Gymnasium
9. The M.I.T. Museum and Historical Collection
10. Pierce Laboratory
11. Pratt School
12. Rogers Building
13. Maclaurin Buildings
14. Bush Building
15. Sloan Laboratories
16. Sloan Laboratory
17. Center for Space Research
18. Information Processing Center
19. Cyclotron
20. Parsons Laboratory for Water Resources and Hydrodynamics
21. Laboratory for Computer Science
22. The Charles Stark Draper Laboratory Inc.
23. Eastman Laboratories
24. Vorrance Building
25. Whitaker Building
26. Ralph Landau Building
27. Dreyfus Building
28. Green Building
29. Hayden Memorial Library
30. President's House
31. Horace Sayford Ford Building
32. Center for Life Sciences
33. Center for Materials Science and Engineering

Sciences. In Nov. 1860, under the chairmanship of Dr. Rogers, this group petitioned the Commonwealth to incorporate the "Mass. Institute of Technology, having for its objects the advancement of the Mechanic Arts, Manufactures, Commerce, Agriculture and the applied sciences generally, together with the promotion of the practical education of the industrial classes. . . ." On April 10, 1861, the "Act to Incorporate the Massachusetts Institute of Technology" was approved by Governor Andrews, and the year after that the Corporation elected as its first president Dr. Rogers. The outbreak of the Civil War delayed the organization of the school, which opened its first classes on Feb. 20, 1865, in the Mercantile Library in downtown Boston, advertising that its courses were "suited to the various professions of the Mechanican, the Civil Engineer, the Builder and the Architect, the Mining Engineer and the Practical Chemist." At that time Dr. Rogers made the following enthusiastic entry in his diary: "Organized the School! Fifteen students entered. May not this prove a memorable day!" In Feb. 1866 M.I.T. moved into its first permanent home, the Back Bay edifice later to be known as the Rogers Building. Dr. Rogers continued to direct the activities of the Institute there until 1870, when ill health forced him to resign. But then a financial crisis at M.I.T. led the Corporation to call upon Dr. Rogers once again, and on Dec. 10, 1879, he was elected president *pro tempore.* Rogers saw the Institute through this crisis, and in the spring of 1881 he gave up the presidency for the final time, just a year before his death.

He was succeeded as president by Francis Amasa Walker, a remarkable man who had distinguished himself in the Union Army during the Civil War, rising to the rank of general at the age of 25. Walker served as president until his untimely death in 1897, by which time M.I.T. had developed to the point where it was generally considered to be the finest institution of its kind in the U.S.

In 1900 the enrollment at M.I.T. reached 1277, and it became obvious to the Corporation that the Rogers Building would soon be inadequate to house the school. By that time Back Bay was completely built over, and so there was no room for M.I.T. to expand. During the decade that followed there was considerable debate about moving M.I.T. to a new site, and there were even proposals that it amalgamate with Harvard. In June 1909 M.I.T. inaugurated as its sixth president the distinguished physicist Richard Cockburn Maclaurin, and under his able leadership the matter of a new site for the university was soon settled. Maclaurin had already looked favorably upon a site on the Cambridge side of the new Charles River Basin, and he began his presidency with an intense effort to raise the funds necessary to relocate and expand the university. In March 1912 a 50-acre site was purchased in Cambridge, largely through funds contributed by M.I.T. alumni, and then a large gift by George Eastman, head of the Eastman Kodak firm of Rochester, enabled Maclaurin to begin erecting buildings on the land. The Cambridge campus, which was called the New Technology, was officially opened in a three-day series of ceremonies on June 12–14, 1916, climaxed when President Maclaurin dedicated the Great Court of the university. The Rogers Building in Back Bay continued to be used by M.I.T. for more than two decades after the move to Cambridge, during which time it housed M.I.T.'s Architecture Dept. In 1939 it was demolished to make way for the New England Mutual Life Insurance Co. Building, bringing the old era to an end. In the years since then M.I.T. has grown and developed tremendously, and today it is renowned as the finest institution of its kind in the world.

The Museum. The M.I.T. Museum, founded in 1971, has a small but very interesting set of exhibits connected with all aspects of the university's history. Among the collections are: scientific instruments and technical apparatus developed or used at M.I.T.; photographs of people, events, and settings in M.I.T.'s history, with background provided in the form of biographical and other written materials; portraits, paintings, and sculptures by prominent American artists of the 19–20C; audiovisual collections, including tapes, disk and video recordings, and films documenting M.I.T.'s history; architectural drawings done by M.I.T. students between 1869 and 1969; memorabilia connected with M.I.T.'s social history, including banners, trophies, and souvenirs. Some of M.I.T.'s historical collections are housed elsewhere in the university, the two most important being the Hart Nautical Museum and the Compton Gallery, both of which are described below.

Continue along Massachusetts Ave, following it as it crosses Albany Ave, then a railroad track, and just beyond that Vassar Ave. One has now reached the main area of the M.I.T. campus, a vast complex of buildings stretching off on both sides of Massachusetts Ave between Vassar St and Memorial Drive, all of it on filled-in land. On the N.W. corner of Massachusetts Ave and Vassar St is an enormous building in the style of a medieval fortress with crenellations. This is the *Metropolitan Storage Warehouse,* completed in 1895 by Peabody and Stearns, the first large building erected on the filled-in land on which M.I.T. now stands. Directly across Vassar St, on the S.W. corner, is another fortresslike structure, originally built in 1902 to serve as an armory, the architects being Hartwell, Richardson, and Driver; this was acquired by M.I.T. in 1958, and after conversion it became the *Dupont Center Gymnasium.* On the l. hand side of Massachusetts Ave one sees in succession two modern M.I.T. buildings; first the *Metals Processing Laboratory,* built in 1950 by Perry, Shaw, Hepburn, and Dean; then the *Center for Advanced Engineering Studies,* erected in 1966 by Skidmore, Owings & Merrill. Opposite, on the r. side of the avenue, is the huge *Julius Adams Stratton Building,* which serves as the M.I.T. student center; this was erected in 1963 by Eduardo Catalano. Now, looking again to the l. side, one sees the most impressive structure on this side of the campus; this is the **Rogers Building,** a domed edifice with a portico of enormous columns capped with Ionic capitals. The building is named after William Barton Rogers, founder and first president of M.I.T., and it was completed in 1937 by Welles Bosworth and Harry J. Carlson. It now houses the *School of Architecture and Planning.*

Inside the lobby of the Rogers Building on the r. is the M.I.T. Information Office; free maps of the campus are available there and free guided tours of the university are given quite frequently. From the lobby of the Rogers Building one can also reach the Compton Gallery and the Hart Nautical Museum, but the complex of buildings here is truly labyrinthine, and one should ask for specific directions in the Information Office. The Hart Museum may also be approached from the entrance at 55 Massachusetts Ave, farther down the street.

The *Margaret Hutchinson Compton Gallery* is open Mon.–Fri. 9–5 (free). This gallery is used for changing exhibitions of objects from the M.I.T. Historical Collection, which includes many works of art. Exhibitions have included "The M.I.T. Etchers"; "M.I.T. Alumnae in Science and Technology"; "Eighteenth-Century Scientific Instruments"; "The Forbes Whaling Collection"; and "Molecular Graphics."

The *Francis Russell Hart Nautical Museum* is open daily 9 a.m.–8 p.m. (free). The museum is under the direction of M.I.T.'s Dept. of Ocean Engineering; it is to a large extent an exhibition of ship and merchant-marine development. On display are rigged models of ships ranging in time from a Viking vessel to those of the present; also exhibited are half-models of yachts and merchant vessels from c. 1850 onward, as well as engine models. Among the exhibits are items from the following special collections: the Captain Arthur H. Clark Collection, which includes half-models and prints and vessels throughout history; the Allen Forbes Collection of paintings and prints pertaining to whaling; and the Charles H. W. Forbes Collection of yachting photographs, 1885–1930. The museum files, open by appointment Tues. and Thurs. 10–5, contain maritime paintings, prints, and photographs, as well as working drawings of yachts and small craft by well-known 20C designers.

Directly across from the Rogers Building a flight of steps leads up to a large plaza bounded to its N. by the Stratton Student Center. The design for this pleasant and lively area was originally done by Eero Saarinen, and although the plans were altered before completion of the space, two of his buildings have been erected there. At the rear of the plaza is *Kresge Auditorium,* which Saarinen completed in 1953. This astonishing building is covered by a thin-skinned concrete dome (only 3.5 inches thick at its peak), supported at the ground by just three very minute points, with the sides formed by segmental sections of thin glass. Within, there is an oak-paneled auditorium that seats 1238, and below that a theater with a capacity of 200. Near the front of the plaza there is a stark building in the form of a windowless red-brick cylinder standing in a shallow pool, an unorthodox structure that Saarinen designed in 1954 for the *M.I.T. Chapel.* Within this nondenominational chapel the walls are undulating rather than circular; the altar is a block of white marble on three circular steps, illuminated dramatically from above through a skylight, and behind the altar is a bronze screen by Harry Bertoia, consisting of small rectangles strung together on wires, looking like a giant wind-harp, altogether a highly unusual and original work.

Now continue along Massachusetts Ave, passing on the l. the long structure that extends from the Rogers Building to the end of the block; this was designed by Welles Bosworth in 1919, and for a large part of its length it houses the *Pratt School of Naval Architecture,* while the corner section is the *Pierce Laboratory.* At the end of the block on the r. stands *Ashdown House,* a neo-Tudor pile which one should really see from Memorial Drive to appreciate its manorial appearance. This M.I.T. dormitory was erected in 1900 by the architect H. B. Ball; it was originally known as Riverbank Court, a sumptuous apartment house which was meant to be part of the affluent residential area that investors thought would develop on the left bank of the newly filled Charles Basin, but the coming of M.I.T. to Cambridge changed all of that. A long line of student dormitories, residence centers, and fraternity houses extends from Massachusetts Ave along Memorial Drive to the western end of the campus, a distance of about 1¼ miles. The most interesting of these is *Baker House,* which is the third large building from Massachusetts Ave, standing just to the l. of the twin-towered complex of *McCormick Hall* (Anderson, Beckwith, and Haible, 1962–67). Baker House was designed in 1949 by Alvar Aalto, in collaboration with Perry, Shaw, Hepburn, and Dean; its most unusual feature is its undulating shape.

Return to Massachusetts Ave and continue walking eastward along Memorial Drive. A short way along, a huge and very attractive court opens up, enclosed on all but the front center by a quadrangle of M.I.T. buildings. The rear of the courtyard is formed by the *Maclaurin Buildings,* named after Richard Cockburn Maclaurin, president of M.I.T. when the university made the move from Boston to Cambridge. The huge structure at the center, surmounted by a low Roman dome and fronted by an enormous colonnade of Ionic columns, was erected in 1913 by Welles Bosworth. In the l. center of the garden court there is a superb abstract bronze by Henry Moore, entitled *Three-Piece Reclining Figure, Draped* (1973).

Farther along is the *Hayden Library,* a two-story building that has large areas of glass for its sometimes bored readers to gaze out over the Charles; this was erected in 1949 by Vorhees, Walker, Foley, and Smith, together with Anderson and Beckwith. This is the central M.I.T. library; free brochures are available here which provide visitors with self-guided tours of this and other libraries of the university. The Hayden Library also has a large and very active art gallery, with changing exhibitions that are open free to the public; part of this exhibition area consists of a central courtyard where larger works of sculpture are exhibited; other large sculptures are exhibited in the courtyard to the l. of the library. Behind the library there is a large double courtyard formed by a complex of university buildings. The most striking of these structures is the 23-story tower with a sphere and spire on its roof; this is the *Cecil and Ida Green Building*, an earth-science center, and it was erected in 1964 by I. M. Pei and Assocs. In the courtyard some distance in front of the Green Building there is a huge and masterful stabile by Alexander Calder, commissioned for this site.

Continuing along, one now passes the *Walker Memorial*, named in honor of General Francis Amasa Walker, president of M.I.T. from 1881 to 1897. This very Roman-looking edifice, with its portico of columns with Doric capitals, was erected by Welles Bosworth in 1916 as a gymnasium and dining hall. On the riverside directly in front of the Walker Memorial is the *Walker C. Wood Sailing Pavilion*, built in 1936 by Harry C. Carlson; this is the entrance to a series of marinas that stretches for some way up the Charles, giving this stretch of Memorial Drive a very sportive atmosphere. Next one passes an ivy-covered villa that serves as the residence of the president of M.I.T., a dwelling put up in 1916 by Welles Bosworth. This is at the beginning of the last block on this side of the campus. The last impor-tant university building is at the beginning of the next block, where Wads-worth St leads in from Memorial Drive; this is the *Sloan Building*, designed in 1938 by Donald Des Granges, and it houses the M.I.T. School of Man-agement and the Faculty Club. Farther along Wadsworth St on the same side there are two other monumental M.I.T. buildings, both designed by Eduardo Catalano. The first of these, midway up the block, is the *Grover M. Hermann Building*, erected in 1964, which houses the Dewey Library and academic offices. Beyond that, where Wadsworth St opens into Kendall Sq, is the 29-story skyscraper known as *Eastgate*, an apartment house for married students and faculty at M.I.T., designed in 1965.

The second part of this itinerary, to the Science Museum and East Cambridge, begins here. Those wishing to postpone that part of the itinerary can walk up Wadsworth St to Kendall Sq, where there is a Red Line T station; from there one can go either to Harvard Sq or downtown Boston. Those who are able and willing to continue the itinerary from here can now go on, crossing over to the river side of Memorial Drive, to stroll along the left bank of the Charles River to the Charles River Dam.

B.   The Science Museum and East Cambridge

The stroll from M.I.T. to the Science Museum takes one along the N. end of the Charles River Basin, providing an incomparable view of the Boston shore and skyline. All of the skyscrapers of Boston are arrayed grandly on the skyline of the city, from Copley Sq to the downtown area; one can make out the spires of the churches in Back Bay, and the golden dome of the State House gleams from among the clusters of red-brick mansions on Bea-con Hill. The stroll along the pedestrian path from M.I.T. to the Charles River Dam is a long but invigorating one, for even on the hottest days there is usually a breeze coming in from the sea, powering the gay flotillas of sailboats that are always skimming to and fro on the Charles.

Halfway between M.I.T. and the Science Museum is the *Longfellow Bridge*, the oldest and most ornate of the bridges across the Charles.

It follows the same course as the West Boston Bridge; this opened in 1793, reducing the traveling-distance between Old Boston and Cambridge from 8 to 3.5 miles, and giving a tremendous impetus to the development of Cambridge. The present bridge was completed in 1900 (Edmund M. Wheelwright consulting architect, and William Jackson chief engineer). It was originally called the Cambridge Bridge, but later it was given its present name in honor of Henry Wadsworth Longfellow. This was the route that Longfellow took on his frequent trips between Cambridge and Boston to see his friends on Beacon Hill, particularly Jamie and Annie Fields and their circle. And it was undoubtedly on his way home from Beacon Hill to Cambridge one night that he was inspired to write the lines in the first stanza of his poem "The Bridge": "I stood on the bridge at midnight, / As the clocks were striking the hour, / And the moon rose o'er the city, / Behind the dark church tower. . . ."

The pedestrian walkway passes beneath the Longfellow Bridge and then crosses Broad Canal. Continue beside Cambridge Parkway; on the last stretch before the Charles River Dam one must leave the riverside to cross Lechmere Canal. A short way farther along on the r. is the **Charles River Dam.**

The Charles River Dam follows the course of Craigie's Bridge, also called the Canal Bridge, opened in 1809. This span took its name from Andrew Craigie, the leading figure in the group of speculators who two years earlier had formed the Lechmere Point Corporation, the other principals being Governor Christopher Gore and Harrison Gray Otis. The purpose of the Corporation was to develop East Cambridge for a quick profit, and the opening of the bridge did lead to the success of that venture. Craigie's Bridge was replaced by the Charles River Dam, completed in 1910. The construction of the dam prevented the tides of Boston Harbor from going beyond this point, and so the Charles was no longer a tidal estuary, bordered by salt marshes and noxious mud flats; instead the banks of the river were drained and filled in, after which they were developed.

Once on the Charles River Dam, one is in *Science Park,* which includes the Museum of Science and the Hayden Planetarium. (Contrary to common opinion, almost all of Science Park is in Cambridge, and only a small part is in Boston.) One then comes to the main entrance of the ****Science Museum,** which is in the 90ft-high central tower.

Admission. The Science Museum is open Mon.–Thurs. 9 a.m.–4 p.m. July and Aug. 9 a.m.–5 p.m.; Fri. 9 a.m.–9 p.m.; Sun. 9 a.m.–5 p.m.; fee; except for Massachusetts teachers. The Hayden Planetarium has its own entrance, but it can also be entered from within the museum. Shows in the Planetarium are given at the following times: Sept.–June, Mon.–Fri. 11 a.m.; Sat. 11 a.m. and 1 p.m.; Sun. 12 noon and 2 p.m.; also Fri. evening at 8 p.m. In addition to the times already given, there are daily shows year-round at 3 p.m., except during the period Sept. 2–18, when the Planetarium is closed for maintenance. Children under five not admitted; fee for shows; otherwise no extra fee beyond that charged to enter the Science Museum.

History. As mentioned earlier, the Museum of Science traces its history back to the inception of the Boston Society of Natural History, founded in 1830, which had its first permanent home in Back Bay (see above). The museum began the move to its present site in 1949, when it received a lease from the Metropolitan District Commission for the nominal price of $1 a year, after which ground was broken that same year. The first permanent unit of the new museum, the East Wing, opened in 1951; followed by the Charles Hayden Planetarium in 1958; the central Countaway Building in 1960; the West Wing in 1972; and the Elihu Thomson Theater of Electricity in 1980. During that period the site on the Charles River Dam was landscaped to create the very attractive Science Park.

Exterior. Outside the museum there is a garden bordered by rock samples from all over the world, including pieces from the Giant's Causeway, Mont Blanc, and the Rock of Gibraltar. Some of these are quite fascinating and a number are very beautiful, in particular a large piece of rose quartz. When approaching the museum, notice the five gold-leafed aluminum plaques on the facade of the tower; these were designed by the Boston sculptor Theodore C. Barbarossa and symbolize the five major fields of science and technology that are explored in the museum and planetarium: Astronomy, Energy, Man, Industry, and Nature.

Interior. After passing the ticket desk, one is in the main lobby; the East Wing and the Planetarium are to the l.; the West Wing and the Theater of Electricity to the r. Immediately to the r. there is a shop with books and other objects concerned with the various exhibits and activities in the museum and the planetarium.

This tour begins in the *basement* of the museum, which is approached by the staircase at the rear of the lobby. On the way down there is a fine view up the Charles River, which in good weather one can enjoy from the pretty garden behind the museum. During summer months a boat leaves from here for a tour of the river as far as the Hatch Shell; the schedule and fares are posted on the dock.

After reaching the basement, cross the terrace lobby to the front of the building to enter the *Peabody Gallery;* this features the Human Body—Discovery Space, where visitors can pump a model lung, build a skeleton with real bones, and examine X-ray images for fractures, etc. After leaving the Peabody Gallery, turn l. to enter the small area of the East Wing in the basement that is open to the public. Immediately to the r. is the *Colby Room.* This is a re-creation of the gun-and-trophy room of the late Colonel Francis T. Colby, which was in his mansion in Hamilton, Mass. The superbly carved and brass-studded "Elephant Doors" at the entrance to this room were once the portals to the Palace of the Sultan of Wita, a coastal village in what is now S.E. Kenya, then part of Zanzibar. In the room are exhibited the heads and skins of 15 African animals shot by Colonel Colby; these can be identified by referring to the chart in the display case beside the door. Also exhibited are Colonel Colby's gun cabinet and a collection of Masai swords and spears.

Just beyond the Colby Room is the *Robb Auditorium,* used for lectures on science for visiting schoolchildren. Across from this there is an area in which are displayed dioramas showing the habitats of small mammals, including the raccoon, mouse, bat, opossum, and chipmunk, along with one showing a water hole in Kenya during the dry season, and another depicting the Great Western Plains of the U.S., c. 1800.

Going back through the terrace lobby, one now enters the West Wing on the basement level. Here one is on the lowest level of the *Bancroft Gallery,* a great central well rising up from the basement through the First and Second Floors. The first area on the r. contains a computer exhibit set up by the Honeywell Corp. This consists of a working Model 316 computer and terminals, with keyboards which visitors can operate. In addition, there are slide shows, films recordings, and push-button displays, all designed to explain the computer, the history of its development, and its applications in the future. In the next area beyond that, on the r., there is an exhibit relating to telephone communications, prepared by the New England Telephone and Telegraph Co. This features a step-by-step demonstration of how the dial telephone transmits its messages, as well as a specially constructed phone in which visitors can hear their own voices. Other exhibits include replicas of early telephones and a painting showing Alexander Graham Bell using his invention for the first time. The next area on the r. is a topographical model of Boston Harbor and its shores, and behind that there is a large diorama of the Pilgrim village of Plymouth as it appeared in 1635. Next to this a number of dioramas depict life in the Bay Colony in colonial times. One shows Paul Revere working in his silversmith shop in 1768, in the act of engraving the Liberty Bowl. Next on the r. there is an exhibit concerned with insects from all over the world. Near the corner of the room on that side is the most striking display in the museum, a life-sized model of the extinct prehistoric monster Tyrannosaurus Rex, a flesh-eating dinosaur with a body 20ft high and a 4ft head. In the corner of the room behind the dinosaur there are minature dioramas, including a battle between dinosaurs; Swiss lake-dwellers, c. 200 B.C.; the building of the pyramids; a Hopi village in Arizona; prehistoric cave-dwellers; and primitive cliff-dwellers.

At the far end of the West Wing in the basement is the lower entrance to the Theater of Electricity (see below). After passing that, one sees a Rollins Steam Engine dating to 1906.

Walking back along the other side of the room, one passes model trains, cars, and horse-drawn vehicles, antique automobiles, and a racing car. Then one passes an exhibit of machine tools, with a master machinist at work on objects used in fashioning the museum's various displays. Also in this area is a hot-air balloon that rises and falls in the great gallery, and an evacuated vertical tube in which a feather and a metal ball are periodically dropped, showing that when there is no air resistance all objects fall with the same acceleration.

An escalator ascends from the basement to the *First Floor mezzanine* of the Bancroft Gallery. Here one can see at closer range some of the exhibits that are suspended from the roof of the gallery. The most important of these is the Gemini 7 Spacecraft; this is the actual capsule that made 206 orbits around the earth in 330 hours, 35 minutes on Dec. 4–18, 1965, with Command Pilot Frank Borman and Pilot James A. Lovell, Jr.

In all it flew 5,716,900 miles; at the time it was the longest manned space flight, and it also took part in the first space rendezvous, when it was guided to within one foot of Gemini 6, piloted by Walter M. Shirra, Jr., and Thomas P. Stafford.

Besides this, there are models of satellites that either orbited the Earth or landed on the Moon. These are: Skylab, Vanguard I, Intelstat IV, Mercury Spacecraft, Apollo 11, the Apollo Command Module, as well as a Moon Globe, a large sphere with an accurate scale-model reproduction of the moon's topography. On the mezzanine of the Second Floor there is an exhibit with a full-sized replica of the lunar module of Apollo 11, flown by the astronauts who made man's first landing on the Moon, along with a mockup of the ascent-stage controls of the satellite.

After reaching the mezzanine on the First Floor, turn r. to visit the large area on the front side of the museum, where an extremely interesting and attractive exhibit entitled Mathematica has been set up. The rear wall of this area features a display outlining the history of mathematics, and elsewhere in the chamber there are fascinating exhibits illustrating the various fields of mathematics, including many beautiful geometrical models.

Walk around to the side of the mezzanine facing the river, starting on the l. The first exhibit is entitled Fluidica, a series of manipulative displays demonstrating various principles of fluid dynamics. Beyond that, in the l. corner of the room, there is a model of the Water Screw invented in the 3C B.C. by Archimedes, and still used by farmers in modern Egypt to raise water into their fields for irrigation. There is also a model of a water pump invented in the 16C by Leonardo da Vinci, and used to pump drinking water up to the castle of the Duke of Milan. Along the rear wall of the mezzanine on this side is the Wave Tank, a 90ft-long tank filled with 2693 gallons of water, used for demonstrating the propagation of waves in fluids. In the center of this area there are the following exhibits: a sand-pattern pendulum used to demonstrate Lissajous figures (the patterns traced out in two-dimensional oscillations); an exhibit on insects, including a giant model of a common house fly, magnified 260,000 times; a section of a giant sequoia tree; and a 900-pound grandiorite rock from Antarctica, estimated to be between 450 and 600 million years old. And in the corner to the r. there is a color organ, a device used to show the relation between the frequencies of musical notes and those of light.

Walking back toward the far end of the mezzanine, one passes *Stearns Hall,* an area devoted to changing exhibitions. Turning r. at the end of the mezzanine and walking toward the opposite corner, one comes to the *Thomson Theater of Electricity,* one of the highlights of the Museum's activities. This theater and exhibition area is named after Elihu Thomson (1853–1937), the electrical engineer and inventor who in 1892 was a cofounder of the General Electric Co. The theater contains a giant Van de Graaf generator, a device capable of generating potential differences of 2,500,000 volts, creating electrical sparks up to 15ft long, a very dramatic demonstration of the electrical phenomenon involved in lightning, along with other effects in electricity.

Behind and to the l. side of the Theater of Electricity there is currently a display concerned with the properties of the human brain. Elsewhere in the environs of the theater there is a case with exhibits connected with the work of Elihu Thomson, and manipulative devices demonstrating various electrical effects.

After leaving the Theater of Electricity, walk back along the front of the mezzanine and through the central lobby into the Second Floor of the East Wing. After passing on the r. the *Visitors' Service Office,* one sees straight ahead a globe, on which are accurately represented the topographical features of the Earth. In the alcove to the l. there is exhibited a Foucault Pendulum, of a type that in the 17C provided the first direct evidence of the rotation of the Earth on its axis.

The long pendulum swings back and forth in the same invariable plane as the Earth rotates beneath it, but to an observer in the museum the plane of its oscillation appears to move around in a circle during the course of a day, its progress clocked by the wooden pegs that its bob knocks over as it reaches them one by one.

On the r. side of the Earth globe there is a gallery with life-size dioramas of New England life zones, as well as samples of exotic rocks, including a piece of petrified wood and another of solidified lava from Mount Vesuvius. Proceeding straight ahead past the Earth model, one comes to a gallery with an egg hatchery to the r. and to the l. a stage for scientific demonstrations. The corridor beyond that has dioramas of animal and bird life in New England. Beyond that is a circular area with more exhibits involving living things, and one concerned with the science of genetics. At the end of this area one turns r. and then l. on the hallway that runs along the river side of the museum. This brings one to the lobby of the **Hayden Planetarium,** where there are a few exhibits concerned with astronomy, which one can examine while waiting for the show in the auditorium to begin.

After leaving the Planetarium, walk back along the riverside hallway to its far end, passing a model of a boar's bridge. At the end of the hall turn

r. and walk across the hallway, where one can take either the stairs or the elevator to the Second Floor.

After reaching the *Second Floor,* one sees first exhibits dealing with the human foot and the human lung. Turn l. on the central corridor to walk back into the East Wing, passing on the r. the Friendly Fast Serve Cafeteria. (There is also a cafeteria on the Sixth Floor, the Skyline Room.) Just beyond the cafeteria on the r. there is a room with bronze figurines of animals done by the sculptress Katherine Lane Weems. Beyond that on the r. is *Pierce Hall,* with exhibits involving medical science, including the chemistry of the human body. On the l. in this area are exhibits relating to human vision and the human heart, as well as a striking model of the DNA model, on a scale 400 billion times its actual size.

Walking back through the East Wing, one crosses a bridge over the central lobby into the uppermost level of the Bancroft Gallery. After crossing the bridge, one comes on the r. to the *Wright Theater;* the featured exhibit here is the Transparent Woman (times of lecture posted outside). The area to the r. of the mezzanine past the Wright Theater is devoted to exhibits concerned with energy. The exhibits here that most interest young people are the series of inclined planes and loop-the-loops, in which rolling balls are put through their motions and collide to illustrate the laws of conservation of momentum and energy. Beyond this, in the right-hand corner of the mezzanine, there is a stage where demonstrations of scientific phenomena are given.

Crossing to the river side of the mezzanine, one finds in the area to the r. the *Warren Shell Collection.* This unique collection of seashells from all over the world was given to the museum by Mrs. Fiske Warren; its themes are: iridescence in nature; the influence of shell design on architecture; and the relation between the geometric perfection of shells and modern scientific design. Behind the shell collection there is a gallery with the theme Design Around Us, with changing exhibits related to the architectural designs and symmetries one finds occurring naturally in the world.

Continuing along that side of the mezzanine, one passes on the r. the *Cahners Theater,* which is used for lectures and demonstrations on natural science. Return to the other side of the mezzanine and turn r. to cross back on the bridge over the central lobby. This brings one back to the stairs and the elevator in the East Wing, ascending to the Third Floor.

Only a small part of the *Third Floor* is open to the public, most notably the *Harrison F. Lyman Library,* which is down the hallway from the stairs and elevator overlooking the river. The library has a very good collection of books, periodicals, and other materials relating to science and technology, particularly those areas that would be of interest to young people. A small area to the r. of the hall leading from the stairs and elevator to the library has a number of ship models, as well as a demonstration of how stroboscopes, a device using a rapidly flashing light, can be used to study high-speed phenomena. There is also an area here which is used for scientific lectures and demonstrations for very young schoolchildren.

The only remaining area of the museum that is open to the public is on the *Sixth Floor;* this is the Skyline Room Cafeteria, where lunch is served every day except Mon., and dinner on Fri. evening. The view from the Skyline Room is superb.

On the Boston side of Science Park there is a fine old engine that once ran on the Boston & Maine Railroad; this is open for inspection at the times posted.

The last part of this itinerary goes through East Cambridge, a quarter of the city that few outsiders ever visit; this is a pity, for it is one of the most interesting and picturesque neighborhoods in the area.

After leaving the Science Museum, go back westward along the Charles River Dam and continue for a short way along Monsignor O'Brien Highway, which crosses Commercial Ave and passes beside Lechmere Canal. Turns off to the l. onto Cambridge St, a thoroughfare laid out by the Lechmere Corporation immediately after the completion of the Craigie Bridge in 1809. The intersection here marks the original high-water mark in colonial times, before the first landfill operations began.

As one walks up Cambridge St between First and Second Sts, one passes on the l. a huge old commercial building that takes up the entire block. This is one of a number of superb structures of this type that have survived in East Cambridge, relics of the tremendous industrialization that took place here in the mid-19C. This building was erected in 1866 by the A. H. Davenport Co., furniture-makers; the upholstered couch manufactured by this firm became so popular in the second half of the 19C that it became a part of the English language. This grand old building now houses the Deran Confectionery Co., the sweet aromas of whose products hang heavy in the air of this part of East Cambridge.

A block farther along Cambridge St is the civic center of East Cambridge, both past and present. On the l. side of Cambridge St, between Second and Third Sts, stands the monumental Victorian edifice that houses the *Registry of Deeds and Probate Court*. In the front yard of the building a History Station has been set up, with maps, prints, and texts explaining the history and topography of East Cambridge.

History and Topography. The original settlement of East Cambridge was on a hill, or drumlin, which was surrounded by water and marshland, so much so that it became an island at times of exceptionally high tides. The first to settle on this hill, in 1629, was Thomas Graves, who surveyed and laid out Charlestown for the Massachusetts Bay Colony. Graves received for this service 126 acres on this hill, which then became known as Graves' Neck. In 1757 the Graves estate became the property of Richard Lechmere, and thereafter the area became known as Lechmere Point, a name it still bears. Lechmere Point was the scene of the first military operation of the Revolutionary War, when, on the evening of April 18, 1775, British troops landed there from Boston on their way toward Lexington and Concord. Later that year the Continental Army built a fortress at Lechmere Point, calling it Fort Putnam, after General Israel Putnam. During the last days of the siege of Boston, in March 1776, the American guns in Fort Putnam were very effective in bombarding British positions in the town.

The opening of Craigie's Bridge, along with the laying out of Cambridge St, began the development of East Cambridge, connecting it with Old Cambridge on one side and Boston on the other. Craigie and his associates in the Lechmere Corporation surveyed the open land in East Cambridge and laid it out into streets and lots in 1811, offering the area for sale to real-estate developers. In 1813 Craigie and his group convinced the officials of Middlesex County to transfer the seat of government to East Cambridge, where the Lechmere Corporation donated land and a courthouse designed by Charles Bulfinch. Next Craigie persuaded industries to relocate in East Cambridge, beginning with the renowned Boston Porcelain and Glass Co., which provided jobs for the European immigrants who began to settle in the town in ever-increasing numbers. As East Cambridge grew and prospered, it rivaled Cambridgeport and Old Cambridge in wealth and political power, and when the three towns amalgamated as a city in 1846, the first mayor was a resident of East Cambridge, a Unitarian minister named James D. Green. By that time the Irish were well established in East Cambridge; in 1842 they founded St. John's, the first Roman Catholic church in Cambridge, and two decades later they established St. John's Institute, which helped Irish immigrants prepare for a better life in the U.S. by teaching them to read, write, and debate, as well as providing a social center for them. By the end of the Civil War almost half the population of East Cambridge was Irish. During the latter half of the 19C and in the 20C there was a large influx of Italians, Poles, Lithuanians, and, most recently, Portuguese, who today have given a very Mediterranean flavor to much of East Cambridge. This flood of immigrants was due to the continued commercial growth of Cambridge, which by the 1930s became New England's third most important manufacturing city, with the greatest part of the industrial activity being carried on in East Cambridge. Despite that, large parts of East Cambridge have remained completely residential till the present day, most notably the pleasant and serene quarter described below.

The majestic old building that houses the ***Registry of Deeds and Probate Court** is the most important extant 19C civic building of Middlesex County. This edifice was built in 1896–98 by Olin W. Cutler in the neoclassical style, with enormous brick columns forming porticoes on all four sides, those to the N. and S. surmounted by pediments and approached by steep flights of steps. The building is still performing the functions for which it was originally designed, the only one of the surviving 19C civic buildings of Middlesex County to continue in service, with the Probate Court on the Second St side and the Registry of Deeds on Third St. Look down the Second St side to see the superb wrought-iron lantern-holders still in place beside the entryway there.

Continue W. on Cambridge St. On the N.E. corner of Third St is the *Middlesex County National Bank,* a little building in the 20C classical style, erected in 1971 by Thomas M. James. In the middle of the next block on the l. side is the quite elegant building in polished Maine granite that houses the *East Cambridge Savings Bank,* built in 1931, another work of Thomas M. James. The lavish carvings on the facade are by Paul Fjelde; the fine Byzantine interiors include pink North African marble walls, carved doors and brightly colored terra-cotta ceilings decorated by Alfred Rasmussen, a Boston artist. It is a very charming building, and one should not pass it by without having a look inside.

Directly across the street, a plaque on the facade of the bank there records that this was the site of St. John's Literary Institute, which from 1862 to 1924 was the center of the intellectual and social life of the Irish residents of East Cambridge. The Church of St. John itself was on the S.E. corner of Cambridge and Sciarappa Sts, where it stood from 1842 until its demolition after its congregation moved elsewhere in Cambridge in the second half of the 19C. On the N.E. side of the same intersection is the *Roman Catholic Church of St. Francis of Assisi.* This was originally a Baptist meetinghouse, erected in 1837, and the campanile was added in 1932, after the present Italian congregation took over the church.

Turn l. on Sciarappa St and follow it to the next corner, where it intersects Otis St. On the S.E. corner, at 80–82 Otis St, there is a very impressive double brick house of three stories dating from 1861. Across from this, on the S.W. corner, there is a huge red-brick structure that houses the *Putnam School,* erected in 1887 by James Fogerty. The school takes its name from Fort Putnam, the fortification that the Continental Army erected here in 1775, on the highest point of East Cambridge.

Walk W. along Otis St. About halfway along on the r. is the *Roman Catholic Church of St. Hedwig,* built in 1939 by F. F. McDonough for a Polish congregation. The present church replaces a 19C Universalist meetinghouse destroyed in the hurricane of 1938. Across the street from the church, at No. 100, is a three-story brick house, built in 1848, but the entrance doors and mansard roof were added later. Just beyond the church, at Nos 103–105, is a wood house in the Greek Revival style built in 1843. Continue along Otis and cross Fifth St; on the l. side of the street are three interesting houses dating from the second half of the 19C: Nos 122–124 (1870); No. 134 (1868); and, on the corner, a wooden Colonial Revival dwelling with two bows flanking a portico, erected in 1895 by John Muldoon, and now used as a funeral home. Turning l. on Sixth St, one sees to the r. the *Roman Catholic Church of the Sacred Heart,* an impressive edifice in blue slate erected in 1874 by P. W. Ford; the belfry to the r. of the church is missing its steeple, which once rose to a height of 170ft. Sacred Heart was erected by the local Roman Catholics after the nearby Church of St. John moved elsewhere in Cambridge, and it is now the only church in East Cambridge still used by the congregation that built it. Next door to the church is its rectory, built in 1885.

At the next corner is Thorndike St, with, on the S.W. corner, a very rural-looking cottage with a side piazza, dating to 1855, with a large garden at its front. On the S.E. corner there is a simple gable-ended house, dated 1829, which is typical of the workers' cottages built in this part of East Cambridge at that time; the smaller house behind it on Thorndike St is of the same type and period.

Now walk eastward along Thorndike, crossing Fifth St. On the next block are a number of fine old workers' houses, which appear still to be owned by local people of the working class; these are, on the r.: No. 116 (1865); No. 96A (1826), once the home of James D. Green, the Unitarian minister who in 1846 became the first mayor of Cambridge; a row at Nos 83–95 (1865); and on the corner to the l., at No. 85, a house dating to 1822, with its garden in front, reminiscent of what this street must have looked like in the early days of East Cambridge. Crossing Sciarappa St, one sees more of these fine old workers' houses; these are, on the r.: No. 18 (1846); and No. 74 (1843); and on the l.: a double house at Nos 71–73 (1844–47); No. 69 (1845); and No. 59 (1827). The house of Thomas Graves, the first settler in East Cambridge, is believed to have stood just to the S. of the dwelling at 59 Thorndike St.

At the N.W. corner of Thorndike and Third Sts is the unique *Roman Catholic Church of the Holy Cross.* This Federal-style meetinghouse was originally built in 1827 for a Unitarian congregation. Later it was acquired by an Episcopal mission, and later still by its present Polish congregation.

Looking down Third St to the r., one sees the former *Third District Courthouse,* a Georgian Revival structure erected in 1931 by Charles R. Greco. The courthouse was closed in the 1970s, as were a number of other public buildings in the immediate area, and it has now been converted by private developers.

Across the way, to the r., is the huge *New Superior Court Building,* completed in 1968 by Edward J. Tedesco Assocs. This edifice, the first skyscraper in East Cambridge, was originally designed to have a complex of satellite structures that would extend from the present structure a full block up to Otis St, and would have caused the demolition of the older public buildings that stand in that area. Fortunately, the skyscraper cost far more than expected and the grandiose plan was scrapped, preserving the older buildings to its N., on the block bounded by Thorndike, Otis, Sciarappa, and Third Sts. The splendid edifice that takes up the W. side of that block, distinguished by its domed belfry, is the *Old Superior Courthouse,* whose present structure was erected in 1848 by Ammi B. Young, with alterations in 1898. The 1848 structure has at its core parts of the original East Cambridge courthouse designed in 1814 by Charles Bulfinch for Andrew Craigie and his associates in the Lechmere Corporation. The courthouse was originally slated for demolition when the New Superior Court Building was completed, but now it is going to be preserved, and it is being converted by private developers. The E. side of the block is occupied by the old *Clerk of Courts Building,* a Victorian pile erected in 1889 by Robert P. Wait and Olin W. Cutter. This fine old building has also been saved from demolition, and it too has been converted by private developers.

Continue eastward along Thorndike, and at mid-block between Third and Second Sts look to the l. in the space between the Old Superior Courthouse and the Clerk of Courts Building, where one sees the S. portico of the Registry of Deeds and Probate Court, one of the grandest spectacles in Cambridge.

Turn l. at the next corner onto Second St, passing the E. facade of the Clerk of Courts Building. In colonial times the waters of the Charles came right up to this point. Before reconstruction began on the courthouse there was a plaque on its E. facade recording that British troops landed here from Boston on the evening of April 18, 1775, on their way to Lexington and Concord.

Now turn r. at the next corner onto Otis St. At the N.E. corner of this intersection, at 30—34 Second St, there is a row of three brick houses dating from 1836—39; and on the S.E. corner, at 36—46 Second St, a row of six wooden-frame houses all built in 1842. This is the densest concentration of early-19C houses in the area, and gives one some idea of what East Cambridge must have looked like in its early days. Continuing eastward along Otis St, one passes on the r. a block-long brick building of four stories; erected in 1869—71, this is a very well-preserved example of an East Cambridge commercial structure of the period.

At the next corner turn l. onto First St, which at the next intersection brings one to Cambridge St. Turning r. there, one finds on the l. the Lechmere station on the Green Line of the T, where one can travel on the subway back to Park St in downtown Boston.

22 Other Places of Interest in Boston, Cambridge, and Downtown Brookline

This last section includes a brief description of other places of interest in Boston, Cambridge, and contiguous areas of downtown Brookline. When major sites are near a T station on the subway or on a bus route, that information will be given; however, because of the need for brevity, detailed instructions are not provided. The best way to locate these places, as well as to find more minor sites, is to consult one of the comprehensive maps of the metropolitan area that have a street index; a good one is the Arrow Metropolitan Map and Street Guide.

A. The Parks of Boston

Boston is justly proud of its park system, which includes a good deal more ground than just the Common and the Public Garden. Besides these two central green areas, the system includes an almost continuous vernal stretch that begins at the Charles River Dam and stretches for a distance of some miles, almost out of the city limits. This so-called emerald necklace comprises six major parks and their connecting highways: these are: the Charles River Reservation, Back Bay Fens, Muddy River Improvement, Jamaica Park, Arnold Arboretum, and Franklin Park.

History. The present Boston Park System is to a large extent the creation of Frederick Law Olmsted, who in 1878 was appointed landscape-architect adviser to the Boston Park Commission, created just three years earlier. At that time Olmsted was the world's most renowned designer of public parks, among which were Central Park in Manhattan and Brooklyn's Prospect Park. By 1875 the Park Commission had already drawn up a master plan for the park system they were going to create. After Olmsted's appointment he worked with the commissioners in refining their plans and also in designing the individual parks. He continued to work on this project until his retirement in 1895, creating most of the emerald necklace that one sees today. The last addition to this beautiful stretch of parkland was the Charles River Reservation, which was landscaped in several stages after the completion of the Charles River Dam, the first part being the Esplanade, begun in 1931 through a gift presented to the city by Mrs. James T. Storrow.

The part of the emerald necklace most familiar to Bostonians is the **Charles River Reservation,** and there is no more pleasant way to spend part of a fine day than to stroll along this exceedingly beautiful stretch of riverside. Starting at the Charles River Dam, the first site of interest on the right bank of the river is the *Hatch Shell.*

The Hatch Shell is due to the generosity of Maria E. Hatch, who at the time of her death in 1926 left $300,000 to the city of Boston, willing that it should be used for the creation of a public work that would serve as a memorial to her late brother, Edward Hatch. The money was finally used in 1940 to pay for the construction of the Hatch Shell, whose principal use is for the Esplanade Concerts given annually in July by the Boston Pops Orchestra. These concerts, one of the highlights of life in Boston, were initiated on July 4, 1929, by Arthur Fiedler, who conducted the Boston Pops Orchestra for a half-century.

The oval lawn on which the audience sits during the Esplanade Concerts is surrounded by a path on the periphery of which there are four commemorative bronze statues. Starting from the Hatch Shell and taking the path on the l. side of the oval, one comes first to a statue of *General George Patton* (1885–1945), the flamboyant commander of the U.S. Armored Forces in Europe in World War II. The statue is by James Earle Fraser (1876–1953); it is a replica of the original, which is at West Point, New York, and was erected on its present site in the 1950s.

The second statue on the l. side of the Hatch Oval is of *Major General Charles Devens.* After distinguished service in the Union Army during the Civil War, General Devens later became a judge in the Massachusetts Supreme Court, and later still he served as attorney general in the Cabinet of President Rutherford B. Hayes. This statue, a work of Olin L. Warner, originally stood behind the State House, but when a parking lot was created on that site the statue was moved to its present location.

At the back of the oval there is a statue of *David Ignatius Walsh* (1872–1947), a work completed in 1954 by the Boston sculptor Joseph A. Coletti (b. 1898). Walsh was a lawyer who served as lieutenant governor of Massachusetts, governor, and U.S. senator.

On the r. side of the oval there is a statue of *Maurice J. Tobin* (1901–53), a work of Emilius R. Ciampa. Tobin was mayor of Boston in 1938–44; governor of Massachusetts in 1946–47; in 1948 he was appointed secretary of labor in the cabinet of President Harry S. Truman.

The most beautiful stretch of the Charles River Reservation begins beyond the Hatch Shell, at the *Storrow Lagoon.* This lovely body of water is named after Mrs. James T. Storrow, whose generosity is largely responsible for the Charles River Reservation. It was created by filling in a long and narrow outer island to enclose the lagoon, which is joined to the mainland by a series of graceful stone bridges. On this part of the stroll the most pleasant route is along the outer island, for there the roar of the traffic along Storrow Drive is muted.

The inner path leads past one of the most unusual monuments in Boston, the *Lotta Fountain,* a stele surmounted by the figure of a dog, whose tail curls around the statue from back to front. The statue was commissioned by Loretta (Lotta) M. Crabtree, whose will (she died in 1924) endowed a fund to set up "beneficial drinking fountains for men, horses, birds and dogs." Beyond the Lotta Fountain there is a memorial to Oliver Wendell Holmes, and after that a large plaque commemorates Mrs. Storrow. A short distance beyond this is the *Harvard Bridge,* the end of the loveliest stretch of the Charles River Reservation. However, one can continue to go for miles beyond this along the Charles in very pleasant surroundings, as countless Bostonians do each day, walking, cycling, or roller-skating, or just taking their ease under a shade tree beside the river.

The "emerald necklace" heads inland from the Charles just beyond the Harvard Bridge, following the highway which along successive stretches is known as the Fenway, the Riverway, the Jamaicaway, and the Arborway. This narrow thread of verdant parkland makes driving along the highway much more pleasant than it would otherwise be; however, there is little along this stretch of the "emerald necklace" to interest visitors. On the first stretch of the Back Bay Fens there is a large area planted with kitchen gardens, a carryover from the "Victory Gardens" of World War II. Farther along, in the area behind the Museum of Fine Arts, there is an exceptionally beautiful rose garden. The prettiest stretch of this winding highway is where it goes around *Jamaica Pond,* the largest body of fresh water in Boston, with an area of 65.5 acres. On the S.W. shore of the pond there is a monument commemorating the historian Francis Parkman, whose summer home stood nearby; this is a work of Daniel Chester French, dedicated in 1906.

After passing Jamaica Pond, one drives along the Arborway for less than a half-mile to come to the main entrance of the ****Arnold Arboretum,** one of the most renowned botanical gardens in the U.S.

Approach. The closest subway T stations are Arborway on the Green Line (four blocks from the Jamaica Plains Gate), and Forest Hills (two blocks from the Forest Hills Gate).

Admission. The Arboretum is open every day throughout the year from sunrise to sunset (tel. 524-1717).

History. The Arboretum is named after James Arnold, a prosperous New Bedford shipping merchant and amateur horticulturist, who died in 1869 and bequeathed over $100,000 to be used by his trustees "for the promotion of Agricultural or Horticultural Improvements, or other Philanthropic purposes at their discretion." After Arnold's death the trustees decided to create a tree garden, signing an agreement with Harvard on March 29, 1872, and turning over the endowment to the university. Harvard, in turn, allotted to the tree garden a 125-acre estate that it had earlier acquired in a bequest from Benjamin Bussey. On Nov. 24, 1873, Harvard appointed Charles Sprague Sargent as the first director of the Arnold Arboretum, a post he held until his death in 1927. Soon after his appointment Sargent contacted Frederick Law Olmsted, who was at that time designing the Boston Park System, and they began to plan the Arboretum. Their discussions eventually resulted in an agreement between Harvard and the city of Boston concerning the status of the Arboretum. According to this agreement, Boston would purchase the grounds of the Arboretum from Harvard, buy some additional contiguous property, and lease it all back to Harvard at a nominal fee for 1000 years; the city also agreed to fence in the land, lay out the roads and paths, and police the grounds, keeping it open throughout the year as part of the Boston Park System. Since that time additional property has been acquired, so that the Arboretum now comprises 260 acres of land in Jamaica Plain, as well as a 150-acre experimental garden in Weston, Mass. At the outset, Prof. Sargent and the staff of the Arboretum undertook to grow specimens of every woody plant that could live outdoors in Boston's climate. Today, the living collections at the Arboretum comprise about 6000 different kinds of woody plants. In addition, there are some 6000 plants of nearly 2000 different kinds growing in the nurseries for study or as replacements for some of the older specimens. In effect, the Arnold Arboretum is an outdoor museum of trees and woody plants, arranged informally within a naturalistic and very attractive park setting.

Interior. The Administration Building and Library are to the r. of the entrance at the Jamaica Plain Gate. Inside this building free maps of the Arboretum are available, and books about the park and its collections may be bought. From this and the other entrances a network of roads and paths takes one through the Arboretum, whose highest and most scenic point is at the Overlook on Bossey Hill.

The Arborway continues beyond the Arnold Arboretum, and in less than a half-mile it brings one to the westernmost corner of **Franklin Park,** the last link in the "emerald necklace."

Approach. Take the Orange Line to the Dudley or Egleston stop; from the Dudley station take the Franklin Park bus, or from Egleston take the bus marked Mattapan.

History. Franklin Park is another work of Frederick Law Olmsted; it is considered to be one of his three masterpieces, the others being New York's Central and Prospect Parks. Olmsted's plan for Franklin Park was published in 1885 and construction began the same year. At the time the park first opened it was out in the country; Olmsted realized that Boston would eventually expand and surround it, and so he planned the 525-acre green area as a verdant haven for city-dwellers. The largest area in his plan was the "Country Park" which was set aside for the enjoyment of natural scenery. Other special areas were the "Playstead" which was reserved for sports; a playground for small children; a zoological garden; and bridle paths and paths for strollers. The "Country Park" is now a golf links; the "Playstead" is the site of a stadium; and the zoological gardens have been closed for some years, though they are now being rehabilitated and will open again in the not-so-distant future.

Interior. (Franklin Park is on the edge of a high-crime area, and it is not advisable to walk through it alone, even in the daytime.) The principal attraction of Franklin Park in the past was the Children's Zoo, which is currently being restored and may once again be opened to the public. When the zoo reopens it will have several new features, including enclosures which will reproduce the environment of a tropical rain forest, a bush forest, a desert, and a veldt. For information about these and other activities in Franklin Park, including the free summer performances of the Elma Lewis Playhouse-in-the-Park, inquire at the Boston Parks and Recreation Dept, One City Hall Sq, tel. 725-4505.

B. Boston Harbor Islands State Park

The **Boston Harbor Islands** are a unique natural resource easily accessible from downtown Boston. The more than 30 islets in this group were in 1970 incorporated into the Boston Harbor Islands State Park, and on a number of them visitors may enjoy picnicking, hiking, fishing, swimming, boating, overnight camping, and the exploration of historic old fortresses.

Approach. Islands with facilities of one sort or another for visitors are Georges, Gallops, Lovells, The Brewsters, Peddocks (special permission needed), Bumpkin, Grape, and Slate. Commercial ferryboats go to Georges Island from Long Wharf, which is located near the Aquarium T station on the Blue Line. The schedule for ferry trips to Georges Island is posted on Long Wharf, or telephone the Bay State and Provincetown Steamship Co. at 723-7800. Free water-taxi service is available during the summer months from Georges Island to Gallops and Lovells; service to Grape and Bumpkin is provided less frequently, and other islands are accessible by private boat. Permits are required for overnight camping and other use; these may be obtained without charge by calling the following numbers; for Georges, Lovells, and Peddocks, 727-5250; for all other islands, 749-7160. During July and Aug. there are interpretive programs on Grape, Bumpkin, Gallops, Great Brewster, and Calf Islands. A self-guided nature trail has been laid out on Lovells Island.

History. Remains of campsites and other archaeological evidence indicate that the Harbor Islands were inhabited by Indians as early as 4000 B.C. When Captain John Smith explored Boston Harbor in 1614 he gave it enthusiastic praise, writing: "Here are many isles all planted with corn, groves, mulberries, savage gardens, and good harbours. . . . The seacoast . . . shows all along large cornfields, and great troops of well-proportioned people." The first English settler on the Harbor Islands was David Thompson, a member of Sir Ferdinando Gorges' abortive colony of 1622, who in 1626 built a house for himself and his family on the island that now bears his name. When Boston was first settled in 1630, a number of colonists established farms, orchards, and vineyards out on the Harbor Islands, most notably Governor John Winthrop, who the following year was given title to what is now known as Governor's Island. During the Revolutionary War fortifications were built on several of the islands, and a few skirmishes were fought in the little archipelago. British amphibious attacks on several towns along the New England seaboard during the War of 1812 stimulated the construction of major fortresses on the islands of Boston Harbor. These fortresses were strengthened during the Civil War, when Fort Warren, Georges Island, served as one of the principal Union prisons for captured Confederates (see below). Throughout World Wars I and II the Harbor Islands were still considered to be strategically important, and they were used for coastal defense and as military encampments. During World War II the entrance to the harbor was fenced off with an underwater torpedo net and was heavily mined. Several additional islands were fortified with rapid-fire batteries and anti-aircraft guns. Remains of these and the earlier fortifications can still be seen today.

Guest houses, inns, and resorts were established on the Harbor Islands in the 18C, with the fresh produce from the farms and abundant seafood used in the restaurants and hotels. Excursions and day trips to the islands were also extremely popular for those seeking a respite from the already congested city. Illegal gambling and boxing matches were also frequent attractions at the inns on a few of the islands. By the late 19C, recreational use diminished, and a variety of public facilities and institutions were built on the islands because of their relative isolation, including hospitals, reformatories, poorhouses, and sewage-treatment plants. The establishment of the Boston Harbor Islands State Park in 1970 has led to their increased use by the public, linking them once more to Boston.

Historic Sites on the Harbor Islands.
Two sites on the Harbor Islands are listed in the National Register of Historic Places. One of these is *Fort Warren* on **Georges Island.**

The U.S. began work on the fort in 1833, when the name Warren was taken from the fortifications on Governor's Island and applied to the works on Georges Island. The construction and arming of the fort continued intermittently until the outbreak of the Civil War, when its defenses were strengthened, a project that was completed in 1863. When completed, the fort complex consisted of a circuit of star-shaped granite walls and earthen bulwarks surrounding a four-acre parade ground, along with an ammunition magazine, a hospital, and, later, a warehouse which during World War I was used to store mines. During the Civil War, Fort Warren served as a prison for captured Confederate soldiers. Two of the most celebrated Southerners imprisoned here during that period were James Mason and John Slidell, envoys from the Confederacy to Great Britain, who in 1861 were seized aboard the British vessel *Trent,* and who were held for a time on Fort Warren. Immediately after the Civil War, on May 24, 1865, Alexander Hamilton Stephens, Vice-President of the Confederacy, was brought to Fort Warren and imprisoned there until Oct. 13 of that year. The fort also had a renowned ghost, the Lady in Black, who is connected with a legend that arose during the Civil War, when a young Southern lady is supposed to have made her way into Fort Warren to join her imprisoned husband. When they attempted to escape, so the legend goes, he was killed and she was executed as a spy, and thereafter she appeared from time to time, garbed in a black mourning gown, to haunt the soldiers on duty in the fortress.

The other historic site on the Harbor Islands is *Boston Light,* on **Little Brewster Island.** According to the town records of Boston, there was a beacon and watchtower on Little Brewster from the earliest days of the settlement.

A lighthouse was built on Little Brewster in 1716, the first to be erected in North America. This lighthouse was destroyed by the British at the time of their evacuation of Boston on March 17, 1776; it was rebuilt in 1783 and has been repaired and altered to a certain extent in modern times.

C.   Historic Houses in Boston and Cambridge

The following is an annotated listing of some of the historic houses in Boston and Cambridge that appear in the National Register of Historic Places, but which are not described in any of the previous itineraries. All of the houses listed in this section are private and are not open to the public except by special arrangement. There are a few houses on the National Register, not visited on previous itineraries, that are open to the public as museums; these will be described in the last section of this chapter.

Boston
Dorchester. (Anyone who wishes to visit the historical houses in Dorchester or to obtain additional information about them should contact the Dorchester Historical Society; tel. 265-7802.)

James Blake House, 735 Columbia Rd; erected 1650, this is a frame, clapboarded house with gabled roof, central chimney, and diamond-paned window casements; one of the few remaining New England dwellings built by an immigrant colonial carpenter; home of James Blake, General Court deputy and deacon of the First Church of Roxbury.

Roger Clapp House, 199 Boston St; a clapboarded and shingled house erected in 1765 by the housewright Samuel Pierce.

William Clapp House, 195 Boston St; a Federal-style house put up in 1806 by the builder Samuel Everett (the Clapp family were responsible for maintaining the surrounding pear orchards, where they developed a particular variety of the fruit that bore their name).

Pierce House, 24 Oakton Ave; erected in 1652; a renovated saltbox house occupied continuously by the Pierce family from the time it was built until 1968.

William Monroe Trotter House, 97 Sawyer Ave, c. 1880–90; from 1899 to 1909 this was the home of William Monroe Trotter, one of the few nationally prominent black leaders in the early 20C who actively fought racial segregation and injustice, and at the same time opposed the accommodationist policies of Booker T. Washington.

Jamaica Plain *Loring-Greenough House,* 12 South St, erected in 1760; frame, clapboarded house, hip roof with balustrade, pedimented porch on N. and S. sides, and framing Corinthian columns on the W.; additions in the late 18C and early 19C; built for Joshua Loring, commander of the British campaign against the French on Lakes George, Champlain, and

Ontario during the French and Indian War, who remained a Loyalist during the American Revolution, eventually moving to England; the house was seized by patriots after British evacuation, serving as General Nathaniel Greene's headquarters and later as a hospital for American soldiers.

Roxbury. The greatest concentration of historic houses in Roxbury is in the *John Eliot Sq District*. This was Roxbury's town center since it was first settled in 1630, located at the early crossroads of highways from inland towns to Boston. The present square is named after the Rev. John Eliot, the first minister of the First Church of Roxbury, renowned for his missionary work among the Indians and for his translation of the Bible into their language. This historic site comprises 19 residential, religious, civic, and commercial structures in and around John Eliot Sq, featuring a wide variety of 18–19C architectural styles. The most notable structures are the First Church of Roxbury, erected in 1809 (see below), and the gambrel-roofed Dillaway-Thomas House, built c. 1750–54, which was the parsonage of the First Church until the 1830s.

Shirley-Eustis House, 31 Shirley St, erected in 1747, remodeled in 1819, and moved to its present site in 1867; a frame, clapboarded structure of 2½ stories with a hip roof, dormer windows, a central cupola, front bays articulated with pilasters, and a pair of pilasters at the corners of the facade; built for William Shirley, royal governor of Massachusetts in 1741–56; used by the Continental Army as a barracks during the Revolutionary War; purchased in 1819 by Dr. William Eustis, surgeon in the Continental Army and twice elected governor of Massachusetts.

Alvah Kittredge House, 12 Linwood St, a Greek Revival structure erected in 1836; built for Alvah Kittredge, an early real-estate developer in Roxbury; later owned by Nathaniel J. Bradlee, a noted Boston architect.

William Lloyd Garrison House, 125 Highland St, a 19C structure which in 1864–79 was the home of William Lloyd Garrison, renowned leader of the Abolitionist movement, editor of *The Liberator*, and founding member of the New England and American Anti-Slavery Societies.

Cambridge

The historical houses listed below are, for the most part, of little architectural distinction, and are listed in the National Register because of their association with the renowned figures who once resided there.

71 Cherry St, a Federal-style structure erected in 1806–7, birthplace of Margaret Fuller, celebrated feminist, critic, and journalist.

88 Garden St, Federal-style house built in 1810, home of Asa Gray, a Harvard professor who was one of America's first great botanists; this building originally stood in Harvard's Botanical Gardens.

196 Prospect St, 1840s; from 1892 to 1922 this was the home of Maria Louise Baldwin, one of the most distinguished black women educators of the late 19C–early 20C, who was master of the Agassiz School in Cambridge and a nationally known lecturer.

22 Craigie St, c. 1870–1900, last home of George D. Birkhoff (1881–1944), one of the world's leading mathematicians of his generation.

10 Buckingham Pl, c. 1920, last home of Percy Williams Bridgman (1882–1961), recipient of the 1946 Nobel Prize in physics for his research in the field of high-pressure physics.

23 Hawthorn St; from 1910 to 1957 this was the home of Reginald Aldworth Daly, internationally renowned geologist.

17 Francis St, c. 1890, from 1898 to 1916 the home of William Morris Davis, whose outstanding contributions in meteorology and geomorphology helped transform geology into a true earth science.

15 Follen St, 1900; from 1900 to 1928 the residence of Theodore W. Richards, whose research in the determination of atomic masses won him the Nobel Prize in chemistry in 1914.

D. Old Buildings in Boston, Cambridge, and Downtown Brookline

The following is an annotated list of old houses, commercial buildings, and public edifices in Boston, Cambridge, and downtown Brookline, not visited on the previous itineraries, that have some architectural interest. Those wishing more information about these buildings should consult the following works, both of which are very informative and extremely inexpensive: *Victorian Boston Today,* edited by Pauline Chase Harrell and Margaret Supplee Smith; and *Guide to Cambridge Architecture,* by Robert Bell Rettig. In the listing that follows, the date of the building is given, together with its architectural style and the name of the architect, if that is known.

Boston

Jamaica Plain. (Originally a small farming village within the town of Roxbury, Jamaica Plain was annexed to Boston in 1874).

Curtis Hall, South St, corner of Sedgwick, built in 1868 as the West Roxbury Town Hall; the interior and the original mansard roof were destroyed in a fire in 1908; remodeled in 1912.

7 Greenough Ave, 1893, Colonial Revival, Blackall and Newton.

15 Greenough Ave, 1880, Queen Anne/Shingle Style, William Ralph Emerson.

73 Elm St, mansard/Stick Style, with its original polychrome roof.

10 Revere St, 1880, Ware and Van Brunt.

701–705 Center St, Romanesque Revival store with panel-brick detailing and brownstone trim (Rogers Drugstore has occupied this building since the day of its construction).

100 Pound St, 1893, Colonial Revival, William Ralph Emerson.

54 Burroughs St, 1896, Colonial Revival, Bali and Dabney.

50 Burroughs St, c. 1845.

9 Brewer St, c. 1850, Gothic Revival.

Eliot Hall, 7 Eliot St, c. 1855, rebuilt 1885; this building was used as a temporary town hall until 1868; since 1878 it has housed the Footlight Club, the oldest amateur theatrical group in the U.S.

The Eliot School, 24 Eliot St, 1832; this was endowed by John Eliot, who in 1689 gave to the town of Roxbury 75 acres for the support of a school and a schoolmaster.

21 Eliot St, 1891, Shingle Style, H. M. Stephenson.

23 Eliot St, 1898, Colonial Revival, H. M. Stephenson (thought to have been patterned on the Hancock Mansion).

28 Eliot St, c. 1874, Greek Revival.

58 Eliot St, 1880, Queen Anne style, Bradlee and Winslow.

48 Eliot St, 1886, Shingle Style.

57 Eliot St, c. 1900; this Greek Rival building once housed the Children's Museum.

"Pinebank," off the Jamaicaway opposite Moraine St, 1870, Sturgis and Brigham, now used as a center for art and drama courses offered by the Boston Parks Department (Arts in the Park); leading down to Jamaica Pond is a flight of stone steps from the Hancock Mansion.

South Boston. (Originally known as Dorchester Neck, South Boston was a part of Dorchester until its annexation by Boston in 1804.)

112–114 Dorchester St, c. 1835, duplex Greek Revival building.

316 Silver St, c. 1835. Greek Revival.

5 Silver St, c. 1865.

440 W. Fourth St, c. 1840.

114–124 W. Fourth St, c. 1873, panel-brick row houses in the style of the French Second Empire.

389–391 W. Fourth St, c. 1846, duplex Greek Revival.

396 W. Fourth St, c. 1850, Italianate.

392–394 W. Fourth St, c. 1855, Italianate.

388 W. Fourth St, early 19C, Federal French style.

380 W. Fourth St, c. 1865, French Second Empire.

368–374 W. Fourth St, c. 1856, transitional Greek Revival and Italianate.

361 W. Fourth St, c. 1830s, Greek Revival.

142 Dorchester St, c. 1850, Italianate villa.

146 Dorchester St, c. 1840s, Gothic Revival.

155 Dorchester St, c. 1830s, Greek Revival.

162–164 Dorchester St, c. 1860, French Second Empire.

176 Dorchester St, c. 1865, French Second Empire.

187 Dorchester St, c. 1830s, Greek Revival.

22 Gates St, c. 1875, French Second Empire.

46 Thomas Park, c. 1875, French Second Empire.

56 Thomas Park, c. 1876, High Victorian Gothic.

69 Thomas Park, c. 1866, French Second Empire.

89–94 G. St, c. 1863, French Second Empire.

82 G. St, c. 1853, transitional Greek Revival and Italianate.

80 G. St, c. 1865, French Second Empire.

Bird Schoolhouse, E. Fourth St, opposite Pacific St, c. 1870; this building has served in turn as a school, a kindergarden, and a synagogue.

505 E. Broadway, c. 1852, Italianate.

509–511 E. Broadway, c. 1840, Gothic/Italianate.

742 E. Fourth St, c. 1855.

746–754 E. Fourth St, c. 1855, Franco-Italianate row houses.

770 E. Fourth St, French Second Empire.

772 E. Fourth St, c. 1891, Colonial Revival.

794–796 E. Fourth St, duplex, 1870, French Second Empire.

838 E. Broadway, c. 1869, French Second Empire.

797–827 E. Broadway, c. 1870, Franco-Italianate row houses.

789 E. Broadway, c. 1864, Franco-Italianate mansion, built for Harrison Loring, a wealthy shipbuilder.

787 E. Broadway, c. 1871, a Franco-Italianate mansion built for the Paige family.

788 E. Broadway, 1868, French Second Empire mansion.

53–57 M St, c. 1873, High Victorian Gothic mansion.

780 E. Broadway, c. 1870, panel-brick style.

766–774 E. Broadway, c. 1873, French Second Empire Style.

The South End

281–293 Shawmut Ave, row houses, c. 1852.

Blackstone Sq and *Franklin Sq,* both of which originated in the original plan adopted in 1801 by the Boston Town Council; Charles Bulfinch is thought to have been the major contributor to the design of these two areas, which were built up in the 1830s and 1840s.

425–435 Shawmut Ave, Greek Revival row houses built in 1847.

35–45 W. Newton St, a row of brownstone town houses in the Italianate palazzo style, erected in the early 1850s.

The St. James Hotel, W. Newton St opposite Blackstone Sq, 1867–68; when this was first built it was considered to be the most luxurious hotel in the South End, and among its notable guests was President Ulysses S. Grant; in the years 1882–1901 it housed the New England Conservatory of Music.

Massachusetts Homeopathic Hospital, E. Concord St, 1875–76; designed by William Ralph Emerson, this red-brick Victorian Gothic structure is now part of the Boston University Medical Center.

Boston City Hospital, Worcester Sq and Harrison Ave, 1861–64, designed by Gridley J. F. Bryant; modern additions have almost completely obscured the original structure.

Aaron Allen House, 1682 Washington St, 1859–60.

Chester Sq was the first and largest of the Victorian squares laid out in the new South End, lined with houses built mostly in the 1850s and 1860s.

558 Chester Sq, 1855.

545–547 Chester Sq, c. 1853, a pair of houses in the Renaissance Revival style.

532 Chester Sq, 1858, designed by Luther Briggs, Jr., now the headquarters of the South End Historical Society.

Chickering Building, 791 Tremont St, c. 1853; constructed for the Chickering Piano Co.; reconstructed in recent years to provide apartments and studios for Boston artists.

3–23 Rutland Sq, c. 1860, a circuit of simple wooden houses built in one of the smaller Victorian squares in the South End.

Cambridge

(The old houses listed for Cambridge are, for the most part, restricted to those that were built before the end of the Civil War. The annotated list that follows lists old houses that are near the itineraries in the Cambridge section, and in the same order as those routes appear in the guide.)

78 Mount Auburn St, 1839, Greek Revival.

6 Ash St, 1848, a cottage in the neo-Gothic style.

12 Ash St, 1846.

14—16 Ash St, 1855.

19 Ash St, a three-story Federal mansion, 1823, attributed to the builder William Saunders.

11 Hawthorn St, 1813, a Federal-style house moved to its present location in 1926.

8 Willard St, a *colonial house built prior to 1765; this was moved from its original site at 83 Brattle St in 1908, and was restored and added to by Lois Lilley Howe, one of the first women architects in the U.S.

22 Larch Rd, a handsome Federal mansion built in 1808, moved to its present site in 1915, with alterations made by Alexander Wadsworth Longfellow, Jr.

17 Fresh Pond Parkway, 1838, a much-remodeled farmhouse that was once the residence of Harvard President Charles W. Eliot.

89 Appleton St, 1862, Stick Style mansard.

80 Sparks St, a mock-Georgian edifice erected in 1858, now housing the Buckingham, Brown and Nichols School.

27 Craigie St, an Italianate mansion erected in 1853 by Henry Greenough.

23 Craigie St, an Italianate mansion erected in 1855 by the builder Oliver Hastings.

3 Craigie St, still another Italianate dwelling, this one put up in 1855 by the builder Isaac Cutler.

22 Berkeley St, designed in 1877 by Griffith Thomas for the historian John Fiske.

20 Berkeley St, 1856.

15 Berkeley St, a towered Italianate villa, 1863.

5 Berkeley St, an Italianate house designed in 1853 by Calvin Ryder.

4 Berkeley St, 1851, once the residence of Richard Henry Dana, author of *Three Years Before the Mast,* now the residence of the dean of the Episcopal Theological School.

6 Berkeley St, an Italianate house erected in 1853 by the builders Moses and Jedediah Ricker.

On *St. John Road* there are three fine old houses that were moved to their present sites in recent years by the Episcopal Theological School; these are: No. 13, a Federal-style house built in 1820 by Joseph Holmes; Nos 11 and 9 were put up by the housewright William Saunders, the first in 1834 and the second in 1845.

44 Follen St, a mansard-roofed house, dating to 1862. Farther along on Follen St are three Greek Revival houses: No. 29, 1837; No. 21, 1841; No 9, 1844.

5 Follen St, an Italianate house built in 1853 by Moses and Jedediah Ricker.

1 Follen St, a handsome granite mansion built in 1889 by the firm of Longfellow, Alden, and Harlow, now housing the Longy School of Music.

58 Garden St, a hip-roofed mansion erected in 1848, with a porch added in 1901.

88 Garden St, a handsome Federal mansion put up in 1810 by the housewright Ithiel Town.

20 Gray Gardens W., a charming *Georgian house dating from the 1790s, moved from Duxbury to this picturesque cul-de-sac in 1930, when it was restored by the architect Clarence W. Brazer.

99 Garden St, a Greek Revival cottage built in 1842.

79 Raymond St, a mansion erected in 1857.

87 Raymond St, an Italianate house built in 1846 and enlarged in 1867.

42—44 Avon St, a double house of 1844 with a charming porch.

38 Avon St, a double house of 1844 with a charming porch.

38 Avon St, 1854.

32 Linnaean St, a mansion known as Gray Gables, 1863.

26 Gray St, an elegant Federal mansion of 1815, moved to its present site in 1886.

35 Bowdoin St, a Federal house built in 1812, and moved here in the 1840s.

22 Arlington St, a mansard-roofed house built in 1862.

11—13 Arlington St, a double Greek Revival cottage erected in 1846 by the builders Nathaniel U. Stickney and Sumner P. Shepard.

42 Trowbridge St, 1842.

1000 Massachusetts Ave, a mansard-roofed house erected in 1857 by Calvin Ryder.

2—4 Hancock Place, built in 1807, the oldest extant house in Dana Hill.
10 Coolidge Hill Rd, 1807.

Brookline

(The old houses listed below are restricted to those in downtown Brookline, in the area contiguous to those parts of Boston and Cambridge covered in the previous itineraries. Those who are interested in a more detailed description of the old buildings of Brookline should consult *Victorian Boston Today,* and also an excellent work put out by the Brookline Historical Commission, *A Guide to North Brookline,* by Carla W. Benka and Leslie S. Larkin.)

Brookline began to develop in the late 18C and early 19C, when wealthy Bostonians started acquiring farms and estates there. The earliest and largest of these estates were "Longwood," which David Sears acquired in 1821, and "Cottage Farm," purchased in 1856 by Amos A. Lawrence and his brother William. During the second half of the 19C, when public transport made Boston more accessible to residents of Brookline, the large farms and estates there were subdivided and developed into suburban residential neighborhoods, inhabited largely by business and professional people who commuted to the downtown area. The following is an annotated listing of some of the more interesting old buildings to be found in that part of downtown Brookline which was once part of "Longwood" and "Cottage Farm."

The oldest surviving house in this area is the wooden edifice known both as *"Aspinwell"* and the *"Sears-Behrend House,"* which appears on an 1844 map of Brookline; this was altered in the late 19C and moved to its present location in 1900.

199 Colchester St, a Shingle Style house built before 1888, when it was remodeled.

7 and 19 Colchester St, two stone houses constructed by the Lawrence family c. 1868—70.

5—11 Hawes St; this block of brick town houses, built by David Sears, appears on an 1855 map of Brookline.

6 Hawes St, 1871, with a Classical Revival portico.

Longwood Mall, laid out and landscaped in 1849 by David Sears, who there planted 14,000 trees, some of which are still standing in the mall.

40 Hawes St, 1897—1900, Federal Revival.

47—49 Monmouth St, a double house with mansard roof, 1855.

12 Monmouth St, a block of brick town houses built in the 1870s by Amos A. Lawrence.

Brookline Arts Center, near the corner of St. Mary's St and Monmouth St; this was originally a firehouse, built in 1886.

74—82 Monmouth St, a row of brick town houses erected 1893—97.

37—45 Carlton St, a row of red-brick and brownstone town houses built in 1891—93.

1043—1071 Beacon St, two rows of town houses completed by 1893.

89 Carlton St and *138 Mountfort St,* two Gothic cottages thought to have been designed for the Lawrence family in 1853 by Nathaniel J. Bradlee.

90 and 96 Ivy St, built for the Lawrence family prior to 1855.

135 Ivy St; this was the Brookline mansion of Amos A. Lawrence; *Ballou's Pictorial Magazine* reported that this "stone house in the English cottage style," was "much admired for its substantial character, harmonious proportions, and its elegant simplicity."

Dexter-Hall House, 156 Ivy St, built in 1850 by the architect George Minot Dexter for his own use.

The Frederick-Sears-Talbot House, 24 Cottage Farm Rd, a Gothic Revival mansion belonging to the Sears family that appears on a Brookline map of 1852.

E.   Churches in Boston, Cambridge, and Downtown Brookline

The following is an annotated listing of some distinguished churches in Boston and Cambridge that have not been described in the previous itineraries. Those who would like to learn more about these and other churches in the area should consult the following two works by Douglass Shand Tucci: *Built in Boston,* and *Church Building in Boston, 1720–1970.* Nearly all of the churches listed below date from the second half of the 19C. Their large number, particularly of the Roman Catholic churches, is evidence of the enormous growth of Boston during that period, with the largest numbers of immigrants being Irish and then Italians.

The largest of all of Boston's churches is deep in the South End, and thus is seen by few visitors to the city; this is the Roman Catholic ****Cathedral of the Holy Cross,** which stands on the corner of Washington and Malden Sts.

The decision to build the cathedral was made in 1860, when Bishop Fitzpatrick decided to sell the original Church of the Holy Cross on Franklin St in the old South End, an edifice designed by Charles Bulfinch, because the neighborhood in which it stood was becoming increasingly commercial, with its congregation moving to the new South End. The church was designed by Patrick C. Keeley and was erected in 1866–75. This immense edifice, constructed of Roxbury pudding stone with granite and sandstone trim, is one of the largest Gothic cathedrals in the world, comparable in size with Westminster Abbey. *King's Handbook of Boston,* published just three years after the cathedral was completed, gives this description of the structure: "The style is of the early English Gothic, cruciform, with nave, transept, aisle and clerestory, the latter being supported by two rows of clustered metal pillars. The total length of the building is 364ft.; width at the transept, 170ft; width of nave and aisles, 90ft; height of the ridge-pole, 120ft. There are two main towers in front and a turret, all of unequal height, and all eventually to be surmounted by spires. . . . The entire interior of the cathedral is clear space, broken only by two rows of columns extending along the nave and supporting the central roof. The pews accommodate 3500 persons. The arch which separates the spacious front vestibule from the church is of bricks taken from the ruins of the Ursuline convent of Mt Benedict. . . . The rose window over the principal entrance is in design a fine specimen of art. The stained transept windows, each 40 by 20ft in size, have designs representing the exaltation of the cross by the Emperor Heraclius, and the miracle by which the cross was verified. The stained windows in the chancel represent the Crucifixion, the Ascension, and the Nativity. . . . There are 24 smaller windows of stained glass, representing biblical subjects, in the clerestory of the transept and of the chancel. The chancel terminates in an octagonal apse. The high altar is formed of rich variegated marbles and is to be surmounted by a fine canopy. On the gospel side stand the episcopal throne, the *cathedra* of the Bishop. On the right side of the sanctuary is the chapel of the Blessed Virgin. . . . There are three other chapels—the chapel of St. Joseph, the chapel of St. Patrick, and the chapel of the Blessed Sacrament. " One need only amend this description in only one respect, and that is, the spires on the two towers in front of the church were never built. The Ursuline convent that King refers to was in Charlestown (the site is now in Somerville), burned to the ground in 1834 by an anti-Catholic mob.

There is another superb church by Keeley in the South End. This is the Roman Catholic ****Church of the Immaculate Conception,** on the corner of Harrison Ave and Concord St. This was built by Keeley in the years 1858–61, in collaboration with Arthur Gilman, who designed the very elaborate interior. Douglass Shand Tucci, in *Built in Boston,* has this to say of Immaculate Conception: "This church is . . . a splendid example of how the best mid-century American architects translated the Classical idiom of their own time just as surely as had the Renaissance architects. . . . It is a remarkable building. One sees the 'Medieval Survival' typical of Italianate design in the tall windows to either side of the central pavilion of the facade and also in the Palladian windows of the central pavilion. Similarly, the pavilion is quoined, though the facade itself is adorned at the corners with pilasters. . . . The exterior of this distinguished ensemble of so many historical forms

. . . nonetheless coheres beautifully in one of the handsomest buildings in Boston."

The Church of the Immaculate Conception was built concurrently with *Boston College,* which stood just beside it. Boston College, the first Roman Catholic institution of higher learning in New England, was founded in 1863 by Father John McElroy, a Jesuit priest, and classes began the following year, conducted by members of the Society of Jesus. Boston College (which is now a university) remained on this site until 1913, when it moved to its present suburban campus in Chestnut Hill, just outside the city limits of Boston.

Immaculate Conception and Holy Cross are just two of about 30 churches that Patrick C. Keeley designed in the Boston area. Other churches by Keeley that are still standing in the city of Boston are the following: *Most Holy Redeemer* (1851), 65 London St, East Boston; *St. Mary's* (1892), Winthrop and Main Sts, Charlestown; *St. Francis de Sales* (1862), 325 Bunker Hill St, Charlestown (this church can be seen clearly from the site of the Bunker Hill Monument; it stands on top of the *real* Bunker Hill, whereas the obelisk commemorating the historic battle is actually on Breed's Hill); *St. Peter's* (1873–75), 309 Bowdoin St, Dorchester; *Holy Trinity* (1877), 140 Shawmut Ave, South Boston; *St. Augustine's* (1859), Dorchester and F Sts, South Boston.

On Dorchester St, a few blocks from St. Augustine's Church, we find *St. Augustine's Chapel,* built c. 1820 and thus the oldest surviving Roman Catholic church in Boston. (St. Stephen's in the North End was built in 1804, but it did not become a Roman Catholic sanctuary until 1862.) Behind the chapel there is a picturesque old graveyard, the oldest Roman Catholic burial place in Boston. Among those buried there is Father Matignon, the French cleric who immigrated to the U.S. in 1792 to become Boston's first Roman Catholic priest.

Another of Boston's old Roman Catholic churches in *St. Joseph's* on Cardinal O'Connell Way in the West End. This was erected in 1823, though it did not become a Catholic sanctuary until 1862. St. Joseph's and the Old West Church on Cambridge St are the only houses of worship still functioning in the West End. Both churches have lost most of their congregations since the redevelopment of the West End, which once had a very numerous and highly diversified mixture of ethnic-religious groups. St. Joseph's stands near the site of the first Roman Catholic Mass celebrated in Boston. This service was held privately in Oct. 1788, when a small group of local Catholics attended a mass in a private house in the West End, the celebrant being the chaplain of a French man-of-war that was anchored in the harbor.

Another old church that has lost most of its congregation is the *First Religious Society of Roxbury,* whose meetinghouse is on John Eliot Sq. This congregation first gathered in 1632 under the ministry of the Rev. John Eliot, the great missionary to the Indians. The present edifice, which now houses a Unitarian congregation, is the fifth house of worship to stand out on this site; built in 1804, it is the oldest wooden church structure in Boston, and hanging in its belfry there is a bell cast by Paul Revere.

Many of the distinguished churches of Boston are rarely seen by visitors to the city, because, like Holy Cross and Immaculate Conception, they are far from the downtown area. One such edifice is the *Mission Church of Our Lady of Perpetual Help,* at 1545 Tremont St, in an area known as Mission Hill in Roxbury Crossing.

The church was dedicated in 1878; King's *Handbook of Boston,* which was published that same year, describes it as: "one of the largest churches in Boston. The church is a basilica, with transepts in the Romanesque style. The church has seats for 2000 people, and affords standing-room for an equal number. . . . The building is of Roxbury stone. Its length is 215ft; width across the transepts 115ft; width of nave and aisles 78ft. THe nave is 70ft high in the clear, and the aisles are 34ft high. Over the intersection of nave and transepts rises an octagonal dome of 40ft inner diameter, to a height of 110ft. This dome is supported by four clusters of four columns each, all of polished granite, with finely-carved capitals. The sanctuary, which is very large, closes with a semi-circular apse, in which is the high altar. Six side altars find room in the chapels at the ends of the aisles and transepts. The Chapel of Our Lady is built out of the west transept. Over the vestibules is the organ gallery, which, like the triforium galleries, is not open to the public."

A very beautiful house of worship in a remote location is the *Church of All Saints;* this is at 209 Ashmont St, in a secluded part of Dorchester called Ashmont. All Saints was built in 1891–94 by Ralph Adams Cram and Bertram Grosvenor Goodhue. In their design and decoration of this superb edifice, according to Douglass Shand Tucci, writing in his *Built in Boston:* "Cram and Goodhue and their artist collaborators realized one of the most distinguished ensembles of Gothic Revival art in the world."

Another exceptional church in a relatively remote location is *St. Mary's,* an Episcopal sanctuary on Cushing Ave in Dorchester. St. Mary's, erected in 1888, is of interest principally because it was built by Henry Vaughan, the English architect who designed the National Cathedral in Washington, D.C. Vaughan's only other church in Boston is *St. Margaret's Chapel* at Louisburg Sq on Beacon Hill.

Two other Boston churches of interest are in Jamaica Plain. One of these is *St. John's Episcopal Church* on Roanoke Ave, completed in 1882 by the architect H. M. Stephenson. The other is the *Unitarian Church* on Center St, at the corner of Eliot St, built in 1854 by Nathaniel Bradlee. The Unitarian Church stands on the site of the first meetinghouse in Jamaica Plain; this was erected in 1769, and its old burying ground is to be seen beside the church.

Cambridge

The *Harvard-Epworth Methodist Church,* on Massachusetts Ave near the N.W. corner of Cambridge Common, was built by A. P. Cutting, who was here very strongly influenced by H. H. Richardson's Trinity Church in Boston.

The *North Avenue Congregational Church,* at Massachusetts Ave and Roseland St, was erected in 1845 by Isaac Melvin.

This Greek Revival edifice, at first known as the Old Cambridge Baptist Church, originally stood on the site of Harvard's Littauer Center. In 1865 the church was bought by its present congregation, who moved it to its current site. After the move the church was raised on a higher foundation, to allow the construction of rooms beneath the building.

The *Prospect Congregational Church,* at Prospect and St. Paul Sts, was erected in 1851; this fine Romanesque Revival edifice is still used by its local congregation. The *First Baptist Church,* on River St just off Central Sq, is a Late Gothic Revival structure erected in 1881 by Hartwell and Stephenson.

The first Baptist church in Cambridge was erected on this site in 1816; this was replaced by a new church in 1866, but that burned in 1881, after which the present building was erected on the foundations of its predecessor.

The *Pilgrim Congregational Church,* at Magazine and Cottage Sts, was built in 1871 by James H. Sparrow and Thomas W. Silloway; a tall spire once adorned the corner tower. The *Grace Methodist Church,* at Magazine and Perry Sts, was erected in 1886 by F. E. Kidder. *St. Paul's A.M.E. Church,* on Columbia and Austin Sts, was built in 1883 by Thomas W. Silloway. *St. John's Church,* at 2254 Massachusetts Ave, near Hollis St, was completed in 1904 by Maginnis, Walsh, and Sullivan. The *Cornerstone Baptist Church,* at 2326 Massachusetts Ave, near Cogswell Ave, was originally erected in 1854 by A. R. Esty; it was rebuilt in 1885 by Van Brunt and Howe, who retained the core of the original building, adding side aisles and a parish hall to the rear. *St. James Church,* Massachusetts Ave and Beech St, was put up in 1888 by Henry M. Congdon; this Romanesque edifice, which is strongly influenced by Richardson's Trinity Church in Boston, stands on the site of a pre-Revolutionary inn known as the Davenport Tavern.

Brookline

St. Paul's Church, on 15 St. Paul St, was built in 1848–51 by Richard Upjohn. This great landmark of mid-19C Gothic Revival architecture was burned down in recent years, but it has since been rebuilt to the original design. *Christ Church,* on Colchester St in Longwood, was built in 1860–62 for David Sears by an unknown architect. This Lombard-Romanesque structure was patterned on St. Peter's Church in Colchester, England, the ancestral home of the Sears family. The *Church of Our Saviour,* on Monmouth and Carlton Sts in Longwood, was built in 1867–68 by A. R. Esty for Amos and William Lawrence, who dedicated it to the memory of their father, Amos. *St. Mark's Church,* at the corner of Park and Marion Sts, is a large Romanesque Revival structure completed in 1862 by the architect George Clough.

F.   Other Places of Interest in Boston, Cambridge, and Downtown Brookline

This last section is an annotated listing of other places in Boston, and Cambridge that *are* open to the public. Some of the sites mentioned here are among the more interesting places in the area covered by this guide, but they were not included in previous itineraries because they were off the route or in remote locations. For the more important of these sites the opening hours and the location of the nearest T stop on the underground will be given; the others can be located on a street atlas; and in the case of sites such as the old burying grounds one can assume that they are open during daylight hours.

Boston

The ***John F. Kennedy (JFK) Library,* Columbia Point.

Approach. Take the Red Line to the JFK–U. Mass. stop; a free shuttle bus operates between the station and the library.

Admission. The library is open daily 9–5; the last film begins at 3:50; fee (tel. 929-4523).

History. The library had its genesis in Nov. 1961, when President John F. Kennedy announced that he would follow the precedent established by Franklin Roosevelt and every chief executive of the U.S. since Herbert Hoover, of donating his papers and memorabilia to the National Archives and asking his friends and supporters to erect an appropriate structure to house them. President Kennedy's original intent was to have his library closely associated with Harvard, of which he was an alumnus, and to build the institution near the university. However, after considerable debate and controversy, it was decided to build the library at Columbia Point, and not to have any administrative association with Harvard. I. M. Pei was chosen to be the chief architect, and in 1975, after several of his designs had been rejected by the trustees, his final plans were accepted and construction of the building began at Columbia Point, with the library being dedicated on Oct. 20, 1979.

Exterior. This highly original and extremely attractive edifice, constructed of gray glass and white concrete, rises to a height of 110ft within a few yards of the water's edge, making it one of the most striking landmarks in Boston. The core of the building is the "great space" a ten-story glass pavilion. On approaching the entrance to the building, one sees first the "dedication wall," which has on it the following inscription: "This Library is dedicated to John Fitzgerald Kennedy, thirty-fifth President of the United States, and to all those who through the art of politics seek a new and better world."

Interior. A visit to the Kennedy Library begins in the theater, where there is a half-hour film on the life of JFK. From there one goes on to tour the museum area of the building. The museum space is arranged in chronological order, with a circulation path moving clockwise around the central area, where exhibits connected with JFK are displayed. There is a double "time-line" through the display area: one giving a chronology of the Kennedy family; and the other listing events taking place in the world at large during the same period. The most popular exhibits are the President's desk, his rocking chair, and the inscribed coconut shell which led to his rescue after the sinking of his boat, PT-100, during World War II. Smaller theaters in the museum area are used to show two shorter films: one containing excerpts from JFK's press conferences; the other being a remembrance of his brother Robert F. Kennedy. In addition, there are TV sets in the museum which replay telecasts of historic events during the Kennedy administration, most notably the Berlin crisis and the Cuban missile crisis. The remainder of the library is chiefly of interest to scholars working on the Kennedy papers or researching U.S. foreign policy, which are the two principal areas of the institution's collection. One area of more general interest is the Hemingway Room; this contains books, papers, and memorabilia of the writer Ernest Hemingway, donated to the library by his widow, Mary Hemingway.

The *Museum of the National Center of Afro-American Artists* (NCAAA), 300 Walnut Ave, at the corner of Crawford St, in Roxbury.

Approach. Take the Orange Line of the T to the Egleston stop. There is a taxi stand at the station, from where it is a short and inexpensive ride to the museum. Those who wish to walk should head toward downtown Boston on Washington St and continue along as far as Cobden St, turn r. there, and follow Cobden to its end at Walnut Ave, where the museum is housed in an old mansion in the middle of a vast area surrounded by a stone wall.

Admission. The museum is open Mon.–Sat. 1–5; fee.

History. The museum is owned and operated by the National Center of Afro-American Artists, which is a multidisciplinary private nonprofit cultural organization founded in 1968 by Elma Lewis. The Center, which has its headquarters in Boston, runs other teaching and performing arts programs; it also operates the Elma Lewis School of Fine Arts, which is two blocks away on the corner of Elm Hill Ave and Seaver St. The Museum of the NCAAA was launched in 1969 through a collaboration with the Boston Museum of Fine Arts. Its director since then has been Edmund Barry Gaither, who is also on the staff of the MFA, and his dedication and vision have created today's fascinating museum. The museum is housed in a neo-Gothic Victorian structure erected in 1873 for the William Aaron Davis family, who originally called it Oakbend Mansion. The mansion passed on to other owners, and c. 1920 it was acquired by Michael James Curley; however, the mayor never lived there himself. In 1921 the mansion was used to house a disciplinary school for boys, and later it became the David A. Ellis Elementary School. The NCAAA obtained title to the building in 1976 from the city of Boston, and repairs and renovations started the following autumn and continue to the present day.

The museum is dedicated to the collection, exhibition, and study of the visual-arts heritage of African peoples throughout the world. It operates programs in five areas: exhibitions, collection and conservation, publications, research, and education. Exhibitions are wide-ranging, covering photography, painting, sculpture, and graphics. Among the strengths of the museum are its African holdings, its collections of Afro-American prints and drawings, and its extensive archive of slides. The museum operates four sets of galleries. They are: the *Special Exhibitions Galleries;* the *Boston Galleries,* devoted to exhibitions from the greater Boston area; the *African Suite,* which has long-term exhibitions of African Art; and *Permanent Collections Galleries,* which display some of the works owned by the museum, including 19C works by black artists. The museum also has jointly produced exhibitions with the MFA and other museums and galleries. For information on current exhibitions in the museum, call 442-8614.

**Dorchester Heights National Historical Site, Thomas Park, Dorchester Heights, South Boston.

Approach. Take the Red Line of the T to the Broadway stop. It is a short walk S. from the intersection of Broadway and G St to Thomas Park, on whose grounds the monument stands.

Admission. During summer months the interior of the monument is open 9–9; in other seasons it closes earlier, around sunset. There are guides from the National Parks Service on hand to describe the monument and its history.

History. Dorchester Heights played a crucial role in the final days of the siege of Boston by the Continental Army in 1775–76. The first act of this drama took place in Nov. 1775, when General George Washington dispatched General Henry Knox to transport captured British cannon from Fort Ticonderoga in New York, so that that they could be used by the American forces then besieging Boston. Knox and his teamsters, driving 80 yoke of oxen, made the 300 mile journey in the midst of winter, bringing 59 cannon. On the night of March 4, 1776, American soldiers and local volunteers steathily fortified the summit of Dorchester Heights. After wrapping their wagon wheels with straw to deaden the sound, they moved the cannon from Roxbury and entrenched them on these hills S. of Boston. When the British spotted the fortifications the following morning, General Howe and his staff immediately met to plan the dislodgement of the Americans from Dorchester Heights, for the cannon there commanded the approaches to Boston Harbor. However, an attempted British amphibious attack on Dorchester Neck, commanded by Lord Percy, was disrupted by a violent storm, and the redcoats were forced to return to Boston. This convinced General Howe that the British position in Boston was untenable, leading him to evacuate his forces and the local Tories on March 17, 1776, after which the Continental Army occupied the town. The fortifications on Dorchester Heights fell into disrepair after the Revolution, but they were rebuilt during the War of 1812. After 1814 the fortifications were allowed to decay once again. During the second half of the 19C the hills of South Boston underwent the same transformation that truncated the peaks of Boston, as they were leveled by real-estate developers. In 1898 the General Court of Massachusetts enacted legislation to build a monument on Dorchester Heights to commemorate the role that it played in the American capture of Boston in 1776. The present monument was built in 1900–2 by the architectural firm of Peabody and Stearns. In 1966 the Heritage Conservation and Recreation Service added the Dorchester Heights Monument to the National Register of Historic Places. Twelve years later the National Parks and Recreation Act authorized the city of Boston to transfer the site to the National Parks Service, which is in charge of the monument today.

The Monument. The white marble tower, which is 215ft high, is designed in the Georgian Revival style. Within, a flight of 76 steps takes one to the observation deck, with a superb view of South Boston, and with the towers of downtown Boston looming dramatically to the N.

Castle Island, which now forms the easternmost tip of South Boston, was first connected to the mainland in 1927, when a causeway was built out to the islet, which has since been joined more substantially to the shore by landfill operations.

The old fortress on Castle Island was known in colonial times as Fort William, and after 1776 as Fort Independence. The first fortification on Castle Island was erected in 1634 by Lieutenant Governor Thomas Dudley, to protect the approach to Boston Harbor. This was destroyed by a fire in 1673, after which it was rebuilt, with other restorations and rebuildings being done in 1705, 1776, 1809, and 1851. The only military operations in which the fort was actively involved was during the last days of the siege of Boston, March 4–17, 1776, when the British artillery on Castle Island bombarded the American position on Dorchester Heights.

Castle Island continued to serve as a military base up until 1962, when the U.S. government ceded it to the Commonwealth of Massachusetts; today it is a part of *Marine Park,* a very pleasant seaside area where the people of South Boston have an opportunity to promenade along the sea front. The fortress is to a large extent the product of the 1851 rebuilding: a single-tiered brick-and-granite pentagon, partly casemented with earthen revetments.

This old fortress has been commanded and manned by a number of renowned figures. During the colonial period the royal governors of Massachusetts were *ex-officio* commanders of Fort William, as were the first governors of the Commonwealth of Massachusetts, most notably John Hancock and Samuel Adams, both of whom took an active part in maintaining the defense works on Castle Island. Among those who served in the garrison of Castle Island were Paul Revere, who commanded the artillery unit of Fort Independence during the latter years of the Revolutionary War; Sylvanus Thayer, the great military engineer, who in 1833 repaired Fort Independence and the other defense works in Boston Harbor; and Charles Francis Adams, who was stationed there for a time during the Civil War. In May 1827 a young recruit named Edgar A. Perry began a six-month tour of duty on Castle Island, later to become renowned as the writer Edgar Allan Poe.

In front of the fortress there is a huge monument erected in 1933 in honor of Donald McKay, the naval architect whose East Boston shipyard turned out the finest of the mid-19C clipper ships. On the front panel of the monument there is a relief portrait of McKay, a list of some of the great vessels that he designed and built, and an inscription recording that he "produced ships of a beauty and speed before unknown which swept the seven seas."
Elsewhere in Marine Park there is a monument surmounted by a large statue of Admiral David Farragut, the American naval hero; this is a work of Henry Hudson Kitson, and was dedicated on June 28, 1863.

The scanty remains of another fortification from the Revolutionary War are to be found in *Highland Park* in Roxbury, at the intersection of Beech Glen St and Fort Ave. This is the site of *Roxbury High Fort,* built in 1775 by Generals Henry Knox and Josiah Winters, on a hill that commanded the only land route that led in and out of Boston.

What remained of the fortress was demolished in 1869 to make way for the construction of a water standpipe, which is contained in the tower now on the site. This tower, designed by Standish and Woodbury, is in the High Victorian Gothic style. The park on which the tower stands was laid out and landscaped in the years 1895–1916, according to plans drawn by Frederick Law Olmsted. The outline of the Revolutionary fortress can be seen in its extensive pudding-stone outcropping, while concrete lines mark the quadrangular earth platform of the works with its corner bastions.

One of the two oldest graveyards in the city is located in Roxbury; this is the *Roxbury Burying-Ground,* at Eustis and Washington Sts. This ancient graveyard dates back to 1630, the same year that the first burials were made in the King's Chapel Burying-Ground. Interred here are two colonial governors of Massachusetts, Thomas and Joseph Dudley, and also the Rev. John Eliot, first minister of the First Church of Roxbury and famed as the "Apostle to the Indians," who was buried here in 1687. The Roxbury Burying-Ground is an outdoor museum of early American funerary art, rivaling in that respect the early graveyards of downtown Boston.

Another ancient Boston graveyard is the *Dorchester North Burying-Ground,* at Stoughton St and Columbia Rd in Dorchester. This graveyard was established in 1633, and buried here are some of the original settlers of Dorchester. Among those interred here are Richard Mather, founder of the renowned Mather clan in Massachusetts; and William Stoughton, lieutenant governor of the Bay Colony in the late 17C, and presiding judge at the Salem witchcraft trials. This graveyard also has a fascinating array of old colonial tombstones and funerary monuments.

One of the most beautifully landscaped burial places in Boston is the *Forest Hills Cemetery,* located just beyond Franklin Park to the S.W. Among the notables buried in this garden cemetery is General Joseph Warren, who was reinterred here in 1855, after his remains were removed from the crypt of St. Paul's Church on the Common; other renowned persons whose graves are to be found here include William Lloyd Garrison and the sculptor Martin Milmore. Adorning Milmore's grave is a monument representing Death Staying the Hand of the Sculptor, a work of Daniel Chester French.

West Roxbury, the most distant from the downtown area of all Boston's districts, has some minor sites with historical associations. One of these is the *Roxbury Latin School,* at 101 St. Theresa Ave.

Roxbury Latin is the second-oldest school in Boston, founded in 1645, though it has been on its present site only since 1927. On the school grounds there is a fine bronze statue of General Joseph Warren, done by Paul Wayland Bartlett (1865–1925). This statue was originally set up in 1904 on Warren St in Roxbury, near the original site of Roxbury Latin. The statue remained on its original site for over 60 years, until changes in the street pattern in Roxbury caused its removal to storage in Franklin Park. As Warren had been a graduate of Roxbury Latin and later a master there, that venerable institution retrieved the statue from storage in the summer of 1969 and set it up on the school grounds in West Roxbury, where it was formally dedicated on May 8, 1970, as part of the school's 345th Convocation.

Another site with historical associations in this suburban district is the *First Church of West Roxbury,* at the corner of Center and Corey Sts.

This is also called the Theodore Parker Church, named after the renowned Unitarian clergyman and Abolitionist, who was minister there in 1837–45. In the grounds of the church there is a seated bronze statue of the Rev. Parker (1810–60), done by Patrick Kraus in 1887. The funds to create this statue were raised by public subscription, on the expectation that it would be erected in Boston's Public Garden. But the Boston Arts Commission refused to accept the statue, whereupon it was put away in storage for a time, until the congregation of the First Church in West Roxbury rescued it in 1902 and erected it on its present site.

The only place in West Roxbury that is listed in the National Register of Historic Places is the *site of Brook Farm,* which is at 670 Baker St.

From 1841–47 this was the location of the Brook Farm Institute of Agriculture and Education, an idealistic socialist experiment inspired by the philosophy of Transcendentalism, established to foster the principles of common ownership of property, fair division of labor, and judicious balance between physical and intellectual pursuits. Led by George and Josephine Riley, the group at one time or another included among its members or supporters such notables as Bronson Alcott, Margaret Fuller, Ralph Waldo Emerson, and Nathaniel Hawthorne. Hawthorne made Brook Farm the setting for his novel *The Blithedale Romance.* The site is hardly worth a visit, except for sentimental reasons, because there is nothing left of the original Brook Farm except a single nondescript building.

Cambridge

Mount Auburn Cemetery, 580 Mount Auburn St. Virtually all of Mount Auburn Cemetery is in Watertown, for the Cambridge boundary merely skirts the northern end of the graveyard. Nevertheless, the cemetery has always been associated with Cambridge and Boston, and some renowned figures from those two cities are buried here.

Mount Auburn was established in 1831 by Dr. Jacob Bigelow, whose intent was to create the first garden cemetery in the U.S. Dr. Bigelow himself planned the layout of the cemetery, working in collaboration with the landscape architect Alexander Wadsworth. The beautiful burial place that they created was so greatly admired that it became the archetype for suburban garden cemeteries all over the U.S.

The entryway to the cemetery, which dates to 1843, was designed by Dr. Bigelow; this is built of Quincy granite and is in the Egyptian Revival style. Within the cemetery one sees the Bigelow Chapel, a Gothic Revival structure erected in 1843 and rebuilt in 1853. Atop the highest hill of the cemetery there is a tower designed in 1853 by Gridley J. F. Bryant. The cemetery is an outdoor museum of American funerary art of the past century, in a superb setting. Interred in the cemetery are such renowned figures as Charles Bulfinch, Oliver Wendell Holmes, Sr., Winslow Homer, Dorothea Dix, Margaret Fuller, and Isabella Stewart Gardner. The most conspicuous monument in the cemetery is probably that of Mary Baker Eddy.

Fort Washington, 98 Waverley St (just to the W. of the M.I.T. campus, a short way in from the river). This little park is the site of a Revolutionary fortification, one of a series of demi-lune batteries that General Washington ordered to be built along the Charles to protect the Continental forces in Cambridge from a river attack by the British. The site was acquired by the city of Cambridge in 1857, at which time three 18-pounders from Fort Warren were installed there, with the grounds enclosed by the elaborate granite and wrought-iron fence that one sees today.

Radcliffe Residential Quadrangle (now shared with Harvard) occupies the block bounded by Garden, Linnaean, Walker, and Shepard Sts. Among the more notable buildings in the quadrangle are the following: *Bertram Hall* (1910), Alexander Wadsworth Longfellow, Jr.; *Moors Hall* (1947), Maginnis and Walsh; and the *Hilles Library* (1965), Harrison and Abramowitz.

The Smithsonian Astrophysical Observatory, entrance on Garden St opposite Linnaean St. Originally known as the Harvard Observatory, this was built in 1844–51 by the architect-engineer Isaiah Rogers, but only the central part of that structure remains today, obscured by later structures. The observatory is of interest principally for the very important role it has played in the development of modern astronomy, for some of the leading astronomers in the U.S. have worked or studied there, contributing many notable discoveries in their field.

The Harvard Business School; this part of the university is actually located in the Allston district of Boston, but it is oriented toward Cambridge, to which it is connected by the Larz Andersen Bridge and the Weeks Memorial Bridge. The original buildings of the school were completed in 1924 by McKim, Mead & White; and the neo-Georgian style has set the pattern for all subsequent structures erected in this part of the Harvard campus.

Harvard Stadium is also in Allston, on N. Harvard St. This was erected in 1902 by George B. de Gersdorff and Charles F. McKim, and was one of the first large structures in the U.S. to be constructed entirely of reinforced concrete.

The following is an annotated list of other sites of some interest in Cambridge: *Immaculate Conception School,* 45 Matignon St; this was originally constructed in 1850 as the Cambridge Almshouse, a work of Louis Dwight and Gridley J. F. Bryant.
Mount Auburn Hospital, 330 Mount Auburn St; erected in 1883 as the Cambridge Hospital, a work of William E. Chamberlain.
The *Cambridge Public Library,* 449 Broadway, a Richardsonian edifice built in 1888 by Van Brunt and Howe, with additions made in 1894 and again in 1901 by the same architects, and a modern wing added in 1966 by Shepley, Bulfinch, Richardson, and Abbott.

Brookline
**John Fitzgerald Kennedy National Historic Site,* 83 Beals St.

Approach. Take the Green Line (Cleveland Circle) to Coolidge Corner; from there walk N. along Harvard Ave as far as Beals St, which is the fourth turning on the r.; turn r. there, and the Kennedy house is on the r. side of the block towards its end.

Admission. The JFK site is open daily, 9–4:45; fee.

History. JFK's father, Joseph P. Kennedy, purchased the Beals St house in 1914 in anticipation of his marriage later that year to Rose Fitzgerald. The Kennedys moved into the house on returning from their honeymoon. Four of their nine children were born during the seven years the Kennedys lived there: Joseph, at Hull, Mass. (1915); John (1917); Rosemary (1918); and Kathleen (1920).

Joseph P. Kennedy, son of a prosperous family from East Boston, had already begun his career in business and finance by the time he married and moved to his house. After his graduation from Harvard in 1912, he became active in the stock market, real estate, and banking. At the age of 25, a year before his marriage, he was made president of the Columbia Trust Co., and in 1917 he became assistant general of the Fore River Shipyards. Rose Fitzgerald Kennedy, who was born in the North End, had grown up in the world of Boston politics. Through her father, John F. Fitzgerald, known as "Honey Fitz," who served as mayor of Boston and also as a member of the U.S. House of Representatives, she had early on come to know the leading figures of her day, and had also received the benefits of an excellent education, both in the U.S. and in Europe. The years during which the Kennedys lived in the Beals St house were quiet ones, typical of a young couple starting their family life. In 1921, when JFK was four years old, the family sold the house on Beals St and moved to a larger residence a short distance away, on Naples Rd (see below). After that the Beals

St house passed to a series of owners. It was repurchased by the Kennedy family in 1966, after which Rose Kennedy supervised the restoration and refurbishing of the house to recreate the appearance that it had in 1917, the year President Kennedy was born there. The Beals St house was designated a National Historic Landmark in May 1965; two years later Congress authorized its inclusion in the National Park System and made it a National Historic Site.

Interior. Visitors are met in the hallway by a Park Services ranger, who gives a brief talk on the house and the life of the Kennedys when they lived here. The ranger will also provide a free brochure which has a plan of the house and a description of all of the rooms. On entering each of the rooms, one presses a button to hear a recording by Rose Kennedy, describing the room and its part in the life of her family.

One begins by visiting the Living Room, which is to the r. of the hallway on the first floor. One then goes upstairs to see, in turn, the Master Bedroom, the Nursery, and the Guest Room, after which one returns to the first floor to visit the Dinning Room and the Kitchen. John F. Kennedy was born in the Master Bedroom on May 29, 1917, and for the first year of his life he slept in the Nursery, which he shared with his older brother, Joseph. When Rosemary Kennedy was born in 1918 she was put in the Nursery, while the two boys were moved into what is now the Guest Room, and after her birth in 1920 Kathleen was also put in the Nursery. Most of the furniture and decorations in the house belonged to the Kennedys, as do all of the personal belongings and memorabilia; other objects are typical of those that the family would have possessed in the years 1917–21. Some of the objects in the Nursery are very evocative, particularly the bassinet in which John and the other children slept when they were infants, and the christening outfit that they wore in turn when they were baptized. The book on the chair in the Nursery, *King Arthur's Knights*, was one of John F. Kennedy's childhood favorites. In the upper hallway there is a fascinating gallery of photographs of the Kennedys and their circle, some taken while they lived in this house, haunting mementos of this extraordinarily gifted family.

The Parks Service brochure also contains a map of the local area, and a guide to four local sites associated with the Kennedys: **1.** *The Naples Road Residence* (private), on the N.E. corner of Naples and Abbottsford Roads. The Kennedys moved here in 1921 after leaving the Beals St house, and remained in residence until 1927, when they moved to Scarsdale, New York. Eunice, Patricia, and Robert Kennedy were born here. Jean and Edward were born after the move to New York. **2.** *St. Aidan's Roman Catholic Church,* where the Kennedys attended Mass, where the first seven children were baptized, and where John and Joseph served as altarboys. **3.** The site of the *Dexter School* (which has now moved elsewhere), which John F. Kennedy and his brother Joseph attended until the family left Brookline. **4.** The *Edward Devotion School,* which both John and Joseph attended in the first year of their elementary education, before transferring to the Dexter School.

The **Edward Devotion House,* 347 Harvard St, near the corner of Stedman St, next to the Edward Devotion School. The Devotion House is the best example of mid-18C architecture in Brookline. The house and the adjacent school are named after Edward Devotion, a French Huguenot who had settled in Brookline by 1645. The present house, a gambrel-roofed structure with a central chimney, dates to c. 1740, but it is believed that it incorporates within it elements of the original 17C dwelling. The house was acquired by the Brookline Historical Society in 1911 and converted into a house-museum, with the rooms restored to their original appearance and furnished with antiques contributed by the old Brookline families, including the Devotions themselves. The house-museum is open Tues. and Thurs. 2–

5; fee. The rooms that are open to the public are the kitchen, parlor, buttery, and an upstairs bedroom, which has among its furnishings a trundle bed.

The *Longyear Museum,* 120 Seaver St; open Tues.—Sat. 2—5, Sun. 1—5; fee. The museum is devoted to memorabilia of Mary Baker Eddy, founder of Christian Science, and of other leaders in the movement.

The **Frederick Law Olmsted National Historic Site,* 22 Warren St, not far from the Brookline Hills T station on the Green Line. This house was acquired in 1883 by Olmsted, at a time when he was designing the Boston Park System, and he resided here until his death in 1903. The house, which was known as "Fairsted," is surrounded by landscaped grounds designed by Olmsted himself, in collaboration with his sons, John Charles and Frederick, Jr. On display in the house are objects associated with the first Olmsted landscape designer's firm and its successors, including drawings, plans, photographs, models, reports, and other project documentation. The archives contain approximately 115,000 drawings distributed over some 5000 individual projects ranging from the 1860s to 1979, a rare and valuable assemblage of work housed in the setting in which it was originally produced. The house and its exhibits are a fitting memorial to Frederick Law Olmsted, a man whose creative genius added much to the beauty of Boston.

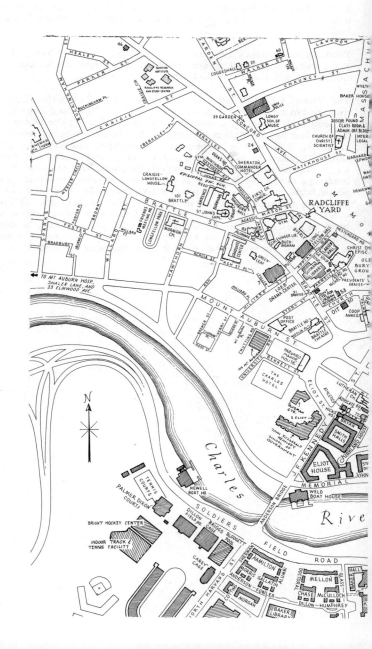

OLD CAMBRIDGE
AND HARVARD YARD

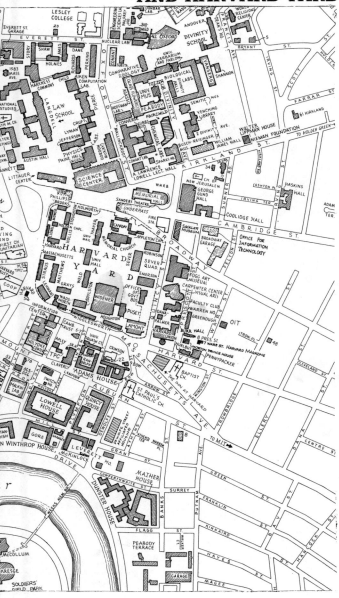

INDEX

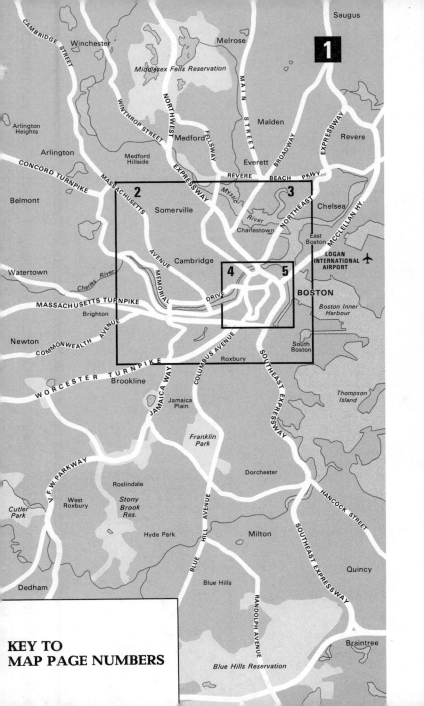

**KEY TO
MAP PAGE NUMBERS**

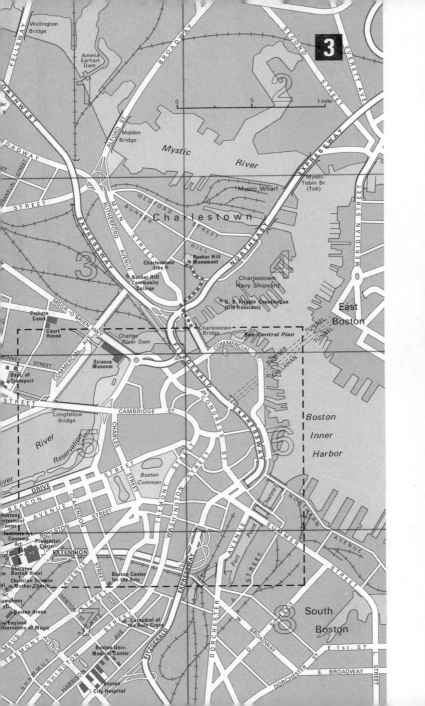

3

Wellington Bridge

Amelia Earhart Dam

Malden Bridge

Mystic River

Mystic Wharf

Mystic-Tobin Br. (Toll)

Charlestown

BUNKER HILL STREET

Bunker Hill Monument

Charlestown Navy Shipyard

Charlestown Libry.

Bunker Hill Community College

U. S. Frigate Constitution (Old Ironsides)

East Boston

Probate Court

Court House

Charlestown Bridge

See Central Plan

SUMNER TUNNEL

CALLAHAN TUNNEL

Charles River Dam

Dept. of Transport

Science Museum

Longfellow Bridge

CAMBRIDGE ST.

River

Reservation

Boston

Inner

Harbor

DRIVE

BEACON

Boston Common

Boston Architectural Center

Institute for Contemp.

Prudential Center

EXTENSION

Sheraton Boston Hotel

Christian Science Mother Church

Symphony Hall

Boston Arena

New England Conservatory of Music

Boston Center for the Arts

Cathedral of the Holy Cross

South Boston

Boston Univ. Medical Center

FITZGERALD

E. 1st. ST.

DORCHESTER ST.

W. BROADWAY

E. BROADWAY

Boston City Hospital

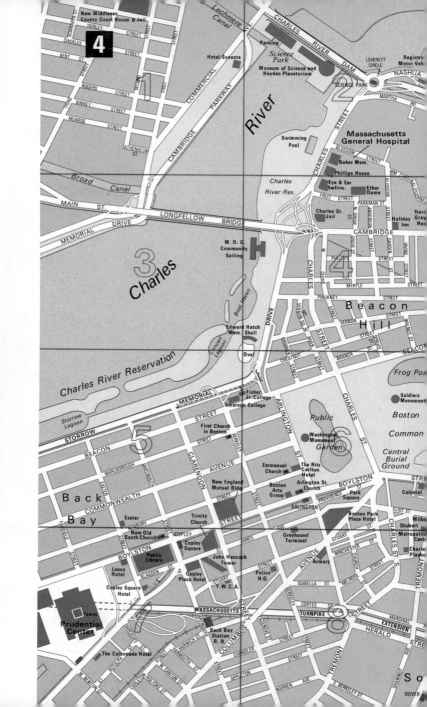

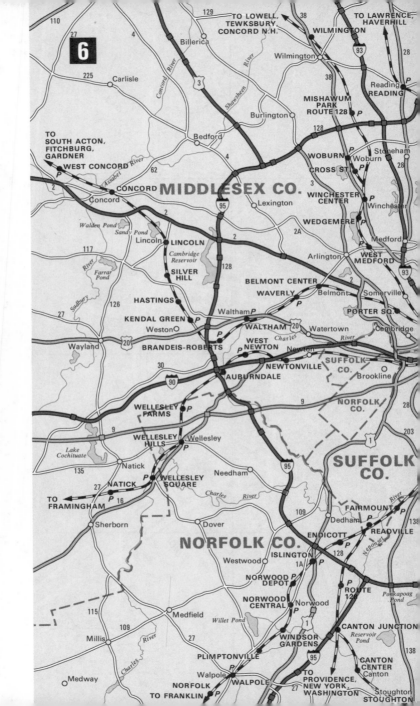